Psychology
for the IB Diploma

Jacob Solomon

Cambridge University Press's mission is to advance learning, knowledge and research worldwide.

Our IB Diploma resources aim to:

- encourage learners to explore concepts, ideas and topics that have local and global significance
- help students develop a positive attitude to learning in preparation for higher education
- assist students in approaching complex questions, applying critical-thinking skills and forming reasoned answers.

CAMBRIDGE
UNIVERSITY PRESS

University Printing House, Cambridge CB2 8BS, United Kingdom

One Liberty Plaza, 20th Floor, New York, NY 10006, USA

477 Williamstown Road, Port Melbourne, VIC 3207, Australia

314–321, 3rd Floor, Plot 3, Splendor Forum, Jasola District Centre, New Delhi – 110025, India

79 Anson Road, #06–04/06, Singapore 079906

Cambridge University Press is part of the University of Cambridge.

It furthers the University's mission by disseminating knowledge in the pursuit of education, learning and research at the highest international levels of excellence.

www.cambridge.org
Information on this title: www.cambridge.org/9781316640807

© Cambridge University Press 2018

First published 2018

20 19 18 17 16 15 14 13 12 11 10 9 8 7 6 5 4 3 2 1

Printed in the United Kingdom by Latimer Trend

A catalogue record for this publication is available from the British Library

ISBN 978-1-316-64080-7 Paperback

Additional resources for this publication at ibdiploma.cambridge.org

Contents

Contents

How to use this book

The coursebook features

This coursebook contains several special features, which are designed to enhance your learning experience. They are outlined below.

KEY QUESTIONS

- These questions indicate the main concepts that you will encounter in each chapter, and why they are relevant.

Learning objectives

- These briefly set out the learning aims for each chapter and will help you navigate the coursebook's content.

Key terms: These terms identify the key vocabulary that you will meet in each chapter, and provide clear, straightforward definitions.

NEWSFLASH

These highlight, analyse and evaluate relevant and up-to-date psychology content, such as that found in the popular media.

INTERNATIONAL FOCUS

These highlight psychology content from international locations, ensuring that the coursebook offers engaging worldwide coverage.

Psychologist profile

These introduce you to important psychologists, providing interesting background information about their lives, as well as the details of their theories.

RESEARCH IDEA

These encourage you to think about your own research, and offer suggestions of topics you could investigate.

Theory of Knowledge

These link chapter content with relevant theory of knowledge (TOK) concepts in order to help build your critical thinking skills.

Critical thinking

These provide opportunities for you to discuss evaluation of studies, ethics and research methods in a critical way.

ACTIVITY

These are hands-on, active tasks that you can do individually, in pairs or as part of a group.

SELF-ASSESSMENT QUESTIONS

These formative questions assess your knowledge of the different topics in the coursebook throughout each chapter.

Chapter summary

These lists sum up the content that you have covered in each chapter.

Exam-style questions

These provide you with an opportunity to practise the topics you have covered in each chapter, and check your understanding and progress through a focus on knowledge and higher-level thinking skills.

Introduction to psychology

'Be not afraid of life. Believe that life is worth living, and your belief
will help create the fact.'
(William James)

1 Psychology for the IB Diploma

KEY QUESTIONS

- How has the centuries-old interest in the human mind developed into the structured, academic discipline of psychology?
- What approaches are applied to psychology at IB Higher and Standard Levels?

Learning objectives

- Describe key debates that underlie much of the current research in psychology. (AO1)
- Explore the development of different approaches to the study of the human mind. (AO2)
- Evaluate how far psychology may be recognised as a science. (AO3)

2

1.1 Changing approaches to psychology

More than a century ago, the first Harvard University professor of psychology, William James (1842–1910), claimed that the greatest discovery of his generation was that the individual could alter his or her own life through a change in attitude, a change in thinking and a change in mindset.

Psychology is deeply involved with the study of all three: attitude, thinking and mindset. Most psychologists today accept that psychology is the disciplined study of mind and behaviour. Here, we will consider whether that idea can be taken a stage further, by defining psychology as the science of mind and behaviour. Is psychology a science?

Psychology is psych+ology, built on two Greek words: 'psyche' meaning 'the mind', and 'logos' meaning 'the science of'. By definition, psychology is the science of mind and behaviour. For millennia, philosophers, religious leaders and those involved with other people have shown deep interest in how the minds of other people work. How far psychology is a science will be considered later in this chapter.

Over the last 140 years, these concerns have acquired two distinctive dimensions that have turned human curiosity and awareness into an academic discipline:

1   **Empiricism**: the understanding of human behaviour needs to be based on findings that can be observed and counted.

2   **Positivism**: theory on human behaviour has to be supported by scientific evidence.

During that period, the means of studying the human mind have developed into increasingly varied and complex approaches.

The advances in research methods available to psychologists have been reflected in the range of increasingly sophisticated means of investigation, which include the following:

1   Focus on studying the conscious mind: separating the person's own mental experiences into visual, tactile and emotional components. In other words, the consideration of the images, sensations and feelings that an individual experiences in order to understand their way of thinking. Developed by Wilhelm Wundt (1832–1920) in 1879 in his laboratory in Leipzig, Germany, the **conscious mind approach** has been criticised for being academic rather than practical.

2   Focus on studying what thoughts and behaviour are meant to do, which is the **functionalist approach** of William James (1842–1910) developed at Harvard in Boston, USA. Influenced by Charles Darwin, the approach that he detailed in *Principles of Psychology* in 1890 was based on the typical pattern that individuals seek to enable the continuation of their lives by successfully adapting to changing circumstances and situations: what is known as the survival of the fittest. Some of his ideas continue to be developed today, especially through the work of biological psychologists who strongly favour evolutionary-based explanations of thinking and behaviour.

3   Focus on studying the unconscious mind to explain thoughts and behaviour. Dreams and word-associations are regarded as indicators of earlier-life, behaviour-influencing experiences that are believed to have a profound influence on the individual's behaviour without the individual being aware of it. It was Sigmund Freud (1856–1939) and his school in Vienna, Austria, that developed this **psychoanalytical approach** in the early part of the 20th century.

4   Focus on studying observable elements in behaviour under the headings of stimulus and response. This is based on data collection, empiricism and the notion that psychology had to be objective in order to be a scientifically acceptable discipline. Using the methodology of natural science, it contrasted with the subjective and introspective approach of Wundt. Among its most famous researchers are John Watson (1878–1958) and B.F. Skinner (1904–90). Known as the **behavioural approach**, it developed during the same decades as the psychoanalytical approach. In contrast to psychoanalysis, it avoided focus on the unconscious and thought processes, as these were not observable and could not be measured.

Psychology: the disciplined study of the mind and behaviour.

Empiricism: the view that the understanding of human behaviour needs to be based on findings that can be observed and counted.

Positivism: the view that theory on human behaviour has to be supported by scientific evidence.

Conscious mind approach: the consideration of the images, sensations and feelings that the individual experiences as a way to understand what that a person is thinking.

Functionalist approach: based on the idea that individuals seek to enable their continuation by successfully adapting to changing circumstances and situations: the survival of the fittest.

Psychoanalytical approach: a means of investigating mental disorders based on the interaction of conscious and unconscious mental elements.

Behavioural approach: focuses on studying observable elements in behaviour under the headings of stimulus and response.

Cognitive approach: focus on how behaviours relate to the way that the mind processes information.

Paradigm: an over-arching way of thinking that accommodates a set of theories.

Brain-scanning techniques: electronic technology making it possible for doctors and researchers to view activities within the brain without using invasive surgery.

Socio-cultural approach: focus on how behaviour relates to the social and cultural contexts in which behaviour is learnt and occurs.

Biological approach: focus on the ways that genetics, the nervous system and the endocrine system influence thoughts and actions.

5   Focus on the way that the mind processes information, known as the **cognitive approach**. Of increasing importance since the mid-1950s, its **paradigm**, or pattern, is that investigating the ways the mind processes stimuli and information is the key to understanding human behaviour. It is true that science only has a limited understanding of the workings of the brain. However, cognitive psychologists hold that it is possible to set up testable models of how the brain processes information, and then compare inputs (stimuli) and outputs (responses) as a means of accessing the ways that the brain handles the information that had previously been difficult to observe directly. Indeed, cognitive psychology makes much use of experimental methods, which are discussed in the next chapter. In addition, the scope of cognitively-based research in psychology has widened considerably with scientific advancements in **brain-scanning techniques** and collaboration with biologically orientated researchers.

6   Focus on social and cultural contexts in which behaviour is learnt and occurs – the **socio-cultural approach** to behaviour. This developed through the 20th century, and tended to concentrate on the way that collective experiences, group identity and language impact the behaviour of the individual. More recently it has considerably overlapped with cognitive psychology when researching how social and cultural inputs can influence the way in which individuals process information.

7   Focus on the ways that genetics, the nervous system and the endocrine (hormone) system influence human thoughts and actions. This is the **biological approach** to behaviour. The more recent findings here are based on research in the areas of the genetic basis of behaviour, the localisation of brain functions (which parts of the brain are responsible for specific human functions), and the role of hormones and neurotransmitters.

These seven approaches may all be applied to explain specific behaviour patterns, such as why a person learns languages quickly, why a person seems unable to fit into a school or workplace routine, why an 18-year-old fears starting a conversation with a stranger, and why a person shows symptoms of depression for a prolonged period.

Sigmund Freud (1856–1939)

Figure 1.1 Sigmund Freud: psychoanalytical approach

Sigmund Freud (1856–1939) was an Austrian medical doctor. His experience in treating patients indicated that many physical symptoms of illness are strongly influenced by the work of the unconscious mind. He became increasingly convinced that it does not just impact on health, but on individual patterns of behaviour as well. Childhood experiences, often long-forgotten, are particularly significant and unconscious contributors to emotional drives, sexual inclinations and behaviours, inner conflict and psychologically abnormal conditions. Freud's approach was to access the individual unconscious mind through analysing dreams and by using word associations: for example, he might choose 'tree' and the patient would say the first word that came to mind. Freud would use these findings to build up the workings of the patient's unconscious mind. From there, he would identify the causes of the disorder and work towards resolving it.

Though Freud's ideas are hard to verify scientifically, they are still much-discussed and influential today.

Figure 1.2 Wilhelm Wundt: conscious mind approach

Figure 1.3 William James: functionalist approach

Figure 1.4 John Watson: behavioural approach

Figure 1.5 B.F. Skinner: behavioural approach

Think of these seven approaches as lenses of a microscope. Each of the seven lenses is focused on the same item. The item is a specific behaviour, as in the above examples. Each will contribute a different perspective to the same situation.

Let's take the first example: *why a person learns foreign languages quickly*. The different lenses may contribute elements as shown in Table 1.1.

1 Conscious mind approach	Feeling good about being able to communicate in a foreign language, enjoying the smiles and hugs of recognition from others.
2 Functionalist approach	Motivated by the belief that speaking foreign languages enables the forming of vital connections with a wider range of people.
3 Psychoanalytical approach	Positive, foreign-language-based encounters in early childhood, though no longer consciously remembered.
4 Behavioural approach	Increasingly high standards of communication in a foreign language have been positively reinforced by previous language-learning success.

Table 1.1 Different approaches in psychology (continued)

5 Cognitive approach	Ability and determination to encode new vocabulary and language structures into the brain's memory structures. May be assisted by a strong self-belief in language-learning abilities that may or may not be based on previous language-learning experiences.
6 Socio-cultural approach	The rate of progress in language learning is determined by the degree of interaction with those speaking that language and the attitudes of the individual's culture and society, towards learning foreign languages
7 Biological approach	The rate of progress in language learning is determined by the density of neurons and associated neurotransmitters in the parts of the brain that handle language learning.

Table 1.1 Different approaches in psychology

The core of the IB at both Higher and Standard Levels focuses on the workings of just the final three approaches. The options for the IB at both Higher and Standard Levels apply these three approaches to specific areas of investigation in psychology.

1.2 The microscope analogy applied to IB psychology

If we use the example of the microscope again, the IB approach may be compared to one that uses just three distinct lenses. These lenses are the biological approach, the cognitive approach and the socio-cultural approach, and they are all focused on human behaviour.

While Chapter 2 introduces the methodologies, which are presented systematically in Chapter 10, Chapters 3, 4 and 5 study the perspectives of each 'lens' in turn. Chapters 6, 7, 8 and 9 apply all three lenses to optional areas of study: abnormal psychology, the psychology of human relationships, health psychology and development psychology. It is therefore vital that you are thoroughly familiar with the elements of the biological, cognitive and socio-cultural approaches to human behaviour before proceeding to apply them to the more specialised branches of psychology.

For now, consider how these various lenses can view and give insight into one particular behaviour. We will choose the specific behaviour of an individual who regularly eats considerably more than necessary to maintain good health.

The biological lens will pay attention to the evolutionary and genetic factors. It will consider that the person's hunter-gatherer ancestors could not rely on being able to access food regularly. For survival, they needed to consume large amounts of food when possible, storing the excess as layers of fat to be turned into energy when food was not available. Being able to store and mobilise excess fat was a crucial factor in surviving to reproductive level. Being able to pass on the essential genes for the capacity to store and utilise fats meant that successive generations would overeat when given the opportunity, converting the excess into fats instead of passing it out of the digestive system. This is irrespective of the fact that for many people today, food is readily available at all times. These biological elements are considered in more detail in Chapter 8.

Switching to the cognitive lens will likely draw attention to the excessive eating possibly happening because of unrealistic expectations from dieting. Individuals enthusiastically put themselves on diets and exercise programmes. However, many soon find themselves on a break-restart, break-restart cycle. As a result, personal weight suffers the yo-yo effect, going up and down.

Figure 1.6 The microscope analogy

Moving to the socio-cultural lens may well reveal the increasingly sedentary lifestyle of modern life, where the individual drives rather than walks to work and uses a computer rather than heavy manual labour in the workplace. Overeating may also be due to higher salaries leaving people with more money left over to pay for non-essentials such as highly tasty but heavily sugared manufactured foodstuffs.

These different perspectives do not necessarily contradict each other. However, a modern psychologist has the task of evaluating the relative importance of the contribution of each element. Strong emphasis on the findings of one lens can indicate a **reductionist** approach, whereas an attempt to integrate the findings of all lenses would demonstrate a more **holistic** perspective.

1.3 How far is psychology a science?

We have already mentioned that empirical and positivist elements are used in psychological enquiry. However, in evaluating psychology's position as a science, these elements need to fit in with the three essential characteristics of scientific investigation:

1   There has to be underlying **theory**, out of which hypotheses can develop. This collective structure is called a paradigm.

2   Testing has to be possible in order to obtain precise data that may support or refute the **hypothesis**.

3   That which is being investigated, and the investigative procedures, need to match reality. The findings should be applicable to explain associated real-world observable phenomena.

Kuhn (1962) proposed that paradigms within a discipline go through three stages:

1   Pre-science stage: where there are many different conflicting approaches to an area of study.

2   Normal science: where researchers work within the same set of paradigms.

3   Revolution: where a conflicting paradigm becomes so persuasive that it creates a paradigm shift within the discipline that becomes accepted by its body of researchers.

Reductionist: explaining a phenomenon in terms of a single cause and/or approach.

Holistic: dealing with or treating the whole of a phenomenon and not just a part.

Theory: a well-substantiated explanation for a phenomenon or relationship.

Hypothesis: a proposed explanation of something observed which may be supported or refuted by evidence.

Kuhn argues that psychology cannot be regarded as completely scientific, as some approaches used in research are not easily measured and quantified. A psychoanalyst and a behavioural psychologist would approach a patient with major depression for example, in different ways. Researchers using quantitative methods are likely to place greater weight on the statistics and what may be inferred from them. Those using qualitative analysis will probably focus on fewer participants, but use detailed interviews or questionnaires designed to enable the participant to inform on individual background circumstances, emotions, other important details not easily reached by quantitative methods. However, Feyerabend (1975) disagrees, holding that the research process is actually hindered when researchers deliberately work within a set of beliefs that are common to those working in that discipline. He argues that scientific progress is actually promoted in situations where researchers work outside their subject's set of beliefs, and their work is strongly attacked and strongly defended.

Under Kuhn, the growing similarities between biological and cognitive psychologists and their shared paradigms may well be moving the subject from pre-science towards normal science. Under Feyerabend's criterion, it may indeed be argued that psychology is a normal science, as it is the wider range of paradigms which are strongly held by the different approaches that characterise the discipline.

We will now visit in more detail the theories and hypotheses that are typical of psychological enquiry. Many of the following ideas can be applied to any discipline that involves theories and hypotheses. We will then introduce the concept of methodologies used to investigate the hypotheses; methodologies themselves being a vital strand that is developed in the next chapters. We will briefly consider how far these methodologies are scientifically based and whether they indeed address the hypothesis of the research.

We have already stated that paradigms in psychology form the area within which theories can develop, which in turn generate hypotheses. Suitable data is required for the support or rejection of the hypothesis, whose nature is more fully explored in later chapters and systematically in Chapter 10.

Karl Popper (1934, translated in 1959) holds that scientific theories and their associated hypotheses must be **refutable**, meaning that the analysis of the data gathered in research can cause the hypothesis to be rejected. Indeed, a typical hypothesis in psychology is commonly expressed negatively, using a **null hypothesis**.

For example, suppose you are researching the effect of background music on success in a memorisation task. The null hypothesis would state that the presence or absence of background music neither aids nor adversely affects the memorisation process. If the data obtained supports the null hypothesis, then the positive hypothesis proposing that background music affects the memory process has been indicated to be incorrect. Hypotheses are reframed as null hypotheses for the following reason: if the theory was framed as a positive hypothesis, it would tempt the researchers towards **confirmation bias**, meaning accepting information that supports the hypothesis and avoiding information that rejects it.

The positive hypothesis is supported where the data indeed rejects the null hypothesis. This is Popper's argument: science progresses through refutation rather than support.

The methodology of research needs to be scientific in order for psychology to be considered as a science. That means that its research methods must be standardised, replicable and, when possible, controlled.

In addition, the hypothesis should relate to the real world as opposed to the laboratory situation. This makes investigation more difficult when it takes place in a simulated environment, and its findings are generalised to the real-world situation. How ecologically valid are the findings? Are the apparently supported theoretical relationships **correlational**? This means that although one variable is shown to affect the other, in fact that can only happen when there is a third element operating in the background which happened in the laboratory simulation but is not always present in real life. Even where investigations are controlled, ecologically valid, replicable and non-correlational, the acceptance of the hypothesis does not mean that behaviour in similar circumstances is entirely predictable. This is because subsequent similar research may produce conflicting results or confine the original discovered relationship to more specific circumstances.

Refutable: able to be rejected, for example where the analysis of data gathered in research has the potential of causing the rejection of the hypothesis.

Null hypothesis: where the hypothesis is expressed in terms of there being no statistical significance between two variables under study. Research involves attempting to discredit it.

Confirmation bias: a heuristic where the individual focuses on information and interpretations that confirm pre-existing opinions and expectations.

Correlational: having connection between two or more things, such as sets of data or situations.

In addition, the investigation must be **ethically acceptable** to be valid research in psychology. Ethics are addressed in Chapter 2.

In reality, the main methodological uneasiness of psychology being considered as a science arises out of the sheer complexity of the issues that the subject addresses: human thinking and human behaviour. Even the simplest actions and behaviour are affected by biological, mental and environmental factors, which vary considerably between locations, cultures and the human processing of stimuli and information. These place serious barriers to understanding and predicting human behaviour.

1.4 Ongoing general debates in psychology

In addition, irrespective of whether the biological, cognitive or socio-cultural lens is used in our microscope, you should be aware that there are up to four debates underlying any theory or research in psychology. These can be illustrated with William, aged ten. William is highly intelligent, popular and athletic, but has a condition called **arachnophobia** (meaning a great fear of spiders).

The four debates are as follows:

1   The nature–nurture debate. Are William's fears related to the working of his genetics and nervous system (nature), or did the words and behaviours of other people communicate to him that spiders are harmful (nurture)?

2   The reductionist–**holism** debate. Is William's fear of spiders due to one particular cause (reductionist), for example hearing a bedtime story of a child being bitten by a spider, or remembering his older brother scream as a large spider suddenly appeared on his shoulder? Or is his situation caused by more than one, or by many, factors?

   Bear in mind that psychology is becoming increasingly holistic in approach. This is particularly the case in developments in social psychology that increasingly overlap with cognitive approaches, and advances in cognitive methods of investigation that incorporate biological methods of investigation.

3   The free will–**determinism** debate. Did William choose to be scared of spiders (free will), or did he not have any option in the matter?

   Taken to extremes, this debate raises the question of, for example, whether criminal behaviour is genetically determined.

Figure 1.7 'Get me away from that thing!'

Ethically acceptable: the research conforms to the professional guidelines binding on psychology investigators.

Critical thinking

Read the research of Kiecolt-Glaser (1984) in Chapter 8. This work investigates whether personal stress may increase the likelihood of susceptibility to infectious disease.

Evaluate how far that research may be regarded as scientific.

Arachnophobia: fear of spiders.

Holism: the explanation of a phenomenon in terms of a variety of causes and/or approaches.

Determinism: where a thought process or behaviour is considered to happen through processes beyond the individual's choice or control.

4   The nomothetic-idiographic debate. May the factors determining William's fear of spiders be generalised to anyone who has encountered similar spider-related events as William (**nomothetic**), or are the elements in William's case exclusively specific (**idiographic**) to William?

Researchers in psychology almost always have to consider how far their findings are valid for populations with different characteristics to those investigated. Frequently, researchers study their most accessible population, which is the undergraduate body of students within their own department. These people are generally young, intelligent, culturally compatible with the department and in good health. The researchers have to assess how far their findings may be generalised to individuals with only some of those characteristics, or none at all.

Nomothetic: where the factors influencing a person's behaviour can be generalised to the behaviour of individuals in similar circumstances.

Idiographic: where the factors influencing a person's behaviour cannot be generalised to others in similar circumstances, but are specific to that individual.

Ethnocentrism: the generalising of the findings on one culture to another culture.

1.5 Cultural issues

In addition to the above debates, the interpretation and validity of theory and research studies in psychology are subject to possible elements of cultural bias which have to be borne in mind, such as the following:

- **Ethnocentrism**: generalising the findings on one culture to another culture. For example, studies on people's willingness to help others carried out in Western societies need to bear in mind that the costs and rewards of helping others may be very different in other cultures. Indeed, about two-thirds of published work in psychology is from North America, which contains only 17% of the world's population. Reviews of research in these countries indicate that only about 5% of those tested are non-white.

- Theoretical bias: for example, the Western evolutionary concept of the survival of the fittest is less applicable to many African societies. They tend to prioritise the survival of the tribe as a whole and think in terms of interdependence rather than independence, and co-operation rather than competition.

- Methodological bias: for example, the Western criteria for diagnosing depression are based on psychological symptoms such as feelings of sadness, worry and guilt, and thoughts of suicide. These criteria are less effective in identifying the symptoms reported by patients in China and the Asian Pacific Rim that might well indicate depression.

- **Gender bias**: for example, the psychological research on anorexia nervosa is largely based on women, who constitute the majority of diagnoses. There are few studies of male anorexia, raising the question of the extent to which the findings on female patients may be generalised to include male patients.

Gender bias: the possibility that a diagnosis or means of treatment of abnormality may be wrongly influenced by perceived gender similarities or differences between the professional and the patient.

ACTIVITY 1.1

Under the heading 'a career in psychology', suggest ten different types of work opportunity that might attract a university graduate in psychology. Bear in mind that some jobs will involve years of specialised training beyond a first degree.

SELF-ASSESSMENT QUESTIONS 1.1

1 a Define psychology.

  b Define empiricism and positivism.

  c What roles do empiricism and positivism have in the discipline of psychology?

2 Distinguish between the following approaches in psychology: biological, cognitive and socio-cultural.

3 What case can be made for and against psychology being regarded as a science?

4 List and briefly describe four key debates in the discipline of psychology as a whole.

5 Academic psychology strives to be academic in approach. State four potential biases that researchers need to be aware of.

1.6 Practical value of psychology

Psychology is far more than an academic activity, however. At best, psychology's continually growing number of discoveries is valuable for helping professional services to improve others' quality of life and relationships. People working in psychology-based callings have to be authorised by the professional body that governs their particular speciality in the field. In addition, those working in **psychiatry** are medically trained with strong backgrounds in biology and neurology, and are able to prescribe drugs. Clinical psychologists typically have doctorates in psychology and specialise in identifying elements in people's lifestyle that could be adversely affecting their mental health, such as spousal and family relationships, work issues, eating routines and ways of thinking. They often use **psychotherapy**, an interactive conversation-based approach.

Psychologists are not only based in hospitals and clinics, but many serve in schools, colleges, senior citizens' services and workplaces including offices, supermarkets and factories. Others, as forensic psychologists, work with adult and young offenders, and are often called on to provide psychological evidence in trial proceedings.

As psychology expands in content and in assisting society, it is likely to involve an increasing number of people. You may well become one of them!

Psychiatry: a branch of medicine that deals with mental and emotional disorders.

Psychotherapy: an interactive conversation-based treatment of mental health problems based on the client's thoughts, feelings, moods and behaviours.

Chapter summary

1 Psychology may be defined as the disciplined study of the mind and behaviour. This discipline tends to be characterised by empiricism and positivism.

2 The IB programme at both Standard and Higher Levels focuses on and applies the biological, cognitive and socio-cultural approaches to understanding the behaviour of the individual.

3 Psychology may be increasingly considered to be scientific, in view of its paradigms, associated theories and hypotheses being subjected to testing based on empirical, positivist and refutable data.

4 Many investigations in psychology are related to underlying general issues affecting psychology as a whole: the nature–nurture debate, the reductionist–holism debate, the freewill–determinism debate, and the nomothetic–idiographic debate.

5 Investigations in psychology need to take into account the dangers of cultural biases such as ethnocentricity, methodological bias and gender bias.

6 Academic experience in psychology can be a gateway to an increasing number of associated career opportunities.

Research methods in psychology

'A wonderful fact to reflect upon, that every human creature is
constituted to be that profound secret and mystery to every other.'
(Charles Dickens, *A Tale of Two Cities*)

Learning objectives

- Explain how psychology is distinguished as a discipline from common sense observations and generalisations on human behaviour. (AO2)

- Explore some of the tools of investigation available for research in psychology. (AO2)

- Evaluate the validity of suitably researched findings in psychology. (AO3)

2.1 Psychology versus psychobabble

Psychology differs from the general interest and observations on human behaviour in the following ways:

- Psychology's findings are based on theory and research that have satisfied the rigorous investigative procedure requirements of the discipline.

- Psychology's claims are based on scientific data gathered during research.

These ideas were introduced in Chapter 1.

The entire discipline of psychology is composed of theory that is supported in varying degrees by findings from research. Some of these methods of research are particular to the biological, cognitive or socio-cultural approaches to behaviour discussed in Chapter 1. Thus the use of neuro-technology to trace the intensity of an emotion, and its path through the brain, is typical in researching the biological approach to behaviour. In contrast, the use of **content analysis** following a long interview in studying an individual's cultural issues in the workplace would exemplify the socio-cultural approach.

Content analysis: the finding of patterns within qualitative data.

The data in those findings may be in different forms. It can vary from the tables and graphs generated from a questionnaire survey distributed to thousands of individuals on different continents, to a few in-depth transcripts of detailed interviews, each lasting an hour or more. It could also be from a series of brain scans or even blood tests.

Much of the work in psychology evaluates how reliable the data is, and how far the patterns found within the data may be generalised to other groups of people. What are the strengths of the findings? What are the weaknesses? How far do those weaknesses impact on the value of the conclusions?

The principles and research in psychology are distinguished from general interest in human behaviour in being supported by evidence of professionally suitable standing.

How many 'psychological' claims like the following have you heard?

'I knew you were having a bad day before you walked in through the door. I am something of a psychologist, you see.'

'Bringing up ten kids has taught me so much about children that I should have a doctorate in psychology.'

'I can tell whether you're lying or not just by looking at you. I know a lot more about psychology than you think.'

'Uncle Jim, aged 45, has just bought a new red two-seater Lamborghini. He must be going through a midlife crisis with romance. He's probably pursuing a young twenty-something supermodel.'

'You're always losing things. You never remember anything. You've got Alzheimer's disease!'

'Our teacher always insists that bags must be put under the desks, students sit in straight rows, in their assigned places, and speak only one at a time. It shows that she suffers from obsessive compulsive disorder.'

Figure 2.1 What challenges might this type of personality face inside and outside the classroom?

Figure 2.2 'I wish I was 20 years younger, but I'm making up for lost time now!'

Psychobabble: the application of the terminology of psychology in a manner that is academically unacceptable.

What all these statements have in common is that they are not grounded in psychology, but in **psychobabble**. In contrast, psychology is a discipline.

In Chapter 1, we considered the idea that psychology is the science of mind and behaviour. Indeed, psychology seeks to study scientifically how we handle stimuli and information, and how the associated mental processes influence behaviour. In contrast, psychobabble is where specialised terms are taken from psychology and instantly applied to what is in front of us.

By themselves, none of the 'psychological' claims on the previous page can be considered as psychological evidence.

None of those statements are necessarily untrue. None are based either on disciplined application of psychological theory or on academically acceptable psychological evidence. That is because none of the assertions and explanations have been researched to the extent that they can accurately account for any of those six scenarios. In order for them to qualify as good psychology, they need to be rooted in substantiated research evidence.

Take 45-year-old Uncle Jim, thought to be going through a midlife crisis. Psychologists would first ask: 'Is there such a thing as a midlife crisis?' They would look at the evidence for and against. They might cite Elliot Jaques (1965) who coined the term 'midlife crisis', claiming that it is in the early 40s that a person begins to come to terms with the fact that he or she will not live forever, and this causes stress. That is behind the almost desperate striving to become young again through taking romantic, financial or physical risks. However, the research of Aldwin and Levenson (2001) indicates that although midlife is often a time for reflection and reassessment, it does not necessarily include drastic and bizarre changes in lifestyle. In other words, psychologists do not all agree that the midlife crisis exists.

In the other examples, psychologists accept that conditions of OCD and Alzheimer's disease do actually exist. They can be diagnosed by clinical psychologists but not by laymen, and most emphatically not by those suffering pedantic teachers, or those who constantly leave things behind.

In addition, assuming that there is such a thing as a midlife crisis, the evidence with Uncle Jim is not sufficient for a diagnosis. Perhaps he always wanted a sports car, but he can only now afford it. Red may just be his favourite colour, or it happened to be the colour of the only car in stock at that price. It does not necessarily indicate romantic designs and risky behaviour.

In other words, the burden is on psychology as a discipline to establish that there is such a thing as a midlife crisis. Having proved that, it would have to show that its typical symptoms include the purchase of two-seater sports cars. The psychologists would also need to demonstrate that the choice of the colour red indicates romantic intentions.

Once all three elements are accepted by the discipline of psychology, the next stage would be applying it to the unique case of Uncle Jim. Even if his behaviour appears to be symptomatic of a midlife crisis, alternative explanations of his behaviour would have to be considered. These would have to be balanced against the midlife-crisis diagnosis.

We will come back to Uncle Jim a little later.

In fact, psychobabble statements are often included in **pop-psychology**. Psychobabble applies the terminology of psychology in a manner that is academically unacceptable. Psychology may not necessarily be more difficult to understand, but it is supported by the evidence of documented and verifiable research. Pop-psychology with psychobabble is not.

Pop-psychology: where popularly-accepted explanations of human thinking and behaviour claim to be supported by psychology, but are insufficiently supported by academic research.

For example, pop-psychology has frequently claimed that complex computer games are good for children as they speed up the workings of the nervous system, enabling quicker and more skilled responses in reacting to real-life situations. However, currently there is conflicting evidence from neuro-psychologists as to whether this claim is biologically valid.

Much of the IB programme in psychology studies research methods commonly used in psychology. Psychology confines our knowledge of the workings of the human mind to claims and relationships that are supported by grounded theory and research. It is indeed the theories and research in different branches of psychology that are the building blocks for the academically acceptable knowledge of human behaviour that we have. And part of your work as a student is to evaluate the claims made by theories and research in psychology which you will meet on your journey through this course.

We will now look at methods of research commonly used in psychology. These will be exemplified by research studies that demonstrate the issues faced by those advancing the frontiers of knowledge in psychology, together with the ethical issues involved.

Just because statements are supported by real psychology doesn't make them less interesting. This is shown by some recent findings, including the following studies:

1 You cannot get to know more than about 150 people properly, however many friends you have on social media (based on Dunbar, 1992).

2 A new resolution takes 66 days of constant practice to be part of your way of life (Gardner et al., 2012). So if you make a New Year's resolution, circle 7 March on your calendar.

3 You cannot always trust your memory. Your mind takes emotionally-charged and unreliable mental photographs at frightening, exciting or horrific events (Loftus and Palmer, 1974).

4 The more choices you have, the less likely you will buy, however much you say that you want variety (based on Schwartz, 2004).

5 Group decisions are less likely to suitably address the realities of the situation than individuals' decisions. They tend to be influenced by the most powerful and emotional personalities in the group (Hughes et al., 2010, based on the Challenger Space Shuttle disaster of 1986).

Figure 2.3 One vote each, but who's going to be listened to when getting up to talk?

In all these five examples, the findings are distinguished from general interest in human behaviour in being supported by evidence of professionally suitable standing.

Select one of the five claims above.

1 Identify what you think there is to discover *and* what we need to know to establish the discovery in the claim of your choice.

2 What methodology would you apply for your investigation of the claim?

3 What problems would you face in enabling your findings to be accepted by professionals in psychology?

2.2 Quantitative research methods in psychology

Research in psychology uses tools from the range of **quantitative methods, qualitative methods** or both.

Quantitative research is based on figures that come from surveys, interviews, observations and questionnaire responses. The information is numerical. It is statistically summarised, and statistically analysed. Quantitative data is also experimental if it involves both a test and a control population. As it typically involves large numbers of people, the evidence it generates is empirical. The **empirical approach** uses findings based on **observation**, experience and experimenting with a suitably large number of people. In this chapter, we focus on Milgram's experiment on **obedience** which may be classified as both quantitative and empirical, although it is also non-experimental as it does not have a control population.

Scientific rigour uses the following principles that are developed in this and in the next chapters of this book. As Figure 2.4 shows, a piece of research should:

- be objective
- be hypothesis-based
- generate empirical evidence for analysis
- be controlled for outside factors
- be replicable
- be readily applicable to explaining real-world behaviours and situations.

It is also required to conform to **ethical guidelines**.

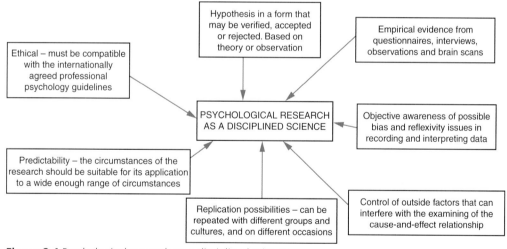

Figure 2.4 Psychological research as a disciplined science

In this book, we will see studies that have been professionally accepted and do not satisfy all the points. For example, the study of Genie is frequently cited despite its being a unique **case study** of one person only.

There are studies where both quantitative and qualitative methods are used to determine the relationship between the same two or more variables. This is called **triangulation**.

Whatever the chosen method, investigation in psychology must be compatible with the professional ethical guidelines for its findings to be admissible to the discipline. The main principles of ethics are covered in this chapter, and are constantly referred to when planning and evaluating research. (That includes the research that you will be conducting for your IB internal assessment.)

Quantitative psychology may be experimental or non-experimental. Qualitative psychology is typically non-experimental.

Quantitative methods: research based on figures that come from surveys, interviews, observations and questionnaire responses. They can be statistically summarised, and statistically analysed.

Qualitative methods: research based on the more extended and descriptive data that typically comes from personal journal entries and interview transcripts. The information does not translate into figures.

Empirical approach: focus on findings based on observation, experience and experimentation with a suitably large number of people.

Observation: in quantitative research this involves recording the nature and the frequency of a given behaviour or other phenomenon in a particular environment.

Obedience: where a person yields to specific instructions or orders from an authority figure.

Ethical guidelines: code of conduct for investigators in psychology to prevent unacceptable exploitation of participants. The guidelines must be satisfied in every piece of research.

Case study: investigation involving a few participants or even one participant in depth, typically in a natural setting.

Triangulation: in research, where more than one method is used to determine the relationship between the same two or more variables. This typically involves both quantitative and qualitative methods.

2.2.1 Experimental methods in quantitative psychology

Experimental psychology involves carrying out the research under both test conditions and controlled conditions. These conditions are identical, except for the one variable that is changed in the experimental condition. That variable is called the **independent variable** (IV). The variable that is studied as being affected in both the test and control condition is the **dependent variable** (DV).

The procedure for scientific experimental approach is likely to follow the flow chart in Figure 2.5.

The participants in an experiment are likely be a sample of the population studied. Let us say that the problem for investigation is the capacity of all 18-year-old students in a city to memorise a set of unconnected objects under different environmental conditions. The sample will have to proportionally represent the different **genders**, cultures and ability ranges of 18-year-olds in the city. Frequently, research in psychology in university departments faces the issue that the participants who are most accessible are the undergraduates of their own department. This creates problems when applying the findings to explain the behaviour of a wider population. How representative are the findings of 18-year-olds in general, and in different parts of the world? In other words, how far may the results be generalised?

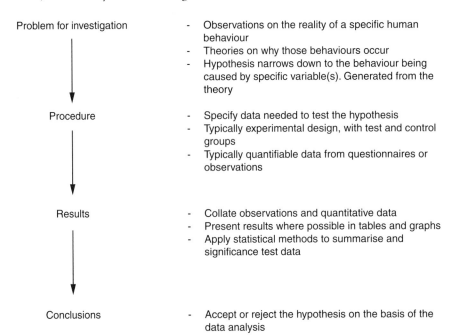

Figure 2.5 The scientific experimental approach

Samples in quantitative research should be large enough to apply statistical analysis. Sampling issues are examined in more detail in Chapter 10. (Appropriate sampling is an essential element in your internal assessment.)

As an example of how experimental methods are used in psychology, let us go back to Uncle Jim and plan to research whether it is indeed true that 45-year-old male purchasers of sports cars may be choosing the colour red for romantic motives.

As it is a research study, it has to open with a **research hypothesis**. The hypothesis is founded on observing and theorising about the phenomenon. It should be justified, on the basis of established psychological theory, related previous research or empirical evidence. Empirical evidence is the data that is accumulated by observation and experience. Empirical observation and experience in this case could be based on practical experience rather than on scientific data: for example, that you know a number of people with red cars who bought them when they were in love.

The hypothesis in this study would therefore be: 'The 45-year-old male purchasers of red sports cars choose that colour because of romantic motives.' The purpose of the study would be to investigate whether the hypothesis would be accepted or rejected. Details on types of hypotheses are contained in Chapter 10.

The hypothesis clearly frames the question that is being investigated through quantitative methods. Remember that quantitative analysis is based on numbers. In this case, a sample of 100 male, 45-year-old purchasers of red sport cars might be given an anonymous questionnaire like the one in Activity 2.2 to complete. The scale used is a **semantic scale**, where the participant circles the number that best fits their response to the question. A semantic scale turns descriptions into numbers. The scores cannot be added up: two people saying that the choice of the colour red for their sports car was 'somewhat important' to them does not add up to one person who says that red was 'most important'.

One hundred questionnaires produce a considerable amount of empirical data.

Let us say that out of the sample of 100 red sports car purchasers aged 45, 80 included at least one romantic-associated motive shown by a score of 3 or 4. This might suggest that choice of red was significant. But perhaps it is not universal to the behaviour of 45-year-olds in that situation. Maybe romantic motives are common to all 45-year-old male sports car purchasers, not just those who buy the red ones. It is therefore necessary to run a control questionnaire to eliminate this possibility. It would be given to the men who bought a sports car other than red. That is the control mode. The results are compared with those who bought red sports cars. That is the test mode.

Thus this investigation is indeed experimental. The DV is the degree of romantic feeling in the colour of the car. The IV is the colour of the car.

Experimental research is distinguished by having a test population and a control population. They are identical except for changing the nature of the IV in the test population.

If within the sample of 100 non-red sports car purchasers aged 45, only 20 included at least one 3 or 4 score romantic-associated motive, it might suggest that there could be a link between the colour red and romantic motives. If the sample revealed 80, then there would be no difference in the degree of romantic motives between those buying red sports cars and those buying non-red sports cars.

It might be suggested that it is the sports car itself that reflects romantic motives rather than its colour. The colour of the car would be immaterial. This is the stage of the analysis of the data in both the test and control conditions, and the analysis of the results. Indeed, it is both actual figures and their interpretations that determine whether the hypothesis should be accepted or rejected. The entire procedure follows the research cycle as indicated in Figure 2.6.

Semantic scale: questionnaire-survey descriptors are turned into numbers. The scale is arranged along a spectrum of possible responses to a question. The numbers cannot be added up.

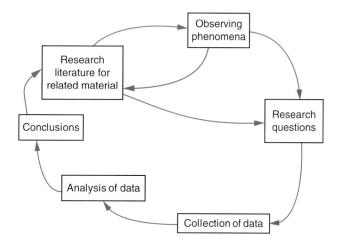

Figure 2.6 The growth of psychology as a discipline – the research cycle

Demand characteristics: the participant responds according to what they think that the researchers want to hear without it necessarily being true.

Hawthorne effect: the research participants' responses are influenced by the knowledge that they are part of a research study.

Screw-you effect: the participant, determined not to co-operate, gives the response that they think the researchers do not want to hear without it necessarily being true.

Briefing: the information given to participants before taking part in the investigation. It is required by the ethical guidelines in psychology.

Debriefing: the information given to participants after taking part in the investigation. It is required by the ethical guidelines in psychology.

Natural experiments: where the background scenario for both the test and the control already exists within the environment. Often associated with quasi-experimental investigations.

Field experiments: where the researcher manipulates the IV, but within a real-life environment rather than a laboratory.

Quasi-experimental investigations: where the researcher imposes the situation of the test and control investigation using the pre-existing natural environment.

The validity of a piece of research in psychology is constantly evaluated in terms of strengths, limitations and the degree to which its findings may be generalised to other populations.

There is room for criticising the conclusions of this study. The survey was based on self-reporting. Maybe people don't really know what made them decide to purchase their car. Maybe the sports car owners gave the responses they thought that the researchers wanted to hear without necessarily being true: that is called **demand characteristics**. Maybe knowing that they are part of a research study influences the participants' responses: that is called the **Hawthorne effect**. The **screw-you effect** is also a possibility, where participants answer in order to sabotage the research. And also, the self-declared, romantically-inclined red sports car buyers might have been affected by an unknown third variable which did not show up in the investigation.

In summary, a piece of experimental research in psychology requires five elements:

1 Grounds for theorising that a psychological relationship might exist between two variables.

2 The setting and justification of a hypothesis.

3 The collection of suitable and sufficiently controlled samples to be statistically significant in testing.

4 The analysis of the data in terms of the hypothesis.

5 The decision of whether to accept or reject the hypothesis.

In addition, as Figure 2.4 shows, the study must be objective, not subject to outside influences, structured to produce results that can predict future behaviour, and replicable for different groups and different occasions. Finally, the study must conform to ethical guidelines for acceptance within the professional community of psychologists, such as those of the British Psychological Society, the American Psychological Association and the Asian Psychological Association. These are considered at the end of this chapter. In this case, the investigators would have to obtain the written consent of the participants, guarantee participant anonymity and give participants as much information as possible on the purpose of the investigation before and after the study is carried out. **Briefing** and **debriefing** refer to the information given before and after the study. Deception at any stage is only permitted as a last resort and where the findings of the investigation are of significant importance to the advancement of the welfare of society.

Experimental psychology is also dealt with at greater length in Chapter 10. (You will have to carry out an experimental investigation as your internal assessment at both Higher and Standard Levels.)

It is important to point out that the above research could be classified as naturally experimental. There was no need to set up a scenario in either the natural environment, or in the artificial environment of the laboratory. It was based on self-reporting, on the already existing situation of 45-year-old men having bought both red sports cars and non-red sports cars. A good example of a **natural experiment** is the Charlton et al. (2002) study in Chapter 5 of the relationship between television viewing and violence. This contrasts with, for example, Bandura's very distinctly laboratory-based experimental research in the same area (Chapter 5).

True experimental research is laboratory-based. Both the environment and the situation are set up by the researcher. **Field experiments** that are based in the natural environment are **quasi-experimental**, in that the natural environment is already there. The researcher imposes the situation of the investigation on the pre-existing environment: the background scenario for both the test and the control already exist within the environment.

SELF-ASSESSMENT QUESTIONS 2.1

1 Distinguish between the following terms:

 a psychology, psychobabble and pop-psychology

 b quantitative research and qualitative research

   c empirical evidence and evidence from triangulation

   d experimental research and non-experimental research

   e independent variable (IV) and dependent variable (DV)

   f true experimental research and quasi-experimental research

   g Hawthorne effect and screw-you effect

2 List the elements required for an item of experimental research in psychology to be valid.

ACTIVITY 2.2

Re-read the sections on Uncle Jim, the midlife crisis and the red sports car. Study the associated questionnaire below.

QUESTIONNAIRE FOR THE RED SPORTS CAR

For the red sports car owners forming the test group.

Why did you choose the colour red for your sports car? Circle one number against each possible reason. 1 = not important at all. 2 = somewhat important. 3 = important. 4 = most important.

Red was the only car available	1	2	3	4
The colour red makes me feel young	1	2	3	4
The colour red makes me feel romantic	1	2	3	4
The colour red reminds me of _____ (fill in blank)	1	2	3	4
Other reason (state here) _____	1	2	3	4

For the non-red sports car owners forming the control group.

Which colour did you choose for your sports car? _____

Why did you choose that colour? Circle one number against each possible reason. 1 = not important at all. 2 = somewhat important. 3 = important. 4 = most important.

The colour chosen was the only car available	1	2	3	4
The colour makes me feel young	1	2	3	4
The colour makes me feel romantic	1	2	3	4
The colour reminds me of _____ (fill in blank)	1	2	3	4
Other reason (state here) _____	1	2	3	4

Figure 2.7 Questionnaire for the red sports car

1 State the hypothesis, the IV and the DV of the red sports car experimental research.

2 Why might the red sports car research be described as

   a experimental

   b natural experimental?

3 Suggest the strengths and the weaknesses of the red sports car investigation. What would your overall evaluation of that investigation be, and why?

It should be clear by now that studies in psychology are rooted in research that carries the appropriate methodology and ethical codes. They also need the support of learned associations in psychology, such as the Association for Psychological Science and the European Association for Research on Learning and Instruction, or the Association for Psychological Science. However, the fact that the study is accepted for publication in respected peer-reviewed publications does not mean that it is unchangeable. It is still subject to critical analysis. How far may the findings based on samples be generalised to whole populations? May the relationship found be generalised to other cultures?

Not all quantitative methods are experimental. Controls are not suitable for all investigations in psychology, for example in Milgram's famous research.

2.2.2 Non-experimental methods in quantitative psychology

Research study: Milgram (1961)

'The social psychology of this century reveals a major lesson: often it is not so much the kind of person a man is as the kind of situation in which he finds himself that determines how he will act.' (Stanley Milgram, 1974)

These words form the background theory of Stanley Milgram's famous research on obedience, which is widely regarded as the most famous and most shocking piece of psychological research in the 20th century. Obedience is the compliance with the commands of those in authority. Studies of obedience belong to the socio-cultural influence on behaviour, which is the subject of Chapter 5.

Stanley Milgram (1933–84)

Stanley Milgram (1933–84) was of Eastern-European Jewish immigrant origin. Of a political science academic background, his application to transition into social psychology at Harvard University at postgraduate level was initially turned down as his scholastic background did not include any psychology. His perseverance and subsequent success at Harvard led to his PhD in 1960 and an assistant professorship at Yale University, followed by a return to Harvard in a teaching capacity. His research on how obedience to authority figures can lead to extreme anti-social and indeed genocidal behaviours earned him a great deal of publicity. Allegedly because of this controversial research, described below, he was denied tenure at Harvard, and accepted an offer for a full professorship with tenure at the graduate college of City University, New York. Milgram died after a heart attack in December 1984.

Figure 2.8 Stanley Milgram

Background to the investigation

Milgram's work was a controversial experiment on the perils of obedience; what can happen if we always do as our authority figures tell us without question.

It was Milgram's background in both political science and psychology that led him to consider the Nazi atrocities against the Jews and other races which took place in the early years of his life. He believed that the Germans who had accepted Hitler as their leader had a fundamental character defect, which was that they obeyed those in authority without question. He initially wished to show that whereas American people followed their own concept of right and wrong, Germans did what they were told: orders were orders. That was the defence used by Nazi war criminals at the Nuremburg Trials of 1945: 'We were only acting under orders.' This defence also featured in the trial of leading Nazi Adolph Eichmann (1906–62). Because of his organisational talents and Nazi ideological reliability, Eichmann was ordered to manage the mass deportation of Jews to concentration camps and death camps in German-occupied Eastern Europe. His activities were key to making possible the extermination of six million Jews. Captured and tried in Israel in 1961, he was found guilty of planned mass murder, and Eichmann became the only person to have been judicially executed in the entire history of the state of Israel.

Eichmann's arguments used at his trial profoundly affected Milgram, and formed part of the background of his own famous research. Chief among Eichmann's defence was that he was a bureaucrat just acting out his duties under orders. Indeed Eichmann himself claimed that he had joined the Nazi SS to build a career rather than because he agreed with its outlook and methods.

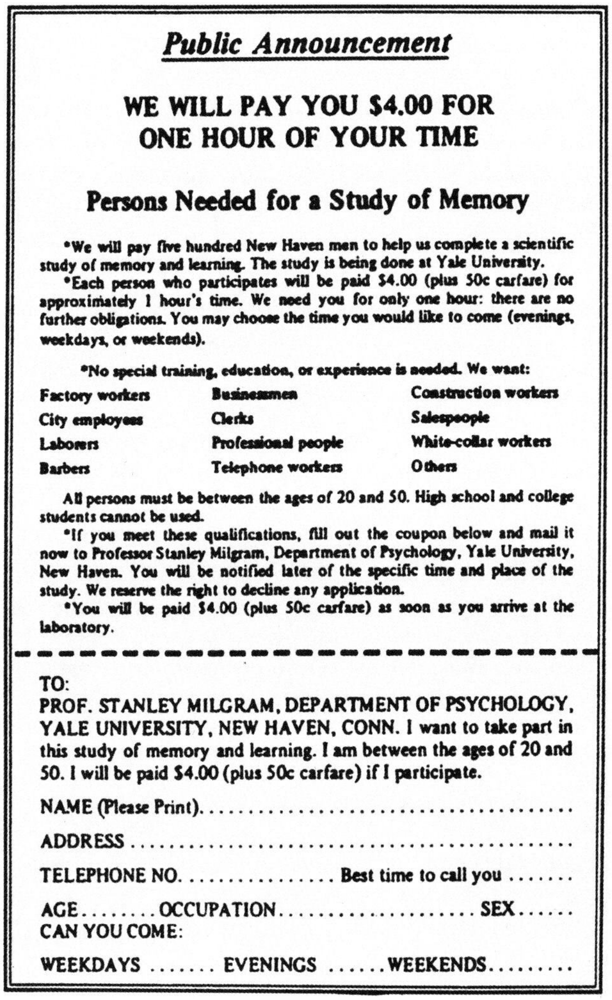

Public Announcement

WE WILL PAY YOU $4.00 FOR ONE HOUR OF YOUR TIME

Persons Needed for a Study of Memory

•We will pay five hundred New Haven men to help us complete a scientific study of memory and learning. The study is being done at Yale University.

•Each person who participates will be paid $4.00 (plus 50c carfare) for approximately 1 hour's time. We need you for only one hour: there are no further obligations. You may choose the time you would like to come (evenings, weekdays, or weekends).

•No special training, education, or experience is needed. We want:

Factory workers	Businessmen	Construction workers
City employees	Clerks	Salespeople
Laborers	Professional people	White-collar workers
Barbers	Telephone workers	Others

All persons must be between the ages of 20 and 50. High school and college students cannot be used.

•If you meet these qualifications, fill out the coupon below and mail it now to Professor Stanley Milgram, Department of Psychology, Yale University, New Haven. You will be notified later of the specific time and place of the study. We reserve the right to decline any application.

•You will be paid $4.00 (plus 50c carfare) as soon as you arrive at the laboratory.

TO:
PROF. STANLEY MILGRAM, DEPARTMENT OF PSYCHOLOGY, YALE UNIVERSITY, NEW HAVEN, CONN. I want to take part in this study of memory and learning. I am between the ages of 20 and 50. I will be paid $4.00 (plus 50c carfare) if I participate.

NAME (Please Print).....................................

ADDRESS...

TELEPHONE NO. .... Best time to call you ....

AGE........OCCUPATION..................... SEX......
CAN YOU COME:

WEEKDAYS .... EVENINGS ......WEEKENDS.........

Figure 2.9 An advertisement for Milgram's research

In the process, though, it was clear that he had lost his moral bearings, and the capacity to question others.

All this created the observational and theoretical elements that were vital to Milgram's research. The original plan was to test his 'Germans are different' hypothesis through a sample of regular German adults with no record of violent behaviour. He would put them into a position where they would be required to obey orders to carry out what appeared to be ultimate crimes against humanity, and observe how far they would comply. How far would people go in obeying an authority figure? His famous experiment at Yale University was intended to be a pilot study only, a rehearsal for his planned research in Germany.

In the event, the pilot study revealed that the 40 American male adults in Milgram's study were also likely to commit atrocities against innocent people. The hypothesis of 'Germans are different' was no longer followed. It was not that Germans were different from Americans. In that respect Americans were the same as the Germans. Perhaps mindless obedience to one's superiors was human nature. Milgram's situational experiments appeared to be able to arouse the same murderous behaviour among random American adults as in the German Nazis.

Aim

The study sought to investigate whether or not individuals would obey orders from an authority figure to inflict harm on another person in the form of electric shocks of graded severity.

Procedure

Forty male adults participated in Milgram's research. They were recruited by newspaper advertisements (see Figure 2.9), inviting people to come forward to take part in research on memory and learning. In exchange for their participation, each person received $4, a considerable sum in 1961 for just one hour's work.

Milgram produced an authentic-looking and convincing, but dummy, shock generator. Its levels of electric shock ranged from 30 volts to 450 volts, in 15-volt increments. The switches were categorised with the labels 'slight shock', 'moderate shock' and 'danger: severe shock'. The final two switches were labelled simply with an 'XXX' which left very little to the imagination. Participants took part individually, were directed according to the standardised procedures set out below and did not meet the other participants.

Each participant was directed through the same experience, the same course of action and in the same environment. On entering the psychology department at Yale University, the participant was introduced to experimenter Mr Williams. He was dressed in a laboratory coat. Mr Williams was specifically selected for his natural air of authority.

Each participant was also introduced to Mr Wallace, presented as someone who was also taking part in the research. The participant was told that his own role would be either 'teacher' or 'student', depending on which piece of paper he drew from a hat. Unknown to the participant, his role was always 'teacher', both pieces of paper being labelled thus, and Mr Wallace, whom most participants found pleasant and likeable, was always the 'student'.

Both the participant and Mr Wallace were then told that the purpose of the session was to study the effect of punishment on learning. The 'teacher' would be giving the punishment. The 'teacher' was given a 45-volt shock from the generator to clear up any doubt as to whether it was real. In fact it was the only shock that was actually delivered. Electrodes were then attached to the 'student' who by then had been moved next door, out of the teacher's sight. Mr Williams, the researcher working under Milgram's instructions, remained with the 'teacher' at the shock generator.

These procedures was set up as Milgram's pilot study was specifically designed to determine how much pain ordinary American people would cause to an innocent person when acting under orders. At what point would they stop and walk out of the study? The maximum level of shock given was the level at which the participant obeyed orders.

The 'teacher' was to read out a series of questions, to which the 'student' sometimes answered incorrectly.

Unknown to the participant, the 'student' (Mr Wallace) was a professional actor who had been scripted to plead for mercy, plead for release, complain about his heart being in danger, pound dramatically on the wall, and demand to be let out at 300 volts, and then to stop pounding and be silent after 315 volts. Any subsequent non-answering would be treated as a wrong response and would be duly punished with further increments of 15 volts, up to the highest level of 450 volts, marked 'XXX'.

During the procedure, most participants asked the Yale lab-coated researcher whether or not they should continue. The researcher issued a series of orders to ensure that the 'teacher' indeed did what the job required of him. The words were scripted, spoken calmly, firmly and with quiet authority. They were graded to urge the participant to carry on with the procedures, despite the 'student's' cries and begging for mercy:

1 Please continue.

2 The experiment requires that you continue.

3 It is absolutely essential that you continue.

4 You have no other choice, you must go on.

Figure 2.10 Licensed to kill under orders with 450 volts?

These were accompanied by the informative: 'Although the shocks will be painful, there is no permanent tissue damage, so please go on.'

Milgram observed the entire procedure for each of the 40 participants through a one-way mirror.

All participants were debriefed at the end of the session. Then, and only then, they were told the true purpose of the study, and their roles in it. And later on, Milgram carried out a survey of the participants and found that more than 80% were actually pleased to have been involved, and only one person expressed regret.

Results

How far indeed did most participants go? Before the research, Milgram asked his students (none of whom took part in his study) how many people out of a hundred would go all the way to giving the full 450 volts, whose label had lethal implications. His Yale students predicted only 3%. In fact, 26 out of 40 had delivered the killer voltage, to the highest point to which the switches would turn: a shocking 65% of the sample.

Many 'teachers' clearly showed anxiety, agitation and discomfort at what they were doing. But when told to 'please go on' by authoritative researcher Mr Williams in the laboratory coat, they did just that. These were the participants who were obedient irrespective of the orders. The other 16 refused to continue, though all had progressed to at least the 300 volts, whose intense shock had elicited the desperate cries and pounding on the wall from professional actor, 'student' Mr Wallace.

This 'pilot' study did not move on to Germany. Indeed, it was not that the Germans were different from the Americans. It was the other way round: the research had shown that the Americans were the same as the Germans. As Milgram observed after the experiment: 'Ordinary people, simply doing their jobs, and without any particular hostility on their part, can become agents in a terrible destructive process. Moreover, even when the destructive effects of their work become patently clear, and they are asked to carry out actions incompatible with fundamental standards of morality, relatively few people have the resources needed to resist authority.' (Milgram, 1974)

And this did not hold true for men only. Later studies including an all-female sample showed that their obedience rate was similar to that of the men.

Conclusion

On the basis of the findings of this research, Milgram put forward his **agency theory**. This means that our faith in those whom we regard as being experts and superiors causes us to put the entire moral responsibility on them when we carry out their instructions. In this case, the individual participants felt themselves as being under their experts and superiors for the following reasons:

- The work took place at the highly respected Yale University.
- The researcher was dressed professionally in a laboratory uniform.
- The researcher quietly and authoritatively maintained his air of superiority by calmly and firmly ordering the participant to continue to impose higher levels of electric torture for incorrect answers in the name of education.
- Despite the 'student's' cries, the 'teachers' accepted the researcher's assurances that the shocks were not dangerous.

It is this 'agentic state' of the participants in the research that indicated that the worst atrocities can be carried out by very ordinary people, as exemplified by the Nazi Holocaust.

On a more everyday level, Milgram distinguishes between being in an **autonomous state of mind** and an **agentic state of mind**. The autonomous state of mind is where we entirely make our own decisions and take full responsibility for the consequences. The agentic state of mind is where we obey those whom we accept as making decisions for us, such as parents, teachers and employers.

If the authority of the superior is weakened, the rate of obedience is likely to fall dramatically. Further investigations by Milgram indicated that the presence of participants who refused to accept the orders dramatically reduced obedience levels. When other people refused to go along with the experimenter's orders, 36 out of 40 participants refused to deliver the maximum shocks.

Evaluation of the investigation

How academically acceptable is Milgram's investigation? Research evidence in psychology is assessed by a balanced judgement that considers the identified strengths of the study against the identified weaknesses of the study. The validity of a piece of research in psychology is constantly evaluated in terms of strengths, limitations and the degree to which its findings may be generalised to other populations.

Strengths of the study

The strengths of the study were its **ecological validity**. Being ecologically valid means that the nature of the environment in which the research took place enables the findings to be more readily applied to real-life situations. The situation of obedience to 'higher and better-informed authority' in Milgram's work appeared to parallel members of death-camp squads, people serving in the military and employees. In all cases, authoritative and superior people were giving the instructions, and those carrying them out were merely employees serving as the employers' agents. The procedure was well-standardised and obedience was accurately measured in determining at what part the participating 'teacher' would stop. Also, the sample contained 40 people who had been selected from many applicants as being a cross-section of the male population aged 20–50.

Agency theory: putting the moral responsibility on people regarded as experts and superiors when carrying out their instructions. Connected to agentic state of mind.

Autonomous state of mind: where a person makes their own decisions and takes full responsibility for the consequences.

Agentic state of mind: where a person obeys without question those accepted as experts or superiors such as parents, teachers and employers. Connected to agency theory.

Ecological validity: where the nature of the environment in which the research takes place enables the findings to be more readily applied to real-life situations.

Figure 2.11 Adolph Eichmann stated that he was only following the wartime orders of his superiors and did not feel himself to be guilty.

Figure 2.12 The agentic state of mind can cause even this?

Limitations of the study

The obedience of 26 out of the 40 people was attributed to the authoritative and agentic situation. It could be argued that there were other non-related factors accounting for that high rate of obedience, such as the conformist nature of those who participated. Additionally, research on the Nazi Holocaust indicates that their enthusiastic participation in the atrocities was quite different from the situation of those having to be prodded by Milgram's experimenter. Eichmann was shown to have used his 'eliminationist anti-Semitism' as his prime motivation to deport millions of Jews to the Nazi death camps. Parallel justifications have been found for those responsible for the mass murders in Bosnia and Rwanda in the 1990s.

In addition, Milgram's work raised serious ethical problems. Milgram carried out the study without **informed consent**, as he deceived his participants in the true character of his research. His pressure on his participants to continue may be argued as taking away their ethical right to withdraw. It also appeared to have caused considerable distress to some participants. Despite debriefing, it could have led to long-term loss of self-esteem and feelings of guilt.

The work was professionally defended because of its extremely important implications in understanding murder and indeed genocide. It was claimed that deception was necessary, as the findings of the study could not have been obtained in any other way. In addition, Milgram argued that the results were entirely unexpected. He had not expected many participants to continue to the point where the apparent electrocution would be causing the student severe distress. In addition, people were not actually prevented from leaving the experiment at any point they wished.

Indeed, 84% of those taking part were very happy to have done so, with 75% reporting it to have been a valuable learning experience. And finally, all participants were examined one year later by a psychiatrist who reported that no participant had shown any signs of having been harmed.

Informed consent: an ethical requirement where participants should normally be made fully aware of the content and context of the research. Their decision on whether or not to take part must be based on full knowledge of the purpose of the work, and where their contribution fits in.

Critical thinking

1 How far may the fact that Milgram made his participants extremely uncomfortable be justified?

2 Why is Milgram's research considered so important in psychology? Is it less important today, bearing in mind that it was carried out about 50 years ago? Explain your answer.

3 Do you see subjects' willingness to administer shock in the Milgram study as the behavioural or moral equivalent of the Nazis' extermination of people in the death camps? Why?

RESEARCH IDEA

Milgram's research focused on the agentic state of mind.

1 Find out about the classic research on a similar theme by Philip Zimbardo (1971).

2 View the following two films:

Experimenter (2015) on Milgram's research

The Stamford Prison Experiment (2015) on Zimbardo's research.

3 Compare and contrast the methods used and the findings on the agentic state of mind in the two experiments.

4 What were the conclusions in each study?

5 How far do you agree with the conclusions on the basis of their findings?

6 Why in psychological research do we tend to say that the results 'indicate' or 'suggest', rather than 'prove'?

Methods commonly used in non-experimental quantitative research

The methods used most often in non-experimental quantitative research are

- observation such as in Milgram's study

- questionnaires.

These methods are not exclusive to non-experimental studies: in fact they may be employed in specific experimental work. Remember: what is not controlled is non-experimental.

Observation in quantitative research typically involves recording how many times a type of behaviour occurs in a particular environment. If you are counting how many times a teacher uses her favourite expression in a class, you are carrying out simple observation. If you are gathering observation-based information in researching how far primary (elementary) school children interact with children from different classes and genders, you are carrying out a more complex observation process. Observation is also used in modern brain-scanning techniques, described in Chapter 3, which can record the varied patterns in the brain as it processes different types of thinking. It may be **overt observation**, when those observed have given their consent. It may also be **covert observation**, which faces the ethical issues of deception and may only be waived when the researcher is suitably experienced, the investigation is of vital importance to understanding human behaviour and the information cannot be obtained in any other way. In other words, deception is only ethically supported when used for a good cause and as an absolutely last resort.

Overt observation: when those observed have given their consent.

Covert observation: when those observed do not know that they are being watched.

Figure 2.13 How far do primary school children interact with children from different classes and genders?

Questionnaires enable the participants in a study to report their reactions, thoughts, opinions and feelings in a manner that the researcher can quantify and apply statistical analysis. With quantitative studies, questionnaires commonly use semantic scales of the type described earlier in this chapter. Although the scores cannot be added up, they yield quantitative data which, like observation frequencies, may be statistically analysed. The questionnaire surveys, however, could produce inaccurate results due to problems inherent in self-reporting. It is possible that participants in the sample will be influenced by demand characteristics, meaning a tendency to give the answer they think the investigator wants, even if it is incorrect. Responses to questionnaire surveys also face cognitive issues in errors with memory recall, as detailed in Chapter 3.

Figure 2.14 How may the interviewer minimise the risk of obtaining incorrect information because of demand characteristics?

Correlation studies: collecting sufficient data on two or more variables to see if there is a direct or inverse relationship between them.

Standard deviation: measure of deviance from the mean that is calculated by finding the square root of the variance.

Correlation studies involve collecting sufficient data on two or more variables to see if there is a direct or inverse relationship between them. For example, the work of Perry and Pollard (1997) showed a negative correlation between the size of the brain of a three-year-old child and the degree of neglect suffered by that child. In this case, the ethical issues were reduced by the neglect having happened entirely in the past. The children suffered no neglect during his psychological investigation.

As emphasised earlier, whether the research is experimental or non-experimental, it uses mathematical data as long as it is quantitative. That means that the findings may be graphed in various ways. They may be summarised in the form of descriptive statistics, such as modes, medians, means, **standard deviations** from the mean and the degree of correlation between two or more variables. They may be tested for significance against the research hypotheses by means of statistical tests.

INTERNATIONAL FOCUS

Have you ever left your phone in a public place? Do you remember that sinking feeling of shock, and wondering whether you would ever see it again?

It depends where you are, according to the research of M.D. West (2005), who put it to the test in the crowded central business districts in two cities. The areas chosen were midtown Manhattan in New York and the Shinjuku district of Tokyo.

Procedure: In each location he dropped 100 phones and 20 wallets with $20 worth of cash inside.

Result: The degree of return was 77 phones and 8 wallets (2 empty) in New York; 95 phones and 17 wallets in Tokyo.

Conclusion: You have a better chance of seeing your property again in Tokyo than in New York.

Discussion: How might psychology explain the differences in the rates of honest behaviour in the two contrasting cultures?

Figure 2.15 Top: Manhattan, New York. Bottom: Shinjuku, Tokyo. Will you ever see your phone and your money again if you lose them here?

2.3 Qualitative research methods in psychology

The later chapters of this book contain research that is qualitative in nature, such as Rosenhan's investigation on correct diagnosis of insanity, in Chapter 6. This section briefly visits the workings of qualitative research in psychology in order to give the framework for the studies described in this book that use that type of research. Detailed and systematic treatment of qualitative research forms the subject matter of Chapter 10.

Qualitative research is based on the more extended and descriptive data that typically comes from personal journal entries, observations, case studies and interview transcripts. The information does not translate into figures. It is analysed on the basis of what the data reveals and implies, and on patterns within the data that are apparent to the researcher. It includes the use of content analysis, which is explored in Chapter 10.

Though quantitative methods are seen as the most scientific, qualitative studies are more suited to situations where the evidence relies on personal experience and emotions that are not easily captured in figures. Qualitative researchers aim to gather an in-depth understanding of human behaviour and the factors that influence behaviour. The main sources of qualitative data are:

- semi-structured interviews
- narrative interviews
- observations
- case studies.

These are typically conducted in a natural, ecologically valid setting.

Semi-structured interview: the use of both closed and open questions to enable the participant to develop responses made. Used in qualitative research.

Narrative interviews: the use of open questions to enable the participant to give detailed verbal responses. Used in qualitative research.

Semi-structured interviews involve the preparation of a list of bases that must be covered, typically using closed and open-ended questions. The closed questions get the participant to talk in a focused way, and the open ones enable them to expand and respond more freely. Open-ended questions tend to reveal deeper insights of the person's experiences of what is being investigated. The **narrative interview** could be on the lines of: 'Tell me what you thought when you were put in the situation and how you coped with it.' The respondents might focus on their coping mechanisms, and what changes the experience gave to their overall ways of coping with the stress. The results might be subjected to content analysis: finding patterns in the data.

Observations involve the detailed viewing of naturally occurring behaviour, in an ecologically natural environment. There exists the compromise between the level of intervention of the researcher, and the validity of the results beyond the specific observational setting. Detailed written observations and video-captured information might be subject to a content analysis, as above.

Case studies, as we have mentioned, involve investigating a few participants or even one participant in greater depth. In some research, as in the example below, there is only one participant who satisfies the criteria for the research. Among the problems involved is assessing how findings related to one or a few people may be generalised to wider populations. Two famous examples of case studies are HM (Henry Molaison) and Genie. HM is discussed in Chapter 3.

Case study: Genie

People have long wondered how and in what language a person will speak if totally deprived of stimuli – if they never have the opportunity to pick up a language from anyone else. Furthermore, is there an age where it becomes virtually impossible to subsequently pick up even a first language, at any rate to native-speaker standard? Susan Curtiss's study of Genie (1977) is a classic case study that partially addressed these questions. It involved one participant only. Indeed, Genie's situation was unique.

Genie was an American child raised in conditions of extreme isolation and deprivation until her discovery in 1970 at the age of 13 years and 7 months. Among other appalling treatment, Genie was beaten if she made any noise, and had learnt to suppress almost all vocalisations, except for a whimper. According to Curtiss, Genie was 'un-socialised, primitive, and hardly human'. Although

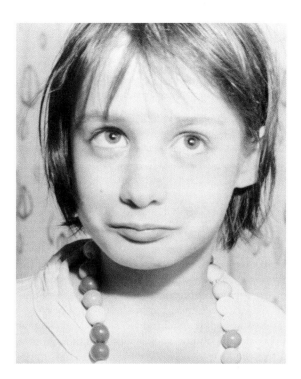

Figure 2.16 Genie

she could understand a handful of words, she essentially had to learn her first language at the age of 14. The case study showed that she had never developed normal language skills, and by age 18, she could only produce short sentences that were grammatically incorrect, including incorrect use of pronouns. Her vocabulary subsequently expanded, but her intonation remained comprehensible only to those who knew her, and Genie herself had great difficulty in understanding complex syntax. The fact that Genie could learn any language at all weakens the claim that there is a critical age-bound period for language learning. However, her linguistic problems extending into adulthood do imply that childhood is the optimal period for language learning.

A series of legal battles between different parties with interests in Genie, including social services, relatives, foster homes and academics, have placed Genie out of touch with the psychology community. Recently turned 60, her last location at the time of writing was in an adult care institution for people with learning difficulties in southern California.

This study was based on Genie's environment and was thus ecologically valid. In this case, it was the only opportunity of studying the effect of total sensory deprivation in childhood on language learning at an older age, as the circumstances of Genie were unique. The study of Genie is a **longitudinal study**, in that it continued for a long period: Genie had been observed over a number of years. The ethical issues are minimised by Genie's sensory deprivation having been completely in the past by the time she had been brought to Curtiss's notice. The study was, however, restricted to that unique case. That raises the question of how far the findings in Genie may be generalised to the process of language learning.

Longitudinal study: research continuing with the same participants for an extended period, typically months or years.

Evaluating qualitative research

The case of Genie indicates that qualitative analysis has the strength of being adaptable to investigating complex and sensitive issues, such as living in a violent relationship. It frequently provides in-depth experience of interest to the psychologist that is not easily obtained by quantitative methods. It helps to explain phenomena, for example why relationships break up. It seeks to identify and evaluate factors that may contribute to solving a problem, such as which initiatives might help couples sustain their relationships. Moreover, it tends towards high ecological validity, as participants typically respond in the context of their own environment.

Additionally, qualitative analysis can allow the researcher to interpret reality on the basis of information that is obtained in the research. This contrasts with quantitative research, whose conclusions are based on its design and methods of data analysis. The strengths and limitations of two approaches to research are considered in more detail in Chapter 10.

This form of analysis can involve time-consuming interviews and observations. It can generate large amounts of textual data, making it difficult to identify patterns. And finally, there are issues in data analysis being **reflexive** and lacking an impartial quantitative, statistical framework.

These themes are dealt with at greater length in Chapter 10.

Reflexive: where the research may be influenced by the viewpoint of the researcher.

2.4 Evaluating theories and research in psychology

Psychology differs from other sciences in that it is not characterised by laws. It does contain principles, which are subject to constant critical review in the light of the most recent findings. Theories are supported or weakened by the findings of research studies. For example, the theory that people obey even the most bizarre orders when those giving them are in positions of high authority would appear to be supported by the research of Milgram. However, this is a theory only, not a law. It does not apply to all individuals. Indeed, Milgram did not claim that every person would impose the maximum or even a minimum amount of pain on an innocent person when acting under orders.

All work in psychology is subject to evaluation, and re-evaluation in the light of further research. Any theory or piece of research is constantly evaluated in terms of strengths and limitations, and overall assessment of its validity and degree can be generalised. As an IB student, much of your work in psychology involves critically evaluating the theories and research that you meet.

As an example, let us return to the simple theoretical relationship theorised by Milgram, which is: 'People of all types obey even the most bizarre orders when those giving them are in positions of high authority.' The following criteria may be applied in assessing how far that theory and its associated research are valid:

1   Is it possible to test the theory through research? Milgram's work was a pioneer piece of research in the field. His initial study of 1963 was repeated 18 times with variations over the next few years.

2   Is it possible to test the theory scientifically, on the basis of empirical data? Was the sampling method appropriate to the research? Empirical data is gathered in suitable quantities from experiments, observations or questionnaires. It is then verified as far as possible with statistical tests, and/or comparison with existing published research. Milgram's 1963 research employed a sample of 40 American males aged 20 to 50, from very different walks of life. The observation was straightforward. It simply required the recording of the stage at which each participant refused to continue carrying out the researcher's orders.

3   Are the theory and associated research practically useful? Milgram's findings from his initial and subsequent research have been applied to understanding how regular members of the law-abiding public became involved in mass-murder programmes in the Balkans and in Rwanda in the 1990s.

4   Is the research associated with the theory ethically acceptable? Professional ethical guidelines have become considerably stricter over the last half-century. A modern ethics review board might well withhold approval on the grounds of the deception involved and the distress likely to be suffered by those taking part. Lack of ethical support would mean that the study would not be published in academic circles, and therefore would not be admitted to psychology.

5   How far is the research ecologically valid? Could the behaviour shown by the participants in Milgram's work be due to the peculiarities of the laboratory at Yale University, and the perceived demand characteristics? If so, could they be less applicable as explanations of real-life involvement in killings and genocide?

Furthermore, Milgram's research has not been fully tested cross-culturally. It might be argued that people are less compliant to authority in at least some parts of the world. They are more likely to walk out if they feel 'cognitive dissonance' (mental conflict and discomfort) in the task they are ordered to carry out. In addition, Milgram's work would almost certainly not be repeated for verification today. That would be due to ethical considerations and the fact that Milgram's research is common public knowledge, particularly through its appearance in popular films, such as *The City and the Self* (Stanley Milgram and Harry From, 1972), and *Experimenter* (2015).

A word of caution. You will almost certainly meet theories and research in psychology that you strongly disagree with, and will immediately want to counter with words like 'ecologically invalid', 'does not show cause and effect' or even 'it is politically motivated', 'it is sexist', 'it is racist', etc. You should avoid this. If you feel that the research is ecologically invalid, show precisely why the laboratory situation did not resemble the real-life situation that it was designed to simulate. If you feel that the correlation study that indicated that an increase in variable A meant a decrease in variable B was incorrect, you will have to justify it. You cannot just dismiss it as 'not necessarily showing cause or effect'. You might, however, make a reasoned suggestion for the reality being much more complex. For example, variable A influences C and D which in turn affect B, rather than variable A directly influences B. And if C and D are not present, there will be no significant relationship between A and B.

Remember that any published research that you study will have almost certainly been approved for academic publication by leading professional organisations in psychology, such as the American Psychological Association (APA) and the Asian Psychological Association (APsyA). The researchers are typically highly experienced, with international reputations in their field. Bear that in mind as you evaluate their work and contributions to the subject. In short, your criticisms should be based on informed judgement rather than on unsupported opinion.

SELF-ASSESSMENT QUESTIONS 2.2

1 Distinguish between the autonomous state of mind and the agentic state of mind. Which term would best describe the participants in Milgram's 1961 research in the light of the conclusions, and why?

2 Identify two strengths and two limitations of Milgram's research.

3 Define the following terms in the context of Curtiss's study of Genie:

   a qualitative study

   b longitudinal study

   c content analysis

   d reflexivity

2.5 Ethical considerations

Research in psychology is required to conform to the code of professional ethics in order to be academically acceptable.

Like all professions, psychology is regulated by a code of conduct that must be satisfied in every piece of research. Its purpose is to prevent unacceptable exploitation of those participating. It is also designed to reassure participants that their privacy and well-being will be respected and safeguarded as far as reasonably possible. That can sometimes have serious consequences for the psychologist. For example, a participant in a qualitative study can go through a long series of time-consuming interviews. The participant is guaranteed anonymity. The participant initially feels comfortable at interview, and reveals information which might be very sensitive and deeply personal. Later on, there are feelings of remorse: 'How could I tell those things to a complete stranger?'

The code of ethics rules that the participant has the right of withdrawal at any stage. If the participant withdraws, the psychologist may not use the information revealed, however useful it is, and however many hours were spent in getting it. It is one of the occupational hazards of research in psychology.

Breaches of ethical rules will, at the very least, result in that research not being published in the professional literature of any regulating academic body in psychology. In addition, the psychologist involved will be putting his or her own professional reputation at serious risk.

Over the last half-century, the ethical codes in psychology have become more stringent and more heavily enforced. Ethical codes have more recently been extended to protect animals used in research from undue suffering and exploitation. Remember that much important investigation work on, for example, hormone injections would be forbidden to try out on humans. But under certain very closely-defined conditions, it could be used on animals, which possess many similar characteristics to humans.

The main ethical guidelines for research with human participants include informed consent, avoidance of deception, protection of participants, the right to withdraw at any stage, debriefing and confidentiality:

1   All participants must give their informed consent. They have to be aware of the content and context of the research. Their decision on whether or not to take part must be based on full knowledge of the purpose of the work, and where their contribution fits in. Children taking part must have their parents' consent.

2   There must be no deception. Participants must not be deceived at any stage of the study. They have to be briefed before the research and debriefed afterwards. However, appropriate degrees of deception may be used where the investigation is of great importance to the understanding of human behaviour. Even so, it has to be kept to a minimum, and may only be used when the information could not be obtained in any other way.

3   Participants must be protected. This includes being safe from physical and psychological pain, and invasion of privacy. That includes covert observation, unless the study's importance justifies it and the information cannot be obtained in any other way.

4   All participants have the right to withdraw during and also after the study. They have the right to insist that their contributions are not used.

Figure 2.17 What message do you think her body language is communicating?

5   All participants must be assured that their input is kept anonymous to the degree that their contribution to the research does not make it possible for others to trace their identity. That can cause serious limitations in follow-up work, and also in peer review (critical assessment of one psychologist's work by others in the field).

6   Research with animals may take place only where the information may not be obtained in any other practical way, where stress and pain is minimised, where the researcher is trained in the field of the use of animals in research, and where the entire project has been given the approval of an ethical governing body.

7   Where research involves members of ethnic groups, due attention should be given to their particular cultural sensitivities. This will often require liaising and working in full co-operation with their elders if appropriate.

Assessing research studies in all branches of psychology includes the ethical considerations as a matter of course. As an IB student, you will have to ensure that your internal assessment research project is ethically acceptable, including obtaining the participants' consent, briefing, informing them of the right to withdraw, and debriefing them at the end. These elements are considered in Chapter 10, which focuses on the internal assessments at both Higher and Standard Levels.

SELF-ASSESSMENT QUESTIONS 2.3

1   State six ethical guidelines for research with human participants.

2   Which is more likely to be in breach of ethical guidelines, overt observation or covert observation? When might its use nevertheless be justified?

ACTIVITY 2.2

Assess the ethical acceptability of the following pieces of research by today's standards, as detailed above.

a   the mock 'red sports car' research

b   Milgram's research.

You should assess the research using the following six headings: informed consent, no deception, protection of participants, right to withdrawal, guarantee of anonymity, and cultural sensitivities. You may then discuss your findings with a partner.

Chapter summary

1 The principles and research in psychology are distinguished from general interest in human behaviour by being supported by evidence of professionally-suitable standing.

2 Research in psychology uses tools from the range of quantitative methods, qualitative methods, or both.

3 Experimental research is distinguished by having a test population and a control population. They are identical except for changing the nature of the IV in the test population. If the research is not controlled, it is non–experimental.

4 The validity of a piece of research in psychology is constantly evaluated in terms of strengths, limitations and the degree to which its findings may be generalised to other populations.

5 Research in psychology is required to conform to the code of professional ethics in order to be academically acceptable.

The biological approach to understanding human behaviour

3

'Serotonin and dopamine are technically the only two things
you will ever enjoy.'
(source unknown)

KEY QUESTIONS

- What does our increasing knowledge of the different parts of the brain contribute to understanding human behaviour?
- How does knowledge of the nervous and endocrine systems help the understanding of human behaviour?
- What are the roles of evolution and genetics in influencing human behaviour?
- In what ways can knowledge of biological influences on animal behaviour be applied to explain human behaviour? (HL only)

Learning objectives

- Outline principles that define the biological approach to understanding human behaviour. (AO1)
- Outline the roles played by different parts of the brain, the nervous system and the endocrine system in influencing human behaviour. (AO1)
- Examine the ways that genes are regulated and behaviourally expressed. (AO2)
- Assess the evidence indicating genetically based determinants of human behaviour. (AO3)
- Evaluate the degree to which the findings from animal research may be applied to the understanding of human behaviour. (AO3) (HL only)
- Discuss the ethical considerations involved in animal research for the specific purpose of understanding human behaviour. (AO3) (HL only)

3.1 Overview of the biological approach to understanding human behaviour

In the nature-nurture debate, the biological approach tends towards nature-based explanations of human behaviour. It focuses on hereditary influences and the individual-specific workings of the **brain**, nervous system and hormone system. In addition, the Higher Level extension considers what animal-based studies have to contribute to our understanding of human behaviour.

The biological approach to understanding behaviour focuses on the combination of two essentials:

- It views particular behaviours. Examples include loss of temper, falling in love and criminal activity.

- It considers **biological phenomena**. Examples include genetic information, the various parts of the brain's intensity of engagement and the levels of **hormones** in the bloodstream.

This approach considers the degree to which behaviours correlate with biology. It strives to examine the ways in which the individual's genes, hormones and nervous system influence behaviour. In the nature-nurture debate, the biological level of analysis strongly emphasises the nature side. Of course, we tend to copy actions, manners and skills from those around us. But the precise way that we do it and to what degree of success, are influenced by our physiology.

This chapter explores the brain and behaviour, hormones and behaviour, genetics and behaviour and, for Higher Level students, the role of research on animals in understanding human behaviour. It considers researchers' use of increasingly sophisticated technology, and at the same time bears in mind the associated ethical issues.

However, much of the data obtained by such an approach is correlational, which does not show cause and effect. For example, a 14-year-old student has exceptionally effective spatial abilities. A brain scan shows an unusually high concentration of nerves in the parts of brain involved in these activities. Was that mental development a product of extensive travel experience which influenced development of the brain's spatial skills, or have natural selection and genes determined the brain's superb geographical capabilities?

Put more generally: does our psychology affect our biology (genes, hormones and nervous system), or does our biology affect our psychology? Or can it be both ways, the relationship between biology and behaviour being a complex one of mutual causality (that both can cause the other)?

Brain: the part of the central nervous system that is enclosed within the skull.

Biological phenomena: the forms that a group or category of living organisms may take.

Hormones: biochemical substances produced by glands within the endocrine system, carried in the bloodstream. Hormones bio-determine the way the body synchronises and adjusts to specific stimuli and conditions.

Figure 3.1 Do we control our genes?

There are psychologists who believe that the biological level of analysis is the dominant field in explaining human behaviour. They believe that cognitive and socio-cultural influences are strictly guided by our own physiology. Thus they will argue that a child will become whatever they will be, despite the influences of parental upbringing and the school attended. For example, the reason that Mateo married Sara is not because Sara is so much like his mother, but because Mateo's genetic structure led him to the same type of woman that his father chose. That would be a biological deterministic, reductionist argument.

It could, however, be argued that Mateo's choice was based on his growing love for his mother. His brain adapted to the norms that he admired in his mother's behaviour. To varying degrees, our biology adapts to the choices that we make and our developing thinking. This is the process of **brain plasticity**, a phenomenon explored later in this chapter.

Today, there is a growing trend to combine biological explanations of behaviour with cognitive and socio-cultural ones. This is the more holistic approach, which is complex and integrative. For example, the reason that Mateo chose to marry Sara was not only because she was the same type of person that his father chose (genetic influences) or due to his growing admiration of his mother's attitudes and behaviours (brain plasticity influences), but because he enjoys her company and finds her physically attractive (see cognitive influences in Chapter 4), and he is pleased that their religion, outlook, interests and circles of friends are compatible (see socio-cultural influences in Chapter 5).

Brain plasticity: the capacity of the central nervous system to develop additional neurons in response to a person's persistent efforts to develop a specific skill.

NEWSFLASH

The Jim twins meet after 39 years!

9 February 1979 was a special day for Jim Lewis. He knew that he had a twin brother and that his unmarried mother had them adopted by different families in Ohio, USA when they were only one month old. After years of searching through court records, he found his twin brother, Jim Springer.

Apart from both twins being named James with a nickname of Jim, they had many other things in common. Both men has chosen identical jobs and worked as sheriffs. They had both been married twice, with a first wife called Linda and a second called Betty. Each twin had a dog during childhood, with the name of Toy. They has chosen the same style of bright blue Chevrolet car. Both chose to take vacations at Pas Grille Beach, Florida. In addition, both twins suffered from regular migraines.

This case, discovered by Bouchard et al. (1990) during the Minnesota twin study, is considered later in this chapter.

Figure 3.2 Twins Jim Lewis and Jim Springer meet at last.

Endocrine system: the biochemical messenger system responsible for generating, releasing and distributing hormones.

Cortisol: a neurohormone active in adapting to stress through pain reduction and improved physical and mental activity, although prolonged high levels weaken immunity to disease.

ACTIVITY 3.1

Using the Newsflash above:

1   Suggest explanations for the similarities between the two Jims.

2   No other pair of twins in the 100+ pairs taking part in the Minnesota twin study showed quite the same degree of similarity. How far does this information modify your response to question 1?

The biological approach to understanding human behaviour has a set of underlying principles and research methodologies that we will introduce in turn.

3.1.1 Principles of the biological approach to the behaviour of individuals

The strengths of the biological approach to the behaviour of individuals include its relatively high scientifically-based credibility, and its associated methodology leaning towards the experimental and the quantitative. It contributes to an understanding of a wide range of phenomena, such as why progress in a difficult skill comes with dedicated practice, why certain groups of people tend to suffer discriminatory behaviour, and what makes people fall in and out of love.

The biological approach to behaviour has effective practical application, such as the use of medication in treating mental conditions. It is nature-based, putting forward strong arguments in the nature-nurture debate. The main principles of the biological level of analysis include:

1 There are biological correlates to behaviour. As already discussed, there is a relationship between our nervous and **endocrine systems**, and the way we feel and behave.

   For example, when we are under stress the body secretes **cortisol**, a major strain-coping neuro-hormone. This hormone helps our nervous system to deal with the current pressures and anxieties. However, cortisol is known to interfere with memory recall. Increased cortisol levels can explain why people get memory blanks, for example, when experiencing stress during an examination, even when they know the material perfectly.

2 Research on animal behaviour can be relevant to understanding human behaviour. This concept is based on the shared physiological characteristics of humans and animals. The approach is grounded in the evolutionary relationship between humans and animals. Current research indicates that chimpanzee DNA is 99% similar to human DNA, with rat DNA slightly less at 98%. This principle is explored through the research studies that appear in several sections of this chapter. The detailed study of the specific role of animal research in human behaviour is a Higher Level requirement only.

3 There is some genetic basis to individual behaviour patterns. Currently, we do not know enough about genetics to identify accurately the types of behaviour promoted by specific genes, although there has been considerable progress in this field over the last two decades. Much of our knowledge of genetics and behaviour comes from studies of the rare instances where twins are brought up separately in completely different environments. These are discussed later in this chapter, in considering evolutionary explanations of behaviour.

4 The biological approach to understanding human behaviour is grounded in the working of two systems, which, as we will see, interact with each other. Detailed knowledge of these systems enables psychologists to understand the mechanisms we use in picking up, processing and reacting to **stimuli** and information. The systems are:

   a The nervous system, consisting of the brain, **spinal cord** and **neurons**. Its major component is the brain itself. Psychologists focus on the workings of different parts of the brain to understand human behaviour. They also study **neural networks** and **neurotransmitters**, which together communicate stimuli and information from one neuron to another, and to and from the brain. Neurotransmitters are substances found in the terminal buttons of the neuron, and are biochemical in structure. They enable stimuli to be processed and reacted to by the **central nervous system (CNS)** (brain and spinal cord).

   b The endocrine system, which functions through hormone**s**. These biochemical substances are released by the various **ductless glands** (e.g. adrenal gland, pineal gland), and are carried through the bloodstream to where they are most needed. Some hormones also function as neurotransmitters, such as **dopamine** and **oxytocin**.

Stimuli: anything that may excite sensory receptors of the nervous system.

Spinal cord: the thick band of nervous tissue that extends downwards from the brain through the spine, forming the central nervous system together with the brain.

Neurons: nerve cells found in both the central and peripheral nervous systems.

Neural networks: a system of interconnecting neurons, for example within the brain.

Neurotransmitters: biochemical substances that travel across the synapses of nerve cells that carry the specific stimuli to the next cell. They are powered by the electricity that the body naturally generates.

Central nervous system (CNS): the part of the nervous system composed of the brain and spinal cord.

Ductless glands: glands that secrete hormones directly into the bloodstream; also known as endocrine glands.

Dopamine: a neurotransmitter that helps to control the brain's reward and pleasure centres. Increased dopamine levels in the brain mean increased pleasurable stimulation.

Oxytocin: a hormone that is discharged through the pituitary gland into the bloodstream, which promotes feelings of love, trust and acceptance of one another. It is also a neurotransmitter.

Brain functions: the multitude of voluntary and involuntary roles that the brain carries out, ranging from controlling heartbeat rate to deep thinking and decision-making.

We have already noted that the exclusive emphasis on biological explanations of behaviour is a reductionist physiological approach. For example, behaviours associated with falling in love are not only influenced by the workings of **brain functions**, neurotransmitters and hormones, but also have cognitive and socio-cultural-based explanations. These are considered in Chapter 7, the optional topic which considers the psychology of human relationships. A holistic, integrative approach, as opposed to a reductionist approach, seeks to balance the physiological explanations and treatments with those from other levels of analysis.

3.1.2 Research methods used in the biological approach to the behaviour of individuals

The leading methods of investigation used within the biological approach to behaviour are laboratory experiments, correlation studies and case studies.

Laboratory experiments

Laboratory experiments at the biological level of analysis are designed to establish the cause and effect relationship. For example, an experiment may investigate whether high levels of the stress-coping cortisol hormone have a negative effect on the memory. Put simply, does the cortisol hormone make us forget things when we are stressed out?

Experimental research involves a hypothesis that may or may not be accepted on the basis of the subsequent findings. The experimental framework includes at least two samples: a test sample and a control sample. The conditions are the same for the test and the control, except that the independent variable (IV) is changed for the test sample. The control sample might be given a **placebo**, a harmless pill, medicine or procedure that the patient incorrectly believes will produce a specific physiological effect. And ethical considerations involving consent and deception have to be addressed satisfactorily for the research study to be accepted.

Placebo: intervention that is designed to have no effect. Any effect that does take place is attributed to a person's expecting a change to take place.

The use of laboratory experiments is exemplified by Baumgartner et al. (2008) (see Section 3.3.1) on the effect of oxytocin on behaviour in economic decision-making. Like all experimental research, it involved a test sample and a control sample to determine the acceptance or rejection of a hypothesis.

Correlation studies

Correlation studies investigate the nature and degree of the relationship between two sets of values.

Correlation studies are exemplified by the work of Perry (1997) who studied the brain development of physically and socially deprived Romanian orphans. Based on brain scans, he found a negative correlation between two variables: the size of the brain and the degree of child neglect. This study indicates that good-quality parental care assists a child's mental development.

Case studies

Case studies typically focus on the condition of one person over a period of time, the findings on whom might be generalised to similar conditions occurring in other people, for example a person's behaviour before and after an accident that caused brain damage, such as HM (Henry Molaison, 1926–2008). Case studies tend to be longitudinal (taking place over an extended time period), relying on regular interviews and observations. In addition, the uniqueness of the details of each case means that greater safeguards are required to protect the participants' anonymity. For example, HM was referred to by initials throughout his lifetime, keeping his identity a secret until he donated his brain to scientific research. Also, the very uniqueness of such studies raises the question of how far the findings may be generalised.

We will now consider how the psychology-related workings of the brain, nervous system and endocrine system affect behaviour.

3.2 The brain and behaviour

Our understanding of the brain is progressing rapidly. **Brain function localisation** – the notion that different parts of the brain carry out different physical and psychological functions – has been known since the mid-19th century.

Brain function localisation: the idea that different parts of the brain perform different functions.

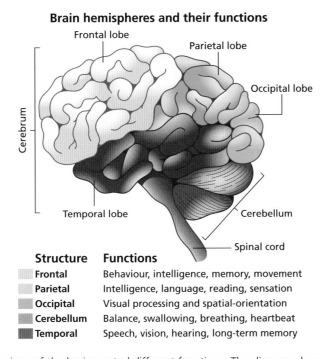

Brain hemispheres and their functions

Structure	Functions
Frontal	Behaviour, intelligence, memory, movement
Parietal	Intelligence, language, reading, sensation
Occipital	Visual processing and spatial-orientation
Cerebellum	Balance, swallowing, breathing, heartbeat
Temporal	Speech, vision, hearing, long-term memory

Figure 3.3 The regions of the brain control different functions. The diagram shows the side view.

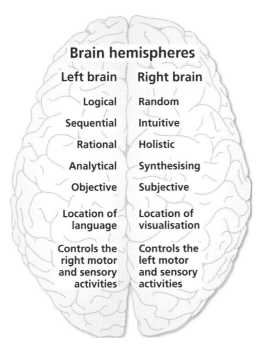

Figure 3.4 The regions of the brain control different functions. The diagram overlooks the top surface of the brain.

47

Brain function lateralisation: the tendency for specific neural and cognitive functions to be more dominant in one brain hemisphere than in the other.

Closely associated is **brain function lateralisation**, where either the left- or the right-brain hemisphere is dominant in a particular physical or psychological function. Left-brain functions include language, and precise and logical reasoning; right-brain functions include intuition, aesthetics and creativity.

Simplified, there are three concentric layers, starting at the central core of the brain and moving outwards. The central core regulates involuntary physical and psychological processes, the next layer controls the limbic system which handles emotions, and the outer cerebrum handles the higher mental processes, which are divided into left-brain and right-brain lateralised.

3.2.1 Methods of investigating the brain's roles in behaviour

The notion of brain function localisation dates back to 1848, with Harlow's famous case study of Phineas Gage.

Case study: Phineas Gage

Gage was a railway foreman worker, supervising the building of the railway route of the Rutland and Burlington Railroad outside Cavendish, Vermont, USA. The powder that was being used in carving out the railway cutting suddenly exploded, which sent a three-centimetre-wide metal pole right through his head. The pole had travelled cleanly through his left cheek, the base of his skull, the forward portion of the left frontal lobe of the brain, and exited through his left eye and through the top of his head. It landed around 25 metres away.

Gage survived the accident. Though blinded in his left eye, he seemed to be able to carry on working as normal. Neither his speech nor his movements had been affected by the passage of the metal pole. However, his character suddenly changed. Previously he behaved like a gentleman, earning a reputation as a popular, respected, hard-working and responsible railway foreman. But after the accident, the railway company refused to employ him in that capacity. Though his physical capabilities (apart from his sight) were unaffected, his mental capabilities were greatly affected. His intellectual level was reduced to that of a child and his ability to control his behaviour to a socially acceptable level was totally diminished. Phineas Gage caused much excitement in the medical profession. His behavior changes after the accident demonstrated that the frontal lobes of the brain strongly influence personality.

His skull is at Harvard University. It has been studied by modern neurologists linking the reports of his behavior with recent discoveries in the workings of the brain, such as Tyler R & K (1982), and more recently Van Horn et al. (2012).

Broca area: part of the brain responsible for speech production, located in the left frontal lobe of the brain.

Broca's aphasia: impaired ability to produce speech, yet able to understand speech.

For the next few generations, brain function localisation studies relied entirely on patients with pre-existing brain injuries. Broca (1861) specialised in investigating the effect of stroke on human mental capacities. His most famous study included a young man who had suffered a stroke, and was nicknamed 'Tan', because that was the only word he seemed able to pronounce in his present condition. 'Tan' had no difficulty understanding speech, but he could not talk. He had the capacity for language comprehension, but not speech production. An autopsy after his death showed that the area damaged by the stroke was within the left frontal lobe of the brain. Indeed, the area of the brain that gives the function of being able to talk is named the **Broca area**. Its non-functioning, as in the case of 'Tan', is referred to as **Broca's aphasia**.

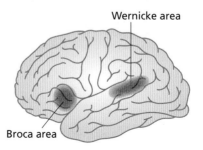

Figure 3.5 The Broca area and the Wernicke area. The diagram shows the side view of the brain.

Wernicke (1874) worked on cases that complemented those of Broca: individuals who, following a stroke, were still able to talk but could not understand what was being said. Autopsies after the deaths of those patients showed that the part of the brain damaged by the stroke was the left posterior superior temporal gyrus. The area of the brain that gives the function to be able to understand speech is named the **Wernicke area**. Its non-functioning is referred to as **Wernicke's aphasia**.

Information obtained from those pioneering cases was foundation material for mapping the brain. Taking part in a conversation activates both the Broca area and the Wernicke area – two very different parts of the brain – and also the very complex connections between them, as well as the auditory nerves and speech muscles.

Case study: HM

However, the case of HM indicates that functions of the brain do not appear to be confined to single locations. HM fell off a bicycle at the age of seven and suffered an injury which was believed to be causing his subsequent, continued serious epileptic seizures. In 1957, doctors removed the tissue from the temporal lobe of the brain (there was no effective drug treatment at the time), including much of the hippocampus. Following the operation, HM could recall information acquired early in life, but he could not form new memories; a case of **anterograde amnesia**. HM's brain was scanned in 1997, showing that the areas that had been damaged included the hippocampus and **amygdala** regions. The fact that HM's memory functioned at all indicated that memory functions are more widely distributed throughout the brain than previously thought, and not just in these two regions.

Brain-scanning techniques

Major breakthroughs in attempting to locate brain functions began in the 1960s with the innovation of electronic brain-scanning techniques. This made it possible for researchers to see images of the soft tissue inside the skull while the person was alive. No autopsy was needed. **Electroencephalography (EEG)** began to be developed in the 1950s, which included EEG topography that made it possible to study the electrical activity taking place across the surface of the brain. **Computerised tomography (CT)** was introduced in the 1960s and 1970s. In practice, this focusing of X-ray beams to give an overall static picture of the brain is used to identify **lesions** (damage to the brain) and atypical structures within the brain. It was succeeded by the higher resolution, second-generation **magnetic resonance imaging (MRI)**, which in turn is continuing to give way to third generation, very expensive **positron emission tomography (PET)** and **functional magnetic resonance imaging (fMRI)**. These two systems not only give details of the brain as it is, but are able to trace activity within the brain, including which parts of the brain are operating when a person is performing a specific task.

PET and fMRI have shown that the different patterns in brain activities are extremely multi-dimensional, with various parts of the brain being coordinated to varying degrees of intensity. The extremely complex brain mapping rules out, for the most part, a single part of the brain being exclusively responsible for a specific function.

The range of brain-scanning techniques continues to develop. Each has its own strengths and limitations. Apart from suitability for the particular task, their use is constrained by cost and availability.

These electronic methods are among the most common techniques used today in researching the way the workings of the brain influence behaviour, and their use will be exemplified in the study below. However, observations from autopsy, stroke, accident victims and brain surgery patients have also contributed to understanding the brain and behaviour, as exemplified by the case study of HM.

Research study: Harris and Fiske (2006)

Like many modern research studies of the workings of the brain, this study on defining the parts of the brain that determine attitudes and resultant behaviours towards others used fMRI. This highly complex technology uses a magnetic field and radio signals to observe a specific process taking place in the blood flow within the different parts of the brain. The process takes place in the haemoglobin (the protein content of the blood) that carries and releases oxygen. The more active the part of the brain, the more oxygen it uses, and the greater the amount of oxygen that will be released. The fMRI scanner sends a series of radio-frequency magnetic pulses that reorientate the hydrogen atoms in the brain. The speed at which they come back to where they were is a measure of the degree of oxygenated haemoglobin in that part of the brain.

Wernicke area: the part of the brain that processes the meaning of language, located in the rear of the brain.

Wernicke's aphasia: impaired ability to understand speech, yet able to produce speech.

Anterograde amnesia: being unable to form new memories after brain damage, but still able to recall memories made before the brain damage.

Amygdala: the part of the brain that integrates basic emotions, emotional behaviour and motivation.

Electroencephalography (EEG): a brain-scanning technique where a large number of electrodes are attached to the head, making it possible to record impulses from the top layers of the brain.

Computerised tomography (CT): scanning technique in which ionised dye is injected in the blood to highlight specific brain tissue. The tissue is then scanned to create an image.

Lesion: a structural alteration to tissues or organs caused by disease or injury.

Magnetic resonance imaging (MRI): a brain-scanning method that monitors the electromagnetic energy released by the brain after it has been exposed to a magnetic field.

Positron emission tomography (PET): an electronic technique that images processes in the brain. Its mechanism is based on the injection of radioactive material into the bloodstream, and the monitoring of the decay-emitted positrons in the brain.

The fMRI scanner creates a series of two-dimensional scans that combine to create a moving picture of activity within the brain, rather than just viewing structures within the brain. Their limitations for use in psychology research are that they are extremely expensive, require costly maintenance, and research budgets enable only a small (and often not sufficiently representative) number of participants to be examined. Moreover, fMRI scanning requires trained personnel in operating the technology, and reading and interpreting the information generated.

Aim

To examine the roles of the **medial prefrontal cortex** and the amygdala in determining undergraduate students' attitudes towards drug addicts and homeless people.

Its wider objective was to investigate the *biological* correlates of **stereotypes** and **prejudice**, which would underlie any discriminatory behaviour. For example, 'Do you have small change to pay for my bus fare?' would be more likely to get a 'yes' from a stranger looking like a fellow-student than from a stranger looking like a homeless person. Is this behaviour biologically generated?

Procedure

Twenty-two undergraduates from Princeton University, New Jersey, USA took part in this study. Each student was connected to an fMRI scanner, medically established as being an entirely safe procedure. They were first shown pictures of a variety of objects. They were then shown pictures of a variety of people. The responses of both the amygdala and the medial prefrontal cortex were recorded by the scanner. The amygdala emits the immediate reaction to a new situation or object. The medial prefrontal cortex assesses more slowly how to react, and has a moderating effect on the response of the amygdala.

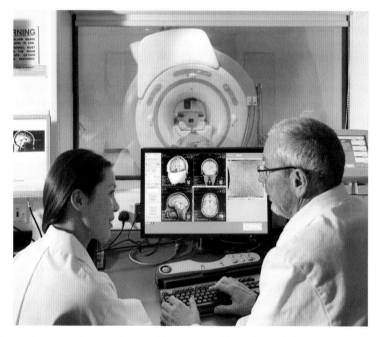

Figure 3.6 Psychologists seek to understand human emotions through fMRI-detected activity in the amygdala and in the medial prefrontal cortex.

The researchers selected images of drug addicts and homeless people because they were extreme out-groups, representing the category of people likely to have the most negative stereotypes in the eyes of the students. Firstly, addicts and homeless people were likely to be social outsiders; out-groups in the eyes of the students. Secondly, as out-groups they had neither the characteristics that were likely to elicit sympathy, such as people with disabilities, nor the characteristics to incite envy, such as wealthy businesspeople.

Functional magnetic resonance imaging (fMRI): a brain-scanning technique that measures the energy released by haemoglobin molecules, using it as a means of determining the amount of blood and oxygen in specific parts of the brain.

Medial prefrontal cortex: the front part of the frontal lobe of the human brain that fully develops during early adulthood. Functions include decision-making.

Stereotype: a person being identified as belonging to a particular group, with the belief that they have the characteristics commonly attributed to that group.

Prejudice: unjustifiably negative attitude towards members of an out-group.

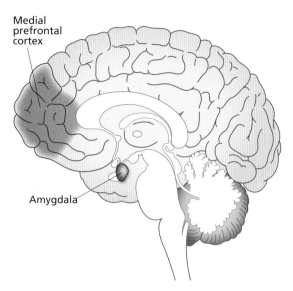

Figure 3.7 The human brain processes the immediate reaction in the amygdala, and the more thoughtful reaction about ten seconds later in the medial prefrontal cortex.

The researchers predicted that the medial prefrontal cortexes would be active when the students were viewing pictures of human beings, but inactive when viewing objects. Thus the students' amygdalas might place a picture of an older person in a wheelchair as an outsider, but their medial prefrontal cortexes would nevertheless generate some empathy. However, a picture of an object such as a dirty white sock would elicit a 'disgusted' response from the amygdala, but no moderation whatsoever from the medial prefrontal cortex.

Results

The fMRI scans of the 22 participants indicated that emotional reactions to pictures of objects were confined to the amygdala. There were no reactions from the medial prefrontal cortex. In contrast, pictures of all types of people showed varying reactions in both the amygdala and the medial prefrontal cortex. There was one exceptional category: the extreme outsiders consisting of the drug addicts and homeless people. There was no reaction in the medial prefrontal cortexes. There was no moderation of the emotion of contempt shown by the amygdalas. Thus the extreme out-groups only succeeded in activating the brain regions registering 'disgust'.

Conclusions

This study indicated that biological mechanisms were capable of dehumanising people stereotyped as belonging to extreme out-groups. The 22 students tended to see the drug addicts and the homeless people as 'contemptuous things' rather than as human beings.

Strengths of the study

It was fMRI-based with the capacity to register activity throughout the brain and not just in a particular region. It is also easily replicable for use with similar and different groups.

Limitations of the study

No cause and effect can be completely determined as the findings are entirely correlational. Additionally, there may well be cognitive and social learning elements that are more crucial in stereotyping, prejudice and resulting discriminatory behaviour.

And as previously explained, fMRI scans have shown that the different patterns in brain activities are extremely multi-dimensional, with various parts of the brain being coordinated to varying degrees of intensity. The extremely complex brain mapping rules out, for the most part, a single part of the brain being exclusively responsible for a specific function. The idea that different, but not all, sections of the brain are simultaneously involved in specific functions is the concept of brain function localisation, which is examined in detail in the next section.

The brain also functions as the central controller of the entire nervous system, including the **peripheral nervous system (PNS)** that extends to all parts of the body. The nervous system's workings and role in psychology are examined in this next section.

3.2.2 The workings of the nervous system

The human brain is made up of at least 100 billion (1 000 000 000 000) neurons, of three main types:

1. sensory neurons responding to touch, light, noise, taste and smell

2. motor neurons carrying messages to organs, glands and muscles

3. association neurons transmitting and consolidating information between other neurons.

The nervous system includes the central nervous system (CNS) consisting of the brain and spinal cord, and the PNS, linking the sensory neurons to the CNS and the CNS to the organs, glands and muscles.

The PNS functions through two systems: first the **somatic nervous system**, which allows the individual to choose reaction to stimuli, and second the **autonomic nervous system**, which connects the CNS to organs and glands without conscious control. For example, you do not voluntarily control the number of times your heart beats every minute.

The autonomic nervous system divides into the sympathetic branch which prepares the body for action (e.g. increasing the heartbeat when running) and the parasympathetic branch which regulates the body's energy (e.g. reducing the heartbeat when relaxed).

Every stimulus and piece of information feels different, because of the way its message is conveyed to the brain, and the way the brain responds to that message. Moving your hand over broken glass feels very different to moving your hand over a silk scarf. That is because within the nervous system lie series of neurons that are separated from one another by **synapses** (gaps between the neurons). Stimuli and information are communicated by electro-biochemical processes from one neuron to another, to and from the brain. Firing across the synapses are neurotransmitters. These tiny substances work in different combinations according to the stimuli, such as moving your hand over broken glass or a silk scarf. Stimuli are processed and reacted to by the CNS. With the broken glass, the reaction is pulling your hand away, fast.

Communication between neurons is an electro-biochemical process. The neural impulse is electric, which stimulates the release of the neurotransmitters. These jump across the **synaptic clefts**, and are absorbed by the receptor cells on the **dendrites**. Dendrites are very thin, branched extensions of the neurons. This process repeats itself from neuron to neuron, and to, from and within the CNS.

Peripheral nervous system (PNS): part of the nervous system that is outside the brain and spinal cord.

Somatic nervous system: this is also called the voluntary nervous system and it enables the individual to choose how to react to stimuli and which movements to make, such as the decision to stand up or sit down.

Autonomic nervous system: this connects organs and glands to the central nervous system and deals with involuntary actions, such as breathing, hormone regulation, and digestion.

Synapse: the gap between the points of connection between neurons.

Synaptic clefts: the tiny gap between the pre-synaptic neurone that fires the neurotransmitters and the postsynaptic neuron that receives the neurotransmitters.

Dendrite: a long, very thin projection of the neuron, which carries electric impulses received from other neurons.

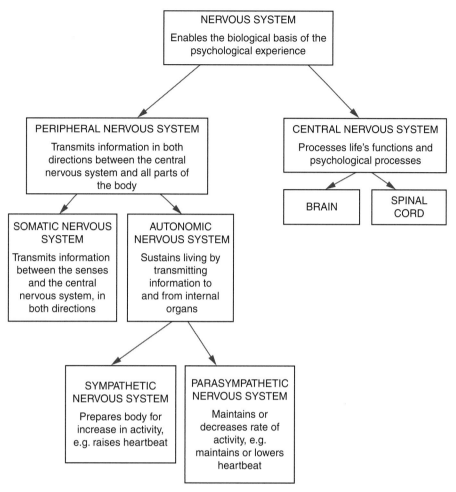

Figure 3.8 The workings of the nervous system

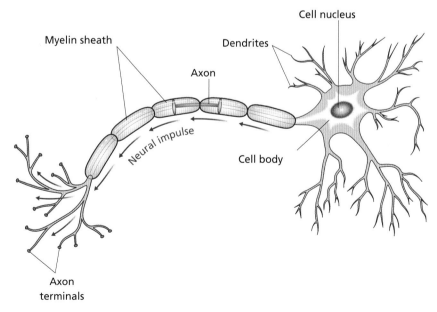

Figure 3.9 A typical neuron

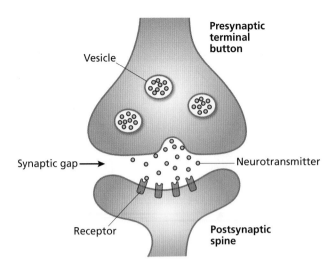

Presynaptic terminal button

Vesicle

Synaptic gap →

Neurotransmitter

Receptor

Postsynaptic spine

Figure 3.10 A typical synaptic gap

Psychology has an important role within the nervous system for the following reason. A person's psychological as well as biological situation can affect the rate of the 'firing', the release, of neurotransmitters. Drugs such as alcohol and nicotine can stimulate and inhibit neurotransmitter activity by covering the ends of the synaptic site. Any one neuron may be working with more than 5000 synapses from thousands of other neurons.

Serotonin and dopamine are the two neurotransmitters readily associated with feelings of pleasure. Serotonin is an inhibitory neurotransmitter, employed by the nervous system in mediation of pain, sleep control and regulation of mood. High levels of serotonin are associated with feelings of well-being and happiness, and of being at peace with the world.

Dopamine, as previously defined, is a neurotransmitter that helps to control the brain's reward and pleasure centres. Increased dopamine levels in the brain mean increased stimulation. For happy experiences, dopamine release sets the pleasure circuit in action. Dopamine is manufactured in the brain and released in the prefrontal cortex.

Dopamine is 'fired' when you see a soft drink advertisement for example, and you immediately experience the pleasure that you associate with that beverage, without actually drinking any of it. This initial pleasure typically creates the desire for the drink.

Neurotransmitters allow the impulse to cross a synapse (excitatory) or stop the impulse and prevent it from crossing a synapse (inhibitory). An example is the contributory excitatory role of dopamine in creating nicotine addiction. Nicotine stimulates **adrenaline** hormones, causing increased heartbeat, which in turn creates feelings of pleasure as it stimulates the release of the pleasure-giving dopamine neurotransmitters. Those feelings also stimulate **acetylcholine** neurotransmitters, creating more acetylcholine receptors sites in the process. Withdrawal means that these newly-formed receptor sites yearn for neurotransmitters, resulting in a craving for more cigarettes. This is what makes smoking difficult to give up, and is covered in more detail in the health psychology option in Chapter 8.

Does falling in love involve the excitatory work of neurotransmitters? Using an fMRI scanner, Fisher et al. (2005) demonstrated on a sample of 17 people who were newly in love, that dopamine activity was very high in the **ventral tegmental area (VTA)** and also in the right **caudate nucleus**. The neurotransmitters of the newly-in-love couples were firing fast! That was reflected in their behaviour: less need for food and sleep. And they could not stop thinking of every tiny detail of the new partner. Craving each other's company caused the same emotional rush of pleasure on meeting as a fix of cocaine for a drug addict (Fisher et al., 2005) – except, as Fisher points out, the cocaine effects wear off rather more quickly.

Serotonin: a neurotransmitter which when fired causes feelings of pleasure. It is an inhibitory neurotransmitter, employed by the nervous system to medicate pain, control sleep and regulate mood.

Adrenaline: a hormone produced by the adrenal glands. When released, it quickens the heartbeat and deepens the breathing, preparing the body for fight, flight, fright or freeze.

Acetylcholine: a neurotransmitter whose many functions include activating other neurons and hormones such as dopamine, creating a feeling of well-being.

Ventral tegmental area (VTA): region that has a role in influencing the intense emotions involved in love.

Caudate nucleus: site that has a role in the decision-making process.

This study indicated that dopamine acting as a neurotransmitter in the brain contributes to the reward and motivation system that enables the individual to focus mating energy on the specific other person: a cross-cultural, virtually universal phenomenon.

However, neurotransmitters in turn are affected by agonists that amplify their effect and antagonists that reduce their effect. These are not fully understood. As a result, neurons working together can produce a large variety of effects resulting in a complex repertoire of behaviours. Therefore any claim of cause and effect should be treated with caution.

In addition, the influence of neurons on behaviour has the additional dimension of changes constantly occurring within the brain, involving **neuroplasticity**.

Neuroplasticity: the development of additional neurons, appropriate in nature to a person's persistent efforts to develop a specific skill.

3.2.3 Neuroplasticity and its effects on human behaviour

Neuroplasticity is the continued development of specialised neural networks over time or after injury. These can increase the range of skills that form the individual's repertoire of behaviours, such as fluency in a newly learnt foreign language or driving a car. Research studies show that such developments in the brain can take place throughout life, and are promoted and supported by continued stimulating and demanding activities. Indeed, neuroplasticity is subject to psychological influences from the environment as well as from genetic elements. There are many aspects of neuroplasticity. We will look briefly here at how neuroplasticity has been indicated to be a feature of adolescence. Later on, in Section 3.5, we will consider how different environments influence brain development: in the pioneering study of Rosenzweig et al. (1972), whose findings using an animal model have been applied to the human brain, and in the more modern research exemplified by Maguire et al. (2000) which employed non-invasive MRI brain scanning.

The concept of neural changes in adolescence is supported by the work of Sowell et al. (1999), which indicates that the commonly-experienced sense of confusion in adolescent age groups corresponds with the changes in the brain's parietal and frontal lobes. This cross-sectional research scanned the brains of the participants of two groups, one of adolescents aged 14 and the other of adults in their 20s. The MRI scans showed that the younger group had a large number and a high density of synaptic connections connected with visuospatial (planning) and executive (self-control) functions. However, the MRI scans with the older group revealed a much lower synaptic density, indicating that 'brains are believed to develop mainly by a pruning of their neural thickets to form orderly processing paths' (McCrone, 2000). In other words, adolescence corresponds with 'biological confusion in the brain': the gradual strengthening of crucial and more frequently used visuospatial and executive-functioning neurons, and neural pruning; and the disintegration and disappearance of the inferior and less-used surplus neurons.

ACTIVITY 3.3

1   Consider the information on how neurotransmitters work in the paragraphs above. Suggest reasons why not drinking enough water may cause confused thinking. Justify your reasons.

2   A teenager who regularly smokes declares they became addicted at the first puff. Suggest a physiological basis for this claim. Justify your answer. You will also find material to help you in Chapter 8.

3.3 Hormones and their effect on human behaviour

Hormones are chemicals released by the various glands into the bloodstream. Affecting the rate at which the body works, their purpose is to activate or deactivate specific cells. Hormones produce reactions by attaching themselves to the receptors of the particular cells that they target, which can increase or decrease their rate of functioning. They take seconds longer than neurotransmitters to become effective, because they are carried in the bloodstream rather than within the nervous system to where they are most needed.

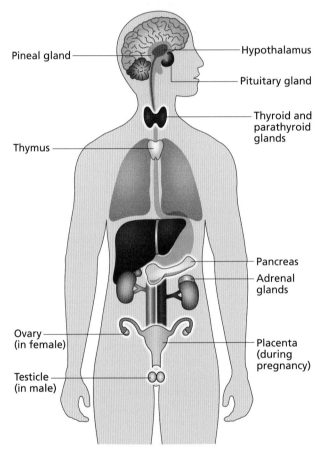

Figure 3.11 The endocrine system

Both neurotransmitters and hormones are highly influential in a wide variety of behaviours. Over 50 types of hormone have been discovered. Among those influencing human behaviour are:

- Adrenaline: secreted by the adrenal glands and influential in fright, flight or fight responses to threatening stimuli.

- **Melatonin**: secreted by the pineal gland and influential in lowering body temperature to induce sleep.

- Oxytocin: produced by the **hypothalamus**, secreted by the pituitary gland and influential in creating trust and also personal attachment between people. It is secreted by the pituitary gland into the bloodstream, functioning as a hormone. It is also produced within the brain and functions as a neurotransmitter by connecting with oxytocin receptors and the end of neuron dendrites. The hormone dopamine can also act as a neurotransmitter.

Melatonin: a hormone secreted by the pineal gland in response to darkness, which aids sleep.

Hypothalamus: a small area at the base of the brain that regulates the endocrine system and the autonomic nervous system.

3.3.1 Research on one hormone and its effect on human behaviour: oxytocin

Oxytocin functions as both a hormone and a neurotransmitter. Oxytocin is involved in creating the trust within which romantic love can flourish, which makes one individual feel very close to another. As pointed out earlier, according to the work of Fisher et al. (2005), romantic love is not an emotion, but a biologically-based motivation system. In that situation, not only dopamine but also oxytocin hormone is released with touches and hugs. This is what is likely to create the craving for each other's company, to enable lovers to mate, feel very close to each other and produce offspring.

The biological approach to human behaviour highlights how oxytocin is secreted by the hypothalamus, the part of the brain that interfaces with the hormone system. Oxytocin is released in two ways. Firstly, it is discharged through the pituitary gland into the bloodstream. In that capacity, oxytocin functions as a hormone. Secondly, oxytocin also appears to be manufactured within the central nervous system where it connects with oxytocin receptors at the end of the neuron dendrites. Oxytocin thus also functions as a neurotransmitter.

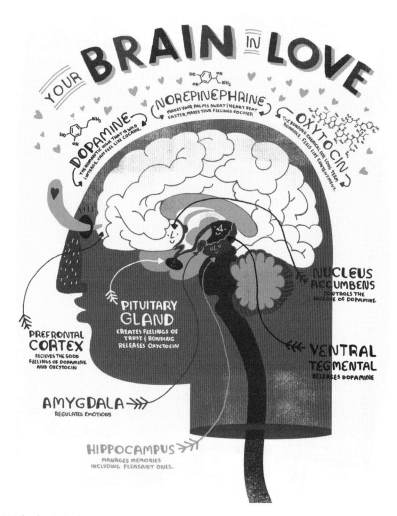

Figure 3.12 The brain in love

These functions of oxytocin help to explain why people tend to remain with one partner at a time, rather than jump from one sexual partner to another. The work of oxytocin in its roles of hormone and neurotransmitter will now be considered in the research work of Baumgartner et al. (2008).

Research study: Baumgartner et al. (2008)

Baumgartner et al. looked at the workings of oxytocin in an experimental framework.

Aim

To investigate the hypothesis that oxytocin as a hormone and as an active brain neurotransmitter positively influences being trusting and forgiving in economic decision-making.

Procedure

The research was carried out in a laboratory situation. The 49 participants received either oxytocin (test group) or a placebo (control group) through a nasal spray. They then took part in a trust game activity on the principle of investors and trustees. In investor-trustee pairs, each investor player received a sum of money and had to decide whether to keep it or share it with the trustee player. The sum was tripled if it was shared. The trustee then had to decide whether the money would be shared, indicating trust or kept, indicating betrayal of trust. The participants played against different trustees and also against a computer. In half of the games, the trust was broken. The players received feedback at once from those conducting the experiment. The dependent variable (DV) was the degree the cheated partner forgave. The IV was the presence of the oxytocin supplement.

The purpose of this research was to enable the researchers to draw parallels that would show the role of oxytocin in causing a cheated partner to forgive and continue the trust that had existed in the romantic relationship. It was far easier to simulate one partner cheating on another in money and apply the results to cheating in love than to simulate directly the act of cheating one's partner in love.

The brains of the participants in both the test and control groups were fMRI-scanned.

Results

Those who had taken oxytocin continued to invest. Their behaviour showed forgiveness and the same degree of continuing to trust despite betrayal. This, however, was true only when playing against people, not against the computer. The trust with people was there even though they knew that they had been cheated. In contrast, the control group given the placebo invested less once they knew that they had been cheated.

The fMRI images generated in the oxytocin-receiving test group showed a significantly decreased response in the highly concentrated oxytocin-receptor amygdala section of the brain, and in the caudate nucleus in the brain. Thus the amygdala's emotional responses to having been cheated were reduced. In the caudate nucleus, recall of the cheating behaviour was also reduced.

Conclusion

It would appear that the higher oxytocin levels would create and enable trust even when money and romantic love were at stake.

Strengths of the study

- It was controlled, as characteristic of an **experimental study**. It appears to provide a biologically-based explanation of why people frequently overlook very serious faults in their partners.

Experimental study: where the researcher uses a test and control population, and has the capacity to manipulate the independent variable in the test population.

- The economic decision-making game appeared to parallel the hormonal and neurological biological inputs to people being forgiving and restoring trust within relationships.

Limitations of the study

- Although the areas of the brain scanned did show decreased action, the connection with oxytocin was entirely correlational. There was no scientific explanation of the physiological work of the oxytocin supplement.
- The effects of the nasal spray oxytocin used in the research, and of the naturally-produced oxytocin, may well differ.
- The researchers assumed that the hormonal and neurological biological inputs to people being forgiving in economics trust-games do indeed parallel those involved in restoring trust within relationships.

The effect of melatonin

Human behaviour is affected by numerous other hormones. Among them is melatonin, produced by the pineal gland, which is located in the centre of the brain. Melatonin is secreted as a reaction to the dark, and inhibited by light. It affects human behaviour as its presence helps us to sleep. Its precise function is to communicate with the pituitary gland, which in turn sends out other hormones which make it difficult to stay awake.

Thus people living in climates with large environmental seasonal variations in the number of daylight hours tend to sleep more during the long winter nights than during the shorter summer nights. They tend to sleep fewer hours if there is a light on in the bedroom. Associated with the seasonal variation in light is **seasonal affective disorder (SAD)**, which is a type of depression occurring at the beginning and end of winter. Those affected by SAD are particularly sensitive to the changes in natural light availability. The changes to and from long hours of darkness seem to cause rises and falls in melatonin levels over a 24-hour period. Associated behaviours include fatigue, irritability, problems concentrating, loss of sex-drive and insomnia. It has been addressed by exposing to artificial light in such a way that the natural changes of more or fewer hours of daylight can be altered so that the individual's sleep rhythms have more time to adjust.

Seasonal affective disorder (SAD): a form of depression as a response to the changing amount of natural light available at the beginning and the end of the winter season.

3.3.2 The role of pheromones in human behaviour

Pheromones are ectohormones. This means that they are biochemical compounds manufactured by the body; they are similar to hormones, but their influence is outside rather than inside the body. Hormones affect the behaviours of the individuals secreting them. Pheromones affect the behaviours of other members of the same species coming in contact with the individuals that are secreting them. Pheromones, widely utilised in the animal population, are typically exuded through the sweat glands.

Among the behaviours that pheromones can stimulate in ants and other insects are to back off, to lay eggs elsewhere, to beware nearby dangers, to follow the trail for food and to become aroused for sexual activity.

Many of these pheromone-role biochemical compounds have been identified. For example, the androstenone that the pig secretes appears to work as a pheromone to simulate both sexual attraction and aggression. The other members of the species detect the pheromones through a specific part of the olfactory system. Known as the vomeronasal organ, it is connected to the hypothalamus in the brain. This organ exists in human beings, but it deteriorates before birth.

Evolutionary arguments would nevertheless suggest that pheromones play similar roles in human behaviour, perhaps being detected and processed by the general olfactory system. However, no conclusive study shows that humans sweat or otherwise use androstenone or any other substance as pheromones.

There are many pheromone products sold for the purpose of attracting the opposite sex. This is despite there being little reliable controlled scientific evidence of pheromones having that effect

Pheromones: chemicals that are produced and released into the environment by an animal species that can affect the behaviours of other members of the species nearby.

in humans. Manufactured pheromone products are, however, highly effective in insect control and are used in, for example, misleading males into a trap to prevent them from breeding.

Research study: McClintock (1971)

McClintock was one of the first to investigate the possibility that individuals biologically influence the behaviour of others through naturally-exuded pheromones.

Aim

To determine whether women living in close proximity will eventually find themselves menstruating at the same time, a phenomenon known as menstrual synchrony. A positive result would suggest the workings of pheromones among human beings.

Procedure

135 female college students living in the same dormitory complex participated. At two-month intervals between September and April, each participant was asked when periods took place. Each also gave information about those with whom they most regularly associated, in order to compare their respective menstrual cycles. Using that information, McClintock compared the data from each participant with that of her closest dorm friend, and also with that of her dorm friends who were less close but still within her social group.

Results

The findings did indicate statistically significant menstrual synchrony for both very close and slightly more distant female friends.

Conclusion

McClintock suggested that pheromones could have influenced the menstrual synchrony that appeared at the end of the time span of the investigation. This synchronisation is sometimes referred to as the **McClintock effect**.

McClintock effect: the hypothesised synchronisation of menstrual cycles that may develop over a time period when a large number of women live and work in close proximity.

Strengths of the study

- The possibility of the synchrony being influenced by pheromones is strengthened by McClintock's finding in the same study that the groups of girls that most regularly associated with male students had the shortest menstrual cycles.

- The sample was relatively large. The investigation compared both extremely close friends and frequent contacts living next to each other.

Limitations of the study

- The findings were based entirely on the participants' self-reporting. No physiological data was used in the investigation.

- There have been many attempts to replicate the study, but significant supporting results have not been found. That could suggest that McClintock's findings were mere chance.

More recent research on pheromones has tended to work on the principle of controlled investigation. Typically, the participating test group is exposed to a substance with chemicals which are suggested to be emitting pheromone effects. The control group is also exposed to a similar substance, but it does not contain the chemicals hypothesised as emitting pheromone effects. All participants are then exposed to the same stimuli. They are then brain-scanned to see whether there are any significant differences between the two groups in regard to the parts of the brain stimulated.

Research study: Gelstein et al. (2011)

Gelstein et al. investigated the possibility of pheromones being activated through human tears. It was based on a previous discovery that the tears secreted by mice not only protect the eye, but contain pheromones that influence the behaviour of other members of the species at the same time.

Aim

To determine whether humans tears generated by sadness emitted pheromones actually reduced the sex-drive of would-be suitors.

Procedure

The study used two solutions. Both had the same smell. One was entirely composed of sadness-produced human tears, generated by two women in their early 30s watching a poignant movie. The other was saline solution. 24 men of a similar age group took part. On smelling the two liquids, they could not distinguish between them.

Placed into two groups, the test participants were constantly exposed to a drop of tears held by a pad close to the nose, while the same was done to the control except that it was saline solution which had trickled down the cheek of one of the women who contributed the tears. Both groups watched a series of ambiguous pictures of attractive and less attractive people of the opposite sex and were asked to rate their attractiveness. They were also connected to an fMRI scanner which registered the parts of the brain that were responding to those stimuli.

The study was repeated soon afterwards, with the test group becoming the control group with the saline solution and the control group becoming the test group with the tears. Thus all participants participated in test and control capacities.

Results

The results indicated that the participants in test mode displayed lower sexual arousal as evidenced by the fMRI scans.

Conclusion

The researchers concluded that there was indeed a possibility that sadness-produced tears could contain pheromones whose chemosignals would lower the sex-drive of would-be suitors.

Limitations and strengths of the study

However, similar studies have not demonstrated positive results, and no human-generated and emitted biochemical substance has been identified as a pheromone. There is still doubt as to whether humans biologically influence others in that way. It is nevertheless an area of considerable interest to those researching biological factors affecting human behaviour, especially because of its widespread functioning in non-human species. Much more may be discovered.

SELF-ASSESSMENT QUESTIONS 3.1

1 Distinguish between:

   a hormones and neurotransmitters

   b dopamine, serotonin and oxytocin.

2 a What do the findings of the case studies Gage, Broca, Wernicke and HM have in common?

   b How do they advance understanding of the workings of the brain?

3 How are PET and fMRI improvements on previous electronic brain-scanning techniques?

4 What does the research of Harris and Fiske (2006) contribute to the understanding of the way the brain processes information?

5 What does the research of Baumgartner et al. (2008) indicate about the roles of the nervous and endocrine systems in forgiving cheating partners?

6 In what ways may pheromones affect human behaviour? What are the limitations of those indicators of evidence?

Critical thinking

'We all love best not those who offend us least, nor those who have done most for us, but those who make it most easy for us to forgive them, and who will forgive us.' (Source unknown)

Critically analyse this idea in terms of the possible presence and absence of the hormone oxytocin.

In addition, the biological level of analysis considers that behaviour patterns can be inherited. It applies biological analysis to genetics and behaviour, as considered in the next section of this chapter.

3.4 Genetics and human behaviour

All organisms including humans are made up of cells. Each cell nucleus contains chromosomes made of DNA (deoxyribonucleic acid). Genes are located along the chromosomes, rather like beads on strings. Each gene is a unique slice of chemically-coded genetic data, which has its own specific location and its own specific task. That task can be the determination of a physical or a behavioural characteristic.

Within humans, each cell nucleus contains 46 chromosomes that are actually 23 chromosome pairs, along which are located approximately 19 000 genes. The father contributes one half of one chromosome pair and the mother contributes the other half.

An individual's genome refers to all the genes that an individual possesses, and it provides the blueprint for the structure and functioning of the human body. It contains all the genetic characteristics that are to be passed from one generation to the next. Some of these characteristics are physically expressed, and some are behaviourally expressed.

The biological approach in understanding human behaviour focuses on the genetic bases for individual behaviour patterns. Not enough is currently known about genetics to accurately identify the types of behaviour promoted by specific genes, although a great deal of research in this field is currently taking place. Some of our knowledge of genetics and behaviour comes from studies of the rare instances where twins are brought up separately in completely different environments.

Our knowledge of the working of genes has been greatly advanced by the Human Genome Project. Coordinating scientific researchers worldwide between 1990 and 2004, the project mapped and sequenced the entire human genome. Discovering the identity and location of different genes has been a significant advance towards understanding the role of genes in observed human behaviour. However, the findings of the Human Genome Project do not extend to the precise role of individual genes in, for example, depressive or eating disorders. This current lack of knowledge limits the ability to apply genetic testing. Nevertheless, research in understanding the roles of individual genes is continuing to be advanced by **linkage analysis**, and by **genome-wide association studies (GWAS)**, as explained below.

There are a range of ethical issues and codes of practice faced by those researching the influence of genetics on behaviour. These are considered at the end of this section.

3.4.1 Principles of the role of genes in influencing behaviour

Psychology's involvement in genetics includes the following three key ideas:

1 Genes influence behaviour. Research in this field focuses on identifying and examining the specific genes that combine to influence human behaviour, using methods such as twin studies, adoption studies, **family studies**, more recently linkage studies and GWAS.

2 Psychological factors may partially determine whether particular genes are active or inactive. Psychology and genetics interact when studying whether a gene is switched on (active), or switched off (inactive). The switching on and off of genes is partly influenced by the work of hormones and by psychological factors, such as environment and culture. The specific area of study that considers **gene regulation** (the factors that switch genes on and off) is called **epigenetics**. A switched-on gene influences the behaviour to occur. This is called **genetic expression**. Genes stop expressing themselves when they are switched off. The switching on and off of genes is distinct from mutations in genes, as genetic expression does not involve changes in the genes' chemical composition. Various signals activate the special proteins that can promote or block the expression of a gene. Diet, exercise and stress can all create or prevent genetic expression. Hormones also affect genetic expression, either

Linkage analysis: where the frequency of particular behaviours is matched up by polymorphisms, or variations within the gene.

Genome-wide association studies (GWAS): the study of specific genetic variants within a large number of individuals to investigate whether a genetic variant or set of variants is associated with a trait.

Family studies: plotting the recurrence of a behaviour over several generations in order to assess the likelihood of it being inherited and passed to the next generation.

Gene regulation: mechanisms that cells use to increase or decrease the production of particular proteins that can affect physical characteristics or behaviours.

Epigenetics: the study of the factors that switch genes on and off. Also known as gene regulation.

Genetic expression: where a gene is switched on and thus can influence a specific behaviour to occur.

by directly entering the cell and interacting with the receptor proteins within, or more indirectly by binding to receptors in the cell membrane and affecting genetic expression through intermediate molecules. Therefore, having a gene for a particular behaviour does not necessarily mean that such a behaviour will occur or will ever occur. Indeed, sometimes genes are permanently switched off, usually due to methylation of the DNA molecule as part of the development process, and may never be expressed in the future. Methylation happens within the life cycle of some genes where methyl groups combine with the DNA molecule, and can change the activity of a DNA segment without changing the sequence.

3   Genetics and psychology connect in determining an individual's opportunity to reproduce. It is the genetic code that contains the genetic blueprint for the physical characteristics of each organism. Evolutionary theory holds that animals and people can only survive to the next generation if those characteristics enable them to live to produce healthy offspring who in turn can survive to reproduce. Physical traits are thus subject to the evolutionary pressures of developing the capacity to survive. However, the survival of the fittest may not be just on the basis of adaptable physical traits, but also on adaptable behavioural traits. Successfully living to survive and breed imposes evolutionary pressure to develop and pass on suitable genes that promote survival behavioural traits, and especially the capacity to attract mates for reproduction purposes. Those who are physically and behaviourally fit enough are rewarded with mating opportunities.

3.4.2 Methods that psychology uses to investigate genetically-based theories of behaviour

The following ways in which psychologists interact with genetics have greatly advanced over the last two decades, although some previously conducted investigations continue to be of value:

1   Twin studies: comparing the specific behavioural traits of **monozygotic (MZ)** and **dizygotic (DZ)** pairs of twins who have been reared together, and/or reared separately. This makes it possible to investigate the relative importance of genetic and environmental factors in influencing a particular type of behaviour.

2   Adoption studies: comparing the specific behavioural traits of adopted children with their natural parents and their adoptive parents. This also makes it possible to investigate the relative importance of genetic and environmental factors on a particular type of behaviour.

3   Family studies: plotting the recurrence of a **phenotype** over several generations in order to assess the likelihood of the behaviour being inherited and the chance of that behaviour being passed to the next generation. A phenotype is an observable physical or behavioural characteristic that is determined by the interaction of genetic and environmental factors.

4   Linkage analysis: where the frequency of particular behaviours is matched up by variations within the gene, called **polymorphisms**.

5   GWAS: involving the study of specific genetic variants within a large number of individuals to investigate whether a genetic variant or set of variants is associated with a trait.

Principles and methods in this field are discussed in the next sections, in examining genetic and evolutionary explanations of behaviour.

3.4.3 The use of twin studies and concordance rates to investigate the role of genes in behaviour

Twins that share the same genetic information, but have been reared separately, provide a distinct opportunity to evaluate the role of different environments on genetic expression. Even MZ or identical twins never have a 100% **concordance rate** in behaviours. The concordance rate is the percentage frequency of the same trait in the two people being researched.

Monozygotic (MZ) twins: formed when two sperm cells pierce the same ovum. The resulting twins will be of the same gender and identical.

Dizygotic (DZ) twins: formed when two sperm cells pierce two separate ova. The resulting twins will be non-identical and may be of different genders.

Phenotype: an observable physical or behavioural characteristic that is determined by the interaction of genetic and environmental factors.

Polymorphism: variations within an individual gene.

Concordance rate: in genetics, the proportion of twins or relatives sharing similar physical or behavioural characteristics.

Research study: Bouchard et al. (1990)

The Minnesota study of twins reared apart involved a longitudinal study involved 137 pairs of twins (81 identical, 56 non-identical, some reared apart and some reared together), and it began in 1979. It has the advantage of being cross-cultural as it involved twins all over the world, and included the Jim twins. It was based on the premise that the relative importance of genes (nature) versus different environments (nurture) can be studied using the rare instances of where twins have been brought up separately from each other.

Relatedness: the degree to which individuals are connected when they share common genetic material.

MZ twins, sharing 100% of the same genetic material and thus the highest degree of **relatedness**, were considered to be more likely to have stronger genetic similarities than DZ twins sharing 50% of the same genetic material. The hypothesis was that the greater the role of genes, the closer would be the levels of intelligence and consequently the degree of sophistication in behaviour. Thus MZ twins were theorised to have higher concordance rates in intelligence. The amount of variance between twins reared together and twins reared apart would also indicate the relative roles of genetic and environmental factors. Lesser variance would point to genetic factors, greater variance would point to environmental factors.

Aim

The Minnesota study was primarily focused on finding the extent to which genes determine intelligence. In linking intelligence to behaviour, a more intelligent person is likely to interact on a deeper level with the environment and society.

Procedure

The participating twins went through some 50 hours of interviewing and testing in the period leading to 1990.

Results

Table 3.1 shows the degrees of similarity in intelligence between twins (mean age was 41).

Identical (MZ) twins reared together	Very high similarity in intelligence
Identical (MZ) twins reared separately	High similarity in intelligence
Non-identical (DZ) twins reared together	Moderate similarity in intelligence
Non-identical (DZ) twins reared separately	Relatively low similarity in intelligence
Biological siblings reared together (control)	Low similarity in intelligence

Table 3.1 Intelligence similarities between twins

Conclusion

Overall, the results of the Minnesota twin study indicated that 70% of intelligence and behaviour appropriate to that degree of intelligence may be attributed to genetic inheritance, and 30% to other factors.

Strengths of the study

The size of that study made it one of the most reliable studies of twins ever carried out. The study did show that the greater similarities in intelligence appeared to be positively correlated with the amount of shared genetic material. It thus contributed findings on the nature-nurture debate in the relative importance of genes and the environment. It has opened the field to possible future twin studies linking specific genes to specific behaviours, and also relating differences in twins to epigenetics (that is, which elements switch genes on and off).

Limitations of the study

The Minnesota twin study has nevertheless been criticised on several grounds. Participants were recruited by media publicity. The data found was correlational and thus unable to establish cause and effect relationships, i.e. how far the differences found were influenced by genetics and how far by different environments. There was no adequate method of ascertaining the frequency of contact between the twins before the study. The data was largely obtained by the self-reporting of participants. Another consideration is that twins raised together do not necessarily **experience** the same environment, which can create variations in genetic expression.

Twin studies have also been used to investigate genetic factors in the eating disorder anorexia nervosa. Several studies, as exemplified by Kortegaard et al. (2001) among 34 000 pairs of Danish twins, found that the concordance rate was 0.18 for DZ twins and 0.07 for MZ twins. With an overall 1% incidence of anorexia nervosa among adolescent females, the DZ propensity for an anorexia nervosa's twin is 18-fold, and the MZ propensity is 7-fold. This indicates a high, though not exclusive, genetic input. This is broadly in line with the slightly earlier work of Strober et al. (2000), which indicated that first-degree relatives of young women with anorexia are more than ten times as likely to develop that condition as their counterparts in the general population.

Research study: Hutchings and Mednick (1975)

Hutchings and Mednick studied the effect of genetics on criminal behaviour. This study contributed to the debate as to how far crime running in families is genetically influenced. The research was empirically-based, focusing on people with criminal records who were adopted as children. It sought to investigate whether criminal behaviour was more likely to have been learnt from the adoption environment, or if it was guided by specific genes towards criminal behaviour.

Aim

To find out if there is a genetic correlation to crime.

Results

This study discovered that if both the biological and adoptive fathers had criminal records, more than a third of the sons would also get criminal records, a relatively high concordance rate. If just the biological father had a criminal record, it would drop to about a fifth of the sons getting a criminal record, a lower concordance rate. Where the adoptive father had such a record, it dropped to 11%. Where neither father had one (the control), 10% of the sons had a criminal record.

Conclusion

On the basis of the concordance rates in these findings, the researchers concluded that genetics played a somewhat greater role than upbringing in influencing criminal behaviour.

Limitations of the study

The study may be criticised on the grounds that children who are adopted are often placed in a similar environment to that of their natural parents. In addition, genes seem unlikely to account for criminal behaviour peaking in the 20s age-group, and then sharply declining. Furthermore the main factor may not be the genes, but environmental circumstances common to both the natural and adoptive parents, such as low socio-economic status and alcoholism, leading to developmental problems with the child. Moreover, legal definitions of different types of crime are unlikely to conform to genetic structures.

Until recently, research into eating disorder behaviours exemplified by anorexia nervosa was based on patients' self-reporting and psychiatrists' judgements according to the professionally-set criteria. The study was based on people with criminal records.

However, today GWAS are being increasingly used, rather than just data showing degrees in concordances in behaviours. This involves the genetic matter (such as blood or saliva samples) of a large sample with the disorder being compared with the genetic matter of those without the disorder. The **alleles** significantly prevalent in the disorder sample only are then stated to be associated with the disorder.

Allele: an alternative form of a gene that can arise by mutation on the same place on the chromosome.

Research study: Scott-Van Zeeland et al. (2014)

Scott-Van Zeeland et al. used genetic material from a sample of some 1200 females with anorexia, and 2000 without. The laboratory analyses showed a significantly higher frequency of the gene EPHX2 in samples from those with the disorder than in those without. EPHX2 appears to influence an enzyme that regulates the metabolism of cholesterol. That enzyme interferes with the normal processing of cholesterol, and can thus disrupt eating behaviour. This has been supported by findings indicating that those with anorexia nervosa have unusually high cholesterol levels which seem to be incompatible with their eating patterns. Further research has suggested that those higher cholesterol levels support an improved feeling of well-being that can be disrupted by eating, which would help to explain why the disorder is being characterised by persistent restriction of food intake.

This study did not use twins. It has opened the field to possible future twin studies linking the frequency of gene EPHX2 to specific behaviours, and also relating differences in twins to epigenetics: which psychological elements switch EPHX2 on and off. This is also related to the **diathesis-stress model**, which is examined in the next section. Applying this model to anorexia nervosa, there is the possibility that an individual with the frequency of EPHX2 may only develop that abnormality if the interaction with the environment causes those genes to switch on (be genetically expressed).

Diathesis-stress model: model which holds that psychological abnormality and its associated behaviours are products of both genotype and environment.

3.4.4 The use of genetic variations studies in investigating the roles of genes in behaviour

Current research on how genetics influence behaviour typically focuses on polymorphisms, where the frequency of particular behaviours is matched to variations within the gene. These polymorphisms are used as genetic markers. This linkage analysis employs GWAS.

Research study: Caspi et al. (2003)

Caspi et al. is a pioneer study on the role of the 5-HTT gene in depression after experiences of stressful events. It examined the roles of the interaction between genes and environment in **major depression**; it is referred to again in Chapter 6. A depression becomes a major depression when its symptoms persist uninterrupted for two weeks. The team's approach applied both linkage analysis and genome-wide association.

This research used the diathesis-stress model. This model holds that abnormal conditions (such as major depression and anorexia nervosa) and their associated behaviours are products of both **genotype** and environment. If a person has a genotype promoting a particular condition such as depression, environmental conditions can enable the expression or non-expression of the condition and associated behaviours.

The study focused on the role of serotonin in depression, which functions as both a neurotransmitter and a hormone. Low activity levels of serotonin occurring when the level of serotonin uptake in brain synapses are high can result in a net decrease in serotonergic neurotransmission. Low serotonin levels adversely affect mood, social behaviour, appetite, sleep and sexual desire.

It was already known prior to the study that the 5-HTT gene influences the level of serotonin. The hypothesis was that a mutation of the serotonin transporter gene 5-HTT, which is associated with a low transmission level of serotonin, creates genetic susceptibility to depression when accompanied by suitable environmental circumstances. The form of this mutation is where either one or both 5-HTT alleles are short rather than long.

Major depression: where the mood disorder of depression continues for an uninterrupted two weeks or more.

Genotype: the genetic make-up of a particular organism.

Aim

To examine whether an individual's susceptibility to depression is influenced by genetic make-up.

Procedure

There were 847 participants aged 26 who were living in New Zealand, all of whom had been biannually assessed for mental health until 21. They were divided into three groups according to whether their 5-HTT alleles were both short, both long, or one long and one short.

All participants filled in a survey that was designed to assess the degree of stress they experienced between ages 21 and 26, in the areas of work, health and relationships. On the basis of self-reporting, they were also assessed for depression.

Results

The team found that people with one or two short alleles showed more depressive symptoms and behaviours than those whose genotype include the long alleles of 5-HTT. Depressive symptoms included idealising suicide in highly stressful conditions.

Conclusion

There is a link between the presence of the short 5-HTT allele and the symptoms of depression.

Strengths of the study

* The study showed a correlation between the presence of the short 5-HTT allele and depression, including depression-associated behaviours.

* The study used the biologically-based linkage analysis and GWAS analysis.

* The study considered a range of environmental conditions that might enable genetic expression.

Limitations of the study

* Although the study showed a correlation between a gene mutation and a behaviour pattern, it did not show that it was the gene mutation that actually caused the behaviour.

* People without the gene mutation have been diagnosed with major depression.

* It is not clear whether it was the stressful events rather than the genetic mutation that influenced the depression and depressive behaviour.

3.4.5 Evolutionary explanations for behaviour: the survival of the fittest

We have already considered studies based on the concept that there are genetic codes for behaviour as well as for physical characteristics. It follows that behaviour and physical traits are subject to evolutionary pressures for survival.

Genetics and evolution are intricately connected. It is the genetic code that contains the genetic blueprint for the physical characteristics of each organism. Evolutionary theory holds that animals and people can only survive to the next generation if those characteristics enable them to live to reproduce healthy offspring who in turn can survive to reproduce. Physical traits are thus subject to the evolutionary pressures of developing the capacity to survive.

The survival of the fittest may not just be on the basis of adaptable physical traits, but also on adaptable behavioural traits. Success in living to survive and breed imposes evolutionary pressure to develop and pass on suitable genes that promote survival behaviours, and especially the capacity to attract mates for reproduction. Those who are physically and behaviourally fit enough are rewarded with mating opportunities.

In the animal kingdom, males fighting one another for access to females is common behaviour. Evolutionary theory argues that the underlying purpose of such behaviour is to procreate and pass on one's genes. Indeed, animals and humans share a lot of similar behaviour when attracted to the opposite sex. The same can apply in modern society with men competing for women and also women competing for men. Young people competing for entry into prestigious and well-paid careers or to be recognised as elite sport achievers may be partially due to the social recognition that can lead to preferred choice of partners, ultimately for mating and procreation.

Figure 3.13 The winner lives to pass on his genes.

However, choice of partner may also be influenced by genetic factors of which we are unaware. The biological approach to behaviour considers that women may well have evolved to gravitate to men whose genes will combine with their own to promote long-term survival by enabling them to breed and rear the healthiest children.

Research study: Wedekind et al. (1995)

Wedekind suggests that the desire to produce healthy children who are resistant to disease is an evolutionary-based, unconscious factor in female human behaviour when it comes to choosing a partner. This is based on the **major histo-compatibility complex (MHC)**. We are the product of those MHC genes that are co-dominant, meaning that both sets of inherited genes have a beneficial effect on the child's immune system. Thus the more varied the MHC genes of the parents, the stronger the immune systems of the children. Wedekind sought to support that principle with his famous experiment.

Aim

To investigate whether or not women were attracted to men with dissimilar rather than similar genes without knowing the reason why.

Procedure

The research involved 49 female and 44 male university students with a wide range of MHC genes. The men wore new T-shirts supplied for two nights in a row, and had no contact with anything that might interfere with their natural body odour. The participating women were at the midpoint of their menstrual cycle, when their senses of smell were at their keenest. Each smelt seven shirts. Each shirt was put in a separate box with a sniffer-hole at the top. The shirts were chosen for each woman according to her MHC. Three shirts were unwashed and of similar MHC; three were unwashed and of different MHC; and the seventh was a control, having not been worn at all. Each woman thus smelt a suitable range of T-shirts, rating the smell of each T-shirt as pleasant or unpleasant.

Major histo-compatibility complex (MHC): sets of cell-surface proteins that help the immune system to recognise foreign substances. The immune system itself protects the body from invading organisms, such as viruses, bacteria and cancerous cells.

Results

The women showed a significant preference for the scent of men with different genes, as long as they were not taking oral contraceptives. Those who were, preferred the scent of men with similar genes.

Conclusion

This seems to indicate that human mating patterns are influenced by evolutionary considerations. The evolutionary model suggests that the ultimate choice of child-producing partner is with the woman, even if she may not be aware of it at the time. A woman is unconsciously attracted to the man who is going to pass on the highest-quality genetic material. That will give her children the best chance of surviving her, and to reproduce in turn.

Strengths of the study

- This experimental study showed that women's choices of the most compatible smells were not random in MHC terms. It has been supported by similar later studies, such as that of Santos et al. (2005) with Brazilian male and female students as participants.

- It supports the general evolutionary theory that mating opportunities are proffered to males with the best-quality genes. Indeed, when males fight with each other over a female, she will choose the winner out of admiration rather than the loser out of pity. The winner's role in her survival and her offspring is likely to give her the greatest chances of her descendants continuing long after her death.

- Support for the study is also indicated by the fact that women on oral contraceptives and therefore out of the reproducing mode preferred men of similar rather than different MHC genes.

Limitations of the study

- Its limitations are that it implies that people with different rather than similar MHC genes are attracted to each other. While there are many children born from parents of very different races and cultures, socio-cultural based studies such as that of Markey and Markey (2007) indicate that on a worldwide basis, couples tend to be similar in age, religion, socio-economic status, intelligence, physical attractiveness, personality and outlook.

ACTIVITY 3.4

A young man may ski-jump to Olympic standards, yet get tongue-tied when asking a young woman he would like to know better for some time together. In the first activity, he risks serious injury and even his life. In the second, neither life nor limb are in danger. What evolutionary-based argument could you suggest for his confidence in the first situation and his fear in the second?

In addition, evolutionary arguments need to be treated with caution for the following reasons:

- The findings are correlational. They do not demonstrate that it is the mutations themselves that affect the evolving characteristics and behaviours.

- They overlook socio-cultural influences on behaviour modifications.

- They assume that genes tend to modify synchronously (at the same time) with changing environments. In reality they may take much longer to mutate and modify in response to particular environmental changes. We do not know enough about human behaviour in previous millennia to trace the genetic modifications which prompted adaptive behaviour changes in response to environmental pressures.

3.4.6 Ethical considerations in research on genetics

Research in genetics shares the standard ethical codes used in psychology. These have been examined in Chapter 2, Section 2.5.

On one hand, genetic research can be highly beneficial to humanity, for example research in human genetics to identify particular genes involved in hereditary diseases. On the other hand, its potential for improving the overall quantity and quality of life has to be balanced with the reality that genetics research involves some very specific and highly sensitive additional ethical issues:

1 Danger of revealing adverse genetic information to the participant. It may distress a participant with depression symptoms to find out that he or she possesses, for example, a short allele mutation in gene 5-HTT. It may reveal biological correlates that can promote depression-associated behaviour as the participant's self-fulfilling prophecy. It could also indicate unanticipated and distressing findings, such as misattributed parenthood. Participants have to be warned clearly and unambiguously of potential distress-causing findings as well as being briefed on the nature of the study before signing informed consent.

2 Genetic information is highly personal and extremely confidential. There can be serious consequences to information leaks to third parties about adverse genetic characteristics. Breaches of privacy can also lead to the **stigmatisation** of members of the participant's family assumed to share genetic material. The passing on of such knowledge can create often insurmountable difficulties for the participant and their family in finding a partner, getting a job or getting better terms for a medical insurance policy. The researcher has to guarantee absolute confidentiality, with a signed consent document showing the participant's clear understanding of the study and its implications. The participant 's confidentiality has to be respected even where it prevents any follow-up study. For this reason, access codes are used instead of names, and participants must be guaranteed absolute privacy.

3 There is a possibility that certain previously unknown, unpleasant facts might be revealed, for example that the participant's believed parents are not his actual parents. This has to be put to the participant before obtaining his consent.

4 The importance of the discovery of a previously unknown genetic disorder might well be over-exaggerated by the researcher and/or the participant. It might also be taken out of proportion and out of context.

5 Genetics issues are extremely sensitive within the cultures of many ethnic groups. In these circumstances, the elders of the society must be consulted for permission to work with members of their groups.

Stigmatisation: the devaluing of an individual or category of people whose behaviour differs from society's norms.

Critical thinking

1 How far do the Minnesota study of twins (1990), and Hutchings and Mednick (1975) indicate that human behaviour is determined by genes?

2 What other possible explanations might be given for the findings in the studies in question 1?

SELF-ASSESSMENT QUESTIONS 3.2

1 How are genetics and evolution connected?

2 What does the research by the following indicate how the behaviour of the individual is influenced by genetics?

  a Wedekind et al. (1995) on choice of heterosexual partner

  b The Minnesota twin study (1990) on levels of intelligence

  c Hutchings and Mednick (1975) on tendency towards criminal behaviour

  d Caspi et al. (2003) on likelihood of symptoms of depression

  e Scott-Van Zeeland et al. (2014) on likelihood of symptoms of anorexia

3 How may the methodologies of the last two studies be distinguished from the methodologies of the first three studies?

4 What ethical issues require special attention when researching genetic influences on behaviour?

INTERNATIONAL FOCUS

McDonald et al. (2012), a study on prejudice and discrimination, suggests that xenophobia and intolerance may well be part of our evolutionary development.

No racist gene has been identified and classified by geneticists. However, the study led by van Vugt of VU University, Amsterdam theorises that the human mind is designed to live in conflict with outsiders.

Feelings of hostility towards outsiders are explained as developing from the time when people lived in tribes: you survived only when you were extremely wary of strangers from other tribes and knew how to protect yourself.

This evolutionary process (whose genetic input has not been identified) is used to explain the negative attitudes that some people have towards people of a different race, nation, school and even football team. Human activities that create barriers between one person and another ignite the wired-up genetic package of negativity towards the out-group and cause discriminatory, racist behaviours.

The solution to racist evolutionary pressure? Extend your circle of friends and associates to include people of different faiths, races, schools, organisations, and yes – football teams.

Figure 3.14 People from all over the world having fun together

Theory of Knowledge

Our studies of the brain, neurotransmitters, hormones and genes indicate that we operate according to physiological laws. Yet, as proposed in the International Focus (right), we can challenge undesirable behavioural patterns even if they are physiological in origin.

1 Based on your studies in this chapter, outline the types of physiological evidence behind the discriminatory behaviour described in the article.
2 'Extend your circle of friends and associates to include people of different faiths, races, schools, organisations, and yes – football teams.' Suggest and justify a scientific basis for this recommendation for behavioural success in overcoming discriminatory behaviour.

3.5 The value of animal models in psychology research (HL only)

Despite marked advances in brain-scanning techniques at the biological level of research, animals continue to be used, any resultant findings being applied to humans with various degrees of caution. This area of study is a Higher Level requirement only.

Animal models in psychology involve imposing particular positions or conditions on an animal or group of animals, and then extending the findings to explain human development and behaviour, such as exemplified in Rosenzweig et al. (1972), described below.

Animals are widely used in both medical and psychological research. According to EU statistics, over 11 million animals were involved in 2011. Three-quarters were rodents, mostly mice, although investigators also used rats and more rarely, guinea pigs. Non–human primates, such as chimpanzees, macaques, baboons, marmosets and other monkeys were less frequently involved. These accounted for 0.05% of the total number of animals used in 2011, which was numerically one-third less than in 2008.

There are many organisations such as People for the Ethical Treatment of Animals (PETA) that are committed to the halt, or at least the sharp reduction, in the use of animals for research.

Figure 3.15 Protesting against the use of animals in research

However, psychologists do continue that practice for the following reasons:

1 Animals, especially mammals, have genetic and physiological similarities to humans. This is especially true of mice and rats, as well as of non-human primates. Indeed, our nervous and endocrine systems work on similar principles to other mammals. Psychological drugs such as anti-depressants can be tested on them and their results will be observed before proceeding to humans, or deciding to reject or refine them.

2 Animals breed quickly. That makes it possible to observe several generations over a short period, which is particularly useful when researching the influence of genes on behaviour patterns.

3 Animals age more quickly than humans. That can, for example, facilitate research on how experiences of enriched or deprived early-childhood environments can affect behaviours in adulthood.

4 Animals can be used in procedures that would be unethical for humans, such as temporary overcrowding or isolation. They can also be killed using humane procedures prior to post-mortem brain studies that may provide more detailed information than human brain scanning. Thus animal models could be suitable to investigate conditions that are unacceptable or inaccessible to human participants, as they can involve unavoidable harm to animal participants. For example the study of Harlow and Harlow (1962) on the effects on a child of being deprived of a mother figure in infancy was not conducted on humans but on rhesus monkeys. The monkeys were materially cared for, but deprived of an attachment figure throughout their early development. Later released into the company of other monkeys, they were unable to interact normally.

5 Animal research continues to focus on projects designed to further the understanding of the nature and the workings of specific brain areas, neurotransmitters and hormones that contribute to healthy function and development. This is vital in designing preventative and stabilising treatments for psychiatric illnesses, including Alzheimer's disease. Knowledge obtained from such studies benefits humanity and can save human and animal lives.

However, the differences between humans and animals raise the question of how far the findings in animal research may biologically be applicable to humans. For example, in Section 3.3.2 it was mentioned that the vomeronasal organ enables pigs to detect androstenone secreted by other pigs, but that organ is non-functional in human beings as it deteriorates before birth. That, as well as other findings, have kept open the question of whether pheromones influence human behaviour.

Applications of animal studies to human cognitive processes can have severe limitations, as the highly developed human prefrontal cortex manages sophisticated processes including reasoning, problem-solving and forward planning, as well as memory. Rats, for example, do not possess the granular prefrontal cortex found in primates.

Animals have been used in the field of neuroplasticity or brain plasticity and its effects on human behaviour. As explained earlier in this chapter, this involves the continued development of specialised neural networks over time or after injury. Every new thing we learn or experience promotes the development of nerve cells and synaptic activity in the brain. Research studies show that such developments can take place throughout life, and are promoted and supported by continued stimulating and demanding activities as well as from genetic elements.

This section considers the use of animal models in three areas of research:

1 The role of different environments in promoting the development of denser neural networks.

2 The role of genetics in promoting high levels of human anxiety and aggressive behaviour.

3 The application of non-invasive ultrasound technology in clearing the brain of protein-based lesions. These are associated with the memory loss and declining cognitive functioning of patients with Alzheimer's disease.

Research study: Rosenzweig et al. (1972)

Rosenzweig et al. studied neural development as a result of stimulating environments, using laboratory rats.

Aim

To investigate whether or not the presence or absence of stimuli in the environment can cause physical changes to the neurons within the cerebral cortex of the brain. Does a more exciting environment enable the brain to engineer a more sophisticated range of behaviours?

Procedure

This study was carried out with rats having the genetic similarities of coming from a common litter. All rats were supplied with the same adequate food and water throughout the study. Each rat was allocated to one of the following groups for at least 30 days:

Group 1: Enriched environments, containing a maze and a variety of toys. A dozen rats were placed in a variety of stimulating conditions.

Group 2: Impoverished environment, each rat being put in an individual bare separate cage with no stimulating items.

Group 3: Controlled environment with three rats to the cage, but no stimulating items.

The IV was the presence of an enriched environment or an impoverished environment. The DV was the weight and the thickness of the participating rats' cerebral cortexes.

The rats were then euthanased to enable the study of the characteristics of their brains.

Results

The researchers found that rats from the enriched environments had significantly thicker and heavier cortexes than those in the impoverished environment. In addition, those from the enriched environments had more active neurons within the cerebral cortex: they transmitted acetylcholine more effectively. Acetylcholine is a neurotransmitter that assists learning and memory.

Conclusions

Prolonged exposure to enriched environments stimulates neuroplasticity, which may be physically identified in terms of additional neurons in the cerebral cortex as well as an increase in the weight of the brain as a whole. This conclusion is based on the evolutionary premise that the principles of neuroplasticity in rats apply to humans as well.

These animal-research-based findings support the provision of stimulating and challenging environments for children, such as Head Start programme in the United States. They also indicate that poor, stimulus-lacking surroundings can limit brain development and lower the range and degree of sophistication of behavioural responses to the environment.

Strengths of the study

- Its results support the view that repeated intellectual stimulation promotes development of increasingly effective and complex neuron development within the brain, leading to a more sophisticated and effective range of responses to the environment in both animals and humans. This finding is supported by later fMRI-based research on neuroplasticity, such as that by Maguire et al. (2000) (see below).

- The study was experimental, and within the controlled environment provided by a laboratory setting. That made it possible to establish cause and effect.

- The study was replicable, and its findings have been supported in follow-up studies. Similar degrees of brain plasticity have been found where the rats have been placed in the enriched environment for just 30 minutes a day rather than kept in that place constantly from day to day.

Limitations of the study

- The enriched environments' contribution to the rats' brain development is unclear. It could have been due to the stimulating environment encouraging the rats to interact with each other, rather than the enriched surroundings themselves. This was not helped when as a follow-up, the experimenters eliminated the social elements. The rats they then placed in enriched but solitary environments tended to ignore the opportunities provided, and behaved as though those facilities were not there.

- The study was carried out on rats and applied to humans. It assumes that brain plasticity works on similar principles with rats and humans.

- There is the ethical issue of undue harm and stress caused to the animals in the study. That may only be justifiable if the findings are worth that suffering.

Research study: Maguire et al. (1972)

In overall evaluation this study, designed to show brain plasticity in response to different environments, was carried out on animals as human brain scanning was insufficiently developed in 1972 for it to be able to pinpoint brain plasticity. Thus the use of rats could be defended. This contrasted with the more modern brain plasticity study by Maguire et al. (2000), which focused directly on humans rather than animals, and non-invasive MRI brain scanning. That study examined whether specific structural developments could be detected in the brains of people who intensely studied spatial navigation. It focused on a test group of 16 male London taxi drivers who passed The Knowledge (the examination required for taxi drivers to enter the profession) and had been subsequently driving for at least 18 months. The scans of the taxi drivers were compared with 50 male non-taxi drivers of similar age. The researchers found significantly more grey matter in the brains of taxi drivers in the right posterior hippocampus, whose volume seemed to correlate positively with the number of months working as a London taxi driver.

Research study: Hendricks et al. (2003)

The role of genetics in promoting high levels of human anxiety and aggressive behaviour is supported by the experimental research of Hendricks et al. (2003).

Aim

To investigate whether the absence of the moderating gene classified as Pet-1 influences abnormally high levels of anxiety and aggression in humans. It could have some bearing on the possible future use of genetic material in the diagnosis of abnormal behaviour patterns.

Procedure

The investigators used a group of genetically-normal mice for the control population, and genetically-modified (GM) mice for the test population. The GM mice had been bred from **knock-out** mice whose Pet-1 gene had been clinically removed, or knocked-out. Knocking out the functioning of a gene can indicate what that gene normally does.

Knock-out: in genetics, where specific genes have been clinically removed.

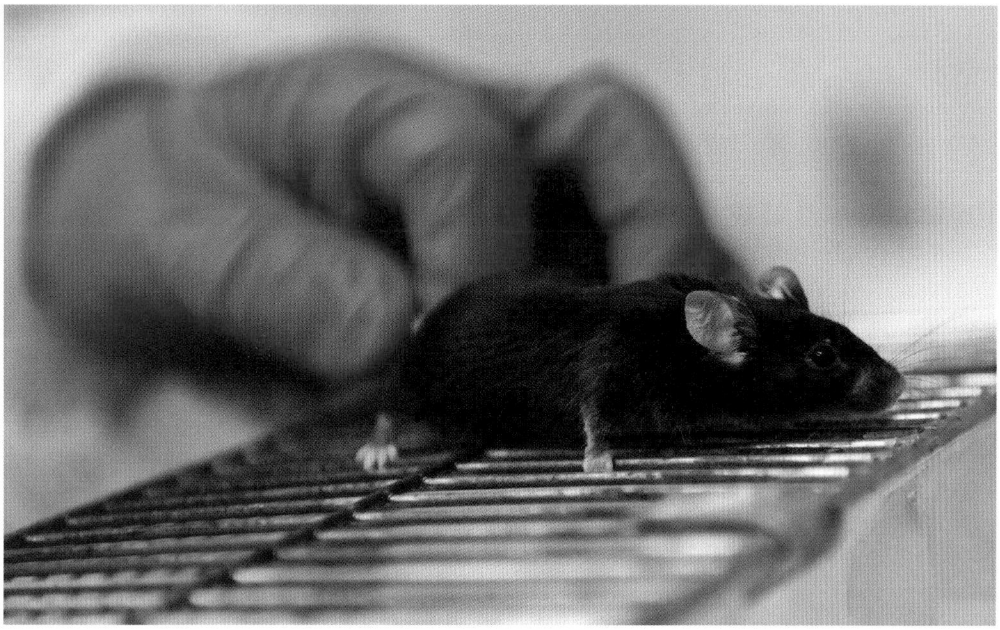

Figure 3.16 A genetically-normal mouse

Results

Observers monitored the levels of the mice's anxiety-associated behaviour in response to changing environmental conditions. Both the test knock-out mice and the control normal mice were placed in a chamber with the opportunity to choose between an unprotected open space and a safer protected space. The test mice were observed to stay longer in the safe area than in the more vulnerable area. When they were assigned a territory, the knock-out mice were quicker to attack an intruder than the normal mice. Thus the GM mice appeared to display significantly higher levels of anxiety and aggressive behaviour.

Conclusion

The researchers concluded that there is significant genetic input in unusually high levels of anxiety and aggressive behaviour in humans. The absence of the moderating Pet-1 gene appears to adversely influence fretfulness and belligerent anti-social behaviour. This state appears to result in inadequate serotonin production, in consequence increasing the risk of mood disorders and abnormal behaviours.

Serotonin functions as both a neurotransmitter and as a hormone in promoting feelings of security and well-being. Indeed, the knock-out mice lacking Pet-1 produced insufficient and poorer-quality serotonin cells.

Strengths of the study

In evaluation, the mice genome is of value because it is very similar to that of humans. It would not have been possible to carry out a similar experiment knocking out the genes of humans. The study's findings seem to indicate a potential role for genetic material in the diagnosis of human abnormality, or at least to predict the likelihood of a patient positively responding to a serotonin-promoting drug such as Prozac. In addition, the controlled use of mice made it possible to observe cause and effect.

Limitations of the study

However, there are substantial differences in human and mouse biology. For example, humans and mice share the same γc gene. A mutation in this gene causes mice to lose B cells, while humans do not. That distinction has substantial consequences in drug development. Furthermore, the presence of Pet-1 may not necessarily mean that the gene expresses itself, which could well be influenced by environmentally-based psychological and physiological factors.

There are also ethical issues involved in the creation and use of knock-out mice, which are considered in the final section of this chapter.

The application of non-invasive ultrasound technology in clearing the brain of protein-based lesions

The excessive accumulation of protein-based lesions is associated with the memory loss and declining cognitive functioning of patients with Alzheimer's disease. Those lesions are associated with neurotoxic amyloid plaques and neurofibrillary tangles that disturb communications between the neurons.

More commonly associated with older people, Alzheimer's disease involves a serious and continuous cognitive decline in quality of life. This decline includes problems in recognising family and friends, carrying out multi-step tasks such as getting dressed and taking part in new situations.

Research study: Leinenga and Götz, 2015)

Aim

Teams led by Götz at Queensland (Australia) Brain Institute have been working to develop a new Alzheimer's disease treatment to restore memory function, focusing on repairing damaged brain cells. It involves the application of non-invasive ultrasound technology designed to clear the brain of the neurotoxic amyloid plaques. This procedure appears to create a path for blood proteins to enter the brain, and clear out clusters of lesions that reduce cognitive functioning. It is designed to open the blood-brain barrier, facilitating drug uptake and thus restoring effective neuronal function.

Procedure

The actual procedure used genetically-modified mice, bred to develop the brain deposits that impair cognitive functioning. The researchers injected tiny bubbles into their bloodstream and then beamed sound waves into the brain tissue. Those sound waves were absorbed by the bubbles and temporarily opened the blood-brain barrier, a natural mechanism that prevents bacteria getting to the brain tissue. That enabled small proteins from the bloodstream to enter the brain, and stimulate the cells that could clear the lesions which caused memory loss and other cognitive malfunction associated with Alzheimer's disease.

The mice were tested in three cognitive tasks before and after the treatment, including a maze, an exercise in enabling them to remember new objects, and another to remember places to avoid.

Results

The results showed substantial cognitive improvement in three-quarters of the mice that went through the treatment.

Conclusion

The study concluded that these treatments showed sufficiently significant improvements in memory for further research, moving towards applying them to animals with thicker skulls and ultimately to human beings. Subsequent research is showing that ultrasound treatment is more effective when combined with antibody treatment in clearing the lesions and reducing Alzheimer's disease symptoms in mice. Its application to people faces the problem of the much greater thickness of the human skull. For treatment to be effective, the ultrasound would have to be structured so that it would not generate a temperature beyond human endurance.

Strengths of the study

The strengths of the study are its opening possibilities to treat Alzheimer's disease, a condition that is increasingly common as people live longer. Currently, Alzheimer's disease-associated conditions affect 44 million people worldwide. The study's use of transgenic mice has induced similar biological conditions as those experienced by Alzheimer's disease patients, and the success rate of the treatments has indicated a substantial possibility that they might be able to address Alzheimer's disease as experienced by humans. The use of transgenic mice could be ethically justified on utilitarian grounds, coupled with the fact that the research could not have been carried out in any other way.

Limitations of the study

However, this treatment is still being developed and has not been applied to people at the time of writing. It is not yet clear how far this animal model is fully applicable to humans, and indeed whether this form of animal research can provide practical insight towards restoring normal cognition and behaviour in patients with Alzheimer's disease. Also, issues with the opening of the blood-brain barrier in human beings undergoing such treatment are still not fully understood.

3.5.1 Ethical considerations in animal research

As already implied, the use of animals in psychological projects that may possibly extend our understanding of human behaviour raises extremely sensitive issues. The scientists, veterinary personnel and others working in such research do not set out to deliberately cause pain and suffering to animals. However, there is no denying that some research, however valuable, involves inevitable suffering to animal participants, such as long periods of isolation and being forced to ingest substances or undergo biologically invasive treatment.

The ethical arguments continue to be strongly debated between two positions: the utilitarian position and the animal rights position.

- The utilitarian position assesses the likely degree of animal suffering in terms of the value of the findings of the research to both humanity and animals. This position will ethically support animal research as long as the likely benefits of the findings outweigh the suffering of the animals.

- The animal rights position holds that all animals have rights, experience pain and are entitled to our protection rather than exploitation. Their inability to indicate participatory consent or withdraw from the study does not enable them to become subjects in research, especially when it involves biologically invasive procedures. Animals are not suitable objects for research.

Many countries have legally-backed guidelines for the ethical use of animals in research. For example, the UK 1986 Animal Act legislated that animal-based research may only take place in approved facilities, procedures must hold the approval of an ethics board and the research cannot take place without animal participation. Animal research in Japan is governed by a series of national legislative directives together with guidelines by various ministries and organisations. These recognise the necessity of using animals for scientific purposes, and at the same time attempt to impose minimum suffering and minimum numbers of animals used. The theoretical position is broadly in line with replacement, reduction, and refining. However, there has been an increasing awareness of the need for an effective independent accreditation system to ensure suitable compliance with existing animal rights legislation.

The EU directive of 2010 for any academic research using animals is required to follow 3Rs, first described in 1959 by Russell and Burch:

1 Replace. Use non-animal-based methods where similar results can be obtained. Possibilities today would include using computer simulations, human volunteers and cell cultures.

2 Reduce. Use the minimum number of animals. Where possible, obtain more findings from the same animals rather than introduce new ones.

3 Refine. Ensure that the research is carried out in such a way that the animals suffer as little as possible before, during and after the research.

Today's standards in humane care and use of animals in research may be exemplified by the guidelines of the American Psychological Association, which include:

• Psychologists make reasonable efforts to minimise the animals' pain and infection, including performing surgery under anaesthesia.

• Psychologists may only cause stress, pain or privation to an animal where the method and goal is justified scientifically and the findings help to relieve human suffering.

• Psychologists working with animals need to be trained in the care and handling of the species used, including humane ways of carrying out euthanasia if necessary.

It is clear that the ethics of the use of animals in research on humans is controversial, even when backed with legislation and professional codes. Reconsider the above four pieces of research, consider other studies and take an informed position on this highly emotive issue.

SELF-ASSESSMENT QUESTIONS 3.3

1 What justifications are given for the use of animals in psychology research?

2 What do the following animal-modelled studies contribute to our knowledge of human behaviour?

   a Rosenzweig et al. (1972)

   b Hendricks et al. (2003)

   c The work of the research teams of Götz at Queensland Brain Institute.

3 What ethical issues require special attention when using animals in psychology research?

Chapter summary

1   The biological approach to behaviour focuses on hereditary influences and the individual-specific workings of the brain, nervous system and hormone system.

2   A huge range of hormones and neurotransmitters bio-determine the way the body synchronises and adjusts to specific stimuli and conditions. The role and existence of pheromones in humans is being studied, but is not yet widely accepted as a reality.

3   Brain functions are localised, e.g. the left frontal lobe for speech, the temporal lobes and hippocampus in memory functions, and the amygdala for emotional reaction. The medial prefrontal cortex region of the brain enables the human being to intelligently modify initial emotional reaction.

4   Modern information on the workings of the brain is mostly obtained by electronic and non-invasive brain scanning. Data from PET and fMRI scans enables complex brain mapping, generally ruling out a single part of the brain being exclusively responsible for a specific function.

5   Evolution tends to enable the opportunity to reproduce to those whose genes promote behaviour patterns that are best adapted to attracting a healthy partner, and producing healthy offspring.

6   Current studies comparing similarities in behaviour with the percentage level of shared genetic material indicate a broad positive correlation.

7   Although research capacity to identify the various individual genes influencing particular behaviours is increasing, the field of how genes influence behaviour largely relies on empirical data based on biological correlations between genes and behaviour, rather than on analysis of cause and effect.

8   Ethical guidelines for research on how genetics influence behaviour are especially stringent in view of the possibility of yielding information highly sensitive to the participant and the participant's family.

9   Common justifications for the use of animals in psychology research include similarities to humans in genes and physiology, short life and breeding cycles enabling life-long and family (generations) studies, and non-practicality of using human participants in research. (HL only)

10 Applications of animal-based findings to human psychology have been widespread, exemplified by fields of designing effective learning environments, identifying genes influencing specific behaviours, and seeking to restore deteriorating cognitive faculties. (HL only)

11 Ethical guidelines for the use of animals in psychology research include conformity to nationally-determined professional guidelines, and avoidance of their use when other equally valid research methods are practicable. (HL only)

Exam-style questions

Short-answer question

•   Outline two principles that define the biological approach to behaviour.

Essay response question

•   With reference to at least one research study, to what extent does genetic inheritance influence behaviour?

The cognitive approach to understanding behaviour

4

'Very little is needed to make a happy life. It is all within yourself, in your way of thinking.'
(Marcus Aurelius)

KEY QUESTIONS

- How is behaviour guided by the different ways we mentally process incoming stimuli and information?
- How closely does our processing of information match reality?
- How does interaction with digital technology influence cognition and behaviour? (HL only)

Learning objectives

- Outline the principles that define the cognitive approach to behaviour. (AO1)
- Outline the nature of cognitive processes, including models of memory and thinking in decision-making. (AO1)
- Explain how and why particular research methods are used in the cognitive approach to behaviour. (AO2)
- Examine the ways in which schemas influence the accuracy of cognitive processes. (AO2)
- Discuss the ways in which emotion may influence cognitive processes. (AO3)
- Evaluate the positive and negative effects of modern technology on cognitive processes. (AO3) (HL only)

4.1 The influence of cognition on the behaviour of the individual

'Nobody understands me! I'm on my own. I can't talk to anyone about it!'

Figure 4.1 Only George the cat understands me.

Cognitive psychology recognises that we understand how **you** behave when we know something about how **you** understand things; how **you** think, how **you** perceive, how **you** learn and how **you** remember. Each one of us relates and reacts to incoming stimuli and information in different and very individual ways. This is explained in the following sections.

Figure 4.2 Look carefully. What has the artist drawn? Did you change your mind as you were looking?

4.1.1 Principles of the cognitive approach to behaviour

The cognitive approach to behaviour focuses on the processes by which sensory inputs are received, processed, stored, recovered and acted upon. People filter, process, store and recall information differently because they are biologically and socio-culturally unique. It is that highly individualised store of information and experience that influences individual behaviour.

For example, two violinists are trained by the same teacher, yet they play the same pieces of music in a different style. This may be because of differences in cognition. The two violinists do not interpret all the teacher's inputs in entirely the same way. Therefore each one plays the same piece slightly differently.

In the mid-1950s, psychologists began to explore cognition to further understanding of human behaviour. The focus in psychology was shifting from behavioural, which considers observable behaviour, to cognitive, which investigates the mental processes behind the observable behaviour, such as perception and memory. It came to include how we interpret our environment, our emotions and our resultant behaviours.

Thus the cognitive level of analysis considers the way that *you* process and understand information. The emphasis is indeed on 'you'. You could be sitting in the same class as 29 other people. Everyone in that class agreed that the lesson was a good one, and that they came out of the room the wiser for the experience. But if you interview each student and ask for an account of the lesson, there will be 30 different versions of that class. It may appear that the teacher simultaneously gave 30 different lessons to 30 different people.

Figure 4.3 One lesson received by 30 students? Or 30 different lessons given by the teacher at the same time?

That is because each of those 30 people, yourself included, processes information differently. Biologically, your genes are different from those of your classmates. Your hormone and nervous systems work in their own individual way. And socio-culturally, you all grew up differently. Some of you spent your first years in environments and cultures with outlooks and values that are not the same as the surroundings you are in now. You may even be living in two societies at the same time, for example the internationally-based one of the IB programme, and the culture of your own family, nationality and religious faith.

The cognitive approach takes those genetic factors, environmental factors and past experiences into account in discovering how your mind and the minds of other people work. It looks at how their behaviours vary as a result.

The cognitive approach suggests that you form internal **schemas**. Schemas are **mental representations** that guide behaviour. If the mind is like a computer, the brain is the hardware and the schemas are the software. The mind-is-a-computer analogy is explored in the final section of this chapter, as an HL requirement. In our example above, the reason each person understood the lesson differently was because each person applied their own, individualised combination of schemas to that lesson.

Schemas and their influence on behaviour are considered in detail in the following sections. Cognitive psychologists have developed a range of research methods to study schemas and examine their reliability.

Cognitive psychologists use traditional research methods, for example experiments and verbal protocols. More recently, there has been an increasing emphasis on the use of technology, which gives biological rather than direct cognitive information, such as PET, CAT, MRI and fMRI scans.

Today, psychologists are moving towards a general consensus that a synthesis of the biological, cognitive and socio-cultural levels of psychological analysis brings us closer to understanding the complex interacting systems that make up the human being. Cognitive psychologists increasingly work together with neuroscientists, social psychologists and cultural psychologists. They recognise that the cognitive approach interacts in many ways with biological and socio-cultural phenomena.

In summary, cognitive psychologists work on the following premises:

1   The human being is an active information processor. Like computers, our brains actively organise and manipulate information and cues from the environment. However, the individual decides which inputs they wish to process and how thoroughly to process them. Thinking things through takes mental computer-processing effort, and there can be a tendency to find short cuts that give less than accurate results. There can also be gender **bias** in what information is attended to and mentally encoded, as in the work of Bem (1981) on gender schemas.

2   The way we mentally process things guides our behaviour. We do not see a reality or situation objectively. Instead, we select and process the inputs from the environment into a mental representation. This brings in our stores of related knowledge and experience, and our own biologically-, socially- and culturally-created schemas. Our reactions and behaviour patterns, guided by those mental representations, are the output.

3   The way we mentally process representations that guide our behaviour should be studied scientifically. Until the rise of cognitive psychology in the 1950s, most researchers focused on inputs called stimuli and outputs called responses. That is the behaviourist approach. It holds that the nature of the actual processing that takes place in the brain is too complex for the focus of psychologists. Cognitive psychology believes that it is possible to infer some elementary knowledge about the processing that takes place in the brain through observation-based research, where variables are manipulated. More recent research increasingly makes use of brain-imaging technology where different cognitive processes can be localised to specific parts of the brain.

4   The way we process information is influenced by the emotions felt at the time of processing. Research into this area is increasingly involving psychologists working primarily outside the cognitive field, such as biologically-orientated cognitive neuroscientists and socio-culturally-orientated psychologists.

5   Cognitive processes are influenced by social and cultural inputs. The individual's schemas are much influenced by interactions with other people, their social norms, their values and their ways of life.

The cognitive perspective as explained in this chapter may be applied to these questions:

•   How can two people watch the same yellows, reds, oranges and pinks in the same sunset and yet feel and act on completely different emotions?

•   How is it possible for a student to quote the details of every single motor vehicle manufactured in the last 20 years, and yet not manage to learn and recite a single poem by heart?

•   Can it happen that a person who lied sincerely believes that they told the truth?

Schemas: individualised mental representations that guide behaviour.

Mental representation: an arrangement of internal cognitive symbols that seek to correspond to external reality.

Bias: supporting or opposing someone or something in an unfair way, due to personal opinion influencing judgement.

85

- Why might arriving an hour late at a social invitation result in a different behavioural reaction in Switzerland and in Saudi Arabia?
- Can our understanding of human information-processing help manufacturers to redesign food packaging to persuade people to buy their products, by tracing the intensity of an emotion and its path through the brain?

Figure 4.4 If French is so hard, how come everyone in France speaks it?

The biological approach to behaviour would emphasise the research on the workings of the brain at different ages. That includes, for example, studies that indicate that different parts of the brain work much harder at learning to speak a language at the age of 16 than in acquiring the ability to speak a first (or second) language at the age of 6.

The socio-cultural approach to behaviour (Chapter 5) focuses on our upbringing and society. Following our example of language learning, many English speakers who struggle to learn and speak a foreign language wonder if it is worth the effort. That is because wherever they are, there will almost certainly be someone who can communicate in English.

The cognitive level of analysis in contrast would look at the nature of the language learning experience. If English is your mother tongue, you may face difficulties speaking German as its nouns change endings depending on where they are used in a sentence, and its adjectives have three genders: masculine, feminine and neuter. These linguistic elements are not present in English, as nouns and adjectives tend to be case-free and gender-free. There might be nothing in your existing language schemas to accommodate them.

4.1.2 Research methods applied in the cognitive approach to behaviour

Traditionally, research methods used in cognitive psychology include quantitative-based, experimental and observational studies, and self-reporting in interviews. Today, cognitive psychology increasingly interacts with the biological approach as it can access data on the brain's processing of information through brain-imaging technologies, as discussed in Chapter 3.

In view of the large range of methods currently available to cognitive psychologists, their approach exemplifies the more complex holistic perspectives that are becoming increasingly important in psychology today.

1   The use of experimental and quantitative methods is typified in the classic study of Loftus and Palmer (1974) later in this chapter. However, the use of quantitative methods for research in cognitive psychology tends to give indirect rather than direct findings. In Loftus and Palmer we do not see the brain cells reconstructing what is remembered through the filter of an existing schema. The experimental method of studying cognitive processes, however, is **inferential**. The results of the experiment form the basis of the theory only. The researchers neither identified specific schema patterns in the brain, nor observed the biologically-structured bases on which previous experiences were reconstructed.

2   Interviews may be used where cognitive issues are investigated in detail. For example, the concept of **flashbulb memory** is a special type of emotional memory that relates to a specific event. It not only recalls what happened, but immediately reconstructs the way the person felt at the time. It is as if the whole thing is incorporated as one, as with a flash picture on a camera. This concept, put forward by Brown and Kulik (1977), emerged through interviewing at the cognitive level of analysis. The events chosen for participant recall, a cognitive function, were the deaths of J.F. Kennedy and Martin Luther King Jr. Participants who were interviewed demonstrated a very clear recollection of where they were, what they did and what they felt when they first heard the news of these important figures' deaths. On the basis of their in-depth interview responses, the researchers suggested that there may be a specialised neural mechanism which arouses emotions and sets off specific behaviours because of the very deep impression made by the event.

Like experimental studies, however, interview-based studies yield information that becomes the foundation of the theory only. They do not give direct information of the cognitive processes actually operating inside the brain. The findings of Brown and Kulik's interviews became the basis of their theory that there is such a phenomenon as flashbulb memory, but the scope of their research was not designed to determine whether a specialised neural mechanism exists.

3   Observational methods were at the forefront of Jean Piaget's studies of the stages of the mental and intellectual development of the child, in an area that today would be called cognitive development. The test for whether the two-year-old child has progressed from the sensory-motor stage to the more complex pre-operational stage is to observe his behaviour when a favourite toy is covered with a blanket. If the child shows distress but does not use his freedom to remove the blanket and recover the toy, then the child lacks object permanence. Once he does recover the toy from under that blanket, he does have the object permanence schema and is thus past the sensory-motor stage. This area of study is detailed in Chapter 9. Again, such recorded observations reveal information on which to construct theory. They do not view cognitive processes in action by observing what goes on inside the brain.

4   More recently, a widening range of brain-scanning techniques have been applied to the scientific study of how the brain processes information, such as the use of CAT, PET, MRI and fMRI scans. Rapidly developing in sophistication and scope of application, they are likely to be more widely used in the future as more is being discovered about the extremely complex biological workings of the brain. Unlike the three previous approaches, these enable researchers to actually observe the presence or absence of specific processes inside the brain. But they do not yet give information on the nature of the actual thoughts that go on inside the brain.

For example, a brain scan can indicate whether or not you are concentrating in class. But it cannot yet show whether the object of your concentration is the content of the lesson or something quite unrelated. Likewise, the work of Sharot et al. (2007) investigated the biological aspect of flashbulb memory using scanned evidence of increased amygdala action, suggesting that there are indeed specific neural structures involved in flashbulb memory. However, the evidence was correlational. It did not explain what parts of the memory could be attributed to the amygdala.

Ethical considerations at the cognitive level of analysis are similar to those for the biological and socio-cultural approaches. Participants must know why the study is being done, that their involvement is voluntary, what the data will be used for, and if necessary be debriefed at the end of the study. In extreme cases, the ethical requirement for informed consent might be waived, when

Inferential statistics: these aim to highlight relationships and trends in the data, and their degree of significance.

Flashbulb memory: an emotional memory that relates to a specific powerful impression-creating event that reconstructs what the person did and felt at the time.

the focus of the study is of public importance and there is no other way to obtain the information. That would be true of Loftus and Palmer's study of the accuracy of memory recall when giving legal testimony. Telling the participants the purpose of the investigation in advance might affect the accuracy of witness testimony of the detail, and so invalidate the study.

Such studies of schematic representations of behaviour are of considerable public importance, as they could seriously affect the weight given by the courts of law to witness accounts of accidents.

As with the biological approach, participants must have the protection of anonymity, even at the risk of reducing the authenticity of the research and of preventing any follow-up study. And additionally, cognitive research involving associated cultural issues is extremely sensitive for many ethnic groups. For example, in the Muslim culture it might be expected that a husband would give permission before his wife participated in a research study.

In IB Psychology, we look at four areas of inquiry in relation to cognitive studies:

1   Cognitive processing: memory, schema theory, and thinking and decision-making processes.

2   Reliability of cognitive processes: reconstructive memory and biases in decision-making.

3   Emotion and cognition: the influence of emotion on cognitive processes.

4   Cognitive processing in the digital world: the interactions between digital technology and cognitive processes. This area of study is a Higher Level requirement only.

4.2 Cognitive processing: memory, schema theory, and thinking and decision-making processes

Although this section considers memory, schema theory, and thinking and decision-making separately, it is vital to remember that they are interrelated. Our schemas influence the ways we process facts, concepts and events into our memory stores, and how we subsequently recall and apply them in the decision-making process. Cognitive psychology theory uses models to frame and present some of these functions.

4.2.1 Cognitive processing: models of memory

Human memory seems complex. It constitutes part of the learning process, as without it human progress would be virtually impossible.

Some things are easy to remember while others are difficult.

For example, you study for a psychology test with music playing in the background. The task of memorising series of concepts, theory and research studies is hard work, requiring sustained and concentrated effort. At the same time, your mind refuses to switch off the tune you hear while you are studying. It carries on playing in your head, even during the test the next day. Not only has it become part of your memory without trying, but it actually interfered with your test memory recall the next day.

Remembering a tune without even trying to memorise it is an example of **implicit memory**. Implicit memory is where information is acquired mainly without conscious effort. Drawing on past experiences, implicit memory contains items that without trying and sometimes unconsciously become part of the **long-term memory (LTM)**, a permanent memory store with virtually unlimited capacity.

Implicit memory also includes **procedural memory**, such as the series of motions required to drive a car, perform a ski-jump or tie a shoelace.

Implicit memory: memory containing information acquired mainly without conscious effort.

Long-term memory (LTM): the permanent human memory store with virtually unlimited capacity.

Procedural memory: part of the implicit memory, handling stages or motions of a particular operation or skill.

In contrast, **explicit memory**, also known as **declarative memory**, is material that is consciously learnt and rehearsed, such as the task of memorising a poem, a scientific formula, or the date and time of your next visit to the dentist. Explicit memory divides into **episodic memory**, focusing on the details of particular events and experiences of one's life, and **semantic memory**, including facts and concepts. The work of Tulving (1989) using brain scans indicates that these two distinct types of memory tend to be retrieved from the LTM by different parts of the brain. His participants carried out a series of mental tasks, some of which were designed to use episodic memory and others, semantic memory.

The scans showed greater activity in the frontal lobes of the cortex when retrieving episodic information from the memory, and greater activity in the posterior lobes of the cortex when retrieving semantic information.

Types of LTM

Our studies of memory will focus on the **encoding**, **storage**, and **retrieval** functions in the explicit memory. Encoding happens where the mind identifies and processes the information. Storing keeps the information, although it may become increasingly distorted over time. Retrieval is where the stored information is recalled as necessary.

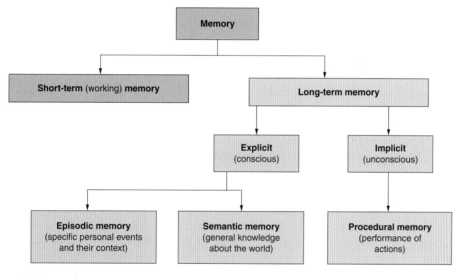

Figure 4.5 Types of memory

Explicit memory: (also referred to as declarative memory) contains facts, concepts and ideas that have been consciously learnt and rehearsed. It divides into episodic memory and semantic memory.

Declarative memory: (also referred to as episodic memory) contains facts, concepts and ideas that have been consciously learnt and rehearsed. It divides into explicit memory and semantic memory.

Episodic memory: the part of explicit or declarative memory that holds the details of events and experiences of one's life.

Semantic memory: the part of explicit or declarative memory that holds facts and concepts.

Memory encoding: where attended-to information is mentally converted into a representation that can be stored in the memory and retrieved later on.

Memory storage: where information mentally converted into a representation is held in the short- or long-term memory.

Memory retrieval: where information held in the memory is retrieved and brought into consciousness.

ACTIVITY 4.1

To illustrate the differences between explicit and implicit memory, try the following. On a piece of paper, write down the 26 letters of the alphabet in the order that they appear on your computer keyboard, from top row to bottom row. Do not look at your computer keyboard.

You may well find that the task of recalling the alphabet from memory in that particular order was hard work, even if you reproduced it completely correctly. It involves memory recall at the explicit, declarative and semantic level.

Now type the following sentence: 'Pack my box with five dozen liquor jugs.'

You probably did it without even trying, maybe without even looking at the keys. Yet you not only remembered but also operationalised the first task, as that sentence contains every one of the 26 letters of the alphabet, requiring you to know the precise location of each key. It involves memory recall at the implicit level.

In addition, modern research is becoming increasingly focused on how implicit memory influences our knowledge, schemas and behaviour patterns. This plays an important part in the decision-making process, which is considered in Section 4.2.3.

There are two models that provide a framework for understanding the conceptualisation of the memory process over time: the **multi-store memory model** and the **working memory model**. Both models provide a framework for an understanding of the memory processes over time.

The multi-store memory model (Atkinson and Shiffrin, 1968)

The multi-store memory model is one of cognitive processing and retention of information. It holds that memory storage and recall are a linear process, within the three stores shown in Figure 4.6.

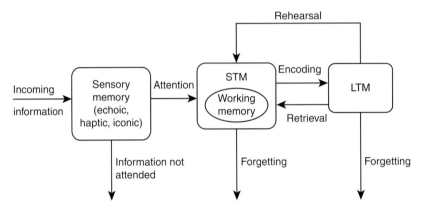

Figure 4.6 The multi-store memory model

1   **Sensory memory (SM).** Sometimes know as the sensory register, the SM is not under cognitive control. It receives inputs in various forms, including sound (echoic), touch (haptic) and visual (iconic). Incoming information not attended to is lost without trace. Whatever we selectively attend to is accepted by the SM and becomes eligible for coding into the STM.

2   **Short-term memory (STM).** The STM temporarily stores a limited amount of information passed on by the SM. The STM holds information for a maximum of 30 seconds. The information needs to be attended to in order to keep it there, or it can be displaced and lost; think of struggling to remember a ten-figure telephone number. Encoding in to the STM may be by auditory means (such as continuously repeating the numbers), visually (imagining the appearance of the numbers in your favourite font) or semantically (through meaning, such as by relating it to another similar set of numbers that you already know). That may undergo further coding into the LTM.

3   Long-term memory (LTM). Coding information into the LTM is usually by semantic means (the giving of meaning, and the use of existing schemas) and the amount varies according to the nature of that information. As already considered, LTM exists in different forms, including types of implicit and explicit memory. Although the information is relatively secure there, it may be lost or distorted by schema interferences, which are considered in Section 4.3.1.

This model regards the memory stores as the structural components of the memory system. It also proposes that the processes of attention, coding and rehearsal activate the mechanisms that decide which information should be encoded in the memory, and which information should be discarded.

Strengths of the model

*   Studies of anterograde amnesia patients show a good recall of instructions given in the last few seconds (good STM), but very poor recall of those given less recently (poor LTM), suggesting different stores. Anterograde amnesia is where brain damage has resulted in being unable to encode new items into the memory.

- In free-recall experiments (e.g. Murdock, 1962) involving memorising lists of words, subjects tend to remember those that are most likely to have been well-rehearsed in the beginning, before the novelty of taking part in an experiment has worn off (the primacy effect), and those at the very end of the list (the recency effect).

- The model has biological support. For example, the work of Newcomer et al. (1999) on how stress adversely affects memory recall indicated that the STM and LTM are separate stores. It was high levels of cortisol, a naturally-produced stress hormone, that interfered with the memory transfer and retrieval between those stores.

Limitations of the model

- The model is too simple. Its emphasis is more on memory stores than on the actual processes of attention and verbal rehearsal. It does not take into account the different levels and motivations for processing information. But we memorise numbers more successfully if they make up the phone number of someone we would like to meet again than if they are mere random numbers.

- The ability to visualise and recall the sound of something at the same time strongly indicates that the STM is not one single store.

The working memory model (Baddeley and Hitch, 1974, 2000)

The working memory model challenges the multi-store's model STM store as being too simple. The working memory model is the theoretical framework referring to the structures and processes used for temporarily storing and manipulating sensed information. The model holds that the STM has three specialised rather than one general structure that temporarily stores and manipulates sensed information. It contains three separate STM components, each of which operates in parallel at the same time, and all three lead to the LTM.

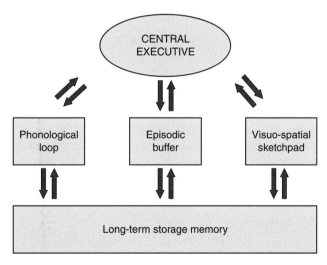

Figure 4.7 The working memory model

1 The **central executive (CE)**: this, the selective SM component, is a controlling attention mechanism with a limited capacity. It decides which information received by the sense organs is picked up, and passed to which one of the three multi-component STM systems that work in parallel, collectively referred to as the working memory. The CE also decides what the working memory pays attention to when two inputs are sensed at the same moment. For example, you are viewing a photograph on your smartphone. A loudspeaker starts to announce the gate number of a flight that may be yours. The CE diverts your attention from viewing the picture to paying attention to the announcement. The CE is on one hand limited in capacity in being only able to cope with one piece of information at a time, but it can also instantaneously switch from one store to another, both in directing information and in collecting responses.

Central executive (CE): sensory memory component of the working memory model. It selects the sensory information that is picked up and passed on to the suitable parts of the three-component working STM system.

2 The three STM subsystems are two-way systems between the CE and the LTM. The CE selectively directs visual and conceptually-based information into those three separate channel components. The information can be operating at the same time: you can visualise and think about a concept simultaneously. (You claim this when you tell your teacher that you pay attention while doodling over your notepad.)

Phonological loop: (also referred to as articulatory loop) the part of the STM within the working memory model that processes auditory information. It consists of a short-term sound store with auditory memory traces that if left alone are quickly lost.

Visual-spatial sketchpad: the part of the STM within the working memory model that processes visual information.

Episodic buffer: the part of the STM within the working memory model that processes narrative-type information.

- The **phonological loop** (or 'articulatory loop'), processing sound or phonological information. It consists of two parts: a short-term phonological (sound) store with auditory memory traces that if left alone are quickly lost, but it is supported by an articulatory rehearsal component, sometimes called the articulatory loop, that can revive the memory traces. This 'inner voice' repeats the series of words or other speech elements on a 'loop' to prevent them from decaying.

- The **visual-spatial sketchpad** or 'inner eye' which holds visual and spatial information. The content of what is stored there can come from two sources: the CE or the LTM.

- The **episodic buffer** is a separate complex memory device enabling you to recall an interrelated set of phenomena, such as a personal story, the sound of your favourite pop group, or how you felt as you came off your first ever roller-coaster ride. It is much like a television recall of an event.

c The LTM receives from, and releases to, the three STM systems above.

Strengths of the model

- In contrast to the multi-store model, this working memory model can accommodate a person's ability to visualise and recall the sound of something at the same time, as it accepts that the STM is not one single store. It could explain how people can multi-task.

- Problems in studying by one method may be put right through studying by another method. For example, those who have difficulties in following a lecture by listening (thereby using the phonological loop) can master the material through the visual-spatial sketchpad by representing the material through a series of diagrams. This explains why the lecture method can fail, where a person is a visual learner rather than an auditory learner.

- The division of memory functions into different stores may help to explain why some brain-damaged patients can recall one type of memory, but not another.

Articulatory suppression: participants are required to memorise and recall a random list of numbers or words, but at the same time have to constantly repeat a specified word while learning the list.

- The model is supported by research on **articulatory suppression**. This is where participants are required to memorise and recall a random list of numbers or words, but at the same time constantly repeating a specified word while learning the list. Landry and Bartling (2011), using experimental methods, found that the test participants in the articulatory suppression condition recalled the items significantly less accurately than the control participants, who memorised the list without any interference. This indicates that the same section of the STM, the phonological loop, is overloaded and significantly less effective when attempting to perform two tasks simultaneously.

- There is biological support. Evidence based on brain-damaged patients and more recently through brain scanning indicates that visual and verbal inputs are processed in different sections of the brain. The work of D'Esposito et al. (1995), using fMRI scans, showed activity in the prefrontal cortex when verbal and spatial tasks were performed at the same time, but not when performed separately. That suggests that the CE function of directing information into and out of the different channels is brain-localised.

- The model can help to explain why it is possible to multi-task in some situations, such as working out a problem and looking at a picture, but not in others, such as working out two problems at the same time.

Limitations of the model

- The nature and role of the CE is still unclear, and with it, the exact way in which the three elements of the STM interrelate.

- The existence of other memory stores need to be incorporated. The episodic buffer was not in the original 1974 model, but added in 2000 on the basis of evidence from brain-damaged patients able to recall anecdotes.

- The model focuses on STM rather than LTM. It does not extend to explaining why memories may become distorted over time.

- It does not incorporate the role of emotions in the stages of the memory process.

SELF-ASSESSMENT QUESTIONS 4.1

1 Define the cognitive approach to behaviour.

2 List the main elements of the cognitive approach.

3 List four research methods commonly used in the cognitive approach. For each, give an example of a piece of cognitive research using this method.

4 Distinguish between the STM and the LTM. How do they relate to each other?

5 In what ways are the multi-store memory model and the working memory model similar to, and different from, each other?

6 What are the strengths and limitations of the multi-store memory model and the working memory model?

7 What are implicit and explicit memory, and how do they differ from one another?

4.2.2 Cognitive processing: schema theory

Cognitive psychology operates on the assumption that our developing schemas guide our behaviour. As mentioned earlier, cognitive schemas are individualised mental representations and mechanisms that process information. They build up from previously acquired knowledge and experience, and they help to organise knowledge, beliefs and expectations. Examples of schemas are the capacity to communicate in French, ride a bicycle, drive a car, pick up on the teacher's mood and interact in a suitable manner. They grow in numbers and complexity through our own experiences of life, education and culture.

Figure 4.8 Schema versus gravity. Schema wins.

Schema processing involves the synthesising of new input from the environment through the mental structures already built. Schemas also appear to influence the memory process at all stages: encoding, storage and retrieval.

They often enable cognitive short-cuts, helping the person to generalise. On one hand, schemas reduce the cognitive energy used to handle big and small situations as they occur. Indeed, schema processing tends to be non-thinking and non-conscious. On the other hand, they can result in non-objectivity, with biases in thinking and memory processes.

Schemas have not yet been scientifically defined in terms of biological entities. However, there are many studies that assess the evidence of the presence and role of schemas in human behaviour. In addition, the study of Loftus and Palmer (1974) later in this chapter considers how questions framed to mislead can trigger schemas that promote errors when reporting past events.

Imagine that your car is being repaired and you rent a different model. The dashboard is unfamiliar. However, the schemas of previous driving experience enable you to work with its different arrangement; something that you would not be able to do if you had never learnt to drive.

How the driving schemas may be applied depends on whether you use **top-down processing**, **bottom-up processing**, or both. Top-down processing is where you bring models, ideas and expectations to interpret new sensory information. That means immediately recognising that dashboards are things you have seen before, and applying the driving schemas to work out how to operate it. Bottom-up processes sense the dashboard as being something new, and then in stages integrate it with existing driving schemas. With top-down processing, it is 'I am processing the information in terms of what I have seen before'. With bottom-up processing, it is 'What am I seeing? What schemas can I apply to work it out?'

Schema processing is a very wide field. As well as top-down and bottom-up processing, it includes:

1 Pattern recognition: a current sensory input being matched with information already held in the memory, or within skills already acquired. An example would be finding the way to use the unfamiliar dashboard.

2 Effort after meaning: trying to match unfamiliar ideas into a familiar framework, with various degrees of success. This is illustrated by the pioneer work of Bartlett (1932), which is considered in this section.

3 **Stereotyping**: schema processing of individuals based on fixed mental representations of the group they belong to. This involves identifying a person as belonging to a particular group, and believing that the person has the characteristics commonly attributed to that group. Identifying a newcomer as belonging to a particular group is the point where the information is processed into a schema. Believing that the person has the characteristics commonly attributed to that group is simplifying the characteristics of the newcomer through the schema, which is a cognitive short-cut: it saves the effort of getting to know the individual. Behaviours flowing from stereotyping can include positive and negative **discrimination**.

The role of schemas in stereotyping may be exemplified by the research of Bargh et al. (1996). It is detailed in Chapter 5, as stereotyping also has socio-cultural dimensions.

In addition, schemas can be culture-influenced and culture-driven. They can also be influenced by the expectations of others.

Attempting to work new ideas into unsuitable but more familiar schemas can promote schema-driven inaccuracies in memory recall. New information is distorted by being made to fit into existing schemas that cannot fully accommodate it (point 2 above), as in the classic study of Bartlett.

Research study: Bartlett (1932)

Bartlett researched effort after meaning, and also the existence of reconstructive memory with a group of participants.

Top-down processing: the bringing of models, ideas, expectations and schemas to interpret new sensory information.

Bottom-up processing: the interpreting of new sensory information as being initially something new and then in stages integrating it with existing schemas.

Stereotyping: a cognitive process where an unknown individual is perceived to have the characteristics commonly associated with the group they belong to.

Discrimination: unjustifiably negative behaviour towards members of an out-group.

Sir Fredric Bartlett (1886–1969)

Sir Fredric Bartlett (1886–1969) was the first professor of experimental psychology at the University of Cambridge, UK. His famous work 'Remembering' is his development of schema theory and constructive memory in which his 'War of the Ghosts' study forms an important part. His childhood involvement in sports stimulated his interest in the psychology of that field, which found expression and development in his explanations of the adaptive coordination of movements that people create in previously unencountered situations. Although cognitive psychology emerged as a distinctive field in psychology in the last years of his life, he preferred to describe himself as 'A Cambridge Psychologist'.

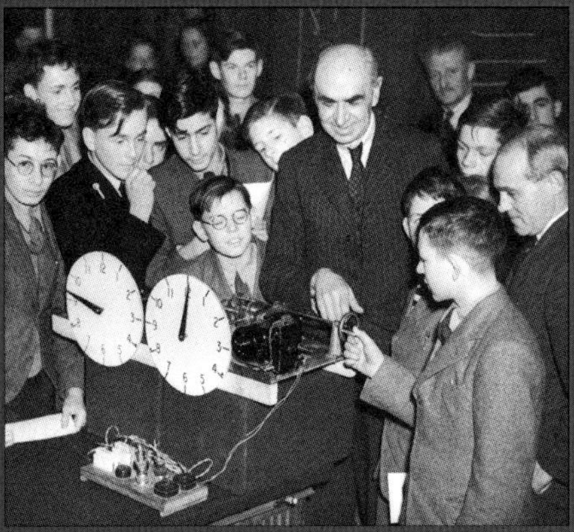

Figure 4.9 Sir Fredric Bartlett

Aim

To investigate whether cultural schemas and previous knowledge would adversely affect the level of accuracy in memory recall.

Procedure

Bartlett worked with a group of British participants with a Western socio-cultural background. The participants were required to read the story below. It was based on a Native American legend. Those taking part were not told the purpose of the experiment.

The War of the Ghosts

One night two young men from Egulac went down to the river to hunt seals, and while they were there, it became foggy and calm. Then they heard war-cries, and they thought, 'Maybe this is a war-party.' They escaped to the shore, and hid behind a log. Now canoes came up, and they heard the noise of paddles, and saw one canoe coming up to them.

There were five men in the canoe, and they said:

'What do you think? We wish to take you along. We are going up the river to make war on the people.'

One of the young men said, 'I have no arrows.'

'Arrows are in the canoe,' they said.

'I will not go along. I might be killed. My relatives do not know where I have gone. But you,' he said, turning to the other, 'may go with them.'

So one of the young men went, while the other returned home.

And the warriors went on up the river to a town on the other side of Kalama. The people came down to the water, and they began to fight, and many were killed. But presently the young man heard one of the warriors say, 'Quick, let us go home: that Indian has been hit.' Now he thought, 'Oh, they are ghosts.' He did not feel sick, but they said he had been shot.

So the canoes went back to Egulac, and the young man went ashore to his house, and made a fire. And he told everybody and said, 'Behold I accompanied the ghosts, and we went to fight. Many of our fellows were killed, and many of those who attacked us were killed. They said I was hit, and I did not feel sick.'

He told it all, and then he became quiet. When the sun rose, he fell down. Something black came out of his mouth. His face became contorted. The people jumped up and cried.

He was dead.

Results

After 15 minutes, Bartlett asked the participants to reproduce the story. He found that although the main themes of the story were largely understood, the details reproduced, employing effort after meaning, tended to be the ones that Western cultural schemas could most readily relate to. With each retelling by the participants, Bartlett found the narratives to be shorter. They tended to leave out details that the participants thought were less significant. Some recollections included details that did not exist in the story, such as 'fishing' in place of 'hunting seals'.

Conclusion

Overall, Bartlett found that reconstructive memory becomes more inaccurate the further the experience is distanced from the person's existing operating schemas. He concluded that people reconstruct the past by trying to fit it into existing schemas, even though it will not be accurate. That is reconstructive memory, discussed in more detail later in this chapter. According to Bartlett and supported by modern research, memory recall is an imaginative attempt to restore the experience without necessarily being accurate.

Strengths of the study

The study is ecologically valid. The story was deliberately chosen as being outside the culture and schemas of those who participated. The findings indicate support for the existence of schemas serving as tools for the processing of new information. Indeed, Bartlett's participants may be said to have been activating their own schemas. The study also supports the notion that the mind tends to reconstruct recalled information within pre-existing schemas.

Additionally, the work of Hunter (1964) replicated Bartlett's work, using the same story with results similar to Bartlett's. He noted that even if incorrectly recalled, the story became more coherent each time it was retold by the participants. It appeared that the recollections were advancing into interpretations of the story rather than recounting the story itself. This showed that the human memory does not always function as a computer. The input entered and the output recalled do not match: there is the element of memory being an imaginative construction of the experience.

Limitations of the study

Bartlett has been criticised for lacking experimental controls, and for being informal. For example, the intervals at which the story was reproduced were not standard for each participant.

Schemas can also be influenced by culture.

INTERNATIONAL FOCUS

Kearins (1981) considered the role of schemas in mental-mapping large expanses of desert territory.

This study compared the ability of white Australians and people of indigenous descent to encode spatial and visual information. The hypothesis was that the children of indigenous Australian origin would perform better than white Australians on tasks requiring those skills, because their societies had depended on their associated schemas for thousands of years. Their lifestyle had been semi-nomadic. Their very survival depended on their capacity to encode and store huge amounts of information about almost-featureless landscapes that they had to orientate to hunt game, gather berries, and locate sources of water. As resources were sparse, distances were large. Failure to encode visual information effectively could mean never finding the way back to the tribe, and almost certain death.

Figure 4.10 Which group will find it harder to find the way home? What important skills will that group need?

Effective schemas for activation of those spatial skills were essential for indigenous people's survival. These abilities were generally not relevant to the experience of city-origin white Australians.

The method of investigation involved a total of 88 boys and girls aged between 12 and 16 living in Western Australia. 44 were indigenous Australian and 44 were white Australian. The groups were matched for age and gender.

The basic task was memorising the position of objects. The researcher placed 20 objects on a board with 20 squares. Both groups of children were to memorise the position of the objects on the board for 30 seconds. The objects were then piled up at the centre of the board. They then had to place the objects in their original location.

For both groups, these tasks were repeated with variations:

- First mode: the 20 different objects were manufactured, including a matchbox and a pair of scissors.

- Second mode: the 20 different objects were natural and commonplace in Australian deserts, such as rock and a small skull.

- Third mode: there were 12 manufactured objects that were similar to each other. All were unlabelled small bottles of different size, shape and colour.

- Fourth mode: there were 12 small rocks. All were different from each other in size, shape, colour and texture.

Kearins found that the indigenous Australian group far more accurately placed the objects in their original squares than the white Australian group. The white Australians were more successful with the first task, using different manufactured objects. The indigenous Australians performed equally well on natural and manufactured objects. However, their frequency of perfect scores was higher when they worked with 12 objects than when working with 20.

The researcher concluded that the indigenous Australians' millennia of desert survival enabled them to develop the spatial and visual-encoding schemas that were crucial for survival.

Critical thinking

1 The findings of this quasi-experiment were correlational. Explain fully what this means.
2 What explanations other than spatial schemas can you suggest for the significant differences in ability between the indigenous Australian and white Australian children in Kearins's study, and how may those explanations be investigated?

The strength of this study is that the findings support the evidence for the existence of culture-driven schemas. Although the participating indigenous Australian children were not hunter-gatherers, it is likely that their upbringing and culture included repeated cues of their traditional culture and lifestyle. Their parents were first-generation settled indigenous Australians. The study is also replicable with similar groups.

However, the scope of the study was its limited application due to it being confined to the 12–16 age group. The study was also quasi-experimental: the variable between the two groups was culture, and that could not be manipulated. Thus the findings were correlational. They did not show a cause and effect relationship in the development of schemas in particular domains.

Strengths of schema theory

Schema theory contributes much to the cognitive level of analysis of human behaviour. It helps us to understand socio-cultural issues such as the mechanisms of bias and prejudice, which are considered later in this chapter. It also gives a framework for understanding how objects and events are not perceived by different cultures in the same way. That is because our individualised schemas enable us to categorise the appearance and behaviour of newcomers in terms of people, groups and values that we already know.

Schemas also enable us to selectively filter and encode newly-encountered information into our memory stores. Schema theory can explain why memories are selective and sometimes inaccurate, as both encoding and retrieval are aided by and filtered through existing schemas. Cognitive psychologists emphasise that memory is reconstructive by nature, and tends to become more inaccurate the further the experience is distanced from the person's existing operating schemas. The ways that existing schemas prompt flawed memory recall are also considered in detail later in this chapter.

Schema theory could additionally account for the common situation of mistaking a stranger for someone who is known. Thus, it reflects the brain's search for meaningful patterns without necessarily checking whether the images produced are accurate.

Finally, a teacher presenting a new concept to you and your class may be applying schema theory. The teacher is likely to relate it to what you already know, to the schemas that you already have. That way the learning process is eased, as you consider the unfamiliar material in terms of the familiar material.

ACTIVITY 4.2

Follow a new concept introduced by a teacher in any class, and list the ways they made it more accessible by explaining it in terms of what you already know.

Limitations of schema theory

Some of the research experiments in this chapter have been criticised for lack of ecological validity. A follow-up on Loftus and Palmer's (1974) experiment using people who witnessed a real accident (Yuille and Cutshall, 1986) did not show any significant influence from leading questions, involving 'smashed', 'collided' and 'bumped', even though those leading questions were deliberately designed to mislead. As discussed in Section 4.3.1, that research study raises the issue of whether the findings on reconstructive memory might have been distorted and exaggerated by the laboratory conditions. These may include demand characteristics, and perceived lack of importance of the study by the participants.

Additionally, individual schemas have not been biologically isolated and defined. Despite rapid progress in brain-scanning mechanisms, it is not currently possible to trace fresh information being processed by the brain, except at a very general level. Therefore, there remains the lack of capacity to identify specific schemas, and to understand how they interrelate with other schemas.

SELF-ASSESSMENT QUESTIONS 4.2

1 Define schemas.

2 What does schema processing involve? List five ways in which schemas process information.

3 What do the following studies indicate on the nature of schemas that influence the behaviour of the individual?

   a Bartlett (1932)

   b Kearins (1981)

4 List the strengths and limitations of schema theory.

4.2.3 Cognitive processes: thinking and decision-making

Thinking involves using information and doing something with it, such as working out a problem or making a decision. Thinking engages our knowledge in interpreting our environment, predicting what may happen and planning how to deal with things. The thinking becomes problem-solving where it focuses on resolving a particular complication. The problem-solving becomes decision-making when the decision-maker already knows the range of possible choices.

Psychologists have applied a range of models of thinking and decision-making, including the cognitive elements of emotion mindset, and reasoned action. This section incorporates these factors into the **dual process model of thinking and decision-making**:

The dual process model of thinking and decision-making

Proposed by Stanovich (1999) and developed by behavioural economist Daniel Kahneman, the model holds that individuals bring two systems of thinking to decision-making:

- **System-1 thinking**: where the thinking is quick, automatic, involves little effort, and is more likely to be influenced by biases.

- **System-2 thinking**: where the thinking involves patience, logic, effort, careful reasoning and application to the particular goal.

System 1 and System 2 were brought into the forefront of national discussion by Professor Daniel Kahneman's landmark book, *Thinking Fast & Slow*, on human decision-making and how people can make erroneous decisions based on rules of thumb, emotion and instincts.

System-1 thinking is more likely to promote bias in decision-making. It often applies cognitive schemas as **heuristics**, mental short-cuts that may or may not be suitable bases for particular decisions. Heuristics may incorrectly apply familiar schemas to situations that do not match them, such as activating stereotypes that do not fit the realities. The use of heuristics can give the 'I've-seen-it-all-before' sense of getting things right, but result in more relevant factors being ignored. The likely biases in System-1 thinking are explored in the next part of this chapter, in its assessment of the reliability of cognitive processes.

Dual process model of thinking and decision-making: individuals bring two systems of thinking to decision-making, known as System-1 and System-2 thinking.

System-1 thinking: the thinking is quick, automatic, involves little effort, and is more likely to be influenced by biases.

System-2 thinking: the thinking involves patience, logic, effort, careful reasoning and application to the particular goal.

Heuristics: mental short-cuts that may or may not be suitable bases for particular decisions, developed in the hippocampus and only then in the amygdala.

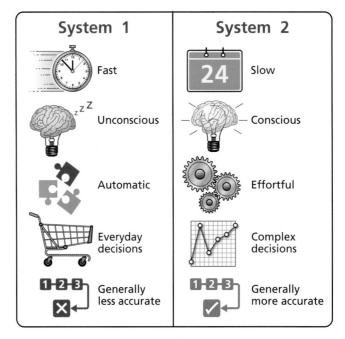

Figure 4.11 System-1 versus System-2 decision-making

System-2 thinking is conscious and effortful. It involves the careful consideration of available information and possible options. The basis of the decision will be better informed, but the decision-maker will probably be less certain of having made the right one. System-2 thinking is particularly challenging to use when under pressure and having to think of many things at the same time. System-2 thinking does not guarantee a correct decision, but it will probably result in a more informed one. Generally, System-2 thinking is more likely to be used where the problem is not an everyday one and the decision-maker regards it as complex and important.

Research study: Alter et al. (2007)

This idea is exemplified in the research of Alter et al. (2007) who found experimental-grounded evidence for the switching over to System-2 thinking when an everyday task such as reading became more difficult than usual.

Aim

To find out whether decreasing the legibility of the font in a standard cognitive test would produce more accurate responses. The reasoning was that the participants would employ the more reasoned System-2 thinking than the more heuristic System-1 thinking.

Procedure

The participants were 40 undergraduates from Princeton University, USA, who were required to complete a standardised cognition reflection test. They were randomly assigned to the control 'fluent' condition or the test 'non-fluent' condition. The IV was the type of font. The text and questions for each individual in the control fluent condition was in easy-to-read black Myriad Web 12-point font. Those in the test non-fluent group received theirs in the difficult-to-read 10% grey italicised Myriad Web 10-point font. The DV was the number of errors made in the standardised cognition test.

Results

The results showed a significantly higher degree of accuracy with the test non-fluent participants than with the control fluent participants. In all, 65% of the participants in the non-fluent condition answered all the questions correctly, whereas only 10% of those in the fluent condition did so.

Conclusion

The researchers concluded that their research supports the view that difficult tasks prompt the use of the more-reasoned System-2 thinking rather than the more-heuristic System-1 thinking.

Strengths of the study

The strengths of the experiment are that it was a simple **independent measures** experimental study that used a relatively homogenous sample. The IV was duly manipulated and the findings indicated cause and effect. It is easily replicable. The findings of this study can help to explain why, for example, a neatly handwritten and easy-to-read piece of work might well be unfairly but more generously marked than the same item produced in an eye-straining, hard-to-decipher script.

Limitations of the study

The limitations of the experiment are in the theory it was designed to support. It may be argued that the test-group participants were not switching from one system of thinking to another, but found themselves thinking more carefully as a natural result of the difficult font slowing them down.

Research study: Goel et al. (2000)

Aim

To investigate whether there is biological support for the dual system model.

Procedure

There were 11 right-handed participants who were given a series of deductive reasoning tasks that fell into two categories. Half were based on concrete, content arguments. The other half were similar, but the content was abstract. In all tasks, participants had to deduce whether or not the inferences given were valid on the basis of the information. All the participants completed all the tasks.

An example of a concrete argument used: (a) All dogs are pets (b) All poodles are dogs, so therefore (c) All poodles are pets. Is (c) valid?

An example of an abstract argument used was: (a) All P are B (b) All C are P, so therefore (c) All C are B. Is (c) valid?

Within the entire task, half the deductions were invalid.

Each participant was attached to an fMRI scanner while carrying out the tasks, in order to investigate whether the different types of thinking in the dual process model engaged different parts of the brain.

Results

The scan findings indicated that many common areas of the brain were active in carrying out all the tasks. Nevertheless, there were significant task-type differences. When their content was concrete and likely to use System-1 thinking, participants tended to engage the left hemisphere temporal lobe. When their content was abstract and likely to use System-2 thinking, the reasoning appeared to be processed through the parietal lobe.

Strengths of the study

The strengths of the study are that firstly, it was set up with standardised tasks designed to elicit the two different types of thinking. Secondly, the brain scan data produced by the study did indicate biological correlates for the two different types of thinking.

Limitations of the study

The limitations of this study are again in the theory it was designed to support. It is possible that the participants may have applied the same system of thinking to both sets of exercises, but the parietal lobe was engaged in the abstract questions because the participants found them harder to respond to rather than due to the transition from one type of thinking to another. In addition, it is not clear that the greater engagement of the parietal lobe indicates System-2 thinking's greater demands.

Independent measures design: where each participant in the sample is involved in either the control condition or in the test condition.

Evaluation of the dual process model of thinking and decision-making

Strengths of the model

- There are biological correlates suggesting that different parts of the brain engage in System-1 and System-2 thinking, exemplified by Goel at al. (2000).

- There are experimentally-based findings indicating that easier and less demanding tasks employ System-1 thinking, while more challenging items will use System-2 thinking, exemplified by Alter et al. (2007).

- There are high **validity** and high **reliability** studies indicating System-1-related cognitive biases in thinking and decision-making. Some of these are explored in the next part of this chapter.

Limitations of the model

- Although there appear to be biological correlates to different types of thinking, they do not define the distinct two systems as the model does, in terms of degrees of speed, effort and reasoned analysis.

- The model does not factor in the emotional condition of the decision-maker.

Validity (of research): how accurately the study measures what it is designed to measure.

Reliability (of research): the degree to which the study in repeated trials using the same methods, design and measurements produces the same results.

SELF-ASSESSMENT QUESTIONS 4.3

1 Distinguish between System-1 thinking and System-2 thinking in the dual process model of thinking and decision-making.

2 State the strengths and limitations of the dual process model of thinking and decision-making.

3 What contribution have the following studies made to our understanding of thinking and decision-making?

   a Alter et al. (2007)

   b Goel et al. (2000)

4.3 The reliability of cognitive processes

NEWSFLASH

University students deluded by Bugs Bunny.

It has probably happened to most of us. We remember an event so clearly that it seems to have happened just yesterday. Then we learn that it actually never happened.

A study has found just how easy it can be to induce a **false memory** in the minds of some people. Subjects in a study recalled seeing Bugs Bunny in Disneyland, California which is impossible because Bugs Bunny is not a Disney character. Researchers had planted a false memory.

Loftus and Pickrell (1995) wanted to see whether misleading suggestions might interfere with memory, using the world of advertising. Would such prompts promote false memories, getting people to recall something they could never have seen before?

False memory: recalling an event that never happened and believing it is true.

The researchers talked to students, asking about their childhood visits to Disneyland, California and about seeing or meeting Bugs Bunny there. In later interviews, around one-third of the participants said that they had seen or met Bugs Bunny at Disneyland.

That was a false memory. Bugs Bunny was not a Disney character. He belonged to Warner Brothers.

This research suggests that it doesn't need something traumatic to adjust our memory: it shows that you can implant a memory for an event that never even happened.

ACTIVITY 4.3

In groups, discuss how far the above factors can explain why so many participants related that they had encountered Bugs Bunny at Disneyland.

Human memory systems are not only complex, but also often inaccurate, unreliable and distorted. The research considered below indicates that memory distortion may happen during storage, processing and retrieval. That may happen for various reasons, such as the emotional state of the individual, and schema interferences. It can result in **confabulation**, where memories are sincerely believed and declared by the person to be true even though they are contradicted by evidence.

Thinking and decision-making are also susceptible to bias: people do not always use System-2 rational thinking, but are often inclined to use the less cognitively-demanding System-1 short cuts by placing emphasis on information that confirms rather than contradicts pre-existing ideas and expectations.

It may be suggested that the students' alleged recall of Bugs Bunny relied on the way that the prompts were processed by their schemas. When the facts interfered with the person's existing schemas, the students' minds may have reconstructed Bugs Bunny's presence according to the schemas, even though he had not been there. This is an example of **reconstructive memory**.

Confabulation: where memories are sincerely believed and declared by the person to be true even though they are contradicted by evidence.

Reconstructive memory: where schemas, beliefs, imagination and gaps in recollection combine to create an individual's inaccurate recall of events.

4.3.1 Reconstructive memory

Reconstructive memory is where cognitive schemas influence memory recall, which in turn may induce inaccuracies in memory processing, storage and retrieval. Inaccurate memories can be caused by changes during the processing, storage and retrieval stages. It can involve the following elements:

- confabulation

- schema processing

- **selective memory**: the ability to retrieve certain facts and events, but not others

- false memory.

One of the main explanations given for inaccurate memory recall is where the new information is distorted by being made to fit into existing schemas that cannot fully accommodate it, as in Bartlett's (1932) study. Although Bartlett has been criticised for being informal and lacking experimental controls, more modern research has supported the concepts of both schema-based information-processing and reconstructive memory, as in Loftus and Palmer (1974).

Selective memory: the ability to retrieve certain facts and events but not others, depending on how easily the inputs coded into memory fit into existing schemas.

Elizabeth Loftus

Elizabeth Loftus (1944–) is a cognitive psychologist and professor at the University of California, Irvine. Her work over the last 40 years has specialised in researching how far we can rely on our own memories. Loftus's work has indicated that people inaccurately reporting information often genuinely believe what they have been saying. Eyewitness memory can often be suspect, and encountered misinformation can prompt inaccurate memory recall.

Her work has also involved training and advising legal professionals in assessing the accuracy of evidence from witnesses in court, most famously in murder cases. The memory, Loftus claims, is malleable. It is wide open to misinforming suggestions that can lead to individuals being wrongly identified, accused and convicted. Memory, she holds, is not a recording device. Rather, it is like a Wikipedia page. You can change it, and other people can change it.

Figure 4.12 Elizabeth Loftus

Research study: Loftus and Palmer (1974)

Loftus and Palmer conducted an investigation on how the use of language, schemas and memory may contribute to inaccurate and reconstructive memory recall. Their study was based on two experiments that were designed to assess how far the participants' estimates of the speed of colliding vehicles could be influenced by misleading **framing** of the questions.

Framing: a heuristic where decision-making is liable to be biased by the way the information is given or the request is made.

Aim

To find out whether participants' estimate of the speed of vehicles would be significantly influenced by the wording of the question.

Procedure

The first experiment involved 45 participating university students who were shown a series of seven movie clips of traffic accidents. After each clip, all participants answered questions designed to recall details of the accident. The critical question was the speed of the cars when the accident took place. It is not easy for an onlooker to estimate the speed of a moving car with accuracy.

The aim of this first investigation was to determine whether increasing the emphasis on description of the collision would influence the participants' recall of how fast the cars were travelling. In separate test-group trials, the word 'hit' in the question was replaced with 'contacted', 'bumped', 'collided' or 'smashed'. The hypothesis was that leading questions suggesting the area of response would influence schema processing. That in turn would affect the accuracy of the recall.

The second experiment involved 150 participating university students, who were all shown the same one-minute video of a car crash. 50 students were asked to estimate the speed of the car that 'smashed into each other', the key word being 'smashed'. 50 students were asked to estimate the speed of the cars that 'hit each other', the key word being 'hit'. The other 50 students formed the control group who were not asked to estimate the speed. One week later, they responded to questions on their memory of the crash, including: 'Did you see any broken glass?' There was no broken glass in the video.

Results

The results of both experiments indicated a significant support for the hypothesis. In the first experiment, 'smashed', 'collided' and 'bumped' got a significantly faster speed estimate than 'hit' and 'contacted', as shown in Figure 4.13:

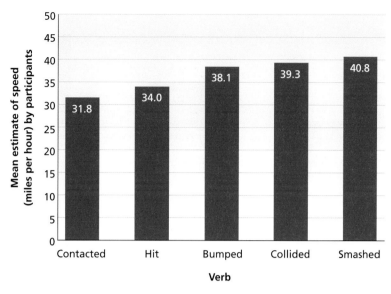

Figure 4.13 The effect of language on the perception of speed

The results indicated that the speed estimates were indeed influenced by the intensity of the verb used to describe the accident.

In the second experiment, more than twice as many participants recollected the false memory of the broken glass.

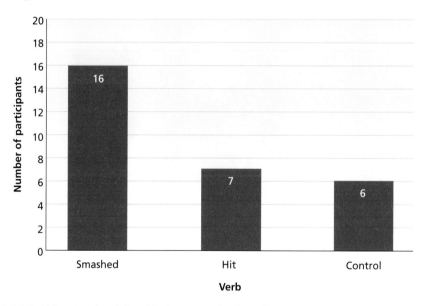

Figure 4.14 Participants who claimed to have seen broken glass

Conclusion

The conclusion was that different words activate different schemas in the memory. Hearing the word 'smashed' caused the memory to reconstruct a more severe picture than hearing the word 'hit' or 'contacted'.

Strengths of the study

The work of Loftus and Palmer was quantitative, controlled and formally-conducted experimental research. It supports the theory that memory recall may be reconstructive and therefore prone to inaccuracies. Its findings can have serious implications where witnesses in good faith could wrongly testify in a court of law, or in police procedures involving a parade where the victim has to identify the accused.

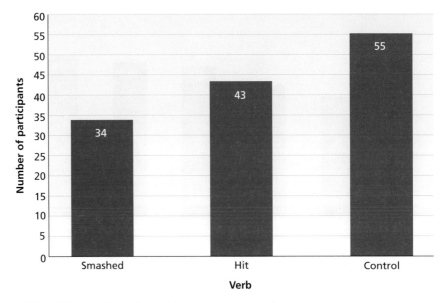

Figure 4.15 Participants who did not claim to have seen broken glass

Limitations of the study

Loftus and Palmer conducted their experimental work specifically in a laboratory situation. It is possible that some respondents responded to 'demand characteristics', giving the responses they thought the interviewers wanted. That means that real-life witness accounts of such a crash might well be more accurate.

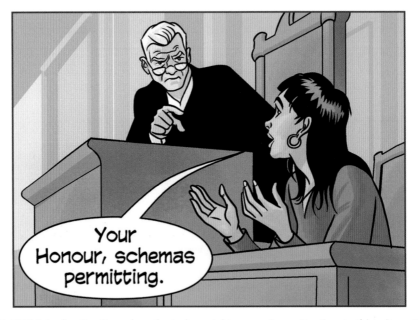

Figure 4.16 Think of a situation when the judge might pay serious attention to this witness's claim. The profile on Elizabeth Loftus could help.

However, the information sought was not perceived to be of the same degree of importance as giving eyewitness testimony on a crime, where the participants might have been more careful. That issue has been investigated in studies such as Yuille and Cutshall.

Research study: Yuille and Cutshall (1986)

The work of Yuille and Cutshall (1986) indicates that real-life eyewitness testimony is indeed likely to be more accurate in a real-life situation than in a laboratory situation. Yuille and Cutshall carried out a similar type of study to Loftus and Palmer, but in a natural setting.

Aim

To determine whether leading questions would reduce the accuracy of memory recall.

Procedure

There was no pre-selected group of participants. They were witnesses to what had happened, and subsequently agreed to take part in the study.

The incident was a robbery of a gun shop in Vancouver, Canada. The attacker immobilised the owner by tying him up, and proceeded to steal money and guns from the shop. The owner managed to break free, but the thief who was still there fired twice. The police who had arrived in the meantime intervened and eventually killed the attacker.

All of this happened outside the shop, and the police interviewed 21 people who witnessed the scene. The researchers contacted them, and 13 agreed to take part in the study.

Each participating witness first recounted the incident, and then responded to a series of questions from the interviewer. Within that procedure, the researchers employed two leading questions, similar to the ones used in Loftus and Palmer. They asked one half of the group if they saw a broken headlamp on the getaway vehicle. They asked the other half if they saw a yellow panel on the car. In fact the car had neither a broken lamp nor a yellow panel. Finally, they rated their level of stress for that day.

Results and conclusion

The eyewitness reports were generally reliable. Much of the detail recounted was confirmed by police reports, with an accuracy rating of approximately 80%. That was considerably higher than in Loftus and Palmer, and appears to indicate that memory recall can be more accurate when the study's design does not pressure the participants to respond with answers they think they want the researchers to hear.

Limitations of the study

Unlike Loftus and Palmer, this study is not replicable, as an incident with precisely the same facts is unlikely to recur. In addition, it is possible that the participants had previously followed up what they had witnessed in the media, thus knowing much more about the crime than the researchers gave them credit for.

4.3.2 Biases in thinking and decision-making

Individuals are not always rational thinkers. The previous section considered the human tendency to rely on intuition and make decisions on the basis of cognitive short cuts. Using the framework of the dual system model of thinking, it looked at the ways that System-1 and System-2 thinking can influence the decision-making process.

System-1 thinking is fast, effortless, susceptible to bias and therefore error-prone, while System-2 thinking is slow, effortful and generally more accurate. Decisions based on System-1 thinking are likely to be less grounded, and decisions based on System-2 thinking are likely to be more grounded. In terms of bias, System-1 thinking tends to focus on a limited amount of information readily available at the time of the decision, and prefers to avoid the mental stress and effort that might lead to a changing perception of reality.

Theory of Knowledge

Discuss the reliability of observation in psychology compared with natural science, considering the following ideas:

1   The research studied in this section indicates a reconstructive element in human memory.
2   Observation in psychology is likely to be influenced by cognitive schemas.
3   Psychology involves cognitive concepts that may not be observed through the physical senses.

This section briefly considers a selection of types of System-1-associated cognitive biases including heuristics that can interfere with effective decision-making. They are based on the research of Kahneman, whose work on the dual system thinking appears earlier in this chapter, and several other researchers in the field. Types of biases include:

1 **Availability heuristic:** the more available information, the more we think it could happen to us. It is based on our perception of how frequent or common something is. For example, people's System-1 thinking biases them towards being typically more scared of being murdered than being killed in a car crash. The availability heuristic may be based on murders taking a bigger proportion of the leading news items than car crashes. As a result, people fear losing their lives to a killer rather than to another driver. In reality, in most countries, murder accounts for far fewer deaths than road accidents.

2 **Peak-end rule:** people's System-1 thinking memories of a good or bad experience focus on three things: how it started, what was the best or worst thing that happened, and how it finished. The peak-end rule enables the easy memory retrieval of bite-sized chunks, which may not accurately represent an entire event. For example, imagine your first skiing holiday. The things recalled may be apprehension of being attached to the skis for the first time, an unexpected bloody-nosed fall after taking things too fast, and that exhilarating feeling of effortlessly gliding down a difficult 'red' run on the last day with the thumbs up from your instructor. The long queues for the ski lifts, the freezing weather, and the exhausted muscles are biased-out when thinking in System-1 mode, only to be recalled when facing the same things on your next skiing holiday.

3 Framing: thinking fast in System 1 indicates that decision-making is liable to be biased by the way the information is given or the request is made. One example is the DMV (the US Department of Motor Vehicles) requiring the driving licence applicant to decide if they would like to donate organs for transplant in the event of death. When phrased on the lines of 'put an X in the box if you would like to donate', relatively few people agreed to donate. But when phrased 'put an X in the box if you do not wish to donate', far more people agreed. One reason may be anchoring (see point 6 below): the implication that wishing to donate is the norm, and people's System-1 decision-making is being centred and anchored within the region of what they think other people do.

4 **Endowment effect:** thinking fast in System 1 can bias an individual to overestimate the value of something simply because they own it; whether it is the home, the car, or the jeans being worn that day. For similar reasons, the potential buyer who is not yet personally connected may apply System-1 thinking to underestimate the value of those items.

5 Confirmation bias: the focusing on information and interpretations that confirm pre-existing opinions and expectations. Individuals with strong opinions on political and social issues who apply System 1 may be biased and inconsistent in their critical thinking. They will accept supporting evidence at face value, and subject opposing evidence to rigorous scrutiny. Confirming data will be reliable; non-confirming data, unreliable.

6 **Anchoring bias:** the reliance on the first piece of information offered (the 'anchor') to make a decision, irrespective of its accuracy and relevance. For example, a watch may be worth $1000. If it is displayed next to a watch priced at $3000, it might sell at a much higher price as the buyer's anchor is $3000. But if it is placed next to a watch priced at $500, it is less likely to sell at $1000 as the System-1 thinker has already judged its value on the $500 anchor. In short, such decision-making happens in reacting to the value of the anchor.

Research study: Lord et al. (1979)

Aim

To investigate the nature of confirmation bias, and the degree that such a bias would lead to inconsistencies in assessing supporting and contradictory evidence.

Procedure

The participants were 48 undergraduate psychology students, 24 of whom were in favour of the death penalty and 24 against. The students were placed into groups and were given a series of cards presenting research on the death penalty, some supportive and some opposed. The students filled in a questionnaire designed to show any attitude change. Then they were given the full details of the procedures and findings of each study. They had to judge how accurate each study was. In light of their reading, they answered the attitude change questionnaire a second time. Finally, they were presented with a further study with opposite results. Once again, they filled in the questionnaire.

Results

The overall findings of this study showed significant polarisation at the end of the study. Although all were exposed to the same stimulus material and detailed information, both the supporters and the opposers of the death penalty ended more convinced that their initial opinion was backed by academic research. And although some participants were initially taking wary steps towards the opposite standpoint, they returned to their original point of view after they examined the evidence.

Conclusion

The researchers concluded that the System-1 confirmatory bias exists within academic circles, where different standards are applied to the evidence supporting their personal standpoint and the evidence contradicting it.

Strengths of this study

Subsequent studies indicate that people can persist in their viewpoint even when the evidence overwhelmingly contradicts it. In addition, this study used psychology students who were academically equipped to handle the findings and details of research studies including critically assessing the evidence.

Limitations of the study

Both supporters and opposers tended to have highly-charged emotions towards the death penalty, limiting the capacity to generalise confirmation bias from that particular study to everyday decision-making. In addition, its laboratory setting brought the opposing information to the participants through written material. Auditory or visual information might have been more persuasive.

Finally, the emotional content of this study may also exemplify how emotion influences cognitive processes: in this case increasing the susceptibility to confirmation bias.

Research study: Ariely et al. (2003)

Ariely et al. conducted an experimental study to investigate whether anchors influenced System-1-type thinking even when they are irrelevant to the decision being made.

Aim

To test whether the last two digits of a person's social security number would affect the amount of money they would bid at an auction for various goods whose average retail price, unknown to the participants, was $70. They included high-quality chocolates, wine, computer accessories and books.

Procedure

The products were introduced to the participants, who were a class of 55 MBA students. They were asked whether they would buy each item for the same number of dollars as the last two digits of their social security number. Each gave the accept or reject response. They were then asked to state the maximum amount they would pay for items.

Results

The results showed a significant correlation between the social security number and the maximum amount prepared to pay for each product. Those with above-median social security numbers gave prepared-to-pay values from 57% to 107% more than those with below-median social security numbers. For example, those in the top social-security quintile were prepared to pay an average of $56 for a cordless computer keyboard, in contrast with those in the bottom quintile whose offers averaged only $16.

Conclusion

Anchors appear to be substantially influential in the decision-making process, even where they are irrelevant to the decision being made.

Strengths of the study

It appears that cognitive psychology has demonstrated that biases and faulty decisions are more likely to occur when the thinking is in the fast, heuristically-based, everyday-default-mode than when it is slower and effortful.

Limitations of the study

However, research shows that experts in a particular field can apply System-1 thinking and achieve similar accuracy to System 2. An expert ski jumper can make all the correct instant judgements for a brilliant performance by applying heuristically-based previous experience, but at the same time be unable to explain how they did it.

Thin slicing: where judgements about the nature and quality of a human interaction are made on the basis of the expert viewing a very small part of the interaction.

This is supported by the work of Ambady et al. (2000) who researched **thin slicing** with students' rating of college teachers. Thin slicing is where judgements about the quality of the interaction are made on the basis of the expert viewing a very small part of the interaction. In this study, students were required to rate teachers they had never met on the basis of video clips. One group gave ratings after watching five-minute clips of each teacher. Another group gave ratings after clips lasting less than one minute per teacher. The ratings of both groups were found to have a high correlation with the ratings given by students who attended their courses, and there was no difference between the ratings given by the five-minute clip group and the less-than-one minute clip group.

SELF-ASSESSMENT QUESTIONS 4.4

1   Define the following:

   a   reconstructive memory

   b   selective memory

2   What key contributions have been made to our assessment of the reliability of cognitive processes by the following?

   a   Bartlett (1932)

   b   Loftus and Palmer (1974)

   c   Yuille and Cutshall (1986)

   d   Loftus and Pickrell (1995)

3   Define the following types of biases in System-1 decision-making:

   a   availability heuristic   **b**   peak-end rule   **c**   framing

   d   endowment effect   **e**   confirmation bias   **f**   anchoring bias

4   What do the following studies contribute to our understanding of biases in System-1 decision-making?

   a   Lord et al. (1979)

   b   Ariely et al. (2003)

5   Define thin slicing. How does the study of Ambady et al. (2000) use this concept to support the use of System-1 heuristics?

Home-brewed lemonade for sale.

With a group of others in your class, brew a supply of lemonade or any other drink. Make sure that you have the permission of the school or any authorities before setting out your sales stand. Hopefully, the weather will be similar on both days. Make sure that you have three sets of paper or plastic cups: small, medium and large.

On Day 1, offer small drinks, medium drinks and large drinks. Price the drinks according to the following pattern in your currency: small: 50c, medium: 90c, large: $1. Calculate the sales percentage for each size.

On Day 2, preferably a week later, offer small drinks and large drinks only, at the same prices as the previous week. Calculate the sales percentage for each size.

Compare the sales percentage of small drinks and large drinks in Week 2 with Week 1. Identify any differences. Then suggest an explanation using thinking and decision-making theory.

4.4 Emotion and cognition

Research in both psychology and neurology indicate that our emotions influence the way we process information. Our emotions and cognitions interconnect.

Emotions, such as happiness, sadness, fear, disgust, anger, surprise or being impressed, influence cognitive processes by enabling the individual to adapt and relate to objects, events and situations in a uniquely personal way. In addition, memories that are emotionally charged tend to be more easily recalled, although not necessarily with a high degree of accuracy. This section examines both of these principles.

4.4.1 The influence of emotion on cognitive processes

Emotions such as anger, surprise and happiness are a combination of biological and cognitive factors. They involve physiological changes, involuntarily arousing the autonomic nervous system and endocrine system, the workings of which are presented in Chapter 3. The emotions influence cognitions that in turn influence situation-adaptive behaviours such as running away smiling or tensing in anger.

LeDoux's model of the brain (1999) shows that it simultaneously processes information along two paths of emotion. For example, someone is extremely annoyed. Their grasp of the situation, the cognitive process, goes simultaneously along a short route and a long route. The short route gives an animal-type response and is immediate. It starts at the sensory thalamus, the pick-up point of cognition. It travels directly to the finishing point, the amygdala, which stimulates the response. There is no rationalisation.

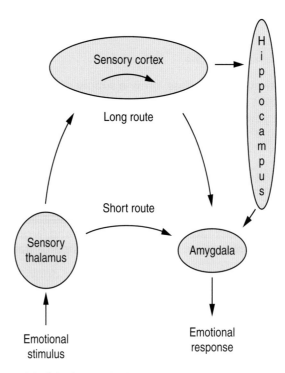

Figure 4.17 LeDoux's model of the brain's dual path processing

At the same time, the information is processed in more depth and in a more rational manner through the long, more complex route. That goes from the sensory thalamus via the sensory cortex and hippocampus and only then to the amygdala. It takes several seconds, but it enables the use of intelligence and experience, System 2-type thinking, before responding. Thus it may be a good idea to count to ten before reacting.

This model shows a vital interrelationship between cognitive and biological factors, and also how emotion influences cognition according to the different paths it takes through the brain. This biological set-up shows two simultaneous processes of cognition. The short route brings less complex, System-1-type schemas into cognitive processing, but is vital in emergencies as it saves the time that could be a matter of life and death. The long route brings more complex schemas into play and allows for a more reasonable and intelligent interpretation of a situation, which can help people to avoid inappropriate responses to situations.

Individuals show their emotions through different ways, including facial expression, physical movements and tone of voice. The effect of voice tone on the means and quality of other people's mental processing is the subject of the next research study.

Research study: Smith et al. (2015)

Aim

To investigate how the emotions communicated in an instructor's tone of voice may affect the performance of a cognitive task.

Procedure

The participants were 15 young adults of both genders between ages 20 to 38, all of whom were either university undergraduates or held at least a first degree. Each individual responded to 80 deductive reasoning questions while attached to an fMRI scanner. Both these deductive tasks and the fMRI scans were conducted on similar lines to Goel et al. (2000) in the thinking and decision-making section, described earlier in this chapter. A typical question, as there, would be: (a) All dogs are pets (b) All poodles are dogs, so therefore (c) All poodles are pets. Is (c) valid? After each task, the participant indicated valid deduction or non-valid deduction by pressing one of two keys.

These 80 tasks were pre-recorded in the voice of the same person throughout and communicated to the participants through earphones. The tone of voice was sad for 20 questions, angry for 20 questions and neutral for 40 questions.

Results

The results showed that the percentage of correct reasoning responses was 73% for angry-voice delivery, 64% for neutral-voice delivery and 66% for sad-voice delivery. There was no significant difference between the tone of voice and the time taken to respond to the questions.

The fMRI scans showed significant differences in the parts of the brain that were activated in response to each emotion within the question delivery. The sad voice correlated with activation of the left and right hippocampuses, as well as within the left inferior temporal gyrus. The angry voice correlated with increased activity in the left superior frontal gyrus and in the right angular gyrus. The neutral voice correlated with less activity in the left hippocampus and more activity in the right posterior **insula**.

Insula: the part of the brain where taste is sensed and integrated with the neural reward systems.

Conclusion

The study indicated that each different emotive tone of voice seems to have stimulated a different pattern of neural responses, that in turn at least partially influenced the degree of accuracy of the responses.

Strengths of the study

- The study indicates biological correlates between different emotions and corresponding reasoning processes in the brain.
- The accuracy levels of the responses were significantly above mere chance.
- The study supports behavioural findings indicating that the quality of reasoning improves in response to a neutral tone of voice becoming an angry tone of voice.

Limitations of the study

- It is possible that the respondents were responding to fear as a motivator rather than anger.
- The findings needed to take into account the pre-existing emotions of the participants at the start of the study.

4.4.2 Flashbulb memory: where past emotions prompt recall

Research study: Brown and Kulik (1977)

Aim

To investigate whether shocking or otherwise deeply emotional events can create such flashbulb memories.

Procedure

A total of 80 males participated: 40 black and 40 white. They filled out a questionnaire on the topic of the death of three people: J.F. Kennedy, Martin Luther King Jr and someone they knew personally. Participants were prompted to recall their circumstances surrounding each event: where they were with whom they were, and what they were doing at the time the events happened. They were also asked to recall how they first heard of the events, the level of emotion they felt on hearing of the events, how important those events were in their lives, and how often they had spoken of those events since. The latter was an attempt to factor in the element of memory rehearsal.

Results

The results showed that 90% of the participants recalled a considerable amount of detail surrounding the death of the individual close to them, but with public figures there was a significant race difference: 75% of black participants but only 33% of the white ones had flashbulb memories of the murder of Martin Luther King Jr.

Conclusion

Brown and Kulik seem to have identified two important determinants of the 'flashbulb memory package': event importance and event emotionality.

Strengths of the study

Its reliability may be determined as it is easily replicable.

There is also biological support. The work of Sharot et al. (2007), designed to investigate the biological aspect of flashbulb memory, used scanned evidence of increased amygdala action as suggesting that there are indeed specific neural structures involved in flashbulb memory.

Limitations of the study

The evidence was correlational. It did not explain what parts of the memory could be attributed to the amygdala.

Flashbulb memory has been questioned by the work of Neisser and Harsch (1992). They argue that flashbulb memory may be a narrative memory. People could be taking later events and putting them back into the memory, mixing them with the 'flashbulb event'. It may be that there is still a special memory mechanism for the 'flashbulb memory package', but if there is, does the memory last any longer than 'normal' memories? Indeed, Neisser and Harsch's investigation, which followed the 1986 space shuttle Challenger disaster, indicated that some 40% of the participants who recalled the event showed distinct memory distortion, which they argued was based on information found out some time after the event that was being fed into the memory of the actual event. In addition, studies of flashbulb memories are non-experimental, in that they do not include control conditions that distinguish between non-flashbulb memories and flashbulb memories.

Finally, the study was biased in terms of both gender (participants were male only) and culture (more recent studies indicate a lower level of flashbulb memories in collectivist societies).

SELF-ASSESSMENT QUESTIONS 4.5

1   What do the following theories/studies indicate about the way emotion influences cognitive processes?
    a   LeDoux's model of the brain's processing of information (1999)
    b   Smith et al. (2015)

2   Define flashbulb memory. What two factors appear to influence flashbulb memory according to Brown and Kulik (1977)?

3   How have the findings of Brown and Kulik been modified by:
    a   Sharot et al. (2007)
    b   Neisser and Harsch (1992)?

4.5 Cognitive processing in the digital world (HL only)

There has been a steady increase in the amount of time that individuals interact with the digital world. One study in the UK estimates that the average 16- to 24-year-old spends more than 27 hours per week on the internet for education, computer games and social media.

Public debate about the positive and negative effects of computer technology continues. Supporters of video games claim that they help to develop multi-tasking abilities, train multi-dimensional thinking and spatial skills, speed up reaction times and are a harmless form of releasing aggression. Others allege that they are addictive, interfere with family life, promote inattention in the classroom and develop virtual rather than real-life social intelligence and skills.

This issue of whether computer use positively or negatively influences cognitive processes and human interactions is a relatively new area of inquiry, but it has already generated much debate among psychologists. There is some evidence suggesting deteriorating functioning of the memory due to people relying on computer storage and search engines such as Google to access information; this is nicknamed 'The Google Effect'. With computer gaming, supporting findings from research indicate positive neurological growth and brain plasticity. This is especially significant with games requiring focused attention, fast tracking of many objects at the same time, avoiding distracting decoys and promoting pro-social interaction with other players.

However, other studies have claimed that although these biologically-supported cognitive developments do occur, they only transfer to real-world life skills when performing a very similar task – for example, the perceptual and multi-tasking skills used in controlling air traffic. One study found that although experienced video-game players demonstrated significantly better online spatial skills than non-experienced players, those skills did not transfer into the real world. The non-experienced performed real-life spatial navigation tasks just as well as the experienced. Yet additional studies point to the nature of the particular computer game. There are studies based on brain scans that indicate, for example, that action video games do enhance visual attention, low-level vision, speeds of information processing and statistical inference skills.

At the same time, some research supports the claim that it is the very speed and intensity of such computer games that can contribute to attention deficit disorder (ADD) behaviours in environments such as schools, where the classroom cannot offer the same quality and intensity of mental stimulation. Furthermore, the immediate reward-for-progress built into the games that frequently results in an accompanying rush of dopamine is not readily compatible with classrooms where the norm is sustained hard work without immediate reward, especially where the content is under-stimulating. Other research-backed claims hold that although violent-content electronic games are unlikely to promote violence in a non-violent user, there exists a concern that such gaming might desensitise the player to the real-life suffering and needs of other people.

The debates on the positive and negative effects of modern technology on cognitive processes are compounded by the validity of research methodologies. For example, comparing the skills of game players to non-game players may be criticised on the grounds that the players may have reached their current performance levels through a high aptitude for computer gaming rather than hours of practice. Also, the baseline for non-players may well be unreliable, due to variations in the already-present skills that they could bring to the game.

This section considers four pieces of research that focus on the positive and negative effects of modern technology on cognitive processes and human interaction.

4.5.1 Effects of the use of digital devices on the human memory

The earlier part of this chapter considered types of LTM including procedural, semantic and episodic memory. Transacting with electronic devices accesses yet another system, an external set-up that can do the memory work for you. This **transactional memory** is where the encoding, storage and recall on command is delegated to a digital device.

Transactional memory: where the human encoding, storage and recall on command is delegated to a digital device.

Research study: Sparrow et al. (2011)

Aim

Sparrow et al. (2011) used an experimental design to research whether the use of transactional memory can adversely affect human biological memory systems. The objectives were to test whether (a) being told to remember the information would influence the accuracy of later memory recall, and (b) whether hearing that the information would be stored by the computer would influence the accuracy of later memory recall.

Procedure

There were four conditions in the study, and the participants were divided into four groups. All participants typed 40 trivial facts into the computer, some of them better known than others. Each was allocated to one condition only; it was an independent measures experiment.

- Condition 1: the computer would store all the information, but their task was to remember it.

- Condition 2: the computer would not store the information, and their task was to remember it.

- Condition 3: the computer would store the information, and they were not specifically asked to remember it.

- Condition 4: the computer would not store the information, and they were not asked to remember it.

Results

The results showed that when told the computer would save the information (conditions 1 and 3), there was no difference in memory recall, whether the participants were told to remember the information (condition 1) or not (condition 3). However, memory recall rates improved by 50% when they were informed that the computer would not save what they typed into it (conditions 2 and 4). It made little difference whether or not they had been told to store the information. Even more significantly, memory recall rates were 50% more accurate in condition 4 (not asked to remember, but told that the computer would not save the information) than in condition 1 (asked to remember, and told that the computer would save the information).

Conclusion

In conclusion, the study seems to indicate that transactional memory has an adverse effect on declarative memory. Confidence in computer and internet storage reduces the motivation and effort exerted for encoding sensory information into LTM.

Strengths of the study

- It was experimental. The results were supported by a follow-up study by the same research team where participants were required to type a series of 10 researcher-supplied trivial facts and then to place each one into suitable folders, with labels such as names, items, data.

- The study found that more than twice as many participants were able to recall the location of the trivial facts (including when prompted with the information where it had been forgotten) than correctly recall the facts themselves.

Limitations of the study

- It had a laboratory set-up.

- There were difficulties in explaining the less effective semantic memory recall. The study's findings suggest less effort is made in remembering data that is stored inside the transactional memory, but it does not explain why the more we use the transactional memory, the less we seek to remember.

4.5.2 Effects of computer gaming on promoting cognition skills and learning efficiency

The earlier part of this chapter also acknowledged the ongoing debate of whether and to what degree computer gaming contributes to the development of the player's cognitive skills. Below and in Section 4.5.3 are samples of two studies within that area of discussion.

Research study: Haier et al. (1992)

Aim

Haier et al. is a pioneer study that aimed to research whether playing the computer game Tetris improves efficiency in visual-spatial ability and motor-coordination. Efficiency in this context means a higher standard of play that engages less effort from the brain.

Figure 4.18 How far does playing Tetris regularly improve the brain's processing skills?

Procedure

There were eight participants, aged 19–32, who were volunteers recruited by advertisement within the university community. Each participant was scanned twice using PET while playing Tetris, at the beginning and at the end of the study. At the start of the study all were new to the game, which involved the speedy mental rotation of objects on the screen. After the first scan, the participants practised this game daily for five days per week over up to a two-month period. They were given their second end-of-study scan on completion of that practice. As a control function, 16 additional participants were PET-scanned while passively viewing visual stimuli.

The PET scan was suitable for this research as it required the participants to be injected with glucose. The scans show the degree that the glucose is metabolised and the parts of the brain that are thus engaged. A relatively low rate of metabolism by fewer parts of the brain would indicate less effort from the brain than a higher rate from more parts of the brain. The lower the rate, the more efficient the thinking.

Results

The results showed that significantly less glucose was metabolised after the weeks of practice than at the start of the study. At the same time, there was a correspondingly significant decrease in the degree of engagement in the cortical and subcortical regions of the brain. In addition, there was a negative association between the individual standard of play at the end of the study and the level of glucose metabolised.

Conclusion

The researchers concluded that the evident decrease in glucose metabolism may indicate that learning and skills mastery can promote a more efficient utilisation of neural circuitry. In the case of Tetris, these circuits may well transfer to spatial skills enhanced by the practice in visual rotation of objects afforded by the game.

Strengths of the study

- The study used brain scanning to obtain correlational evidence for different patterns of processing in the brain.

- It used the absence of similar rates of metabolism from the control sample to support the findings that such game play can enhance particular cognitive skills.

Limitations of the study

- The study by itself does not show how far, if at all, the apparent changes in neural circuitry promoted by this training are likely to transfer to valuable real-world skills.

4.5.3 Effects of computer gaming on children's attention span in the classroom

The influence of children's regular and prolonged television viewing on their attention spans has interested generations of psychologists. Studies have associated television viewing for more than two hours a day with attention problems for children in the classroom. More recently, research has examined the possibility of a similar association with video games.

The question of whether long hours playing video games harm children's attention spans or not is of public interest. It especially concerns those with responsibility for children, such as parents, educators and psychologists. That is because there is much speculation over whether over-exposure to the powerful socio-cultural influences of the television and the games screen interfere or do not interfere with attention span. Attention is a cognitive function that is used when actively encoding into the memory the information given by the teacher in the classroom. That attention means that the brain is less likely to respond to any other sensory information, such as the sound of heavy trucks passing by the school.

Research study: Swing et al. (2010)

Aim

To investigate whether video gaming had a negative effect on children's attention spans.

Procedure

The participants were 1323 children aged 8–11. The study was longitudinal, extending for a period of 13 months. It included reporting from parents, teachers and children on at least three (but no more than four) occasions within that period. The children self-reported about their television and video gaming routines. These were compared with their parents' descriptions of their children's viewing and gaming habits. Their school teachers gave information on the attention levels typical of each child. At the same time, a group of 210 college students (mean age 19.8 years) participated, through self-reporting on their television viewing, video game exposure and attention problems.

Results

The results indicated that the children who spent more than two hours per day playing video games were more likely to have attention difficulties in class than those spending less than two hours. These findings supported earlier research that associated similar levels of prolonged television viewing with attention problems in children. Similar results were found for the college students.

Conclusion

The researchers accounted for their findings through the particular nature of the content and rhythm of video games. Video games popular with children tended to be fast, dramatic, highly colourful and changing extremely rapidly. Their producers typically work with teams of electronic multi-media experts, and multi-million-dollar budgets. They insert the powerful stimulations of quick and rapid changes in camera angles, flashing lights and sound-pitch. These are thought to make the brain's cognition functions become dependent on that ultra-powerful level of stimulation. School teachers working at a more human pace do not find it easy to compete.

Strengths of the study

- It involved a large sample.

- Its longitudinal dynamic nature was able to monitor increased and decreased involvement with video games with changes in child attention spans.

Limitations of the study

- It relied on self-reporting from parents, teachers and students.

- It did not involve, for example, researchers observing the child participants in the classroom.

- The child participants were recruited from ten schools in two Midwest states in the USA.

- It is not clear how far the findings of the study may be generalised.

4.5.4 Effect of the use of digital technology on human interactions

Communication using social media and online interactions is widespread. There is a growing body of research on the positive and negative benefits on human reactions. It has long been recognised that real-life, face-to-face, offline quality friendships can cognitively enhance human well-being. Whether digital social media can achieve the same positive cognitive effects has been of continuing interest to the public as well as to psychologists. Indeed, the average Facebook user spends just under one hour per day on the site, according to the company's 2016 statistics.

Research study: Shakya and Christakis (2017)

Shakya and Christakis investigated the relationship between social media use and personal well-being. Personal well-being included physical and mental health, but also incorporated the cognitive dimension of feelings of life satisfaction.

Aim

To investigate the degree of similarity between the personal benefits of online and real-life friendships.

Procedure

The participants were a total of 5208 adult Facebook users. Recruited from a national panel in the USA, they had given permission for their Facebook accounts to be accessed for this research process. The study was longitudinal in design, extending over a two-year period using three waves of their Facebook data, in 2013, 2014 and 2015.

The foci of the investigation were the following measures of well-being: life satisfaction, self-reported mental health, self-reported physical health and body-mass index. For each participant, the inputs from Facebook included liking ('likes') for other posts creating their own posts and clicking on links. And for each participant, the measures of real-life social networks included being asked to name up to four friends with whom they discussed important matters, and up to four friends with whom they spent their free time.

Results

The results showed the following correlations to be significant. The number of real-life friends correlated positively with personal well-being as defined by the four measures. In contrast, the number of clicks 'liking' other posts and also the number of Facebook links clicked-on, correlated negatively with life satisfaction, mental health and physical health. The negative correlation was particularly strong for the level of mental health.

Conclusion

The study concluded that Facebook relationships did not replace the real-life relationships needed for a healthy life. Indeed, it strongly suggested that Facebook use actually contributed to a reduction in the overall quality of life. The study also indicated the possibility that other people's selective disclosure about special events in their lives might well lead to negative self-comparisons. In addition, attempts to keep pace with the large feeds of social media might distract from the very different skill of cultivating relationships which might be fewer in number, but mutually far more rewarding and meaningful.

Strengths of the study

- The longitudinal design allowed the measures of Facebook use and personal well-being to be monitored over a two-year period for each participant, indicating dynamically that an increase in the quantity of Facebook use associated with users' compromised well-being.

- The researchers used the evidence from the participants' Facebook accounts rather than interview and relying on self-reporting.

- The study attempted to monitor the individual's well-being and face-to-face social networks at the beginning, middle and end of the two-year period. That strengthened the evidence of association between the increase in the rate of Facebook use and deteriorating well-being.

Limitations of the study

- The participants' data on their personal well-being was based on their self-reporting.

- The required confining the research to those who gave the researchers permission to access their Facebook data may have created a not fully representative sample of the community being studied.

SELF-ASSESSMENT QUESTIONS 4.6

1 Define transactional memory.

2 What key contributions have been made to understanding the effect of the use of digital technology on cognitive processes and human interactions by the following studies?

  a Sparrow et al. (2011)

  b Haier et al (1992)

  c Swing et al. (2010)

  d Shakya and Christakis (2017)

Chapter summary

1 The cognitive approach to behaviour focuses on the processes where sensory inputs are received, processed, stored, recovered and acted upon by the individual.

2 A schema is a mental representation that guides behaviour. If the mind is like a computer, the brain is the hardware and the schemas are the software.

3 Methods of investigation in the cognitive approach to human behaviour include quantitative methods, interviews, observational studies and, increasingly, brain scanning.

4 Memory models include sensing input from the environment, STM and LTM functions; these involve the selective attention, rehearsal and retrieval of information.

5 Cognitive schemas are individualised mental representations and mechanisms that process information. They build up from previously acquired knowledge and experience, and they assist in organising knowledge, beliefs and expectations.

6 Thinking and decision-making may use the quick, automatic but more bias-susceptible System-1 thinking, or the more deliberate, effortful, goal-orientated and generally more accurate System-2 thinking.

7 Pre-existing schemas may adversely affect accuracy in the recalling and reporting of past events, especially when prompted by cues designed to mislead, or by various categories of System-1 heuristics.

8 Emotional elements involving flashbulb memory and different processing paths through the brain can influence the nature and accuracy of cognitive processes.

9 (HL only) How far the use of digital technology positively or negatively influences cognitive processes and human interactions has already generated much debate among psychologists. Areas include human memory, learning efficiency, attention spans in the classroom and quality of human social interaction.

Exam-style questions

Short-answer question

• Explain how one research study reflects on the reliability of one cognitive process.

Essay response question

• With reference to two research studies, evaluate the influence of schematic influences on behaviour.

The socio-cultural approach to behaviour

5

'Give me a dozen healthy infants, well-formed, and my own specified world to bring them up in and I'll guarantee to take any one at random and train him to become any type of specialist I might select – doctor, lawyer, artist, merchant-chief and, yes, even beggar-man and thief, regardless of his talents, penchants, tendencies, abilities, vocations, and race of his ancestors.'
(John Watson, 1930)

Learning objectives

- Outline the principles that define the socio-cultural level of analysis. (AO1)
- Outline the ways in which elements of socialisation can influence behaviour. (AO1)
- Examine the ways in which culture can influence individual attitudes and behaviour. (AO2)
- Explore the ways in which globalisation affects our personal identities and our consequent attitudes and behaviour. (AO2) (HL only)
- Evaluate research on how social identity theory and social cognition may influence behaviour. (AO3)
- Discuss the ways in which individuals endeavour to come to terms with the fundamental differences between global culture and local culture. (AO3) (HL only)

5.1 Overview of the socio-cultural approach to understanding human behaviour

Socio-cultural psychology emphasises that we interact with different people and varied surroundings from birth. We acquire from others the language(s) we speak, the games we play, the values and ideals we feel comfortable with, even the way we cut up our food. The socio-cultural approach is based on the following principles that underlie how our behaviour is strongly influenced by those we interact with.

5.1.1 Principles of the socio-cultural approach to understanding human behaviour

1 Social and cultural environments influence behaviour. As individuals, we tend to adjust our manners and conduct to the norms of where we are, and who is there. The influence of society on our behaviour is always present, and involves issues grounded in social identity and social cognition which are both explored in this chapter. In addition, our behaviours (as well as our identities and attitudes) are increasingly influenced by global socio-cultural values. The detailed exploration of globalisation on behaviour is a Higher Level requirement only.

2 Individuals want to connect and identify with others. This can sometimes mean going through persistent and tough qualifying processes in order to be accepted by the group of your choice, whether in appearance or in actions. It can involve changing your opinions, outlook and values. It might be because of **majority influence**: 'everybody does that.' It might be because of **minority influence**, if we aspire to be like a particular individual in the chosen group. It might even take the form of a high level of **self-efficacy** and **reciprocal determinism**, by behaving as one who influences the norms of the environment and society.

Majority influence: where the individual follows the thoughts, behaviours and attitudes that are the norms of the group.

Minority influence: where a persuasive minority group successfully exerts pressure to change the attitudes or behaviours of the majority.

Self-efficacy: the degree to which the individual believes they can participate in particular social activities.

Reciprocal determinism: where individuals can communicate and influence new norms to society.

The socio-cultural approach may be applied to any issues concerned with understanding how aspects of society and culture influence the behaviour of individuals. The approach can also give insights into how society and culture modify the behaviour of individuals when in groups. Examples of such issues are how far people copy examples of behaviour observed from people around them, how people make adjustments from one social group to another, and how the behaviour of one leading individual may influence the interactions within a group.

In the preceding two chapters, you learnt about the biological and cognitive approaches to individual attitudes and behaviour. It is important to understand that the socio-cultural level of analysis does not replace them. Rather, it gives further dimension to these other two perspectives. Indeed, psychologists today are moving towards a general consensus that a synthesis of the biological, cognitive and socio-cultural approaches to individual behaviour brings us closer to understanding the complex interacting systems that make up the conduct of a human being.

5.1.2 Research methods used in the socio-cultural approach to behaviour

As with other approaches to behaviour, leading methods of investigation used within the socio-cultural approach to behaviour are laboratory experiments, correlation studies and case studies.

Laboratory experiments

These are designed to establish the cause-and-effect relationship. For example, an experiment may investigate whether people's cognitive stereotypes can be activated to influence behaviour. For example, do your movements slow down when thinking about elderly people?

125

From the findings of Bargh et al. (1996) (discussed later in this chapter) and similar laboratory simulation-based research, the researchers concluded that stereotypes can subtly and easily be activated to influence behaviour, overriding our conscious mind in the process.

Experimental research involves a hypothesis that may or may not be accepted on the basis of the subsequent findings. In Bargh et al. (1996) the hypothesis was that people's actions are unconsciously influenced by the stereotypes that they hold of individuals and situations. Here, the IV was a series of hardly noticeable prompts designed to stealthily arouse the stereotyped slow motion of the senior citizen. The resultant behaviour of the test group was a slower walk to the next destination than the control group which had received neutral and non-age-related prompts.

In addition, ethical considerations involving consent and deception have to be addressed satisfactorily for the research study to be accepted.

Correlation studies

In all branches of research, correlation studies investigate the nature and degree of relationship between two sets of values already in existence.

An example is Lueck and Wilson (2011) who investigated the impact of socio-cultural factors on difficulties experienced by Hispanic migrants to the USA. It found that having no choice about migrating, lack of English language proficiency, weak social networks and personal experience of discrimination in the USA all contributed to stress in being able to function optimally in their new environment. The relationship between these factors and stress levels was correlation instead of the use of an IV to show cause and effect.

Socio-cultural psychologists also use behaviour observation, such as in Tajfel's investigation of behaviour between **in-groups** and **out-groups**, and case studies, such as Curtiss's study of Genie in Chapter 2.

In-groups: groups with which an individual identifies.

Out-groups: groups with which an individual does not identify.

INTERNATIONAL FOCUS

People are selfish. They think of themselves only, 24/7.

That's what I once believed. But now I've changed my mind. During the last 12 months, my van broke down three times. On each occasion, I drew a big sign asking for help and put it in the window. Every time someone stopped to help me.

Last week the tyre burst when I was on a lonely stretch of highway. I posted on my back windscreen, 'Need a jack, will pay'.

A car stopped. It was driven by a powerfully-built Central American man who didn't speak much English, with his wife and four children.

I didn't need to say anything. The man took one look and knew exactly what to do. Yes, he communicated through his daughter who spoke some English, he did have a car jack, but it would have to be supported as it was too small for my van. There was a log on the roadside. Using the saw in his toolkit, he cut off a slice, and mounted the jack on it. He passed me his tyre iron, but I broke it trying to remove the wheel.

No problem. His wife took the broken iron, drove off, and soon returned with a new one from the nearby garage.

By the time the wheel was changed we were hot, sweaty and exhausted. I tried to put a $20 note into his hand, but he just shook his head. While he wasn't looking, I passed it to his wife.

I thanked them in the few words of Spanish that I knew. Their daughter told me that they were here in Oregon, USA, to help with the cherry harvest.

They would then move on to picking peaches in California before going back home. She asked me if I had eaten. No, I replied. She disappeared for a moment and then came back with a delicious tamale.

I thanked her, and unwrapped it just when the car started to move. Out slipped the $20 note!

He wouldn't take it back. Instead, he put together four words in English, enunciating them slowly and clearly: 'Today you, tomorrow me.' And rolling down his window, he drove away.

As I sat down to enjoy the tamale, I thought to myself: the person who stopped was one of the poorest on that highway. He was here for one purpose only, to work. And yet, he found the time to help me.

Since then, I've helped people whenever I can. I've changed a few wheels, and yesterday I saw an elderly lady struggle with her shopping and drove her home. And whenever I'm helping, I feel that I'm doing something to repay that kindness and the $20.

Figure 5.1 There are people who do care.

5.2 The individual and the group

The socio-cultural approach looks at how other people affect our behaviour, even when we think we are acting independently. The key topics of study are:

- the role of social identity theory in explaining behaviour
- the role of social cognitive theory in explaining behaviour, including the role of stereotyping.

5.2.1 The role of social identity theory in explaining behaviour

Social identity theory: the ways individuals think about who they are and evaluate themselves in relation to groups.

Social categorisation: a cognitive process where the individual divides the social world into those who belong to their particular group and those who do not.

Social identification: where individuals adopt the identity and behavioural norms of the in-group, or groups.

Social comparison: determining where your in-group stands relative to rival out-groups.

Self-concept: the way people think about themselves as individuals.

Intergroup behaviour: relating to someone as a member of the in-group would to an outsider, rather than as one human being to another.

Interpersonal behaviour: relating to someone as one human being to another, and not specifically as a member of an in-group would to an outsider.

Social identity theory refers to the ways that individuals think about who they are and evaluate themselves in relation to groups. The position proposed by social identity theory is that an individual's sense of who they are is based on being a member, or not, of specific social groups.

Tajfel and Turner (1979) developed social identity theory. They proposed that there are three mental processes involved in evaluating others as 'us' or 'them', the in-group and the out-group. These take place in a particular order, and are **social categorisation**, **social identification** and **social comparison**.

Social categorisation

Social categorisation is a cognitive process where the individual divides the social world into those who belong to their particular group (the in-group) and those who do not (the out-group). It focuses on the common ground between people inside the group, and highlights the differences from people outside the group.

In-groups and out-groups are found in many areas of life, such as politics. In the USA, there are two main political parties: Democrats and Republicans. A member of the Democratic party sees the Democrats as their in-group, and the Republicans as an out-group. For a member of the Republican party, this is the other way round. Similarly, in-groups and out-groups can be constructed on the basis of ethnicity, nationality or class. Groups can also form around leisure or intellectual interests. Supporters of sports teams see themselves as members of an in-group, with supporters of rival teams being the out-groups.

Social identification

Social identification, the second stage, is where individuals adopt the identity and behavioural norms of the in-group, or groups. Social identification is a behavioural as well as a cognitive process. For example, a 15-year old with ambitions to serve in the police force may see him or herself as a police-person despite being too young to train and serve in professional practice. Such an individual is likely to adopt the identity of a police officer and behave in the ways that they know such a person would behave, and conform to the norms of the group. They will define appropriate behaviour by the norms of the group or groups they belong to. Social identification can extend to the socio-cultural cognitions of bias and prejudice, and to the behaviours of positive and negative discrimination.

Our social identification and social identity is based on **self-concept**, meaning the way we think about ourselves as individuals; for instance, 'I have a good sense of fun' or 'I find it difficult to talk to strangers'. Social identification can express different behaviours in different environments. A teacher, for example, might be a warm, friendly and accommodating person outside school. She is quite different in school when punishing late work with a low grade and an after-school detention. That is because she identifies herself as a teacher in her teaching environment, and she acts as teachers normally act in the classroom.

The teacher's insistence on homework being handed in on time is **intergroup behaviour**, part of her social identification. She is a member of the in-group teaching profession. As such, she practises the in-group's belief that effective teaching of the out-group requires consistent and firm discipline. That is within her professional, in-group identity.

Yet two hours later, she greets the same student with a smile in the local sports club. That is her **interpersonal behaviour**. It comes from her own self, not from the norms of being a teacher, the group she identified with earlier in the day.

Your social identity allows you to see yourself having a place in the particular groups that you value. Social identity theory explains how people sometimes try hard to change their lifestyles to fit into a particular group, such as an exclusive sports club or a college society. They identify themselves with a group's outlook and objectives. They see their ideal selves as part of the group.

Social comparison

Social comparison determines where our in-group stands relative to rival out-groups. Members of the in-group emphasise the **positive distinctiveness** of the in-group, and why it is good to belong to it. This stage is important. Once we have identified with a specific group, we try to see how favourably our in-group compares with the other out-groups. If our self-esteem is to be maintained, our group needs to compare favourably with other groups. For example, you might be proud to be a member of your school, because you believe that your school is the best of its kind.

This kind of social comparison can lead to **fundamental attribution errors** when explaining the behaviour of groups you identify with. You might remain proud to support your school sports teams even if they lose, attributing their lack of success to **situational** rather than **dispositional factors**.

Social comparison is the final stage of social identity theory. Once we have categorised ourselves as part of a group and have identified with that group, we then tend to compare that group with other groups.

Social comparison helps to explain prejudice and discrimination. When groups identify themselves as rivals, they need their members to feel that belonging to their group continues to support their high esteem, in order that they will continue to support it. Competition and hostility between groups can also be important factors in competition for resources.

Research study: Tajfel (1970)

Aim

To demonstrate that people show bias to individuals in in-groups and prejudice to individuals in out-groups, even where there is nothing of objective importance that distinguishes the in-group from the out-group.

Tajfel conducted two sets of experiments to show that groups can form on the flimsiest bases. And once groups do form, there is basis for bias towards the in-group members, and prejudice towards the out-group members.

Procedure

The study involved two quantitative, experimental studies on schoolboys aged 14–15, living in Bristol, UK. The basis of the groupings was random. In the first experiment, the 64 boys had to estimate the number of dots on slides that had been projected on the screen. Some boys overestimated, others underestimated. In the second experiment, there were 48 boys taking part. They were shown works of art painted by Kandinsky and Klee. Some boys preferred Kandinsky. Others preferred Klee.

The boys were then divided into groups. In the first experiment it was supposedly over-estimators who were put into one group, and the under-estimators put into the other. In the second experiment it was supposedly those who preferred Kandinsky and those who preferred Klee. The key word is 'supposedly'. In reality, and unknown to the boys, the groups were entirely at random. Neither the estimation of dots nor the preferences in art had any basis in reality to distinguish between the groups. That is what the experimenters wanted. They needed two groups of boys, already known to each other, to be put into groups without any real basis whatsoever. They had no idea who was also in their own group, or what they had to gain.

The experimenters then proceeded to find out whether such randomly constructed groups would show in-group favouritism and out-group discrimination. Each participant was required to award points to others who deserved them in various follow-up procedures. The identity of those 'others' was hidden. All they knew was whether they were part of the in-group or out-group (over-estimators versus under-estimators; Kandinsky versus Klee), depending on which group they were in.

Results

The results showed that when awarding points in activities between two members of the in-groups, there was no pattern of bias and discrimination. When awarding points between members of the out-groups, there was also no pattern. But when one person was in-grouped and the other was out-grouped, the points were heavily weighted in favour of the in-group. Statistically, the results indicated

Positive distinctiveness: what makes the in-group special, enabling its members to feel proud to belong to it.

Fundamental attribution error: overestimating the role of dispositional factors and underestimating the role of situational factors, or vice versa.

Situational factors: where you understand a person's behaviour as a product of their own circumstances, rather than being directed personally at you.

Dispositional factors: where you understand a person's behaviour as being directed personally at you, and not a product of their own circumstances.

bias to the in–group and discrimination to the out-group. None of the boys knew the identities of those they were judging apart from which group they belonged to. And those who observed indicated that the boys were trying to judge as fairly as possible.

Conclusion

The study's conclusion was that indeed, once groups form for any reason whatsoever, or even for no reason, there develops bias towards members of the in–group and discrimination towards members of the out-group. Just categorising people into in-groups and out-groups is enough to set up intergroup discriminatory behaviour.

Strengths of this study

- It is replicable. This classic, controlled experimental study has been repeated in different forms with similar results.

- It demonstrated the minimal group concept: that in–group/out-group discriminatory behaviour can occur even between groups that are formed on the slightest base.

Limitations of this study

- It may have limited application. The participants were British schoolboys in their early teens. Schoolboys divided into groups by adults could have interpreted them as 'teams', which would have put them into competition mode.

- It showed discriminatory behaviour only in the particular situation of being required to make decisions. Tajfel's juvenile participants only showed preference when having to choose between rewarding an in-grouper or an out-grouper. There was no evidence of hostility between the groups.

ACTIVITY 5.1

Jane Elliot's blue-eyed / brown-eyed classroom activity for third grade children (1968)

After the assassination of Martin Luther King Jr in 1968, schoolteacher Jane Elliot wanted to explain to her class of eight-year-olds about the problems of racism. She divided her class into blue-eyed and brown-eyed children. Brown-eyed children were given more rights, and blue-eyed children were seen as inferior and less able.

Almost immediately, Elliot observed that the brown-eyed children became domineering and more confident in their abilities. Blue-eyed children became much less sure of themselves and became frightened of the brown-eyed children. Even the brightest blue-eyed students became unable to perform.

Jane Elliot's lesson is not presented in an academic journal. It is therefore unsuitable for use as a research study in coursework or in an exam response. Despite the worldwide publicity (for example *ABC*'s documentary: 'The Eye of the Storm' in 1970), the earliest published academic follow-up is Byrnes and Kiger (1990). That study supported Jane Elliot's classroom exercise to the degree that virtually all participants found the exercise meaningful in approaching prejudice, although moderately stressful.

Figure 5.2 Jane Elliot's class united, soon to be divided

1 How were the self-concepts of the blue-eyed and the brown-eyed children different from one another during the experiment?

2 How were the concepts of in-group and out-group reflected in the behaviour of the children of the two groups?

3 Where do you think in-group conflict was greatest: in the experiment of Tajfel, or in Jane Elliot's classroom? Explain the reason for your choice.

4 Create a table of the social identity issues in both the Tajfel and Jane Elliot scenarios under the following columns: social categorisation, social identity, and social comparison.

5 Identity two in-group/out-group situations in your own environment. Create a table for each situation under the following columns: social categorisation, social identity and social comparison.

5.2.2 The role of social cognitive theory in explaining behaviour

Social cognitive theory seeks to explain how people process information about the world (including other humans) on the basis of cognitive elements such as schemas, attributions and stereotypes. This is also true of cultural cognition.

Schemas are considered in Chapter 4. Attribution theory and stereotyping are key cognitive elements in the socio–cultural approach to behaviour, and are presented in this chapter.

The principles of social cognitive theory include the following:

1 Individuals learn the social norms, skills and habits that enable participation in society by observing and imitating others. This is **social learning theory**, a key contributor to social cognition.

2 Individuals' social cognition contains diverse elements, including schema development, attribution and stereotyping.

3 Observing and involvement with others can communicate society's norms to individuals with cues for **conformity** and **compliance**.

Social cognitive theory: how people process information about the world (including other humans) on the basis of cognitive elements such as schemas, attributions and stereotypes.

Social learning theory: the individual acquires behaviour patterns through observing, imitating and modelling the behaviour of others.

Conformity: adjusting thinking and behaviour to fit in with the perceived norms of the environment, without being told to do so.

Compliance: adjusting behaviour to fit in with overt demands.

4 Individuals can communicate new norms to society: this is reciprocal determinism.

5 Individuals' self-efficacy influences the degree to which they can participate in society. Self-efficacy is considerably, though not totally, cognitively built up through past experiences.

Our study of social cognitive theory explores elements belonging to the above principles of social cognitive theory.

1 Individuals learn the social norms, skills and habits that enable participation in society by observing and imitating others

'Set the right example!'

'Choose the right people to make friends with.'

When you first go to high school, you look up to the students who have been there for some years, and take your cues on how to act from them. When you are in your final year, you in turn are being looked up to by new arrivals.

Social learning theory explains that the individual acquires behaviour patterns through observing, imitating and **modelling** the behaviour of others. Modelling involves learning through observation of other people (models), which may lead to **imitation** if the behaviour observed appears to lead to reward. So our interaction with other people affects the way we behave.

When social learning takes place, the learner pays attention to the model, remembers the behaviour that was observed, and subsequently replicates the action. There is a good feeling in demonstrating what has been learnt, because it models the behaviour of others. This is **vicarious learning**.

It also gains the approval of others, according to the results of following that behaviour. As you become competent in a new skill, for example skiing, you enjoy the encouraging looks from the ski coach and other skiers.

Modelling: where behaviour is learnt from the example of someone else.

Imitation: where behaviour is learnt through observing and modelling the actions of other people.

Vicarious learning: a behaviour modelled on the example of others.

Figure 5.3 'I've done it. Who's next?'

People can model someone they have never met. For example, many believed that the human being could not run a four-minute mile before Roger Bannister (1929–2018) succeeded in 1954. He was the model. Within the next few months that record had been broken several times, as leading athletes had learnt by his example that it could be done.

In fact, models may be categorised under two headings: **positional models**, people we see but do not interact with directly, for example, cartoon characters and famous people; and **personal models**, people with whom we are in frequent contact, for example parents, teachers, peers and community leaders. Personal models are more likely to be sources of long-term developments of social behaviour.

Research study: Bandura (1965)

Aim

Bandura's et al. (1961) classic study in social learning theory aimed to demonstrate that learning can occur through mere observation of a model, and that imitation can take place in the absence of the model. The learning behaviour in this experiment was aggression.

Bandura's team investigated whether children would imitate the aggression modelled by an adult, and also whether children were more likely to imitate same-gender models.

Procedure

The participants were 36 boys and 36 girls aged three to six, who were divided into similarly composed groups. Group 1 was exposed to adult models who showed aggression by bashing an inflatable 'Bobo' doll. Group 2 observed a non-aggressive adult who assembled toys for ten minutes. Group 3 was the control and did not see any model. In groups 1 and 2, some watched same-sex models and others watched opposite-sex models. All groups were then placed in a room with toys.

Once the children had settled down to play, the toys were taken away. The children were told that those toys were for other children. That was the provocation to manipulate the participants into an aggressive state of mind. The children were then left with the 'Bobo' doll.

Results

The results showed that those exposed to aggression at the earlier stage showed significantly more aggression towards the Bobo doll than those who had not been exposed to aggression. Also, boys were more likely to imitate the physical aggression they had seen from men, and the girls were more likely to imitate the verbal aggression they had seen from women.

Positional models: people that you do not know but who influene your behaviour, such as political leaders and celebrities.

Personal models: people that you know who influence your behaviour, for example parents, teachers, peers and community leaders.

Albert Bandura (1925–)

Figure 5.4 Albert Bandura

Albert Bandura (1925–) was raised in a small village in Canada where his father laid railway track and his mother worked at the local store. He studied in a very small high school with 20 children and only 2 teachers. Graduating at the University of British Columbia, he developed his interest in learning and behaviourism at the University of Iowa where he obtained his doctorate in 1952. Very soon afterwards, he was appointed to the faculty of Stanford University with which he has been associated ever since.

Bandura is most famous for his theories and studies on how behaviour is acquired, and particularly the concept of modelling behaviour. His social learning theory focuses on the attention the learner gives to the stimulus of the ways others behave, the impression it makes for it to be retained, the reproduction of that behaviour, and that the motivation for that behaviour to continue will depend on the feedback from others.

He is currently Professor Emeritus of Social Science in Psychology at Stanford University, USA.

Figures 5.5 and 5.6 The sudden frustration and readiness to copy violent behaviour of the children taking part in Bandura's study.

Conclusion

The conclusion was that aggression is learnt; it is not part of the child's nature.

Strengths of the study

The study does appear to support social learning theory, that we copy the behaviour learnt from others. The models performed aggressive acts that were not likely to be within the children's repertoires. And although it was in a laboratory setting, it was not substantially different from an occasion when the nursery teacher has to give the class some disappointing news, for example to put away the toys quickly because another class needs them immediately. Thus, the laboratory situation did relate to real life as experienced by those children; it had some ecological validity.

Limitations of the study

The children might not have related beating the doll that bounced back with a smile to actual aggression. Also they were likely to be frustrated when the toys were taken away, whether they witnessed the aggressive scenes or not. There was a very brief encounter with the model, which contrasted to the long hours that children sometimes spend watching aggressive scenes on television. There was no follow-up study to assess the long-lasting impression made on the children by the violence. Finally, there was the issue of demand characteristics: the children might have acted aggressively in order to please the researchers.

By today's ethical standards, there would be the issue of the merits of provoking very young children and exposing them to violence for research purposes.

The findings of Bandura et al. seem to contrast with the later research of Charlton et al. (2002), which was an ecological rather than a laboratory study. This compared the observed levels of elementary school violent behaviour on the island of St Helena, before and for five years after the 1995 introduction of television. The content level of violence on the island was approximately the same as in the UK. Contrary to hypothesised expectations, the levels of violence remained the same as in the pre-television era. In contrast with Bandura et al., these findings would downplay the role of social learning theory.

Research study: Markey and Markey (2010)

Aim

Many computer games – as human-designed products – contain violent themes. The work of Markey and Markey (2010) aimed to investigate how effective they are as agents of social learning. Do they cause the individual players to model violence in real life? Bandura's work focused on how far such modelling was done by television, Markey and Markey's by computer games. Both television and computer games are positional rather than personal models.

Figure 5.7 Virtual life – or rehearsal for real life?

Procedure

Markey and Markey's experimental research factored in the issue of personality traits. With a sample of 118 teenagers, they took into account that certain types of children might be more likely to learn violence from computer games than others. They aimed to determine whether computer games would have no effect on child violence, negatively affect all children irrespective of personality trait, or just affect those with susceptible personality traits.

Markey and Markey created their own psychological model to highlight personality traits. They included the following three characteristics:

- high neuroticism – easily provoked to anger, very emotional, often distressed and depressed

- low agreeableness – not caring about other people's feelings, little concern for others

- low conscientiousness – acts thoughtlessly, doesn't keep promises.

Results

Each participant played a violent or a non-violent video game while their hostility levels were observed and assessed. The teenagers who were highly neurotic, less agreeable and less conscientious tended to be most adversely affected by violent video games, whereas participants who did not possess these personality characteristics were either unaffected or only slightly negatively affected by violent video games.

Conclusion

Computer games with violence were more likely to affect those who were already highly neurotic, less pleasant and less responsible. In other words, it was not the game, but the player.

As Markey and Markey put it: 'Those who are negatively affected have pre-existing dispositions, which make them susceptible to such violent media.'

2 Individuals' social cognition contains diverse elements, including schema development, attribution and stereotyping

The previous chapter considered the idea that we process information though a matrix of cognitive schemas. As explained, cognitive schemas are individualised mental representations based on past similar experiences that we apply to interpret the environment and guide our interactions with the environment. Social and cultural elements contribute in varying degrees to the formation of the individual's cognitive schemas, which are not precisely identical in any two people.

People often appear to act in unexpected ways, and we try to understand their behaviour. For example, on the way to school you meet someone that you know, but the person continues walking as though you did not exist. Your social cognition immediately applies **attribution theory**: you strive to interpret that particular event. Maybe you think they dislike you; that would be dispositional, where you interpret the other's behaviour as specifically connected with you. Maybe you think they were feeling upset and just weren't in the mood to talk to anyone. Your attribution interpretation would then have been situational – everything to do with them and nothing to do with you. Attribution theory thus enables us to apply our previous experiences to make sense of our environment, without necessarily being correct.

> **Attribution theory:** how the individual attempts to explain why people behave in a particular way.

Our schemas and attributions also come into play in social categorisation (discussed in Section 5.2.1), particularly when applying stereotypes in attribution. For example, a person is stopped for driving through a red light. The attribution may be influenced by a negative gender stereotype. If it's a woman: 'Women are bad drivers.' If it's a man, a more tolerant attribution on the lines of: 'Too much testosterone behind the wheel.'

Not all stereotypes are bad, and not all are completely wrong. Psychologists are frequently stereotyped as people who are there to analyse you and tell you what to do. That stereotype could prompt you to be wary and cautious, but it is often correct; many of them do that work for a living.

Research study: Bargh et al. (1996)

Aim

Bargh et al. (1996) conducted a series of experiments to investigate whether stereotyping can influence discriminatory behaviour **without our being aware of it**. Can certain cues **automatically** activate stereotypes, prejudices and discriminatory behaviour **without our knowledge**?

Procedure

In one of the experiments, 30 participants were divided into two, one with 'old age' stereotypes and the other with neutral words unrelated to age. Each group was given a word puzzle to unscramble. The 'old age' group's puzzle included words such as 'wrinkled'. These were designed to automatically activate old people stereotypes without the participants being aware of them. The control group's puzzle contained neutral, non-age-related words.

Once they finished, the participants had to go to the lift by walking down a short corridor just under ten metres in length. Would the 'old age' slow-motion stereotype modify the thinker's behaviour into slower motion?

Results

The researchers' findings indicated that the stereotype would modify behaviour. Those having worked on ageing-associated words were observed and timed to have walked significantly more slowly to the lift than the control group.

Conclusion

This study concluded that the automatic activation of one's stereotypes of aging can prime and promote behavior resembling people who have aged.

Strengths and limitations of the study

This study had the strength of being experimental in design, with the independent variable being manipulated in the test sample for the priming and activation of the 'old age' stereotype. However, it could be argued that the slow walking in the test sample may have been influenced by factors other than stereotypes of the elderly, which vary from participant to participant. In addition, the sample was made up of university psychology students who were not necessarily representative of the general population.

Bargh et al. immediately followed the study that used age stereotypes with a similar one using racial stereotypes. Whereas in the previous experiment the participants might have been aware of the activation of the old-age stereotype, the cues in the following study were designed to happen too quickly for the participants to be consciously aware of them.

In that experiment, 41 participants were given an unstimulating and dull computer task. While working, an image of a young man was periodically flashed on the screen. On some screens the young man was a Caucasian, and on other screens the young man was an African American. This choice was based on previous research indicating that people stereotype African Americans as being more aggressive than Caucasians. The images were flashed for about 1/50th of a second: too fast for the conscious brain, but possible for the unconscious brain to capture.

On completing the task, the experimenter told the participants that the computer system failed to save the data and they would have to repeat the task. Independent observers closely watched the reaction of each participant, rating the viewable facial signs of annoyance on a scale of 1 to 10 with each participant. (Once that had been done, the participants were informed that the computer actually had saved their work and nothing else needed to be done.)

The results showed a significant difference in the level of the flicker of emotion: those unconsciously activated by the African American young male rated at nearly three out of ten and those activated by the Caucasian young male at just over two.

From the findings of this and similar experiments, the researchers concluded that stereotypes can subtly and easily be activated to influence behaviours, overriding our conscious mind in the process.

3 Observing and involvement with others can communicate society's norms to individuals with cues for conformity and compliance

Compliance behaviour is where a person carries out a request under direct pressure. This is even though that pressure may not necessarily be perceived by the person. The request may be made by someone asking you to do a favour, for example to return the ball that was thrown into your back garden. It may also be made by the media, for example where an advertisement or a free sample urges you to buy a certain product.

Complying is not quite the same as conforming or obeying. Conformity differs from compliance as the situation does not use direct pressure targeted at the individual, but pressure is often perceived by individuals, and as such influences their behaviour. A student conforms by attending school according to the dress code. A student complies by going home to change into school uniform when told to do so by the school authorities.

An 11-year-old child entering the classroom for the first time after being homeschooled may be completely 'lost'. They could suffer months of painful adjustment for having gone without the social and cultural aspects of conventional schooling.

Figure 5.8 Due compliance with school norms

Reciprocity: where people comply out of feeling obliged to return a favour.

Foot-in-the-door: compliance technique asking for a small favour which is easy to grant, with a view to requesting a much larger favour.

Door-in-the-face: compliance technique asking a larger favour than required, getting it turned down and proceeding to the much smaller favour required.

Low-balling: compliance technique getting the person initially committed, and then upping the requirement at the last moment, knowing that the person won't change their mind.

There are a number of ways in which behaviour can be influenced to make a person comply:

- **Reciprocity** – where people comply out of feeling that they need to return a favour. Advertisers frequently give free samples of their food products in the expectation that people will reciprocate through buying their goods. Compliance through reciprocity is exemplified by Berry and Kanouse (1987), who found that people are more likely to comply with a demanding request when paid in advance rather than when paid only on completion. This could be because they feel the need to reciprocate the goodwill. Berry and Kanouse conducted their research through the post, with two sample groups of doctors. The doctors in both samples were paid $20 to fill in a demanding questionnaire. The test group received payment in advance, together with the questionnaire. Those in the control group were told that they would receive their payment on receipt of the completed survey. There was a substantial difference in the number of returned completed questionnaires. The test sample who were paid in advance complied 78% of the time, in contrast with the lower 66% in the delayed-pay sample.

- **Foot-in-the-door** technique – opening with a small request that is easy to comply with as an opener to further compliance with the intended bigger request. So instead of asking a parent to borrow the car for the weekend, foot-in-the-door technique would start with the smaller request of 'Can I borrow the car to go to pick up my new computer?' and on getting a 'Yes' response, would be followed by 'Can I borrow the car for the weekend?'

- **Door-in-the-face** technique – making a first request which will be turned down, because it is obviously too big. Then making a second smaller request, which was in mind in the first place. The person might comply out of feeling guilty for having turned down the initial request.

- **Low-balling** – typically used by salespeople: offering the subject an item at a lower price, only to increase the price at the last moment for perhaps 'something better', which was the object of the sale. The buyer is more likely to comply despite the price change as they had already made up their mind to buy the product.

The low-balling compliance technique may be explained by the theory of commitment. This means that once you decide to buy something, you buy it even if the conditions change somewhat. You have also convinced yourself that you need the product.

- **Hazing** involves a series of initiation rites required to join a group that is perceived as exclusive, such as a college society. In deciding to join, the individual complies with the often dramatic and stringent ceremonies. This initial degree of compliance leads to a greater degree of compliance later on, within the group activities.

Hazing: compliance technique requiring a newcomer to go through a difficult and seemingly pointless procedure to gain acceptance with the group.

Figure 5.9 Comply and be one of us.

The study of Aronson and Mills (1959) involved asking female students to join a sex discussion group. They were placed into two groups. The first had to go through an embarrassing initiation procedure to join. The second was allowed in straight away. Once both groups were in the meeting, the activity involved accomplices who were instructed to conduct an extremely boring programme. Those who went through the initiation commented on the meeting being valuable and instructive. Those who were admitted straight away found the meeting to be a waste of time. Thus early compliance demanding initial sacrifices appears to lead to a greater commitment to comply by putting maximum effort into the proceedings of the meeting.

The theories do not clearly explain why some people do not comply – or are able to resist such tactics. Studies in compliance tend to rely on self-reporting devices in order to determine why the individuals made their decisions.

ACTIVITY 5.2

1 Carefully distinguish between compliance and conformity.

2 In a table, summarise six compliance techniques. Use as headings: name of technique, description.

3 Divide into groups of three or four students. Each group selects a different compliance technique. Act out a scenario lasting no longer than four minutes, showing the strengths and limitations of the chosen compliance strategy.

4 What ethical issues may be involved in the use of compliance techniques?

The effectiveness of the door-in-the-face technique in getting someone to comply might be a suitable theme for class investigation. One possibility would be to pick a classroom in your school that needs a change in display material. List the participating students in two separate groups, the test and the control. Approach each participant individually during the next couple of days. Request those in the control group to give up a lunch-break to help to change the class display material. Request those in the test group to come into the school on Sunday morning to help change the display material, and immediately follow up that larger request with the smaller one – to help during lunch-break. Then compare between the test and control groups the number of people who actually came to help to redecorate the classroom.

Society can communicate its norms to individuals with cues for conformity. The group norm is established by the way the majority behaves. There is no actual request to act according to those norms.

Conformity is encouraged by the cues of others in the environment. It might be majority influence (individual follows the thoughts, behaviours and attitudes that are the norms of the group) or minority influence (individual follows the ways of those whose behaviour does not fit in with group norms).

Research study: Asch (1956)

Solomon Asch (1907–96)

Figure 5.10 Solomon Asch

Solomon Asch (1907–96) developed his interest in majority influence in group conformity out of an experience he had as a child in Poland. On participating in his first Passover home-ceremony, he saw his grandmother putting out an extra glass of wine on the table. His uncle told him that it was for the Prophet Elijah, who would participate invisibly at the family festivities. Asch was fascinated, and he believed he saw the level of wine in the glass go down slightly.

By 1939, Asch was studying the effects of propaganda and indoctrination at Brooklyn College. He felt that propaganda was most effective in an atmosphere of fear and ignorance, as typified in Nazi Europe. Asch's fame grew in the 1950s, following a set of experiments which showed that majority-influence social pressure can make a person say something that is obviously wrong.

Aim

Asch's study of conforming with the majority had an impact on psychology to the degree that it is known as the 'Asch conformity' or the 'Asch paradigm'. The investigation's purpose was to determine whether individual participants would conform to majority influence. Majority influence was designed for the giving of incorrect answers in a situation where the correct answers were clearly evident.

Procedure

Each target participant entered a room where there were six other participants, dressed formally in business suits. Participants were told that they were going to take part in 'a psychological experiment on visual judgement'. Unknown to the target participant, the six others were accomplices of the experimenter.

All participants went through a series of exercises, involving a series of single lines on individual cards, and three comparison lines of different lengths on a second card. Participants had to say, in turn and out loud, which line on the second card was the same as the one on the first cards. The target participant was placed towards the end of the group. Confederates, dressed formally in businesses suits, gave the same wrong answers on 12 of the 18 trials. The purpose of the confederate in this study is to help the researcher to deceive the participants.

This study was controlled, where the participants were given the same 18 trials with no one in the room except the experimenter. In total, they gave the correct answer in more than 99% of the trials.

Results

The results showed that more than one-third of the participants agreed with the confederates' responses in half or more of the trials. Nearly three-quarters conformed at least once, but just over a quarter never conformed. In follow-up, some conforming participants claimed to have seen the same as the majority. Others conformed because they did not want to be ridiculed by the group. The majority who conformed did so because they thought that their perception of the lines must be inaccurate, and the majority's accurate.

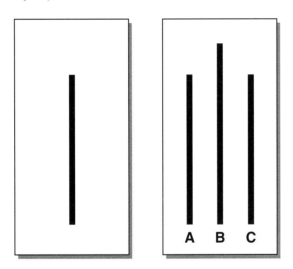

Figure 5.11 An example of the lines used on the cards in Asch's experiment.

Conclusion

Thus it seems that even in unambiguous situations, there is still pressure to conform to a unanimous majority. Asch concluded that some people experience social influence and conform to avoid rejection. Others experience informational influence and conform because they doubt their own judgements. Follow-up experiments indicated that a majority of three with no accomplice dissenters was more effective in producing conformity than a majority of eight with one accomplice dissenter.

Strengths of the study

The overall conformity rate was 32%, which shows that less than a third conformed to majority influence when it seemed to be wrong. It is likely that the formal and serious atmosphere confronting the target participants created an environment where conformity was expected.

Limitations of the study

The time and the place that the research was carried out might have affected the findings. In the 1950s, the USA was very conservative and in the grip of McCarthyism, an anti-communist witch-hunt. That placed greater pressure on people to conform.

The work of Perrin and Spencer (1980) repeated the Asch experiment with British university students on science and mathematics courses. Few of the students were taken in by minority influence and almost none of them were deceived. They then repeated the experiment, but this time with participants who were young offenders and accomplices of the researcher who were recruited from probation offices. There, they found similar rates of conformity to the original Asch experiment.

It may be argued that maths and science students were less likely to let themselves be led in the wrong direction. In contrast, the young offenders might have conformed because the experience of being institutionalised promotes conformity to authoritative influence.

Additionally, there are ethical considerations. The original Asch experiment would, by today's standards, have raised the issue of the participants being deceived and made to feel anxious about their performances. However, it could be argued that there was no other way to obtain the information as participants would have not been taken in for one moment had they known that deception was going to happen.

Research study: Schultz et al. (2008)

Aim

To determine how far the setting of a norm by an environment could enable others to conform to it. The norm was communicated as being the established standard of behaviour within that setting.

Procedure

This experimental study was set in a hotel in California. Would a norm be set that would successfully promote the reusing of towels after the first night in order to save the energy and water (in short supply) in machine washing? The research team researched 794 stays in 132 units of the hotel: 102 units were in the experimental mode, and 30 in the control.

Both the experimental and control hotel rooms had a well-presented written request on the table to reuse the towels by hanging them on the rail, rather than placing them in the basket for washing. However, the request was expressed differently. In the experimental rooms, it was framed as being part of the group norm. Here, it is the norm for people to conserve and save resources. There was also a request in the control room. But it was phrased as a simple request to save on the washing rather than implying that it was the majority behaviour to save on the washing.

Result

The researchers counted the number of towels put in the wash after the first night, for all 794 stays. 25% more guests from the test group complied with the request to reuse their towels than from the control group.

Conclusion

The study concluded that higher levels of conformity occur when the environment presents the desired behaviour as an explicit norm for that setting rather than as a request.

Strengths of the study

Schultz differed from Asch in that the research was carried out in an ecologically valid situation. It is quite normal for a hotel to request guests to reuse towels where possible. The request was framed differently in the test and control situation. Majority influence, in the form of normative social influence, was clearly indicated in the letter to guests in the test rooms.

Limitations of the study

The conformity influence was not very strong. Some hotel guests simply don't bother to read the literature, however elegantly presented. Even where they do, the request may be out of their mind by next morning. They will put the towels into the wash-basket out of habit.

Watch the film *Twelve Angry Men* (1957). The dissenting juror in a murder trial slowly convinces the others that the case is not as clear as it seemed in court. Pay attention to the arguments to both convict and acquit the defendant.

1 On the basis of the movie, identify and list the evidence both to convict and acquit the defendant.

2 Would you have voted guilty or not guilty on the basis of the evidence alone? Explain your verdict according to your assessment of the balance of evidence in question 1.

3 The verdict of the jury was that the defendant was not guilty. Do you think that it was based on the balance of evidence in 1, or can you state other factors involved? Explain your answer.

4 Individuals can communicate new norms to society: reciprocal determinism

Majority influence explains some, but not all, conformity in human behaviour. There are certain situations where people might follow a charismatic and influential minority rather than the majority of the group. These people are communicating their new norms to the environment. That can occur in minority influence. Examples include the struggle for women to vote in Britain during the early years of the 20th century, and the various green movements' early programmes getting people to change their lifestyles to minimise damage to the environment. Hochstetler et al. (1985) in the next section shows how one individual, in that case a cyclist on a video, can influence the cognition and behaviour of many individuals.

5 Individuals' self-efficacy influences the degree to which they can participate in society

The expression of minority influence is an aspect of the concept of self-efficacy, which is part of social cognitive theory. The theory proposes that an individual's perception of the possibility of success in a given area is related to previous associated experiences. For example, you are a native speaker of French, but from eight years old you learnt Spanish in school and can now happily converse in Spanish. Then, when you are 16, your parents are offered a two-year contract in Russia. Because of your success in Spanish, you believe that you will eventually learn and master Russian. If, however, your experience of learning Spanish was less successful, moving to Russia will seem like bad news rather than an opportunity to absorb a new language.

Self-efficacy theory was proposed by Bandura (1977). It emphasises the role of observational learning that is at the core of social learning theory. However, it takes social learning theory further, incorporating the roles of previous social experience and reciprocal determinism in perceiving and responding to situations faced. That raises social learning theory to social cognitive theory. As Bandura puts the cognitive element: 'People who believe they have the power to exercise some measure of control over their lives are healthier, more effective, and more successful than those who lack faith in their ability to effect changes in their lives' (Bandura, 1997). In other words, people will try to do what they think they can do, and will avoid a challenge in which their cognition and past experience indicate that they will not succeed. Self-efficacy is therefore 'the belief in one's capabilities to organise and execute the courses of action required to manage prospective situations' (Bandura, 1995).

People with strong self-efficacies believe that they can successfully tackle difficult assignments, handle problems and disappointments incurred as learning experiences, and develop deeper interests in their work and other activities through increased participation and commitment. Self-efficacy ideally develops from childhood through adulthood.

The reverse typifies those with poor self-efficacy. A significant negative experience causes loss in confidence and expectation of negative outcome.

Bandura identifies four major sources of self-efficacy:

1   previous personal success in a similar task

2   modelling: seeing others managing the task, making it appear achievable

3   verbal encouragement and expressed confidence from others

4   emotional arousal: capacity to interpret the situation that minimises the stress and elevates the mood.

An example of a field requiring self-efficacy is sports. This can be positively developed by mental attitudes and coaching in the following ways:

• Previous experiences: winning against the same team after a severe battle last season.

• Modelling: the person in your lane swims the 25-metre pool in 20 strokes, and you take 25. Watching her style persuades you that your stroke efficiency can also reach her standard.

- Verbal encouragement: someone who knows you well convinces you that you can take part in the sprint triathlon. You swim and run well, but you haven't ridden a bicycle since your 11th birthday.

- Emotional arousal: how you interpret the feedback – you run a 10k race and show a higher-than-expected pulse rate at the end of the event. You could attribute it to your doubting whether you are designed by nature to be a long-distance runner. Therefore you will not train for the half-marathon next season. Or you might attribute it to your feelings of excitement at your first long-distance run, so you will train for the half-marathon next season.

Research study: Hochstetler et al. (1985)

Aim

To investigate whether it was possible to improve success in cycling by manipulating self-efficacy.

Procedure

Forty women took part, divided into two groups. The first group was shown a video of a woman riding a cycling challenge with great difficulty. The second group was shown a video of a woman facing the same challenge easily and effectively.

Both groups then performed the same cycling task.

Results

The first group found the task difficult and exhausting, but those in the second group managed the task in the same spirit as the model in the video.

Conclusion

The results suggest that modelling has a key role in self-efficacy-motivated achievement in sport. However, it was a controlled experiment, with the associated issue of ecological validity. Furthermore, the experiment was restricted to women, raising doubts of generalisation to both genders.

Strengths of self-efficacy theory

- Studies, such as that of Hochstetler, have indicated that perceived self-efficacy is a good predictor of individual athletic performance.

- There is much anecdotal evidence from celebrities who attribute their sporting success to the forces that aroused their cognitions of self-efficacy.

- The strong sense of self-efficacy of even one individual can exert minority influence on the cognition and behaviour of many individuals.

Limitations of self-efficacy theory

- Studies of self-efficacy tend to focus on one of the above components, rather than on self-efficacy as an integrated whole.

- Self-efficacy by itself does not take into account individual physiological factors. These might be more closely related to sporting success or lack of it.

5.2.3 Ethical considerations in socio-cultural research

Ethical guidelines to prevent the unacceptable exploitation of those participating are as relevant to investigating the socio-cultural approach to behaviour as to any other domain in psychology. These include the ethical principles discussed at the end of Chapter 2: informed consent, anonymity, avoidance of deception, protection of participants and the participant's right to withdraw at any stage. In addition, many socio-cultural studies of minority groups need to tackle culture-bound sensitivities, and to obtain the goodwill and co-operation of the gatekeepers of their communities.

SELF-ASSESSMENT QUESTIONS 5.1

1   Define social identity theory.

2   Name and outline the three mental processes involved in evaluating others as belonging to in-groups or out-groups.

3   What was the main conclusion of Tajfel's (1970) classic study in social identity theory?

4   Define social learning theory as an influence on behaviour.

5   Distinguish between personal and positional models.

6   On what basis did Bandura et al. (1961) conclude that social learning theory accounts for aggressive behaviour in children?

7   How do the findings of Bandura (1965) and Charlton et al. (2002) appear to conflict?

8   On what basis do Markey and Markey (2010) reject the hypothesis that computer games cause violent behaviour?

9   Define attribution theory.

10   Distinguish between stereotyping, prejudice and discrimination.

11   On what basis did Bargh et al. (1996) conclude that certain cues can activate stereotypes, prejudices and discriminatory behaviour without the awareness of the individual?

12   Distinguish between compliance and conformity.

13   Distinguish between majority influence and minority influence in conformity.

14   Define the following influences seeking compliance: reciprocity, low-balling, hazing, foot-in-the-door and door-in-the-face.

15   What is the Asch paradigm?

16   What limits does Schultz's (2008) study place on the Asch paradigm?

17   Define self-efficacy.

18   Describe what the findings in Hochstetler et al. (1985) contribute to understanding the following concepts:

   a   minority influence

   b   self-efficacy

5.3 Cultural origins of behaviour and cognition

This section considers how our culture affects the way we behave, the way we think, and what we remember.

Culture can be understood as a set of common beliefs that hold people together. These common beliefs give rise to social practices, and social practices are filled with meaning. In psychological terms, culture has been defined by Hofstede (2001) as the mental software common to the members of the socio-cultural group.

Cultural cognitive schemas have been internalised, so they influence thinking, emotions and behaviour. Members of the same group learn them through daily interactions and from feedback. For more detail on cognitive schemas, see Chapter 4.

Cultural norms are behaviour patterns that are typical of specific groups. They are passed down from generation to generation, through social learning by the group's 'gatekeepers' (guardians of culture). These are parents, teachers, religious leaders, peers and, to a greater or lesser extent, the media. Exposure to cultural inputs creates systems of values that may be applied to issues such as choice of marriage partner, rights of animals, physical punishment of children and alcohol consumption.

Cultural norms reflect the ways that different peoples have survived in their environment, how they have organised life in social groups, and the resulting beliefs, attitudes and norms that shape their specific behaviours.

Psychology's interest in culture is based specifically on how it affects the behaviour of people. In applying culture to psychology, it is necessary to find out how specific cultural factors relate to behaviours such as initiation rites, witch doctors, infanticide (killing babies in specific circumstances) and honour-killings.

Cultural dimensions are the issues and perspectives of a culture based on values and cultural norms. They influence the attitudes and behaviours the individual brings to specific situations.

For example, if you're making a business deal in the Middle East, it could be a longer and more informal process than in the West. Family photos may be shared, as well as home hospitality, long before talking about the deal. In the Middle East, the handshake can mark the opening of the serious stage of the business deal, rather than the conclusion of it.

In addition, the degree of personal space versus closeness is an issue. British people tend to keep a slightly greater personal space from one another than North Americans; both cultures tend to keep a further distance from each other than in sub-Saharan African and Central Asia.

Cultural norms: behaviour patterns which are typical of specific groups.

Cultural dimensions: the issues and perspectives of a culture based on cultural norms and values.

INTERNATIONAL FOCUS

A language student, Janice, who lives with a Spanish-speaking family in Mexico, reports on a recent experience:

'The family are fun to be with, and they always have time for me. I was getting on so well with them that I invited the parents and their two children for dinner on a summer Saturday night to a tasteful but expensive restaurant. On arrival, an aunt and her three children immediately joined us, the youngest being a three-year-old who wouldn't sit still. Never mind, I thought, family is everything in Mexico. But when the time came to pay the bill, I expected the relatives to contribute their share: after all, I hadn't invited them. They didn't. I ended up paying for everything, and I felt that they had come for a free meal at my expense.

Was it cultural or personal? Janice later found out that in Mexico, inviting one person of the family is assumed to include other members when they hear about it. She discovered this when the family took her along to a similar event and the host, who was a complete stranger, paid for everyone, including her.

Figure 5.12 'I wish he'd told me in advance.'

ACTIVITY 5.3

Arrange yourself into groups of three or four. One of you reads out Janice's report above. Then discuss these questions:

1 How might you have behaved in a similar position?

2 What culture-demanding situations have you encountered when in a different group or country, and how did you fit in with them?

The key areas of study in origins of behaviour and cognition are:

1 culture and its influence on behaviour and cognition

2 cultural dimensions and behaviour

3 the effect of **enculturation** and **acculturation** on human cognition, identity and behaviour

4 **universalist** and **relativist** perspectives

5 **etic** and **emic** perspectives.

5.3.1 Culture and its influence on behaviour and cognition

We have already emphasised that cultures are made up of a set of attitudes, behaviours and symbols shared by a large group of people, and usually communicated from one generation to the next. Cultural groups are characterised by different norms and conventions. There is a distinction between **surface culture** and **deep culture**.

In the introduction to this section, you read about Janice's cultural learning experience when she found herself paying the restaurant bill for a group of strangers. There, she encountered the national culture on two levels. The surface culture, the behaviour, was the invited person extending the invitation to friends and relatives unknown to the host. The deep culture, the mental software, was the cognitive schema of mutual dependence. Cognitively, Mexican individuals feel profound concern and responsibility for the welfare of immediate family, extended family and friends.

Enculturation: the acquisition of the necessary and appropriate norms and skills of your own culture of origin.

Acculturation: where people change or at least adapt due to contact with another culture, in order to fit in to that culture.

Etic approach: this approach views behaviours across cultures, and attempts to find out if specific behaviours are culturally determined or universal.

Emic approach: this approach views behaviour within one culture and examines it within the parameters of that culture rather than within a worldwide norm.

Universalist: a perspective which assumes that cognitive and emotional psychological mechanisms are generally similar throughout the human race, even though they may be expressed behaviourally in different ways.

Relativist: a perspective which views psychological processes as being so different that they cannot be compared across cultural groups.

Surface culture: the behaviours, customs, traditions and communication patterns of a culture that can easily be observed.

Deep culture: the beliefs, values, thought processes and assumptions of a culture that are more easily understood by members of that culture but are less accessible to members of other cultures.

However, Janice's uninvited guests are not completely culturally isolated. Global influences such as travel, the media and the internet can cause cultures to change, or at least allow for more accommodation for expressions of different cultures. These are examined in the HL section later in this chapter.

In influencing cognitive schema, culture has an impact on cognitive processes, affecting what we remember and how we process information and stimuli. These link the cognitive and socio-cultural approaches, and are the subject of the work of Kulkofsky et al. (2011). This study extended the research of Brown and Kulik (1977) on flashbulb memory studied in Chapter 4, towards examining how socio-cultural elements might influence the extent and nature of flashbulb memory.

Research study: Kulkofsky et al. (2011)

Aim

To examine how far culture influences the cognitive phenomenon of flashbulb memory.

Procedure

The study involved 274 middle-class adults from the USA, the UK, Germany, Turkey and China who responded to written questionnaires provided in each native language. Firstly, they had five minutes to recall and write down as many public events as possible that had happened more than one year ago, such as the terrorist attack on the World Trade Center in New York (2001). Secondly, they were asked to recall where they were when the events happened, and what they were doing when the news reached them. Thirdly, they responded to questions about what each event meant to them, how they felt on hearing about each event, and how often they had subsequently talked about each event. Bilingual research assistants translated the responses back into English.

Results

The researchers found that there were no cultural differences in the nature of flashbulb memories as long as the event was of national importance. Cultural differences did appear when the events were not specifically of national importance. Participants from a Western, individualist culture appeared to feel more involved on the personal level, and thus appeared to have rehearsed their memories of such events and their own surrounding circumstances at the time of the event.

Conclusion

The extent and nature of flashbulb memory does seem to be culturally influenced. The cognitive facility of flashbulb memory appears to develop more strongly in individualist cultures than in collectivist cultures. A possible explanation is that in collectivist cultures, such as in China, the individual's experiences are culturally regarded as less important. Therefore its accompanying schemas are less likely to frequently rehearse the recalling of the event.

Strengths of the study

- The study used a large sample of participants chosen from a similar socio-economic group.

- The researchers took care to ensure that the questions were clearly communicated to the participants, and that the participants' responses were communicated to the researchers. They ensured that the translators were familiar with the culture as well as the language of the participants.

- The study indicates that deep culture, in this case individualism and collectivism, can profoundly influence the extent and nature of memory recall.

Limitations of the study

- The study assumed that the participants shared the cultural characteristics attributed to their nationalities.

- It also assumed that the participants fully and accurately reported their memories and experiences, and that the degree of frankness in reporting was not culturally influenced.

5.3.2 Cultural dimensions and behaviour

Cultural dimensions underlie cultural cognition. Cultural dimensions are the values held by people living within a particular culture.

Identifying and applying cultural dimensions are the focus of Geert Hofstede's ongoing studies, which began in 1967 and have extended into the present century. These focused on survey-based written responses on morale in the IBM workplace, a multi-national company employing people of many nations and cultures. Hofstede carried out a content analysis of the responses received from the 53 countries and three regions in the survey. The findings were presented as four different key trends between IBM workers from different countries. These work-related trends were named cultural dimensions. Since then the work has extended to other industries and firms, which by 2010 had added the two further cultural dimensions of long-term/short-term orientation and indulgence/restraint, bringing the total number up to six.

Each cultural dimension is a spectrum. Not all countries lie at the extremes, the countries that participated in the original study being rated on a scale between 1 and 100. Some of the countries that were added later surpass this scale.

These six cultural dimensions are as follows:

1   Individualism/collectivism. Workwise, are you an individual working for the company, or are you personally a part of the company? As an individual member, you might readily transfer to a rival company offering better conditions. You would be less likely to leave if you were part of the group: how could you behave in such a way as to let the side down? The collective view sees the group's destiny as your destiny.

    The USA is an example of a culture with individualist leanings, where the focus tends towards the individual first and the immediate family second. By contrast, with collectivist cultures, for example the Middle and Far East, people tend to be integrated into strong, cohesive groups, represented by the extended family and the socio-cultural group from birth to death. These on one side give support and connection to the individual member. However, not fitting in and striking a decidedly individualist course can result in severe sanctions, exclusion from the group and even honour killings.

    This is also reflected in work ethics: in the USA you can leave a job as soon as another one with better prospects and benefits comes up. In Japan, there is group and company loyalty; you stay with the company you are part of. In the USA, a mistake costing the company millions of dollars will almost certainly mean that the boss instantly dismisses the employee concerned. In Japan, the boss may well accommodate the error and cover up for the employee, especially if they are established as trustworthy and 'one of the company'.

2   Uncertainty-avoidance index, or degree of tolerance for avoiding uncertainty. This refers to the society's willingness to stray out of its comfort zones to reap the potential rewards. North America's culture is that constructive risk-taking is a necessity for developing academic and social maturity, and that learning from mistakes is a positive experience. Going bankrupt, as long as the business has been run in good faith, is part of the learning process for a first-time businessperson in the USA. In contrast, in Europe, going bankrupt can have serious connotations, such as difficulties with gaining credit in the future. Similarly, companies have faced uncertainty-avoidance cultural issues when promoting online purchasing as an alternative to conventional shopping. For example, in 2015 the average customer in Spain spent the equivalent of $849 on online purchases, but only $678 in Belgium, despite Belgium's annual income per person being more than 25% higher than Spain.

    The more extreme uncertainty-avoidance cultures attempt to keep the society as safe and secure as possible. They are often comforted in the belief that theirs is the only society that has the Truth.

3   **Power Distance Index.** This refers to the difference between how people are treated in a culture, depending on whether they are high or low in the power structure of that organisation. The greater the power distance, the greater the deference shown by those lower

Power Distance Index: the measurement of the amount of deference shown by someone lower down the power pyramid to someone higher.

down the pyramid to those up above. How do individuals in your school or company behave towards those higher up or lower down in the organisation?

For example, in the UK teachers have been traditionally addressed as 'Sir', 'Ma'am' or 'Miss'. Teachers today address all students by their first names. Fifty years ago, the cultural norm was to call boys by their surnames and girls by their first names, even in a mixed-gender school. Teachers called boys by their first names in the final two years of high school. That is significant. Many students in those years were then high up in the school pyramid of power, serving as prefects and thus part of the school disciplinary system.

By contrast, in schools in Denmark, Finland and Israel, students are on first name terms with all their teachers. The more conservative schools use the title 'teacher' before the teacher's first name.

On the whole, power distance levels tend to be high in Asian, Arab and Latin American countries and low in Western European countries such as Denmark and Austria.

4   Masculinity/femininity. This dimension refers to how much a culture emphasises gender differences. How are you expected to behave in the workplace? What qualities should you show in order to win the respect of those sharing your environment? Some cultures such as Japan strongly promote qualities traditionally associated with the male gender: competitive cutting-edge performance and achievement. Other cultures such as Norway and Sweden emphasise a balance between work and family, a culture of caring, and minimising differentiation between the genders.

Figures 5.13, 5.14 and 5.15 Lesson number one: power distance

Figure 5.16 In how many cultures would separate entrances be acceptable today?

5   Short-term/long-term orientation. This was the fifth cultural dimension that Hofstede added in 2001. It refers to a culture's tendency to have an outlook that delays gratification to the future or demands immediate gratification. Nordic countries tend towards the short term, East Asian countries are culturally more in tune with the long term.

6   Indulgence/restraint. Added in 2010, an indulgent society accepts enjoyment of life as long as it is does not interfere with the lives of others, whereas countries characterised by restraint strictly regulate fulfilment of the need for enjoyable activities. Africa, Latin America and Western Europe tend towards indulgence, whereas East Asian and the Middle Eastern cultures are far more restrained.

This complex model of the six cultural dimensions is particularly important in issues such as cross-cultural leadership in firms, awareness of cultural differences in business deals (see below) and in the marketing of products. Adverts for high-powered motor bikes would stress self-image in short-term orientation countries such as the USA, but are more likely to emphasise reliability and safety in East Asia.

Critical thinking

1   Find out why Hofstede chose IBM to be the focus of his research on cultural dimensions.
2   How useful might Hofstede's study be to IBM? Justify your response.

Geert Hofstede (1928–)

Figure 5.17 Geert Hofstede

Geert Hofstede (1928–) has a background of mechanical engineering, service to the Dutch Army as technical officer and managerial service to three large Dutch companies. His training as an engineer at the University of Delft combined with his growing psychological interests shaped his research in the field of personnel management. In 1967 he graduated cum laude from the University of Groningen in social psychology. He made full use of that combination when he served as management trainer and manager of personnel research at IBM International. That gave him the base to carry out his initial research in the 1970s, based on some 100 000 completed questionnaires from IBM employees and a large number of work-based interviews in Europe and the Middle East. His findings from IBM and other companies indicated that employees in general showed work-attitudes and behaviours specific to the cultures of their country rather than specific to the company they worked for.

ACTIVITY 5.4

Examine how far the outlook 'It's my life and I will choose how to live it' is typical of the societies that you belong to, and the societies that you know.

5.3.3 Culture and identity

Socialisation is a key cultural process. Socialisation is where the individual learns to behave compatibly with social and cultural norms, and through them acquires a sense of identity. Starting at pre-school age, socialisation continues throughout life, as the individual learns and refines the behaviours, skills and habits necessary for optimum participation and social acceptance within their own culture.

Socialisation involves enculturation, which is the acquisition of the necessary and appropriate norms and skills of one's own culture of origin. Enculturation happens under the influence of direct tuition (guidance by parents and later peer groups towards acceptable behaviours), by observing others and participating in cultural-specific activities which are then applied to wider situations. For example, Pakistani Muslim children born in the UK tend to grow up among family, religious and social elements of enculturation that in many ways contrast strongly with traditional British cultural norms. It is that enculturation that greatly contributes to a sense of personal identity.

Acculturation, in contrast, takes place when people change or at least adapt due to contact with another culture, in order to fit in with that culture. This may happen where the individual is a student at a foreign university, a professional person on a work contract abroad, married to someone from another country, or an asylum-seeker.

Acculturation may also be a result of increasing exposure to global culture, via travel and the media. It can also occur when the person may never have travelled, but grew up in a minority group with different cultural norms to the majority group in which they now wish to participate. In sum, enculturation may be viewed as first-culture learning, acculturation as second-culture learning.

An individual's acculturation rarely completely replaces the original enculturation, but tends to modify it. The fact that people worldwide identify with particular personalities and products associated with global culture does not mean that they abandon their own cultural norms. Their enjoyment of popular music from another part of the world does not detract from their love of the music of their culture. Enculturation does tend to contribute much to the person's identity, even when modified to various extents by acculturating influences.

Both enculturation and acculturation develop on two levels: behavioural and cognitive. Behavioural includes choice of music, means of addressing people in an older generation and ways of spending leisure time. Cognitive can involve attitudes towards education and the workplace, members of the opposite sex and elements associated with globalisation. The individual's enculturation may be modified by the acculturation that can occur through migrating to different cultures or exposure to a different culture, including global culture.

Cultures are generally dynamic: they change over time at both the deep culture level and the surface culture level. For example, deep Western culture has moved to the positive values of gender equality over the last century. That has been expressed in the surface Western cultural changes of women's participation in traditionally male professions and occupations.

Cultures can also change as a result of globalisation forces, or the influence of migration. One example is culinary tastes. American-style fast food is becoming widespread in India and China. Indian and Chinese foods have for decades been popular and culturally accepted in the UK.

People living within societies whose norms differ from their enculturation experiences use a variety of acculturation strategies. Berry (1974) identified these strategies:

1 **Assimilation**: where an individual strives to adopt the attitudes and behaviours of the majority culture and exits the original culture in the process.

2 Integration: where the individual fits in with the majority culture, but still maintains the original culture.

Socialisation: where the individual learns to behave compatibly with social and cultural norms, and through them acquires a sense of identity.

Assimilation: where an individual strives to adopt the attitudes and behaviours of the majority culture and exits the original culture in the process.

3 Separation: where the individual minimises contact with the majority culture, but strives to maintain the original culture.

4 **Marginalisation**: where the individual is excluded from the majority culture and cannot maintain the original culture. That can be due to situational factors within the new culture, such as a language barrier or discriminatory behaviours.

Often, acculturation is not easy. Individuals desire and seek the company of others, which can be in short supply when they are not able to take part in social activities because of problems with fitting in. This creates **acculturation stress**, which is the psychological strain of striving to adapt to a different culture. In some cases, the stress can be avoided through contacts and activities within the expatriate community, for example Turkish people who have migrated to Australia. Many such people have only superficial contact with the local community, spending time with people who speak their language and know their culture. Other individuals experience acculturation stress, particularly when having no choice but to integrate, such as in the world of work. For example, even though English is widely understood in Sweden, work essentials generally include being able to converse in Swedish and fit in with the social norms.

Acculturation challenges can promote persistent, powerful and pervasive stressors that in turn can activate psychological disorders including anxieties and depression. This is especially common where the cultural differences are very large, such as new Hispanic immigrants to the USA. The problem can be compounded when families migrate and generational differences occur in rates of acculturation, called acculturation gaps. Immigrant children enter the school system and generally learn the language and culture quickly. In contrast, the immigrant parents tend to have poorer-defined scope for contact with the new culture, and take much longer to acculturate to the social norms, often with the help of their children. That frequently creates family stresses – children feel that their parents do not share their world, so tend to turn to their peer group for guidance in situations where they would normally have turned to their parents.

Research study: Lueck and Wilson (2011)

Aim

To investigate factors that predict acculturative stress in Hispanic migrants to the USA.

Procedure

The study involved 2059 participants of Hispanic origin who migrated to the USA. This number included 946 who were first generation migrants and grew up in their countries of origin, including Mexico, Cuba, Colombia and other Spanish-speaking countries. The rest of the sample had experienced the USA from their childhoods.

Each participant was assessed for the following: native language proficiency, English language proficiency, language preference, discrimination, family cohesion, social networks, socio-economic status and reason for migrating to the USA. They were also assessed for acculturative stress. The information was obtained by semi-structured interviews that were conducted by a team of interviewers face to face or over the internet. Those conducting the interviews were of similar cultural and linguistic backgrounds to the participants. Interviews averaged 2.4 hours per person.

Results

The following factors were found to be statistically significant predictors of acculturation stress:

1 Higher native language proficiency as opposed to bilingual proficiency.

2 Migrating to the USA being forced, for example because of persecution, rather than being voluntary.

3 Weak social networks, often a result of language barriers. Those with more limited English skills tended to suffer difficulties building support networks outside their communities. Those with a lack of native language skills found it difficult to relate to older family members, especially in personal matters.

4 Experience of substantial discriminatory attitudes and behaviours.

Marginalisation: where the individual is excluded from the majority culture and cannot maintain the original culture.

Acculturation stress: the psychological strain of striving to adapt to a different culture.

Conclusion

On the basis of empirical evidence, the study indicates that specific factors contribute to acculturation stress.

Strengths of the study

- A large sample of over 2000 people took part, who were interviewed by people familiar with the Hispanic culture as well as the context of the investigation.

- The results were supported by a previous study yielding similar results on Asian migrants to the USA (Lueck and Wilson, 2010). However, the researchers argue that Hispanic children face additional acculturation stress in schools on linguistic grounds. Asian children speak different languages and need to use English as a common language. Hispanic people speak a common language, and the use of Spanish was perceived as a potential threat to the English-only policy in schools.

- The use of the semi-structured interview enabled the interviewers to probe more detailed information.

Limitations of the study

- The results were correlational, with the standard difficulties of identifying cause and effect.

- Some of the stresses reported may have been due to non-culturally-related elements rather than acculturation difficulties.

5.3.4 Emic and etic approaches to understanding cultural influences on individual attitudes and behaviour

Western psychology traditionally looked for universal behaviours, and took for granted that they would apply to human beings worldwide. This is the etic approach. It views behaviours across cultures, and attempts to find out if specific behaviours are culturally determined or universal. In contrast, the emic approach looks at individual behaviour from the standpoint that it is culturally specific. It views the behaviour in terms of the society that it is part of.

For example, different schools have different cultures, expectations, written rules and unwritten norms of behaviour. Comparing schools using uniform criteria in academic achievement, sporting and music facilities, standards of classroom discipline and how happy the students are uses the etic approach. It assumes that all schools are in the same cultural framework, and that they share a universal culture. However, there are subtle cultural differences between schools. The students feeling educationally and socially fulfilled in School A might score that school highly on the happiness scale, according to etic criteria. But the culture of School B where individual students are clearly not having a good time is that good schooling is not meant to be enjoyable. Their experience will score low on etic criteria. However, an emic approach would identify the individual student's situation on its own terms and set the criteria as appropriate to the school's specific culture. Thus service to the community or stringent religious conformity might be closer to the school's culture and perception of success.

The following principles characterise the etic approach:

1 Human behaviour is fundamentally universal, not culturally specific. The etic approach takes the universalist perspective which assumes that cognitive and emotional psychological mechanisms are generally similar throughout the human race, even though they may be expressed behaviourally in different ways. An emic approach is likely to take a relativist perspective, with the view that psychological processes in contrasting societies are so different that they cannot be compared across cultural groups.

2 An etic approach is **deductive**. It determines what **research questions** are to be investigated before understanding the culture of the local people. The research is planned according to the theory and methods of the investigators' culture, and then applied to a different local culture.

Deductive (in etic/emic context): where research is conducted according to the theory and methods of the investigators' culture. It is then applied to a local culture, which may or may not be similar. Typically used in etic rather than emic studies.

Research question: what a study is seeking to answer, but not in the form of a testable statement.

Two research team studies both led by Levine (Levine et al., 1994; Levine et al., 2001) are considered in Chapter 7. These teams researched the cross-cultural differences in helping strangers, exemplifying the etic approach. Their investigation was to assess how helpful people were in 36 cities in the USA and 23 cities in other countries. Both studies included three different scenarios requiring simple and short-time assistance from local people: returning a dropped pen, helping a blind person at a busy junction and aiding an injured person to retrieve a fallen magazine.

In combining the two studies, the results within the USA showed that the chance of being helped by a stranger was inversely proportional to the size of the city. Outside the USA, there were instances where, contrary to expectations, faster-pace cities actually rendered more assistance than the less-hurried urban environments. People in Copenhagen and Vienna proved far more helpful than in Kuala Lumpur.

Underlying Levine et al. is the etic framework implying that human beings share universal psychological perceptions and mechanisms. That assumption means that the investigation can be replicated among different cultures using standardised methods and materials, which increases the study's validity. The investigation could have found similar results irrespective of geography and culture, paving a way for a global-scale application to enable people to give more assistance to strangers in need of help. However, the standardised methods applied by Levine et al. indicated a cultural element involved in the degree of willingness for strangers to give assistance when needed.

The following principles characterise the emic approach:

1 Human behaviour is fundamentally culturally specific. The emic approach takes the particularist perspective which assumes that psychological mechanisms greatly differ between cultural groups.

2 An emic approach is **inductive**. This means determining what research questions are to be investigated only after getting to understand the culture of the local people. It would incorporate their local cultural and linguistic knowledge in their investigation. Thus the approach of Levine et al. to studying how different cultures help strangers might not have been a suitable investigative tool to apply to societies with very non-Western values. By contrast, an emic approach could pave the way for a local-specific application to enable people to give more assistance to strangers needing help, building up trust on terms of the culture under study.

Inductive (in etic/emic context): determining what research questions are to be investigated only after getting to understand the culture of the local people. Typically used in emic studies.

The findings of the emic study tend to be limited to the community being investigated. That means that their reliability is not easy to establish, as they are not readily replicated.

Relatively few studies are solely emic. An example of one having emic elements is Parker et al. (2001) in Chapter 6, a leading study designed to investigate cultural considerations in the diagnosis of major depressive disorders.

SELF-ASSESSMENT QUESTIONS 5.2

1 Define culture.
2 Distinguish between cultural norms and cultural dimensions.
3 List Hofstede's six cultural dimensions.
4 Give examples of cultures towards the extremes of each cultural dimension.
5 Distinguish between enculturation and acculturation.
6 List and briefly explain four possible strategies a person living in a culture different from their own might use.
7 List the socio-cultural factors indicated by the research of Lueck and Wilson that contribute significantly to migrants' higher levels of acculturation stress.
8 Distinguish between etic and emic approaches in psychology investigation.
9 Give an example of research that is etic and explain what is etic about the study.

5.4 Globalisation and identity (HL only)

Globalisation: the growing interdependence of countries worldwide through the increasing volume and variety of cross-border transactions in goods and services and of international capital flows, and through the more rapid and widespread diffusion in technology.

The IB programme uses the International Monetary Fund (IMF) definition of **globalisation**:

'The growing interdependence of countries worldwide through the increasing volume and variety of cross-border transactions in goods and services and of international capital flows, and through the more rapid and widespread diffusion in technology'.

You are globally involved as an IB student. The programmes you follow are shared by around 3000 schools in over 130 countries. You might well be globally involved in a Community, Action and Service (CAS) or a Model United Nations (MUN) programme in another country.

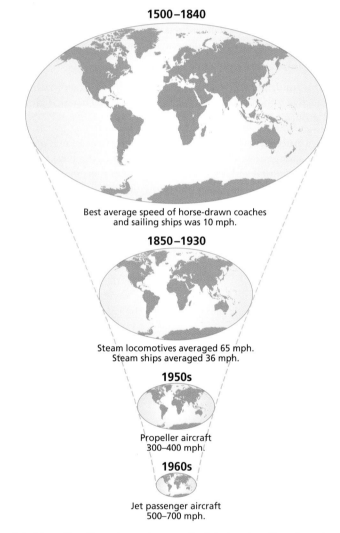

1500–1840

Best average speed of horse-drawn coaches and sailing ships was 10 mph.

1850–1930

Steam locomotives averaged 65 mph.
Steam ships averaged 36 mph.

1950s

Propeller aircraft
300–400 mph.

1960s

Jet passenger aircraft
500–700 mph.

Figure 5.18 As global travelling times have decreased, global connections have increased.

Globalisation involves the compression of the world – in practical terms, the time to travel between two places is greatly reduced: this is time-space compression. It involves the increasing speed at which people, goods, services and finance can cross international borders. Today, you can connect by the internet in zero time and at almost zero cost. Indeed, globalisation brings greater consciousness of the world as a whole. It also gives the individual more opportunity to connect with individuals from different social groups and cultures worldwide. Global culture can create a global world view. In terms of social identity theory, it can psychologically extend entry-eligibility to one's in-group to include a wide range of geographically-dispersed different people on this planet. The elements shared between members of the global in-group are mutual accessibility through global networks, enjoyment of a wide range of products that have global associations, and sharing a common openness (if not always practice) towards outlooks with a Western cultural bias, such as individualism, increasing economic opportunities and freedom of choice in lifestyle.

Yang et al. (2011) conducted a cross-cultural study designed to find out how lay people perceive globalisation. The research included respondents from the USA, China, Taiwan and Hong Kong. The results showed that 26 items were perceived as features and symbols of globalisation. They included the United Nations (UN), the World Trade Organisation (WTO), global warming, McDonald's and Facebook. The research put the items into five categories: global consumer brands (e.g. McDonald's), information technology (e.g. Facebook), human mobility (e.g. encounters with local people on foreign vacations), natural disasters and international aid (e.g. the Haiti earthquake of 2010), and international trade and regulatory bodies (e.g. the WTO and the UN).

In addition, evidence for the impact of global influences worldwide includes the following points:

- Though four times as many people speak Mandarin Chinese than English as a first language, English is understood by more than a third of the world's population. And worldwide, two-thirds of university academic papers are in English.

- 'OK' and 'Coca-Cola' are the most widely understood words on the planet.

- One study showed that more people on the planet correctly identified the golden arches of McDonald's than the cross as a symbol of Christianity.

- In Latin America, most of even those living in small communities have access to what's going on in the world through television, and can identify current international conflicts and world-class celebrities. They know the lyrics of the latest English pop songs even if they don't understand them.

- Urban and wealthier young people in Middle Eastern countries now date rather than wait to meet their spouse through arranged marriage. However, there have been **exclusionary reactions** in some quarters, such as within the more fundamental Muslim countries and groups.

Exclusionary reactions: viewing globalised culture with suspicion and as a threat.

The reality for people of widely varying cultures is often on two different and often conflicting levels. On one level, people want to enjoy the improving technology, range of products and entertainment provided by globally accessible media. Young people from all but the most non-democratic or most theocratic countries will enjoy the economic opportunities, entertainments and products available through the wider global community. On another level, the cultural values associated with many of the global interactions and values are perceived as a threat to the strong and very different cultural values in traditional societies. This is especially true where it touches on religious belief, cultural practice and the expectations of women in society.

It has been argued that global forces over which individuals have no control are destabilising life in their own localities. They are taking away the security people get from their own familiar surroundings, from their sense of locality and from their sense of place. As Bauman (1998) writes:

Figures 5.19 and 5.20 'This isn't where I grew up. I could be living anywhere in the world.'

'Being local in a globalised world is a sign of social deprivation and degradation. The discomforts of localised existence are compounded by the fact that with public spaces removed beyond the reaches of localised life, localities are losing their meaning-generating and meaning-negotiating capacity and are increasingly dependent on sense-giving and interpreting actions which they do not control.'

Political scientists, economists, sociologists and geographers have continually studied the influence of globalisation on individuals and societies. In comparative terms, psychologists are newcomers to this area of study, as observed by Bandura in 2001: 'revolutionary advances in electronic technologies and globalisation are transforming the nature, reach, speed, and loci of human influence'. He believes that psychology is well placed to examine how these fundamental processes in society affect the way people view globalisation. He also claims that psychological theory and investigation methods may be effectively applied to understanding how globalisation affects the behaviour of individuals and societies. These can focus on the nature of people's interactions within an increasingly widening social and cultural matrix.

Nevertheless, psychology-based studies of individuals' reactions to exposure to foreign cultures are relatively few. Globalisation's effect on psychological phenomena and processes is a new field for investigation. Some recent work on the influence of globalisation on individual attitudes and behaviour has come from researchers of Chinese background. China's increasing exposure to international trade and tourism has attracted studies on how the individualist American culture and the more conservative and collectivist Chinese culture interact globally.

5.4.1 Globalisation's influence on attitudes, identity and behaviour

Do individual attitudes and behaviour welcome or at least accommodate globalised culture, showing an **integrative reaction**? Or do they view non-native inputs with suspicion and even outright rejection, showing an exclusionary reaction?

Louise Frechette, ex-UN Deputy Secretary-General, presented globalisation with both outlooks:

'[Globalisation] brings up many opportunities to learn from each other, and to benefit from a wider range of choices, but it can also seem very threatening … Instead of widening our choices, globalisation can seem to be forcing us all into the same shallow, consumerist culture giving us the same appetites but leaving us more than ever unequal in our ability to satisfy them. Many millions of people have yet to feel its benefits at all.' (Address to UN delegates, 1999)

The reactions and resultant attitudes, identities and behaviours may vary according to the positions discussed below. However, it is important to bear in mind that positions also vary according to the nature of the particular global inputs. Some may be perceived as beneficial. Others can be viewed as threats. For example, Saudi Arabians welcome the improved technology that global initiatives have brought to their country, but are very uncomfortable with movies beamed by satellite that threaten Islamic standards of modesty and behaviour. Thus the same individual may show an integrative reaction to one global element and an exclusionary reaction to another.

Individual reactions to globalisation may fall into the following positions:

1 Integrative accommodation of globalisation: the individual accepts the global inputs as compatible with the local culture. The global and local cultures join together as complementary parts of the individual identity. These in turn affect attitudes and behaviour. Thus the individual feels comfortable as a member of the local or cultural community, and as a citizen of the world. There is a local-global accommodation or even local-global synthesis in personal identity formation. There is no perception of cultural intrusion. The reactions are mostly integrative towards both globalisation and local culture.

Such an outlook was found in Inuit communities in Northern Canada, through the pioneering study of Richard Condon (1988). His investigations found that people of the Inuit society appeared to comfortably accommodate two cultures simultaneously – their own, and the wider Canadian and global community. Their access to television (and today to the internet) gave them the sense of being members of a much wider entity, as evidenced in their support for

Integrative reaction: where people welcome or at least accommodate globalised culture.

Canadian hockey teams and long-distance travel for higher education and training. However, their distinctly Inuit identity remained intact. They did not see the widening global experiences as challenging their cultural values of shyness and deep family ties with a high degree of mutual support. Nor did it threaten their continued enjoyment of snowmobiles or ice-fishing.

Figure 5.21 Through global networks, his family can expect fresh fish for dinner.

2   Global citizen. The global culture is the preferred lifestyle over the local culture. The global citizen will view some of the traditional local and cultural ways as secondary to their lifestyle, and may move to reject them, a process referred to as culture shedding. The attitudes and behaviours indicate integration towards global culture, and some exclusion from local culture.

Culture shedding is exemplified by the emerging adulthood of middle-class urbanised young adults in developing countries. Emerging adulthood is the increasingly common prolonged time gap between childhood and marriage/parenthood. As the work of Saraswathi and Larson (2002) observes, in emerging adulthood, middle-class youth in India and South-East Asia have increasingly modern and secular identities. They are more similar to their counterparts in Europe than to the traditional rural people in their own countries who have their families at a younger age. Education and training continue well into their 20s and even beyond, postponing and even avoiding the traditional path of marriage and family. And this trend appears to be growing as the professional and business classes in those countries expand.

3   Exclusionary responses to globalisation. Here, the individual puts their own traditions first and globalisation second. In extreme cases, they reject globalisation altogether. Reactions to globalisation may intensify respect for local cultural icons, and for getting more involved in the local and cultural community. Global culture may be seen as a threat and even rejected outright as an unwelcome force.

Such attitudes indicate moving away from the globalised stereotype of the middle-class younger generation in Western-style baseball caps, blue jeans, designer shoes and the latest smartphone. They may even turn to traditional and religious values, in the belief that they contain the eternal truths instead of what they see as the temporary, passing fashions of the materialistic and spiritually-void globalisation process. In doing so, they frequently join groups that reject the secular nature of globalism, and promote religion in a fundamentalist movement designed to give access to eternal truths and at the same time exclude non-like-minded people.

This is exemplified by Debra Kaufman's (1991) study, 'Rachel's Daughters: Newly Orthodox Jewish Women'. Kaufman interviewed 150 mainly middle-class well-educated American women who grew up in culturally-open secular Jewish backgrounds. On reaching young adulthood, each individual had chosen to connect and identify with more conservative rather than more mainstream Jewish roots. Like most fundamentalist movements, they moved into neighbourhoods populated with traditionalist followers who lived by 'an adherence to a rigorous code of conduct, a belief in a sacred past superior to the present, a sense of being besieged by the rest of the world, and a belief in a hierarchy of authority, with men over women, adults over children, and God over all' (Marty and Appleby, 1993). In other words, an uncompromising rejection of many important aspects of globalised society including equal opportunities, empowerment of women and sexual liberation.

Repeated themes in Kaufman's study showed the sense of security and fulfilment these women found in the shared order and meaning of deeply fundamentalist Jewish life. They shared an identity and exclusionary stance that not only minimised contact with non-Jews, but with Jews who did not share their outlook. The outlook was that Torah teaching and tradition is the ultimate, and anything else would undermine its spiritual integrity. Many of those interviewed claimed that their living within that framework was actually more liberating. The religious guidelines gave them the space for their femininity to blossom. Those guidelines included strict modesty norms in dress and behaviour, and were maintained by a male-dominated authoritarian social structure. They also deeply valued the feelings of the existential certainties rooted in their truths of eternal values that they chose.

Similar reactionary choices are made in other communities. For example, the study of Wu et al. (2014) highlights exclusionary trends among individual Hui-Muslims in China. They increased their commitment to fundamentalism and especially separatist dietary practices in their endeavours to exclude Han-Chinese influences.

Many religious extremist groups include people who have withdrawn from global influences into the security of the exclusionary community of their choice. Though nervous of outside influences, they typically handle outsider encounters with pro-social behaviour. Terrorists with agendas to strike at representations of global culture (e.g. the attacks on the World Trade Center in New York, 2001) are exceptions.

4 Marginalisation, or disorientation: such individuals sense conflicting identities and cannot easily resolve them. 'Where do I belong?' They find conflicts between local/cultural and global inputs hard to reconcile. They neither feel comfortable in global circles nor in local/cultural circles. They sense confusion with behaviours that are neither integrative nor rejectionist.

The work of Norasakkunkit and Uchida (2011) highlights the maladaptive situation of a substantial number of disorientated young adults in Japan. Economically, the higher rate of global interactions has brought increased competition in world markets. As a result, the very firm job security enjoyed by the Japanese professional is not as common as in their parents' generation. At the same time, they see the more individualistic nature of global, cross-border transactions as a vague challenge to the vitality of their society. Thus, these individuals have felt marginalised by the changes in society. Their identities are confused. Their disorientation and consequent lack of focus on long-term goals has made them choose to shift from the business and professional centres of society to the edges. They are not motivated to pursue long-term goals. They feel neither at ease with the local culture that emphasises self-improvement and independence, nor with the more individualistic nature of global society.

This chapter concludes by looking at globalisation's influences on individuals' attitudes and behaviour in specific situations.

5.4.2 The effects of the interaction of local and global influences

There are a huge number of ways in which globalisation may influence the way we feel and act in a particular circumstance or setting. We will examine the following through the research described below:

- The individual experiences a simultaneous interaction with global and native culture. Will that promote exclusionary or integrative attitudes and behaviour?

- The individual experiences globalisation through foreign travel. How may that affect the level of trust shown towards strangers?
- The individual senses strong and varied global inputs. How might they enhance or detract from the individual's level of creative thinking?

Foreign travel can enable a person to experience globalisation by widening their experience and meeting individuals and groups that would not be encountered in the home environment. How far may the globalisation experience affect the degree of discrimination shown towards strangers? Does travel open the mind to trusting strangers?

Research study: Cao, Galinsky and Maddux (2013)

Pro-active interaction with strangers is a key element in globalisation. This is because a substantial level of trust is essential for any international business deal to work. Trust comes at the price of risk-taking and making ourselves vulnerable to members of the global community from very different social and cultural backgrounds.

Cao, Galinsky and Maddux's research simulated an investment exercise, designed to obtain empirical evidence.

Aim

To investigate whether travel opens the mind to trusting strangers.

Procedure

The study used a mixed-gender sample of 237 American university undergraduate students.

The students first completed a questionnaire survey that was designed to determine their own personality types and their degree of foreign travel. Their degree of trust was then measured by taking part in an investment game. They were to be randomly assigned to the role of 'sender' or 'receiver'. Unknown to the participants, every individual was designated as a sender. The assignment was to agree to send a sum of money not exceeding $10 to the receiver, a person they did not know. The receiver would 'invest' it and 'triple its value'. The receiver would then decide how much of the money would be given back to the sender. The idea was that the more money the senders would invest, the greater generalised trust they would be showing.

Results

The results showed that these two variables were positively correlated. The researchers found that the greater the breadth of individual foreign travel, the greater the general willingness to trust rather than to withdraw.

Conclusion

Travel experience has a positive influence in enabling the individual to extend integrative attitudes and behaviour by risk-taking and lowering the discriminatory barriers of mistrust.

Strengths of the study

This study used a large sample and sought to control for different personality types, thereby identifying the extent that each participant tended to trust other people in general.

Limitations of the study

Its limitations include the correlation-indicated greater willingness to trust among those more widely travelled possibly being influenced by other elements. Such a factor could be the interest in other cultures that promoted the travel in the first place, rather than the actual travel itself.

However, personal identity clash can sometimes occur between elements within the global entity and elements within the native culture entity.

Research study: Torelli et al. (2011)

This experimental work placed 125 American students of European origin in a simultaneous two-culture situation.

Theory of Knowledge

'Does travel open the mind to trusting strangers?'

Pick a country you visited (or moved to) for the first time.

1 What did you know about the country and feel towards it before your visit?
2 In what ways did your knowledge and feelings towards that country change after your visit? Explain what experiences helped you to change your mind.
3 Looking back, how far has your knowledge about what really goes on in that country been improved by your having been there? Explain your response.

Aim

To determine how students would react when a valued icon of their local culture was under threat in a different, global setting. The hypothesis was that the participants would identify far more intensely with their icon when it was set in the background of a very different culture. Indeed, in such circumstances they would protect their icon with exclusionary attitudes and behaviour.

Procedure

The first group was culturally primed by being shown three iconic items that were strongly identified with the USA: running shoes, jeans and breakfast cereals. The second group was also primed, but with items that were less iconic of the USA: table lamps, bread toasters and umbrellas. These created the psychological conditions in the first group in which national identity and global identity would be both strongly represented in a conflicting situation.

Half of the first group was told that the strongly iconic running shoes, jeans, and breakfast cultures were made by local companies in China; the companies being 'Qinjin' for the running shoes, 'Xenshi' for the jeans and 'Chenxiao' for the breakfast cereals. The other half of this group were given the American-sounding names of 'Aspire', 'Nine-Zero' and 'Uncle Bob' for the running shoes, jeans and breakfast cereals respectively.

Then half of the second group was told that the less-iconic table lamps, bread toasters and umbrellas were made by Chinese companies; 'Zhongyan' for the table lamps, 'Beihua' for the toasters and 'Wufeng' for the umbrellas. The other half of the group were given American-sounding names for the same products: 'Schonbek', 'Robin' and 'Murray' for the table lamps, toasters and umbrellas respectively. All participants rated their assigned products using three criteria, on a 1–9 scale: bad-good, unappealing-appealing and unfavourable-favourable.

Results

The results showed significantly lower ratings for products that were Chinese-made brands of highly iconic American products than for any other type of products.

Conclusion

Individuals tend towards exclusionary reactions to a foreign culture when it conflicts with a cherished icon associated with their native culture.

ACTIVITY 5.5

Figure 5.22 Starbucks opened in the Forbidden City, Beijing in 2000

The Forbidden City in Beijing, China:

- A leading cultural iconic site for the people of China. As an icon, it rivals the Great Wall of China.

- China's largest palace complex, with similar past status to the White House, the Kremlin, Buckingham Palace and the Palace of Versailles.

- Built in 1420, closed in 1911.

- Home to 24 emperors of the Ming and Qing dynasties.

- Any unauthorised visitor found on its premises during its operation was put to death.

- Surrounded by a 10 metre-high wall, under heavy guard from surrounding watchtowers.

- Contains 90 palaces and 980 buildings. Nearly 9000 rooms.

In 2000, Starbucks took up residence in the Forbidden City. Starbucks duly offered its world-renowned menu to the tens of thousands of weary visitors passing by daily.

Starbucks, originating in Seattle, Washington State, USA:

- A leading cultural icon for Americans, rivalling McDonald's.

- On average, a new Starbucks opens every 12 hours.

- If you don't like dairy, you can choose between soy milk and coconut milk.

- The maximum 'trenta'-sized cup holds more liquid than the human stomach.

- The average customer visits Starbucks six times per month.

- There are 87 000 possible drink combinations.

- Online dating website Match.com offers starbucks dates online.

Following local protests, Starbucks agreed to close down operations at that location in 2007.

1   Identify and explain the social identity issues likely to have been involved in the debate as to whether or not to close down Starbucks in the Forbidden City.

2   The number of Starbucks outlets in China today is steadily growing, and has nearly reached 1000. Suggest and justify reasons for its success in China generally in the light of its having been closed in the Forbidden City.

SELF-ASSESSMENT QUESTIONS 5.3

1   Define globalisation and time-space compression.

2   Distinguish between integrative and exclusionary reactions.

3   List four studies that show different attitudes and behaviours towards global inputs. Classify the findings of the studies in terms of integrative/exclusionary tendencies.

4   Name a research study showing how exposure to global inputs affects reactions to simultaneous exposure to local cultural icons. What were its findings?

5   Name a research study that shows how an individual's previous exposure to foreign travel may affect the level of trust shown towards strangers. What were the findings of that study?

Chapter summary

1 The socio-cultural perspective emphasises that the individual's attitudes and behaviour are modelled on other people within the environment, whether or not those people are personally known to the individual.

2 Social identity theory holds that an individual's sense of who they are is based on a sense of belonging or not belonging to specific social groups.

3 An individual's social cognition develops from the elements of social learning theory, schema development, stereotyping, social attribution, social norms and self-efficacy.

4 The degree of the transmission of social norms is evidenced in the degree of conformity and compliance of the individual. Perceived pressure to conform to the majority opinion or to particularly strong individuals within the group can influence the individual to submit to their judgement to avoid dissent.

5 Culture can be understood as a set of common beliefs that hold people together which give rise to social practices imbued with meaning. It may be passed on by enculturation, and weakened by acculturation and assimilation with a different society.

6 Cultural dimensions are the issues and perspectives of a culture based on its values and cultural norms which influence the attitudes and behaviours that the individual brings to specific situations. Understanding cultural dimensions is important for international exchanges, business deals and the marketing of products.

7 Research studies in socio-cultural psychology may be of emic character, framed within the norms of a culture. In contrast they may be of etic character, investigating whether specific behaviours are culturally determined or universal.

8 (HL only) Local culture meeting globalisation can result in various degrees of integrative or exclusionary behaviour towards globalisation on the part of the individual.

9 (HL only) Higher degrees of exposure to globalisation appear to positively affect the levels of trust shown towards strangers by the individual, while higher degrees of identification with our own culture tend to weaken globalisation influences.

Exam-style questions

Short-answer question

- Explain the influence of two cultural dimensions on individual behaviour.

Essay response questions

- Evaluate the role of social learning theory on influencing the behaviour of an individual.

Abnormal psychology

'If you think people in your life are normal, then you undoubtedly have not spent any time getting to know the abnormal side of them.' (Shannon L. Alder)

KEY QUESTIONS
- How may abnormal behaviour be defined and accurately diagnosed?
- What are the causes of behaviour abnormalities, and how may they be influenced by cultural and gender variations?
- What are the range of treatments available to therapists for the treatment of abnormalities?

Learning objectives

- Outline the criteria used in defining and diagnosing abnormality. (AO1)
- Explain the role of genetics in causing psychological disorders. (AO2)
- Evaluate the use of medication and placebos in aiding recovery from abnormal conditions. (AO3)
- Evaluate the different cognitive and socio-cultural-based methods for the treatment of abnormal conditions. (AO3)

6.1 Introduction to abnormal psychology

Psychologists do not agree on what abnormality actually is. The consensus accepts that abnormality is a cognitive or behavioural state that impairs interpersonal functioning and/or creates distress for others.

Psychologists dispute the **aetiology**, or causes of abnormality. Psychiatrists emphasising the biological approach to behaviour typically explain abnormality in terms of hormonal or neurological imbalances. The cognitive approach focuses on issues of the individual's perception and processing of information, exemplified by treatments such as **cognitive behavioural therapy (CBT)**. Socio-culturally-based therapists tend to view individual behaviour in terms of deviation from social and cultural norms.

Aetiology: the study of the causes of a disorder.

Cognitive behavioural therapy (CBT): psychotherapeutic treatment based on the theory that thinking patterns strongly influence many behaviour patterns.

Figure 6.1 Wim Hof, 'The iceman'

Figure 6.2 Michel Lotito, the consumer of indigestible objects

ACTIVITY 6.1

Research the behaviours of the individuals shown in Figure 6.1 and 6.2. How far do you think that their behaviours could be classified as abnormal?

Our studies in abnormal psychology apply the biological, cognitive and socio-cultural approaches to understanding behaviour in defining, explaining and viewing treatments for specific types of abnormal behaviour.

Abnormal psychology focuses on the classification, causes, diagnosis and treatment of impairments in important areas of normal mental functioning.

Normality is defined by Jahoda (1958) as enjoying ideal mental health, which includes the following characteristics:

- positive self-esteem irrespective of personal qualities and achievements

- sense of direction in working towards positive goals of one's own choosing

Abnormal psychology: the classification, causes, diagnosis and treatment of impairments in important areas of normal mental functioning.

Normality: the enjoyment of mental health, whose parameters are to some degree culturally determined.

- having the self-confidence to interact competently with people, situations and the environment

- being able to form deepening relations with other people, including romantic relations

- sense of integrity in being able to fit into the surroundings without sacrificing one's identity.

Not enjoying a way of life that is continuously defined by those characteristics does not mean an abnormal behaviour pattern. Virtually all people go through short periods and even phases when they sense that they are not functioning at their best. However, serious and consistent deviations from any of those norms may suggest abnormality.

In reality, Jahoda's list would be more valid as a list of characteristics of a minority of very well-adapted individuals rather than the opposite of abnormality. Were these criteria applied rigidly, most people would not qualify as being normal. In addition, there are people whose unrealistically high self-esteem causes them to think that they are more successful than they really are. Such delusions would hardly be a qualifying criterion for normality.

Moreover, this list has a culturally Western bias. The norm in traditional societies tends towards individuals turning to elders and superiors for guidance and advice. In collectivist societies, a sense of high self-esteem that is persistently unlike one's peers and colleagues might point towards abnormality rather than normality.

By contrast, Rosenhan and Seligman (1984) apply seven criteria to determine whether a behaviour pattern is normal or not:

1 Is any suffering involved?

2 Is the person's behaviour the source of their own troubles?

3 Does the person manage to communicate feelings in a rational and reasonable way?

4 Is an unpredictable pattern shown in dealing with situations?

5 Is a particular situation experienced quite differently from the ways others go through it?

6 Is the behaviour causing awkwardness and embarrassment to others?

7 Is the person's way of doing things in violation of their accepted cultural standards?

Psychopathological: concerning mental disorders and associated behaviours that may be the result of a mental abnormal condition(s).

This list does directly address abnormality. It also shows a careful balance between the mental well-being of the individual and the realities of society at large. It views abnormal conditions as **psychopathological**, meaning illness in the mind. This dimension places much of abnormal psychology into the clinical domain of the psychiatrist, whose framework considers mental health disorders as requiring treatment in a structure that parallels physical health disorders. One of the psychiatrist's tools is the diagnostic manual, whose nature and use is considered in the next section.

However, the task of defining abnormality needs to take into account that social realities change, as in the following circumstances:

1 Behaviour may be categorised as abnormal when it is seen to threaten powerfully backed regimes and interests. For example, Soviet Russia categorised dissidents as mentally abnormal and forced them to undergo clinical treatment.

2 Behaviour previously considered abnormal in Western society would not be considered so today. Examples include a sexual interest in a person of the same gender, and a woman deliberately choosing to be single rather than to marry.

3 Many behaviours at odds with the dominant culture are normal behaviour within the minority culture that the individual identifies with. This is exemplified in the manual of the American Psychiatric Association, which classifies various disorders as culture-bound syndromes.

4   The over-diagnosis and under-diagnosis of a particular condition within different groups. For example, a gender bias is shown when early teenage boys rather than girls are more readily diagnosed with attention deficit disorder (ADD) because they fit the associated gender stereotype of being disruptive in class and unable to focus.

These factors make it difficult to classify what behaviours are abnormal. There exist possibilities of clinical bias, gender bias, culture bias and socio-economic status bias. All these greatly complicate the process in the diagnosis of a particular condition in an individual, and in determining whether or not it is indeed abnormal. They are also factors that can influence the professional's decision on the form of the patient's course of treatment.

In addition, cultural factors tend to influence the way the individual patient interacts with the mental health profession. In the USA, the complex ways in which society and culture influence mental health were investigated within the US Department of Health and Human Services Report of the Surgeon General (2001). This study recognised the following key socio-cultural-bound variables involved where a very wide range of people interact with professional diagnosis, treatment and service delivery:

1   the means used by the patient to express mental health abnormalities

2   the coping strategies used by the patient, including willingness to undergo treatment

3   the overcoming of social barriers – generally, minority groups face greater cultural stigmas in actively seeking help than majority groups

4   the means and degrees of support given by family and community

5   the means and degrees of support given by professional service providers

6   the culture of the family, community and professional service providers

7   the degree of mistrust of mental health services, especially in the sensitive areas of miscommunication between patient and mental health professional, stereotyping and clinical bias.

Added to which can be the fear of confidentiality leaks. Some of these points are expanded in Section 6.1.2 in the context of cultural bias.

This leads us into the next section, which considers the strengths and limitations of the diagnostic processes commonly used in advanced Western-type societies.

NEWSFLASH

Is fantasising a form of abnormal behaviour?

Dream success and you will live success. Think positively, and all those great things will happen to you. Set high expectations, and realise your brilliant success.

Modern psychology agrees, but only partially. Studies indicate that your mind needs to be set to visualising your future, not fantasising about it. There is a crucial thin line between fantasy and expectation.

One study (Oettingen and Mayer, 2002) looked at four challenges people face: finding a good job, finding a partner, exam success and successfully undergoing surgery.

The study looked at how much each participant fantasised about and expected a positive result.

The results found a difference between fantasy and expectation. Those who merely fantasised about the job they wanted had applied for fewer vacancies. If they were employed, they were among the lower paid. But those who visualised job success with high expectations achieved a relatively high degree of job success. The study also identified a correlation between those with successfully realised high expectations of success at work and similar expectations of success in three other areas of life: in examinations, finding the desired partner and recovering from surgery.

Positive fantasies are bad for the fantasiser. Enjoying a fantasy world gives an instant sense of achievement that is false. It is an escape from reality. Living with expectations, on the other hand, is based on past experiences. You expect to find a new quality partner because your previous partner was someone special. You expect to excel in the exam because you recall past experiences where hard preparation gave you the success you wanted. If your past experiences were less than reassuring, your expectations guide you to modify your approach in striving towards achievement.

Oettingen and Mayer and other similar studies have shown that entering a fantasy world is likely to sabotage our real goals in life because it falsely simulates the sensations of success.

ACTIVITY 6.2

Debate whether fantasising is abnormal behaviour as it can harm the individual, as described in the Newsflash.

6.1.1 Identifying abnormality: validity and reliability of diagnosis

Pathological: the study of the nature of disease and changes that it can cause.

Diagnosis manual: a professionally-compiled and comprehensive collection of abnormalities with standardised guidelines and criteria for diagnosis.

DSM-5: the diagnosis manual for abnormalities used in the USA.

ICD-10: the diagnosis manual for abnormalities used in the UK, as well as in the World Health Organisation.

Validity (of diagnosis): how accurately the diagnosis procedures correctly identify the condition of the patient.

Reliability of diagnosis: the degree that the diagnosis is confirmed by another independent psychiatrist.

Some abnormal behaviour patterns, such as dementia, may by diagnosed by electronic brain scanning. However, despite advances in brain-scanning technology, most psychological disorders cannot by traced to **pathological** sources.

Much diagnosis today relies on the psychiatrist's judgement of the symptoms fitting the criteria of an abnormal condition as defined by the **diagnosis manual**. Two of the most used manuals are **DSM-5** (Diagnostic and Statistical Manual, fifth edition) in the USA, and **ICD-10** (International Classification of Diseases, tenth edition) used by the World Health Organisation and also in the UK.

Not all the factors affecting the **validity of the diagnosis** are entirely in the hands of the psychiatrist. Validity refers to the likelihood of the diagnosis being correct. **Reliability of diagnosis** depends on the degree that the diagnosis is independently supported by one or more of the psychiatrist's professional peers.

Pathological evidence for an abnormal condition is usually not available due to the limited understandings of the workings of the brain. Therefore, the psychiatrist has to rely on personal impressions of the patient during clinical interviews, self-reporting from the patient and/or clinical observation to identify the symptoms. Diagnoses may be given on the basis of these identified symptoms collectively qualifying for a specific abnormal condition.

In addition, the validity of a diagnosis can in practice be affected by the other factors that psychiatrists need to take into account. A diagnosis could cause the patient to suffer a stigma of mental illness, which can have serious social and economic consequences. It could involve job loss, and being shunned by former friends and even family. Additionally, a patient diagnosed as mentally ill may no longer be held fully responsible for violent or anti-social behaviour, and their movement might have to be institutionally restrained.

6.1.2 Problems affecting the validity of diagnosis

Ideally, two different psychiatrists should reach the same diagnosis if they apply the same standard manual-based diagnostic criteria of DSM-5 or ICD-10. In reality, the reliability of diagnosis depends on several factors beyond the definitions and classifications of the manuals. Underlying some of these factors are the possibilities of clinical bias.

Potential issues affecting reliability in clinical diagnosis

1 The clinical interviewer's perception of the patient's situation

The individual psychiatrist has to decide whether the degree of severity of the patient's symptoms actually meets the criteria for the diagnosis. For example, a diagnosis of **schizophrenia** can be substantially based on the patient's self-reporting, which may be flawed. This can involve serious professional and ethical dilemmas. A wrong diagnosis could negatively label the patient, affecting employment, medication and even resulting in compulsory hospitalisation. In reality, the individual may be enduring a difficult temporary phase coping with, for example, colleagues and clients at work. Conversely, the non-diagnosis of an under-reporting patient could result in that person not receiving vital support and treatment.

Schizophrenia: a disorder that can involve delusions, hallucinations and disturbances in emotions and behaviour.

Figure 6.3 Do they already know about me in the diagnosis manual?

This argument might well be less important with the advance of brain-scanning technology, especially in the diagnosis of conditions such as Alzheimer's disease, attention deficit hyperactivity disorder (ADHD) and ADD.

2 The clinical interviewer's approach to the patient

Psychiatrists bring their distinctive professional styles, theoretical orientations, cultural backgrounds (considered later in this section) and personalities to the clinical interview. Value judgements are involved in psychiatric diagnosis. It can also include a possible gender bias. Thus diagnosis can depend on the values and the culture of both the interviewer and the patient, in contrast to the more objective criteria of medical diagnosis based on data from, for example, a blood test.

For example, the work of Cooper et al. (1972) sought to investigate reliability in the diagnosis of depression and schizophrenia. It involved American and British psychiatrists observing films of clinical interviews of patients, whom they had to diagnose. Twice as many of those viewed were diagnosed as schizophrenic by the American psychiatrists as by the British psychiatrists, raising the possibility of a cultural bias.

However, there are studies that indicate an overall improvement in diagnosis. The research of Jakobsen et al. (2005) used ICD-10 criteria in diagnosing schizophrenia in 100 Danish patients with a history of psychosis. They found a concordance rate of 98% between two psychiatrists working independently on each case, suggesting that modern criteria may be applied with much greater accuracy. This does not necessarily mean that a manual-based diagnosis of schizophrenia is accurate just because two psychiatrists agree in applying the same diagnostic tool. The diagnosis of schizophrenia depends on several symptoms being present at the same time, which could lead to over- or under-diagnosis. The definitions also work on the basis that there is no state of **co-morbidity**, meaning that the patient has more than one abnormal condition.

Co-morbidity: where the patient is diagnosed as having more than one abnormal condition.

3 The clinical interviewer's difficulties in distinguishing between normal and abnormal behaviour

This aspect was investigated by Rosenhan (1973).

Research study: Rosenhan (1973)

Aim

The work of Rosenhan 'On being sane in insane places' sought to test the reliability and validity of the diagnosis of schizophrenia in an ecologically valid setting. Could psychiatrists distinguish between 'normal' and 'abnormal' behaviour?

Procedure

Each of the eight participants (including Rosenhan himself) was required to gain admission to a specific psychiatric hospital within the USA. Their ruse was to claim to have heard 'voices', but otherwise giving a normal background. The deception worked. All instances were diagnosed as schizophrenia under the then current DSM-2 manual, except one person who was classified as manic-depressive.

Once admitted, their task was to seek to be discharged as soon as possible. That depended on their convincing the staff that they were sufficiently mentally healthy. Thus the 'patients' acted normally once hospitalised, except for taking notes. That was vital. All the participants were covert participant observers, watching the hospital staff without their knowledge.

Results

In fact, the act of note-taking was interpreted as evidence of insanity by the staff members, who did not seem to pay much attention to the content of the notes. On average, it took 19 days for them to be released, most commonly with a diagnosis of 'schizophrenia in remission'. Not surprisingly, the publicity given to the team's findings created considerable embarrassment to the psychiatric profession. That became all the more acute when the participants revealed that nearly one-third of the other patients suspected that the participants were sane. The patients were revealed to have been more accurate in diagnosis than the professionals.

The follow-up study took place when the staff at one psychiatric hospital were told that some fake patients would present themselves, and they should be on the lookout for them. Out of 193 patients, 83 were suspected of being imposters by at least one member of staff. In fact, all the patients were genuine.

Conclusion

The study concluded that the psychiatrists' failure to distinguish between genuine and fake patients seriously questioned the professionals' competence in diagnosing schizophrenia.

Strengths of the study

The study highlighted psychiatrists' need to improve their application of diagnostic tools, however precise those tools are. The study was ecologically valid as issues determining cause and effect were present. All 'patients' had been hospitalised on the basis of their self-reporting of hearing voices. It also indicated that the label of schizophrenia is hard to remove, despite the apparently poor reliability of diagnosis.

Limitations of the study

However, the study may be criticised on the grounds that psychiatrists are trained to diagnose on patient-reported facts in order to help them, rather than suspect that their motives are not genuine and turn them away. For comparison, there were no fake patients in the high concordance rate in Jakobsen et al. (above). Additionally, the very fact that the participants presented themselves as patients to the psychiatrists created their expectation of needing treatment. Moreover, the later diagnoses of 'schizophrenia in remission' were correct to the degree that the 'patients' displayed no sign of that condition on release. So the hospital staff had made the correct diagnosis in the end. Finally, some of the participants might have been nervous; they were not professional actors.

There was also the ethical issue of covert **participant observation**. It may be justifiable in this case as the findings were of paramount public importance and could not have been obtained in any other way. However, informing the psychiatrists that imposters would be present in the follow-up study does raise the ethical issue of genuine patients not receiving necessary treatment as a result.

4 Gender considerations in diagnosis: the possibility of gender bias

The rate of diagnosis of depression in women is about twice that of men. That raises the question of whether there is gender bias in identifying depression with women. The study of Bertakis et al. (2001) supported the hypothesis that both male and female populations fundamentally have similar rates of depression. However, that study indicated higher female diagnosis rates as being influenced by the male-stereotype gender bias, as well as the reality of women seeking help more frequently and reporting symptoms more thoroughly. In addition, the study of Brommelhoff et al. (2004) supported the view that gender biases are not entirely clinical. Social pressure in families to seek help for handling depressed feelings tends to be more persuasive for women than for men.

5 Cultural considerations in diagnosis: cultural variation

The differences in cultures between the psychiatrist and the patient may create severe difficulties in effective psychiatric diagnosis.

There is a fear of giving a diagnosis of, for example, depression, as it can create stigmatisation and disproportionate harm to the patient in their own society. It can make the patient extremely wary of reporting affective (mood-related), behavioural, and cognitive symptoms. There is the possibility that the distress that the person experiences is a product of their belief system. Such an individual may see the suffering as a divine-imposed consequence of a past misdeed, rather than a fundamental underlying disorder. This may influence the patient to play down the symptoms and be at risk of not receiving appropriate diagnosis and treatment.

Additionally, the work of Cochrane and Sashidharan (1995) indicates some tendency for psychologists of Western culture to treat people according to the norms of the majority white populations of their country. For example, a non-white patient suffering bereavement may claim to hear voices from their recently deceased relatives. That might well be classified as an abnormality under DSM-5 criteria, yet perfectly normal and acceptable within the person's minority culture.

Indeed, Fernando (1988) has shown similar types of clinical bias in race stereotyping among psychiatrists in the UK. Black patients diagnosed with abnormalities associated with violent behaviour are significantly more likely to be detained against their will in a mental institution than any other group. This racial bias fits in with a stereotype that black people with violent tendencies are unlikely to respond to outside treatment.

There is also the possibility of the psychiatrist not being able to identify signs of (for example) depression where they are expressed in a non-recognisable way within a different ethnic group. Some cultures tend to play down emotionally expressed disorders, and only address them when they are expressed physically. For example, the study of Zhang et al. (1998) reported that only 16 out of over 19 000 people from 12 different regions in China reported suffering from a mood disorder at least once in their life. This might indicate that depression hardly exists among Chinese people. However, many did report **somatic** (relating to the body rather than to the mind) symptoms that indicated depression, such as 'a weakness of the nerves', 'fatigue' and often 'lower-back pains'. That fits in with the Chinese emphasis on disease arising out of disharmony in the body between the energy flow and the different organs in the body. Indeed, the work of Kleinman (1982) argued that the somatisation of symptoms makes it difficult to 'join the dots' and identify a depressive situation, even where one exists. Conversely, there is also the danger of accepting physical pain by itself as a symptom of depression with Chinese patients.

Participant observation: involves the researcher(s) becoming part of the target group that is being studied. The investigator is working from within those being observed.

Somatic: relating to the body rather than to the mind.

Depressive episode: a period of symptoms of depression, which becomes major depression if it persists continually for at least two weeks.

INTERNATIONAL FOCUS

The work of Parker et al. (2001) is a leading study designed to investigate cultural considerations in the diagnosis of abnormality, in this case major depressive disorder. Major depressive disorder includes experiencing one or more major **depressive episodes**. The criteria for the diagnosis of a depressive episode is a depressive mood lasting at least two weeks that contains five symptoms including: lack of interest or pleasure in most activities, loss of energy, marked gain or loss of appetite, marked increase or decrease in hours of sleep, sudden agitated movements or slowing down of movements and speech, more difficulties than usual in decision-making, unjustified and excessive feelings of guilt, and recurrent thoughts of death and suicide.

The focus of this cross-cultural study was on individuals seeking professional help for that condition in two contrasting societies: Australian patients of Western ancestry and culture, and Chinese patients living in Malaysia. The purpose was to investigate the ways in which each group of patients identified cognitive and somatic symptoms as reasons for seeking professional help.

The participants were 100 outpatients diagnosed with major depressive disorder. There was an equal number of Australian and Chinese participants. No patient had been diagnosed for any other condition, for example schizophrenia, that might influence the results of the study.

The participants were required to report on their experience of major depression with a 39-point questionnaire listing two sets of symptoms: psychological and somatic. The psychological symptoms were Western-based, reporting on mood and cognition. The somatic symptoms were those commonly observed by Singaporean psychiatrists with experience of Chinese patients. The individual patients were given two tasks. Firstly, they reported on each symptom listed on the questionnaire: whether it was experienced all the time, most of the time, some of the time or not at all. Secondly, they ranked the symptoms from the most distressing to the least distressing. Additionally, they specified the main symptom that persuaded them to seek help.

The study found that the 60% of the Chinese patients stated that they sought help because they experienced a symptom that was somatic. In contrast, only 13% of the Australians described their major depression in somatic terms.

Based on the survey results below, the Chinese patients affirmed significantly fewer cognitive and emotional symptoms of depression.

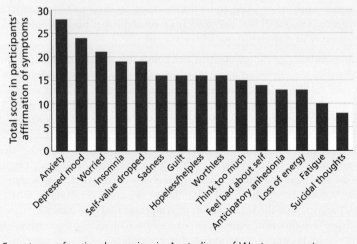

Figure 6.4 Symptoms of major depression in Australians of Western ancestry

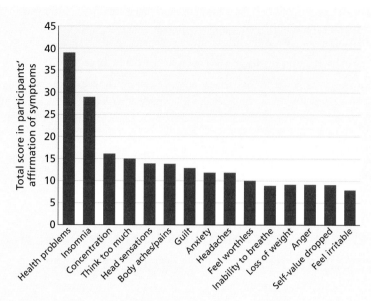

Figure 6.5 Symptoms of major depression in Malaysian-based Chinese

Both groups listed a similar number of somatic symptoms connected to their depressions. However, the Chinese patients indicated significantly fewer cognitive or emotional symptoms.

The study indicates that expressing depression in terms of personal thinking, emotions or any way that suggests mental problems, may be significantly less socially acceptable in Chinese culture than in Western culture.

The strengths of the study are that psychiatrists who understood the Chinese community were involved in the planning of the questionnaire, which was designed to incorporate somatic elements that were not included in the standard DSM-4 (today DSM-5) criteria for the diagnosis of major depression. Additionally, the questionnaires had been translated into Malay and Chinese and then back-translated into English for the purpose of maximising accuracy in working with the participants in Malaysia; 80% of those people did not speak English as a first language.

The study is limited by several factors. Firstly, Chinese communities living in Malaysia are participating in a far more globalised society than most of their counterparts in mainland China, where the cultural differences in reporting might well have been more extreme. Secondly, the Chinese participants had been diagnosed with major depression under the Western criteria stated in DSM-4. Lacking an emic approach, it may have excluded from the sample some people with a form of depression that is not reached by Western diagnostic tools.

Additionally, the study was based on self-reporting. There could have been memory inaccuracies and cultural differences in perceived demand characteristics. Both could be influenced by what they believe is the most socially acceptable way of describing their individual conditions.

The psychiatrist working together with a bilingual and bi-cultural person trained in mental health may address these cultural issues. Such a person can relate and present the various symptoms reported by the patient to the framework of the psychiatrist's understanding.

6 Cultural considerations in diagnosis: socio-economic bias

Abnormal conditions of financially poorer patients may be given more extreme diagnoses than similar abnormal conditions of richer patients. They also had a greater chance of being confined to mental institutions, and for longer periods. In addition, the treatment for poorer patients would more probably be interventionist, such as drugs or ECT therapy. Both drugs and ECT treatment disempower rather than empower the patient to address the abnormality. In defence, some psychologists justify the socio-economic differentiations in treatment as it is the wealthier classes that would have had the higher level of education to benefit from non-interventionist and empowering verbal one-to-one and group therapies.

6.1.3 Ethical considerations in diagnosis: the issues of stigmatisation and culture differences

The reality of psychiatric diagnosis is that it gives the patient a new identity, which can be a label for life, such as 'schizophrenic' or 'depressive', rather than 'a person with schizophrenia' or 'a person with depression'.

This is a stigma that can continue after the symptoms are over: 'schizophrenia in remission' and 'depression in remission'. It is very likely to affect marriage prospects, job prospects and an individual's sense of personal identity. The work of Doherty (1975) points out that those who reject their mental illness label tend to improve more quickly than those who accept it.

The ethical difficulties are all the more serious where members of certain groups are at higher risk of receiving a stigmatising diagnosis than others. Examples of such situations include:

1 In the UK, a patient is nine times as likely to be diagnosed as being schizophrenic if coming from an Afro-Caribbean background rather than from a white British one. Morgan et al. (2006) accounted for this with racially-biased diagnostic error rather than genetic propensities to schizophrenia.

2 Women are more likely to be diagnosed with depression. This has already been discussed in the earlier framework of gender bias. The work of Rosser (1992) additionally proposes that gender bias may be partially due to the large number of male psychiatrists in the profession who might 'over-diagnose' and stigmatise a woman as being depressed. In reality she could perhaps be bored and frustrated with her role as a mother and homemaker, and miss her honoured role in the workplace.

3 Ethically, there remains a serious risk of over-diagnosis and the unjust consequences flowing from stigmatisation (including 'in remission' conditions) needing to be balanced with the potential denial of treatment to those who need it, which can prevent a suicide or significant harm to a third party.

In addition, the differences in cultures between the psychiatrist and the patient may create severe difficulties in effective psychiatric diagnosis, as examined earlier.

Critical thinking

Since Rosenhan's 1973 study 'On being sane in insane places', there have been improvements in methods of diagnosing abnormality. How likely would it be that repeating that study today would give similar results to those in 1973?

SELF-ASSESSMENT QUESTIONS 6.1

1 What does abnormal psychology focus on?

2 List Rosenhan and Seligman's seven criteria for determining abnormality.

3 Distinguish between validity and reliability in diagnosis.

4 List the problems affecting the validity of diagnosis.

5 How have the following studies contributed to assessing the validity of diagnoses made in psychology:

    a Rosenhan (1973)

    b Jakobsen et al. (2005)

    c Parker et al. (2001)?

6 State three ethical issues in diagnosis.

Theory of Knowledge

Read the following passage by Giana, a 15-year-old Italian girl:

I stared at myself in the mirror and rolls of fat stared back at me.

Nothing in my life was right when I was 14. My father lost his job, my parents were talking about divorce, and I felt alone because my best friend left school and moved to another part of the country. I envied the slim and fit people who seemed to have a lot of fun and I wished I were one of them. So I stopped eating fats, carbohydrates and milk products and lived on lean meat, raw carrots and apples. I ran 10 kilometres every day on the gym treadmill. My weight dropped by more than a third. One Sunday morning I went running in the park and I collapsed. I woke up in hospital. They said that I was seriously underweight. They gave me a diet sheet instructing me to eat more high-calorie foods. But when I stared at myself in the mirror, rolls of fat stared back at me. My mother took me to the doctor, who immediately referred me to the psychiatric ward in the town hospital. I have been there for the last three months. After a course of treatment, I started to eat more food.

1 What are the psychiatrist's ways of knowing Giana's abnormal condition?
2 How far is the psychiatrist's diagnosis of Giana's condition likely to be based on scientific evidence?
3 Explain the types of possible bias that could influence the validity of the diagnosis of Giana's condition.
4 Are the methods of diagnosis you have discussed likely to be the ones used in 40 years' time? Explain your answer.

6.2 Abnormal psychological conditions

Abnormal psychological conditions form a very wide area of investigation. The purpose of the next sections is to focus on just two commonly occurring conditions: major depression which is an **affective disorder**, and **anorexia nervosa** which is an **eating disorder**. The following elements are considered within the study of each disorder: symptoms, prevalence in terms of cultures and genders, aetiologies and approaches to treatment.

Aetiology involves explaining the cause of the abnormal behaviour. These are complex, and the relative importance of contributing factors are debated by psychologists. Aetiology connects to psychiatry in that the treatment given should take into account the causes of the disorder. These may be biologically, cognitively and/or socio-culturally rooted.

Affective disorder: a category of mental abnormalities whose symptoms include mood disorders.

Anorexia nervosa: disorder evidenced by severely limited food intake, together with extreme concern about body image and body weight.

Eating disorder: a category of mental abnormalities whose symptoms include problems with food intake.

6.2.1 Prevalent symptoms for affective disorders: major depression

For a disorder to be classified as affective, it has to relate to mood. Examples of such mood-related abnormalities are bipolar disorder, major depression and extreme/inappropriate emotions. Major depression is the most common of these. Indeed, anxiety and depression were estimated to have been responsible for one-fifth of days off work in the UK in 2016 and more generally, recent polls have indicated that 17% of Canadians and 20% of Australians have taken time off work/school due to mental health issues.

The symptoms of major depression may be placed under the following headings:

1 **Affective symptoms**: feeling continuously sad for at least two weeks without a clear reason. There is a lack of interest and pleasure in enjoyed activities.

2 **Behavioural symptoms**: not wishing to be together with other people, difficulty in sleeping at night, difficulty in getting through a normal day's work, observable agitated or unusually slow movements, self-destructive and even suicidal behaviour.

3 **Cognitive symptoms**: difficulties in being focused on what is going on, inappropriate feelings of guilt, and negative attitudes to oneself and one's surroundings.

4 **Somatic symptoms**: fatigue, loss of appetite and significant weight loss/gain.

A significant number of these symptoms consistently persisting over two weeks may be diagnosed as major depression.

At any one moment, almost 4% of the world population suffers major depression. The prevalence of major depression is a subject of many studies. Approximately 15% of people in the developed world and (significantly less at) 11% of people in the developing world will be affected by major depression at least once in their lifetime. Specifically and for different countries and cultures:

1 In the USA, the rate is 13% for men and 20% for women (Kessler et al. 2005).

2 In Japan, the prevalence is 3%, only about one-sixth of that of the USA (Andrade et al., 2003). However, it has been argued that Japanese people are likely to place a non-depression interpretation on depressive symptoms.

3 In the city of Chennai, southern India, the overall rate is 16%. It is more than three times as high for those on lower incomes than with those who have high incomes. Over a quarter of those divorced had suffered or were suffering from major depression. That was higher than those widowed (one-fifth), and those currently married (just over one-seventh) (Poongothai et al., 2009, using a sample of 25 000 people and a self-reporting questionnaire).

4 There are very low rates for depression in the Middle East and China, where those suffering symptoms are more likely to report in somatic terms than in psychological terms in order to avoid a severe social stigma and social avoidance (Sartorius et al. 1983).

5 The work of Marsella (1995) indicates that depression is more prevalent in urban cultures than in rural cultures. Possible explanations are greater degrees of anonymity and lack of social support, housing difficulties, overcrowding, unpleasant working conditions and fear of approaching the psychiatric profession for help.

6 Women with depression outnumber men with depression by 2:1. The exception is among Jews, where men and women sufferers have similar prevalence (Levav et al., 1997).

There is considerable debate among psychologists over this apparent prevalence of major depression in women. Arguments given include:

a Women are more likely to suffer poverty, single parenthood, personal abuse and sexual discrimination (McGrath et al., 1990, Nolen-Hoeksema, 2001).

Affective symptom: an indication of a mood disorder.

Behavioural symptom: an indication of a mental abnormality based on the patient's behaviour.

Cognitive symptom: an indication of a mental abnormality based on the patient's reporting of their perception of the environment or an event.

Somatic symptom: an indication of a mental abnormality based on the patient's reporting of their physical feelings.

b Gender bias in reporting: men tend to under-report due to a higher pain threshold for the symptoms of depression (Barsky et al., 2001).

c Men are more likely to over-indulge in alcohol as an antidote to depression. In support, men and women seem to show similar prevalence for depression within cultures where drinking is strictly forbidden (Egeland and Hostetter, 1983).

d There appears to be no clear support for biological changes in female puberty influencing the development of major depression. However, the meta-analysis of Kessler et al. (2001) suggests that the biological changes at puberty may combine with culture-specific social responses to increase a woman's vulnerability to depression.

e Women feel more vulnerable in the workplace than men, and fear that assertive behaviour will lower their standing with their employers and colleagues (Costrich et al., 1975).

f Women are less likely to mentally distract themselves from depressing thoughts and situations (Nolen-Hoeksema, 2000).

Higher female prevalence of major depression has been alleged to be due to gender differences in diagnostic procedures, but extensive literature review has shown that the male/female differences are genuine (Piccinelli and Wilkinson, 2000).

6.2.2 Prevalent symptoms for eating disorders: anorexia nervosa

Eating disorders, for example anorexia nervosa, are where a person feels loss of control and self-disgust over eating too much high-calorie food. They avoid putting on weight by dieting, using laxative tablets and/or taking excessive exercise. Anorexia nervosa's main symptoms are:

1 Affective: including disliking the shape of one's body, fear of putting on weight.

2 Behavioural: including desperate attempts to get rid of excess weight through under-eating and over-exercising.

3 Cognitive: including a negatively distorted body image and low self-esteem, often accompanied by a depressed mood.

4 Somatic: including nutritional deficiencies leading to hormonal imbalances, muscle cramping, tiredness and disruptions in the menstrual cycle. The last, however, is not a deciding criterion as anorexia has been diagnosed in patients with the other symptoms, and is clearly inapplicable to males and to post-menopausal women.

At any one moment, the prevalence of anorexia nervosa worldwide is between 0.5% and 1% of adolescent and young adult females. The prevalence is greatest among advanced Western cultures, although it is growing in Latin American and Middle Eastern societies as well. However, this condition has been observed in every region in the world (Keel and Klump, 2003). They argue that its prevalence is universal, although it might be increasing due to the slimness ideal promoted by Western cultures.

In the USA, the work of Rowland (1970) found significant ethnic differences in prevalence. There was a high prevalence of anorexic patients who were Caucasian, and an even higher representation of people with Italian and Jewish roots.

There is relatively little research on male patients. Women appear to outnumber men with anorexia nervosa by about ten to one, although there is an increase in male patients where the age of onset is between eight and fourteen (Seligmann et al., 1994). There is considerable debate among psychologists over this apparent prevalence of anorexia nervosa in women. Among the many arguments given for the gender bias are the following points:

1 Men may be under less social pressure to conform to a particular physical appearance (Rolls et al., 1991).

2   High pressure to be thin has been especially noticeable among females whose activities are perceived to depend on it, such as ballet dancers and models (Currin et al., 2005).

3   Women are more likely than men to exaggerate the differences between their own body shape and their ideal body shape (Fallon and Rozin, 1985).

4   Women are more likely to work towards having a perfect figure, over-attending to the marginal elements in which they differ from their ideal model (Southgate et al., 2009).

Anorexia nervosa has the highest fatality rate of any psychiatric disorder, rising to 20% among serious cases in adolescent girls. However, some 90% of patients respond positively to the various approaches to treatment discussed in the final sections of this chapter.

An understanding of the aetiologies of the disorders is vital so that suitable treatment is applied.

6.2.3 Aetiologies of major depression

It is vital to bear in mind that affective conditions such as major depression and eating disorders such as anorexia nervosa have extremely complex aetiologies. The causes of those disorders are constantly debated among psychiatrists and other mental health professionals. Included here are just a selection of elements which are supported by recent research.

As previously discussed, although feelings of helplessness and being unable to cope from time to time are normal, they become the abnormal condition of major depression when they persist constantly and daily for a period of two weeks.

The aetiologies are complex, with valuable contributions from the biological, cognitive and socio-cultural perspectives.

Biological aetiologies

Genetic factors: the role that biological heredity plays in determining cognition and behaviour.

Hormonal activity: the work of chemical substances secreted by endocrine glands that determine the rate at which the body works.

Biological aetiologies focus on two influences: **genetic factors** and **hormonal activity**.

Genetic factors in major depression

Several studies, as exemplified by Nurnberger and Gershon's review of seven twin studies (1982), have shown a 65% concordance rate in depression for MZ twins and 14% for DZ twins. Bearing in mind that a major depressive condition is not present in most humans, the researchers estimated that this disorder has a high genetic input.

Until recently, research in affective disorders exemplified by major depression was based on patients' self-reporting and psychiatrists' judgements according to the professionally-set criteria. Although empirical evidence pointed towards the presence of genetic elements, conclusions have been correlational and unable to establish cause and effect.

However, today GWAS are being increasingly used. This involves the genetic matter (such as blood or saliva samples) of a large sample with the disorder being compared with those without the disorder. The genetic variations significantly prevalent in the disorder sample are only then stated to be associated with the disorder.

Currently, there are over ten genetic variations (called genetic markers) that appear to have a higher frequency in major depression. These markers are exemplified by the study of Caspi et al. (2003) (see Chapter 3) on the 5-HTT gene. Each person inherits two of these genes, one from each parent. The 5-HTT gene affects the serotonin transporter protein, which in turn influences the amount of serotonin in the brain. Low levels of serotonin are associated with depression. The study found that two distinctly short 5-HTT genes adversely affect the serotonin transporter protein, meaning there is a low level of serotonin in the brain. Frequencies of major depression were significantly less where one of the 5-HTT genes was long, and even more uncommon where they were both long. These findings are confirmed by the longitudinal study of Wilhelm et al. (2006), which found that in the DNA samples of 127 individuals, 80% of those with two short 5-HTT genes became depressed after three or more negative and stressful life events, in contrast to only 30% of those with two long genes.

These two studies indicate that genes influence the degree of vulnerability to major depression.

Hormonal activity in major depression

Among the hormones associated with depression is cortisol. This hormone is naturally released to cope with a stressful situation. Those suffering from chronic stress (stress prolonged over a long period) have high cortisol levels, which are associated with depression. High cortisol levels lower the density of serotonin receptors, and the functioning of receptors for noradrenaline. This situation is associated with major depression.

Low levels of cortisol are also associated with low levels of enjoyment, including major depression. When in constant demand during a long period of chronic stress, cortisol begins to run out. The work of Fernald et al. (2008) surveyed over 600 Mexican mothers and their children, in different socio-economic groups. It found that those living in the worst poverty were producing the least stress-coping cortisol. Their stress-coping biological mechanism tended to be worn out, leaving the children open to depression and also to autoimmune diseases, such as multiple sclerosis.

Figure 6.6 Poverty in a shanty town in Mexico. Do such stresses make people more vulnerable to depression?

The biological aetiologies have the following strengths:

- Twin studies persuasively indicate the presence of genetic elements.
- GWAS-based research has enabled the identification of genetic variants in people with major depression.
- Low serotonin levels in depressed people seem to be consistent with the behaviours observed in those with major depression.

However, the limitations of biological aetiologies include these points:

- Possibilities of a high degree of co-morbidity with those diagnosed with major depression. That may include other affective conditions such as bipolar disorder.
- Twin samples may be unreliable due to the small samples and the possibility of the twins being socio-culturally influenced by each other's behaviour patterns. In addition, they are likely to have been brought up together.

- The genes associated with depression appear to increase the vulnerability to depression rather than promote the depression itself. Genes may predispose a person to depression but cognitive and socio-cultural factors may actually trigger the depression.

- The genes thought to influence the likelihood for depression are increasing in number, making this condition harder to explain in genetic terms.

Cognitive aetiologies

Cognitive aetiologies of major depression focus on two influences: **faulty thinking** through negative thinking, and **learned helplessness**.

Faulty thinking

Beck's cognitive theory of depression (1976) is based on depression being caused by faulty thinking developing out of **negative schemas**. These schemas can be the products of negative experiences in childhood and early adolescence, often connected with parents and other people of importance.

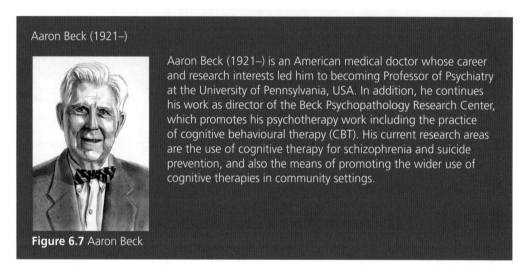

Aaron Beck (1921–)

Aaron Beck (1921–) is an American medical doctor whose career and research interests led him to becoming Professor of Psychiatry at the University of Pennsylvania, USA. In addition, he continues his work as director of the Beck Psychopathology Research Center, which promotes his psychotherapy work including the practice of cognitive behavioural therapy (CBT). His current research areas are the use of cognitive therapy for schizophrenia and suicide prevention, and also the means of promoting the wider use of cognitive therapies in community settings.

Figure 6.7 Aaron Beck

Beck's work proposed that there are three cognitive elements contributing to depression. Beck's cognitive triad is where depressed people see themselves, the world and their futures in a negative light. This mind-frame is the default position of the depressed person, and may be described as automatic negative thinking. Beck observed that depressive patients show evidence of being affected by a distorted cognitive set of schemas about the self, the future and what is going on all around.

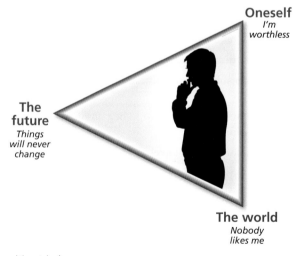

Figure 6.8 Beck's cognitive triad

Faulty thinking: thinking based on schemas that do not match reality.

Learned helplessness: where past experience of insoluble problems or inescapable and intolerable physical conditions has reduced the individual to apathy in facing similar situations in the future. Believed to be a possible cause of depression.

Negative schemas: an individual's mental matrix of processing information that interprets the environment as being hostile or non-negotiable.

Examples of unpleasant life experiences that both develop and switch on negative, depression-fostering schemas might be rejection by the university of first choice, or not being on a party guest list.

These depression-fostering schemas may include the **ineptness schema** (that my academic or social skills are not good enough), the **self-blame schema** (what went wrong was my fault) and the negative over-generalising **self-evaluation schema** (that I'm good for nothing).

In addition, negative schemas can promote faulty depression-promoting **selective abstraction**. The person may have a quality and mutually-supportive circle of good friends, and at the same time just one colleague who is critical and cynical. The selectively abstractive schema will promote negative self-assessment based on that one detractor and ignore all the positive messages from the many friends.

Cognitive bias is where the depressed person is negatively attributing bad experiences to personal failings. For not getting the university place: 'I'm not clever enough.' For being off the guest list: 'I'm not popular enough.' In reality, the wanted university programme had an excess of suitable applicants. Also in reality, the hosts did not know that the person was interested in coming to the party. That thinking is based on automatic negative thoughts which are generally not based on reality or, even if valid, could be dealt with in a suitable way.

Learned helplessness

Learned helplessness is when negative previous experiences have convinced a person that they are powerless to handle similar situations. It is that feeling of being unable to cope and resigning to suffering that is a significant cognitive aetiology of depression. Depression indeed can paralyse by depriving people of their ability to respond effectively to their troubles.

Seligman's (1974) theory of learned helplessness was based on his work with dogs. As shown in Figure 6.9, each dog was placed into a cage divided by a barrier. When the floor on the dog's side of the barrier was electrified to give a sharp, though not dangerous, shock, the dog quickly learned to escape by climbing over the barrier. When restrained and shocked, as in the second illustration, the dog eventually stopped trying to escape. When freed from the restraint as in the third illustration, the dog did not attempt to cross the barrier, although physically it could easily have done so.

The study concluded that it was the dogs' learned helplessness schemas that prevented them making the escape when they could have easily done so. This suggested that humans may well behave similarly as a result of past negative experiences. This prompted Seligman to view learned helplessness as an aetiology of depression.

The cognitive aetiologies have the following strengths:

• They create a framework to show how those suffering depression think more negatively about themselves and the world even when they are not actually depressed. Their depression-promoting schema remains.

• The fact that CBT has a significant success rate in the treatment of major depression suggests that faulty thinking and learned helplessness may well be key aetiologies of the disorder.

However, the limitations include these points:

• Beck's negative cognitive triad can be a product of major depression rather than a cause of major depression. It can be the depression itself rather than specific events that powered the schemas.

Ineptness schema: an individual's mental matrix of processing information that sees them incapable of competently handling a particular situation.

Self-blame schema: an individual's mental matrix of attributing negative experiences to their own faults rather than to outside factors.

Self-evaluation schema: an individual's mental matrix based on how they judge themselves that is applied to interpreting interactions and events.

Selective abstraction: focusing excessively on a particular aspect of a social interaction or event, ignoring other aspects that are of at least equal importance and could result in a different overall interpretation.

Cognitive bias: the inaccurate processing of information due to the over-focus on some elements and the under-focus on others of equal or greater importance.

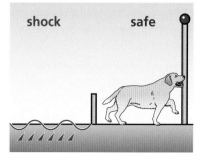 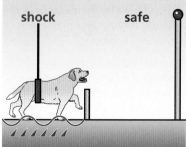 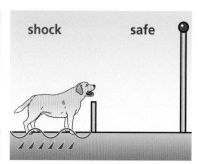

Figure 6.9 The stages of creating learned helplessness with dogs

- Applying the experience of dogs to human learned helplessness does not explain why many humans (unlike dogs) can suffer highly unpleasant experiences without learning to be helpless. Indeed, Seligman subsequently modified the learned helplessness theory of depression to factor in the person's way of thinking. Learned helplessness would be more likely to account for depression in a person with cognitions leaning to pessimism rather than with cognitions leading to optimism.

- It does not account for genetic and neurological elements that influence the individual's potential to suffer major depression.

Socio-cultural aetiologies

Socio-cultural aetiologies of depression focus on how stressors in one's circumstances and environment might promote that condition. These can include elements such as poverty, an unsatisfactory relationship with one's spouse or lack of social support. They also look at resources available in the community for addressing these stressors.

Today, there is increasing awareness that social stress may activate biological predispositions for major depression, especially where the individual lacks coping resources and strategies. Biological elements strongly increase the potential for depression. Socio-cultural elements activate the potential into reality.

The role of social stress and stressors on causing depression has been investigated in the classic work of Brown and Harris (1978) in south-east London, UK. The semi-structured interview-based study was confined to two groups of women. The first contained those who had sought/received help for depression. The second was a general sample of 458 women between 18 and 65.

The findings of the study included these points:

- Over four-fifths of the first group had suffered a major life-cycle event such as the death of a close relative, or a prolonged severe difficulty, for example coping with a large number of children at home, compared with only a third of those who were not in a depressed group. Such stressors greatly increased the individuals' vulnerability to depression.

- There were poverty-linked tendencies to depression in the second group. 23% of the poorer working-class women claimed to have been depressed at least once in the last twelve months. That contrasted with just 3% in the more affluent middle class.

- Substantially higher rates of depression were found in women who were separated, divorced or widowed, than those who were married. These and other provoking factors were found to cause hopelessness in vulnerable women lacking personal connections and social support.

- The strong presence of family and community were seen as supporting higher levels of individual esteem and finding means of coming to terms with provoking situations.

It has also been argued that depression as an abnormal condition is a Western construction. Other world areas place the reality of what Westerners would diagnose as depression into their own cultural frames. The work of Okello and Ekblad (2006) among the Baganda population in Uganda showed that local people see depressive symptoms as products of thinking too much about their personal positions instead of easing into situations as they occur. Symptoms the West associates with depression are viewed by the Baganda as illness of thoughts. The initial remedy is to spend time with the family. If symptoms persist, it is likely to mean that the person is being troubled by ancestral spirits or evil spirits.

Until recently, depressive symptoms in Japanese culture were seen as indications for the need of spiritual guidance, time with the family and paying attention to the moral compass bearing. Framing depression as a disorder rather than as an indicator has only become important in Japan on its being increasingly open to Western ideas.

The socio-cultural aetiologies have the following strengths:

- They indicate that environmental elements do influence the development of major depression. Indeed, the semi-structured interviews in Brown and Harris (1978) enabled the researchers to identify the detailed stressors with more reliability.

- They help to explain why major depression is more common among those living in poverty.

- They also accept that not all cultures interpret the standard Western depressive symptoms in the same way. Some do not view those symptoms as abnormal, but as part of life and as an indicator of the need to attend to certain aspects of one's life.

- They afford the possibility of using emic approaches towards interpreting the meanings of depression symptoms in non-Western cultures.

However, there are limitations:

- The findings from the classic study of Brown and Harris (1978) are limited in application as it was composed exclusively of female participants.

- Social aetiologies generally have difficulties in explaining why within the same environment some people are more likely to develop major depression than others.

- There are difficulties in establishing cause and effect. In Brown and Harris (1978), was it the poverty that created the depression, or was it the depression that created the poverty?

- The realisation that interpreting the Western symptoms of major depression as indications of abnormality may be limited in application in other cultures.

6.2.4 Aetiologies of anorexia nervosa

Anorexia nervosa has the following DSM-5 listed characteristics: persistent restriction of food intake, intense fear of gaining weight, and a distorted view of body image. There will be undue focus on body shape and weight on self-evaluation, or a non-acceptance of the life-threatening potential of starvation. This disorder involves starvation, and has the highest mortality rate of any psychiatric disorder (Arcelus et al., 2011).

Anorexia nervosa is most common in young women, often starting in mid-adolescence. It is also being diagnosed increasingly in young men and middle-aged women.

As with major depression, the aetiologies are complex, with valuable contributions from the biological, cognitive and socio-cultural perspectives. These will be considered in turn.

Biological aetiologies

Biological aetiologies focus on two influences: genetic factors and **biochemical imbalances in the brain**.

Genetic factors in anorexia

There have been several studies in this area, as exemplified by Kortegaard et al. (2001), who found among 34 000 pairs of Danish twins that the concordance rate was 0.18 for DZ and 0.07 for MZ twins. With an overall 1% incidence of anorexia nervosa among adolescent females, the DZ propensity for an anorexia nervosa's twin is 18-fold, and the MZ propensity is 7-fold. This indicates a high, though not exclusive, genetic input. This is broadly in line with the slightly earlier work of Strober et al. (2000), which indicated that first-degree relatives of young women with anorexia are more than ten times as likely to develop that condition as their counterparts in the general population.

Until recently, research into eating disorders exemplified by anorexia nervosa was based on patients' self-reporting and psychiatrists' judgements according to the professionally-set criteria. Although empirical evidence pointed towards the presence of genetic elements, conclusions have been correlational and unable to establish cause and effect.

The work of Scott-Van Zeeland et al. (2014) used genetic material from a sample of some 1200 females with anorexia, and 2000 without. The laboratory analyses showed a significantly higher

Biochemical imbalances in the brain: where there is an abnormality in the degree of concentration of neurotransmitter receptor sites in the brain, for example a low concentration of dopamine receptor sites in the brains of anorexic patients.

frequency of the gene EPHX2 in samples from those with the disorder than in those without. The gene EPHX2 appears to influence an enzyme that regulates the metabolism of cholesterol. That enzyme interferes with the normal processing of cholesterol, and can thus disrupt eating behaviour. This has been supported by findings indicating that those with anorexia nervosa have unusually high cholesterol levels that seem to be incompatible with their eating patterns. Further research has suggested that those higher cholesterol levels support an improved feeling of well-being that can be disrupted by eating, which would help to explain the disorder's being characterised by persistent restriction of food intake.

Biochemical imbalances in the brain

Dopamine receptor sites: located on the post-synaptic neuron. They receive the pleasure-giving dopamine neurotransmitter that is fired by the pre-synaptic neuron.

Using PET scanning, the work of Bailer and Kaye (2010) found a relatively low concentration of **dopamine receptor sites** in the brains of those who developed anorexia. At the same time, brain-imaging studies showed that a high level of serotonin tended to be associated with this condition. High serotonin levels suppress appetite and increase obsessive behaviour, expressed in the undue focus on body image. The combination of the imbalances in serotonin and dopamine could explain why people with anorexia are powerfully driven to lose weight, but gain little happiness and sense of achievement in having done so.

Using fMRI brain scanning, the work of Oberndorfer et al. (2013) found that the 14 recovered anorexic females in the test sample had a low feel-good response to sweet tastes, compared to the 14 non-anorexic females in the control sample. These differences appeared in the test groups' weaker neural responses in the insula brain area. This part of the brain is where taste is sensed and integrated with the neural reward systems.

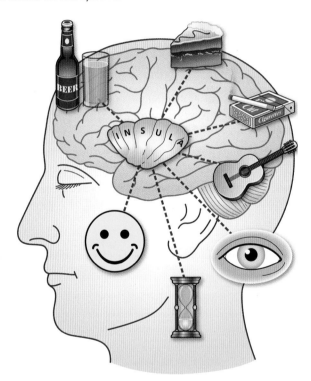

Figure 6.10 The position of the insula, the part of the brain that rewards pleasurable experiences

The biological aetiologies have the following strengths:

- Twin studies persuasively indicate the presence of genetic elements.
- GWAS-based research has enabled the identification of genetic variants in people with anorexia.
- High serotonin levels and disrupted dopamine function seem to be consistent with the behaviours observed in those with the disorder.
- Experimental investigation can be controlled to a considerable degree for confounding variables. In Oberndorfer et al. (2013) both the test and control groups fasted overnight and ate the same 604-calorie breakfast.

However, the limitations include the following points:

- Possibilities of a high degree of co-morbidity with those diagnosed with anorexia. That may include affective disorders such as major depression. It also incorporates other eating disorders including bulimia, which involves food purging as well as restricting food intake.

- Twin samples may be unreliable due to the small samples and the possibility of the twins being socio-culturally influenced by each other's behaviour patterns.

- It is possible that it was the malnutrition itself that affected the serotonin and dopamine disorders.

- The genes associated with anorexia appear to increase the vulnerability to anorexia rather than promote the condition itself. The genes may increase the potential for the condition, but other factors including cognitive and socio-cultural are more likely to activate the condition.

- The biological research of Oberndorfer et al. (2013) does not show whether the biological imbalances in the brain system cause anorexia or are caused by anorexia. This might be improved by repeating the research with an additional population at risk of anorexia.

- Much of the research (e.g. Scott-Van Zeeland et al., 2014) is based on exclusively female participants, raising the question of whether it can be generalised to males.

Cognitive aetiologies

Cognitive aetiologies of anorexia focus on two influences: faulty thinking and **attentional bias**.

Attentional bias: excessive focus on one element in a scenario, at the expense of another operative element.

Faulty thinking

Faulty thinking in this context means that the self-image the person sees in the mirror is distorted rather than accurate.

Fairburn (1997) drew attention to anorexia being caused by faulty personal schemas on body shape and body weight. It is these that cause the distorted self-image. Such schemas may originate in low self-esteem and the desire to increase self-worth, or hearing remarks from other people on the importance of getting thin and staying thin. The result of these schemas is the individual's self-viewing a distorted body image. What she, or less commonly he, sees is not what other people see.

Research study: Fallon and Rozin (1985)

Aim

To investigate body-image distortion at a general level, and to find out whether the faulty cognition on personal body type was gender-related.

Procedure

Using a sample of 475 American undergraduates of both sexes, they showed two series of nine body images, from very thin to very heavy, as in Figure 6.11.

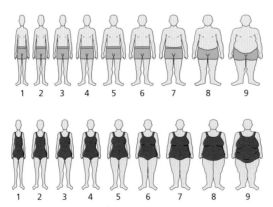

Figure 6.11 Body shapes used in researching faulty cognition

The participants were required to show (a) which body shape most accurately represented their own, (b) which body shape was their ideal body shape, and (c) which body shape of the opposite sex they would be most attracted to.

Results

The study showed significant gender differences. Men tended to choose similar if not quite the same figures for (a) and (b), though with (c) a significant number believed that women would prefer them to have a thinner figure than they had, and that they idealised. In contrast, women had a strong though not universal inclination to choose a larger and heavier body shape than their own. They also selected a much thinner figure for what the opposite sex would find most attractive, and a still thinner one for their ideal body shape.

Conclusion

The study concluded that American women are much more likely than men to have worryingly faulty schemas in personal body shape and body weight. This may well be a cause of eating disorders including anorexia. In addition, the faulty thinking may lead to attentional bias.

Attentional bias

Attentional bias is where a person focuses on certain elements and avoids considering other important elements. With anorexia, the desire is to perceive a perfect body self-image. It is a cognitive characteristic of perfectionism. The anorexic overlooks the dangers involved in self-starvation, including bone thinning, kidney damage and heart problems.

Indeed, the attentional-bias cognitive aetiology argues that attention to the detail of the perfect body shape together with neglecting the overall picture of personal health helps to explain this eating disorder.

The work of Southgate et al. (2009) aimed to investigate whether this perfectionist element in female anorexic patients was stronger than in the general female population. Using the same method for the test and control participants, the researchers showed a series of original images. Each original image was accompanied by a series of eight similar pictures. The task with each original image was to select the similar image that most closely matched it.

The results indicated a significantly greater accuracy among those with anorexia than the general population. That could indicate that it is the perfectionist attention to detail on reaching the ideal body weight that drives the anorexic patient to achieve a goal that causes the attentional bias, placing the overall picture in the background. In short, it is the all-or-nothing focus on a perfect figure that causes the attentional bias. It is also likely to result in body-image distortion.

The cognitive aetiologies have the following strengths:

- The research helps to explain the greater prevalence of anorexia in females than in males.

- The fact that CBT has a significant success rate in the treatment of anorexia suggests that faulty thinking and attentional bias are key aetiologies of the disorder.

However, the limitations include these points:

- It is difficult to determine whether faulty thinking and attentional bias are causes of the disorder, or symptoms of those who have already developed that condition.

- Cognitive arguments by themselves do not explain why not all people dissatisfied with their body shape develop eating disorders, including anorexia nervosa.

- Not all participating anorexics have the condition with equal severity.

Socio-cultural aetiologies

Socio-cultural aetiologies of anorexia focus on two influences: social learning theory and cultural norms.

Social learning theory

Social learning theory holds that social norms strongly influence the individual's behaviour patterns. Ideal body images of peers and people in the media frequently persuade young women in particular to work hard towards obtaining a similar 'ideal' body shape.

Social learning theory as an aetiology of eating disorders was researched by Becker et al. (2002). The team studied girls in two schools in the Nadroga province of the Pacific island of Fiji, which until 1995 had no access to broadcast television. Before 1995 eating disorders were virtually unknown, as the Fijian ideal body shape was a fuller figure. From then onwards, there was greater exposure to Western social norms. The participating girls of secondary school age in the two schools identified the rate of eating disorders on two occasions; in 1995, and three years after broadcast television in 1998. The results showed a significant rise in all eating disorders over that three-year period. The researchers concluded that television indeed promoted a new social norm by setting an ideal Western-style body image.

Groesz et al. (2002) carried out a meta-analysis of 25 studies on the theme of how levels of women's body-image satisfaction were influenced by exposure to different female models. The results indicated that participants showed no change in personal body satisfaction level after viewing models that were average size or plus size. However, exposure to thin models appeared to have introduced a social norm whose impact resulted in increased body dissatisfaction, which became more pronounced when the period of exposure was substantially increased.

Cultural norms

This socio-cultural aetiology suggests that cultures create the model for the disorder to be acceptable in terms of age and gender.

Brooks-Gunn et al. (1988) studied sport-associated cultures in terms of aetiologies of eating disorders, including anorexia. In total, 424 girls aged between 14 and 18 participated in the study. There were four groups. Figure skaters, ballet dancers and swimmers formed the three test groups, with non-athletes making up the control group. Each group was given a survey on attitudes to eating. The results showed significantly more negative nutritional attitudes among the skaters and dancers than with the swimmers and non-athletes. The researchers concluded that this trend reflected the subcultures of the different activities.

The socio-cultural aetiologies have the following strengths:

- They indicate that environmental elements influence the development of eating disorders, including anorexia.
- They help to explain why anorexia is most common in industrialised countries where being slim is idealised and food is plentiful.

However, the limitations include these points:

- It cannot explain why within the same environment some people are more likely to develop anorexia than others.
- Socio-cultural arguments by themselves do not explain why people go from health-promoting changes in diet and exercise to unhealthy extremes in both.

As previously pointed out, understanding of the aetiologies of the different psychiatric disorders is vital in order to match the treatment to the condition. This chapter proceeds to consider various approaches to the two disorders studied: major depression and anorexia nervosa. Although the various treatments discussed are rooted in aspects of the biological, cognitive and socio-cultural approaches, they are not necessarily mutually exclusive. Indeed, some programmes involved eclectic treatments, incorporating elements from a variety of approaches; for example, medication may be combined with counselling.

SELF-ASSESSMENT QUESTIONS 6.2

1 Define the following terms:

   a aetiology   b affective disorder

   c major depression   d anorexia nervosa

2 List symptoms of major depression and anorexia nervosa.

3 List two biological, two cognitive and one socio-cultural aetiology of major depression. Support each one with a research study.

4 List two biological, two cognitive and two socio-cultural aetiologies of anorexia nervosa. Support each one with a research study.

6.3 Approaches to treatment of disorders

The main purpose of research into the description and aetiology of psychological disorders is to develop the most suitable treatment to improve and maintain people's mental health. This is where the following two disciplines converge:

1   Psychiatry: a branch of the medical profession that is concerned with diagnosis of the condition and interventionist treatments. These **biomedical approaches** typically involve chemotherapy, using drugs such as anti-depressants, **anxiolytics**, and antipsychotics (such as tranquillisers). They can also use **electroconvulsive therapy (ECT)** as a means of treating depression. ECT's current use is far from the popular image of electric shock being used as punishment to abate undesirable behaviour. It nevertheless remains a controversial treatment.

2   Counselling psychology and psychotherapy: although these terms are often used interchangeably, there are specific differences.

Counselling focuses on the client's present issues. The purpose of counselling is to guide the client towards the best-fit approach in order to achieve their objectives. Past experiences will, at the most, play only a minor part in the therapy.

However, the psychotherapy approach uses the past tense to a considerable degree. This is because the objective of psychotherapy is to resolve the underlying issues that promote the current problem. Thus, psychotherapy helps the individual to work through and resolve past experiences in order to function optimally.

The success of psychotherapy does depend on the relationship and the degree of trust between the client and the therapist. The client may disclose deeply personal and previously unshared information, and describe recurrent feelings. Typically, effective psychotherapy treatment involves about 20 meetings, and sometimes many more. Each session is designed to progressively enable the client to open up, explore the past, consider how it impacts on the present, and locate the relevant factors that enable the therapist to help the client to deal effectively with the issue.

Most of the following discussion is focused on the example of major depression, probably the most common and widespread abnormal condition.

6.3.1 Biomedical approaches to treatment of disorders

As previously stated, biomedical treatment involves the use of drugs to restore the body to mental health where the aetiology of the condition indicates biological causes.

The affective condition of depression may well be biologically influenced through low serotonin levels. The eating disorder of anorexia nervosa could have been strongly influenced by biological imbalances in the brain.

This section considers two approaches to disorders: use of drugs exemplified by **serotonin re-uptake inhibitors (SSRIs)** and the use of ECT.

Use of SSRI drugs

The biomedical approach almost always involves the use of drugs, typically anti-depressants. SSRIs (such as paroxetine and fluoxetine (Prozac)) are commonly used to treat affective disorders arising from low serotonin levels. SSRIs are not neurotransmitter supplements; they make each unit of neurotransmitter serotonin more effective. Instead of the serotonin being immediately reabsorbed, it stays longer in the synaptic gaps, and is therefore more effective as a unit of pleasure. Effectively, they make more serotonin available. The purpose of SSRIs is to improve serotonin-based energy and create an overall sense of feeling good. This is particularly applicable to depressive conditions with aetiologies of low serotonin.

Biomedical approach: biologically-interventionist treatment to treat mental disorders, such as drugs or chemotherapy.

Anxiolytics: medication that reduces anxiety.

Electroconvulsive therapy (ECT): a controversial treatment where electrical stimulus is designed to promote chemical changes in the brain in order to abate the disorder.

Serotonin re-uptake inhibitors (SSRIs): medication enabling each unit of neurotransmitter serotonin to be more effective.

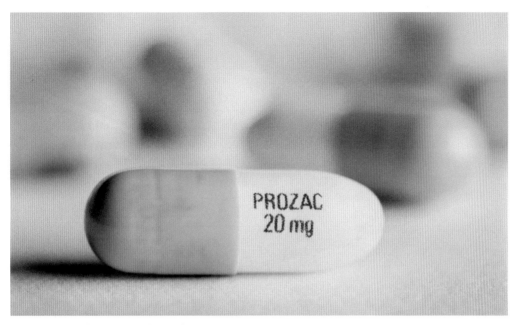

Figure 6.12 Is this drug likely to relieve or cure?

SSRIs are frequently prescribed for major depression, though less so for anorexia nervosa unless it is accompanied by depressive or other symptoms of affective disorder.

Leuchter et al. (2002) assessed both the use of SSRIs and placebos in helping recovery from depression. This study divided 51 depression patients into two groups. The first group was given SSRIs. The second was given placebos. Both groups were EEG brain-scanned. The scans showed substantial frontal-cortex activity with those taking placebos. Those on SSRIs did not show the same frontal-cortex activity, but both groups recovered from depression.

This study indicates that although the SSRIs address only the symptoms of the depression, the belief that they are genuine treatments may well set the brain off into depression-recovery mode. The same could be said of placebos, although the differences in frontal-cortex activity indicate that the depression-recovery process is by a different route. This also fits in with the findings of Kirsch and Sapirstein (1998) in their meta-study designed to assess how effectively Prozac, as opposed to placebos, alleviates depression. It found placebos to be 25% less effective than Prozac, which suggests that the specific parts of the brain that are stimulated in depression-recovery mode influence the rate of recovery.

The findings of Leuchter et al. (2002) on the use of SSRIs and comparisons with the use of placebos do have scientific support from the brain-scanning results, and are quantitatively supported by the sample size. However, such drugs directly address the existence of low-serotonin conditions, rather than the reasons as to why the serotonin levels are low in the first place. Their strengths and limitations are included in the evaluation of biomedical approaches later on in this section.

Use of ECT

ECT has been conveyed in the popular media as an abusive, cruel and mind-controlling form of psychosocial control. As late as 1985, the National Institute of Health in the USA observed that ECT had been unjustifiably used for the behavioural control of disruptive patients in mental institutions.

However, in today's reality, it is a painless medical procedure carried out under general anaesthetic without the patient feeling any sensation at all. Although originally developed in the 1940s for the treatment of schizophrenia, its most common use today is for depression. Regulated under professional procedures, it is commonly used in the USA, Canada and the UK, and less frequently in Japan and in some other European countries. There is no evidence that its present form causes structural damage to the brain. Patients wake up after a few minutes without any recollection of the treatment.

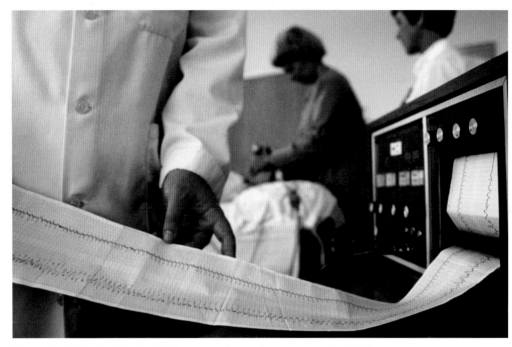

Figure 6.13 How justified is ECT for major depression when all else fails?

ECT involves the use of electrical stimulation to create a seizure in the patient's brain. The psychiatric profession is not clear on how exactly seizures relieve and sometimes even abate depression. The empirical evidence however is that ECT is sufficiently effective in relieving (as opposed to curing) depression to be commonly used where the abnormal condition is resistant to drugs, or when the patient's condition is too extreme to wait for the drugs to take effect. There are many documented instances where it is claimed to have been lifesaving. However, long-term relief from depression generally requires a series of sessions, typically ten given over a three-week period.

According to the American Psychiatric Association, ECT can be safe and beneficial in the treatment of bipolar disorder and suicide risks, as well as major depression that has resisted other treatments.

More recently, the less invasive **transcranial magnetic stimulation (TMS)** has been developed as an alternative to ECT. TMS creates a magnetic field to induce a much smaller electric current in a specific part of the brain without causing seizure or loss of consciousness. The current is caused by a magnetic field created by an electromagnetic coil that delivers the pulses through the forehead. Approved by the American FDA (Food and Drugs Administration) since 2008, it can be applied to the patient when fully conscious and it promotes gentle stimulation to the brain rather than inducing seizure. However, it does require more frequent administration over a longer period, typically almost daily over five weeks. Although safe and effective for depression, it appears to be less powerful than ECT.

Transcranial magnetic stimulation (TMS): creation of a magnetic field to induce a small electric current, as treatment to the specific part of the brain associated with the disorder.

Critical thinking

Investigate the ethical issues involved in the use of ECT, and in TMS. Critically assess how far the apparent benefits of these psychiatric treatments justify their use.

Evaluation of biomedical approaches to treatment of disorders: the example of major depression

The strengths of the biomedical approaches in treating major depression include these points:

- In terms of outcome, ECT and TMS give quicker results than counselling and psychotherapy, and have not been shown to create permanent damage when applied professionally and correctly.

- These treatments can provide short-term relief from the symptoms of depression to the degree that the patient would be responsive to counselling and psychotherapy.

- The safe use of ECT requires the patient to be given a medical examination, with special attention to the heart by means of an electrocardiogram (ECG), a device that measures the heart's electrical activity using electrodes placed on the skin. That is to ensure that there are no other medical conditions that could interfere with ECT treatment.

- The work of Folkerts et al. (1997) with 39 participants suffering treatment-resistant depression indicated a 71% recovery success rate at the end of a four-week period for those given ECT, but only 28% for those given antidepressants.

The limitations of the biomedical approaches in treating major depression include:

- The work of Heninger et al. (1996) questioned the serotonin hypothesis, that depression is caused by low levels of serotonin in the brain. Their work did not show that reducing serotonin in healthy individuals causes depression.

- SSRI users face the risk of the side-effects of nausea, headaches, insomnia and sexual problems. ECT treatment can include some short-term nausea, headache, fatigue, confusion and slight memory loss. However, these risks must be balanced against the real dangers of major depression worsening through lack of treatment.

- Further research such as the meta-study of Kirsch et al. (2008) have indicated that placebos have broadly similar effects as SSRIs, with only a small difference in reducing depressive symptoms between the placebo and the real drug. Thus the success of the medication may be based considerably on the cognitive factor of the patient's belief rather than on the biochemical merits of the drug itself. However, the findings in the earlier controlled, measured-outcome study of treatment for depression by Elkin et al. (1989) indicated that depressed patients given anti-depressants plus normal clinical support showed a 50% recovery rate, whereas those given a placebo plus normal clinical support showed only a 29% recovery rate. For comparison and within this study, those given psychotherapy in the form of CBT but no drugs also showed a 50% recovery rate. An **outcome-based study (in abnormal psychology)** tests the effectiveness of the therapy by finding out how many patients recover from the condition.

- In contrast with psychotherapy, both SSRIs and ECT treatment appear to address the symptoms rather than the causes of major depression. Both types of treatment have to be repeated at regular intervals to be effective.

- It is not fully understood how ECT biologically affects depression. Breggin (1997) argues that it may work by actually causing a form of brain damage that causes **anasognosia**, a condition where the patient denies their difficulties. Indeed, Szasz (1971) argued more generally that 'electricity as a form of treatment requires the sacrifice of a patient as a person, [and] of the psychiatrist as a clinical thinker and moral agent'.

Outcome-based study (in abnormal psychology): where the degree of improvement in the patient's condition is judged on completion of the treatment, rather than during the process of the treatment.

Anasognosia: where the individual suffering a disorder is unaware of having that disorder.

RESEARCH IDEA

Choose three famous personalities from the world of politics or the media who, on experiencing an abnormal condition, have successfully been helped by the psychology profession. Investigate the reasons for each person's success in overcoming the limitations resulting from the abnormal condition.

6.3.2 Individual approaches to treatment of disorders: counselling and psychotherapy

Virtually all cultures practise some form of counselling and psychotherapy designed to relieve emotional pain.

Counselling therapy and psychotherapy are designed to enable patients to address their own depression-provoking cognitions. They operate on the premise that depressed patients have to break their habits of negative thinking.

This section considers two non-biological approaches to disorders: the use of individual approaches exemplified by CBT and the use of group therapies. CBT was originally developed as a means of helping depressed patients. However, today it is widely applied to other conditions including obesity, which is considered in the Health Psychology option.

Individual therapy: use of CBT for treatment of disorders

Originally developed by Beck, this approach holds that negative thinking is a primary aetiology not only for depression, but also for a wide range of other psychological disorders including bipolar disorder, schizophrenia, various eating disorders, obesity and gambling addictions. It has even been successfully applied to help individuals abate prejudice towards other people. The purpose of CBT is to enable the patient to successfully deal with the **automatic negative thinking** which creates a series of schemas that promote a false set of **self-limiting beliefs**. The faulty thoughts that are often rooted in childhood are either totally untrue or grossly over-generalised, such as 'everyone hates me', 'I am a good-for-nothing' and 'I'll never be able to date the type of person I would really like to know better'. These automatic negative thoughts are not only about oneself, but also about the world and about the future.

Beck and other psychologists of a similar outlook developed CBT in the light of these observations. It is designed to train the patient to handle their distorted schemas about the self, environment and future, which in turn dissolves the depressed feelings.

For example: Alessandro is being treated for depression, which seems to be connected with his worry about failing his forthcoming professional examinations. His CBT therapist works to change his mind-frame to: 'You do indeed have the power to qualify. You are intelligent and able. You can achieve the success that you deserve. Work on planning your methods and set clear targets for each 45-minute period of study, period by period.' The goal is to enable him to change his self-schema and regard himself in a far more positive light.

Alessandro's CBT therapist also tells him that he should do eight suitably-disciplined study sessions a day, and record his successes in a journal. It is those rewarding feelings along the way that help the client to improve the self-schema, alleviating the symptoms of the depression.

CBT therapy operates on a one-to-one basis. Developed in the 1960s through to the 1980s, its overall objective is **cognitive restructuring**. CBT views the task of the therapist as reshaping the faulty schemas of the patient. Cognitive restructuring is designed to enable the client to:

- identify what the negative beliefs and thinking patterns are
- test out whether these beliefs are actually true (this is called validity testing) and
- accept that parts of the thinking patterns are flawed.

The CBT programme moves on to **cognitive rehearsal**, where the patient selects a past difficult situation and works in a warm and supportive atmosphere with the therapist to structure a coping strategy to handle the problem. Such exercises simulate real-life situations likely to be encountered when the client is without the support of the therapist. These activities are supported by homework sessions that reinforce the progress made in the coping strategies learnt in the one-to-one meetings. The whole process of CBT for a major-depressed patient can involve as many as 20 sessions.

For eating disorders such as bulimia nervosa, the treatment typically involves:

- identifying the negative beliefs and thinking patterns about the mental distortions on body shape
- identifying the negative behaviours of binge-eating and vomiting
- moving on to activities that produce more positive feelings about one's physical appearance: replacing binge-eating and vomiting with three planned meals and two planned snacks per day
- working with people who are close and supportive to the patient to offer encouragement
- maintaining the programme to prevent relapse into bulimia.

CBT has been less commonly used to treat anorexia nervosa, as it has proved extremely challenging for the therapists to promote change in the client's underlying schemas.

Interpersonal therapy (IPT) is similar to CBT in that they are both designed to help people cope with depression and several other disorders, but IPT is based on the principle that mental health depends on people's often faulty ways of communicating and interacting with one another. There is a very close relationship between human relationships and mental health. In terms of the cognitive triad, the focus is on the environment: that is, other people. IPT therapy concentrates on helping clients to communicate feelings and expectations in relationships as well as to develop strategies for handling relationships.

Automatic negative thinking: a false set of self-limiting beliefs promoted by a series of negative schemas.

Self-limiting beliefs: patterns of thinking that prevent people from functioning at maximum potential, which are supported by negative schemas about oneself.

Cognitive restructuring: a form of cognitive therapy focusing on adopting more rational and constructive ways of dealing with stresses and problems.

Cognitive rehearsal: a form of cognitive therapy where the client imagines being in a difficult situation that happened in the past. The therapist works with the client to practise effective management of the problem.

Interpersonal therapy (IPT): psychotherapeutic treatment based on the theory that thinking patterns associated with current difficulties in relationships strongly influence some behaviour patterns.

Evaluation of individualised therapy to treatment of disorders: the example of treating major depression with CBT

The strengths of this approach in treating major depression include these points:

- CBT highlights the idea that thoughts create depression rather than depression creates thoughts. Depressed people have erroneous schemas that cause automatic negative thinking. The therapy provides clients with the means of coping with it.

- CBT is personalised to the specific situation and support needs of the client, in contrast to the biomedical methods that are generically applied.

- CBT can be very effective where there is mutual trust and warmth between therapist and client.

The limitations of this approach in treating major depression include these points:

- There has been no study that demonstrates clearly that negative thinking creates depression. There is also no serious claim that negative thinking is the only cause of depression. CBT is less likely to be effective when the cause of the depression is biological.

- CBT has been criticised for not sufficiently taking social factors into account (Champion and Power, 1995), such as the patient's domestic and work situation. Outcome-based studies may be unreliable as positive or negative changes in the patient's life can occur during the several months of the therapy. The patient's depression-feeding domestic and work issues can suddenly resolve themselves reasons not directly related to the therapy, such as falling in love.

- The outcome-based study of Elkin et al. (1989) indicates that drug treatment and counselling show similar recovery rates in the order of 50%.

- CBT developed out of the experience of the Western individualistic culture. Its one-to-one nature may create problems for patients in collectivist cultures.

- Outcome-based studies do not continually observe the effect of the treatment. This may be addressed by watching the patient from session to session, which would be a process-based approach. That would help to control elements not connected with the treatment that are affecting the client's recovery or lack of recovery.

Research study: Leu, Wang and Koo (2011)

Aim

To investigate the extent that feelings of serenity, joy, confidence and attentiveness were inversely correlated with feelings of being depressed, feelings of being stressed, loss of appetite, and difficulties in falling asleep at night.

Procedure

Six hundred and thirty-three college students of Asian-immigrant, Asian-American and European-American background participated in this study based at the University of Washington, Seattle, USA. The researchers used a questionnaire, the data coming from the participants' self-reporting.

Results

European-American participants showed the hypothesised strong negative correlation between their rankings in the number of positive emotions, and their frequency and intensity of depressed and stressed feelings. Asian-Americans showed a weaker correlation, but Asian immigrants showed no significant correlation between positive emotions, and depression and stress.

Conclusion

The study concluded as supporting the hypothesis that Asians interpret and react to positive emotions differently in connection with their mental health from people of European-American background.

Thus treatment of abnormalities does appear to have cultural dimensions. These findings recommended that mindfulness therapies that encourage clients to focus on both the good and the bad might well be more suitable for helping Asian clients, than the standard CBT therapy focusing entirely on positive emotions, which could be counter-productive.

Elkin et al. (1989) showed that both medication and psychotherapy work to some degree, but the outcome-based, empirical results do not address the serotonin hypothesis that low serotonin levels cause depression. Nor did the similar success rates with psychotherapy methods demonstrate an exclusively cognitive or social cause of depression. It could be argued that their success worked together with a natural healing of the condition.

There is a growing trend of using **eclectic treatment**, meaning that health professionals combine methods such as medication and counselling if they are likely to assist the patient's recovery.

Eclectic treatment: where health professionals combine methods, such as medication and counselling, that together are likely to assist the patient's recovery.

Riggs et al. (2007) investigated the effectiveness of combining CBT with SSRI medication or a placebo. One hundred and twenty-six teenage participants took part in the study, many already known to the social services and the juvenile courts. All had been diagnosed with depression as well as substance abuse or conduct disorder. Divided into groups of CBT plus SSRI drugs, and CBT plus placebo drugs, the results after four months of treatment showed success ('improved' or 'much improved'): 76% for CBT plus medication, and 67% for CBT plus placebo.

The outcome difference between SSRIs and placebos was broadly in line with Elkin et al. (1989). The study, though limited in application due to the entirely teenage participant population, does indicate over 50% substantial improvement rate in contrast to non-combined medication or CBT treatments.

6.3.3 Group therapy for treatment of disorders

Individual therapy is one-to-one, between therapist and client. Group therapy is one-to-several, typically between the therapist and six clients at the same time. The same therapies may apply, such as CBT and IPT.

Those in group therapy take part in a range of activities that address their condition, such as brain-storming, situation-simulation exercises, role-playing, giving feedback and building up trust within the group. Often these exercises do not directly address depression at all. They are designed to create common experiences that develop bonds of trust between the participants, with the therapist acting as facilitator. This can create an atmosphere where the members of the group will speak openly and frankly about their situations in future sessions. It is also possible that the success of one member of the group in successfully negotiating depression will inspire other participants to do likewise.

Figure 6.14 In what ways may this form of therapy help recovery from major depression?

In order for group treatment to work, the participants have to be chosen with care. Groups can work where, for example, the participants have been experiencing similar levels of major depression and are undertaking professional treatment for the first time. However, groups can also be composed of past and present sufferers taking part in therapist-coordinated activities together. That can help those currently depressed to focus on recovery by relating to people who have been in a similar position.

Thimm and Antonsen (2014) is an outcome study of CBT group therapy treatment of depression. It retrospectively examined the degree of improvement and recovery of 88 patients treated in this way, in a psychiatric clinic in northern Norway. The Beck Depression Inventory scoring system was used to measure progress and recovery rates. This tool was used twice: at the end of the programme of group CBT treatment, and three months later. Post treatment, 44% of the patients showed significant improvement, including 30% who recovered. Three months after treatment, 57% of the patients showed significant improvement, with 40% who recovered. However, one patient in six dropped out and did not complete the treatment.

In conclusion, this relatively small-scale study showed the success rate of group therapy results to be comparable with individual therapy such as in the study of Elkin et al. (1989).

Evaluation of group therapy to treatment of disorders: the example treating major depression with CBT

The strengths of this approach in treating major depression include the following points:

- The openness of the more communicative members of the group can encourage the shyer person to talk more frankly than in a one-to-one session with the therapist.

- Group CBT is cheaper than individual therapy as clients can share the cost.

- Group CBT can be very effective where there is mutual trust between the members of the group, and between the therapist and the members of the group.

- The outcome study of Thimm and Antonsen (2014) has shown comparable success rates between group CBT and one-to-one CBT therapy.

- Toseland and Siporin (1986) reviewed a series of studies that compared individual treatment and group treatment. Three-quarters of the participants reported group therapy treatment of depression as being equally effective to individual treatment, with the other quarter claiming that group treatment was even more effective. All preferred group treatment to one-to-one sessions.

The limitations of this approach in treating major depression include these points:

- However carefully groups are put together, there can be serious blocks to progress, such as: cultural inhibitions of speaking in the company of strangers, fear of one of the group breaking confidentiality, and one or two people who dominate the proceedings to such a degree that the others fear participating or do not wish to participate.

- Some groups have high drop-out rates or individuals who feel that they will not be missed if they sometimes miss sessions.

- Not all participants in group therapy for depression have similar causes, forms or intensities of depressions.

- The outcome-based study of Thimm and Antonsen (2014) on improvement and recovery rates was based on collected data over a ten-year period. It did not continually observe the effect of the treatment. Group therapy may be addressed by watching the patient from session to session, which would be a process-based approach. That would help to control for elements not connected with the treatment that are affecting the client's recovery or lack of recovery.

SELF-ASSESSMENT QUESTIONS 6.3

1. Distinguish between psychiatric and psychotherapeutic approaches to treatment of disorders.

2. Describe two biomedical treatments for disorders.

3. List the strengths and limitations of the biomedical approaches in treating major depression.

4. Describe two cognitive treatments for disorders.

5. List the strengths and limitations of the cognitive approaches in treating major depression.

6. Describe one eclectic study in the treatment of major depression.

ACTIVITY 6.3

This activity is suitable for individuals and groups.

Imagine you are working as a fully-qualified psychiatrist. One of your diagnosed major-depressed patients tells you that he plans to commit suicide later that week. He asks you not to tell anyone. Suggest the possible options, and assess their relative merits.

Chapter summary

1   Abnormal psychology focuses on the classification, causes, diagnosis and treatment of impairments that have adverse effects on the individual and/or on other people.

2   Diagnosis of any disorder is under the psychiatric criteria for the specific condition as defined in professional manuals exemplified by DSM-5 and ICD-10. The psychiatrist obtains the patient information by observation and clinical interview.

3   Validity is the likelihood of the diagnosis being correct, which can be adversely influenced by differences in the psychiatrist's cultural background, perception, style, gender and theoretical orientation.

4   The reliability of diagnosis depends on how far it is independently supported by one or more of the psychiatrist's professional peers.

5   The symptoms for any disorder including major depression and anorexia nervosa may be classified under affective, behavioural, cognitive and somatic.

6   Among the possible aetiologies of major depression are the biologically-based GWAS correlates (e.g. length of the 5-HTT genes) and cortisol levels which are too high or too low, cognitively-based faulty thinking and learned helplessness, and the socio-culturally-based stressors from one's personal circumstances and the environment.

7   Among the possible biological aetiologies of anorexia nervosa are genetic influences evidenced by biologically-based genetic correlates from twin studies, GWAS correlates and biochemical imbalances in the brain. Cognitive aetiologies incorporate faulty negative thinking and attentional bias. Socio-cultural aetiologies involve idealised media-promoted body images, and social cultures creating the model for the disorder to be acceptable in terms of age and gender.

8   Psychiatric treatment is medically based, which for major depression can involve types of drugs (typically SSRIs), ECT treatment, TMS treatment and other biologically-based interventionist procedures. Placebos have generally been found to be significantly less effective.

9   Psychotherapy is physically non-interventionist. For major depression, it can use CBT, IPT or other therapies in one-to-one or group sessions. Its development in Western society is based on Western clinical experience and is likely to require modifications in serving people of other cultures.

10 A patient may follow an eclectic programme of treatment which employs both biological and psychotherapeutic procedures.

Exam-style question

Essay response question

*   Discuss the validity and reliability of the diagnosis of abnormality.

The psychology of human relationships

'A real friend is one who walks in when the rest of the world walks out.'
(Walter Winchell)

KEY QUESTIONS

- What makes us want to connect or not connect to another specific individual?
- What behaviours are commonly observed within group situations, and how may their challenging aspects be identified and resolved?
- What is the nature of pro-social behaviour, and how may it be promoted?

Learning objectives

- Outline the roles that culture plays in the formation and maintenance of relationships. (AO1)
- Examine cognitive and socio-cultural explanations of prejudice, discrimination and conflict. (AO2)
- Examine the biological influences on intra-group and inter-group behaviours. (AO2)
- Evaluate the role of genetic compatibility in the choice of a partner. (AO3)
- Evaluate the effectiveness of cognitive-based strategies in conflict resolution. (AO3)

7.1 Psychology and human relationships

Psychologists become involved in studying human relationships in order to understand and enhance the ways in which people connect with one another.

Our lives touch the lives of others with varying intensity and involvement which is often, but not always, mutual. Situations where that takes place include:

*   deciding whether to step forward to help a stranger in immediate need

*   interacting with different generations, such as at a great-uncle's 70th birthday party

*   interacting with authority figures, such as teachers, employers and police officers

*   meeting that special person.

All three core approaches to behaviour address this complex field. This chapter considers three of the above human relationship situations: social responsibility such as helping a stranger in need, personal relationships such as interacting with that 'special' person, and group dynamics such as discriminatory behaviour in refusing help when needed.

The biological approach to the behaviour of the individual would emphasise the role of genetics and human biochemistry. It would examine the individual's assisting the stranger in need in terms of genetically-based **kin-selection theory** and the closeness of the relationship. Falling in love would focus on evolutionary and hormonal systems, with emphasis on oxytocin and **vasopressin**. The ways that prejudice and discrimination may affect those targeted may focus on the function of cortisol and its levels in the bloodstream.

Kin-selection theory: the innate, evolutionary desire to promote the survival of the part of the human race that has the highest amount of shared genetic material. This is a means of promoting one's own virtual survival beyond death.

Vasopressin: a hormone released during sex that powers long-term commitment between the couple.

Figures 7.1, 7.2, 7.3 and 7.4 What psychological elements do the interacting people in these photographs bring to each other?

The cognitive approach to the behaviour of the individual would apply schema theory and emphasise the way the brain processes and interprets information from other people. Thus the individual may step out to help the stranger in trouble because not doing so would create cognitive dissonance. The couple fall in love because they see in each other special things that they deeply value. An individual suffering prejudice and discrimination may adapt to the unpleasantness of the situation through a schema making comparison with other people: 'many have suffered more than me'.

The socio-cultural approach to the behaviour of the individual might consider the pro-social behaviour of helping the stranger as an expression of the individual's social or religious upbringing, the falling in love as a product of enjoying a newly-found degree of openness and acceptance, and suffering discrimination in terms of the victim displaying behaviours that arouse prejudicial feelings.

7.2 Interpersonal relationships

We need the company of other people, whether or not we get on with them.

One of the more extreme prison punishments in the USA and the UK is solitary confinement, more commonly referred to as security housing units. That means no contact with other people, being kept alone in the cell for up to 23 hours a day, with one hour's exercise walk within a confined space. The Pelican Bay (North California) prison study in 1993 showed that lack of human contact over even just a few days caused severe psychiatric disorders such as panic attacks, obsessive thinking and heart palpitations.

Figure 7.5 Humankind needs fellow humans irrespective of past behaviour towards them.

Maslow's hierarchy of needs: the forces motivating our behaviour are those of the most basic need currently not being satisfied. From most to least basic, these are physiological survival, personal safety, love and belonging, esteem and self-actualisation.

This indicates the need to enjoy the company of others for both mental and physical health. According to **Maslow's hierarchy of needs**, relationships are vital to leading a fulfilled life. Maslow (1943) proposed that the forces motivating our behaviour are those of the most basic needs currently not being satisfied. From most basic to least basic, these are physiological survival, personal safety, love and belonging, esteem, and self-actualisation. For instance our personal safety comes before our need for love and belonging, but our need for love, belonging and human relationships needs to be satisfied before self-esteem. Those lacking love, or at least a feeling of being valued and accepted, will face huge challenges in progressing to the greatest personal fulfilment of achieving self-actualisation. Our very fundamental needs for love, belonging and sexual intimacy may be realised through friends, family and sexual intimacy.

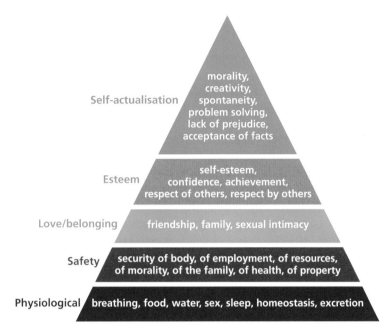

Figure 7.6 Maslow's hierarchy of needs

People interact with others on many different levels: within families, schools, workplaces, and cultural and recreational gatherings. This may include interaction with people we know nothing about, such as in the social media.

Our studies, however, will focus on the one-to-one interpersonal relationship that may well become permanent, including:

- initial attraction in finding each other
- communication in supporting the relationship
- cultural elements that each person brings to the relationship
- possible change, decline and termination of the relationship.

Each area continues to attract considerable theory and research studies.

7.2.1 What causes one person to be attracted to another?

The biology perspective

Biologists emphasise that the forces of attraction and falling in love are for the ultimate process of combining one's genes with the partner who will produce the best offspring.

In addition, women unknowingly tend to gravitate to men with different, but potentially co-dominant genes. It was demonstrated by the 'dirty shirt' experimental research of Wedekind et al. (1995), which indicates that the desire to produce healthy children that are resistant to disease is an evolutionary-based, unconscious factor in female human behaviour when choosing a partner. This is based on MHC, as explained in Chapter 3. We are the product of those MHC genes that are co-dominant, meaning that both sets of inherited genes have a beneficial effect on the child's immune system. Thus the more varied the MHC genes of the parents, the greater the likelihood of stronger immune systems of the children.

INTERNATIONAL FOCUS

Buss et al. (1990) conducted the International Mate Selection Project, a multi-lingual questionnaire-based study involving nearly 10 000 people from 33 different countries. Its purpose was to identify what characteristics individuals most sought in potential mates, worldwide.

Their research showed that biologically-associated factors were most important. The need for cultural compatibility, however, reduced the range of biologically-desirable partners available. Both genders placed the highest value on mutual attraction and love, a finding that questioned the widespread belief that romantic love is a Western phenomenon. Irrespective of culture, men placed a premium on physical attractiveness and youth, though within the boundaries of cultural acceptability. Also irrespective of culture, women placed a premium on social status, financial prospects and ambition. In fact, virginity was the only significant culturally-influenced element, being unimportant in the Netherlands and Scandinavia, but tending towards essential in Iran, India and China.

The findings of Buss et al.'s questionnaire indicated the high degree of biological determination in choosing a partner. Males will compete for the females in the best physical condition to rear children, in whom they will have combined their genetic material. Females prize the security and support that can be maximised by selecting the best male.

Figure 7.7 'With you, I'm the woman I want to be.'

What Buss et al.'s study also showed was the vital importance the respondents gave to romantic love. Biologists identify those feeling as being generated through a combination of neurotransmitters and hormones, which in combination put lovers into heart-throbbing, head-spinning worlds of their own. These include:

- adrenaline, giving the courage to make an initial approach to 'that special person'; it can also mean less need for food and sleep

- serotonin, speeding up the nervous system

- oxytocin, a powerful hormone released by both genders during touching and sex

- vasopressin, another powerful hormone released during sex, which powers long-term commitment.

The cognitive psychology perspective

Cognitive psychologists stress that on the whole, we tend to select friends and partners who process information in similar ways and have similar or at least compatible ranges of schemas. In other words, they are similar to ourselves.

Research study: Markey and Markey (2007)

Aim

To assess how far people's choice of partner was based on similarities.

Procedure

The participants were recruited by advertisement: 66 male and 103 female undergraduate students who were single but interested in finding a partner, and also 106 couples who had been together for more than a year. The questionnaire contained questions for the single participants under the headings of: (a) what characteristics and attitudes the respondent would like the ideal partner to have, and (b) the actual characteristics and attitudes of the respondent. Similar questions to these were adapted and given to the 106 couples that had been together for more than a year.

Results

The results indicated that generally people do seek, and do settle down with partners like themselves; and where they differ they tend to complement each other.

Strengths of the study

It used a relatively large sample.

Limitations of the study

The study required self-reporting on hypothetical situations. Successfully-matched couples tend to mirror the behaviours of each other as they idealise the behaviours of each other (Davis and Rusbult, 2001). In other words, it may not just be that similarity promotes attraction, but that attraction promotes similarity.

Research study: Kiesler and Baral (1970)

Cognitive psychology also places emphasis on self-esteem in forming relationships. This is exemplified by this experimental study.

Aim

To investigate whether a man is most likely to make the first approach to a woman when he feels really good, whether or not she is likely to say 'yes'.

Procedure

Kiesler and Baral gave an IQ test to two groups of men, and then gave them scores that were entirely untrue. Each member of the first group was told that he achieved the highest ever scores, individually and in private. Each member of the second group was told that his scores were very low and something must have gone wrong, individually and in private. Both groups were then asked to proceed to the waiting room, where they would be paid in due course for taking part in the study. While waiting, a very attractive young lady walked into the room.

Results

Those with the high scores engaged in conversation with her. Those with the low scores did not.

Conclusion

The study concluded that men with high self-esteem mindsets seek and actively pursue high-quality female partners.

The study was ecologically valid to the degree that the participants were likely to have stretched their mental capacities to maximise performance in the IQ test. On hearing that they did well, they would have felt self-satisfaction. On hearing that they did badly, they would have experienced disappointment.

However, it could be argued that the sudden and temporary rise and fall in self-esteem promoted by the unexpected results of the IQ test does not necessarily resemble the behavior flowing from a similar-but-long-term level of self-esteem that the individual may apply to his search for a partner.

The socio-cultural perspective

Socio-cultural perspectives in attraction include a wide range of attractiveness-creating elements, which include the following aspects:

- Familiarity. Seeing people more than once helps to reduce the initial suspicions associated with strangers. More frequent exposure tends to increase trust (Zajonc, 1971).

  This was supported by the work of Jorgensen and Cervone (1978), who found that people gave higher ratings to the photographs of strangers the more times they saw the photos. This is in line with the study of Festinger et al. (1950) on friendships and community life in a housing project for 260 married veterans at MIT, which indicated that those who live, study and work near to us are more likely to make suitable partners and friends.

- Social comparison. A person appears more attractive to those who have been less exposed to extremely good-looking people than to those who have. This is illustrated by the experimental work of Kenrick and Gutierres (1980). The control group was asked to rate the attractiveness of an average-looking woman. The test group was given the same task after watching *Charlie's Angels*, a television programme starring three very attractive women. Those seeing the programme rated the average woman as less attractive.

- Cultural compatibility. As previously-considered, Buss et al.'s (1990) cross-cultural study of attraction indicated that while most factors were universal and biologically grounded, there were two elements that showed cultural variations. They were the importance or lack of importance of chastity, and the maximum acceptable age gap between the man and the woman.

Attraction, however, is usually the beginning of the relationship. Psychologists consider elements other than attraction in understanding how relationships can successfully mature. We will look at two of them in detail: communication and culture.

7.2.2 Maintaining a relationship: communication and accommodation

The biology driving the excitement of falling in love typically fades with time. The work of Duck (1998) shows that conflicts occur sooner or later, and are the norm in relationships. Whether the relationship survives and flourishes or goes into terminal decline depends to a great degree on the communication strategies used by the couple, and their capacity to accommodate the increasingly noticeable differences between them.

The research of Canary and Stafford (1994) identified and highlighted five communication strategies that enable a relationship to continue successfully:

1 Doing unpredictable things that make your partner feel good. A surprise dinner with her favourite food, a flower casually picked when walking hand-in-hand, something exciting in the bedroom.

2 Self-disclosure: being able to share deeply personal thoughts and feelings at the right moment with the right person. Opening up makes the partner feel comfortable and valued, especially when accompanied by good listening skills. However, opening up too early in the relationship can have the reverse effect. The work of Altman and Taylor (1973) indicated that disclosing over-intimate personal information in the initial stages generally caused the other to think less, not more, of the person. It suggested a lack of confidence and security. However, self-disclosure is welcome once intimacy is established. The cross-cultural study of Kito (2010) showed that both American and Japanese students showed more intimate disclosure of personal thoughts within the romantic relationship than with friends of either gender.

Figure 7.8 Opening up makes a partner feel valued and loved.

3   Tuning into the other person's feelings at a particular moment, giving the feeling of being present with him or her, makes the partner feel loved and respected.

4   Keeping a social network by doing things together with a wide circle of family and friends.

5   Sharing some of the household tasks together, perhaps taking turns to cook.

In addition, the interpretation of the partner's communication may enhance or deteriorate the relationship. For example:

He burns the steak. Her verbal reaction can reflect the character of the entire relationship. Where the relationship is positive, she might smile with 'Next time, watch the meat and turn it over at the right time!' There, the communication is situationally grounded; he was daydreaming. But when the relationship is going through difficulties, it might be, 'You don't care for me! You would never have let the steak turn black if your boss was coming for dinner!' There, the communication is dispositionally grounded. He burnt the meat, she thinks, because he doesn't love her any more. Indeed, the research of Bradbury and Fincham (1992) indicated that where wives made dispositional judgements in communicating blame to the husband, they were more likely to have generally ambivalent feelings towards the husband.

Other things being equal, good sex releases oxytocin as both a neurotransmitter and a hormone. Oxytocin can enable one's partner to be more forgiving and generous in interpretation, as indicated by the experimental research of Baumgartner et al. (2008), which is detailed in Chapter 3.

This leads to the role of **accommodation in maintaining a relationship**. Accommodation is the capacity for one to handle and adapt to the other's tolerance-straining behaviour once a friendship or intimate relationship is already there. You may even spot it in a classroom. For example, a teacher may more readily grant an assignment time-extension to a well-meaning but occasionally forgetful student who has been in her classes for several years, than to another who only joined that term.

> **Accommodation in maintaining a relationship:** the capacity to handle and adapt to the other's tolerance-straining behaviour according to the degree of friendship or intimate relationship already present.

Research study: Rusbult et al. (1991)

Sooner or later, partners face annoying things about the other's behaviour patterns.

Aim

To investigate the correlation between the level of commitment within a relationship and the capacity to accommodate, if not actually tolerate, bad behaviour.

Procedure

The investigation involved 144 male and female American undergraduate psychology students, all of whom had or were having close relationships. Their task was to consider a series of scenarios where one person behaved badly to the other. The IV was the level of interdependence, meaning the degree of closeness between the two people. These were on four levels going from low level to high level of interdependence: casual acquaintance, casual dating regular dating and seriously involved with each other. After each scenario, they answered questions on the DV, which was how they would respond, and which centred around the following reactions:

- exit: Goodbye!
- neglect: keeping quiet and valuing the partner less, allowing the relationship to deteriorate
- loyalty: keeping quiet and hoping that things will improve
- voice: actively working together to improve things.

Results

The results showed a significant relationship: the higher the level of interdependence, the greater the level of accommodation. These findings form the basis of what is known as Rusbult's **Investment Model of Commitment Processes**.

Conclusion

This model indicates a direct relationship between the degree of closeness between the couple, and the capacity to accommodate bad behaviour within the relationship in a constructive manner. It indicates that problems occurring within relationships are more likely to be proactively and effectively handled when there is established interdependence between the couple. The study also indicated that women tended to be more accommodating than men.

Strengths of the study

The relatively large number of participants in the sample all of whom self-reported themselves as being in or having been in a relationship. That could well have put them in a relatively good position to judge how they might have acted in the scenarios provided.

Limitations of the study

The degree to which the research may be generalised: do the workings of personal relationships of psychology undergraduates apply to the wider population? Also, the research was not in the natural environment; there is no evidence that psychology students are any better at predicting their own behaviour in hypothetical situations than other people.

> **RESEARCH IDEA**
>
> Two people who have just fallen in love present themselves to a psychologist. On what bases can the psychologist predict the relationship's long-term potential, and what guidance might be offered to promote its maximum chance of success?

7.2.3 Cultural elements in human relationships

We have already considered the work of Buss et al. (1990) in Section 7.2.1, and their investigation into the role of cultural compatibility in choosing a partner. It may also be argued that the study, though cross-cultural in focus, did not include those in more traditional and rural societies that are home to two-thirds of India's and nearly half of China's populations. In fact, those from rural, less educated and lower socio-economic status backgrounds tended to be unrepresented in the sample.

Arranged marriages are common in traditional and rural societies, whereas marriage based on romantic attachments is largely Western. This model does not represent the whole truth. Duck (1998) points out that non-romantic elements in choice of partner are observed in individualistic societies as well as traditional ones. These elements include religion and opportunities to improve wealth and social position.

Investment Model of Commitment Process: problems occurring within relationships are more likely to be proactively and effectively handled when there is interdependence between the couple.

Theory of Knowledge

'I'm in love. I just can't stop thinking about him/her!'

1 What possible approaches would a psychologist use to assess whether that person is in love or not?

2 Some psychologists explain human behaviour through reductionist approaches (one main determinant) and others through holistic approaches (several or more widely different determinants combining together). Which approach in your opinion is best for determining whether or not a person's claim to be in love is true?

The merits of love matches versus arranged marriages continue to be debated by psychologists. Gupta and Singh (1982) studied 50 couples in India. Half of them married for love, and half of them had their marriages arranged. The overall results based on self-reporting were that those who chose their partners reported diminishing love after five years, but those with arranged marriages reported increasing love. This is supported by the work of Fiske (2004), whose research claimed that romantic marriages are likely to break up more quickly than arranged marriages. However, Fiske qualified that claim by arguing that arranged marriages in traditional societies can effectively be means of alliances between two extended families, and it is these social and economic pressures that place an extremely high price tag on separation and divorce.

Levine et al. (1995) put forward the view that the need for passionate love before marriage is of prime importance in individualist Western societies only. They based it on the findings of their cross-cultural study of college students who reported on whether they would marry a person whom they did not love, but had all the other qualities that they desired in a partner. The students in individualist countries overwhelmingly said 'No' (96% in the USA, 95% in Australia and 92% in the UK). In contrast, half the students from the less individualistic India and Pakistan reported being prepared to marry on that basis.

It may be argued that both types of marriage find common ground, in that many do continue to flourish into old age. The bases for long-term success are likely to be deepening friendship, effective communication within the relationship and an accumulated past of shared experiences and challenges.

7.2.4 When relationships change and end

The research of Levinger (1980) proposed that relationships go through five ABCDE stages are: initial **A**ttraction, **B**uilding by dating and making the relationship permanent, **C**ontinuation once things become routine, **D**eterioration on finding interests outside the marriage framework, and finally **E**nding the relationship in break-up or divorce.

Levinger's work suggests that the relationship becomes at risk when the continuation stage slowly and silently fades into the deterioration stage. The couple will endeavour to find the vital commitment to keep the relationship together. Some manage, successfully. Others feel unmotivated to make the effort, and let the relationship just drift. Then, the threat to the relationship may increase through situational elements, such as pressure of work, clashes in working hours and availability of other partners.

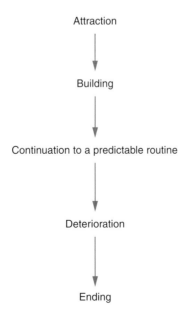

Figure 7.9 Are some love matches destined for long-term failure, however hard the couple try to keep together?

Psychologists draw attention to other elements to explain the breakdown in relationships:

- Negative patterns of accommodation of tolerance-straining partner behaviour (Rusbult et al., 1991), as examined in Section 7.2.2.

- One partner feeling overburdened relative to the other. Hatfield et al.'s study (1979) of 2000 couples showed that those who felt that they suffered from an unfair division of duties were most likely to cheat on the relationship.

- Fatal attraction, where the very element that attracted the two people to each other becomes the very element that pushes them apart (Femlee, 1995). For example, she fell in love with him because he talks excitedly about his around-the-world travel adventures, but that love can slowly fade when she faces the reality that he is unavailable for months at a time for that very reason.

Duck's (1982) relationship dissolution model

In spite of best intentions, relationships do not always survive the many changes experienced over time. Duck (1982) proposed a relationship dissolution model on the basis of a series of longitudinal studies which identified the following factors that put marriage and long-term relationships at risk:

1 Pre-existing incompatibilities not always obvious at the beginning of the relationship. These include carefully hidden behavioural abnormalities, and also personal attributes and cultural differences that can have charm in the short run, but become grating, exasperating and unbearable later on. Examples are lack of social privacy, and presence of the partner's family and friends.

2 Mechanical failure where a once-compatible couple becomes incompatible as each partner matures in ways that become harder to bridge.

3 A trauma-creating behaviour or event such as infidelity, a sudden discovery or realisation about one's partner, or a verbally or physically violent argument.

Duck identified several other contributory factors behind the three general reasons for relationship dissolution: resenting unequal division of household tasks, spending too much time away from one another, irreconcilable sexual issues and the tendency of blaming the other when things go wrong.

Duck's theory of relationship dissolution indicates that there is often, though not always, a time lag between the failure of the relationship and the final separation. A typical breakdown goes through the following four stages:

1 **Intra-physic stage:** private perception of being unhappy with the relationship, and focus on its negative aspects and the attractions of sharing life with someone else. Evaluates cost of break-up in terms of outside factors, such as what other people might think. The cognitive frame would be: 'I can't continue in this relationship.'

2 **Dyadic stage:** confronts rather than avoids partner over the benefits and losses involved in break-up, which might lead to reconciliation and a new beginning, but could also phase into stage 3. The cognitive frame would be: 'In withdrawing, I would be doing the right thing.'

3 **Social phase:** face family, friends and communities with a socially acceptable story on why they are no longer together. The cognitive frame would be: 'I'm serious. It's going to happen.'

4 **Grave-dressing phase:** typically each partner will produce their own story of the breakdown, commonly blaming the other for all that went wrong. The cognitive frame would be: 'It's inevitable. Get it over, present yourself in a good light, and begin a new chapter in life.'

Strengths of Duck's relationship dissolution model

- The model is supported by the many people who see it as a framework for their own experiences of broken relationships. The work of Hatfield et al. (1979) indicates that it is the feelings of getting less out of the relationship that promote the initial intra-physic stage.

- The model does accommodate repair and reconciliation possibilities.

Intra-physic stage (of relationship break-up): primary stage of relationship break-up involving private perception of being unhappy with the relationship, and focus on its negative aspects and the attractions of sharing life with someone else.

Dyadic stage (of relationship break-up): secondary stage of relationship break-up involving confronting rather than avoiding partner over the benefits and losses involved in break-up, which might lead to reconciliation and a new beginning, but could also phase into complete break-up.

Social phase (of relationship break-up): tertiary phase of relationship break-up involving facing family, friends and communities with a socially acceptable story on why they are no longer together.

Grave-dressing phase (of relationship break-up): the final phase of relationship break-up where typically each partner will produce their own story of the breakdown, commonly blaming the other for all that went wrong.

Limitations of Duck's relationship dissolution model

- This model needs to accommodate gender differences. Argyle (1988) found that men became unhappy with the relationship when they had less fun, and that women became unhappy with the relationship when they felt that their partner was becoming less supportive. Also, in the final break-up stage, men preferred a clean break whereas women were prepared to remain friends.

- It needs to accommodate cultural differences: the model appears to have a Western bias that cannot always be generalised to other cultures where family intervention and cultural stigmas may form barriers to break-up.

- This model does not extend to the sudden trauma-creating behaviour or event that prompts the abused partner to leave the relationship instantly, never to return.

SELF-ASSESSMENT QUESTIONS 7.1

1 Explain the meaning of the following concepts:

  a accommodation in maintaining a relationship

  b Investment Model of Commitment Process.

2 Describe the explanations offered for the physical attraction of one person to another by:

  a biological psychologists

  b cognitive psychologists

  c socio-cultural psychologists.

  Show how one study supports each explanation.

3 List the communication strategies that help a relationship to continue successfully.

4 How may the interpretation of the partner's communication enhance or deteriorate the relationship?

5 Explain the contributions to understanding cultural elements in human relationships made by:

  a Gupta and Singh (1982)

  b Levine et al. (1995)

7.3 Group dynamics

You have already been introduced to issues of group dynamics in Chapter 5, through the social identity theory developed by Tajfel and Turner (1979) which focuses on different attitudes and behaviours shown to members of in-groups and out-groups.

The in-group/out-group behaviours examined in that chapter can involve conflict between the groups, which in extreme cases can result in war and even **genocide**. War-based conflict involves institutionalised and systematised forms of violence between different groups. Genocide is where the ultimate objective is to destroy a whole race of people. There are even cases where conflict resulting in genocide is not rooted in a deliberate policy of human annihilation, but inadvertently through in-group self-interests combined with prejudicial thinking and discriminatory behaviour, as in the case below.

Genocide: violent behaviour with the ultimate objective of destroying a whole race of people.

213

INTERNATIONAL FOCUS

Truganini and Fanny Cochrane Smith were the last Tasmanians.

Lying 240 kilometres south of Australia, Tasmania and its long-established indigenous population of about 5000 became a British colony soon after Captain James Cook's landings in 1777. Their resistance to the British for using their ancestral lands for agricultural and mining purposes, and consequent inter-tribal warfare, meant that few survived to the 1830s.

Unlike the Nazi Holocaust directed against the Jews, British colonialism had no systematic plans to destroy the indigenous Tasmanian people. There was no Wansee Conference, death camps or mass poison-gas killings. Nor were there plans to set up a museum solely comprising artifacts from the race that the killers were proud to have exterminated. The Tasmanians' 'crime' was simply being in the way of British colonial interests. There was conflict rather than co-operation over the use of scarce resources between the conquerors and the indigenous population.

In 1833, the few hundred remaining indigenous Tasmanians were persuaded to co-operate with the British forces, on the understanding that they would be taken care of and eventually have their ancestral lands returned to them. Resettled by the British on Flinders Island, they did not survive long in their new surroundings. Many were killed by the germs of their own conquerors, to which they had no physical resistance. The British attempt to introduce them to Christianity, a way of life quite beyond their cognitive assimilatory capacities, is claimed to have caused the quiet misery that helped to take away their desire to reproduce. The last individual people of solely indigenous Tasmanian descent were Truganini (1812–76) and Fanny Cochrane Smith (1834–1905). Her real name is unknown due to the policy of anglicising the names of all remaining Tasmanians.

TRUGANINI.

Figures 7.10 and 7.11 Unintentional genocide? Truganini, and Fanny Cochrane Smith, the last people of solely indigenous Tasmanian ancestry

7.3.1 Origins of conflicts

Among the socio-economic explanations of the origins of conflict are power differences between different social groups, subcultures with elements of conflict and even violence, and deindividuation, the viewing of those involved in the conflict as part of the faceless other. We will consider each one in turn.

1 Power differences between social groups

One group being more powerful than another gives the potential for conflict, and often violence is shown towards the weaker group. That can enable members of the group to activate their prejudices into discriminatory behaviour against the weaker out-group, especially where there is perceived competition for scarce resources. The powerful/weaker scenario exists in many forms: better-armed (British colonialists against indigenous Tasmanians), racial (Nazis against Jews), tribal (Tutsis against Hutus in Rwanda), gender (males against females) and generational (adults against children). These are supported by prejudicial and discriminatory social norms among the dominant group. For example, during the genocide in Rwanda, Tutsi youngsters had been taught that killing Hutus was not murder, but the right thing to do. Thus much violence rooted in power difference comes from at least tacit support from the dominant group, which can also include dominance from a violent subculture.

2 Subcultures with elements of conflict and violence

Wolfgang and Ferrcuti (1967) theorised that subcultures enforce particular behaviours because **violent behaviour** is a requirement to be accepted as a member of each group. Indeed, many subcultures have prolonged initiation procedures where the newcomer has to persistently demonstrate physical violence and attitudes of violence in order to be identified as a successful recruit to the group: to be accepted as 'one of us', a member of the in-group.

Violent behaviour: where aggression is used to dominate or harm another person or group.

Research study: Totten (2003)

Totten (2003) conducted a study in Canada on gender-based abuse by in-depth interviewing 30 male youths aged 13 to 17 who were gang members or belonged to violent male peer groups.

Aim

To investigate the ways in which such marginal youth used violence to construct their masculinity specifically through their behaviours of girlfriend abuse.

Procedure

The qualitative data was obtained through semi-structured interviewing.

Results

The data showed similarities in the boys' backgrounds. They had all been exposed to violent role models, substantiating Bandura's theory that people learn violent attitudes and behaviour from direct experience and observing role models. This is in line with his research on violence towards the Bobo doll considered in Chapter 5. In addition, the interviews showed that their fathers all held rigid ideas of gender roles and honour, and they used violence to enforce them. The boys expected their girlfriends to do as they told them, and to expect violent consequences if they did not comply.

Conclusion

The study concluded that families and peer groups significantly contributed to the acquisition of violent norms of behaviour as part of acquiring a masculine gender role.

Strengths of the study

All the participants satisfied the criteria for being identified as having the specifically contentious and violent social characteristics. The semi-structured interviews enabled in-depth interviewing. The data and its interpretation afforded the potential to design educational programmes to combat violent behaviour.

Limitations of the study

Its applications are limited as the self-reporting might well have been a series of exaggerated self-presentations of masculinity for the interviewer. Further, urban subcultures among the young vary considerably, restricting the degree to which the findings may be generalised. Additional problems in applying its findings are due to the problems in distinguishing between violent, anti-social behaviour and commonly observed physically-emphatic interactions between teenage boys.

3 Deindividuation theory

Deindividuation theory is making a person less accountable for contentious and violent behaviour because the victim is unidentifiable, faceless or 'not one of us', just part of the opposition crowd. Wearing uniforms can clearly distinguish us versus them, for example in the different colours worn by football supporters of rival teams. Those supporting the same team tend to constitute the in-group, those with the rival team, the out-group.

> **Deindividuation theory:** a person feels less accountable for violent behaviour where the victim is unidentifiable, faceless or part of the opposition crowd.

Figure 7.12 Deindividuation in action: the faceless other?

In short, you are deindividualised when you as a member of the out-group are 'the faceless other' in the eyes of the violent aggressor.

Research study: Zimbardo (1969)

Zimbardo (1969) conducted an experiment similar to that of Milgram in Chapter 2, using female student participants throughout.

Aim

The study aimed to determine whether levels of aggressive behavior would be influenced by deindividuation.

Procedure

The individual participants in the test category were deindividualised by being uniformly dressed in lab coats and hoods that covered their faces. The experimenter addressed them as a group only. The individual participants in the control category were individualised by wearing the clothes of their choice, and displaying personal identity on name tags. Members of both groups were assigned the role of learning promoter.

Their 'victims' were other female participants, the 'students'. 'Information' was given to the promoters on each student, such as 'she has a warm personality' or 'she is conceited and critical'. As in Milgram, questions proceeded to be asked of the students, and the participating female questioners were instructed to apply electric shocks for every error.

Results

The test deindividualised faceless group delivered twice as much electric shock as the control, individualised group. The test participants did not appear to have used the victims' descriptors at all. One wrong answer and the shock was instantly given. In contrast, the control group gave far fewer shocks, showing evidence of having varied the punishment according to previous character reports.

Conclusion

The study concluded that people were more likely to behave aggressively if they knew they could not be identified.

Strengths of the study

It was experimental in structure, with an additional control removing the likelihood of an alternative explanation. It indicated that deindividuation appeared to lower the perpetrator of conflict's sense of self-control and accountability. Thus the findings of Zimbardo might give an insight on, for example, politically- or racially-motivated killings and brutality from and towards the police. Again, this could fall under the heading of prejudicial thinking and discriminatory behaviour to the 'faceless' out-group.

Limitations of the study

Zimbardo's electric shock study was carried out in a laboratory situation. The participants were middle-class young female students, raising questions about the degree to which the findings may be generalised. There were also ethical concerns over the considerable stress suffered by the participants, making the replication of such a study today unlikely given subsequent stricter professional ethical guidelines.

In proceeding from origins of conflict to resolution of conflict, bear in mind that both fields are vast, and that the theory and research discussed is a sample rather than a comprehensive study of this extremely important focus of psychology.

7.3.2 Strategies for conflict resolution

Conflict can occur in virtually all societies. An extremely common type is based on **bullying** and peers' abuse of power.

Indeed, concern over bullying in schools reached presidential level in the USA. President Obama worked with interest groups including members of his cabinet, researchers, school officials, parents and young people to put together a national strategy to address this problem. Among the recommendations in the 2011 report, teachers were advised to:

- create the atmosphere of trust where students could come forward and disclose vital information on bullying at the school

- be aware of which students seemed to be disliked, and which ones did not seem to be in the main friendship groups

- enable students to gain the necessary social skills to achieve their personal goals through assertiveness rather than by bullying.

Strategies for reducing violent conflict below will consider two areas in detail:

1 community involvement: peer counselling in schools

2 super-ordinate goals reducing conflicts between groups.

Bullying: where a person is repeatedly exposed to negative actions of others, which may be physical, verbal or psychological.

Peer counselling: fellow-students serve as trained mediators between the bully and the victim, with the background support and supervision of the teaching staff.

1 Community involvement: peer counselling in schools

Peer counselling is where students serve as mediators with the background support and supervision of the teaching staff. This involves the co-operation rather than the competition of different sections of the school community. It typically works in the following way. Older students are chosen and briefed in communication techniques, anger management and conflict-resolution skills to serve as peer counsellors. When bullying-associated tensions make themselves felt, the bully and victim are brought together by peer counsellors who act as mediators. Both the bully and the victim sign an agreement that commits them to following what they have agreed to do if any further bullying takes place. The mediators inform the students that a copy of the agreement is passed on to the peer-mediation coordinator and the teacher responsible for school discipline. Further recurrences are then dealt with by the school disciplinary procedures.

Figure 7.13 What co-operative skills do you think the students need to succeed as peer counsellors?

It is vital that the largely preventative peer counselling happens before the tension and conflict spiral violently out of control, by which time such procedures will invariably be too late. Peer counselling is designed to prevent violence, rather than tackle it when it takes place. It also uses student knowledge: bullying that does happen is often known to the students, but unknown to the school authorities.

The efficacy of peer counselling is difficult to assess due to the problems involved in setting up large-scale and effective controlled situations. A longitudinal study of such a school mediation programme in Stow, Ohio which began in 1994, showed that it was well-received by students, administrators, teachers and parents because of its being well-organised and recognised as part of the school's way of doing things. In 1998, the school resource officer helped the student mediators confront and resolve over 100 conflicts, ranging from hallway confrontations to dating relationships. The Stow experience demonstrated the positive aspects of coordination between the school authorities and the community.

Research study: Houlston and Smith (2007)

Aim

To investigate the impact and effect of a peer counselling programme in a north London all-girls secondary state school. In the UK, the premier legislative tool concerned with violence in school is The Children's Act (2004), which mandates the schools to ensure the safety of the students. Official school inspectors are required to report the level of student-to-student bullying.

Procedure

Data was collected from years 7, 8 and 9 (children aged 11 to 14), with year 10 peer counsellors and non-peer counsellors. The researchers conducted a one-year longitudinal study, acquiring quantitative and qualitative data for assessing the success of the programme.

Results

The year 10 students gained very much from their experience in peer counselling in terms of the widely transferable proactive and co-operative social skills from their training and experience.

Conclusion

However, the researchers concluded that peer counselling's impact on the nature and degree of bullying actually going on was not clear, and they felt that older students might well have been less open to the programme.

Strengths and limitations of the study

The programme's success in its main objective of reducing bullying was hard to judge. Self-reported bullying continued at the same rate, though it could be argued that there may have been an overall reduction that was not apparent because more victims were prepared to come forward due to their confidence in peer counselling. That would fit in with the students reporting their feeling that the school was doing more about the bullying situation, with year 7 showing the most positive changes.

2 Super-ordinate goals reducing conflict between groups

A goal becomes **super-ordinate** when it requires two or more people or groups to co-ordinate rather than compete against each other. This results in rewards to all the co-operating parties.

This principle was investigated by Sherif (1954) in his Robber's Cave study.

Super-ordinate goals: where a goal requires the co-operation of two or more people or groups, which results in rewards to all the co-operating parties.

Muzafer Sherif (1906–1988)

Muzafer Sherif (1906–88) was born in Izmir, Turkey, and obtained his doctorate at Columbia University in 1935. Sherif was a founder of modern social psychology, specialising in the areas of social processes, social norms and social conflict. Many of his original contributions to social psychology are well-known and taken for granted today, to the degree that his role in their development is not often remembered.

Figure 7.14 Muzafer Sherif

Research study: Sherif (1954)

Aim

To assess the impact of super-ordinate goals as a proactive approach to violent group conflict, as well as towards reducing prejudice and discrimination.

Procedure and results

Sherif selected a group of 22 white 11-year-old boys who were unknown to each other. They were taken to a remote summer camp in Robber's Cave State Park in Oklahoma, USA. The boys were randomly put into two groups, neither knowing of the existence of the other. The first week was dedicated to team-building activities. The boys hiked and swam together. Each group chose a name for itself – they became the Eagles and the Rattlers. They reinforced their identity by stencilling their group name on their shirts and flags.

Then they were introduced to each other for four days, through a series of competitions. There were trophies and prizes for the winners; nothing for the losers. Tensions rose between the two groups where they showed discriminatory behaviour. They were singing derogatory songs about the 'other' out-group, burning each others' flags, raiding each others' cabins and even refusing to eat with the other group in the same dining hall.

The third stage was the integration phase. The two groups watched movies and lit fireworks together. The hope was that these face-to-face encounters would reduce tensions. They did not. Meetings broke up with the two groups throwing food at each other.

In the fourth and final stage, the researchers arranged situations in which a problem arose which threatened both groups at the same time. The researchers created the situations for two super-ordinate goals, where co-operation between the two groups was vital to their well-being. The first was a blockage of the supply of drinking water to the camp. The two groups managed to work together to remove it, and they celebrated when they succeeded. Later on, the bus on which they were travelling broke down. The boys had to work hard together to push it. By the time these trials were over, they stopped having negative images of the other side. On the final bus-ride home, the members of one team used their prize money to buy drinks for everyone.

Conclusion

- Competition over scarce resources is a vital element in the active dislike of another group, including violent discriminatory behaviour between the groups.

- A super-ordinate situation that threatens both groups equally creates the need to co-operate by combining together, and thus ends the inter-group violent behaviour and negative stereotypes.

Strengths of the study

The small-scale study highlighted the role of social categorisation leading to inter-group prejudice and resultant behaviour, even when the two groups were deliberately set up to be similar. The team of researchers carried out their work in a natural setting of a summer camp rather than a laboratory and could thus claim high ecological validity.

Limitations of the study

There are limitations in terms of describing and analysing behaviour flowing from social categorisation. The conflicts between the Eagles and the Rattlers may well have arisen from the high degrees of group identification and loyalty deliberately engineered by the researching team. In addition, the friendships made between the two groups at the end of the proceedings may have been due to the successful resolution of the final goal. The researchers did not test the scenario of what would have happened if their combined efforts had failed to resolve the problems.

SELF-ASSESSMENT QUESTIONS 7.2

1 Define deindividuation. How does it increase the likelihood of violent conflicting behaviour according to the study of Zimbardo (1969)?

2 Which other two socio-economic explanations on the origins of conflict are commonly used?

3 Define these terms, referring to the research of Sherif (1954) and Houlston and Smith (2007) to explain how they may be applied to conflict resolution in communities:

   a peer counselling

   b super-ordinate goals

Alan is in year 8 and regularly eats lunch with his classmates at the same table in the school canteen. On returning to school after a week's absence, he finds that his place has been taken by Jimmy, a powerfully built and much-feared new student. One angry glare from Jimmy, and Alan moves to the table of a rival class, whose occupants tell him to go away. Alan leaves the canteen and eats lunch alone in the corridor. He feels so sick that he is ready to vomit. As other students wait in the corridor for the next class, Jimmy laughs at Alan with: 'Like your place, kid.'

1 Outline psychological theory and/or research that relates to the behaviour of:

   a Alan's classmates at the school canteen table

   b the students at the table of the rival class

2 What first-stage psychological intervention would you recommend to deal with Jimmy, and why?

3 Evaluate the effectiveness of your suggestion.

7.4 Social responsibility

Social responsibility is a concept frequently used in the business world. It promotes the idea that firms' profit-making activities should advance the welfare and interests of societies in which they operate. In psychology, it would focus on **pro-social behaviour**; able people assisting those who have difficulties. An example would be stepping forward to help a stranger when in need. The biological approach to behaviour would explain such actions in terms of closeness within the human species (Madsen et al., 2007). Cognitive psychologists would place emphasis on being encouraged by unpleasant perceptions of self-deprecation for failing to help (as in Piliavin et al., 1969). Those with socio-cultural leanings may consider the religious elements in the individual's upbringing. Bear in mind that these explanations can be combined; they are not mutually exclusive.

Pro-social behaviour: acting in a way that helps another person or group.

7.4.1 Pro-social behaviour

Your behaviour is altruistic when you help another person at your own cost, without the expectation of any benefit or reward. In contrast to self-centred behaviour, your focus is solely for the other person, even at your own expense. There is no prospect of reciprocity, which means getting a favour in return.

Suffering from stomach cancer, Anna Joyshot was practically sentenced to death by bureaucracy.

Aged 45 with five children, her only 'crime' was that her permanent address was registered in New South Wales (NSW), Australia.

Anna's one chance for survival was an immediate operation. Unfortunately, the medical profession limited the number of stomach cancer operations that surgeons were allowed to perform. There were already too many people above her on the waiting list.

18-year-old high-school student Chloe O'Halloran heard of Anna's situation from a mother whose children she babysat. At once, Chloe opened an online petition, asking the Minister of Health to intervene and save Anna's life. It was signed by nearly 100 000 people, including some national celebrities.

As a result, the NSW health authority very soon announced that they would create two new stomach cancer centres.

After her operation, Anna declared: 'I felt that my life meant so much as people I don't even know took time out of their busy lives to help me, and the other people on the waiting list. I cannot thank them enough.'

Altruism: helping another person at one's own cost, without expectation of benefit or reward.

Altruism is a subset of pro-social behaviour. For example, an old lady gets off the bus, struggling with two heavy baskets of shopping. You're extremely tired after playing in an after-school rugby match, and are just desperate to get home. Nevertheless, you decide that the old lady comes first. You spend the little energy you have left by helping to take her shopping to wherever she wants to go.

What makes your behaviour altruistic as well as pro-social is the motivation. If it is to make a good impression on the people with you, your behaviour is certainly pro-social. Nevertheless, your wish to get their approval makes it pro-social only, not altruistic. However, your act may well be classified as altruistic if your sole interest is in helping a person in need who does not know you, and who you will probably never see again.

RESEARCH IDEA

Find an example of an incident that showed altruistic behaviour on the part of the individual. It may be at your school, in your locality or further afield. What particular aspects of that behaviour would classify it as altruistic rather than just pro-social?

Research study: Piliavin et al. (1969)

Aim

To investigate the incidence of pro-social behaviour when the person in need was male, aged 25 to 35, drunk **or** movement-challenged, and found on the New York subway between 11am and 3pm.

Procedure

This experimental research used fake, set-up crises with covert recording human observers at different subway locations. At each place the person who fell down was either intoxicated and smelling of alcohol, or sober and needed a cane for support. A covert member of the research team was to assist if no member of the public would step forward and help within 70 seconds.

Results

The results of this scenario (enacted 103 times) showed an overwhelmingly positive response from the public. The disabled victim received help in all instances. The drunk victim was helped in more than three-quarters of the incidences. More than one helper was involved in more than half the incidences.

Conclusion

This study appeared to show that people do possess qualities that promote altruistic behaviour, though this would be tempered by the possibility that at least some have stepped forward to avoid the unpleasant feeling of having not helped when being in a position to do so.

Figure 7.15 Is the helper behaving altruistically?

Strengths of the study

The standardised 'need for help' simulations in real-life locations made it ecologically valid. Additionally, the observers were instructed to not only record the quantitative data of frequencies of assistance, but also include notes on the way help was given and any other relevant qualitative information.

Limitations of the study

These were mainly procedural, such as suspected errors in recording the overall picture of members of the public tending to move forward or move away. In addition, the number of drunk-person scenarios formed much less than half of the total.

Finally, by today's standards this research would be ethically accountable for deception of the public, causing anxiety to members of the public, and lack of debriefing.

ACTIVITY 7.2

Find three examples of instances of pro-social behaviour in the media. For each example, assess how far those giving help acted altruistically.

7.4.2 Explanations of altruistic and pro-social behaviour in people

People helping others in need at their own cost without expecting any benefit or reward is one of the happier and probably much-unreported aspects of human conduct. There are many theories offering explanations of altruistic behaviour. We will consider three of them, one each from the biological, cognitive and socio-cultural perspectives.

1 Kin-selection theory

Evolutionary biologists exemplified by Richard Dawkins in *The Selfish Gene* have argued that altruism may well have an element of selfishness in it. It is because every person belongs to the collective of the human race. That means that we have an innate desire to promote the survival of the human race, as humanity is an extension of ourselves. Within that, the higher the element of kin – the closer the person is related to us – the more intense that desire becomes. This is because they share more common genetic material. That is kin-selection theory. Underlying kin-selection is our innate desire to live forever. As that does not happen, the next best thing is that we altruistically support those whose genes most resemble our own, as they are intrinsically our collective long-term, evolutionary survival.

In evaluation, kin-selection theory addresses the reality of parents making huge sacrifices for the welfare of their children, perhaps exemplified by instances in Nazi death camps of parents willing to suffer the most extreme torture if it held the remotest possibility of saving the life of their child. In addition, studies with animals have indicated kin-selection behaviours. For example, the work of Sherman (1980) on squirrels shows that they are more likely to warn relatives than non-relatives when predators are approaching.

However, it does not fully explain why a person may choose to help a person in distress who is a complete stranger, and of a different race and culture. In addition, people show pro-social and even altruistic behaviour towards others in situations when their lives and capacities to produce new generations are not under threat.

Research study: Madsen et al. (2007)

Kin-selection theory appears to be supported by this study.

Aim

To investigate the degree to which individuals are likely to show higher levels of unselfishness and self-sacrifice to those they are biologically related to, than to complete strangers.

Procedure

The participants were students of both genders in two countries, the UK and South Africa. Each student supplied the researchers with a list of blood relatives and their degree of biological closeness, a sister being closer than a cousin for example. The researchers selected just one relative from each list.

Each student had to sit in a highly uncomfortable position: back to the wall, and thighs parallel to the ground. A small sum of money would be paid to the selected relative for every 20 seconds of painful endurance.

Results

The participants indeed suffered pain for longer periods when the recipient was a closer relative, and this was especially significant with the male participants. However, the degree of closeness was less significant among Zulu participants. That could have been because their culture tends to put siblings and cousins on a similar level.

Conclusion

The study's conclusion supported kin-selection theory: that the greater the biological closeness of the relationship, the greater the degree of help offered.

Strengths of the study

This study does appear to support kin-selection theory to the degree that closer relatives seemed to be in a better potential situation to receive help. In addition, the study was cross-cultural, suggesting biological determination at work.

Limitations of the study

The inferences on genetic influences on kin selection were based on researcher observation, and as such were correlational. In addition, there was no control for the different pain thresholds among the participants. Finally, the study probably lacked ecological validity as the sums of money offered were relatively trivial, and probably not enough to determine survival in terms of the family budget.

2 Empathy-altruism theory

The **empathy–altruism theory** in psychology suggests that pro-social and altruistic behaviour is based on **empathy**, a genuine desire to improve the perceived situation of another person. Observing the suffering of another person creates personal distress and empathic concern (Batson et al., 1981). Personal distress is when we suffer watching others suffer. Empathic concern is when we feel the other's pain when we put ourselves in their position.

Empathy-altruism theory: the observation of the suffering of another person creates personal distress and a consequent desire to help.

Empathy: the capacity to understand and share the feelings of others without necessarily being in agreement with them.

Batson et al. argue that the likelihood of altruistic behaviour increases where there is a degree of closeness between the potential helper and the sufferer, such as having once been in a similar situation (cognitive), personally knowing the sufferer or the observer being prompted to imagine what that suffering would be like if it happened to them (both situations are cognitive and arguably socio-cultural).

Research study: Toi and Batson (1982)

Aim

To investigate whether help would be offered if there was a good chance that the people would never meet again. This was an experimental study.

Procedure

This study involved female psychology students listening to tape-recordings of fellow-student Carol, who recorded herself as injured in both legs following a road accident. She spoke earnestly, saying how anxious she was to complete the course. Would students come forward and help her by contacting her, meeting up and helping her with the material of the missed classes?

The students were divided into two groups. The first division was into a high empathy group and a low empathy group. The high empathy group was instructed to listen to the tape and focus on how Carol was feeling. The low empathy group was told not to pay attention to Carol's expressed feelings. The researchers then divided the whole group into two again. One was told that Carol would be returning to the class. They would see her again. The other heard that Carol would no longer appear, as she would be completing her studies out of class. So with high empathy, help would be offered even if they would never see Carol again.

Results

The students who were prompted to focus on the empathy-stimulating content were far more likely to volunteer to assist Carol. It made little difference whether or not she would return to the lecture group. Those whose instructions were to ignore the empathy-stimulating content showed much less interest in helping Carol, even where they were told that she would return in due course.

Conclusion

The findings appear to support the theory that the likelihood of altruism depends on the degree of empathy the helper has for the person in need.

Strengths of the study

The researchers manipulated the groups so that they could rule out the possibility that the decision of whether to help was based on whether she would come back to class. Additionally, the study had female participants only, to reduce volunteering for non-academic purposes.

Limitations of the study

There was a possibility that some of the participants correctly guessed the purpose of the experiment and responded on the basis of demand characteristics, with what they thought the researchers wanted to hear. In addition, this study neither looked at the backgrounds and dispositions of the individual participants, nor considered the possibility that the responses might be biologically based.

3 Pro-social behaviour based on socio-cultural dispositional and situational considerations

Socio-cultural psychology explains altruistic behaviour in terms of:

- dispositional motives – behaving altruistically because concern for others is part of one's upbringing or religious practice
- situational motives – behaving altruistically being more likely in a moment of leisure than when in a hurry to get to somewhere else.

Research study: Darley and Batson (1973)

This is known as the 'Good Samaritan' study. It involved 40 male Princeton theological seminary participating students.

Aim

To find out what was more important in deciding to help another in distress: dispositional or situational motives.

Procedure

The participant in the role of needing help was placed sitting in a doorway, head slumped downwards and coughing.

The participating students answered questionnaires designed to determine their degree of personal religiosity. In the next stage, they were divided into two groups. One group was given a high empathy-generating task: to prepare a short talk on the parable of the Good Samaritan who helped the injured person abandoned and left for dead by the important people of the established community. The other group was given a task that was not designed to create empathy at all: to prepare a short talk about careers for seminary graduates. Each member of each group was treated separately by the researchers.

Each student was then told individually to go over to another building to deliver the talk. One-third of all the students were put into high time pressure: 'Get there at once, they are waiting for your talk'; one-third were put into medium pressure: 'Please go to the other building as soon as possible'; and the remaining third into low pressure: 'You may now leave and make your way to the other building.' All students were let out at separate times, so each student was by themselves when they saw the person in need of help.

Results

The individual decisions appeared to depend on one thing: in how much of a hurry the student was to get from one building to the other. Only 10% of the students under high pressure stopped to help; 45% of the moderate pressure group did, and that figure rose to 63% within the unpressured group. These were situational factors. Dispositional factors such as degree of religiosity or immediately previous involvement in the parable of the Good Samaritan did not seem to be significant.

Conclusion

The study concluded that thinking and even getting ready to present ideals does not mean one will necessarily act on them if in a hurry and occupied with other things.

Figure 7.16 'I am happy to please God and help others with this single action, as my holy teachings instruct.'

Strengths of the study

This was a controlled experiment, with the participant in need of help and the time pressure elements being fairly typical of real life. It was well set up, with due care taken to ensure that the students did not pass the person in need of help in pairs or in groups.

Limitations of the study

It only investigated the conflict situation, where the likely desire to help faced competition from the urgent need to be in a certain place immediately. It did not assess dispositional factors behind the decision to help in the absence of adverse situational factors. There was also the possible ethical issue of deception.

Studies have shown that pro-social behaviour in general and altruistic behaviour in particular may be influenced by cultural and religious norms. For example, giving to charity is voluntary in North America and Western Europe. Western society does not view people who avoid giving to charity as moral delinquents, whereas Muslims believe that passing on some of one's wealth to those in need is one of the Five Pillars of Islam (known as 'Zakat').

This leads on to the more specific issue of what happens if a person is in immediate danger, but there are many others in the immediate environment. Will the competent individual still step forward out of the crowd to help? Or will they hold back as a bystander, in the expectation that someone else within the crowd will intervene?

INTERNATIONAL FOCUS

Levine et al. (1994) and Levine et al. (2001) together researched the cross-cultural differences in helping strangers. Their investigation was to assess how helpful people were in 59 cities; 36 in the USA (1994 study) and 23 in other countries (2001 study). Both studies included three different scenarios requiring simple and short-time assistance from local people: returning a dropped pen, helping a blind person at a busy traffic junction and aiding an injured person to retrieve a fallen magazine.

The results within the USA showed that most help was offered in the south, where the cities were smaller, and least help in the much larger mega-cities of the north east and California. Overall, the chance of being helped by a stranger in the USA was inversely proportional to the size of the city.

The findings for non-US cities were more complex. In the blind person scenario, help was offered every time in Rio de Janeiro (Brazil), San José (Costa Rica), Lilongwe (Malawi), Madrid (Spain) and Prague (Czech Republic). That contrasted with Kuala Lumpur (Malaysia) and Bangkok (Thailand), where the blind person received stranger assistance less than half the time. There were also instances where, contrary to expectations, faster-pace cities actually rendered more help than the less-hurried urban environments. People in Copenhagen and Vienna proved far more helpful than in Kuala Lumpur. The results for non-native city residents seemed to parallel local norms: for example, Brazilians more readily offered help in Rio than in New York.

Among the possible explanations are cultural norms. It appeared less appropriate to seek help from complete strangers in Kuala Lumpur than in Copenhagen. Additionally, India, Malawi and Latin American countries have a cultural tradition of helping complete strangers, despite themselves being no strangers to poverty. It may also be argued that in the larger cities, the local inhabitants feel more anonymous and thus less connected to their surroundings.

In evaluation, Levine et al. (1994) was a real-world simulation with real, everyday situations, and thus had high ecological validity in examining the frequency of pro-social behaviour in different urban and national environments. However, the study may be criticised as the scenarios of the dropped pen, the blind person and the fallen magazine may have aroused the suspicions of some of the locals in sophisticated city environments, who have had negative experiences with scammers.

7.4.3 Bystanderism and its causes

In 1964, Kitty Genovese was stabbed to her death with a hunting knife by a serial murderer and rapist in Queens, New York. Thirty-eight of her neighbours were reported to have witnessed the scene, but not one intervened, or even telephoned for help.

The **bystanderism** of those present in this widely-publicised tragedy attracted researchers Darley and Latané. Their work indicated that bystanderism behaviour's main causes are:

Bystanderism: where individuals do not step forward to help a victim when others are present.

Diffusion of responsibility: the likelihood of a capable individual not volunteering to help where other similarly-able people are present.

Pluralistic ignorance: where people look around at others to see their reactions, as cues for how to act in an emergency situation. The fewer the cues, the less likelihood of an individual intervening.

- **diffusion of responsibility**: the more people present, the more likely the capable individual will rely on someone else to step forward

- **pluralistic ignorance**: people look around at others to see their reactions, as cues for how to act in an emergency situation. The fewer the cues, the less likelihood of individual interventive action.

Research study: Darley and Latané (1968)

Aim

To discover the diffusion of responsibility. This was an experimental study.

Procedure

Darley and Latané interviewed 79 psychology student-participants through headphones on the topic of living in a high-pressure urban environment. Some participants were told that they would be on their own, others were told that there would be a smaller number of co-interviewees, and further participants were told that it would be a larger number. Thus the IV was the number of bystanders, the number of other people the participant believed were in the same discussion loop.

During the intercom proceedings, there was a series of loud choking noises indicating an immediate, life-threatening emergency. That was designed to activate the DV, which was the frequency of the participant alerting the experimenter on hearing the choking noises.

Results

The degree of 'help' dropped where others were believed to be present: 85% of the participants left the room to offer help when it seemed that there was no-one else. But less than two-thirds interrupted their work when there appeared to be a few others, and that fell to less than a third when the participants thought that there were more than four possible helpers present.

Conclusion

The study supported the concept of diffusion of responsibility: that the more people present, the more unlikely capable individuals are to step forward to offer help.

Strengths of the study

The experiment was set up with a convincing state of emergency. Each participant was clearly told whether or not co-interviewees would be participating at the same time, and if so, how many.

Limitations of the study

The experiment lacked full ecological validity due to its laboratory setting. The participants were all psychology students, raising the question of whether the findings could be generalised to wider populations. Additionally, the research did not completely simulate the circumstances of the Kitty Genovese murder, as the participants only heard and did not see the victim.

The study also raised the ethical points of deception, and being placed in an anxiety-creating situation.

7.4.4 Promoting pro-social behaviour

We have already considered promoting pro-social behaviour earlier in the chapter, by referring to community involvement and peer counselling in schools (Houlston and Smith, 2007), and super-ordinate goals reducing conflicts and promoting co-operation to common, beneficial goals between previously conflicting groups (Sherif et al., 1961).

INTERNATIONAL FOCUS

Overcoming the bystander effect.

Two-year-old Wang Yue died after a white van hit her in a small lane in the city of Foshan, China. For seven minutes she lay bleeding as 18 seemingly indifferent people walked or cycled by. Then another vehicle ran the toddler over. An elderly lady then picked her up and moved her towards safety. It was too late. Despite efforts to treat her, she died of brain failure a week later in hospital.

One of the ways in which the bystander effect can be prevented is by requesting help from individuals rather than from groups. Unless they are assigned a certain task that distinguishes them from the group, people will wait for someone else to fulfil that responsibility. For this reason, psychologists encourage someone to step up and take command by singling out people in the crowd to carry out specified essential tasks.

This person should quickly assess the situation and give out emergency orders, such as:

'You in the red peaked cap – find the address of the nearest house so emergency services can find us.'

'You in the blue jeans and white top – call the ambulance.'

'If you know first aid, put up your hand!'

They should then ensure that everyone is doing what they should be doing until the services arrive and fully take over.

Sadly, this did not happen in the case of Wang Yue.

Governments have wrestled with legislation in order to promote pro-social behaviour, as in the case of China in 2017. Wang Yue's death shocked the world – had she been helped at once, she might have lived.

Unfortunately, there is a concern in China that acting in a socially responsible manner in such situations might create problems for the people who stop to help. There have been cases where the helpers have been caught up in lengthy bureaucratic processes and have even been extorted after being accused of being the culprit.

However, the Chinese government is drafting a law to ensure that those who come forward and offer help will not be liable for medical costs. But many commentators hold that protective legislation is not enough: what is needed is a change in attitude, promoting the values and ideals of social responsibility.

SELF-ASSESSMENT QUESTIONS 7.3

1 Define these terms:

a social responsibility

b bystanderism

2 Distinguish between these behaviours:

a pro-social behaviour and altruism

b diffusion of responsibility and pluralistic ignorance

3 Name and explain three theories for pro-social behaviour.

4 Compare and contrast the findings of Piliavin et al. (1969) and Levine et al. (1994) on pro-social behaviour.

5 List three ways in which pro-social behaviour might be promoted.

Chapter summary

1 The psychology of human relationships focuses on pro-social behaviour including altruism, anti-social behaviour including conflict, and inter-personal relationships including co-operation, friendship and romance.

2 Psychologists become involved in relationships to focus on the forces underlying positive relationships, and to facilitate the handling of ambivalence and breakdown in problem relationships.

3 The reasons that couples fall in love can be explained using biological (nervous systems, hormones and genetic composition responding to suitable partner), cognitive (mutual recognition of highly desirable physical and behavioural characteristics) and socio-cultural (familiarity and cultural compatibility) perspectives.

4 Existing relationships have the best chance of continuing to flourish and the least chance of permanent breakdown and separation where communication and accommodation skills are optimal.

5 The merits of culturally-traditional arranged marriages versus romantic-attachment marriages are largely dependent on the interpreting of available evidence.

6 Socio-culturally, conflict-driven anti-social behaviour (whether physical, verbal or psychological) directed at individuals or groups may be based on power differences between groups, subcultures with elements of violence and deindividuation.

7 Conflict and bullying can increase the victim's susceptibility to infectious disease, lower self-esteem and willingness to trust people, and promote the consideration of suicide in extreme cases.

8 Conflict in the form of bullying, especially in schools, continues to be an official concern at national level in many countries. Among the many strategies used to reduce bullying are peer counselling and super-ordinate goals to reduce conflict between groups.

9 The frequent occurrence of pro-social behaviour and its subset altruistic behaviour may be explained by kin-selection theory, empathy-altruism theory, and dispositional and situational considerations. Pro-social behaviour may be promoted through supportive legislation, peer counselling, and co-operation between groups in facing super-ordinate goals.

10 The decision of a competent bystander not to intervene when the safety of a stranger is in immediate danger may be based on diffusion of responsibility, pluralistic ignorance or potential lack of legal support.

Exam-style question

Essay response question

- Analyse why relationships may change or end.

Health psychology

'Health is a state of complete harmony of the body, mind and spirit. When one is free from physical disabilities and mental distractions, the gates of the soul open.'
(B.K.S. Iyengar)

8

KEY QUESTIONS

- What contributions may psychology make to the understanding and promotion of health?
- Why do behaviours occur which are barriers to health?
- What are the nature and value of health promotion models and strategies?

Learning objectives

- Outline the research on the long-term relationship between poverty and ill health. (AO1)
- Explore the evidence for increased stress lowering resistance to disease. (AO2)
- Examine the role of social support as a means of coping with ill health. (AO2)
- Discuss how addiction to an unhealthy lifestyle may form a barrier to quitting. (AO3)
- Evaluate the role of genetics in obesity caused by overeating. (AO3)
- Evaluate models of health promotion. (AO3)

8.1 Determinants of health

Remember that you are applying the biological, cognitive and socio-cultural perspectives to specific issues within the field of health psychology.

Health psychology looks at how issues such as stress, substance abuse, **addiction**, obesity and health promotion may have an impact on a person's physical welfare.

Human physical conditions are traditionally treated by conventional medicine. However, there is a growing realisation that non-biological factors are influential. Indeed, **determinants of health** include not just factors that are biological, but also socio-economic, environmental and psychological. All these can influence the health status of individuals or populations.

How far do psychological conditions determine physical health? Over the last 40 years, health psychology has been serving a vital role in preventing adverse medical conditions, not just in helping those with unhealthy lifestyles to stop their bad habits. At the treatment level, an understanding of the role of health psychology can involve considering the patient's living situation, such as a high-stress situation at home, in school or at the workplace. Modern treatments often take into account the individual's lifestyle as well as the biological disease.

For example, people who are stressed often claim that they are unable to work because they are unwell. Are they really sick, or is it just in the imagination? The framework for addressing this and questions of a similar nature may lie in the **biopsychosocial model** of health and well-being.

8.1.1 The biopsychosocial model of health and well-being

Proposed by Engel (1977), the biopsychosocial model holds that the psychological elements of thoughts, feelings and behaviours, as well as the biological factors of health and disease, influence the physical condition of a person. For example, an individual's chance of developing coronary heart disease is not only increased by a high-cholesterol diet, but by having certain personality attributes, including being constantly hurried, impatient, tense rather than relaxed, and finding it difficult to switch off from work. With this model, clinical practice can include preventative counselling in helping an individual to use better coping strategies when facing stressors and seeking to stop addictive behaviours.

In a similar frame, the work of Reed et al. (1999) showed that HIV-positive people with more pessimistic expectations develop HIV-related symptoms more easily. Wayment et al. (2006) took it further, showing that pessimistic expectations may simply lead to people giving up, which by itself weakens the immune system. That implies that the psychological position of optimism can help the person to survive for a longer period.

Against these strengths, this model has been criticised as the psychological conditions of the individual are often not easy to quantify. This model places considerable emphasis on individuals taking responsibility for their own health in the face of severe challenges, which may not be an option for those with long-standing overeating, tobacco or alcohol addictions or for those unable to leave high-stress situations. And finally, principles flowing from this model have involved extended conventional medical training as new generations of doctors are required to gain experience in professionally interacting with patients at the counselling level.

The biopsychosocial model: the example of stress

Stress is a reaction to a stimulus that disturbs our physical or mental equilibrium. We sense stress when we feel that we cannot easily mobilise the resources needed to cope with the demands that are put on us. Stress becomes the concern of psychology when it is distinguished from **eustress**, the normal degree of stress that is beneficial and positively motivational for the individual. It becomes a health problem when the degree of stress is at the level of being detrimental to the health of the individual.

Addiction: a compulsion to use a substance in order to avoid discomfort in its absence, such as the smoker's craving for a cigarette.

Determinant of health: biological, socio-economic, environmental and psychological factors that influence the health status of individuals or populations.

Biopsychosocial model: the psychological elements of thoughts, feelings and behaviours as well as the biological factors of health and disease influence the physical condition of a person.

Stress: a reaction to a stimulus that disturbs our physical or mental equilibrium. Ordinary stress is a higher level of stress than eustress.

Eustress: the normal degree of stress that is beneficial and positively motivational for the individual.

For example, the environment in which the IB programme is delivered can be stressful, especially in the following circumstances:

- Coordinators and teachers are overworked and frenzied.
- Deadlines are irregular. Six deadlines in three days, with no evidence of coordination between different departments.
- Constant pressure of family and friends who have unrealistically high expectations.
- Constant pressure from a university place-offer requiring a very high IB point score.
- Some administrators, teachers and fellow-students are hard to talk to.

Businesspeople, professionals, skilled workers, semi-skilled workers and unskilled workers all experience stressors from time to time. Stress can develop where there is a mismatch between the perceived demands made on a person and their ability to cope with them. One example is the under-confident teacher with a difficult last class on a Thursday afternoon. Another might be having to finish a company research project within a very tight deadline.

Figure 8.1 Finish by 18:00 on Thursday, or lose our jobs

Some of the main work stressors that have been identified by the UK National Work-Stress Network include: working under constant deadlines, no recognition or reward for good job performance, harassment or bullying at work, new management 'making change for change's sake', and the sudden introduction of new technology. These may be at least partially traced to poor management or communication of the methods to be applied to the task.

One application of the biopsychosocial model can be made by considering the following question:

- People who are stressed often claim that they are unable to function normally because they are unwell. Are they really sick, or is it just in the imagination?

In response to the question raised above on whether people are actually unwell because of stress or whether it is in their imagination, consider the following. Jim is 19 years old. A serious, first-year university engineering student, he's struggling to keep up with the high standard of work that his course demands. With end-of-year exams in just three weeks' time, Jim faces not being allowed to continue the programme unless his work reaches the required standard.

Two days ago, Jim became ill with flu. He had to stay at home. Constantly fretting about approaching exams, things went from bad to worse. Today, his body temperature rose to 40°C (104°F). Feverish and sick, getting out of bed to go to the bathroom or drink a glass of water was an enormous effort which caused him to vomit.

Mid-afternoon, his phone rang downstairs and was answered by his flatmate who called up to him.

'Jim, it's June!'

Jim had met June at a rock-climbing event the previous Saturday. Tall, attractive and positive, she radiated a strong and yet sweet air of determination. Just his type, or rather the type he wanted, but he thought she was 'much too good' for him. On Saturday, he had just about managed to open with a few stammering words, but had come to a stop as her friends appeared and took over the conversation.

'June?'

He ran down the stairs and eagerly picked up the phone.

'Jim, are you free tonight?'

They had a wonderful evening together. When Jim finally got home very late that night, his temperature was down to a normal 37°C (98.5°F). And he wasn't in the least bit tired. He returned to his studies as normal the following morning, and felt fresh and invigorated in his work.

Let's look at the details of Jim's story. Jim was increasingly distressed with the low grades and the possibility of never becoming an engineer. Those feelings plagued him every time he attended a lecture, every time he took part in a tutorial, and every time he was together with participants performing better than he was. This situation was creating the state of chronic stress. As his pre-exam panic level rose, he was infected by influenza and a continually rising feverish body temperature. The totally impartial thermometer proved his fever. He also had plenty of evidence of vomiting. Then, unexpectedly, the girl of his dreams telephoned him. The vomiting stopped and his body temperature dropped back to normal without any medication. And it stayed normal – he felt great!

ACTIVITY 8.1

In groups, discuss a situation where you or someone you know found that good news encouraged good health.

Research study: Kiecolt-Glaser et al. (1984)

This anecdote parallels the findings of a study by Kiecolt-Glaser et al. with 49 male and 26 female first-year medical students. The relationship between stress and infectious disease is the subject of this study, with medical students at Ohio State University College, USA as participants.

Aim

To investigate the effect of the stress of important examinations on the functioning of the system that protects us from disease.

Procedure

The physiological relationship between stress and disease-susceptibility works in the following way. Biologically, a person's endocrine and blood systems work together to confront **antigens**, such as bacteria, viruses and cancerous cells. Being stressed can make the individual more vulnerable to disease, as higher levels of the stress-associated cortisol hormone reduce the effectiveness of the immune system. The bloodstream carries **T-cells**, which are a subtype of white blood cells that have the power of locking themselves onto antigens, multiplying and destroying them. However, a high level of stress-induced cortisol lowers the level of T-cell production, putting the person at far more risk of antigen attacks.

This is the first major biological investigation of the effect of stress on the weakening of the immune system in which the participants were human. Until then, this relationship had been investigated with animals only.

In this study, the **acute stressor** that was the subject of the investigation was the forthcoming first-year examinations taking place in a month's time. Would T-cell counts be substantially lower during the high-stress examination period?

The students gave two blood samples, the first a month before the exams, and the second immediately after completing the first two examinations. It was hypothesised that the T-cell count would be significantly lower in the second sample. That would mean a poorer functioning immune system as a result of exam stress.

All 75 participating students were in good health and were volunteers; there was no coercion to get involved. In order to reduce the intervention of pre-existing conditions, each student

Antigens: harmful bacteria, viruses and cancerous cells.

T-cells: subtype of white blood cells that have the power of locking themselves onto antigens, multiplying and destroying them.

Acute stressor: a stress-causer that does not last long, and might require immediate attention.

was given a questionnaire to determine whether they lived high- or low-stress lives apart from their studies, and whether they had suffered loneliness to a substantial degree. Both these factors tend to increase cortisol levels, and would have to be taken into account before establishing the immediate exam situation as the cause of stress.

Figure 8.2 What hormones are at work to give them every possible chance?

Results

The results showed a significantly lower T-cell count in the post-exam blood samples. This showed that the acute exam stress did indeed reduce the power of the students' immune systems. It was also shown that those reporting higher-stress lifestyles and loneliness had even lower T-cell counts than the other participants. That appeared to support the evidence that both long-term stress and lack of social support made people more susceptible to illness. As such, it strongly supports the biopsychosocial model's incorporating psychological as well as somatic elements as determinants of health.

Conclusion

This study indicates that persistent and seemingly never-ending stress causes an increase in cortisol, which not only leads to depression and memory problems, but also to a decrease in the number of T-cells that cause the immune system to weaken.

Strengths of the study

Its longitudinal and empirical nature: the same people were the source of data for the control and the test situation. The study also sought to take into account the stressful realities of individual participants that were independent of the acute stress of the examinations. Additionally, the study was ecologically valid as the exam was part of the students' real-life situation. Moreover, the degree of stress was established by the clinical markers of T-cell counts rather than observing whether or not people were unwell.

Limitations of the study

There are problems of generalising it to a wider population, as it was conducted on young people who were very likely of well-above average health levels and cognitive capacities to cope with acute stress. It is possible that a sample that represented the national population would have shown even lower T-cell counts immediately after an equally stressful event. In addition, although the study was designed to show cause and effect, it may have not completely taken into account the differences in individual students' cognitive perception of stress and their capacities for coping with stress.

Can stress be measured?

People often say that they are stressed when dealing with sudden changes in their routines, circumstances and lifestyles. The changes can be profound, such as personal injury, being fired from a job and getting married, or they may be less disturbing, such as changing eating habits, going on a foreign vacation or a family get-together.

Does such stress cause illness? The work of Holmes and Rahe (1967) focuses on the observation that stress does frequently cause illness. This is especially true when stress involves strong shifts in the ways and circumstances that people do things.

The purpose of Holmes and Rahe's research was to determine which particular life-changing situations were perceived as major stressors and which were more minor stressors. Major stressors would be likely to result in illness even when occurring in isolation. Minor stressors would also be likely to result in illness when occurring in combination with a major stressor or several other minor stressors.

The **Holmes–Rahe Social Readjustment Scale** measures the degree of stress-severity that specific stressors cause to the typical individual. It works on the basis of comparing the stressor with what is perceived to be the greatest stressor an average person will face: the death of a spouse.

The scale was devised by giving participants a very wide range of stressful events and asking them to tick those which they had recently experienced. They then rated the events according to how much time they thought it would take to readjust and accommodate the stressor.

The researchers found a high degree of participants' agreement in perceptions of the degree of stress. That was also true of different cultures within the USA, including African and Hispanic people. Similar patterns were found with Japanese and Malaysian groups in their own countries.

The maximum stressor score went to the most stressful event – death of a spouse (100). Divorce rated at 73, marriage at 50, dismissal from work at 47, outstanding personal achievement at 28, and Christmas, 12.

The higher the score, the greater the stress. 150 points over one year puts the person at risk for stress-related illness. High risk occurs at 300 points and over.

Holmes-Rahe Social Readjustment Scale: the degree of stress-severity that specific stressors cause to the typical individual.

Life Event	Value	Life Event	Value
Death of Spouse	100	Trouble with In-Laws	29
Divorce	73	Spouse Begins or Stops Work	26
Marital Separation	65	Begin or End School	26
Jail Term	63	Change in Living Conditions	26
Death of Close Family Member	63	Revision of Personal Habits	25
Personal Injury or Illness	53	Trouble with Boss	23
Marriage	50	Change in Work Hours	20
Fired at Work	47	Change in Residence	20
Marital Reconciliation	45	Change in Schools	20
Retirement	45	Change in Recreation	19
Change in Health of Family	44	Change in Church Activities	19
Pregnancy	40	Change in Social Activities	18
Sex Difficulties	39	Change in Sleeping Habits	16
Gain New Family Member	39	Change in Eating Habits	15
Business Readjustment	39	Vacation	13
Change in Financial State	38	Christmas	12
Death of a Close Friend	37	Minor Violations of the Law	11

Figure 8.3 Holmes-Rahe Social Readjustment Scale

Cognitions: the ways in which the individual mentally processes stimuli and information.

Dispositional attribution: the degree to which people attribute their own health-detrimental realities to their own personality.

Health beliefs: the degree to which an individual believes they are capable of being able to make the necessary behavioural changes to improve personal health.

ACTIVITY 8.2

Working in groups of three or four, estimate your general level of stress on a scale of 0 to 10. Suggest a descriptor for your level.

Next, work out your level of stress on the Holmes-Rahe Scale.

Then, in groups, compare results and discuss how far the levels of stress estimates correspond with the levels on the Holmes-Rahe Scale.

Show two strengths and two weaknesses of the Holmes-Rahe Scale that have come out of the group experience.

The findings of the Holmes-Rahe research on stressors showed broadly similar findings among those interviewed. However, they are not always true for every individual. For example, there are people who find being in prison less stressful than indicated on the scale. For some, the predictability and stability of life in jail could be a relief when compared with the stresses of the uncertainties in the outside world.

Having considered the workings of the biopsychosocial model and measurement of stress, we proceed to consider its operation in the next two sections: the nature of dispositional factors and health belief, and risk and protective factors.

8.1.2 Dispositional factors and health beliefs

The concepts of dispositional factors and health beliefs stem from a person's self-efficacy, meaning the degree to which the individual believes they can participate in society in particular activities. Self-efficacy beliefs are **cognitions**, which determine whether pro-health behaviours will be initiated, how much effort will be expended, and how long they will be sustained when facing changes, obstacles and failures. Generally, the higher the self-efficacy, the higher the **dispositional attribution**. This means the degree to which they will attribute their own health-detrimental realities to their own personality, whether in stress or addictive habits, and apply positive **health beliefs**, taking and persisting in the necessary steps to maintain behavioural change. In contrast, individuals with a relatively low level of self-efficacy will tend to attribute their health-detrimental lifestyle to situational or external factors, such as the inability to distance oneself from stress or stop addictive behaviour.

Within the area of stress, dispositional factors influencing health beliefs include the following:

- Perception of the stressor: how you perceive the stressor that you face (primary appraisal).
- Self-efficacy: how you assess the coping skills and resources that you can use to deal with the stress (secondary appraisal).
- Your degree of capacity to relate to past-experienced stresses. If those stresses were chronic and negative, this element could form serious psychological barriers to health improvements.
- Your perceived degree of social support: the encouragement of a friend or confidante that you can trust can promote positive health beliefs.
- Your level of desire to effect positive health change: for example, studies indicate that people working in lower-grade positions in huge bureaucracies for a long time are likely to experience chronic stress as they have a lower dispositional attribution stemming from a low self-efficacy. They will tend to resign themselves to the stressful situation and reluctantly accept the health consequences.

Perceptions of stressors and self-efficacy: primary and secondary appraisals

Cognitively, it is not the actual stressor that determines how your physiology will respond, but your overall assessment of it. Your reading of the situation will also affect your emotional and behavioural reactions.

An exemplary situation would be a full-day, demanding cross-country hike with your school or sporting community. As you make your way to the bus, it starts to rain heavily. Consider the two scenarios:

- You do not like hiking, but you feel that you have to go because everyone else is taking part. The rain 'stressor' will arouse the emotions of resentfulness and sulkiness, with the behavioural reaction of looking for ways to stay in the bus rather than hike.

- You do like hiking and have been looking forward to the trip. The rain 'stressor' will arouse the emotions of 'let's do it anyway' and your behaviour will direct to persuading the less enthusiastic to join in.

In deciding to discourage the hike

In deciding to encourage the hike

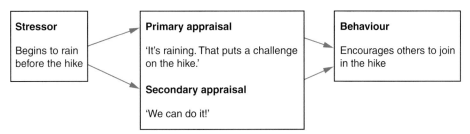

Figure 8.4 Transactional model

The **transactional model of stress** (Lazarus and Folkman, 1984) structures these interactions between stress appraisals and stress responses. The cognitive assessment of the stressor influences the extent and nature of the response, whether it is physiological, cognitive and/or behavioural. As Figure 8.4 shows, the model sees the cognitive stress-coping mechanism as a two-way transaction between the individual and the environment.

Thus, in the rain's interfering with the hiking arrangements, the individual in the first scenario sees the rain and appraises it as an unwelcome source of stress. That is the first part of the transaction. The environment lashing rain against the window is the second part of the stress transaction, from the opposite direction. Then comes the 'I can't deal with this' secondary appraisal, from the same direction as the first.

The individual in the second scenario also sees the rain, but primary-appraises it as a bearable if not an actually welcome source of stress. There is the same environment lashing the same rain against the same window. But the secondary appraisal applies confidence in self-reliance, resilience and a desire for adventure, rather than self-doubt, apprehension and reticence.

Research study: Evans and Kim (2013)

Aim

To investigate the long-term relationship between the **chronic stressors** of past-experienced childhood poverty, and the present adult capacity of the same people to regulate their emotions. These faculties are located in two parts of the brain: the prefrontal cortex and the amygdala.

Transactional model of stress: the cognitive stress-coping mechanism is viewed as a two-way transaction between the individual and the environment.

Chronic stressors: stress causers that are constant, create worry and last for a long time.

Procedure

A total of 54 adults aged 24 years participated. They included those who had suffered poverty aged nine, but were not living in needy circumstances at the current time. There were also people who were currently on very low incomes, though they were not economically deprived at the age of nine.

All were shown a series of images that were designed to arouse negative emotions. The participants were then given exercises in emotional control, which were being monitored electronically by the use of fMRI imaging.

Results

Those who suffered poverty when aged nine were significantly lacking in the ability to control emotions as a 24-year-old. In contrast, those suitably provided-for at nine were far more successful in the fMRI-monitored emotional-control exercises, even though some them were currently experiencing poverty as adults.

Conclusion

The long-term effects of chronic stress experienced through childhood poverty were likely to include emotional disregulation with negative psychological health consequences. This study thus indicates that chronic stresses experienced through childhood may well create a high capacity to relate to childhood-experienced stresses, which in turn weakens dispositional elements that can promote a strong health belief.

Strengths of the study

The study's strengths include the relatively large number of 24-year-old participants given the expensive fMRI technology used, and that the recorded biological correlates in the pre-frontal cortex and amgydala indicated different degrees of control of emotions in response to the images.

Limitations of the study

The study depended on the accuracy of the childhood memories reported by the young adults. In addition, not all children react to similar degrees of poverty in the same ways.

Figures 8.5 and 8.6 They live in the same country, but which child is likely to be under a higher level of chronic stress?

Degree of perceived social support

Resilience means recovering reasonably quickly after an unpleasant and painful situation, such as moving to a new school in a different country, failing an important examination and losing a university place, being a victim of crime, breaking up a romantic relationship or the sudden death of a loving pet. Even very resilient people do not recuperate instantly from such situations, but they adapt to their new realities in a reasonable timeframe and then manage to continue with life. In other words, they absorb the pain, and presently 'pick themselves up' and 'bounce back'.

Previous research has shown that resilience in belonging to a group can help to give a more balanced perspective and the capacity to come to terms with such difficult circumstances.

Research study: Graber et al. (2015)

Aim

To research the role of social support as a stress–coping strategy and thus health-promoting strategy. Does having a best friend during hard times make a substantial difference and make a person more resilient?

Procedure

This study surveyed 409 students of both genders aged 11 to 19 in a poor socio-economic district of Yorkshire, UK. All students completed self-reporting surveys. These had three main objectives:

1   to provide a detailed assessment of the nature of their closest friendship

2   to indicate their levels of resilience in unpleasant situations such as those above

3   to investigate their means of coping with their problems. Did they 'bounce back' in a reasonable period of time and if so, what means did they use towards recovery? Did the presence or absence of a best friend make a substantial difference?

Results

The results showed that there was indeed a positive correlation between the perceived quality of the best-friend relationship and the degree of resilience. Those perceiving higher-quality levels of friendship had a greater degree of social support and thus coped with stress more easily. They were more inclined to talk things over rather than use an externalised coping strategy that used the situational frame in blaming their misfortune on others. They were thus able to bring a more positive set of health beliefs to cope with their circumstances.

Unexpectedly, the study found a small but significant difference between male and female participants. In contrast to the boys, the girls in best-friend situations were somewhat more likely to experiment with risky behaviour such as alcohol or drugs. Boys in established male–male friendships were able to discuss personal concerns with each other, with mutual trust and supportiveness. Friendships typically grew out of activities together, and were based on mutual respect. That indeed increased their resilience and coping strategies.

Conclusion

The higher the quality of the friendship, the greater the resilience. This work suggested that having a best friend was a resource for coping with stress that was accessible to most young people.

Strengths of the study

• Its ecological validity. It was carried out in a lower socio-economic region, where young people face more uncertainties and setbacks in academic achievement, employment prospects, and physical and mental health.

• The sample was substantially large.

Limitations of the study

- It was correlational, raising the issues of cause and effect. It may be that those with a higher degree of pre-existing resilience were best placed psychologically to attract best friends in the first place. It was that resilience that attracted the best friend, not the best friend that built up the resilience. Conversely, those without a best friend may have had inherently poorer coping capacities that in turn would have made them a poorer best friend.

- It was based on self-reporting, with the possible issues of demand characteristics affecting the responses.

- The age group and the relatively homogenous socio-economic status of the participants would limit the study's capacities for being applied to situations with different age-ranges, financial resources and cultures.

Level of desire to effect positive health change

The Whitehall I and Whitehall II studies examined below indicate that it is not the employee's actual workload and responsibilities that increases the chance of coronary heart disease, but their perception of being a mere operative in a huge bureaucracy. This may well indicate negative dispositional factors, together with low self-efficacy leading to poor health beliefs giving little desire to improve one's working environment.

Research study: the Whitehall Studies

At the Palace of Westminster, national policy is formed and decided in the people-elected House of Commons and modified by the upper-chamber House of Lords. Their directives are carried out at nearby Whitehall and its satellites throughout the UK and even beyond. Whitehall is the street and district of central government departments. Its work includes administrative activities, such as aspects of foreign policy, border controls, education, health, livestock and agriculture, and patents.

Figure 8.7 Putting British government policies into practice

The civil service recruits according to ability. Those wishing to enter on the fast track to promotion face very stiff competition. Over a quarter of those on the fast track are Oxford or Cambridge University graduates and selection is much prized. However, only a small minority are accepted for the fast track. Most employees work within the civil service's well-defined hierarchy, which is a complex multi-faceted system to put government directives into practice and is ultimately answerable to the Queen.

Typical work in the civil service involves producing and modifying policy documents, generating reports, and associated research tasks and data analysis. Much of it requires face-to-face dealing with the public. And within each department is the usual range of work found at any large business, including human resources and finance.

As within all organisations there are a number of stressors that those who work for the civil service typically experience, which include the following points:

- Constant working within the bureaucratic community and mentality means that people 'talk the same' despite differences in cultural background and skin colour. That has been linked with social stressors.

- The risk-aversion and slow-moving pace of government work encourages effective conformity rather than diversity and creativity. That has been associated with cognitive stressors.

- There are frustrations in imposing the policies of the government of the day when you do not agree with them. As an employee, the civil service demands that your face shows complete policy neutrality. For example, you are working on border controls. You suffer chronic stress in regularly refusing people you think are worthy of asylum, but whose particular circumstances do not match the official government criteria of an asylum seeker. These issues are likely to create both cognitive-based and socially-based stressors.

- Civil servants can be moved to an entirely different department at very short notice, typically over a six-month period.

- Not all cohort leaders sufficiently support those working under their direction.

- A feeling, mainly in the lower civil service grades, of being a cog in the machine, just another person who carries out orders according to specifications. In short, there is a lack of job autonomy, with no sense of being part of the decision-making process. This final stressor is very much cognitively-rooted.

These realities made the British civil service the object of study in researching how the chances of a worker having a long and healthy life depend on their position in the work hierarchy.

There were two studies, which were carried out by Marmot and team at University College, London. These are currently referred to as Whitehall I (1967–77) and Whitehall II (1985 onwards).

Aim of Whitehall I and Whitehall II

To investigate the relationship between position in the civil service hierarchy and the likelihood of heart failure.

Procedure for Whitehall I

Data was collected from nearly 20 000 male employees over ten years. The data used came from the participants' self-reporting which was framed within a very detailed questionnaire, eliciting information on medical treatment, respiratory symptoms, smoking and physical/leisure activities. Each participant additionally went through a thorough physical procedure to supplement medical data.

Results

The risk of death from coronary heart disease was twice as high among the lowest grades in jobs such as doorkeepers and messengers than at the highest levels with senior policy-makers and administrators.

That was counterintuitive. The findings went against the popular wisdom that more responsibility carries more life-threatening stress. Whitehall I indicated the opposite. It revealed an inverse social gradient in health. The higher up the occupational ladder, the *smaller* the chance of a heart attack. Fast-track promotion would promote health rather than menace health.

Conclusion

The researchers found that those in the lower grades of the civil service were reporting their stress in terms of lack of job autonomy. With that would have followed a relatively low level of disposition to effect positive health change (the cog-in-the-machine feeling described above). In contrast, those with a level of control and predictability within the work situation suffered a much lower degree of stress, with an accompanying higher degree of self-efficacy promoting a higher level of disposition to effect positive health practice and change.

Strengths of the study

This was a well-monitored longitudinal study, with a large number of participants. It used questionnaires designed to elicit detailed data on the health situation of each participant.

Limitations of the study

Whitehall I was criticised for its correlational base. It showed the inverse social gradient of health, but did not demonstrate cause and effect. That was one of the reasons for the follow-up study Whitehall II.

Procedure of Whitehall II

Beginning in 1985, the study is a longitudinal work still in progress and is being moved from phase to phase every few years.

Unlike Whitehall I, all the sample 7000-plus participants were screened to ensure that they had no record of heart disease prior to the study. Thus Whitehall II was designed to be a cause-and-effect study. It would be harder to argue that heart attacks were due to pre-existing conditions.

Data on the health of each of the participants was obtained though self-reporting questionnaires and health screenings, in co-operation with the UK National Health Service. That was particularly important for verifying participant self-reporting on personal medical conditions, which were based on a questionnaire sent home every five years.

Results

The final data is continuing to show a significant inverse social gradient in health, with the lowest grades having a 50% higher frequency of heart disease than the upper grades. None of the participants had heart problems before joining the civil service.

Conclusion

In analysing the questionnaires, some of the differences were found to be due to the higher rates of smoking, unsuitable nutrition and lack of vigorous exercise among the lower grades. However, the significantly recurring factor emphasised by those participants was the feeling of a lack of job autonomy in the frequently changing nature of the bureaucratic work. Those in the higher grades had a greater sense of being in control of their work, which in turn had a positive impact on their health. They did not have to take orders on how and in what timeframe tasks had to be performed. Indeed, a follow-up study on Whitehall II participants compared the early morning cortisol levels of workers in different grades. On awakening, the higher grades and lower grades showed similar cortisol levels. But within half an hour, especially on a work day, the lower grades showed a significantly higher level than the higher grades. Again, the reverse social gradient.

Strengths of the study

The participants were selected on the basis of no pre-existing heart maladies at the start of the study in 1987. It was, and is continuing as a longitudinal study, with the oldest participants now in their 80s. It incorporates elements that show that cognition and social factors are intricately bound up with human physiology. Indeed, the study was set up to highlight the elements that would make it easier to show cause and effect. Thus unlike Whitehall I, Whitehall II is not entirely correlational. In addition, all participants belonged to the same hierarchical organisation governed with similar rules, conventions and codes of conduct. Thus they would have been subject to similar levels of stress arising out of strictly imposed controls in carrying out their duties. Moreover, all share common access to similar quality healthcare through the British National Health Service.

Critical thinking

The findings of the Whitehall research studies indicate that people with a greater level of responsibility have a lower risk of heart failure. Yet other jobs with responsibility have higher risks of heart failure. They include doctors, bartenders and emergency service workers such as fire-fighters. Suggest reasons why that might be so.

Limitations of the study

These include some remaining correlational issues. There may well have been other pre-existing factors encouraging heart disease even though the participants showed no symptoms of them at the start of the study in 1987. These could have included poorer nutrition in childhood and stresses unrelated to work. Although these elements were covered in the questionnaires, the researchers were dependent on the accuracy of the self-reporting of the participants. Furthermore, not all the medical records of the participants were actually made available to the researchers, so in many cases they had to rely on the accuracy of the self-reporting.

Finally, there remains the question of how far the Whitehall reverse social gradient for stress-related diseases in the workplace may be generalised to less hierarchically-structured workplaces. The strict pecking order of the Whitehall situation might have actually generated the stress in the first place.

Associated with the study of determinants of health, dispositional factors and health belief, are risk and protective factors. These are considered in the next section.

8.1.3 Risk and protective factors

How likely may an individual be to develop health-threatening behaviours, such as through smoking tobacco, or unprotected sex? Smoking has a high risk of lung cancer, while unprotected sex carries the risk of sexually transmitted diseases.

Risk and protective factors are health determinants that vary from person to person. A **risk factor** is a condition or a variable that promotes undesirable health outcomes, while a **protective factor** is a condition or variable that promotes desirable health outcomes, or at least reduces the risk of negative outcomes.

In teenage experimentation with sexual intercourse, examples of risk factors may be the influence of sexually active peers and high levels of testosterone/oestrogen. Protective factors could include the ability to say no, and living in a culture that does not tolerate extra-marital sexual experience.

This section looks in more detail at risk and protective factors in smoking tobacco. There has been a great deal of research into which are the significant risk factors that increase the likelihood of a teenager taking up smoking. Conversely, the absence of these elements may be considered to be protective factors, decreasing the likelihood that the teenager will start smoking. Current findings include the following points:

- Biological, genetic: the research of Weiss et al. (2008) identified six genes that can affect the brain's likelihood of becoming addicted to **nicotine**.

- Biological, physical: including the degree of discomfort experienced after the effect of nicotine has worn off. These can include feeling irritable, difficulties in falling asleep and craving for another cigarette.

- Biological, cognitive and socio-cultural: childhood experience of high levels of stress, such as physical or verbal abuse, parental separation and the mental illness or imprisonment of a close member of the family (Pampel et al., 2015).

- Biological/cognitive: teenage boys tend to use cigarettes with higher nicotine content, and inhale more deeply than teenage girls. They are also less likely to use e-cigarettes (Johnston et al., 2016).

- Cognitive, desire to avoid weight gain: some teenagers start smoking in the belief that it will reduce their appetite, and that quitting will prompt them to put on weight (Hong and Johnson, 2013).

- Cognitive, perception of risk: this increased a great deal in the present millennium, contributing to the decline of teenage conventional smoking and the increase of e-cigarettes which are perceived as much lower risk (Johnston et al., 2016).

- Cognitive/socio-cultural: not planning to continue school education at college level (Johnston et al., 2016).

Risk factor: a condition or variable that promotes undesirable health outcomes.

Protective factor: a condition or variable that promotes desirable health outcomes, or at least reduces the risk of negative outcomes.

Nicotine: a stimulating substance that attaches itself to the acetylcholine receptors, creating many more such receptor sites in the process and an accompanying craving for more nicotine.

- Socio-cultural: having parents who smoke (Gilman et al., 2009).

- Socio-cultural: having friends who smoke (O'Loughlin et al., 2009).

- Socio-cultural: having parents who are relatively poorly educated (Johnston et al., 2016).

- Socio-cultural: being white, though black teenagers are more likely to smoke cigars (Singh et al., 2016).

In reducing risk, there are protective factors that involve social intervention. We will consider two of them: degree of interaction with programmes designed to combat smoking, and presence of incentives to stop smoking.

One of the main protective factors can be the influence of school-based programmes. These commonly strive to promote an atmosphere where not smoking is the valued and accepted social norm: 'Not smoking is cool.'

The study of Wiborg and Hanewinkel (2002) on primary prevention of child smoking ('Be smart. Don't start') went further and incorporated competition. With over 2000 12- to 13-year-old students in Germany participating from over 100 classes, the test groups entered a competition, with special benefits for classes that would decide to be non-smoking for the six-month period of the study. The result showed that a third of those in the control group smoked, while only a quarter did in the test group. This experiment showed that competitive social pressure has some significant success at preventing young people from beginning to smoke at the age they are judged to be most vulnerable.

Financial incentives have also been shown to be of protective value. This is exemplified by the work of Halpern et al.

Research study: Halpern et al. (2015)

Aim

This study sought to assess the effect of individual-based and group-based incentive programmes in enabling people to quit smoking.

Procedure

Based in the north-eastern states of the USA, participants were 2500 people about to stop smoking. They were employees of healthcare-company CVS Caremark and their relatives and friends. They were randomly assigned to one of four incentive programmes, or to the usual care for stopping smoking. Two of the incentive programmes were individual-based and two were group-based, each group containing six people.

One of the individual-orientated programmes and one of the group-orientation programmes involved an outright reward, paid in conjunction with the research. The sum was $800 for permanently stopping, in practical terms as long as one year. The other two programmes involved each participant depositing $150, non-refundable if resuming smoking within the 12-month period. If successful, the $150 would be returned, plus an additional $650 payout, making $800 in all.

All participants had free access to aids and information on smoking cessation. This included nicotine-replacement therapy.

Results

Those who had invested the initial $150 showed the highest cessation success, at 52%. In contrast, those who had put nothing into the programme were, at 17%, two-thirds less successful, even though they received a larger net payout. The results showed little variation whether the participant was in the individual therapy or in the group therapy.

Strengths of the study

The study included a large number of participants, each of whom reported the desire to quit smoking.

Conclusion

The health incentive programmes used were of particular value to employers as well as employees, particularly where health insurance payments form part of the salary, as they do at CVS. Typically, non-smoking health profiles save companies several thousand dollars per employee.

Limitations of the study

All the participants were employees of one company concerned with healthcare, who may not be representative of the situation of those working in non-healthcare employment. Moreover, it is not easy to accurately determine the pre-existing motivation for cessation prior to participation in the study.

Conclusion

As Halpern concluded: 'The fact that people actively seek to minimise loss is one of several psychological insights that can help supercharge incentive [to stop] programmes without [heavily] increasing their costs.' This research not only opened a way for the company's employees to live more healthily, but also showed a way that the company could reduce its overall costs of its employee health benefits.

SELF-ASSESSMENT QUESTIONS 8.1

1 Define:

   a determinants of health

   b self-efficacy

2 Distinguish between the following:

   a stress and eustress

   b dispositional health attribution and situational health attribution

   c risk factor and protective factor

3 What does the Holmes-Rahe Social Readjustment Scale measure, and on what basis?

4 What, according to the study of Kiecolt-Glaser, were the effects of stress on immunity from infectious diseases?

5 List four dispositional factors that positively affect health belief. Support each factor by a theory or research study.

6 Name two interventionist-based protective initiatives to reduce the risk of starting or continuing to smoke. Show how each factor is supported by research.

Having considered health determinants, the next section considers in more depth why health problems occur, and how prevalent they are.

8.2 Health problems: the example of obesity and its prevalence

Examining the contribution of psychology to identifying and tackling health problems is a huge field. Health issues include those that are rooted in stress, addictions, obesity, chronic pain and sexual behaviours. We will consider **obesity**: the IB requires a study of the explanation and prevalence of one health problem.

Taking the USA as an example, its population divides into three sectors of approximately equal numbers: those with an ideal body weight, those who are merely overweight, and those who are obese. Ideal body weight is commonly measured as a **body-mass index (BMI)** score. This is calculated by dividing the weight of the person in kilograms by the square of the height in metres. A BMI of between 18.5 and 25 is ideal. Above 25 is overweight, and over 30 is obese.

Unlike tobacco intake, nutrition is a necessary function and characteristic of life. The simple cause of obesity is eating more food than the body uses.

Physiological causes of obesity include hormone imbalances such as an underactive thyroid gland, genetic predispositions and pregnancy. Cognitive elements can involve overeating as a means of coping with stress, or to compensate for stopping smoking.

Socio-culturally, sedentary lifestyles including hours on the computer, watching television and travelling by car all consume far less food-supplied energy than manual labour, playing football, and going from place to place by bicycle or on foot. General work and travel-related tiredness encourages the use of packaged food typically high in sugar, starches, and fat, rather than home cooking using fresh and balanced ingredients.

Like smoking, excessive food intake has its own biological, cognitive, and social causes. We proceed to consider each in more detail.

Biological explanation of the development and prevalence of obesity: genetic predisposition

It has been hypothesised, but not absolutely proven, that humans are genetically programmed to overeat when food is available in order to store excessive food as body fat for times of shortage. This worked well during evolutionary, natural selection. Then, the human race was a species of hunter-gatherers and could not rely on a regular supply of food. Personal survival depended on the capacity to live without eating for a long time. Those who could not eat and biologically store excessive quantities of food might not survive. The capacity to overeat and biologically store was essential to grow to the maturity needed to reproduce.

But today that situation is physiologically inappropriate as in relative terms, food is abundant in the developed world. However, easy access to food has been too recent for the associated genes to adapt.

That genes have some role in human propensity to obesity has been shown by the empirical study of Stunkard et al. (1990). Stunkard's team researched 93 pairs of twins who were reared apart, and compared their BMIs. They found that genetic factors accounted for about two-thirds of the variance in their body weight. The conclusion was that there were strong genetic factors in the development and prevalence of obesity, and that genetics played an even greater role in those twins who were slim. There was also a significantly higher BMI similarity among identical (MZ) twins than fraternal (DZ) twins.

However, this study does not locate the precise genetic factor in obesity. It is not clear how far the main factor is the role of genes in metabolism, or the role of genes in generating the number of fat cells. In addition, critics of the role of genes in obesity argue that the phenomenon of widespread obesity has occurred over too short a period for the genetic make-up of the population to have changed substantially.

Today, research in the effect of genetics on obesity is increasingly based on advances in interpreting genetic molecules. This takes into account that scientific understanding of the precise manner in which individual genes affect obesity is in its infancy.

The study of Claussnitzer et al. was designed to test the hypothesis that a variant of the FTO gene has a considerable role in making it difficult for the body to burn off fat.

Figure 8.8 Are we all secretly fighting the same fat-storing gene?

Research study: Claussnitzer et al. (2015)

The knowledge base for the study included the recently discovered importance of the fat mass and obesity-associated FTO gene on chromosome 16 as being part of a chain. Specifically, FTO works as a master-switch that activates two other genes, IRX3 and IRX5. These determine **thermogenesis**, the body's capacity to burn off energy. Previous research indicated that IRX3 and IRX5 switch on in times of shortage, in order to conserve fat when needed. When they are switched off, they allow the body to burn off the excess fat. Thus, a faulty heredity-based FTO gene set-up will keep the fat storage mode switched on and make it more difficult to lose weight.

That had been found after experimental work with mice on a high-fat diet. The test group had their fat-storing genes artificially blocked. They became 50% thinner than other mice. They continued to burn considerable energy when asleep.

Thermogenesis: the capacity of the body to burn-off energy from nutrition, rather than store and accumulate it.

Procedure, results and conclusion

Using a large number of human fat samples carrying both the normal FTO gene and the 'obesity-variant' gene, the researchers found that biochemically blocking the gene's effect did increase energy burning in the human fat cells, and appeared to restore normal metabolism within those cells.

Strengths of the study

It appears to show cause and effect, through genetic modification of the fat-storing genes in the laboratory. It is not based on empirical observation, but actually locates the genes that demonstrated a role in obesity. It also appears to open the potential for ultimately combating obesity through drug-induced genetic-activity modification.

Limitations of the study

The presence of the 'obesity-variant' gene showed significant variations in prevalence. It was found in over 40% of the white European human fat samples, but only in 5% of the fat samples from black people. That suggests that other as yet undiscovered genes may be at work. In addition, the potential of putting this knowledge to work in the form of an obesity-treating drug in humans has the ethical issues common to genetic modification.

Cognitive explanation of the development and prevalence of obesity: unrealistic expectations from dieting

Many obese people use the simple equation:

weight gain = the amount eaten − the amount of energy burnt off.

Their realisation that they are obese prompts them to get to ideal weight with all possible speed. They enthusiastically put themselves on diets and exercise programmes. However, they soon find themselves on a break-restart, break-restart cycle. As a result, their weights suffer the yo-yo effect, going up and down.

The work of Polivy (2001) shows that this cycle is rooted in too immediate and too unrealistic expectations. When on a diet, especially one that goes to below 1500 calories per day, a person becomes extremely responsive to external cues such as the smell of food, or feeling emotionally down. That can result in a small breach in the programme, such as having an ice cream or missing a session at the gym. Polivy refers to the spirit of the initial mistake as the 'what the hell' effect. That little 'transgression' leads to an all-out binge on high-calorie items with a feeling of utter failure, and restarting the diet only to end on the same cycle.

This combination of false hopes and unattainable criteria for success can explain lack of achievement in dieting and an overall weight gain rather than weight loss.

Polivy's work stresses the importance of moderation in a weight-losing programme. It also includes developing the patience to work towards ideal weight through a series of moderate, attainable goals. These have to be combined with suitable coping skills for dealing with the virtually inevitable small breaches of the programme that will occur.

Socio-cultural factor explanation of the development and prevalence of obesity: sedentary lifestyles and overindulgent relatives

The work of Prentice and Jebb (1995) studied changes in physical activity in a UK sample. The researchers acknowledged that there had been a significant decrease in food intake since 1970. Yet the population as a whole was gaining rather than losing weight. The increase in obesity appeared to be in line with aspects of the increasingly sedentary lifestyle: increase in car-ownership and hours of television viewing. However, the data they used was correlational and thus unable to show a cause-and-effect relationship.

The Prentice and Jebb research was followed by a wider study conducted by the British Foresight Report on Tackling Obesities (2007), which concluded that obesity was an inevitable consequence of a society flooded with energy-dense cheap foods, labour-saving devices, motorised transport and sedentary work.

In addition, obesity is fast becoming a problem within developing countries that are experiencing a modest rise in standards of living. More money means more access to obesity-promoting foodstuffs, as exemplified by the work of Li et al. (2015) in China.

INTERNATIONAL FOCUS

Grandparents and child obesity in China: Li et al. (2015).

Health authorities in China are alarmed at the growing rate of child obesity. Is that the fault of the grandparents?

Most research into child obesity is based on Western populations and tends to emphasise the role of the parents. In contrast with the USA, where 34% of the adult population is obese with a BMI of 30+, China is relatively low at around 5% in rural areas, but rising to over 20% in some cities. This is likely to rise with increasing rural-urban migration and access to Western-type fast-foods and labour-saving convenience devices.

The study of Li et al. focused on the role of grandparents in China. Grandparents were important for three reasons. Firstly, there is a national cultural tendency for grandparents to be heavily involved in the day-to-day bringing up of the children. Secondly, they were born early enough to remember the widespread famine and outright starvation in China, especially during the farming disasters in the Great Leap Forward of 1958–61. Thirdly, child health-promotion programmes tended to be directed towards parents and teachers, rather than the grandparents who were essential child care figures. Bear in mind that ageing grandparents tend to stay within the family home as China has no compulsory national pension system.

This was a largely qualitative study conducted in a total of four elementary school districts across the socio-economic spectrum in two cities. Its purpose was to examine the degree of association between children's objectively-measured weight status and reported health behaviours, and the presence and role of grandparents within the household.

The children were randomly selected and were between eight and ten years old. There was a total of 17 focus groups, and they involved parents, grandparents, school staff and people selling food within easy reach of the school.

The results of the study showed that children who were mainly looked after by their grandparents were significantly more likely to be obese and consume sugary processed foods than those more under the care of their parents or other adults. And where the children were mainly cared for by the parents, the probability of obesity rose substantially if two or more grandparents lived in the household.

The study concluded that grandparent involvement in child care is a major factor promoting childhood obesity in China. It highlighted the widespread situation of the grandparents' attitude being in conflict with parents and teachers, such as minimising child involvement in energy-consuming household chores. The study recommended that government initiatives for tackling child obesity should also be directed at the grandparents. This is especially important as it is considered culturally unacceptable for a child to say no to a grandparent.

The study's strengths are that it incorporated schools of different socio-economic status. By using focus groups and in-depth interviewing, it was possible to establish cause and effect within data that otherwise might have been correlational. It also sought to filter out any other stakeholders (such as local food salespersons) whose interests have had an impact.

Its limitations include its cultural background where in China grandparents take a comparatively large role in child care. Also, it shared the common problems associated with demand characteristics at interview and reluctance on the part of stakeholders interviewed to admit their role in the problem; it put blame on the grandparents.

NEWSFLASH

Pacific nations should consider a 'fat tax' on junk food, says leading doctor.

Not so long ago, a visitor to island of the southern Pacific would be sharing fresh fish, breadfruit, root crops, and local fruits and vegetables with the physically active, hard-working local population.

Today's Pacific islanders want highly-processed imported foods with white flour, sugar and fat. Soft drinks, low-grade fatty meat, instant and canned food; whatever, so long as it's tasty. It won't help to promote the traditional healthy island diet. Imported food is fun.

Cook Island has the world's highest obesity rate. At 46%, that means that almost every second person has a BMI over 30. Not far behind are the islands of Palau and Tonga.

Figure 8.9 Should the market sport the green flag for healthy food?

By 2015, more and more leading Pacific doctors were actively supporting the proposal to place a fat tax on junk food. Their statistics showed that nearly half the region's adult population has symptoms of hypertension, heart disease and diabetes. It was also observed that schools were sending out mixed messages: teaching good eating habits as part of health education and then selling sugared soft drinks and junk food in the school canteen.

There is growing pressure on the islanders' governments to tax junk food and drink. Their national healthcare systems are small, with limited funds and resources.

Fiji, Samoa and Nauru have shown the way by taxing soft drinks. They are now considering regulating the advertising of junk food on television.

Figure 8.10 Should the processed food shelves sport a red flag and a government warning for unhealthy food?

Find two countries other than those in the Newsflash, one developed and one developing, where governments have attempted to regulate obesity. For each country:

1 describe the prevalence of obesity

2 explain the ways in which the government attempts to reduce the national rate of obesity

3 assess how successful the government initiatives have been, and are likely to be.

We will now consider how health may be promoted and evaluate existing initiatives.

8.3 Health promotion

Health promotion may be defined as the encouragement of people to change their lifestyle to reach their optimum level of health. Health promotion empowers people to choose, manage and maintain a healthy lifestyle.

Any health promotion programme is likely to have the components of education and support to improve physical activity and nutrition, and avoid threats to health such as alcohol or drugs.

Psychology has a distinct role in health promotion for the following reasons. It is accepted that healthy living is in the interests of the public. Sickness and general ill health cause suffering and reduced quality of life for the individual. They also affect the community by causing absence from work, and medications are far more expensive than keeping healthy. Health promotion also takes into account that in general, people want to be healthy and want their family, friends and associates to be healthy as well. This is especially the case if they perceive prolonged suffering in not being so. With suitable encouragement and continued support, many will strive to change their lifestyles to include taking regular exercise, and stopping smoking and excessive intake of unhealthy food and alcohol.

Although all people want to have a high quality physical lifestyle, many face considerable cognitive barriers. Health psychologists endeavour to identify the barriers and why they exist.

Some of those barriers are:

'I'm too busy, and my children or grandchildren come first.'

'Every time I dieted, I ended up putting on more weight than I lost.'

'I just hated physical education at school.'

'Does that mean no fast food?'

'I get irritated quickly. When I feel like that, a cigarette is very soothing.'

8.3.1 The work of psychology in promoting health

The health psychologist will seek to help individuals negotiate their cognitive barriers towards better health. That will include helping the person to face unpleasant and failed attempts to improve health.

A health psychologist usually works as an educator, counsellor and supporter on a regular basis. Education enables the patient to open their mind to the need for a positive change of health habits. Counselling will focus on identifying the barriers, bearing them in mind when planning an individual health improvement programme. It may well be based on CBT. Regular support will strive to maintain these initial lifestyle improvements until they become part of the patient's way of life. That can take many months, especially when the patient's initial enthusiasm begins to fade.

Although every individual's journey towards health maximisation is different, the psychological framework for improvement can be placed within health-promotion models. We will focus on two of them that are widely in use: the **Health Belief Model** (Rosenstock et al., 1988) and the **Stages of Change Model** (Prochaska and DiClemente, 1983).

The Health Belief Model (Rosenstock et al., 1988)

The Health Belief Model focuses on two simultaneous sets of forces that motivate the individual to address behaviour adverse to health, such as smoking.

The first set of forces comes from the person. With smoking, for example, how far do you believe your well-being is in danger by smoking? Do you believe that you should give up smoking? Do you see benefits by not smoking? Do you believe you can give up smoking, given the benefits?

The second set of forces comes from the environment. Many societies radiate a clear anti-smoking message with heavy taxes on cigarettes, strict limitations on smoking in public places and government health warnings on the cigarette packet.

The Health Belief Model holds that a person is most likely to stop an anti-health practice where the two sets of forces are at their most powerful. That is where high motivation to give up smoking combines with a powerful message from the environment to stop smoking.

This has been shown by the work of Quist-Paulsen and Gallefors (2003). This experimental study focused on two groups of heart patients that were stopping smoking. The control group was given supportive group counselling. The members of the test group were given additional individualised phone support from the nursing staff, who aroused fear by warning about the serious heart-disease-related dangers of relapsing into smoking. The result was that 57% of the test group, but only 37% of the control group, managed to stop. The rest could not avoid relapsing into smoking. The ethical issues of fear arousal in the test group were justified by the substantially higher rate of successful stopping at the end of the programme, and the support offered by the nurses such as advising medication to stop the craving.

Health Belief Model: a person is most likely to stop an anti-health practice when they have high self-motivation and receive powerful messages from the environment.

Stages of Change Model: a person must go through six stages of change to permanently break an anti-health habit: pre-contemplation, contemplation, preparation, action, maintenance and termination.

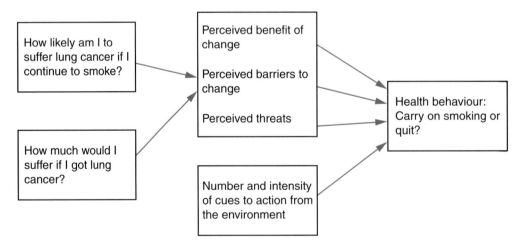

Figure 8.11 The Health Belief Model as applied to smoking

The strengths of the Health Belief Model include the emphasis on identifying the paradigms that need to shift in order to make a health-improvement programme effective. The paradigms behind the perceived barriers to change may be identified and focused on by psychologists. The model, which may be applied to a wide variety of health-adverse behaviours, also emphasises the importance of being in an environment that consistently supports maintaining cessation and the journey towards improved health.

The Health Belief Model, however, assumes that people make rational choices on matters concerning their health. It has the limitations of reaching out only to those who can access the relatively expensive services needed to support a personal or group programme. Those on smaller incomes may not be able to afford the subscriptions to a suitably supportive environment, such as a fitness centre.

The Stages of Change Model (Prochaska and DiClemente, 1983)

The Stages of Change Model (revised since 1983) focuses on six stages of change that a person must go through to permanently break a habit. With the example of needing to lose weight:

1   Pre-contemplation: 'I know I'm overweight, but that's me.'

2   Contemplation: 'I do need a programme of diet and regular exercise, but I'm not quite ready for it yet.'

3   Preparation: 'I will join a thrice-weekly programme at the local gym, and I'm booking an appointment with a dietician.'

4   Action: 'I'm going to an exercise class in the gym on Mondays, Wednesdays and Fridays immediately after work. And it's five regular small meals and three litres of fresh water per day instead of snacking all the time. The kilos of fat just roll off.'

5   Maintenance: 'I've stopped snacking on junk food and soft drinks. I get very tired after weight-training, but the results are worth it. It's willpower and persistence every hour, every day. I'm still thinking about chocolate biscuits, but the pleasure isn't worth suffering the weight-losing exercises all over again.'

6   Termination: 'My weight is ideal. I look great. Unhealthy food and sugared drinks don't interest me anymore.'

A serious person on a dieting and exercise programme will try to progress from stages 1 to 5. However, willpower and persistence might keep them on track during the busy week at school/work, only to relapse into eating more and not exercising during a lonely weekend. That might mean regression to contemplation or even pre-contemplation.

The Stages of Change Model has the following strengths: like the Health Belief Model, it is adaptable to a wide range of behaviours that threaten good health, and gives a framework for the patient's progress and regressions to be identified and targeted by psychologists. Unlike the Health Belief Model, it does take into account the formidable willpower and persistence needed to maintain a fundamental change in lifestyle.

The model's limitations are that it does not readily include the social and cultural factors that might be involved in habit-changing decisions. Like the Health Belief Model, it assumes that people make rational decisions in matters affecting their health. Unlike the Health Belief Model, it does not place enough weight on the environment cues. These can strongly influence an individual to make an immediate decision to change eating habits, join an exercise class, or stop smoking. The individual senses that it is a case of changing now or facing catastrophe.

The importance of the sudden realisation of facing catastrophe is strongly indicated by the research of West and Sohal (2006).

Research study: West and Sohal (2006)

This study compared the process of change involved in ex-smokers, and those who seriously attempted to stop but relapsed at least once. They found limited evidence to support the spectrum of change from stages 1 to 5 above. Indeed, they found that it was the unplanned efforts to give up smoking (like the cue from the environment that it's 'stop now or die soon', or the influence and support of friends who successfully gave up) that were more effective than those attempts that followed the spectrum. This will now be explored in more detail.

The West and Sohal study was an empirical study carried out in the UK. Adult smokers as a percentage of the adult population had been steadily falling over the previous generation by more than a half, from just under 40% in 1980 to the time of the study, and the number was continuing to fall.

Aim

West and Sohal investigated the precise point at which the smokers most commonly made the decision that resulted in a successful cessation. Was it a long-term plan based on the Stages of Change Model that was behind that decision? Or was giving up smoking more spontaneous, perhaps even based on a sudden, instant decision to stop at that very moment?

This question is of particular value to public health authorities that target their anti-smoking campaigns on the smoking community. Their understanding of the psychology of the giving-up process enables them to interact with it more effectively, encouraging smokers to give up with the greatest success.

Procedure

West and Sohal planned their study on the basis that:

1 One-third of all British smokers tried to stop each year. Most, but not all, soon regressed to smoking.

2 Success in giving up increased the quality of life, and also life expectancy by up to ten years.

3 Anecdotal evidence from the medical world indicated that many successful quitters did not plan giving up in advance. Many decided one day to stop, and they instantly did. They did not go back. That evidence placed doubts on the value of the Stages of Change Model, which promotes the need for passing through cognitive stages to successfully change a health-threatening habit.

West and Sohal interviewed a sample of over 5000 households representative of the different socio-economic groups. Questions for ex-smokers and smokers who had made an attempt to give up were designed to place the respondent on a spectrum, showing the time lag between the decision to give up and the actual achievement. Possible responses ranged from 'I just did it without planning in advance' through to 'I planned to give up quite a few days beforehand' up to 'I planned to give up a few months beforehand', with also a 'don't know' option. They also indicated whether or not they were in the 'still not smoking' category.

Results

The results showed that nearly half the attempts to give up were spontaneous, without advance planning. They also indicated that the attempts that were planned were less successful than those that had been unplanned. Those who were most likely to give up spontaneously were the 55+ age group. Those more likely to give up as a result of planning were in unskilled and semi-skilled occupations rather than in professional and managerial positions.

This does not mean that the Stages of Change Model did not apply to some quitters, but the high propensity of spontaneous giving up prompted West and Sohal to propose an alternative model. That would be applied to encourage those who were potential quitters to do so, suddenly and at once.

Indeed, the nature of the responses prompted West and Sohal to propose that health authorities target giving up smoking on the basis of their proposed model, which they based on 'catastrophe theory'.

Catastrophe theory is where tension has already built up, and a press on the trigger can cause 'the catastrophe' which is a fundamental change out of proportion to the triggered stimulus. In that case, it is the decision to give up. The pre-existing pressure would have become greater because of the negative, anti-smoking messages in the environment, and in conversation. West and Sohal express this as the smoker being psychologically on the 'cusp' of giving up, even though they may not be aware of it. As the mention of smoking arouses accumulated pre-existing anxiety, it takes only one small push (the trigger) to activate a major change (the catastrophe) in the smoker's behaviour, and that is the decision to give up at once. What is happening is not a planned campaign to give up, but a sudden decision to do so, immediately acted on. No smoking from now on!

Thus, the Catastrophe Model is accumulated tension – cusp of giving up – one small anti-smoking prompt – trigger action – gives up smoking (the catastrophe) – soon afterwards needs and uses the support of physiological treatment such as nicotine patches and/or counselling.

Conclusion

Public health campaigns should take the Catastrophe Model as well as the Stages of Change Model into account when getting smokers to give up. West and Sohal recommend that the focus should be on the 'Three Ts':

1 Tension – motivational tension to give up

2 Trigger – final stimulus that fired the smoker into the action of giving up

3 Treatment – immediate access to physiological and psychotherapy support.

Strengths of the study

The strengths of the study included:

- the relatively large sample being duly subdivided into a realistic representation of the nation's population, taking into account the UK's regional and socio-economic variations

- the lengthy interview procedures gave participants the chance to provide details of their journey through the process of giving up.

Limitations of the study

The limitations of the study included the following points:

- The research took place when anti-smoking campaigns and legislation were already very much in the British news, being newly applied to workplaces, public transport and some other areas open to the public. That might have temporarily increased the general awareness of and 'tension' relating to the health-dangers of smoking, causing a higher than usual percentage of the spontaneous among those who decided to give up.

- Many people interviewed were uncertain about what actually triggered the act of giving up, claiming they were in the 'don't know' category. This raises the possibility that many of those who did give a definite response might have acted on demand characteristics to cover up uncertain memory recall.

8.3.2 How effective are various health promotion strategies?

Health promotion is typically conducted by national campaigns, with the environment, the mass media, the workplace and communities all taking part. Many schools insist on healthy food being served at meals and in the school shop. Many schools also forbid smoking on the premises at all times, even by visitors.

We have already seen from the work of Quist-Paulsen and Gallefors (2003) that rates of stopping smoking among heart patients indeed rise when the environment's message to give up becomes more powerful; in this case where counselling sessions are followed by the nursing staff's regular and frequent reinforcing phone calls home.

As well as smoking, tackling widespread obesity is at the forefront of many national and municipal health budgets, and is a key issue for the World Health Organisation. It includes preventive strategies and methods of treatment. These involve promoting healthy eating habits from primary school age, such as Britain's 'Eatwell Plate' and Australia's 'Go for your Life' campaign, succeeded by 'Get Set for Life'. Australia's national initiative is discussed below; it is also supplemented with taxes on highly processed foods, also seen in Hungary and Denmark.

Figure 8.12 Britain's 'Eatwell Plate'

Australia's 'Go for your Life' anti-obesity campaign is primary prevention. Targeted at children under 12 years of age not to become obese in the first place, it promotes the habits of:

- drinking tap water rather than a sugary drink
- decreasing time spent at the screen – on computer games and watching television
- including fruit and vegetables in the lunch box
- limiting 'sometimes' food items, such as chocolates, soft drinks and ice lollies
- daily active physical exercise and play
- walking at least some of the way to school and other activities, such as 'Stride and ride'.

The programme involves local government-funded health professionals working together with primary schools, with an award system. It also provides information to the parents, in order to get their support in enabling optimum nutrition and physical activity in the home.

However, early reviews of the study, such as de Silva-Sanigorski et al. (2010), are not conclusive on this campaign's overall success in combating potential obesity in children.

As well as schools, many companies worldwide run health promotion programmes. It is very much in their interests to do so. Health promotion through the workplace benefits both the company and the employees. It reduces sick-leave absences, employee-borne health-insurance costs, and workers' compensation costs. In addition, having a fitness club in the workplace enables people to meet in a less formal environment. Many places of work have benefits that include sports facilities (often on the premises) and specialised counselling available through human resources.

Figure 8.13 Better health = better work

These programmes tend to include health promotion material on eating habits, smoking and alcohol intake, as well as on exercise and stress management.

A meta-study by Chapman (2005) combined recent studies of health promotion in a large number of very different workplaces. In generalising the findings, he found significantly positive results where the workplace was actively involved in promoting employee health. They included more than a 25% fall in worker sickness and absence from work. That saved the companies considerable sums of money as well as improving the quality of life for the workers. Everybody seemed to have gained.

Beyond the workplace, public initiatives have targeted specific age groups throughout the entire community living within a geographical area. One of the most successful of these projects was the Truth campaign in Florida, USA. Designed to prevent the 12–17 age group from starting to smoke, the campaign went under the theme of 'Truth, a generation united against tobacco'. It was designed by Governor L. Chiles and 600 young people at his Teen Summit on Tobacco Education, and ran from 1998 to 1999. The idea was that teenagers would identify with the successful young people of their age group reaching to potentially successful young people, rather than a campaign imposed from above.

Its purpose was to get young people to believe that smoking was for losers. With a $25 million budget from state sources, it ran a series of posters, billboards and television commercials which showed that the tobacco industry was the way a few greedy business people made their fortunes by destroying the health of young people. Tobacco promotion came from manipulative adults who only cared about money. Tobacco control came from successful young role models who made plenty of appearances within the programme.

Within six months, a telephone survey found that 80% of young people in that state had been reached by the campaign, and that the smoking rate had dropped by 20% in middle schools and 8% in high schools. That placed Truth as one of the most successful campaigns ever to be launched in the USA.

The work of Schum and Gold (2007) studied the Truth campaign, and cited the following reasons for the campaign's success.

1   It was conducted at grass-roots level – being planned by teens for teens, it spoke to teens in ways to which they could readily respond. Their passion for the campaign caught others' attention, very quickly.

2   It established a youth social norm: 'It's not cool to smoke.'

3   It made use of teens' own social networks, which were out of reach of more conventional approaches. It was indeed the teenagers who delivered the message. This highlights the potential of social media health promotion programmes at grass-roots level.

These are vital points to note when planning future health promotion initiatives and strategies.

Although the campaign lost power soon afterwards because of a lack of funding, in 2014 Truth was re-launched as 'Finish it', an ambitious programme enthusing young people to be the generation that completely stops smoking.

RESEARCH IDEA

Choose a child-obesity prevention programme. It may be at your school, in your locality or further afield. Find out its objectives, and examine the resources it uses to achieve its objectives. What are the strengths and weaknesses of the programme? How effective is it overall? What suggestions do you have for improving the programme?

SELF-ASSESSMENT QUESTIONS 8.2

1   What do the following studies indicate about the causes of obesity?
   a   Stunkard et al. (1990)
   b   Claussnitzer et al. (2015)
   c   Polivy (2001)
   d   Prentice and Jebb (1995)
   e   Li et al. (2015)

2   What role does psychology play in the field of health promotion?

3   Describe the contributions made by the following models to health promotion:
   a   the Health Belief Model
   b   the Stages of Change Model

4   Explain what the following studies contribute to understanding health models:
   a   Quist-Paulsen and Gallefors (2003)
   b   West and Sohal (2006)

Chapter summary

1   Health psychology looks at how issues such as stress, substance abuse, addiction, obesity and health promotion may have an impact on the individual's physical welfare.

2   The purpose of health psychology is to enable the physically healthy to stay as healthy for as long as possible, and for those with health issues to begin and regularly continue with suitable treatments. Psychology attempts to understand the barriers to living healthily. It seeks ways to motivate the person to identify the barriers, deal with them and attempt to overcome them effectively.

3   Determinants of health include not just biological but also socio-economic, environmental and psychological factors. All these can influence the health status of individuals or populations.

4   Both dispositional factors and health beliefs tend to stem from a person's self-efficacy.

5   Desirable health outcomes tend to be negatively influenced by risk factors and positively influenced by protective factors.

6   Psychology addresses stress in many ways, including the use of medication, and the encouragement of strongly-supportive human relationships.

7   Means of assistance to enable stopping smoking include nicotine-replacement therapy, financial incentives, and programmes from the workplace and the wider community.

8   Genes can be a severe though not an absolute barrier to tackling obesity. Other roadblocks include unreasonable expectations from dieting, a sedentary lifestyle in the workplace and at home, and the recent mass-availability of unhealthy nutrition in developing countries.

9   Models of health promotion provide some framework for the more effective and personalised delivery of individualised assistance.

Exam-style question

Essay response question

•   Evaluate two health promotion strategies.

Developmental psychology

9

'The lucky ones are those who take every opportunity and turn life experience onto truth seeking adventure. They end up fulfilled with deeper dimensions of pleasure and spirit satisfaction.'
(Sameh Elsayed)

- How do peers, the environment and childhood experiences and circumstances influence cognitive and social development?
- How do attachment figures, gender and social roles, and cognitive maturing affect the individual's development of a sense of personal identity?
- How do cognitive and brain development affect the individual's development as a learner?

Learning objectives

- Outline the roles of diet and human interaction on brain development. (AO1)

- Explain how childhood trauma and resilience may affect young people's social development to various degrees. (AO2)

- Examine how childhood attachments may affect the subsequent forming of human relationships. (AO2)

- Evaluate the different cognitive theories of child development as a learner. (AO3)

- Evaluate socio-cultural theories of factors influencing personal identity. (AO3)

9.1 Developmental psychology: an introduction

Psychologists show a special interest in the process of how and why people develop throughout life. Modern developmental psychology does not focus only on childhood and **adolescence**, but also looks at stages within adulthood and the ageing process. The focus of the IB syllabus, however, is on the early rather than later years.

Our journey through the psychology of human development applies the biological, cognitive and socio-cultural lenses to viewing three specific issues within the field of the human life span.

Developmental psychology is a theoretical and increasingly scientifically-based focus on how children and adults change over time. Developmental psychologists are working towards three goals:

1 To describe the processes in human development that are **normative**, meaning common to humanity rather than specific to an individual.

2 To explain the reasons for those processes.

3 To proactively guide and intervene where needed, enabling the individual to get the best experiences from these changes. Many people's development processes are not normative, but **idiographic**, meaning that they are not easily explained by application of the standard models including those considered in this chapter.

Adolescence: the development period between puberty and adulthood, typically between 12 and 20 years.

Normative human development: where an individual's development processes are within the normal range of the human experience, and may be explained by the application of the standard models.

Idiographic human development: where an individual's development processes are not easily explained by application of the standard models.

Figures 9.1, 9.2, 9.3 and 9.4 How do these activities contribute to the individuals' ongoing personal development?

People change throughout their lives. They change in the way they think of themselves, the people they choose to spend time with, the things they wish to do, and in what gives them satisfaction and pleasure. This chapter considers areas of the theoretical framework behind these changes, and ways in which psychology can assist those changes to become positive ones.

9.1.1 Elements influencing cognitive and social development: the role of peers and play

Peer influence is traditionally associated with teenagers rather than with small children, whose primary social influence is likely to come from their families. In reality, however, many children interact with their peers in nursery-school establishments.

Until the 1950s, it was generally thought that play was a worthless and frivolous children's activity. It was also believed that children essentially think the same way as adults, but with much less competence. Jean Piaget, whose work is examined in Section 9.3.1, proposed that on the contrary, play actively assists the child's cognitive development. This is based on his research indicating that children do not think like inexperienced adults, but in a qualitatively different way from adults.

Piaget understood play as being mainly part of the process of **assimilation** of ideas, which is a vital stage in the learning process. Assimilation is where a child tests out the environment in activities such as climbing a tree or building a sandcastle, according to concepts previously encountered. A child who pretends to put on a policeman's uniform and runs to protect his teddy from an imaginary thief is actively assimilating what he already knows about strangers who enter into homes to steal. These exploratory and role-playing activities involve consolidating ideas in a pleasurable way rather than learning something new.

In addition, children do not passively receive their knowledge, but they are curious, self-motivated and deeply interested in discovering and interacting with their environments. The cognitive benefits of play include the enabling of children to create and operate a world that they can master. The social benefits of play include the experience of working in groups, dealing with conflicts and children learning to speak up for themselves.

Lev Vygotsky (1896–1934), who researched the same area as Piaget, put forward the idea that play can promote as well as consolidate development, in a rich **zone of proximal development**. This means that children learn when mixing with relatively dynamic and experienced peers close by. It is their activities that prompt new areas for exploration: 'Play not so much reflects thought as it creates thought' (Vandenberg, 1986). It is the play that cognitively and socially advances the child's development as well as supports it. Examples include joining in a playground game of more complexity than usual, or joining in with peers who are building and modifying model boats that will sail on the pond without turning over.

Play involves enjoyable activities that are unrelated to survival, production or profit. Parten (1932) classified young children's play modes and activities on the basis of observing American pre-school age children. She identified six categories that related to how the individual child relates to their peers. The further up the scale, the greater degree of involvement, and thus the greater peer-based cognitive and social development:

1 Unoccupied, but observing.

2 Solitary, occupied though unaware of or indifferent to peers. More common in the under-four years rather than the four-plus age group.

3 Onlooker: watches activity and interacts by talking to peers about what is happening rather than actually joining in.

4 Parallel play: similar activities played separately from others. Mimicking rather than play interaction.

5 Associative play: attempted interaction between the individual and the peer group, without fluent social coordination with the group.

6 Co-operative play: where the individual fluently interacts with both the peer group and with the activity.

Assimilation (Piagetian concept): the applying of an existing schema to deal with a new situation.

Zone of proximal development: Vygotskian concept, referring to the area between what the child can achieve without help, and what the child can achieve when stretched by an educator or fellow-student with more knowledge and skills.

These categories are still widely referred to today. Cognitive development can be stimulated in all categories; social development from categories 3 to 6.

Given that interaction with peers at play forms a large part of pre-school child interaction, there have been various studies to investigate whether the child's success in adjusting to formal kindergarten may be correlated with their success in having good relationships with peers.

Research study: Ladd (1990)

Ladd's study looked at the idea of children having, keeping and making friends, and being liked by peers in the classroom.

Aim

To investigate the degree that the quality of children's peer relations can affect their adjustment to school at kindergarten level.

Procedure

The study involved 125 kindergarten children and their teachers. Each child's peer relationships were measured three times: at the beginning of the school year, during the second month, and at the end of the school year. The measures of adjustment on the second and third assessment were based on the child's performance level, anxieties, avoidances and overall feelings about the school. The research controlled for degree of pre-school peer interaction, mental age and gender. The measures of the child's classroom peer relationships were used to predict how well they would continue to fit into the school.

Results

Children with more classroom friends at the beginning of the year were enjoying school significantly more by the second month than those with fewer peer connections. Those who maintained those relationships increasingly enjoyed school and performed better as the year progressed. Those who experienced early peer rejection showed signs of disliking the school situation, a desire to avoid school and poorer performance levels.

Conclusions

The quantity and quality of both pre-school peer relationships and kindergarten peer relationships appear to positively correlate with the quality of school performance, the desire to attend school and the enjoyment of the school experience. Effectively, positive peer relationships (often rooted in playtime when peers interact more freely) positively influence cognitive and social development within the school setting.

ACTIVITY 9.1

Look back on your previous years of schooling. For your first year of schooling, give a mark out of ten for each of the following: quantity and quality of friendships with peers, degree that you enjoyed school and quality of your school performance. Then do the same for all your other years of school. Present your figures as a table. Finally, attempt to find whether your experience shows a correlation between these three variables.

9.1.2 Elements influencing cognitive and social development: childhood trauma and resilience

A child is suffers **deprivation** when their basic physical, emotional and social needs are not taken care of. These can include unsuitable diet due to poverty or parental ignorance, inadequate attention from parents who are struggling with their own issues, and the lack of a primary

Deprivation (child): where the child's basic physical, emotional and social needs are not taken care of.

Attachment: where the bond between two people is strong and long-lasting, and substantial separation causes distress.

caregiver in the first three years. A child can also suffer deprivation when placed in an otherwise supportive institution if it has a high turnover of caregivers, making it physically impossible for the child to form a lasting **attachment** to an adult.

Figure 9.5 Does compulsory schooling create an opportunity for this child to ultimately escape poverty?

The effects of deprivation can lead to the following:

- Physiological changes: the CT scan-based work of Perry and Pollard (1997) showed that the brain sizes of three-year-old children who had suffered deprivation were significantly below average.

- Cognitive impairment and attachment disturbance: demonstrated by the work of Rutter et al. (2004). This study involved 144 six-year-old children who until a maximum age of three and a half years had experienced substantial deprivation in Romanian orphanages, and were then adopted into households in the UK. Information on each child's behaviour was obtained by home interviews with the adopting parents, and cognitive testing and observations of the child. The most significant cognitive deficits and attachment disorders were found with children who had been living in deprivation that included severe malnutrition, and extended for more than two years. The commonly found attachment disorder was a lack of preference for adult caregivers and not turning to them when feeling afraid or anxious. However, the data of even the most deprived children indicated some degree of psychological recovery, suggesting that the consequences of maternal deprivation were not absolutely irreversible.

Trauma (child): where the child experiences a sudden and adverse change in circumstances.

Post-traumatic stress disorder (PTSD): an abnormal condition that can develop after a person has suffered a traumatic event. Typical symptoms include feelings of isolation, poor memory skills and a sense of being emotionally dulled.

A child suffers **trauma** when experiencing a sudden and adverse change in circumstances, such as the death of the primary caregiver, war and dislocation as a refugee, or physical and sexual abuse.

The effects of trauma are not always distinguishable from the effects of deprivation. Trauma also often involves deprivation, such as violent killings in the presence of the child being followed by months of struggling to safety as a refugee. Thus the cognitive and attachment behaviours for trauma are often indistinguishable from deprivation.

However, the sudden nature of the trauma can lead to **post-traumatic stress disorder (PTSD)**. This is a mental illness that can develop after a person has suffered a traumatic event. Children with PTSD were the focus of the fMRI-based research of Carion et al (2009). The scans showed the PTSD symptoms of decreased hippocampal activity. The individuals also demonstrated poorer memory skills (including being unable to recall the horrific situations they had experienced), and feelings of isolation and being emotionally dulled.

Research study: Hodges and Tizard (1989)

Aim

To investigate whether maternal deprivation by itself results in attachment disorders that are irreversible.

Procedure

The researchers studied children whose history had included being placed in children's homes with too rapid a turnover of staff for any primary attachment to be made. A caregiver was typically in contact with the same children for two weeks only. This was institutional policy, designed to avoid the inevitable situation where a caregiver would leave and the children would be traumatised. Better for such attachments not to happen in the first place.

The children participating in the survey had subsequently been adopted or returned to their natural parents between the ages of two and seven.

Results

By age eight, most of the adopted children had formed close attachments to their adoptive parents, despite their having never had the opportunity to form an attachment earlier in life. Those returned to their natural parents showed a substantially lower rate of effective attachment formation. This appeared to be due to the adoptive parents accepting the children out of choice, whereas the returned children were often taken in through the parents' feelings of obligation and in circumstances of poverty and competition from other siblings.

These attachment patterns persisted in the 1989 study, when the children reached age 16. Those adopted mostly formed successful attachments, raising doubts on Bowlby's maternal deprivation hypothesis (Section 9.2.1.) which holds that it is in the first three years only that the child makes the vital mother or mother-substitute attachment. Those who had been returned to their parents often continued to suffer problem relationships within the family.

However, both adopted and returned children showed similar problems outside the family compared with a control group of young people. They included difficulties in forming close relationships with peers, and a desire for adult attention and approval. This would support Bowlby's maternal deprivation hypothesis.

Conclusion

Adversity in childhood is likely to interfere with healthy mental and even physical development. The child's capacity to withstand and recover from deprivation and trauma is resilience.

Resilience and resilience-building strategies

A person shows **resilience** in successfully adapting to problem conditions or to a difficult environment. It is the 'ability to thrive, mature, and increase competence in the face of adverse circumstances' (Rouse et al., 1998). It is the capacity to 'bounce back' from deprivation and trauma, such as poverty, family breakdown or the death of a close relative.

Resilient individuals are often members of families that are caring, but limited in resources. Despite poverty, they are encouraged to access opportunities for personal and social development (Rutter, 1995). An example is the child in their early teens who has had to take on parental responsibilities at home because of the parents' long and badly-paid working hours, but still manages to keep up with school and has developed a network of peer friendships.

Resilience in the face of adversity can develop through the support and trust of the key attachment figure, such as the mother. It can also be promoted by someone with a special relationship with the child, such as a sibling, grandparent, close friend, teacher or youth leader. Much also depends on the temperament of the individual.

A child that is easy-going, friendly and proactive will create cognitive schemas for resilience more readily than the child who is more inflexible and deeply sensitive.

Resilience: where a person successfully adapts to problem conditions or to a difficult environment.

The factors promoting resilience were the subject of the study of Schoon and Bartley (2008). Based in the UK, it used information from previous studies totalling around 40 000 individuals with experience of adversity. The findings confirmed the importance of support from family and the social environment, but they also indicated the factor of the child developing a sense of achievement and confidence in their own learning and social abilities. Previous successes motivated such individuals to raise their aspirations and strive towards more fulfilling academic, sporting and social objectives and experiences. Despite past traumas and deprivations, many of them looked towards the future with confidence.

Figure 9.6 Will the trophy promote resilience as well as celebrate victory?

Research study: the High/Scope Perry Pre-school Project

A child is likely to be very much at risk where race, poverty and low IQ combine against them. This is the focus of the ongoing longitudinal study of the intellectual and social development of 123 African-American children that started in 1962.

Aim

To investigate how the community fostering of early resilience may prevent juvenile delinquency in a high-risk population.

Procedure

As a controlled investigation in the USA, it started with 123 participants aged three to four years old, split into the test group which received special treatment and the control group that did not. The test group had a daily active-learning pre-school programme for two years, supported by regular home visits and parent-staff consultations. The rates of educational, social and economic progress of the child participants were followed up at regular intervals.

Results

The findings revealed substantial evidence of resilience in the treatment sample population who formed the test group. Compared to the control, over the years they demonstrated greater educational success, higher incomes and more stable households. There was less welfare-dependency, and there were fewer teenage pregnancies and criminal convictions.

Conclusion

This ongoing investigation has indicated that providing programmes of early years active learning with parental co-operation may create later adolescent and adult resilience in the face of socio-economic high risk.

Strengths of the study

It was a longitudinal study where the progress of the child participants was regularly monitored.

Limitations of the study

Not all the elements (for example, subsequent schooling) could be controlled, and the findings between the two groups tended to be correlational rather than causal.

9.1.3 Elements influencing cognitive and social development: poverty and nutrition

Many children grow up in circumstances where overcrowding, inadequate and unsuitable nutrition, poverty, and family instability are ever-present hazards. That is not only true in economically less-developed nations, but also in the urban decay and ill-conceived rehousing schemes of inner cities in economically developed nations. Nevertheless, some individuals do succeed in developing resilience.

This section focuses on a research study that investigates how improvements in nutrition may assist individual cognitive and social development.

INTERNATIONAL FOCUS

The work of Pollitt et al. (1995) was designed to investigate the possibility of a relationship between diet in early life and fulfilment of intellectual potential.

Pollitt chose four economically very poor villages in Guatemala, Central America. There were around 2000 participants in total, including children under seven years and pregnant mothers. It was theorised that it was the lack of protein in the diet that caused many children to die in infancy, and that the surviving children's learning capacities would be much weaker than the age-group norms.

Pollitt's study was both experimental and longitudinal. It used an independent samples design, so each participant was either part of the test or part of the control. The participants of two of the villages were designated as the test group. Their diet remained similar to the village norms, except that they were regularly given Atole, a diet supplement with high protein content. The participants of the other two villages were the control group. Their diet remained similar to the village norms, except that they were regularly given Fresco, a diet supplement that did not include protein. Thus the IV was Atole, and the DVs included the rate of decrease in infant mortality and, later on, the children's levels of performance in language, numeracy and information-processing skills. The diet supplements were given over eight years, between 1969 and 1977. The follow-up cognitive tests took place in 1988, 11 years after the diet-supplement programme.

The results were that the test group receiving Atole showed a 69% drop in infant mortality, compared with 24% on Fresco, and that those on Atole also showed a faster rate of recovery from infections.

On the follow-up psycho-educational tests, children whose early diets included Atole scored significantly higher on tasks involving knowledge recall, literacy skills and numeracy skills.

They also showed faster reaction time in information-processing tasks.

As evaluation, the investigation was ecologically valid. The diet supplements were given in the participants' natural settings. Additionally, the diet-enriching supplement that did not have protein was given to the other group, to cover the possibility that infant mortality and poorer cognition were caused by the lack of nutrients other than protein. The findings of this study could be generalised to, for example, strengthen the case for free school meals programmes in regions of poverty.

However, the study is limited by poor diet not being the only cause of educational deficiencies. The cognitive levels of the children receiving the superior Atole supplements were found to be well below those in middle-income and more prosperous areas of Guatemala. This indicates that diet is only one factor influencing the acquisition of learning skills. Also, there may be problems in generalising the findings to communities where there may be a similar lack of protein, but where the overall diet contains different nutrients.

SELF-ASSESSMENT QUESTIONS 9.1

1 **a** Define play.

  b What do Piaget's and Vygotsky's theories in early child development contribute to the roles of peer and play?

  c What did the more recent research of Ladd (1990) contribute to the role of peer and play?

2 **a** Distinguish between childhood trauma and childhood deprivation.

  b List the likely effects of childhood trauma and childhood deprivation. Quote research evidence for each effect.

  c What evidence does the study of Hodges and Tizard (1989) contribute to whether or not maternal deprivation results in irreversible attachment disorders?

3 **a** Define resilience.

  b List the factors that are indicated to promote resilience in coping with deprivation and trauma, according to these studies:

    i Schoon and Bartley (2008)

    ii the High/Scope Perry Pre-school Project to prevent juvenile delinquency

4 What does Pollitt's study of the effect of improved diet contribute to understanding cognitive development?

RESEARCH IDEA

Some students regularly eat breakfast before school whereas others tend to miss it. Compare the academic performance of non-breakfast eaters with breakfast eaters during the first two classes of the school day. Research methods may be quantitative or qualitative, and can include observations, questionnaires and interviews.

9.2 Developing an identity

Development of resilience in adverse circumstances helps the individual to get a sense of identity. Our personal identity focuses on two things: who we are, and how we fit into society. This self-concept is something that we constantly revise throughout our lives, in the face of cognitive development and social experience (Schaffer, 2004). As children grow older, they tend to become more aware of their strengths and limitations, including those they perceive as socially-imposed by their immediate environment. With age, other people's responses come to play a more central role in shaping the nature of that awareness.

The elements contributing to personal identity and the way they change is a vast field within developmental psychology. We will look at the development of three characteristics in forming one's personal identity: attachment, gender identity and social roles, and the capacity to see things from the point of view of other people.

9.2.1 Development of attachment

This section considers three main themes:

1 The importance of primary attachment in infancy. This focuses on the work of John Bowlby (1907–90) and his critics. Bowlby's observational studies prompted him to conclude that the intense mother and child attachment is an evolutionary-adaptive behaviour to promote survival.

2 The evidence for the formation of a primary attachment, and the characteristics and causes of the different types of attachment behaviours. This makes use of the classic observational studies of Mary Ainsworth (1913–99).

3 How far attachment patterns in childhood influence the nature of attachment styles and behaviours in adulthood.

John Bowlby and the importance of primary attachment in infancy

The work of Bowlby puts forward an overall model on how particular elements influence child development. With Piaget, it is the age and development-appropriate provision and facilitation of educational experiences. With Bowlby, it is the primary attachment figure presence of a mother or mother substitute, especially in the first three years of life, which he sees as the critical attachment period.

Figure 9.7 According to Bowlby, life's loving attachments begin with the child's primary carer

The main principles of Bowlby's attachment theory are:

1   The strong emotional relationships between the child and the primary caregiver give the child the security from which to interact with other people and situations, and serve as support and shelter when things go wrong.

2   The precise nature of the attachment between child and primary caregiver will show continuity in the child's social behaviours throughout life. Early attachments with parents continue in later relationships, as the early attachments create the schematic **internal working model**. It is these early schemas that set the pattern for further attachments during infancy, childhood, adolescence and finally adulthood.

3   Where the child feels loved, they will tend to grow up with feelings of security, and will continue to feel worthy of affection and attention. In contrast, where the child feels that the primary attachment figure is continually inaccessible, attachment-based disorders could be a problem later in life. These include **affectionless psychopathy** (inability to show affection), social deviance, depression and even a reduced rate of physical growth. This is Bowlby's **maternal deprivation hypothesis.**

4   Deprivation of primary maternal or maternal-substitute attachments are likely to have the short-term effects of initial anger and frustration, despair, and indiscriminate superficial attachments with others, which can develop into the more long-term effects of wanting to be alone and reduced resistance to disease.

Bowlby's attachment theory has attracted considerable research both supporting and modifying its claims. The classic supportive study by Harlow and Harlow (1962) on social deprivation in infancy was conducted not on humans but on rhesus monkeys. The monkeys were materially cared for, but deprived of an attachment figure throughout their early development. Later released into the company of other monkeys, they were unable to interact normally. They could not even form attachments with their own offspring that had been produced through artificial insemination. In addition, the work of Cockett and Tripp (1994) indicated that children showed less long-term attachment deprivation symptoms where they remained at home with constantly quarrelling parents than when they were placed in a more peaceful environment but without a principal attachment figure, following the parents' divorce.

Internal working model: where early-learnt schemas set the pattern for behaviours in later life.

Affectionless psychopathy: inability to show affection; a likely consequence of deprivation or trauma.

Maternal deprivation hypothesis: Bowlbyian concept, where the mother's being consistently inaccessible in infancy creates attachment-based disorders in later life.

However, Rutter (1981) in 'Maternal Deprivation Reassessed' concluded that young children retained the potential to form crucial primary attachments beyond the age of three, the limit given by Bowlby. Also, unlike in Bowlby, there could be more than one primary attachment figure, including father and siblings. Bowlby also needed to take into account the development of resilience in the child and the considerable environmental stimulation present in some of the adopting institutions.

Research study: Mary Ainsworth's observation-based classification of different types of primary attachments

Aim

The work of Ainsworth (1969, 1971 and 1978), herself influenced by Bowlby, focused on the nature of different types of attachment shown between mothers and their one- and two-year-old infants.

Procedure

The 1969 study was conducted with 28 families in Uganda, and it was repeated in 1971 on 26 families in the USA.

Ainsworth conducted a nine-month longitudinal study that involved a series of laboratory-type observations. The nature of the child's attachment to the mother was investigated by the 'Strange Situation', a series of eight scenarios in an unfamiliar room with each lasting no longer than three minutes, including the following examples:

- A stranger was introduced to the child in the presence of the mother.
- The mother left the infant with the stranger.
- After the mother returned and resettled them, the infant was left alone.
- The stranger entered and interacted with the lone infant.
- The mother returned again and picked up the infant.

Results

The pooled evidence following these studies enabled Ainsworth and her team to conclude that the nature of observed infant attachments belonged to one of three types: anxious-avoidant, securely-attached and ambivalent/anxious-resistant. The most frequently observed was Type B, the securely-attached, which in the American study was 70% of the sample. The infant was observed playing contentedly when the mother was present, was distressed by her parting and although not adverse to contact with strangers, treated them differently from the mother.

Type A, the detached-from-the-mother or anxious-avoidant, was characteristic of 20% of the American sample. The infant ignored the mother and did not react when she left, or desire contact when she returned. Although distressed when alone, the child was easily comforted by the stranger.

Type C, the ambivalent/anxious-resistant, was characteristic of 10% of the American sample. There, the infant showed distress when the mother left the room, did not readily accept the stranger, and sought but at the same time rejected contact on the mother's return.

Conclusion

Ainsworth et al. (1978) concluded that there was a significant relationship between the degree of maternal sensitivities towards the child on one hand, and the nature of the child's attachment on the other hand. Type B children, the majority, had experienced emotionally close and responsive mothers. Type A children seemed to indicate emotional distance and less responsiveness from the mother, while Type C children appeared to reflect inconsistencies in degrees of emotional closeness and responsiveness by the mother. In short, there are three types of attachment: secure, avoidant and ambivalent.

In addition, factors other than a lack of maternal sensitivity may help to explain the emotional distance shown by the child towards the mother, such as current stresses experienced by the mother that are temporarily distancing the child. For example, the child may temporarily receive less support because of family bereavement or sudden financial troubles.

Strengths of the study

Ainsworth's study has been widely replicated and broadly similar cross-cultural results (the securely-attached Type B scenario) have been the most frequently observed. The study of Van Ijzendoorn and Kroonenberg (1988) based on the results of 32 cross-cultural studies broadly supported Ainsworth's findings.

Limitations of the study

There have been some notable exceptions. For example, German parents had a higher proportion of avoidance contacts, which Grossman et al. (1985) suggested was a product of the national tendency towards greater interpersonal distance.

We have considered the nature and varieties of attachments in childhood. A key area of research in psychology is how far childhood experience of attachments set the pattern for attachment styles in adulthood.

Research study: Hazan and Shaver (1987) and Shaver and Hazan (1987, 1988)

The subject of investigation by Hazan and Shaver was the influence of childhood primary attachments on personal attachments made in adulthood.

Aim

To determine whether adult attachments divided into similar distributions of secure, avoidant and ambivalent. And if so, were they sequels to the individual's childhood attachment histories?

Procedure

The researchers used a series of tick-box questions designed to generate data on present adult attachments and childhood attachment history. The survey was printed in a local newspaper, and elicited 620 responses with a mean age of 36. Two-thirds were from women.

Results

The returned surveys reported the participants' current adult relationships as 56% attachment-secure, with love and trust; 25% were attachment-avoidant, with fears of intimacy and jealousy; 19% were attachment-ambivalent, with severe emotional swings and also feelings of jealousy. The surveys also reported the participants' quality of relationship with each parent. These showed a positive correlation between the adult attachment patterns. Those with secure childhoods tended to progress to secure adult relationships. Those with colder and more distant relationships with the mother or other primary caregiver in childhood tended towards relationship avoidance and ambivalence.

Conclusion

This led the researchers to view the quality and nature of adult romantic relationships as a product of the attachment process in early childhood (Hazan and Shaver, 1988).

Strengths of the study

It supports Bowlby's theory that the nature of the attachment between child and primary caregiver will show continuity in an individual child's social behaviours throughout life. It fits with the theory that early life experiences with the mother figure contribute strongly to the individual's expectations from adult relationships.

Limitations of the study

The survey's being placed in a local newspaper, and the participants containing considerably more women than men, may place limits on the degree to which the results from the study may be generalised. Also, the questionnaire format being composed entirely of tick boxes meant that the respondents had to estimate the best-fit response, which may not have accurately summed up their own situations.

Finally, the correlation between the nature of childhood and adult attachments may be related to the innate personality of the infant. Easy-going babies who are easier to handle are likely to bring out the more nurturing side of the mother figure, and are also likely to progress in life towards bringing joy to future attachments. Those with more difficult temperaments may well cause strain for the mother figure, and could proceed to place similar strains on later attachment relationships.

Critical thinking

Read the following scenario:

I had an awful childhood! My parents always put their lives before mine. They were both busy in their different careers, and they hardly had time even for each other. Whenever they were together, they were quarrelling. I always had everything I needed, but I was very lonely. I felt that our cat George was the only one in our household that took the time to understand me. I didn't exactly enjoy school, but at least there, there were fun people and we did a lot of things together. It's not that my parents meant any harm. But I felt that I belonged to a house, not to a home. I'm 30 now, and I work as an electronic engineer. I'm single, and have not spoken to my parents for the last four years. I want to just put them out of my mind, get on with my life and make my children the first priority when I find the right woman to have them with.

1 Outline psychological theory and/or research that may account for the attitude of the writer towards his parents.
2 Examine the difficulties the writer might face in finding a suitable partner.
3 Evaluate two factors that may enable the writer to give his future children a more caring environment.

Theory of Knowledge

In addition to personal attachments, parental figures can also influence their children's learning about their environment.

Much of a child's early learning about the world is based on what parents and other adult figures tell them. The very young tend to accept what they hear, possibly reasoning 'Mum always knows best, so of course she's right' and 'the teacher must know or he wouldn't be a teacher'.

As people grow up, they have experiences that may cause them to question intelligently or even reject the beliefs and teachings of the authority figures of their childhood, and especially their parents. Is their acceptance, rejection or rethinking of what they learnt from their parents influenced by whether their parental upbringing was authoritarian, authoritative or permissive?

1 Talk to ten different people over 30 years of age. Ask them individually to talk of the type of parenting they had. As you listen, classify their response as **authoritarian** (based on strict rules, obedience often out of fear) **authoritative** (based on the child's needs, firmly, fairly and consistently enforced) or **permissive** (child-centred as far as possible, affording maximum opportunity for risk-taking and making independent choices).
2 Ask each person to specify three beliefs/principles that their parents constantly emphasised. Possible responses are 'honesty is the best policy', 'our way of life is the best way of life', 'it's best not to date until age 21' and 'the better your grades, the better choice of career and the happier you'll be'.
3 Ask them whether they agree with each of the three items. If so, why? If not, why not?
4 Review and/or tabulate your results. Is there any pattern between parental style of upbringing on one hand, and the acceptance, rejection or rethinking of parental beliefs in adulthood on the other?

Having looked at the development of attachment in childhood and its role in the formation of relationships, we now consider how identity develops through gender and social roles.

Authoritarian parenting: characterised by high demands and low responsiveness. Parents have very high expectations of their children, yet provide very little in the way of feedback and nurturance, and mistakes tend to be punished harshly.

Authoritative parenting: characterised by high expectations and emotional responsiveness. It incorporates clear limits and fair discipline as well as warmth and support.

Permissive parenting: characterised by the setting of few boundaries and a reluctance to enforce rules. These parents are warm and indulgent, but they do not like to say no or disappoint, and their children can grow up lacking in self-discipline.

9.2.2 Development of gender and social roles

Part of the way the individual sees themselves is in terms of gender. At the very base, the sex of a person is determined biologically, depending on whether the chromosomes are XX for female or XY for male. How one's sex is expressed in terms of processing information and means of interaction with others is a function of gender. Gender includes the social and psychological characteristics of being male or female. **Gender roles** are the norms that dictate the types of behaviour that are considered to be acceptable within a given society in terms of the sex of the individual.

Among the determinants of personal gender identity are awareness of physical changes taking place particularly around the age of puberty, and social expectations of how boys and girls should behave. Indeed, when a boy is regarded as becoming a man is often socio-culturally determined. Typically, in hunter-gatherer type societies he is becoming a man when he can kill large, meaty wild animals, build a shelter, and sustain those in his group in the face of other humans and animals competing for the same resources. He can cross the boundary between a mere boy and a man who can make a powerful contribution to society in just one act of initiation. That takes many forms and varies from culture to culture. For example, in traditional Vanuatu society his role as a fully-competent male is initiated in a public-ceremony bungee jump from a 30-metre platform. It becomes valid when he just touches the ground with his head. He will face exclusion if he fails to conform to that social expectation.

However, being regarded by others as a man can be more complex in Western society. There is often a wide gap between the legal age of adulthood, commonly fixed at 18, and earning a professional salary on completion of training and education, which can be as late as age 30.

Psychologists accept that gender roles exist, that some are virtually universal throughout humanity, and that others vary according to different socio-cultural norms. However, the more influential causes of differences in gender roles are debated between psychologists. They consider the relative importance of the biological, cognitive and socio-cultural factors.

Psychologists debate the degree to which the differences between males and females are due to innate biological differences on one hand, and socialisation differences on the other. For example, does a boy who demonstrates the masculine stereotype do so largely because it is within his hormonal structure, or largely because he was brought up that way?

Factors influencing gender roles

Biologically-based theory of gender role development

This perspective holds that males and females are physically programmed for activities and behaviours that are compatible with male and female roles in society. Hormones, such as higher levels of testosterone for boys and oestrogen for girls, are of primary importance, with socialisation only taking a secondary role. For example, rough and tumble play is common with boys of all ages. Complex and emotion-laden social interactions are more typical of girls. According to biologists, testosterone-fired boys' rough and tumble play anticipates the male real-life competition for scarce resources, including for members of the opposite sex. With girls, oestrogen-fired complex social interactions anticipate their adult real-life nurturing role with their own children.

Biological explanations in gender identity also point to evolutionary theory, which claims that gender roles developed out of the needs of early societies. The male advantage was physical strength. Men were required to be tough and competitive in order to attract a desirable female partner with whom to reproduce, pass their genes to the next generation and demonstrate the capacity to supply food resources for their children. Women focused on nurturing themselves in order to attract a quality male. They continued as nurturers of the children, leaving the men to compete in bringing home quality resources.

Biologists point to the persistence of the genes that encourage those behaviours, even though the needs of modern society have changed: most means of earning a living are open to both genders; some marriages continue happily where the wife has a higher income and the husband carries out many of the household tasks.

Gender roles: the norms that dictate the types of behaviour that are acceptable within a given society in terms of the sex of the individual.

The strengths of the biological approach in the promotion of gender roles are that hormone-driven differences in gender roles are also observable in non-human species, for example in dogs. In addition, hormone-driven differences in the womb appear to affect gender roles in life. The longitudinal study of Money and Ehrhardt (1972) studied 25 girls with **adrenogenital syndrome** whose symptoms show a higher-than-normal level of male-associated hormones. The study showed their marked preference for activities fitting the male rather than the female stereotyped gender roles.

However, the link between higher testosterone level and male aggressive behaviour is correlational. The higher testosterone levels may be a result rather than the cause of the dominant behaviour. In addition, the large differences between different societies' male and female gender roles (such as in Mead's study, below) suggest that biological elements may be greatly modified by socio-cultural norms.

Cognitive-based theory of gender role development

This perspective focuses on **gender schema** theory. Gender schemas are rooted in society's beliefs about how boys and girls are expected to behave. Children form and develop their gender roles as they receive affirming or disapproving feedback on how their behaviour fits what is socially desirable for their gender. Such schemas influence the way the child processes subsequent information in terms of which behaviours are gender-compatible and which are not.

They also influence the child's self-esteem, where behaviour that fits with the schema-generated gender roles receives the approval of those around the child. That includes peer pressure. Sroufe et al. (1993) found that the 10–11-year-old children who did not conform to their gender stereotype were the least popular. Thus peer pressure, which is a social element, reinforces the gender stereotype, and from there the gender schema, which is a cognitive element.

Gender schemas can determine how boys and girls process the same information. The work of Martin and Halvorson (1983) showed a group of five- to six-year-olds some pictures of children's activities. Some were in line with the gender role (e.g. a boy playing with a gun), and some went against the gender role (e.g. a girl playing with a gun). The children's recall was tested a week later. Those scenes with out-of-gender roles tended to be remembered incorrectly. The picture of a girl playing with a gun was frequently recalled as a boy playing with a gun. Thus the error in recall appeared to be because it was outside the framework of the children's gender schema.

However, the value of explaining gender roles in terms of cognitive behaviour may be queried because small children show marked preferences for toys associated with their gender before acquiring complex gender-role schemas. In addition, schema development may be prompted by socio-cultural rather than cognitive elements, such as peer pressure in the study of Sroufe at al. (1993).

Socio-cultural-based theory of gender-role development

This perspective tends to connect with social learning theory (see Chapter 5). Social learning theory holds that gender roles are learnt and developed through interacting with the environment and modelling those of the same gender. In the case of gender-role development, the theory is that

Adrenogenital syndrome: where a female's endocrine system shows a higher-than-normal level of male-associated hormones.

Gender schema: the mental processing of a person's behaviour in terms of compatibility with their gender.

Figures 9.8 and 9.9 Are these two scenes powered by gender-role schemas or gender-specific hormones?

children observe role models of the same sex and imitate their behaviours if they can see them leading to gender-role-associated desirable consequences.

Bandura, whose work on social learning theory we examined in Chapter 5, subsequently expanded his approach to include the child's more active participation in gender-role development (Bussey and Bandura, 1992). It is not that society gives cues for the desirable roles for each gender, but that the child decides what role they would like, and chooses the role models to imitate. For example, a six-year-old girl is passionate about fast cars and wants to be a Formula 1 racing driver. She observes male racing champions on television and declares that she wants to be one when she grows up. As a result, she may pick up cues from the people she chooses to emulate even if they are of the opposite sex rather than people of her own gender. How far that might be encouraged or even tolerated varies between different socio-cultural environments. She may face some social disapproval from her own peers, particularly if she is in the pre-teen age group (Sroufe et al., 1993). She is likely to face more disapproval in a traditional collectivist culture than in a forward-looking modern urban environment. On the other hand, she might enjoy approval if she is the only child of a distinguished Formula 1 champion.

Figure 9.10 The racing driver Susie Wolff: successful despite or because of gender role?

Research study: Margaret Mead (1935)

Socio-cultural-based theory of gender-role development tends to connect with culture type, a concept also studied in Chapter 5. Cultural elements refer to distinctive beliefs, values and practices within a specific group that are passed down from one generation to the next. This is powerfully illustrated by the work of anthropologist Margaret Mead (1935 and 1949) on gender roles in a total of seven different tribes in New Guinea.

The findings from Mead's 1935 study of the first three tribes indicated that gender roles were culturally determined. The first three tribes were within the same region, but their cultures showed dramatically different gender roles. The Arapesh tribe reared both boys and girls to be gentle, kind, and affectionate, which are traditional feminine stereotypes. The Mundugumor tribe were the complete opposite. They reared boys and girls with impatient resentment. Babies were placed in rough-fibred baskets and left in dark places. Crying was not welcome; it was sharply discouraged by adult painful scratching of the baby through the basket. Adult males and females were equally powerful, fierce and conflicting, which are traditional male stereotypes. The Tchambuli tribe reared girls to sustain the tribe, including gathering and trading. Contrary to most civilisations, men were regarded as incapable of taking on such responsibilities. They spent their days sitting around in groups, gossiping and making themselves look good.

However, Mead's later 1949 findings from the other four tribes showed strong tendencies towards the traditional female gender roles, including personal fulfilment through sensitive and creative child-rearing. Mead moved away from the view of cultural determinism of gender role, towards the belief that societies based on non-traditional male/female roles were acting against nature.

The socio-cultural influence in gender-role development is reflected in the work of Engle and Breaux (1994), which found that fathers have become more involved in child-rearing where they have participated in parenting and child-development programmes. The socio-cultural influence may also be reflected in the success of the rising number of females in traditionally male professions.

However, in contrast to biological theories, the socio-cultural approach does not easily account for gender roles being a constant and driving force behind the child's behaviour. Additionally, social factors may be biologically influenced, such as Mead's findings that men were more forceful than women in almost all cultures.

9.2.3 Development of empathy and theory of mind

This section extends studies of developing an identity to include recognising and interacting with the identities and realities of other people.

Empathy is putting yourself mentally in the other person's position. It is where you can understand and share the feelings of the other, even if you do not agree. For example, you like mountaineering, but your friend is scared of heights. You are both hiking together and are about to cross a ridge: a narrow path with steep drops on both sides. Your friend takes one look and begins to tremble. Your empathy will therefore prompt you to turn back because you have taken their position into account, however disappointed you may be.

Such empathy is found in few animal species. Even human beings are not born with empathy; the research below shows that it develops as part of the emotional maturing process.

Theory of mind is the capacity to attribute thoughts, feelings and beliefs to other people that are different from our own thoughts, feelings and beliefs. Identifying and understanding the mindset of others enables one to predict their behaviour. This involves the skills needed to perceive and interpret social cues and emotions. That makes it possible to put ourselves in the position of the other, enabling empathy.

> **Theory of mind:** the capacity to attribute thoughts, feelings and beliefs to other people that are different from our own thoughts, feelings and beliefs.

Theory of mind may be said to be a cognitive process, which displays itself in empathic social behaviour.

Our studies of theory of mind and empathy focus on two areas: firstly, at what age theory of mind develops; secondly, how far theory of mind and empathy are norms in human behaviour.

Infants can intentionally communicate with one another before their first birthday, but empathy arising out of theory of mind in simulating or working out what others may be thinking develops later. Being able to understand the identity of others can be seen as an essential marker of development.

Research study: Wimmer and Perner (1983)

Wimmer and Perner conducted a study to investigate at what age theory of mind develops, by involving small children in the following **false belief** tasks. The false belief is being able to recognise that the other person has a different viewpoint even when you are certain that the viewpoint is wrong.

> **False belief:** being able to recognise that the other person has a different viewpoint even when certain that the viewpoint is wrong.

Aim

To find out the age at which a person develops theory of mind to behave empathically and see an event from the point of view of another person.

Procedure

The study included three groups of young children at a summer camp programme: three- to four-year-olds, five- to six-year-olds, and seven- to nine-year-olds.

The researchers used puppets to tell and act out the story of Maxi to the children. There were two cupboards, one green and the other blue. Maxi put some chocolate into the blue cupboard and left the room. His mother took the chocolate out of the blue cupboard and placed it in the green cupboard. After that act, each child was asked: 'Where would Maxi look for the chocolate?' They were not asked in which cupboard the chocolate was.

Responding with the green cupboard would indicate that they witnessed the event from their point of view, but not Maxi's. They would not have passed the false belief test. They did not see the chocolate from Maxi's viewpoint even though he was obviously wrong.

Responding with the blue cupboard would indicate that they correctly witnessed the event from Maxi's standpoint and thus demonstrated theory of mind and empathy, even though Maxi was obviously wrong.

Results

The three- to four-year-olds failed the test. Just over half of the five- to six-year-olds passed the false belief test, as did nearly all of the older children. Those who passed indicated a vital achievement in cognitive development: that someone else could hold a belief that is wrong.

Conclusions

The results indicate that theory of mind starts to develop between the ages of four and six. At this age children can see things from the points of view of others, and recognise that those people can hold beliefs that may be wrong. Being able to think critically in this way is a basis for social success in reading people's patterns of thinking.

Strengths of the study

- The children were concentrating, not guessing. This investigation was followed up by asking the children to think carefully before responding. The answers of the youngest children were still inaccurate.

- It indicates that theory of mind and empathy are largely age-bound biological norms of human development. Subsequent studies have debated whether theory of mind switches on suddenly at age four or develops more gradually over the next two years.

- Puppets realistically acted out the story. None of the children appeared to have difficulties in following it.

Limitations of the study

- The younger children may not have clearly understood the task even though they did not show it. A younger child may not be able to distinguish 'Where did Maxi look for the chocolate?' from 'Where is the chocolate?'

- Children in that age group have been observed in games that do require theory of mind and empathy, such as in 'let's pretend' activities.

Research study: Baron-Cohen et al. (1985)

Wimmer and Perner (1983) and this similar study have been applied to understanding **autism**. Autism is a mental condition involving difficulties in communicating and forming relationships with other people.

Autism: a mental condition involving difficulties in communicating and forming relationships with other people.

Aim

To investigate the extent that autistic children have a theory of mind.

Procedure

The research of Baron-Cohen et al. was a natural experiment: the participants were 27 normally-developed child participants (average age 4.5 years), 14 children with Down's syndrome (average age 11 years, average verbal mental age 3 years) and 20 autistic children (average age 12 years, average verbal mental age 5.5 years). Each viewed the Sally and Anne puppet show. Sally put a marble in her basket and walked out. Anne took the marble and put it in her box. Sally returned. The children were asked three questions: where the marble really was, where the marble was in the beginning, and (the crucial false belief question) where Sally would look for the marble. The correct answer, in her basket, would attribute a false belief to Sally. Success in the Sally/Anne test indicates theory of mind.

Results

Nearly all the normally-developed group and the Down's syndrome group answered the crucial false-belief question correctly. In contrast, only 4 out of 20 of the autistic children answered correctly.

Conclusion

The study concluded that not having developed a theory of mind could explain autism, whose symptoms include social difficulties arising out of an inability to develop theory of mind and empathy. Implied in the study is that theory of mind and empathy are indeed norms in human behaviour.

SELF-ASSESSMENT QUESTIONS 9.2

1 a Define attachment.

   b What, according to Bowlby, is the relationship between attachment in infancy and the pattern of later attachments in life?

   c What, according to Ainsworth, are the three most common attachment types shown in infancy?

   d What are the likely causes of the three attachment types in (c)?

   e What relationship is likely to exist between the individual's infant attachment experience and the attachment the same person makes as an adult, according to Hazan and Shaver (1988)?

2 a Distinguish between a person's sex, their gender and their gender role.

   b List biological, cognitive and socio-cultural factors influencing gender role, citing supporting research with each factor.

3 a How do empathy and theory of mind relate to one another?

   b What do the studies of Wimmer and Perner (1983) and Baron-Cohen et al. (1985) contribute to the understanding of theory of mind?

9.3 Developing as a learner

How do children learn?

And for that matter, how do adults continue to learn? Learning is a lifelong process.

For example, within groups of young people seeking to understand child development, different students will learn its concepts in different ways. One will claim that it was the teacher's clearly structured series of explanations that communicated the ideas. Another will say that the class was a waste of time, but they found a certain story-based movie particularly helpful. A third may declare that they learnt it through the act of reading a text and making notes. In short, the way that people learn varies from individual to individual.

This final part of developmental psychology looks at the cognitive and biological learning development processes that seem to underlie the learning progress of most individuals. As you read, consider how your own learning has advanced and try to judge how much of what you read here applies to you personally.

9.3.1 Cognitive development

We have already considered cognitive processes in Chapter 4. One major reiterated theme is that our behaviours are influenced by mental representations. Our mental representations form through our processing information into our own individualised pictures of understanding.

A cognitive approach becomes a **cognitive developmental approach** when we add a new element to cognitive psychology. That is studying how these mental representations change and become more sophisticated as we grow up and mature.

Psychologists agree that the nature of the processing of information and the resultant behaviours do change over time. The points of debate are what those changes are, whether they take place gradually or suddenly, what causes the changes and how they affect human behaviour.

Cognitive developmental psychology may be seen as a specialised area of cognitive psychology. As with cognitive psychology, it is based on mental units of thoughts, ideas and schemas (cognitive structures), but it views them from the perspective of personal development within the growing up and ageing processes. These changes are expressed in age-related changes in attitude, decision-making and behaviour.

Studies in human cognitive development are of considerable value to education and to criminology. In schools, they enable teachers to structure both the classroom environmental design and classroom practices to maximise student progress. In the courtroom, they can relate the age and mental development of the accused to the degree that they can understand and be held responsible for the crime.

Cognitive developmental approach: where growing up and maturing results in mental representations changing and becoming more sophisticated.

Jean Piaget (1896–1980)

Figure 9.11 Jean Piaget

From an early age, Jean Piaget (1896–1980) was an enthusiast in biology, publishing his first paper on his observations of the albino sparrow at the age of ten. Graduating from university, he came in to contact with Alfred Binet, famous for the Binet Intelligence Test. It was in his work of marking those tests that Piaget noted a consistency in the errors made by younger children. This guided him towards his theory that children naturally process information in different ways from adults. The presence of the recurrence of those errors within specific age groups indicated that children inherently do not think in the same way as adults. That includes ideas of number, quantity, time, causality and justice. Piaget's work was pioneering in that it was the first work that systematically related biological growth to cognitive development. His research was based on detailed observational studies of his own and other people's children, and a series of simple but well-framed tests that were designed to show the level of children's cognitive abilities.

His work has been highly influential in policies and practices within educational and criminological communities.

Our study in human cognitive development will consider the fairly sophisticated contrasting classic models of Jean Piaget and Lev Vygotsky, which both focus on the learning process. Although both are cognitively-based, the foundations of Piaget's model are substantially biological, whereas Vygotsky's model leans towards the socio-cultural. Both models continue to be highly influential, especially in the world of child education. Their works have not yet been superseded by an established and comprehensive brain-scanning-based model of the learning process, and it remains to be seen whether one will emerge in the future.

Piaget's theory of cognitive development

Piaget's theory is that it is the physical process of personal mental development that enables the capacities for learning to take place. To that extent, his model is biologically grounded.

Piaget's theory is detailed in five sections to show how the range of elements in his model integrate with one another. His fundamental principles of cognitive development are as follows:

1 Development precedes learning.

The stages of cognitive development are fundamentally age-bound, which are in turn determined by the biology of mental growth. The biological level of mental growth sets the age-appropriate approach to learning.

2 The child's intellectual development occurs as a series of processes.

Before Piaget, it was generally accepted that children think in the same way as adults, but with less experience and less competence. In contrast, the fundamental concept of Piaget's model is that children think in qualitatively different ways from adults.

Figure 9.12 What does this suggest about the way this young child relates to the environment?

Children's intelligence, knowledge and understanding develop in stages. Children cannot be pushed to function at higher stages of cognitive development before they have passed through the earlier stages.

3 The child's intellectual development occurs through active interaction with the world.

Children do not passively receive their knowledge; they are curious and self-motivated. Children build up their knowledge through the experiences of experimentation.

4 The child assists their learning progress by being actively involved in the learning process.

Activity enables the growing child to build increasingly complex schema to understand and interact with the world. For example, the infant is born with certain reflex actions, such as sucking or gripping.

These initially innate schemas continue to develop and increase in their complexity. The child will apply these schemas to more complex operations, such as gripping a cup with milk inside. The child will make early learning mistakes; first attempts will probably spill the liquid, but experimentation will transform the simple innate schema into the more complex learning-based schema. It will enable the child to drink from any cup without leaving a damp mess behind. This activity is an example of an **operation**, where several schemas co-operate in carrying out a specific task.

5   There are four biologically-determined stages of development.

Schema development operates within the four biologically-determined stages of development. No stage can be missed out. However, not all individuals fully reach the final stage.

Schemas adapt in scope and complexity

Schemas adapt in the following manner:

1   Assimilation is the using of an existing schema to deal with a new object or situation. For example, two-year-old Suzie already knows how to grip a rattle and make a noise. She then finds a toy rubber hammer that makes a loud squeak every time she grips, shakes and squeezes it. That action fits in with her existing schema of gripping an object to achieve the desired purpose with that object. Suzie thus realises equilibrium, a sense of balance. New information has been integrated into the existing schema.

2   **Disequilibrium** is when the existing schema does not work in the new situation, and the schema needs to be modified to deal with it. The new situation before her is drinking milk from a cup. Here, Suzie does grip the cup, but she does not position it correctly. Holding the object correctly is not crucial with the rattle or the squeaky toy rubber hammer, but it is vital with the cup of milk. So the milk pours over her instead of her drinking it. Disequilibrium! Frustration!

3   **Equilibration** is where the existing schema becomes sufficiently modified and complex to deal with most situations. Until that happens, the individual remains in a confused state of disequilibrium, being unable to fit the current situation into an existing schema. Thus Suzie cannot understand why she cannot drink milk from a cup. Soon, however, she will find that she can drink the milk effectively by gripping the cup handle correctly and holding it at the correct angle. That means that she has advanced her gripping session to the next level, from the capacity of shaking the rattle to the much more complex level of being able to hold the cup and drink from it without making a mess.

    Very soon afterwards, Susie finds that the cup-holding schema applies to any cup and any drink that it might contain. Suzie has modified her drinking schema, so she can use a variety of drinking vessels. She has thus assimilated her competence in drinking from a cup.

4   **Accommodation** is where the existing schemas have been developed to the level of complexity where the person can handle similar objects and situations without thought. In this example, it is Suzie's having successfully modified her drinking schema so that she can drink cleanly out of different cups.

Overall, learning takes place when facing situations that our schema cannot easily process, creating disequilibrium. The mind re-equalises by developing more complex schemas as a result of the learner acquiring new skills or new information.

However, the process of bringing the schemas to the next level of complexity requires two elements:

- The child actually faces situations where existing simpler schemas do not work. One way this may be achieved is by putting the child in a more complex and creative play environment:

- The child is sufficiently physiologically developed with the capacities to modify the existing schemas, and to create new ones. According to Piaget, that only happens where the child is within the appropriate stage of cognitive development, which we shall proceed to investigate. Development precedes learning. Piaget also holds that each biological progression from one stage to the next is a relatively quick transition, rather than a steady process.

Operations: where several schemas co-operate in carrying out a specific task.

Disequilibrium: Piagetian concept, where a person finds that an existing schema does not work in a new situation, and that the schema needs to be modified to deal with it.

Equilibration: Piagetian concept, where the person's existing schema becomes sufficiently modified and complex to deal with most situations.

Accommodation (Piagetian concept): the existing schemas have developed to the level of complexity where the person can handle similar objects and situations without thought.

Piaget's biologically-determined stages in his theory of cognitive development

1 **Sensory–motor stage (from birth to two years)** is where the baby goes from reflex, instinctive actions such as breastfeeding to constructing a sucking schema based on experience of what can and cannot be sucked.

By the time this stage is completed, the child will have a sense of **object permanence**. That means that if you take their teddy and place it under the blanket, they will have created a schema of the teddy being in permanent existence whether visible over the blanket or invisible under the blanket. Until then, they will be in distress if you put the teddy under the blanket and it disappears from view, even if they are watching. They will think that the teddy has gone forever.

Figure 9.13 'I can't see the ball, but I know that it's still there.'

2 **Pre-operational stage (two to seven years)** is where the child's thinking is **egocentric**. It is based on what they sees, and from their point of view only. The child will not be able to describe what another person sitting in a different place from them can physically see from their viewpoint.

The child will also show lack of **conservation**. Conservation means that an object or substance remains the same in quantity even though it is worked into a different shape. Lack of conservation will be indicated where, for example, an adult pours water from a short wide glass into a narrow tall glass, and the child says that there is more water in that second glass because it is taller. Another example of lack of conservation is where a stretched-out line of seven objects will be perceived to have more items than when seven identical objects are in a short line.

3 **Concrete operational stage (seven to eleven years):** in this stage the child will be able to look at objects from the point of view of others when prompted. Thus egocentrism will have declined. They will also understand conservation, appreciating that the volume of a substance has not changed even where its shape has. With liquid, this develops by six to seven years, quantity and length by seven to eight years, weight by eight to ten years, and volume by 11–12. However, the child can only do that where the objects are physically present, hence this stage is the concrete operations stage.

4 **Formal operational stage (from 11 years):** is where thinking and processes involving a combination of schemas can be carried out mentally without the support of representing objects being physically present. People at this stage can work things out logically without the support of concrete examples. They can also apply existing schemas to situations they have never previously experienced. In short, the child in this stage can mentally manipulate ideas, reasoning and numbers without having to reconstruct them physically. The child can think and reason like an adult.

Sensory-motor stage (from birth to two years): Piagetian concept; cognitive stage where the infant goes from reflex, instinctive actions such as breastfeeding to constructing a schema such as through the experience of what can and cannot be sucked.

Object permanence: understanding that objects still exist even when out of view.

Pre-operational stage (two to seven years): Piagetian concept; where the child's thinking is limited by lacking the dimensions of conservation, and is unable to see a physical situation from the view of another person in a different position.

Egocentric: thinking of yourself only, without consideration for others.

Conservation: Piagetian concept where an object or substance is perceived as remaining the same in quantity even where it is worked into a different shape.

Concrete operational stage (seven to eleven years): Piagetian concept where the individual can perform mental operations, but only when the objects are physically present.

Formal operational stage (from 11 years): Piagetian concept where thinking and processes involving a combination of schemas can be carried out mentally without the support of representing objects being physically present.

Not all people reach this stage at age 12, and those who can work through an abstract set of ideas in one area of thinking will not necessarily be able to achieve it in another. Some individuals will only reach the stage of formal operations in their later teens, and some will never reach it. Piaget regarded the achievement of this stage as being far less uniform than the earlier ones.

Evidence of progression from one development stage to another

The evidence Piaget used for each stage was based on his observations of his own and other children, and on the basis of simple and highly replicable tests.

From sensory-motor stage to pre-operational stage (typically at age two)

Hiding the child's toy with a blanket in their presence. If the child shows distress, but does not use their freedom to remove the blanket and recover the toy, then the child lacks object permanence. Once they do recover the toy in that blanket, they do have the object permanence schema and are thus past the sensory motor stage.

Figure 9.14 Playing ball is part of Jakub's learning experience.

Figure 9.15 Sensory-motor stage: cannot see the ball, so it does not exist.

Figure 9.16 Object permanence: cannot see the ball, but knows it is still there.

From pre-operational stage to concrete operational stage (typically at age seven)

Represented by: The Three Mountain Task (Piaget and Inhelder, 1956) egocentricity test and Piaget's own conservation test.

In the first task illustrated in Figure 9.17, the child is asked to describe what she sees from her own point of view. Then, she is asked what the doll sees from its point of view.

Figure 9.17 Can the child see the landscape from just her position, or also from the doll's position?

The child has progressed from the egocentric pre-operational stage to the concrete operational stage when she correctly and non-egocentrically sees the landscape from the position of another person, represented in this case by the doll.

In the second task, illustrated in Figure 9.18, there are three beakers. A and B are cube-shaped, filled with water. C is empty, tall and narrow, but with the same capacity as A and B. The adult pours water from B, the cube-shaped beaker, into the tall, narrower beaker C, and places full beaker C next to full beaker A. The child is asked which holds more water: beaker A or beaker C.

Figure 9.18 Does the child appreciate that the volume remains the same even where the shape changes?

Until the age of about seven, children will almost always respond with beaker C even though beakers A and C are holding precisely the same amount of water. The child shows evidence of having moved from the pre-operational stage to the concrete operational stage when they correctly state that both beakers contain the same amount of water, thereby displaying an appreciation of conservation.

From concrete operational stage to formal operational stage (typically at age 11+)

Represented by: transitive inference tasks and deductive reasoning tasks without the use of visual support material.

A transitive inference task requires being able to follow abstract concepts and arguments. A simple illustration: if John is taller than Jim who is taller than Josh, who is taller, John or Josh?

A deductive inference task requires being able to work out an underlying relationship between two objects or factors. This may be exemplified by the pendulum task. In this exercise, the person receives a set of different weights and a piece of string, and is required to experiment to find out what determines the distance of pendulum swing. The response would require evidence of logical investigative thinking.

Figure 9.19: What determines the distance of pendulum swing?

Many older people will not succeed in these types of tasks. Not all individuals reach the abstract operations stage. Those who need visual support in transitive inference tasks, for example, tend to be visual rather than abstract thinkers.

Applications and evaluation of Piaget's theory

Piaget's model of age-related biological development of increasingly complex schemas has wide application in educational practice. It had a major theoretical role in the Plowden Report (1967) for UK primary schools, whose principles remain very influential even today. These include the following:

- Learning should be a process of active discovery. Children learn best when carrying out their own investigations, whose frameworks have been skillfully devised by the teacher. Their findings ideally should create initial disequilibrium, and then promote more sophisticated assimilation and accommodation. The results are increasingly advanced and effective schemas and operations.

- Taught concepts and tasks should be compatible with the stage of the child's biological maturation and not beyond it.

- The teacher's role is to create a physical and social environment that facilitates learning, rather than conveying information by direct tuition. It should encourage the learner's purposeful collaboration with other members of the class, for example by arranging the seating in blocks, so that the students may work in groups.

Strengths of Piaget's theories on child development

- They have demonstrated that children of different age groups process information differently, and certainly not in the same ways as adults.

- They have placed emphasis on the teacher being a facilitator to enable the child to learn through their own discoveries, rather than being a dispenser of knowledge.

- They have become the basis for a great deal of critical research that has vastly increased the understanding of cognitive development.

- They have been highly influential in educational policies and practices, as exemplified by the Plowden Report in the UK.

Limitations of Piaget's theories of child development

- Piaget's methodologies using observation, scenario exercises and interviews used small sample sizes that did not represent the general population.

- Child development may be seen as a continuous process rather than a series of distinct stages. For example, the work of Baillargeon et al. (1985) indicates that children can show an understanding of object permanence even in the first year of life if the conditions are appropriate. In fact, towards the end of his career Piaget viewed the stages as being more continuous.

- Piaget's research methods place too much emphasis on deducing conclusions from the child's mistakes. Consequently, he may have overlooked abilities that children do possess, and he may have wrongly deduced the reason for their failure. The mistakes could have been due to weaknesses in the child's memory span, motivation, impulsiveness, social issues involved in relating to Piaget's test scenarios, demand characteristics (giving the responses they think the researcher wants) and linguistic ability.

- The child-as-an-experimenter model seems to underestimate the importance of the involvement of adults and more knowledgeable peers in the process of learning

- Vygotsky and Bruner claim that it is possible to speed up cognitive development provided that suitable support is used. This is discussed below. The aligning of educational programmes to Piagetian stages of development may be claimed to be holding back more gifted children.

- Knowledge of the biological functioning of the brain through brain-scanning techniques has advanced since Piaget's day. Future influential research on cognitive development in children is likely to be increasingly based on studies of the physiological development of the central nervous system rather than deduced from empirical observation of children carrying out specific learning tasks.

The work of Piaget emphasises the importance of active interaction with the world, and that the learning process is compatible with the child's level of biological development. In contrast, the learning models of Lev Vygotsky, and later Jerome Bruner, emphasise the importance of the learning environment and socio-cultural factors within the learning environment. They claim that young children can understand relatively difficult concepts if they are broken down into suitable units, a practice subsequently called **scaffolding** (Wood et al., 1976). We will proceed to consider Vygotsky's model of cognitive development which contrasts in several ways with Piaget's.

Scaffolding: where relatively difficult concepts can be made accessible by breaking them down into suitable units.

9.3.2 Vygotsky's theory of cognitive development

Vygotsky's theory is that the learning experience precedes and promotes mental development. This idea fundamentally disagrees with Piaget, who holds that mental development precedes learning. To that extent, Vygotsky's model is socio-culturally grounded.

Vygotsky identified the following elements that are crucial in the child developmental learning process:

1 The zone of proximal development is the area between what the child can achieve without help, and what they can achieve when stretched by an educator or fellow-student with more knowledge and skills. It is the learning process that occupies the zone of proximal development, and that in turn creates mental growth. The zone of proximal development continues to extend outwards as the child's learning progresses.

2 High-quality teaching and interaction with other students enriches the zone of proximal development, enhancing the learning which in turn promotes mental development and progress towards higher-order skills.

Figure 9.21 What are the benefits from being in a small, teacher-led group, rather than working alone?

3 The skilled educator breaks down the new concept, skill or task into suitably structured units for the student to grasp, a process later known as scaffolding (Wood et al., 1986). Scaffolding seeks to reduce freedom in carrying out the specific task so that the child can focus on reaching the specific challenging learning objective. In that way, scaffolding will limit learning errors to within a particular range.

4 High-quality constant social interaction with more skilled and experienced individuals enables the learner to acquire the cultural tools to survive in their society. In Norway, it might be the capacity to ski with great skill from an early age. In today's global society, it would include the use of a hand-held computer to find the way between two places.

5 The use of language is a vital factor in the learning process. Although children speak before age three, their speech is public, meaning addressed to the other. Once the child reaches three years, the speech can also be private. Three is the age when thinking and talking converge. By then, the child uses the language they have learnt in talking to themselves as they think things through. Their thinking process involves verbalising thoughts even though they are self-directed; in other words, thinking out loud. The thoughts are shaped by the degree of sophistication and cultural aspects of the language that the child has learnt through continuous interaction with others.

By the time the child reaches seven, the thinking 'goes underground' as inner speech. The language and its cultural aspects continue to shape our thinking, but speech is for the purpose of communicating with others only, not usually with ourselves.

The learning model developed by Jerome Bruner (1915–2016) is similar to Vygotsky's, although he expresses it in terms of **modes of representation**, which are the ways in which knowledge and understanding are encoded and stored in the memory. There are three stages for any concept: enactive, iconic and symbolic. The **enactive representational stage**, where one sees action and becomes familiar with it, can start soon after birth. The **iconic representational stage**, where the concept forms a picture in the mind, can form in the early years. Finally, the **symbolic representational stage**, where information is stored as an increasingly complex set of codes based on flexible-to-apply language or mathematics, is accessible from around the age of seven. Even though each stage is an advance on the previous one, they readily translate into each other. Even adults approach entirely new areas of interest through these three stages.

With that background, Bruner adds an additional element to Vygotsky's approach:

6 The **spiral curriculum** means revisiting previously encountered concepts repeatedly at more complex levels, making the learning process an upward climb on the same base. This also applies to adult learners. Thus Bruner, in sharp contrast to Piaget, claims that even a very young learner can learn almost any material as long as it is organised appropriately with suitable scaffolding, and revisited and developed at suitable intervals in a high-quality and suitably simulating learning environment.

Applications and evaluation of Vygotsky's theory

Vygotsky's theory, that it is the challenging yet achievable learning experience that promotes learning development, has wide application in educational practice:

- The practice of group collaboration in the classroom. Each group should include more advanced students who form the zone of proximal development for those at a more basic level.

- The use of scaffolding to present a concept. An example would be the teaching of the law of gravity to a class of nine-year-olds. Telling the children 'The attraction between two bodies is directly proportional to their combined mass divided by the square of the distance between them' will probably not communicate to the class. Instead, the teacher might open with 'Twenty-two well-built Earthmen playing their weekly football game on the surface of the moon will need a field so large that the spectators will have to use binoculars to watch the game'. The children will have the cognition and imagination to relate. They probably know about football and they have all seen the moon from afar. They will want to know why the match on the moon will occupy so much space. Through further scaffolded stages, they will arrive at the correct scientific representation of gravity, which will correctly incorporate the original idea about the attraction between two bodies. In addition, scaffolding may also be used to structure a student task to ensure greater degrees of accessibility for the lower-ability and less experienced students.

- Devising programmes of learning that build on previously learnt concepts and advance them to a higher level. An example would be the spiral curriculum developed by Bruner.

Strengths of Vygotsky's theory on child development

- To a great extent, it frees the educational process from Piaget's age-related constraints. The model claims that it is the quality of the zone of proximal development that develops much of the learning capacities, rather than the biological process which is outside the learner's control.

- It stresses how the learning process can be speeded up through good teaching and purposeful learning interaction with peers.

- It addresses the means of creating a suitable educational and social environment to advance higher-ability children.

- It has been highly influential in educational policies and practices, in ways described above.

Modes of representation: Brunerian concept; the ways in which knowledge and understanding are encoded and stored in the memory, including enactive, iconic and symbolic stages. Each stage is readily transferable into the next.

Enactive representational stage: Brunerian concept where our mental encoding of a concept is in the elementary form of a physical action fundamental to that concept.

Iconic representational stage: Brunerian concept where our mental encoding of a concept is in the form of a picture fundamental to that concept.

Symbolic representational stage: Brunerian concept where our mental encoding of a concept is in the form of increasingly complex sets of codes based on flexible-to-apply language or mathematics.

Spiral curriculum: Brunerian concept; designing a programme of learning to enable the regular revisiting of previously encountered concepts at more complex levels. The learning process is an upward climb on the same base.

9 Psychology for the IB Diploma

Limitations of Vygotsky's theories of child development

- Much of Vygotsky's work is theoretical. His model lacks the tests that parallel Piaget's scenario tasks.

- Its heavy emphasis on social interaction places relatively little emphasis on underlying biological processes such as those described by Piaget.

- His model incorporates the importance of verbal instruction as part of the zone of proximal development. That may be less effective than observation and practice. Verbal interaction may also work better in some cultures than others, particularly where the teacher is a more authoritarian figure.

NEWSFLASH

I have always loved games. All types. But the best ones were the role-playing games, where I was the bold and determined adventurer, far away from the ordinary, everyday life of my hometown near New York. Carrying on playing as an adult turned me into a teacher of seven-year-old children.

Within half an hour of meeting the class, we were deep in imaginative inquiry.

Figure 9.22 Knowing what to do in rescue situations can be a matter of life and death

In our imaginations, we were high up in the crags of South America. Without warning, a violent earthquake struck. We survived, but the village ahead suddenly vanished under the debris of a collapsing mountain.

We turned ourselves into life-saving rescuers. We planned our rescue like a military operation. Mobile phones and landlines were useless, and all radio and electricity networks were out of order. Children, the normally enthusiastic and the reluctant learner alike, arranged themselves in groups to put together urgent plans of action. Some were hotly debating, some were writing furiously, others were producing army-type diagrams. This was no traditional classroom with children working under the eagle eye of the teacher. The reality of the world's natural disasters was captured within the four walls of the classroom.

Learning was happening so fast that I could not keep up with ticking the boxes of the curriculum objectives. Drawing maps, creating signs and notices, investigating the characteristics of rocks and soils, the use of addition, subtraction, multiplication and division in maximising use of limited locally-available resources, making breathing possible in tight spaces, producing light so that rescue operations could continue at night …

Later on, they produced newspaper reports of their rescue operations and safety leaflets for the local people on what to do and what not to do during an earthquake. Three of the students spoke Spanish at home, so they eagerly translated the newspaper reports into Spanish. They responded to letters of thanks from those they had saved in the village. They also compared their work to real-life natural disaster rescue attempts shown on video: the 2002 Indian Ocean tsunami, the 2005 Hurricane Katrina, the 2010 Haiti earthquake,

296

and more recently in 2017 the huge mudslide in Sierra Leone and the torrential monsoon rainfalls in Sri Lanka.

Yes, we completed the entire year's curriculum as bold and determined world-class life-saving adventurers! Most importantly, we were simultaneously building the leaders and decision-makers of the next generation.

ACTIVITY 9.2

Ensure that you are familiar with Piaget's, Vygotsky's and Bruner's approaches to development in learning. Then complete the following tasks, working in groups and referring to the Newsflash above:

1 Suggest which learning capacities the teacher engaged in the students.

2 Identify the elements in the teacher's approach that incorporated the cognitive development models of Piaget, Vygotsky and Bruner.

3 Which features of the teaching method occur in neither of the above cognitive models?

4 Invent a suitable name of the approach to learning characterised by the Newsflash. Then present its principles in a paragraph or diagram.

Critical thinking

Evaluate the teacher's rescue simulation in terms of being a teaching model for children in *either* the seven-year-old age group, *or* any other age group of your choice.

9.3.3 Development as a learner: brain development

Neuroplasticity as explored in Chapter 3 is the continued development of specialised neural networks over time or after injury. The brain has the lifelong capacity to change, especially in childhood. Research studies show that such developments in the brain are promoted and supported by continued stimulating and demanding activities. Chapter 3 viewed brain plasticity happening through neural development promoted by engaging environments, neural changes in adolescence and neural development occurring through repeated, specialised activities.

Our studies in developmental psychology expand these principles to investigate the relationship between brain development and development as a learner. Research in this field of neuroscience investigates what are the norms of human brain development. It also examines the factors that can interfere with optimal brain development and thus optimal cognitive functioning.

In the normal process of development, we know that the following changes occur in the brain:

1 The brain doubles in size between birth and young adulthood. By age six, 95% of its structure is complete. The areas in the pre-frontal cortex start growing again in the early-to mid-teens, and their maturing process can extend into the mid-20s. Those parts of the brain process impulse control, assessing evidence, decision-making and planning.

2 Throughout the period from birth to adulthood, the folds on the brain's surface become far more complex. It is those areas that process cognitive and emotional information.

3 Neurons within the brain grow in complexity, degree of connectivity and speed in processing stimuli. The neurons develop a white myelin covering which accelerates the speed of transmission of information within the nervous system. This enables neurons to process more complex stimuli to greater effect.

4 Differences in personal learning experiences affect the rates of growth of different learning-associated networks in the brain. This is the process of brain plasticity, discussed in Chapter 3.

Biologically, it follows that normal cognitive development and progress in learning is age-related. This was investigated by Waber et al.'s study into brain development and behaviour.

Research study: Waber et al. (2007)

Aim

To track the stages through which a biologically normal brain develops. Understanding the norms of biological development would enable deviations from normal development to be more easily identified. Such brain abnormalities could be caused by heredity-based disease, and prenatal exposure to smoking or drugs.

Procedure

The study involved 450 young people aged 6 to 18, from different geographical, socio-economic and ethnic backgrounds in the USA. All were in good health.

This was a longitudinal study that started in 1999. MRI brain-scanning the participants on several occasions obtained the biological information. A series of tests to measure intelligence, cognitive functioning (reading, memory, calculating and mental processing speed) and social functioning obtained the cognitive information. The study thus generated the biological and cognitive data required for the study.

Results

The data from the tests indicated that the standard of cognitive performance was very much age-bound. Income and gender variables were less important. Participants from low-income families had poorer IQ scores and showed more behavioural problems, but scored equally well as their socio-economically better-off peers in memory and verbal exercises as well as on measures of social adjustment. There were also few significant gender differences in development as a learner, including in verbal and mathematical skills.

Age and performance on all the measures of cognitive functioning seemed to be positively correlated. That was indicated particularly by the steep increase in cognitive functioning between ages 6 and 11, which had the biological correlates of increasing complexity of the folds in the surface of the brain, increasing neural connectivity and increasing myelinisation of the neurons.

Conclusions

This study indicates that the increase in the effectiveness of learning capacity in a wide range of domains is age-bound in normally healthy children.

Strengths of the study

- The study was composed of biological, cognitive and social data from a comparatively large number of participants who were screened for healthy physical development. It enabled the tracking of the norms of cognitive and learning development against biological elements.

- It was a longitudinal study, enabling the learning development of the participants to be assessed on more than one occasion.

- It highlighted that age predicts performance on all measures of cognitive functioning, suggesting that learning ability is strongly influenced by the biological development of the brain.

Limitations of the study

- The concordances between the biological-based and cognitive-based data were correlational.

- The data provided snapshots of the development in different children at different times, rather than the study being long enough to follow the development process all the way through.

It is consistent from the findings of this study that processes interfering with physical development of the brain are likely to have an adverse effect on development as a learner. This has been supported by the studies of Perry and Pollard (1997), and Rutter et al. (2004), already covered in Section 9.2.1.

More recent studies as exemplified by Barkley-Levenson and Galván have given biologically-supported indications that the teenage brain also experiences development phases, which may well help to explain distinct behaviours associated with that age group.

Research study: Barkley-Levenson and Galván (2014)

Aim

To investigate the influence of different stages of brain development on risk-taking behaviour.

Procedure

It placed teenagers (aged 13–17) and young adults (aged 25–30) into identical gaming situations in which they would have to decide whether or not to take risks. Would the subjective teenage-evaluation of an objective risk be more inclined to take that risk than the older young adult?

The researchers hypothesised that teenage people would indeed be more likely to take that risk for the following reason. If the gamble worked, the reward would be expected to create an intense biologically-based, dopamine-influenced feeling of pleasure: greater than for an adult in the same situation. It is that expected greater intensity of pleasure (called the EV, or expected value of pleasure) that would powerfully prompt the teenager to take the risk.

The researchers sought to find out whether or not there was support for their expectations. This was done by investigating whether the teenagers would accept more researcher-devised, potentially advantageous gambles than adults, and whether the ventral striatums (VS) deep inside their brains would show more activity: teenagers' expected sense of the pleasurable reward in the form of making money being thought to be greater than in adults. This heightened sense of pleasure that teenagers would sense in their brains would correspondingly show greater activity on the fMRI scans of each VS of every teenage participant than in every adult participant.

The research also hypothesised that any adults who took the same degree of risks as teenagers would show less VS activation, being influenced to make those decisions for reasons other than high EV.

The participants in the study were 22 adults and 22 teenagers of both genders. All took part in an extended briefing session in order to become familiar with the task ahead, and to receive the $20 gambling money received from the experimenters in the knowledge that it would be employed in decision-making tasks at the next meeting in which they would individually be fMRI-scanned. The overall purpose of the initial session was to prepare them fully for all aspects of the gambling task one week later.

In that following fMRI session, the participants were given a series of different trial situations where they had to decide whether or not they would be willing to take a gambling risk if it were real money. They were informed that one of the tasks in which they would make a decision would indeed be played for real money; the $20 that they had received.

Results

The higher the EV for each situation, the more likely the teenager was to take the gambling risk. This was supported by accompanying correlational biological findings. The fMRI scans indicated a more powerful VS response in the teenage sample, as well as less activity in the amygdala (indicating correspondingly less fear), and more activity in the medial prefrontal cortex decision-making region of the brain.

This was also correlated with greater activation in the ventral striatum in teenagers than with adults who responded at the same level of risk.

Conclusion

The heightened range of expectations and emotions within the teenage VS neural stage of development prompts teenagers to advantageously take risks to a higher degree than adults.

Strengths of the study

- The format of the gaming situations and the fMRI scanning procedures were in a laboratory situation, where the risk-taking scenarios were standardised and replicable.

- The investigation is pioneering in demonstrating significant biologically-supported correlates in risk-taking behaviour.

- Its results may help to explain risky behaviours with higher frequencies among young people, such as impulsive behaviour, dangerous driving, substance experimentation and extreme sports.

- It highlights the need for educators to be aware of teenagers' predisposition for sometimes ill-advised and dangerous risks when planning activities for that age group.

Limitations of the study

- The study was quasi-experimental: not fully experimental as the participants did not have an equal chance of being allocated to either the test group composed of teenagers or the control group composed of adults. The study had an independent measures design: its very nature did not make it possible for the same participant to be involved in both the test and control situations.

- The findings were correlational: the independent measures design characteristic of the research did not enable the manipulation of the IV with the same participants.

Critical thinking

The IB promotes risk-taking as one of the positive qualities of its ideal students. How far do the findings of Barkley-Levenson and Galván (2014) suggest that being a risk-taker is not actually a good thing?

SELF-ASSESSMENT QUESTIONS 9.3

1 Distinguish between a cognitive approach and a cognitive developmental approach.

2 List the fundamental principles in Piaget's theory of cognitive development.

3 State the four ways in which schemas adapt in scope and complexity through childhood, according to Piaget.

4 Complete a copy of the following table showing Piaget's biologically-determined theory of cognitive development.

Stage 1 –	Transition from Stage 1 to Stage 2:
Stage 2 – Pre-operational stage (ages 2–7)	
	Transition from Stage 2 to Stage 3:
Stage 3 –	
	Transition from Stage 3 to Stage 4: Capacity to reason abstractly without visual support
Stage 4 –	

5 Explain how the following elements are involved in the learning process according to the learning model of the Vygotsky school:
   a zone of proximal development

   b scaffolding

   c use of language

6 What is the meaning and significance of the spiral curriculum proposed by Bruner?

7 a State three recent findings in how brain development affects the learning process.

   b What do the studies of Waber et al. (2007)) and Barkley-Levenson and Galván (2014) contribute to the understanding of how brain development affects the learning process?

Chapter summary

1   Developmental psychology is a theoretical and increasingly scientific-based focus on how the thinking and behaviour of children and adults change over time.

2   The quantity and quality of pre-school and kindergarten peer relationships appear to positively influence children's degrees of enjoyment and success in their early years of schooling.

3   The cognitive benefits of play include the enabling of children to create and operate a world that they can master. The social benefits of play include the experience of working in groups, dealing with conflicts and children learning to speak up for themselves.

4   The adverse effects of childhood trauma and deprivation in cognitive development can be offset by resilience-promoting strategies.

5   Key social and environmental factors promoting cognitive development are home stability without sudden traumas, suitable nutrition and an authoritative parenting style.

6   Bowlby holds that it is the emotionally-intense mother and child attachment made in the first three years of life that sets the nature of the person's future attachments throughout life.

7   Gender roles have biological, cognitive and socio-cultural determinants that vary from society to society.

8   Empathic behaviour and theory of mind normally start to develop between the ages of four and six. The absence of these cognitive and behavioural qualities in older children may indicate autism.

9   Cognitive developmental psychology studies how mental representations change and become more mature with age and experience.

10 The fundamental principles in Piaget's theory of cognitive development are that biologically-driven mental development precedes learning, the child's intellectual development occurs as series of processes, and the child's intellectual development may be promoted through active interaction with the world.

11 Piaget holds that schemas adapt in scope and complexity through the processes of assimilation, disequilibrium, equilibration and accommodation.

12 Piaget holds that a child processes information differently from adults, and in a manner that is determined by the stage of mental development as well as interaction with the environment. These stages are sensory-motor, pre-operational, concrete operational and formal operational. Transition between stages happens over a relatively short period of time.

13 Vygotsky holds that the elements that promote the learning process are language, breakdown of the concept studied into student-manageable units and a suitably enriched zone of proximal development.

14 Bruner holds that a spiral curriculum enables programmes of work to be designed so that students revisit concepts and ideas at intervals throughout their schooling, each time at a more sophisticated level. Even a very young student can learn almost any material as long as it is suitably developed, scaffolded and revisited.

15 Biologically, normal cognitive development and progress in learning is largely age-bound. Learning can additionally be promoted by regular stimulating and demanding activities that encourage the development of more complex neural networks in associated localities in the brain.

16 Recent fMRI-based research indicates that the teenage stages of brain development enable risk-taking activities that become markedly fewer in adulthood.

Exam-style question

Essay response question

- Discuss any two theories for gender roles in developing a personal identity.

Approaches to researching behaviour

'Research is creating new knowledge.'
(Neil Armstrong)

10

KEY QUESTIONS

- Which methods are suitable for investigating phenomena in psychology?
- In which ways may the evidence for claims made by theory and research studies in psychology be assessed?
- What are the scopes and limitations of quantitative and qualitative approaches to researching behaviour?
- How may the research process be designed to optimise validity and reliability?

Learning objectives

- Outline the methods that are suitable for investigating phenomena in psychology. (AO1)
- Examine the ways in which the evidence for claims made by theory and research studies in psychology may be assessed. (AO2)
- Examine the ways in which research processes may be designed to optimise validity and reliability. (AO2)
- Discuss the scopes and limitations of quantitative and qualitative approaches to researching behaviour. (AO3)

10.1 Introduction to research methods in psychology

Chapter 2 introduced some vital elements in research methods in psychology. Core Chapters 3 to 5 the option Chapters 6 to 9 all include the application of a wide range of research methods. In using them, you will have engaged critical thinking skills in evaluating the strengths and limitations of the research studies by challenging their assumptions, designs, methodologies, findings and conclusions.

Approaches to research can be reductionist in focusing on just one approach in investigating a particular behaviour, or holistic where the focus is on the behaviour itself and the consideration of the biological, cognitive and socio-cultural influential elements.

Our integrated framework for researching behaviour includes:

1   the types of quantitative and qualitative research methods used in psychology

2   the elements of researching behaviour, including **research designs**, hypotheses, IVs and DVs, **sampling techniques** and ethical considerations

3   analysing quantitative data and qualitative data

4   drawing conclusions: causation, replication, generalisation for quantitative research, transferability for qualitative research

5   evaluating research, assessing its reliability and validity, credibility, biases and any use of triangulation.

Research design: means of coherently and logically planning a study so that it addresses the research problem.

Sampling technique: method of sampling chosen so that it is most representative of the population being studied.

10.1.1 Quantitative methods used in psychology

There are five quantitative methods commonly used in psychological research.

1 Laboratory experiments

There is one control population and at least one test population. As explained in Chapter 2, in the test mode the researcher manipulates the IV to see its effect on the DV. This manipulation allows causality to be established.

Laboratory experiments may be exemplified by the studies of Loftus and Palmer (1974) (Chapter 4) on reconstructive memory and confabulation. There, as in other such laboratory experimental studies, the environment was controlled, the procedures were standardised and the participants were randomly allocated to experimental or controlled groups.

Laboratory experiments need to take into account possible **extraneous variables**, which are variables other than the IV that might affect the DV. For example, a reproduction of the Loftus and Palmer investigation would have to ensure that the participants in the different groups were of similar age and intelligence. Where such variables are controlled, they are extraneous. Where inadequate control could significantly affect the results of the study, these extraneous variables become **confounding variables** that can result in the findings of the investigation being worthless.

Loftus and Palmer investigated five IVs, which were manipulated by the researchers. Your Internal Assessment requires a **simple experiment**. A simple experiment is where only one IV is used in the experiment.

Extraneous variables: variables other than the IV that might affect the DV.

Confounding variables: where extraneous variables not being adequately controlled could adversely affect and therefore invalidate the results of the study.

Simple experiment: where only one IV is used in the experiment.

2 Field experiments

As in laboratory experiments, the researcher manipulates the IV but within a real-life environment.

This method may be exemplified by the research of Rosenthal and Jacobson (1968) which was set in a Californian elementary school. In co-operation with the school authorities, the

305

researchers gave the students an IQ test. They then gave the teachers a list of students comprising 20% of the school who would strongly improve during the coming year. Unknown to the teachers, the students were randomly selected with no reference to the test. On being retested nearly a year later, those selected (the test group) gained an average of 12 IQ points, in contrast to an average of only 8 for the rest of the school (the control group). The researchers concluded that student progress is significantly influenced by teacher expectations.

Field experiments occur in the real-life environment, and are therefore likely to have a high ecological validity. On the other hand, it is harder to control extraneous variables than in a laboratory. It is also harder to replicate, as field conditions in different locations are seldom identical.

3 Quasi-experiments

Where the IV being studied occurs naturally (e.g. gender, age group, race or scores on a depression-classification table). The variable is pre-existing. No experimenter manipulation takes place.

An example of a **quasi-experiment** is Baron-Cohen et al. (1985) (Chapter 9) on understanding autism, a mental condition involving difficulties in communicating and forming relationships with other people. This study involved 27 participants who had neither Down's syndrome nor autism as the control, with 14 children with Down's syndrome and 20 children with autism in the test groups. It differed from a natural experiment as the DV within the Sally/Anne puppet show was the experimenter's creation; it did not occur naturally. In this, as in other quasi-experimental studies, the researcher can neither freely manipulate the IV, nor allocate the participants to random groups.

4 Natural experiments

Where the researchers find naturally occurring variables and study them. The experimenter is not able to manipulate the IV as it occurs in circumstances beyond their control. An example is Charlton et al. (2002) (Chapter 5), where the introduction of television in St Helena occurred independently of that research.

Natural experiments are likely to have greater ecological validity than laboratory experiments. However, the extraneous variables in such settings may not be possible to control.

5 Correlation research

Correlations research focuses on the degree to which two or more variables are related to each other, and how statistically significant that relationship is. It is non-experimental: there is no IV or DV. Although correlation studies may well be quantitative, such research is designed to investigate the direction (positive or negative) and strength of the relationship between the factors rather than demonstrate cause and effect. An example is the Minnesota Study of Twins Reared Apart (Bouchard et al., 1990) (Chapter 3). This focused on MZ and DZ twins who had been reared separately. It researched the degree of concordance between the twins' amount of shared genetic material, and the degree of similarities in intelligence and behaviour patterns, but it was not designed to show how and why one influenced the other.

Correlation research has the advantage of allowing researchers to collect far more data than the experimental method, and also over a more extended period of time. It enables the study of the effect of phenomena, such as genotypes, that may be difficult or even impossible to manipulate as IVs. It also lends itself more widely to the natural environment rather than being confined to the artificial laboratory setting.

Its limits are that the elements studied are no more than co-variables. Correlation research hypothesises that factors are related, but it is not designed to demonstrate cause and effect. At best, correlation research shows an existing relationship to be statistically significant. However, it lacks elements that can be manipulated to show why those relationships exist.

Quasi-experiment: where the IV being studied occurs naturally, for example gender, age group, race or scores on a depression-classification table. The variable is pre-existing. No experimenter manipulation takes place.

Correlation research: where the research focuses on the degree to which two or more variables are related to each other, and how statistically significant that relationship is.

ACTIVITY 10.1

For each of the following pieces of research, state the method of research used and explain how each study exemplifies that method of research:

1 Bargh et al. (1996) (Chapter 5)

2 Becker et al. (2002) (Chapter 6)

3 Harris and Fiske (2006) (Chapter 3)

4 Lueck and Wilson (2011) (Chapter 5)

5 Markey and Markey (2010) (Chapter 5)

RESEARCH IDEA

Literature, politics and history can tell us more about human behaviour than quantitative scientific method. How far do you agree?

10.1.2 Qualitative methods used in psychology

Qualitative research strategies include the use of naturalistic observations, interviews and case studies.

Sampling methods used in qualitative research are significantly different to those used in quantitative research. **Purposive sampling** rather than random sampling is preferred in qualitative research; participants are selected for having the characteristics that fit in with the research aim.

Purposive sampling: where participants are selected for having the characteristics that fit in with the research aim.

The qualitative approach needs to be transparent in the description of the methods that it uses since this adds to its credibility. Credibility improves when researchers are reflexive; they attempt to make readers of their research aware of their own potential researcher bias. In addition, it should be acknowledged that participants in the research may change their minds as the research proceeds.

Qualitative research has the capacity to obtain in-depth information that is not always readily available to quantitative methods. It can also be used for in-depth exploration of relationships already established by quantitative data.

There are three main qualitative methods commonly used in psychological research: interviews, observations, and case studies.

1 Interviews

At the qualitative level these include unstructured, semi-structured (which both involve one person at a time) and focus-group interviews. They are designed to gain an insight into people's thoughts, opinions and feelings. In certain cases they may be followed up by quantitative questionnaire surveys distributed to a larger sample, as a means of supporting or modifying their findings. Conversely, they can also be used to follow up quantitative studies by working with a small number of the participants to obtain an in-depth understanding of the thinking behind their responses. An example of such a study is Totten (2003) (Chapter 7), whose research on gender-based abuse involved in-depth interviewing of 30 male youths aged 13 to 17 who were gang members or belonged to violent male peer groups.

Semi-structured interviews

These involve the preparation of points of interest that have to be covered, which use both closed and open-ended questions. The closed questions are designed to encourage the participants to relate to the focal points of what is being researched, and the open ones enable them to expand and respond with more depth and freedom.

Semi-structured interviews also have the strength of enabling the researcher to pursue themes of importance that arise during the interview that until then may have not been considered by the researcher. Their limitations include being time-consuming, demanding to analyse, and raising the need to tackle the possible influences of reflexivity on the part of the researcher as well as demand characteristics affecting the participants' responses.

Unstructured interviews

Unstructured interviews tend to be narrative in content: typically, 'Tell me what you thought, how you acted and how you would act now when in that situation.' An example would be investigating what it is like to transfer from the state system of education to an international school in another country at age 16. The respondents might focus on uncertainties in expectations, stress-coping mechanisms and how far their new realities matched their anticipations and apprehensions.

Like the semi-structured interviews, they do enable the participants to convey an in-depth experience from their own viewpoint, often with the more general implications of how they construct meaning in their lives. They share similar limitations to semi-structured interviews as well as the lack of structure, making it possible for the respondent to give a great deal of information that has little relevance.

Focus groups

Focus groups typically consist of six to ten people where the researcher acts as facilitator. The researcher introduces the participants to each other, presents the areas of investigation together with their boundaries and keeps the group discussion on focus. Group members are likely to be asked to respond to issues raised by others, which can help to identify areas of agreement and disagreement among group members.

Unlike semi-structured and structured interviews, focus groups enable data to be generated from several people at the same time. This set-up may reduce the possibility of demand characteristics and improve ecological validity as there is no one-to-one pressure. However, focus groups need to be carefully put together, as there can be clashes of personality, shy participants might prefer to leave the talking to others, and there might be majority or minority influence (Chapter 5).

Common to all three methods, interviewers need to be of a manner, age, gender, ethnicity and disposition that can establish a suitable rapport, where the participants feel relaxed and secure. The ethical guidelines presented later in this chapter need to be scrupulously observed, including simply presenting the objectives of the research in advance and offering the respondents a transcript of the interview as debriefing. The interview should include listening actively, summarising and restating the respondent's views in different words so as to keep the investigation on track, and avoiding the **interviewer effect**, where the interviewer's attitude and demeanour could bias answers; for example, giving a smile that could prompt a response influenced by demand characteristics. Finally, the interviewer has to accept the real risk that the respondent might regret divulging sensitive information and may decide to use the right to withdraw the information given.

2 Naturalistic observations

In quantitative as well as in qualitative research, **naturalistic observations** involve measuring naturally-occurring behaviour with as much precision as possible. This method tends to have high levels of ecological validity, although there are often problems in assessing how far their findings may be generalised to environments that are not the same as the one observed. In the quantitative study of Charlton et al. (2002) (Chapter 5), a series of naturalistic observations were made to record the degree of violence in a St Helena elementary school playground before and after the introduction of television on that island.

Unstructured interviews: designed to draw out in a conversational style how the individual thinks, behaves and would react in a particular scenario. Tend to be narrative in style.

Focus groups: typically consist of six to ten people where the researcher acts as discussion director and facilitator, aiming for data to be generated from several people at the same time.

Interviewer effect: where the interviewer's attitude and demeanour could bias answers from the respondent.

Naturalistic observations: a quantitative and qualitative research method involving measuring naturally-occurring behaviour with as much precision as possible.

Commonly used techniques for recording observations are field notes, which are often coded to facilitate standardisation. For example, aggressive displays of behaviour in the school playground might be recoded as number of incidents observed, those involved (each participant according to gender, e.g. MMMFF), the severity of the aggression on a semantic scale of 1 (relatively mild) to 3 (relatively severe), and a figure showing the time span of the incident in seconds. The results might then be classified into observed behaviour categories, where the coded findings are divided into subsets of behaviour.

Naturalistic observations can be participant or non-participant, and overt or covert.

- Participant observation involves the researcher(s) becoming part of the target group that is being studied. The investigator is working from within those being observed.

- Non-participant observation is where the researcher watches the people being studied without active involvement in the situation being watched.

- Overt observation is where the participants know that they are being observed.

- Covert observation is where the participants do not know that they are being observed.

Rosenhan (1973) (Chapter 6) 'On being sane in insane places' involved both participant observation and covert observation. In contrast, the data in Charlton et al. was compiled through non-participant observation (the observers were not allowed interaction with the children in the playground) and overt observation (the study had the approval of the school authorities and the parents).

Naturalistic observation has the strengths of:

- potentially high ecological validity as it takes place in the natural environment for the participants' daily lives and routines

- potential for the accumulation of data that has depth and detail

- potential of building up trust between researcher and participants more easily than when in an laboratory environment

- less likelihood of participants showing demand characteristics than when in an artificial setting. These are particularly true when the observations are covert.

However, naturalistic observation may be limited by the following aspects:

- Difficulties in recording data accurately and objectively in the field. This problem may be reduced by employing several (rather than just one) researchers, standardising the method of measuring and recording observations, and afterwards moderating the findings so that the observation criteria have been uniformly applied.

- Possibility of interference from extraneous variables: atypical behaviour may be erroneously generalised as being the norm.

- Ethical issues involved in covert observations that have to be justified, as this method invariably involves deception. Deception is only likely to be ethically approved if the investigation is of high public importance and no other suitable method is available. In addition, the participants will need to be suitably debriefed.

- The Hawthorne effect (Chapter 2): where behaviour of those observed improves significantly from the norm when they perceive that they are being watched. This is based on research carried out in the 1920s at a factory of the same name in Chicago, which indicated an improvement in output following a change in environmental conditions. The researchers hypothesised that such changes would prompt the workers to perceive that they were being observed more intensely than usual, and they would work harder than usual for that reason.

- The **Rosenthal effect**: where perceived higher expectation leads to a higher level of performance than the norm while being watched. The Rosenthal effect is based on Rosenthal and Jacobson (1968), whose findings indicated a substantial improvement in performance of those elementary school students whose teachers communicated high expectations.

Rosenthal effect: where perceived researcher-communicated higher expectations lead to a higher level of performance than the norm while being watched.

3 Case studies

These involve the detailed analysis of one individual or a small group, usually over a period. They can be used to investigate a problem in an organisation or group, taking into account the particular context and setting. Case studies thus tend to produce context-dependent knowledge.

An example of a case study would be where a researcher focuses on a single class taught by one teacher as a means of investigating whether specific teaching strategies motivate students from ethnic minorities.

Data collection could use participant observation where the researcher works as teacher-assistant for the period of the observation. It could be followed up with semi-structured interviews and focus groups with minority students, and a content analysis of student writing. Analysis might use **inductive content analysis** (examined later in this chapter) to develop new theory. The findings could be followed up and the theory examined through further cases studies, indicating the degree of generalisation that might be valid from the combined findings.

Case studies may also be an in-depth study of an individual, for example Curtiss's study of Genie (1977) (Chapter 2).

Case studies have the strengths of:

- enabling data-rich, highly detailed and in-depth study, such as the social processes operating in a particular group

- where the study is reproduced, for example with similar groups, it may be possible to transfer the findings to other people whose contexts are similar to the case study

- being the only method of studying a unique context or form of behaviour, for example Curtiss's study of Genie.

However, the use of case studies may be limited by:

- their transferability being reduced to situations sharing similar contexts

- possibilities of researcher bias in methods of interpretation and reflexivity issues

- being difficult or even (as in the case of Genie) impossible to replicate.

Those researching by qualitative methods have to tolerate a degree of uncertainty. Human behaviour is frequently complex; the meaning of similar experiences may be interpreted differently by individuals. For example, chronic injury may have a devastating effect upon elite athletes and their immediate family members since it may involve the end of a playing career and a substantial fall of income; but for others, the same injury could offer an opportunity to retire gracefully from the continual demands of their sport and start a new career in a different area.

It is important to realise that qualitative and quantitative research complement each other. They may both be used in one focus of psychological study.

> **Inductive content analysis:** a qualitative method of analysis that aims to generate new theory based on the data.

10.2 Elements of researching behaviour

Once the method is chosen, the study has to choose the best research design for the task, may set hypotheses, (if experimental) specify the IV(s) and DV(s), select the participants using a sampling technique, control for any confounding variables and demonstrate that the study is ethically acceptable. Each of these elements will now be explored.

10.2.1 Research designs

This section considers three types of experimental design that are used in psychology: independent measures design, repeated measures design and matched pair design.

1 Independent measures design

The independent measures design uses two or more separate groups of participants. One may form the test group and the other the control group. There may be more than one test condition, in a situation where the IV is manipulated in more than one way. Each participant is involved in one condition only.

An example of an independent measures design is the study of reconstructive memory by Loftus and Palmer (1974) (Chapter 4), where the word 'hit' used in the control group was the manipulated IV in the test groups. 'Hit' was replaced with 'contacted', 'bumped', 'collided' and 'smashed'. Each participant was assigned to one condition only.

The strengths of independent measures design include reducing the interference of demand characteristics, as participants being assigned to one condition only are less likely to perceive the purpose of the study and give the responses they think the researcher is looking for. There is also no **order effect** (the responses or behaviour in the earlier stage being likely to influence those given in the later stage). Its main limitation is the possibility that statistically significant, hypothesis-supporting differences between the test and control groups may arise due to differences between the participants in each group, rather than the manipulation of the IV.

Repeated measures design

The **repeated measures design** uses the same participants in both the control and test condition(s) of the experiment. There is one group of participants only.

An example of a repeated measures design is Harris and Fiske (2006) (Chapter 3), which examined the biological correlates of stereotypes and prejudice. The same fMRI-attached participants were shown pictures of objects, pictures of a variety of people and finally pictures of people who were homeless or addicted to drugs, with the researchers observing different processing patterns in the amygdala and medial prefrontal cortex.

The main strength of the repeated measures design is that it avoids the possibility of differences between the groups, as all participants are assigned to the same series of conditions. Its limitations include possibilities of the order effect, the greater likelihood of demand characteristics, and declining participant interest as the study proceeds.

Matched pair design

The **matched pair design** involves different but similar participants being used in each condition. Each participant of a matched pair is assigned to a different condition. The matching of the pairs is on the basis of what is crucial for the study, such as age, gender and cultural background. Twin studies are also an example of a matched pair design.

An example of a matched pair design study is Kearins (1981) (Chapter 4), which considered the role of schemas in mental mapping. The method of investigation involved boys and girls, half of whom were of indigenous Australian descent, and half were white Australian. The groups were matched for age and gender.

As each participant is assigned to one condition only, there is no order effect, and there are lower chances of demand characteristics and group differences. However, it is not always easy to find a large enough population of potential participants from which matched pairs may be selected, and there may be difficulties in matching pairs accurately.

10.2.2 Hypotheses

The hypothesis is a statement that may be tested and falsified on the basis of data obtained by the researcher. The null hypothesis (H_0) proposes that the researcher's intervention will have no effect on the phenomenon being studied, for example human behaviour. If the data supports the null hypothesis, it will not be rejected. If the data does not significantly support the null hypothesis, it may be rejected. The relationship stated in the **alternative hypothesis (H_1)** that the investigator thought might exist will have been supported.

Order effect: where the participants' responses or behaviour in the earlier stage are likely to influence those in the later stage.

Repeated measures design: the same participants are used in both the control and test condition(s) of the experiment. There is one group of participants only.

Matched pair design: different but similar participants are used in each condition. Each participant of a matched pair is assigned to a different condition.

Alternative (experimental) hypothesis (H_1): alternative to the null hypothesis; proposes that the researcher's intervention will have an effect on the phenomenon being studied, for example human behaviour. It is a testable statement of what the researcher seeks to find.

An example is used in Bandura et al. (1961) (Chapter 5), where the null hypothesis is that exposing young children to violent scenes does not significantly increase their observed degree of violent behaviour.

The alternative hypothesis (H_1) in this case would state that exposing young children to violent scenes will increase their observed degree of violent behaviour. It is the findings of the research study that will determine whether the null hypothesis will be rejected or not.

A hypothesis can either be a **one-tailed test** or a **two-tailed test**, whether null or alternative.

- A one-tailed test predicts the direction of the relationship. The direction expressed in the alternative hypothesis is: 'Exposing young children to violent scenes will significantly increase their observed degree of violent behaviour.'

- A two-tailed test predicts that a relationship exists, but could be in either direction. In the above example, it could be: 'Exposing young children to violent scenes will cause a significant change in their behaviour.' That change could be an increase of the degree in violent behaviour because violence must be acceptable if adults behave that way, or a decrease in violent behaviour because beating a harmless doll does not seem to be a nice thing to do.

A hypothesis is not a research question. A research question is what a study is seeking to answer. For example: 'Does exposing children to violent scenes encourage children to behave violently?' The experimental hypothesis is a testable statement of what the researcher seeks to find, such as: 'Exposing young children to violent scenes will increase their observed degree of violent behaviour.'

10.2.3 Independent and dependent variables

As previously explained, the experimental method is designed to show cause and effect. The researchers manipulate the IV in the test sample.

The variables have to be **operationalised**, meaning that both the IVs and DVs need to be measurable.

In Loftus and Palmer, for example, the IV was operationalised, as a measurement on a semantic scale. The five groups all received the question 'About how far were the cars going when they _____ into each other', but the IV filling the blank was manipulated for each group, the verb variously being 'contacted', 'hit', 'collided', 'bumped' and 'smashed'. The DV was operationalised on an arithmetical scale. Each participant checked the box that best corresponded with the estimated speed.

The researcher needs to bear in mind the need to control any extraneous variables, to make it a fair test.

10.2.4 Sampling technique

Sampling is used to select participants for a study. The investigator's aim is that the sample represents the **target population**, the population being researched. There are several methods, each with its own strengths and limitations:

1 Random sampling

Random sampling is where each member of the population has an equal chance of being selected. A computer program can generate a random list from the target population. The names of the target population can be written on pieces of paper, put into a container and the sample drawn by lottery.

The strength of the method is that the findings of such a sample may readily be generalised to the target population, as random sampling minimises the chance of bias. Its limitations are that it is necessary to determine that the people available for participation do actually represent the target population. In addition, small samples may not contain a sufficient variety of participants to represent the different elements within the target population. Furthermore, any participant withdrawals may leave the final sample as less representative.

One-tailed hypothesis test: the direction of the relationship between the IV and DV is predicted, forming part of the hypothesis.

Two-tailed hypothesis test: it is predicted that a relationship between the IV and DV exists, but it could be in either direction.

Operationalisation: a statement of how the IVs and DVs are to be measured.

Target population: the population being researched through a sample.

Random sampling: where each member of the researched population has an equal chance of being selected.

2 Stratified sampling

Stratified sampling is where the target population is divided up for sampling purposes into different sections, such as age groups or income groups. If, for example, 30% of the target population is aged 18–30, 40% is 31–55 and 30% is over 55, then 30% of the sample will be selected from the younger age group, 40% from the middle age group and 30% from the older age group.

This method's strength is that it reduces the chance of bias. It seeks to identify and represent different groups within the target population. A stratified sample is likely to more accurately represent the target population than a random sample. However, the researchers may not have sufficient knowledge of the differences within the target population that would be needed to select a stratified sample.

3 Opportunity (convenience) sampling

Opportunity (convenience) sampling is where the selected sample is made up of participants who are able and willing to take part in the study at a given time. University researchers are likely to invite undergraduate students, as they tend to be the most accessible. IB psychology students working on their internal-assessment simple experimental study may well confine their participants to students at their own school.

The strength of this method is that less effort will be needed to find enough people who are eligible to take part in such a study. The limitations are similar to those of random sampling: likely to be unrepresentative of the target population, and problems created by participants who initially take part and subsequently use their ethical right to withdraw.

4 Volunteer (self-selected) sampling

Volunteer (self-selected) sampling is where the sample is made up of participants who wish to take part rather than being selected by the researcher. An example is the participants in Milgram's study of obedience (Chapter 2), who were recruited by newspaper advertisement.

Such a sample has the obvious strength of being easy to form. People who volunteer might be less likely to want to undermine the study, making such a screw-you effect less likely. On the other hand, the same people might show demand characteristics, giving the response they think the researchers want. In addition, the sample is less likely to be representative, as those who volunteer may tend to have traits that are not common to the target population.

5 Purposive sample

Purposive sampling is where the sample is made up of participants who possess the particular characteristics that are being researched. An example is the study of the efficacies of various treatments for depression in Elkin et al. (1989) (Chapter 6), whose participants were all people diagnosed as depressed.

A purposive sample may become a **snowball sample**, where participants already in the study help the researcher to recruit more participants through their social networks.

The sample will have the strength of excluding participants without the characteristics being researched. In addition, depressed people are likely to know other depressed people, which may be useful in recruiting the sample. The sample may, however, not be representative. For example, all people diagnosed with depression may be eligible to take part. However, the sample may not necessarily represent the entire population of clinically-diagnosed depressed people. The severely-depressed may be under-represented, with the more mildly-depressed being over-represented.

10.2.5 Ethical considerations

The main purpose of the ethical codes in psychology is to protect the well-being and dignity of the participants. They apply whether the study is quantitative or qualitative. However, qualitative studies require additional precautions, as the typically longer-term association between researcher and participant can reveal personal information, which has the potential of interfering with

Stratified sampling: where the target population is divided up into different sections for sampling purposes, such as age groups or income groups.

Opportunity (convenience) sampling: where the selected sample is made up of participants who are able and willing to take part in the study at a given time.

Volunteer (self-selected) sampling: where the sample is made up of participants who wish to take part rather than being selected by the researcher.

Snowball sample: where participants already in the study help the researcher to recruit more.

researcher objectivity. In addition, it could be harder to ensure anonymity with the smaller number of participants.

Research ethical practices are framed within the purpose of the study and its benefit to society, and the researchers' moral, political and personal position and interest in the study.

It is usual practice that a professionally-conducted research project receives the approval of an academic ethics committee at the early stages, particularly if any deception may be involved. The following areas of ethical concern have to be satisfied before the research may proceed.

Informed consent

This means that the participants have to know the purpose of the study, their roles in the study, and that their agreeing to participate is entirely voluntary. The researchers have a duty to communicate all those elements clearly, and in a manner that is fully accessible to all the participants.

Consent is normally obtained from the participants though the use of a written consent form. The permission of parent or legal guardian is required where the participant is under the legal age of consent.

Sometimes fully-informed consent at the outset of study would involve revealing information that would affect the outcome. Such a study may still be ethically acceptable as long it does not harm the participants, and the participants are fully debriefed at the end of the study.

A research study planned to gather and use covertly-obtained data will probably require approval from an academic ethics approval board before it takes place. Favourable opinion is likely to be granted as long as the researchers demonstrate that the knowledge to be gained from the project is of value to society and cannot be obtained other than covertly. It is unlikely to be given where the investigation could endanger the well-being of the participants.

The protection of participants from harm

This, above all, needs to guarantee anonymity, confidentiality, protection of privacy and protection from anything that might cause discomfort or distress during the investigation. At the outset, the researcher needs to communicate to the participants their right to withdraw during and after the study. The right to withdraw includes respecting the participant's wish that the information given prior to the withdrawal is not used.

In the rare cases where full anonymity is not possible, the participants should be fully informed of the realities, on which basis they may decide whether to take part.

Precautions should be taken to ensure that the data will not be revealed to anyone. Typically, written data is stored on private premises or locked inside a safe. Material stored electronically should be on a password-protected disc or be encrypted. The researcher must have the exclusive use of the device used to record the data; a shared university library computer is not ethically acceptable. After the research is completed, the research material would normally have to be destroyed.

The protection of participants from being exploited

Analysis must be conducted in good faith, with due attention to elements that might detract from the integrity of the study, such as researcher bias and reflexivity. This is especially important when the participants belong to the more vulnerable sections of society. It is normal to inform participants that they will be given access to a copy of the research when it is completed. However, this may have to be balanced against the possibility that a participant's reading the findings of the final research report might adversely affect their psychological well-being.

The research must also follow the standard ethical research practices of assessing in which circumstances the data can be revealed to other researchers not directly involved with the study.

10.3 Analysing data

Data analysis is the stage where the researcher processes the raw data in order to discover possible trends. That data can be in different forms, including interview transcripts and numerical outputs.

10.3.1 Inductive content analysis

Inductive content analysis is a qualitative method of analysis that aims to generate new theory based on the data.

Inductive content analysis uses classification codes to reduce volumes of recorded material, such as transcripts or field notes, into more manageable and typically hierarchically-structured data from which the researcher seeks to identify patterns and gain insights. Inductive content analysis arrives at meanings that are drawn out of the data provided by the interviewee. There is no pre-existing theoretical framework. It differs from a deductive approach, where the researcher will have a pre-existing theoretical framework to accommodate the participant's response. In inductive content analysis, the focus is what emerges from the data.

Inductive content analysis may be carried out by **interpretative phenomenological analysis (IPA)** which typically involves:

- working through the transcripts or field notes, using colour or other coding

- identifying emergent themes

- deciding how those themes relate to each other through placing them in clusters and hierarchies (e.g. the effect on a parent of the first child leaving home would be placed in the 'child leaving home' cluster)

- producing a summary table of the themes and relevant details according to the interviewed participant(s).

Inductive content analysis has the strength of also being suitable for the analysis of **post-modern transcripts**. A post-modern transcript does not only contain the words said, but also the gestures, hesitations, fillers such as 'OK' and 'um', body language and changes in tone of voice. Inductive content analysis also has sufficient flexibility to make it possible for investigators to identify and explore relationships that were not envisaged at the time of planning the research.

Its limitations include reflexivity issues: determining how far the findings are actually grounded in the data as opposed to the personal situation of the researcher. Is the researcher seeing what there is or what they would like to see? This difficulty may be partly overcome by enabling several rather than just one researcher to analyse the data, using a pre-agreed standardised set of codes and comparing the findings.

Interpretative phenomenological analysis (IPA): a means of carrying out inductive content analysis, typically involving colour coding, identifying emergent themes and seeking to organise them into a framework from which theory may be generated.

Post-modern transcript: where the interview transcript does not only contain the words, but also the gestures, hesitations and fillers.

10.3.2 Statistics

This section is a summary of rather than a guide to the use of statistics in psychological research.

Descriptive statistics

Descriptive statistics describe the centre and spread of the data. These are efficient ways of summarising and graphing the data. Descriptive statistics in psychology are drawn from the sample and then critically applied to the situation of the target population. The statistics included in this section - measures of central tendency and measures of dispersion – are most effective at summarising data.

- The **measure of central tendency** is a single value that shows the degree that data clusters around the central value, which may be the mean (average), median (number at the midpoint of the data-range), or mode (number occurring most frequently).

- The **measure of dispersion** is the extent that the values within the data differ from the mean.

Descriptive statistics: these describe the spread and range of the data. An efficient way of summarising and graphing the data.

Measure of central tendency: a single value indicating the degree that the data clusters around the central value.

Measure of dispersion: the extent that the data is spread around the mean.

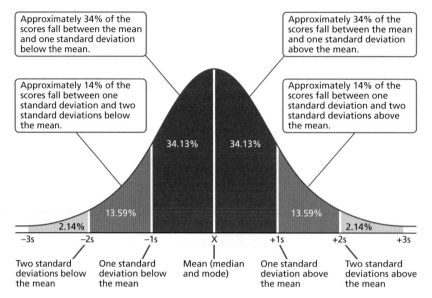

Figure 10.1 A normal distribution

Dispersion can be shown by using quartiles which divides the rank-ordered data into four equal parts, named Q1, Q2, Q3 and Q4. The **inter-quartile range** is a measure of variability, showing the range of scores within each quartile.

However, the most commonly used measure of spread is the standard deviation from the mean, which is calculated by finding the square root of the variance.

The **normal distribution** forms a symmetrical bell-shaped curve. A normal distribution for any particular attribute features a central tendency: most scores of individuals are at or close to the mean, with the number of scores decreasing the further from the mean. For example, it could be that most 18-year-olds need seven hours of sleep per night, but a considerable number cannot manage on less than eight hours, and yet a similar number need only six. There will be fewer who require less than six, and as few who require more than eight. If that is the case, the number of hours of sleep required by 18-year-olds follows the normal distribution.

A distribution is skewed when the median is not the same as the mean. Such a distribution will produce an asymmetric curve. For example, if most 18-year-olds need seven hours of sleep per night, but a greater number require eight than can manage on six, the distribution will be positively skewed. Where more need only six and fewer require eight, the distribution will be negatively skewed.

Presentation of quantitative data

Collected data may be summarised as a data table, in which each row represents a different participant and each column represents a different variable as exemplified in Table 10.1.

Hours of sleep needed per night	Number of participants	% of participants
Less than 5	2	0.35
5–6	18	3.15
6–7	63	11.0
7–8	118	20.6
8–9	120	21.9
9–10	72	12.6
10–11	19	3.33
More than 11	3	0.53

Table 10.1 Data table showing variation in the hours of sleep per night needed at age 18

Inter-quartile range: the range of the middle 50% of the scores Q3–Q1.

Normal distribution: where the distribution of particular values have a bell-shaped tendency; most scores of individuals are at or close to the mean, with the number of scores decreasing further from the mean.

The type of graph used to illustrate the results depends on the nature of the data, and whether the variable being graphed is continuous or discrete.

A **continuous variable** has an infinite number of possible values, even within a range. For example, hours of sleep for an individual could be 7, 7.4, 7.39, 7.398 and so on. There is no restriction on precision to any measurement. Histograms are used to represent continuous data, in which the bars are not separated, but joined together.

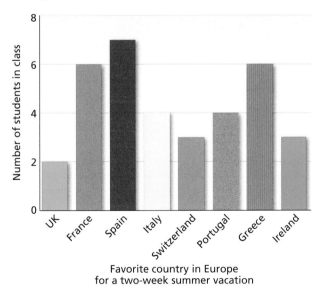

Continuous variable: where a variable has an infinite number of possible values, even within a range.

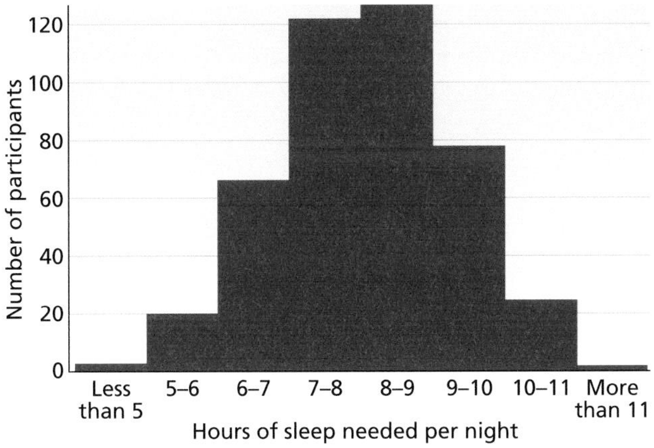

Figure 10.2 Example of a histogram

A **discrete variable** has a limited number of possible values, of countable numbers. An example is where the data on the appraisal of a performance is in the form of a semantic scale of 1 to 5 representing strongly disliked, disliked, neither liked nor disliked, liked or strongly liked. No value can be other than one of those possibilities: there cannot be a 3.5 or 3.49. Discrete variables are restricted in precision for measurement. They are represented by bar charts, in which the bars are not joined together, but separated.

Discrete variable: where a variable has a limited number of possible values.

Figure 10.3 Example of a bar chart

Pie charts may be used to present the frequency of categories as percentages.

Inferential statistics aim to highlight relationships and trends in the data, and their degree of significance. They are the tools used to infer patterns in the sample and determine whether or not these indicate similar patterns within the whole population.

Correlation studies measure the degree to which two or more variables appear to relate to one another. Data from correlation studies can be analysed by calculating the **correlation coefficient**, typically by using the Spearman's rho or Pearson product moment statistical tests.

Pie charts: a circular graphic divided so that the relative size of each slice illustrates a numerical proportion.

Inferential statistics: these aim to highlight relationships and trends in the data, and their degree of significance.

Correlation coefficient: a value that shows the degree to which the variables correlate, and the likelihood of the found degree of correlation occurring by chance.

Both of these show the degree to which the variables correlate, and the likelihood of the found degree of correlation occurring by chance. Which one of those two statistics is suitable depends on the nature of the data, considered later in this section. A coefficient of 0.0 indicates no correlation; 0.3 or −0.3 shows a weak correlation, 0.4–0.7 or −0.4 − −0.7 shows a medium correlation, with above 0.7 or −0.7 showing a strong correlation.

Experimental studies that are quantitatively-based are designed to generate two (or more) sets of data, from the control group and from the test group(s). Inferential testing is applied to determine whether there is a mathematically-determinable and significant difference between the data generated from the control and the test groups. It is on that basis that the researcher can make an informed judgement as to whether the data indicates significant differences or not.

In all cases, the researcher:

1 sets a hypothesis

2 selects an inferential statistical test

3 uses the data and test's formula to calculate a value

4 looks up the value in a distribution table for that particular test to see whether differences have or do not have the mathematical support of being significant.

The **significance level** α is the amount of tolerated error. The significance level of 0.05 is commonly used, meaning that there is a 5% chance that such a relationship might have occurred by chance. The lower the α value, the greater the chance that a real difference exists between the two samples.

Whatever the significance level set, there is the possibility of the null hypothesis being wrongly accepted or wrongly rejected.

For example, α is set at 0.05. The actual result is 0.04. The results would be found to be statistically significant. The null hypothesis would be rejected. If the distribution found was in fact due to mere chance and unrelated to the variables being studied, there would have been **Type 1 error** (the difference in data between two or more samples is accepted as being real, but is actually not).

If, however, the actual result is 0.06, the results would be described as being not statistically significant. The null hypothesis would be accepted. If in fact the differences between the samples was real, there would have been a **Type 2 error** (the difference in data between two or more samples is wrongly found to be insignificant).

Whether to minimise Type 1 or Type 2 errors depends on the context of the research. The researcher has to bear in mind that the two error types are interlinked, so when one is increased the other is decreased.

These error possibilities may be reduced by replicating the research several times and comparing the distribution. They may also be more simply reduced by calculating the standard error, a value that indicates how confident the researcher can be that the sample mean is similar to the true mean of the population.

The correct choice of the inferential statistic to be calculated and applied depends on the nature of the data, the research design and whether the hypothesis proposes a difference between two or more data samples or a correlation between two or more data samples.

The data can be in four forms:

1 **nominal**: for example, types of music enjoyed, ways in which students travel from home to school

2 **ordinal**: for example, positions in a competition: first place, second place

3 **interval**: for example, scores in competition: the person in first place may have a score of 93%, the second 92%, the third 84%

4 **ratio data**: for example, the difference between 1 and 2 is the same as the difference between 3 and 4.

Significance level: probability level (α) set by the researcher at which the null hypothesis will be rejected.

Type 1 error: where the difference in data between two or more samples is accepted as being real, but is actually not. A true null hypothesis is rejected, when it should not be.

Type 2 error: where the difference in data between two or more samples is wrongly found to be insignificant. A false null hypothesis is rejected when it should not be.

Nominal data: where data is categorical; neither measured nor ordered, but placed into distinct categories.

Ordinal data: where data is ordered, but the distance between those categories is unknown.

Interval data: where distance between the values within the data is known.

Ratio data: quantitative data that can be measured on a scale. It may be multiplied and divided, and has a non-arbitrary zero.

The research design also determines the range of suitable inferential statistics, depending on whether it is an independent measures design or a repeated measures design. For this purpose the matched pair design follows the same range as the repeated measures design, as similar rather than random participants are in the control and test conditions.

There is a range of suitable tests:

- The independent t-test: used where the data is in an interval form, the research is independent samples design, and the hypotheses propose a difference between two data samples.

- The repeated t-test: used where the data is in an interval form, the research is repeated samples design, and the hypotheses propose a difference between two data samples.

- The Mann–Whitney U test: used where the data is in an ordinal form, the research is independent design, and the hypotheses propose a difference between two data samples.

- The Wilcoxon (signed-matched ranks): used where the data is in an ordinal form, the research is repeated measures design, and the hypotheses propose a difference between two data samples.

- The chi-squared test: used where the data is in a nominal form, the research is independent design, and the hypotheses propose a difference between two data samples.

- The sign test: used where the data is in a nominal form, the research is repeated design, and the hypotheses propose a difference between two data samples.

- Spearman's rho: used where the data is of interval or ordinal (but not nominal) form, the data is in the form of paired scores from each participant, and a significant correlation is predicted between two samples.

- Pearson product movement: used where the data is of interval form, the data is in the form of paired scores from each participant, and a significant correlation is predicted between two or more data samples. In addition, the data has to follow the normal distribution.

10.4 Evaluating research

Research is evaluated in terms of reliability, validity, credibility and possibilities of different categories of bias.

Reliability

Reliability is the degree to which the study in repeated trials using the same methods, design and measurements produces the same results.

A research study's reliability may be assessed by the **test–retest method**, which requires giving the same test to the same participants on two different occasions, and correlating the scores. A stronger correlation means a greater reliability. When several researchers conduct the investigation by observation, correlating all the observers' scores may similarly assess **inter-observer reliability**.

Validity

Validity assesses how accurately the study measures what it is designed to measure. A study that consistently gives the same wrong results is reliable, but it is certainly not valid.

A study is internally valid when the differences between the test and control samples have been caused entirely by the manipulation of the IV, with all extraneous variables rigorously controlled. **Internal validity** is supported where standardised instructions are followed consistently, and where the possibilities of **investigator effects** and demand characteristics are minimised. Investigator effects happen where the researcher's attitude and demeanour influence the responses and behaviours of the participants.

Theory of Knowledge

In reflecting on the range of methods used in this chapter, how far do the approaches in psychology resemble or differ from those used in natural science?

Test-retest method: reliability is assessed by giving the same test to the same participants on two different occasions, and correlating the findings or scores.

Inter-observer reliability: reliability is assessed in observational studies by employing several observers and correlating their findings or scores.

Internal validity: this is achieved where the differences between the test and control samples have been caused entirely by the accurate manipulation of the IV, with all extraneous variables rigorously controlled.

Investigator effects: where the researcher's attitude and demeanour influence the responses and behaviours of the participants.

External validity: where the results of a study can be generalised or transferred to a different environment, population or time period.

Credibility: used in qualitative research, it establishes how far the results of the research are in agreement with the phenomenon under study, and with the participants' perceptions and experiences.

Bias (research): factors that can adversely affect the accuracy of a study.

Researcher bias: elements that could influence the investigator to analyse the data in a non-objective manner.

Participant bias: where those taking part may answer or behave in the way that they think fits in with the researcher or with other participants.

Sampling bias: where the sampling procedure does not accurately represent the target population.

A study is externally valid where the results of a study can be generalised or transferred to a different environment, population or time period. For example, Asch's study (Chapter 5) on conforming to majority influence lacks **external validity** as more recent replications have shown significantly lower degrees of conformity.

A research study's validity may be judged by assessing how far the research remains valid over time. Validity may also be determined by correlating test scores with another test that has been established as valid.

Credibility

Credibility, used in qualitative research, serves the same purpose as internal validity in quantitative research. Credibility is maximised where the study produces the truest possible picture of what is being investigated. Credibility is also supported where researcher reflexivity possibilities are suitably addressed and the proceedings of the research are carefully documented, making it possible for other investigators to critically follow the entire research process. Overall, credibility establishes how far the results of the research are in agreement with the phenomenon under study, and with the participants' perceptions and experiences.

Possibilities of bias

Bias (research) refers to factors that can adversely affect the accuracy of a study. Commonly-studied biases are researcher bias, participant bias and sampling bias.

Researcher bias includes elements that could influence the investigator to analyse the data in a non-objective manner. It may include the investigator's beliefs, ideals and hoped-for findings. It can also involve confirmation bias: over-considering information and interpretations that confirm pre-existing opinions and expectations, and under-considering those that contradict them. The findings may be more likely to reflect the researcher's hopes and expectations than the position and ideas of the participants. This is investigated in Lord et al. (1979) (Chapter 4), which considers the nature of confirmation bias, and the degree to which such a bias would lead to inconsistencies in assessing supporting and contradictory evidence.

The problem of researcher bias may be addressed by reflexivity. The idea of reflexivity is that the researcher needs to reflect on their own background and beliefs, and how these could influence the research process. It acknowledges that background and beliefs can influence the way research is conducted and how the findings can be interpreted. Good practice requires researchers to provide sufficient details about issues that might bias the investigation, such as political ideology or cultural background.

Participant bias involves the possibility that those taking part may answer or behave in the way that they think fits in with the researcher or with other participants. They do not wish to give away information that may be perceived as being socially undesirable. It can happen that a participant contradicts himself or herself later on in the interview, on feeling more accustomed to the situation. The interviewer would need to check the two responses with the participant, exploring the possibility of a higher level of participant wariness during the earlier stages of the interview.

Sampling bias occurs where the sampling procedure does not accurately represent the target population. In quantitative research, it may occur in a stratified sample, where minority communities or particular age groups could be over-represented or under-represented in the sample. It could also happen in qualitative research, where the selection criteria may, for example, recruit people already known to the researcher or the researcher's department.

10.5 Drawing conclusions

The conclusions are likely to state that the study has supported the researchers' hypothesis if the null hypothesis has been rejected. That is likely to happen if the differences between the control and test populations are statistically significant after manipulating the IV.

However, good practice in psychology at this stage will consider these questions:

1   How far can **replication** be applied to the study? Is it likely to show the same significant relationships with different researchers, in a different location and/or at a different time of the year?

2   How far can **generalisation** (quantitative data) be applied to the study? How far does what the researchers concluded from their sample study apply to the target population, and possibly wider populations?

3   How far are findings of the study transferable (qualitative data) to settings and/or populations outside the study? A study's transferability can considerably widen if it is supported by findings from similar studies.

4   Do the findings of the research show a comparable level of significance if different methods are used to investigate the same phenomenon, such as a content analysis of the participant's written reflections, participant observation and a series of one-to-one semi-structured interviews? This practice is called triangulation, where a study's credibility can be improved by the application of several separate methods to check whether they yield similar results.

Replication: repeating a study with a view to investigating whether it is likely to show the same significant relationships with different researchers, in a different location and/or at a different time of the year.

Generalisation (quantitative data): assessing how far what the researchers concluded from their sample study applies to the target population, and possibly wider populations.

SELF-ASSESSMENT QUESTIONS 10.1

1   Name and describe five quantitative methods commonly used in psychological research. Name a research study exemplifying each.

2   Name and describe three qualitative methods commonly used in psychological research. Name a research study exemplifying each.

3   List and briefly explain eight possibilities of bias in psychological research.

4   List, describe and exemplify three different common quantitative experimental research designs.

5   List and describe six methods of sampling.

6   List and describe three main categories of ethical considerations.

7   Define inductive content analysis, and describe the four stages of carrying out an inductive content analysis of qualitative data.

8   Differentiate with examples the difference between descriptive and inferential statistics.

9   Distinguish between the validity (internal and external), reliability and credibility of a research study.

Critical thinking

Discuss the extent that the following studies may be:

1   replicated among other groups and cultures of your choice
2   generalised (if quantitative) / transferred (if qualitative) to other groups and cultures of your choice.

In your response, identify and assess any possible ethical issues:

a   Asch (1956) (Chapter 5)
b   Loftus and Palmer (1974) (Chapter 4)
c   Yuille and Cutshall (1986) (Chapter 4)
d   Totten (2003) (Chapter 7)
e   Alter et al. (2007) (Chapter 4)

Chapter summary

1 Quantitative research requires the collecting and analysis of numerical data. It may or may not be experimental in design. It is likely to involve a relatively large number of sample participants who will typically be required to perform similar tasks. The data analysis will involve statistical testing and an assessment of how far the findings may be generalised. The study can be experimental, non-experimental or correlational. It can take place in the laboratory or in the natural environment.

2 Qualitative researchers aim to obtain an in-depth understanding of human behaviour and the factors that govern such behaviour. They make use of naturalistic observations, interviews and case studies. The qualitative method investigates the **why** and **how** of behaviour, not just **what**, **where** and **when**. Hence, smaller but focused samples are more often used than large samples. Sometimes the research may be based on one single detailed case study.

3 Quantitative research designs may take the form of independent measures, repeated measures and matched pairs.

4 Experimental studies have a testable hypothesis that is operationalised. It is usually expressed as a null hypothesis.

5 A sample of participants is designed to represent the target population. The sample can be random, stratified, opportunity, volunteer, purposive or snowball.

6 Research in psychology is subject to professionally-based ethical guidelines primarily designed to protect the well-being and dignity of the participants.

7 Qualitative data is typically processed by content analysis, which may be deductive or inductive.

8 Quantitative data is typically processed by statistical methods, at the stages of describing, presenting and analysing the data. The precise statistical methods used will depend on whether or not the data is normally distributed, whether the study is experimental or correlational, the experimental design if the study is experimental, and whether the data is in interval, ordinal or nominal form.

9 Significance levels in inferential statistical analysis are set by the researcher, to indicate whether the null hypothesis should be rejected or not rejected.

10 Research is evaluated in terms of reliability, validity, credibility and possibilities of different categories of bias.

11 In concluding that the study's findings are significant, good practice in psychology will consider the study's scope for replication, generalisation (quantitative), transferability (qualitative) and the use of method triangulation to enhance credibility.

Exam-style question

Short-answer questions

The stimulus material below is a study on the reasons that students drop out of high school.

This research aimed to investigate the reasons that young people fail to complete their high school (secondary) education. The investigators conducted this study in the hope that understanding the causes of student dropping out at some point during the last two years of school could inform new approaches to developing more attractive and personally-relevant school programmes that would encourage such students to continue at school until age 18.

The researchers used a purposive sample in a city of 400 000 people. It was recruited through online social media, youth clubs and places in the city centre that regularly attract young people. The sample consisted of males and females from a variety of ethnic groups, and had a total of 24 participants aged 16 to 18.

Before the interview, each participant was told that their input would be anonymous and that they would have the right to withdraw at any stage. Their response would be audiotaped for the sole purpose of transcription and inductive content analysis, after which the recordings would be destroyed. Each participant was interviewed separately, and signed a consent form.

The semi-structured interview covered possible factors influencing dropping out of school, such as employment opportunities, influence of friends, and personal issues including boredom and unhappiness at school.

The results showed that the reasons for dropping out of school varied. Fewer than expected were working full-time in paid employment and in various productive, income-generating online activities. A few reported unhappiness at having constantly received poor grades. But the most common reasons were that they found school boring, repetitive, predictable and bound by rules that made them feel like small children.

The investigators concluded that schools should view each dropout case as complex and influenced by a gradual build-up of various factors in the last years of schooling. Consideration should be given to enabling the specialist teaching of student-centred programmes such as basic financial literacy, home and car repairs, and food preparation, as well as school-connected work-experience programmes. They recommended further research into the form that such programmes might actually take, given the schools' budgets and range of resources.

Answer all the following three questions.

1   **a**   Identify the method used and outline two characteristics of the method. [3 marks]

    b   Describe the sampling method used in the study. [3 marks]

    c   Suggest an alternative or additional method, giving one reason for your choice. [3 marks]

2   Describe the ethical considerations that were applied in the study, and explain if further ethical considerations could be applied. [6 marks]

3   Discuss the possibility of generalising the findings of the study. [9 marks]

Answers

Answers to exam-style questions in the coursebook are annotated with sample comments from a teacher. Look out for this guidance in the answers for any short-answer questions or essay response questions.

Chapter 1

Self-assessment questions

Self-assessment questions 1.1

1   a   Psychology is the disciplined study of the mind and behaviour.
   b   Empiricism holds that the understanding of human behaviour needs to be based on findings that can be observed and counted. Positivism holds that theory on human behaviour has to be supported by scientific evidence.
   c   Both empiricism and positivism aim to give structure and scientific credibility to the development of theory and research in psychology.

2   The biological approach is concerned with the ways that genetics, the nervous system and the endocrine system influence human thoughts and actions. The cognitive approach focuses on the ways that the mind processes information. The socio-cultural approach considers the ways that collective experiences, group identity and language impact on the behaviour of the individual.

3   Scientific credibility is achieved where the research is based on paradigms, whose underlying theory promotes the development of hypotheses that can generate the necessary precise data to refute the hypothesis. Barriers to scientific credibility may include ecological validity: problems with laboratories sufficiently resembling the real life situations they are designed to replicate. They may also include correlational data, where cause and effect cannot be established as there may be other factors operating on the variables studied.

4   Four of the debates underlying much of psychological theory and research are:
   a   the nature-nurture debate – are the dominant influences on behaviour the genetic and nervous systems or the influence of people and the environment?
   b   The reductionist-holism debate – are behaviours caused by one dominant factor or the interaction of several differing factors?
   c   The freewill-determinism debate – do we have relatively strong or relatively little control over our behaviour patterns?
   d   the nomothetic-idiographic debate – do the findings in the study of person's behaviour patterns apply to that person only or may they be generalised to other people in similar conditions and situations?

5   Four potential causes of bias in research in psychology are: ethnocentrism and generalising its findings from one group or culture to another; theoretical bias and generalising the theory from one group or culture to another; methodological bias and generalising the data–analysis criteria from one group or culture to another; and gender bias and generalising the findings from research on one gender to another.

Chapter 2

Self-assessment questions

Self-assessment questions 2.1

1   a   Psychology is a discipline composed of theories of human behaviour based on scientific evidence. Pop-psychology is where human behaviours are explained by popular opinion, but insufficiently supported by research. Psychobabble involves the application of the terminology of psychology in a manner that is not academically acceptable.

b Quantitative research is based on figures that are generated from surveys, interviews, observations and questionnaire responses. They can be statistically summarised, and statistically analysed. Qualitative research is based on the more extended and descriptive data that typically comes from personal journal entries and interview transcripts. The information does not translate into figures.

c Empirical evidence uses findings based on observation, experience and experimentation with a suitably large number of people, but typically will be applying the same chosen method to the data. Triangulation in research is where more than one method is used to determine the relationship between the same two or more variables. This typically involves the use of both quantitative and qualitative methods.

d Experimental research is distinguished from non-experimental research in that experimental work carries out the research under both test and control conditions. These conditions are identical, except for the one variable that is changed in the experimental condition.

e The independent variable (IV) in experimental psychology is what is changed in the test condition, but held constant in the control condition. The dependent variable (DV) in experimental psychology is what is being affected in both the test and control conditions.

f True experimental investigations are within a laboratory setting. Quasi-experimental investigations are where the researcher imposes the situation of the test and control investigation using the pre-existing natural environment.

g Hawthorne effect is where the participant senses the unfamiliar environment and is determined to co-operate with the researcher, giving responses they think the researcher wants to hear without necessarily being true. Screw-you effect is where the participant, determined not to co-operate, gives the response that they think the researchers do not want to hear without it necessarily being true.

2 The five elements required for an item of experimental research in psychology to be valid are:
   a grounds for theorising that a psychological relationship might exist between two variables
   b the setting and justification of a hypothesis
   c the collection of suitable and sufficiently controlled samples to be statistically significant in testing
   d the analysis of the data in terms of the hypothesis
   e the decision of whether to accept or reject the hypothesis.
   In addition, the work must be objective, replicable, not subject to outside influences and structured to produce results that can predict future behaviour. It also has to satisfy the professional ethical criteria.

Self-assessment questions 2.2

1 The autonomous state of mind is where a person makes decisions and takes full responsibility for the consequences. The agentic state of mind is where a person obeys without question the instructions of those accepted as authority figures, such as parents, teachers and employers. The conclusions of Milgram's study indicated that most of his participants were agentic as they followed their instructor to the degree of inflicting believed-to-be extreme suffering and even death on a fellow participant in the study.

2 Two strengths of Milgram's research:
   a ecological validity for the situation of obedience to 'higher and better-informed authority'
   b procedures were well-standardised and obedience was accurately measured. The sample contained 40 people who had been selected from a cross-section of the male population aged 20-50.

Two limitations of Milgram's research:
   a The obedience of 26 out of the 40 people did not come out of enthusiasm for the task, but through having to be prodded by the instructor.
   b It could have also been due to the conformist nature of the participants who had been selected on the basis of having answered a newspaper advertisement.

3 Curtiss's study of Genie:

   a It was a qualitative study as it relied on observing her behaviour after being discovered at the age of 13, and noting the quality of her speech and social interaction. It was not quantitative as she was the only participant.

   b It is a longitudinal research study as it continued with Genie for an extended period from 1977.

   c Content analysis was used by the researchers to find patterns within the qualitative data obtained from interactions with Genie.

   d Reflexivity raises the issue of whether the interpretations of the findings on Genie may have been influenced by the viewpoint of the researcher.

Self-assessment questions 2.3

1 The six principal ethical guidelines for research with human participants are informed consent, avoidance of deception, protection of participants, the right to withdraw at any stage, entitlement to debriefing, and confidentiality. In addition, the use of suitable approaches towards ethnically-sensitive groups.

2 Covert observation is more likely to involve more issues with ethics than overt observation, as not only have the participants not given informed consent but there is an element of deception. Covert observation may only be considered where the information sought is of high value to the public welfare and it cannot be obtained in any other way.

Chapter 3

Theory of Knowledge

1 Responses may include:

- The behavioural-based observation that prejudice is genetically influenced even though no such gene has been found.
- The amygdala section of the brain registering negative emotions and motivations towards people different to us, observable in fMRI scans.
- Possible lower levels of oxytocin, dopamine and seratonin neurotransmitters brought to a strange social situation, observable in fMRI scans.
- Possible stressed feelings in a strange situation being combated by the cortisol hormone, detectable in a blood sample.

2 Responses may include:

- The medial prefrontal cortex interpreting rather than merely negatively reacting to the strange situation, observable under fMRI brain scanning.
- The capacity of the prefrontal cortex being able to generate some empathy when dealing with a fellow human being, as in Harris and Fiske.
- Non-biological elements within the cognitive and socio-cultural approaches to behaviour that are interacting with and modifying biological responses.

Self-assessment questions

Self-assessment questions 3.1

1 **a** Hormones are biochemical substances produced by glands within the endocrine system, carried in the bloodstream. Neurotransmitters are biochemical substances produced within the nervous system and travel across the synapses of neurons that carry the specific stimuli to the next neuron. Both hormones and neurotransmitters bio-determine the way the body synchronises and adjusts to specific stimuli and conditions.

b Dopamine is a neurotransmitter that helps to control the brain's reward and pleasure centres. Increased dopamine levels in the brain mean increased pleasurable stimulation. Serotonin is a neurotransmitter which when fired causes feelings of pleasure. It is an inhibitory neurotransmitter, employed by the nervous system to medicate pain, control sleep and regulate mood. Oxytocin is both a neurotransmitter and hormone that is discharged through the pituitary gland into the bloodstream. It promotes feelings of love, trust and acceptance of one another.

2 a All four studies showed brain function localisation.

b Gage introduced the concept of brain functions being localised. The pole travelling through his brain left some of his mental capacities intact, but reduced or destroyed others. Broca's case study showed that the functions of specifically the left frontal lobe of the brain included the capacity to create speech. Wernicke's case study showed that the functions of the posterior superior temporal gyrus included the capacity to understand speech. The HM study showed that the temporal lobes and hippocampus are involved in memory functions.

3 PET and fMRI scans produce sufficiently multi-dimensional data to show the various parts of the brain being coordinated to varying degrees of intensity. Their data enables extremely complex brain mapping, and generally rules out a single part of the brain being exclusively responsible for a specific function.

4 Harris and Fiske's (2006) fMRI-based research indicates that the medial prefrontal cortex region of the brain has the capacity to enable empathy and reason to modify the initial emotional response of the amygdala. This happens when dealing with human beings rather than objects, other than the human beings who are socially dehumanised through cognitive stereotyping as belonging to extreme out-groups.

5 The research of Baumgartner et al. (2008) indicates that high levels of the hormone and neurotransmitter oxytocin are usually present in loving relationships. They increase the capacity to trust, overlook and forgive, and also not pay attention to the other person's faults.

6 Pheromones affect the behaviours of other members of the same species, including possibly humans, through contact or proximity to the individuals that are secreting them. Behaviours may include significant menstrual synchrony in women sharing living and working space, and mood-related degree of sexual interest stimulated in nearby potential suitors. However, current studies suggesting the presence of pheromones have not been supported when reproduced, nor have human pheromones been identified as biological entities.

Self-assessment questions 3.2

1 Evolution tends to allocate mating opportunities to those whose behaviour patterns are adapted to attract a healthy partner. These behaviour patterns are likely to be genetically influenced. This in turn should produce healthy offspring.

2 a Wedekind et al. on choice of heterosexual partner (1995): the female human tends to be unconsciously attracted to the man who is going to pass on the highest-quality genetic material that is different from her own, yet co-dominant. Based on major histo-compatibility complex (MHC), this improves the offspring's physiological immunity to disease.

b Minnesota twin study, on levels of intelligence (1990): there are broad positive correlates between levels of intelligence and degree of shared genetic material between twins, which become stronger when they are reared together rather than separately.

c Hutchings and Mednick on tendency towards criminal behaviour (1975): there are broad positive correlates between propensity towards criminal behaviour and degree of shared genetic material. These correlations are higher than the non-genetically-based propensity towards criminal behaviour through growing up in a criminal-tending environment.

d Caspi et al. on likelihood of symptoms of depression (2003): participants with one or two short 5-HTT alleles showed more depressive symptoms and behaviours than those whose genotype included two long 5-HTT alleles. It indicated a link between the presence of the short 5-HTT allele and the symptoms of depression.

  e Scott-Van Zeeland et al. on likelihood of symptoms of anorexia (2014): females with anorexia showed a significantly high frequency of gene EPHX2. This gene appears to influence an enzyme that regulates the metabolism of cholesterol. That enzyme interferes with the normal processing of cholesterol, and can thus disrupt eating behaviour. This has been supported by findings indicating that those with anorexia nervosa have unusually high cholesterol levels that seem to be incompatible with their eating patterns.

3 Unlike the first three studies, the more recent research of Caspi et al. and Scott-Van Zeeland et al. both used genome-wide association studies (GWAS) to investigate whether specific genetic variants within a large number of individuals are associated with particular behavioural traits, which might indicate psychological abnormalities.

4 Ethical issues requiring special attention when researching genetic influences on behaviour would include: the need for absolute confidentiality in view of serious consequences of information on adverse genetic characteristics, the need to brief the participant of the possibility of encountering highly unpleasant previously unknown personal information, the danger of over-exaggerating the findings or taking them out of context, and particular sensitivities of specific cultural groups towards evolutionary and genetics-based research.

Self-assessment questions 3.3 (HL only)

1 Common justification for use of animals in psychology research include similarities to humans in genes and physiology, short life and breeding cycles enabling life-long and family (generations) studies, and non-practicality of using human participants in research.

2 **a** Rosenzweig et al. (1972): exposure to interesting, challenging and engaging environments appears to promote brain plasticity through the physical development of denser neural networks.

  b Hendricks et al. (2003): the nature of the individual's genotype seems to influence the propensity towards anxiety and aggressive behaviour.

  c Research teams of Professor Jurgen Götz at Queensland Brain Institute: the application of non-invasive ultrasound technology together with anti-body drug treatment appears to have potential in clearing the brain of protein-based lesions. These are associated with the memory loss and the declining cognitive functioning of patients with Alzheimer's disease.

3 The use of animals and any associated suffering must be justified in terms of the value of the research to the welfare of society. Any use or suffering must also conform to nationally-determined professional guidelines for the use of animals in research, such as within approved facilities. Animal models may only be used when the research cannot be carried out by other methods such as computer simulations, human volunteers and cell cultures.

Exam-style questions – sample answers

Short-answer question

Among the core principles that the biological approach applies to studying behaviour is that the nervous and endocrine (hormone) systems enable the body to adapt to psychologically-perceived changes in circumstances or environment. This approach holds that there are biological correlates to behaviour, indicating that the nervous and endocrine systems influence the way that the individual feels and behaves.

Could open more directly along the lines of 'A major principle of this approach is that there are biological correlates to behaviour'.

For example, the body secretes the strain-coping cortisol neuro-hormone when under stress. That helps the nervous system to be less anxiety-causing, and less sensitive to pain. It thus enables the human body to cope more calmly with the perceived increased pressures and anxieties. However, cortisol is known to interfere with memory recall, which can give an insight as to why people get memory blanks in examinations, even when they know the material perfectly.

Correct term: cortisol is not a neurotransmitter.

Good term, better than the inaccurate 'has been proven by'.

Unnecessary description: better to go straight to the point with 'autopsies of the brains of the rats placed in the test stimulating environments showed a thicker layer of neurons in the cerebral cortex sections of the brain than those in the control group who were placed in boring and non-stimulating surroundings'.

An example would help.

A second principle defining the biological approach to behaviour is that research on animal behaviour can assist in understanding human behaviour. This concept is based on the existence of shared physiological characteristics of humans and animals. It is also grounded in the apparent evolutionary relationship between humans and animals.

For example, our knowledge of the capacity of the human brain to develop more complex neuron development in specific parts of the brain due to constant and enthusiastic involvement in intellectually demanding activities is supported by the experimental work of Rosenzweig et al. (1972), which used rats. The test group of rats was put in a cage with many exciting and stimulating devices to attract their curiosity and engage their interest and involvement. The control rats were put in an ordinary cage with nothing special to do: boring, non-stimulating surroundings. The rats were killed after being in their new environments for a couple of months. Those in the test groups showed a thicker layer of neurons in the cerebral cortex sections of the brain than those in the control group.

The biological approach to behaviour has effective practical applications, such as clinically-based interactions with the nervous and endocrine systems by the use of medication in treating mental conditions.

Overall, a good response. The response is directed to the question and meets the command term requirements. Good knowledge and understanding is present, which is supported by suitable (if a little dated) research. However, there are some rather descriptive sentences that reduce the focus on the relevant principles.

Essay response question

This needs to be expanded, as psychology makes increasing use of GWAS studies to investigate whether specific genetic variants within a large number of individuals are associated with particular behavioural traits.

Though the findings from studies using twins continue to contribute data, modern studies increasingly employ GWAS studies, as commented above.

Research in how genetic inheritance influences behaviour is largely empirically based. That is because the scientific knowledge required for identifying specific combinations of genes that produce tendencies towards specific behaviours is only in the earliest stages of development.

Currently, leading studies still seem to be based on the biological correlates between genes and behaviour. They often focus on twins who share a relatively large amount of genetic material, as well as siblings who share a relatively small amount of genetic material. They strive to filter out the common socio-cultural influences by looking at the rare instances of twins being reared apart.

The Minnesota twin study (Bouchard et al.) is a longitudinal study of over 100 twins from all over the world, in progress since 1979. This research is based on the principle that the relative influence of genes as opposed to different environments can be studied by focusing on the infrequent instances of twins reared separately from each other.

The Minnesota research aims to examine the extent that genes determine intelligence. Intelligence does link with behaviour; a more intelligent person is likely to interact on a deeper level with the environment and society.

The initial participating sets of twins, some of them monozygotic (MZ) and others dizygotic (DZ), went through around 50 hours of interviewing and testing in the period leading to 1990. The findings showed a very high similarity in intelligence between MZ twins reared together, and a lower, but still high similarity in intelligence between MZ twins reared separately. DZ twins reared together showed a moderate similarity in intelligence, and those brought up separately only a relatively low level of similarity. However, all the above categories showed greater similarity in intelligence than siblings, even where they had been brought up together.

Here, the response attempts to fit in with the question on assessing the influence of genetic inheritance on behaviour.

Response incorporates suitable knowledge of the chosen research. However, 'behaviour appropriate to the degree of intelligence' is vague – examples of such behaviours would help.

Overall, the findings of the detailed sets of interviews from the Minnesota twin study indicated that 70% of intelligence and behaviour appropriate to the degree of intelligence may be attributed to genetic inheritance, and 30% to other factors.

The strengths of the study are that its size made it one of the most reliable studies of twins ever carried out. The researchers operated it as a cross-cultural study, as it included participating twins from all over the world. The study did show a broad relationship in that the greater similarities in intelligence appeared to be correlated with the larger amount of shared genetic material.

Its limitations include the fact that participants were recruited by media publicity. The study did not contain a framework that established the frequency of contact between the twins before the study. It also did not investigate the degree to which the twins raised together cognitively experienced the same environment. Finally, the results were based on observation and self-reporting. Identifying the degree of biochemical commonalities in genetic structures was beyond the scope of the study, and indeed beyond the then technical range of scientific investigation.

Whereas the Minnesota study was designed to investigate the extent that intelligence (and by extension intelligence-based behaviour) is genetically based, the work of Hutchings and Mednick studied the degree to which genes influence specifically criminal behaviour. Indeed, this study contributes to the debate over how far crime running in families is genetically influenced.

This research was empirically-based, focusing on people with criminal records who were once adopted children. It sought to investigate whether criminal behaviour was more likely to have been learnt from the adoption environment, or if it was guided by specific genes towards criminal behaviour.

This study discovered that if both the biological and adoptive fathers had criminal records, more than a third of the sons would also get criminal records. If just the biological father had a criminal record, it would drop to about a fifth of the sons getting a criminal record. Where the adoptive father had such a record it dropped to just over 10%. Where neither father had one (the control), 10% of the sons had a criminal record.

On the basis of these findings, the researchers concluded that in influencing criminal behaviour genetics played a somewhat greater role than upbringing. That would parallel the findings of the Minnesota study that was based on intelligence. However, the study may be criticised on the grounds that children who are adopted are often placed in a similar environment to their natural parents. In addition, genes seem unlikely to account for criminal behaviour peaking in the age group of 20-year-olds, and then sharply declining. Furthermore it may not be the genes, but environmental circumstances common to both the natural and adoptive parents, such as low socio-economic status, alcoholism or even maternal stress during pregnancy leading to developmental problems with the child. Moreover, legal definitions of different types of crime are unlikely to conform to genetic structures. And finally, the results of both Minnesota and Hutchings and Mednick were largely based on data correlation.

In conclusion, both studies show various levels of considerable statistical significance in the degree to which genetic inheritance influences behaviour. However, neither of them rule out the probabilities of other factors that are operational in influencing the behaviour of the individual, especially socio-cultural and environmental elements that may well vary in importance from individual to individual.

This study is suitably focused on behaviours, but it is rather dated. At least one of the studies could have been more recent, such as Caspi et al. (2003) on behaviour patterns indicating depression or Scott-Van Zeeland (2014) on behaviour patterns indicating anorexia.

Again, the response incorporates relevant detailed knowledge.

Effective analytically-presented contrast between biological and socio-cultural elements.

Conclusion answers question.

Overall, an effective and well-focused response, but needs to show knowledge of recent as well as more classical research in the rapidly advancing field of how genetics might influence behaviour.

Chapter 4

Theory of Knowledge

Reliability of reporting based on observation in psychology

Responses will vary widely, but may include ideas such as:

- findings from research such as Loftus and Palmer (1974) suggesting inaccuracies in reconstructive memory
- findings from research such as Yuille and Cutshall (1986) indicating that there may be a substantial difference between the accuracy of information recalled in a laboratory situation with misleading prompts, and the accuracy of memory recall in real life
- discussion of the role of schemas in research such as Bartlett (1932) on influencing memory recall
- experimental nature of psychology indicating findings that are not readily observable in real life, such as the extent to which misleading prompts can promote erroneous reconstructive memory.

Self-assessment questions

Self-assessment questions 4.1

1   The cognitive approach to behaviour focuses on the processes by which sensory inputs are received, processed, stored, recovered and acted upon.

2   Principles of the cognitive approach to behaviour include:
    a   The human being is an active information processor.
    b   Behaviour is influenced by cognitive representations called schemas.
    c   The cognitive representations that guide human behaviour should be studied scientifically.
    d   Cognitive processing is influenced by the emotions.
    e   Cognitive processes are influenced by social and cultural inputs.
    f   Interaction with digital devices and data may influence human memory and cognitive processes.

3   Four research methods commonly used in the cognitive approach to behaviour are:
    a   the use of experimental and quantitative methods, e.g. in Loftus and Palmer (1974) on reconstructive memory
    b   interviewing, e.g. in Brown and Kulik (1977) on flashbulb memory
    c   observational methods, e.g. in Jean Piaget's studies of the stages of the mental and intellectual development of the child
    d   brain-scanning involving the use of CAT, PET, MRI and fMRI, e.g. Sharot et al. (2007) on biological support for flashbulb memory.

4   The sensory memory (SM) receives inputs from the environment and processes attended-to inputs into the short-term memory (STM). The STM holds a limited amount of information received from the sensory memory for a maximum of 30 seconds. That information needs to be attended to in order to encode it into the LTM, the permanent human memory store with virtually unlimited capacity.

5   Both models of memory include SM STM and LTM functions. In the multi-store model, the SM attends to the information and passes it to an STM memory store, which it turn encodes it into the LTM. In the working memory model, the sensory function is represented by the central executive which additionally diverts each piece of information into the most suitable one of three STM components, each of which operates simultaneously in parallel, and all three lead to the LTM.

6   Strengths of the linear multi-store memory model include: evidence of existence of STM as separate from LTM by non-ability of anterograde amnesia patients to process information from one to the other; evidence of STM in primacy and recency effects in memorising lists of words; indications that memory is not a single store; biological evidence of the function of cortisol interfering with information transfers between the stores. Limitations include non-consideration of motivation factors in the memorising process, and that the ability to visualise and recall the sound of something at the same time strongly indicates that the STM is not one single store.

Strengths of the working memory model include: being able to accommodate a person's ability to visualise and recall the sound of something at the same time; ability to explain how different people study by different methods; ability to explain why some brain-damaged patients can recall one type of memory but not another; being supported by research on articulatory suppression (Landry & Bartling, 2011), and fMRI-based biological findings indicating that verbal and spatial inputs can be processed simultaneously in different sections of the brain (D'Esposito et al., 1995). In addition, the model can help to explain why it is possible to multi-task in some situations, such as working out a problem and looking at a picture, but not in others, such as working out two problems at the same time.

Limitations of the linear multi-store memory model: it is too simplistic, focusing more on memory stores than on the actual processes of attention and verbal rehearsal. It does not take into account the different motivations for processing information; for example, we can more readily memorise numbers if they are related to people we would like to meet again than if they are just random numbers. The ability to visualise and recall the sound of something at the same time strongly indicates that the STM is not one single store.

Limitations of the working memory model include lack of precise information on the nature and role of the CE and the exact way in which the three elements of the STM interrelate; and current uncertainty on whether additional STM stores exist. It does not explain the distortion of memory over time, or the role of emotion in the memory process.

7   Implicit memory is where information is acquired mainly without conscious effort, such as in recalling a tune. Implicit memory also includes procedural memory, such as the series of motions required to drive a car, perform a ski-jump or tie a shoelace. In contrast, explicit memory, also known as declarative memory, involves material that is consciously learnt and rehearsed, such as the task of memorising a poem or a scientific formula. Explicit memory divides into episodic memory (focusing on the details of particular events and experiences of one's life) and semantic memory (including facts and concepts).

Self-assessment questions 4.2

1   Schemas are individualised mental representations and mechanisms that process information. They build up from previously acquired knowledge and experience, and they help to organise knowledge, beliefs and expectations.

2   Schema processing involves the synthesising of new input from the environment through the mental structures already built, involving:
   a   top-down and bottom-up processing
   b   pattern recognition
   c   effort after meaning: trying to match unfamiliar ideas into a familiar framework with various degrees of success
   d   stereotyping
   e   cultural influences.

3   a   Bartlett (1932): effort after meaning; that individuals seek to match unfamiliar ideas into existing schemas with various degrees of success.
   b   Kearins (1981): schemas can be culturally influenced, developing according to the needs facing the particular society. Aboriginal Australians' millennia of desert survival enabled them to develop the spatial and visual-encoding schemas that were crucial for survival.

4   Strengths of schema theory include:
   a   framework for understanding bias and prejudice
   b   framework for understanding the selective filtering, encoding and retrieval of memory with various degrees of accuracy
   c   framework for understanding the nature and workings of reconstructive memory
   d   explaining how a new idea may be understood in terms of previously learnt ideas.

   Limitations of schema theory include:
   a   lack of ecological validity for evidence in reconstructive memory
   b   current inability to identify individual schemas biologically
   c   need to understand how cognitive schemas interrelate with emotions.

Self-assessment questions 4.3

1   System-1 thinking: where the thinking is quick, automatic, involves little effort, and is more likely to be influenced by biases. System-2 thinking: where the thinking involves patience, logic, effort, careful reasoning and application to the particular goal.

2 Strengths of the dual process model of thinking and decision-making include:
   a biological correlates suggesting that different parts of the brain engage in System-1 and System-2 thinking, exemplified by Goel at al. (2000)
   b experimentally-based findings indicating that easier and less demanding tasks employ System-1 thinking while more challenging items will use System-2 thinking, exemplified by Alter et al. (2007)
   c presence of high validity and high reliability studies indicating System 1-related cognitive biases in thinking and decision-making.

Limitations of the model include:
   a lack of precision in defining the two types of thinking
   b not factoring in the emotional condition of the decision-maker.

3 a Alter et al. (2007) found experimental-grounded evidence for the switching over to System-2 thinking when an everyday task such as reading became more difficult than usual.
   b Goel et al. (2000) found biological evidence that System-1 and System-2 thinking involved different parts of the brain: more concrete tasks using System-1 thinking tended to engage the left hemisphere temporal lobe; more abstract tasks are more likely to use System-2 thinking and tended to engage the parietal lobe.

Self-assessment questions 4.4

1 a Reconstructive memory is where schemas, beliefs, imagination and gaps in recollection combine to create an individual's inaccurate recall of events.
   b Selective memory is the ability to retrieve certain facts and events from memory, but not others.

2 a Bartlett (1932): reconstructive memory is likely to be more inaccurate the further the experience is distanced from the person's existing schemas.
   b Loftus and Palmer (1974): reconstructive memory can be inaccurate where external prompts promote schemas that can interfere with accurate recall.
   c Yuille and Cutshall (1986): reconstructive memory is more likely to be accurate in real-life eyewitness testimony, even where external prompts promote schemas that can interfere with memory recall.
   d Loftus and Pickrell (1995): adult reconstructive memory of childhood events can be inaccurate where elicited by graphic external prompts promoting false but plausible information.

3 Biases in System-1 decision-making include:
   a availability heuristic: the more available information on a particular possible happening, the more people think it could happen to them
   b peak-end rule: people's System-1 thinking memories of a good or bad experience focus on how it started, the best or worst thing that happened, and how it finished
   c framing: where thinking fast in decision-making is liable to be biased by the way the information is given or the request is made
   d endowment effect: where thinking fast in System 1 can bias an individual to overestimate the value of something simply because they own it
   e confirmation bias: where thinking fast can prompt over-focus on information and interpretations that confirm pre-existing opinions and expectations
   f anchoring bias: where fast thinking prompts the reliance on the first piece of information offered (the 'anchor') to make a decision, irrespective of its accuracy and relevance.

4 a Lord et al. (1979) investigated the nature of confirmation bias, concluding that System-1 confirmatory bias exists within academic circles, where different standards are applied to the evidence supporting the personal standpoint and the evidence contradicting it.
   b Ariely et al. (2003) concluded that anchors appear to be substantially influential in the decision-making process, even where they are irrelevant to decision being made.

5 Thin slicing is where judgements about the nature of a situation are made on the basis of the expert viewing a very small part of the interaction. Ambady et al. (2000) who researched thin slicing with students ('expert level' of experience with teachers) found similar ratings for previously unknown teachers by those who watched less-than-one minute clips of each teacher as those who watched five-minute clips of each teacher.

Self-assessment questions 4.5

1   a   LeDoux's model of the brain (1999) indicates that the brain simultaneously processes information along a shorter route of emotion via the response-stimulating, non-thinking amygdala, and a longer route via the thinking-facilitating sensory cortex, hippocampus, and only then to the amygdala. The long route brings more complex schemas into play and allows for a more reasonable and intelligent interpretation of a situation, which can help people avoid unsuitable responses to situations.

    b   Smith et al. (2015) gives biological support to the way tone of voice may affect the performance of a cognitive task. The fMRI scans showed that a task's questions delivered in a sad voice correlated with activation of the left and right hippocampuses, as well as within the left inferior temporal gyrus. An angry voice correlated with increased activity in the left superior frontal gyrus and in the right angular gyrus. A neutral voice correlated with less activity in the left hippocampus and more activity in the right posterior insula. The angry voice stimulated a significantly more accurate performance of the cognitive task. Each different emotive tone of voice seems to have stimulated a different pattern of neural responses, that in turn at least partially influenced the degree of accuracy of the responses.

2   According to Brown and Kulik (1977), two factors appearing to influence flashbulb memory are:

    a   event importance: how personally important the event was to the individual recalling it

    b   event emotionality: the intensity of personal feelings at the event that subsequently prompted memory recall.

3   a   Sharot et al. (2007) indicated biological support to flashbulb memory, on the basis of increased amygdala action when brain scanning was activated.

    b   Neisser and Harsch (1992) argue that flashbulb memory may be a narrative memory. People could be taking later events and putting them back into the memory, mixing them with the 'flashbulb' memory.

Self-assessment questions 4.6 (HL only)

1   Transactional memory is where encoding, storage and recall on command is delegated to a digital device.

2   Findings on the effect of the use of digital technology on cognitive processes and human interactions include:

    a   Sparrow et al. (2011): transactional memory has an adverse effect on declarative memory; confidence in computer and internet storage appears to reduce the motivation and effort exerted for encoding sensory information into long-term memory.

    b   Haier et al. (1992): specific video games may affect learning and skills through a more efficient utilisation of neural circuitry.

    c   Swing et al. (2010): regular and prolonged video gaming is likely to adversely affect children's and adolescents' attention spans.

    d   Shakya and Christakis (2017): use of social media exemplified by Facebook as a replacement for face-to-face personal interactions contributes to a reduction in overall quality of life.

Exam-style questions – sample answers

Short-answer question

State that the research study was experimental and used independent measures in design.

'Various degrees of exposure' is vague: details of the way that the false prompt was used in the test conditions are needed here.

How was the control designed?

To what extent? Not all the members of the test groups were deceived by the false memory prompts.

More emphasis needs to be placed on the cognitive process: memory recall. The response needs to address the concept of reconstructive memory.

This final evaluative paragraph is not necessary. It goes beyond the scope of 'explain', the command term of the question.

The original 1974 studies of Loftus and Palmer would have been ideal for use in this question.

Good introduction.

Like the earlier classic study of Loftus and Palmer (1974), the study of Loftus and Pickrell (1995) was designed to investigate whether misleading suggestions could interfere with memory recall, and specifically the accurate reporting of a witnessed event.

The participants in this experimental study were 120 university students, each of whom had visited Disneyland, California as a small child. Their task was to recall their trips in detail. Each participant received a guided questionnaire for the task. Its purpose was to prompt them to recall details of their visits. The test groups' materials contained memory prompts that included various degrees of exposure to a fake Disneyland advertisement that prominently displayed Bugs Bunny.

The results showed that Bugs Bunny featured within the accounts of childhood visits to Disneyland in approximately one-third of the test groups, but not within the control group. Bugs Bunny was a false memory, as he belonged to Warner Brothers, not Disneyland.

The study showed that verbal and visual prompts can indeed encourage the creation of false memories.

It was ecologically valid to the degree that all the participants had visited Disneyland in childhood. Its limitations are the focus on memories of childhood events rather than recent events experienced as an adult. In addition, the information sought may not have been perceived by the respondents as being of the same degree of importance as giving eyewitness testimony on a crime. In such a situation, the participants might have been more careful, such as indicated by the findings of Yuille and Cutshall (1986).

Essay response question

The study was not truly experimental, but quasi-experimental. This is because the variable between the two groups was culture and thus could not be manipulated by the investigator. This should be mentioned here, not just in the evaluation.

Cognitive schemas are individualised mental mechanisms that process information. These mental constructs include a network of knowledge, beliefs and expectations about particular aspects of the world. These grow in numbers and complexity through the individual's experiences of life, education and culture. Schema processing involves the individual relating new input from the environment to the mental structures based on previous experiences that the individual has already built. Examples of schemas are the capacity to communicate in English, ride a bicycle, pick up on the teacher's mood and interact in a suitable manner, and to drink out of a cup without leaving a mess.

These schemas often use cognitive short cuts, helping the individual to link a particular input from the environment to previous similar situations.

Schemas have not yet been scientifically defined in terms of biological entities. However, there are many studies that assess the evidence of the presence and role of schemas in human behaviour, including Kearins (1981) on spatial schemas specific to geographical environments and Loftus and Palmer (1974) on how questions framed to mislead can trigger schemas that cause errors when recalling past events.

Kearins (1981) considered schemas involved in mental-mapping large expanses of desert territory, by experimentally comparing the ability of white Australians and Australians of indigenous descent to encode spatial and visual information. The experimental hypothesis was that the children of indigenous Australian origin would perform better than white Australians on tasks requiring those skills, because their nomadic societies' survival had depended on their associated schemas for thousands of years. These abilities were generally not relevant to the experience of city-origin white Australians.

Using a matched-pairs sample from both populations of children aged between 12 and 16 years, the researcher gave a series of spatially-focused memory tests to both groups that required the participants to memorise the position of a series of objects placed on a board and later reassemble them in their original position. Kearins found that in all tests, the indigenous group far more accurately placed the objects in their original squares than the white Australian group.

The researcher concluded that it was the spatial and visual encoding schemas developed by the indigenous Australians' millennia of desert survival that gave them the spatial and visual abilities that enabled them to excel in this task.

The strength of this study is that the findings support the evidence for the existence of culture-driven schemas influencing behaviour. Although the participating aboriginal children were not hunter-gatherers, it is likely that their upbringing included repeated cues of their traditional culture and lifestyle as their parents were first-generation settled native Australians.

The strengths of the design of the experiment could be argued here.

However, the study had the limitations of being quasi-experimental: the variable between the two groups was culture, and that could not be manipulated. Thus the findings were correlational, in not showing a cause and effect relationship in the development of schemas in particular domains.

The second study, the experimental study of Loftus and Palmer (1974), investigated how questions worded to prompt memory recall can influence the degree of accuracy in reporting past events.

All participants were shown video clips of a traffic accident and then answered a series of questions where they reported back what they had seen in the video. Only one memory-recall question interested the researchers: how fast did they remember that the cars were travelling when the accident took place. The researchers attempted to influence the memory recall of the participants in the following way. The verb 'travelling' was changed for each test group to 'contacted', 'bumped', 'collided' and 'smashed'. The study found that that more energy contained in the verb in the question, the faster speed estimate given by the respondents.

Could explain this experimental study using suitable terminology by explicitly naming the independent variable and showing how it was manipulated in the different test situations.

The researchers concluded that people tend to reconstruct memory from the prompts other people give them. This in turn can cause inaccuracies in the telling of a past event, which is reconstructive rather than accurate memory.

In evaluation, schema theory gives a framework for understanding how phenomena are perceived, focused on and arranged by different cultures in different ways. Schemas also enable people to selectively filter and encode newly-encountered information into their memory stores.

Limitations of Loftus and Palmer could be included here, such as its laboratory set up, and the contrasting findings of real-life Yuille and Cutshall (1986). Both studies are suitably focused on how schemas may influence behaviour.

However, and in conclusion, individual schemas have not been biologically isolated and biologically defined. Despite rapid progress in brain-scanning mechanisms, it is not currently possible to trace fresh information being processed by the brain, except at a very general level. Therefore, there remains the lack of capacity to identify specific schemas, and to understand how they interrelate with other schemas.

The conclusion does not synthesise the points discussed in the main body. The points in the paragraph could be mentioned as 'additional' to show that there are dimensions to the issue beyond those presented in the main response.

Chapter 5

Theory of Knowledge

Twelve Angry Men

1 Evidence to convict the defendant may include the following points:
   a Jurors 7 and 10 referring to the boy's story of losing his switchblade was indicative that he possessed the weapon with which he was accused of murdering his father.
   b Testimony of the woman across the street, saying that she witnessed the murder.
   c Testimony of the old man – he heard the boy yell at his father that he was going to kill him, immediately followed by a thud; in the next moment he saw the boy run out of the house.
   d The accused was unable to support his alibi that he was at the movie theatre at the time of the murder.

Evidence to acquit the defendant on the grounds of reasonable doubt of the boy's guilt may include these points:
   a Carrying offensive weapons such as a switchblade was the norm in the slum area where the boy lived.

    b   The woman across the street lived in the same slum area as the boy, and in the eyes of the jury should have carried the same dishonest stigma as the boy. Both she and the accused belonged to the same social class that lied. Why believe her rather than the boy?

    c   The woman across the street made the doubtful claim that she could see the murder from where she was standing, through the windows of the train that was passing at that very moment.

    d   That the accused could not support his alibi did not mean that he had not been at the movie theatre at the time of the murder, as not everyone saves movie ticket stubs.

2   Your response should bear in mind that proving innocence was not required as under the Fifth Amendment of the US Constitution, the accused is innocent unless actually convicted. The evidence should be weighed within the framework of the judge's direction: it was for the jury to decide whether or not there was reasonable doubt on the boy's having committed the murder. The reasoned balance of assessed evidence on both sides should be within that framework.

3   Although answers may vary, your answer should contain the following three fundamental elements:

    a   All jurors apart from one initially wished to convict the accused on the basis of general impression. The accused appeared to be the slum-dweller guilty type, and typical of a low and threatening social class.

    b   The jury wanted to arrive at a quick decision as they had other things to do.

    c   The dissenter, Juror 8 (played by Henry Fonda), was a particularly strong character, and his minority influence was gaining increasing support as the jury discussion continued.

(HL only) 'Does travel open the mind to trusting strangers?'

1   Responses will vary, but your answer will probably reflect the national stereotypes gleaned from literature and from the media.

2   Within a Theory of Knowledge context, your response could be framed within 'ways of knowing'. It could focus on paradigm shifts, and that all five senses can only interact with a society and environment when the person is physically present. Your response could contrast that with an image of the country portrayed by the media and by literature.

3   Your response might include reflections on the country following the visit, and development of ideas within paradigms mentioned in **2**. It should also include the role of global interactions in ways of knowing.

Self-assessment questions

Self-assessment questions 5.1

1   Social identity theory refers to the ways that individuals think about who they are and evaluate themselves in relation to in-groups and out-groups.

2   The three mental processes are social categorisation, social identification and social comparison. Social categorisation is a cognitive process where the individual divides the social world into those who belong to their particular group and those who do not. Social identification is where individuals adopt the identity and behavioural norms of the in-group, or groups. Social comparison determines where our in-group stands relative to rival out-groups.

3   Tajfel's study concluded that once groups form, there develops bias towards members of the in-group and discrimination towards members of the out-group. Just categorising people into in-groups and out-groups can be enough to set up intergroup discriminatory behaviour.

4   Social learning theory involves the study of the individual acquiring behaviour patterns through observing, imitating and modelling others.

5   Personal models are people whose behaviour has influenced our own, and who we know, for example a parent or teacher. Positional models are people whose behaviour has influenced our own and we don't know them personally, for example a political leader or pop star.

6   The test group exposed previously to aggression expressed their frustrations with significantly more violence towards the Bobo doll than the control group that had not been exposed to aggression.

7   Both Bandura and Charlton et al. investigated the extent to which the exposure of children to aggressive behaviour promotes a higher level of violent behaviour. Bandura's laboratory study seemed to support the relationship, whereas Charlton et al.'s observational study did not show any significant relationship.

8   Markey and Markey controlled for personality traits. That study found that violent-content computer games tended to incite violence only in those who were already relatively neurotic, less agreeable and less reliable.

9   Attribution theory is where people use their own reasoning to explain the happening of events or the workings of the environment without necessarily being correct.

10 Stereotyping involves a generalised and rather fixed way of thinking about a group of people, or an assumption that an individual connected with the group possesses the same behaviour patterns as popularly attributed to that group. Stereotyping can result in prejudice which is a negative, preconceived opinion formed on the basis of the unknown person's race, nationality, age and gender. Discrimination occurs where feelings of prejudice influence behaviour in negative ways.

11 Bargh et al. concluded that certain cues can unconsciously activate stereotypes, prejudice and discriminatory behaviour on the basis of his experimental research indicating that: subtle prompts with old-age stereotypes promoted significantly slower walking, and that subtle Afro-Caribbean-laden prompts elicited significantly more aggressive reactions to frustrating experiences.

12 Compliance is where the individual behaves according to what they understand is required. Conformity is adjusting behaviour to fit in with the norms of the environment without being told to do so.

13 Majority influence is where the individual finds themself conforming to the norms of the group, even where wishing to disagree. Minority influence is where the individual finds themself conforming to the views held by strong and authoritative personalities that are not the majority of the group.

14 Compliant behaviour may be promoted by:
    a   reciprocity: complying because of a feeling of having to return a favour, e.g. Berry and Kanouse (1987)
    b   low-balling: easily getting compliance with a small request in order to get the person to comply with a larger request
    c   hazing: willingly given high-degree compliance for a much-wanted objective, leading to a greater degree of compliance later on, e.g. Aaronson and Mills (1959)
    d   foot-in-the-door: complying with a larger request, having already agreed to comply with smaller request
    e   door-in-the-face: getting the other to comply to a small request out of guilt for having refused a bigger one.

15 The Asch paradigm is where a person wrongly conforms to majority influence even though they would have acted correctly alone. The paradigm is based on Asch's experimental research on conformity to majority influence (1956, based on an initial study in 1951).

16 Schultz's (2008) study shows that the Asch paradigm is limited to where majority influence does not have competition from a significant disagreeing minority.

17 As part of social cognitive theory, self-efficacy theory proposes that an individual's perception of the possibility of success in a given area is related to previous associated experiences (Bandura, 1977).

18 The findings of Hochstetler et al. (1985) indicate that:
   a an individual's strong sense of self-efficacy can exert minority influence on the cognition and behaviour of many individuals
   b an individual's perceived self-efficacy is a contributory predictor of their athletic performance.

Self-assessment questions 5.2

1 Culture is a common set of beliefs that holds a group of people together.

2 Cultural norms are the behaviour patterns that are typical of specific groups. Cultural dimensions are the issues and perspectives of a culture based on cultural norms and values.

3 Hofstede's six cultural dimensions are:
   a individualism/collectivism
   b degree of tolerance for avoiding uncertainty
   c power distance
   d masculinity/femininity
   e short-term orientation/long-term orientation
   f indulgence/restraint.

4 Examples towards the extremes of cultural dimensions:
   a individualism – USA / collectivism – Japan
   b degree of tolerance for avoiding uncertainty – North America to a greater degree than Western Europe
   c power distance – high in Latin American, East Asian and Arab countries, lower in Demark, Austria and Israel
   d masculinity – Japan / femininity – Norway, Sweden
   e short-term orientation – Scandinavian countries / long-term orientation – East Asian countries
   f indulgence – African, Latin American and Western European countries / restraint – East Asian and Middle Eastern countries

5 Enculturation is the acquisition of the necessary and appropriate norms and skills of your own culture of origin. Acculturation takes place where people change or at least adapt due to contact with another culture, in order to fit in with that culture.

6 Strategies a person living in a culture different from their own might use:
   a Assimilation: where an individual strives to adopt the attitudes and behaviours of the majority culture and exits the original culture in the process.
   b Integration: where the individual fits in with the majority culture, but still maintains the original culture.
   c Separation: where the individual minimises contact with the majority culture, but strives to maintain the original culture.
   d Marginalisation: where the individual is excluded from the majority culture and cannot maintain the original culture.

7 Socio-cultural factors which contribute significantly to migrants' higher levels of acculturation stress:
   a difficulties with the language of the majority community.
   b where leaving the country of origin was forced rather than voluntary.
   c older migrants being unable to build strong social networks.
   d experience of substantial discriminatory attitudes and behaviours.

8 The etic approach views behaviours across cultures, and attempts to find out if specific behaviours are culturally determined or universal. The emic approach views behaviour within one culture and examines it within norms of that culture rather than within a worldwide norm.

9   An example of an etic study is the Sartorius et al. (1983) investigation into the incidence of depression in four widely-differing cultures. It used identical methods of study and criteria for identifying depression in those four societies.

Self-assessment questions 5.3

1   Globalisation is the increasing interdependence of countries in the exchange of goods, services, finance, technology and tourism. Time-space compression is the increasing speed at which people, goods, services and finance can cross international boundaries.

2   Integrative reactions are where people welcome, or at least accommodate, global interactions and culture. Exclusionary reactions are where people view globalised culture with suspicion and as a threat.

3   Richard Condon's (1988) study of the Inuit communities of northern Canada and Saraswathi and Larson's (2002) study of emerging middle-class adulthood in developing countries both show integrative tendencies towards globalisation. Debra Kaufman's (1991) research on newly Orthodox middle-class Jewish women, and Norasakkunkit and Uchida's (2011) study of disorientated young adults in Japan tend towards exclusionary tendencies towards globalisation.

4   Research studies could include Torelli et al. (2011), which showed exclusionary tendencies where people were primed with a strong icon of local culture, and then an icon of global culture was allowed to intrude into the local culture icon's space.

5   The experimental study of Cao, Galinsky and Maddux (2013) indicated that an individual's previous exposure to foreign travel may positively affect the level of trust shown towards strangers.

Exam-style questions – sample answers

Short–answer question

Cultural dimensions are the issues and perspectives of a culture based on its cultural norms and values, the behaviour patterns that are typical and expected of specific groups. They influence the attitudes and behaviours that the individual brings to specific situations.

— Clear definitions.

Cultural norms are the behaviour patterns that are typical of specific groups. Among the cultural dimensions of Hofstede's studies (1984, 2001) are individualism versus collectivism, and power distance.

The individualism/collectivism cultural dimension can influence an employee's relationship with the place of work. Is the individual working for the company, or is the individual personally a part of the company? As an individual worker, the person would leave for employment in a rival company if it offers better conditions. This individualist outlook is identified as high in the USA. The person is less likely to leave if he culturally feels part of the group, as in Japan, where leaving in those circumstances would feel like an act of betrayal.

Addresses the point of the question: the influence of a cultural dimension on the behaviour of an individual.

The collective view sees the group's destiny and the individual's destiny as one. The argument that 'it's my life and I'll use it to do what I like, and in my own way' has a clear boundary between the individual and society, and is distinctly Western in its cultural orientation. It contrasts with the connectedness of many traditional societies.

Fits the command term: the explanation requirement of the question.

Power distance is a measure of how individuals in a company or school behave towards those higher up or lower down the pyramid of power. The greater the power distance, the greater the deference shown by those lower down the pyramid to those up above. For example, in Britain, teachers are addressed by the students as 'Sir' or 'Miss'. Teachers of all ages normally address each other by first names, though sometimes more formally within the students' hearing, though the principal is still likely to be addressed formally.

A good response that is directed to the question and does meet the command term requirements. Knowledge and understanding are present, supported by suitable examples. However, there could be stronger emphasis on the reality that cultural dimensions within individual cultures tend to fall on a spectrum rather than within a distinct category. Also, a concluding remark tying up the content would help.

By contrast, in Israeli schools all teachers, principal included, are on first-name terms with the students. The more conservative schools use the title 'teacher' before the teacher's first name.

On the whole, power distance levels tend to be high in Asian, Arab and Latin American countries and low in Denmark and Austria.

Essay response question

Good introductory paragraph. Concepts clearly defined, though could have been explicitly grounded in social cognition. Direction set with focus on violence, one particular behaviour.

The concept of social learning theory is that the individual's behaviour patterns are a product of their observing, imitating and modelling others. Modelling involves observing other people and replicating their behaviours. These people may be both personal models and positional models. Personal models are people we know, for example parents, teachers and sports coaches. Positional models may not be known to us personally, e.g. heads of state and film stars, and may even not exist in real life, e.g. cartoon characters. This response will focus on one particular behaviour of the individual: violence. The socio-cultural perspective considers the degree to which the social learning through exposure to violence can lead to violent behaviour.

The violent scene should be specified as the independent variable.

The classic study of Bandura et al. (1961) indicates that young children learn violence; it is not a behaviour that comes naturally to them. In his experimental research involving very young children, both the test and control groups were put through the disappointing and temper-provoking experience of having their toys removed as they were settling down to play with them. However, only the test group was already primed with a violent scene, which was watching an adult attack a Bobo doll, before having their toys taken away. Each group of children was put with the Bobo doll after suffering that provocation. The observed level of violence towards the doll was substantially higher in the test group than in the control group. The conclusion was that aggression and violence are learnt from interaction with other people demonstrating aggressive and violent behaviour. These behaviours are not naturally part of a child's nature.

Suitable contrast between two pieces of research, with different methods acknowledged. However, Charlton et al. needs to be explicitly grounded in social learning theory.

The findings of Bandura et al. seem to contrast with the later research of Charlton et al. (2002), which was an ecological rather than a laboratory study. This compared the observed levels of elementary (primary) school violent behaviour on the island of St Helena, before and for five years after the 1995 introduction of television. The content level of violence on the island was approximately the same as in the UK. Contrary to hypothesised expectations, the levels of violence remained the same as in the pre-television era. In contrast with Bandura et al., these findings would downplay the role of social learning theory.

As with Charlton et al., Markey and Markey needs to be explicitly presented in terms of social learning theory.

The findings of Charlton et al. appear to be substantiated by the more recent research of Markey and Markey (2010), which focused on the issue of whether violent-content computer games cause violent behaviour in teenagers. Unlike Bandura et al., Markey and Markey controlled for pre-existing tendencies in those participating in the quantitative experiments by fitting participants within the categories of susceptible or non-susceptible to the influence of violence. Susceptible individuals were identified as having general tendencies of neuroticism, disagreeability and/or unreliability. The results of the research indicated that those observed to be most adversely affected by violent computer games had the above pre-existing anti-social traits. It was not the violent game by itself that provoked violence. It was the pre-existing disposition of the player that created susceptibility to violence.

However, an evaluation of the conflicting evidence can distinguish between the three pieces of research designed to show how modelling in social learning theory may promote violent behaviour in individuals. Bandura et al. took place in a laboratory setting. It is possible that the children may have shown patterns of violence other than that flowing from their dispositions due to observer demand characteristics; they knew they were being watched. There was also only a very brief observation with the violent input with the Bobo models. The set-up of the experiment was not designed to record the long-term exposure to violence and the long-term impact on the individual's behaviour. On the other hand, the provocation to violence with both the test and control groups was ecologically valid as it was not unlike that experienced in children's daily life, such as being told to put the toys away when they are fully involved in having a good time.

Balanced evaluation, with a suitable depth of critical thinking.

Charlton et al.'s significance was that it took the ecologically valid form of covert observation during the children's normal playtimes in the school playground. However, the violent input through newly-available access to television may not have substantially added anything to the child's experience of violent scenes from books and movies. Furthermore, unlike Bandura et al. where the models had been personally introduced to the children, the models in Charlton et al. were wholly positional and thus more remote from the children's reality.

All three studies were quantitative and experimental (Charlton et al.'s control group being children in pre-1995 observations, Markey and Markey's control being children without pre-existing tendencies to violence). However, the works of Bandura et al., and Markey and Markey were over a very short term involving a violence-provoking stimulus within the confines of the experiment. Only Charlton et al.'s study viewed social learning theory over a long enough period to be representative of real-life learning in the long term.

On the basis of the above evidence, it would appear that social learning theory may be used to explain violent behaviour in the short term, especially where the individual has a pre-existing disposition towards it. However, that cause-and-effect relationship is unclear in the long term.

Conclusion needs to show the role of social learning theory in influencing the chosen violent behaviour. Here, it is confined to whether or not social learning theory might influence behaviour.

Overall, a detailed and focused response, with suitable application of both classical and more recent research.

Chapter 6

Theory of Knowledge

Diagnosis of abnormality

a   Responses may include:

- application of professionally-determined criteria for diagnosis of patient's condition (DSM-5, ICD-10)
- assessment of how far the patient's symptoms fit the condition's descriptors in the manual
- brain scanning currently possible in only a few conditions, such as Alzheimer's disease (most conditions not currently determinable through brain scanning)
- self-reporting by the patient
- observations by the psychiatrist
- content analysis of patient's self-reporting.

b   Responses will vary, but may include:

- Brain scanning is scientifically based in showing whether the brain is responding normally or abnormally to stimuli.
- Validity of interpretations of brain-scan results can depend on the psychiatrist's analytical skills and professional judgement.
- Observations made by the psychiatrist can be flawed (Rosenhan, 1973).
- Diagnosis depends on the accurate self-reporting of the patient.
- Reporting and interpretation of symptoms may be culturally influenced.
- Patient's condition may not easily fit into a professional-manual diagnosis of psychiatric abnormality, especially where there is a possibility of co-morbidity.
- Scientific reliability can be improved where other psychiatrists give independent diagnoses of the same patient's condition.

c   Responses will vary, but may include cultural bias, racial bias and gender bias on the part of both professionals and information provided to professionals by the patient and the patient's family.

d   Responses will vary widely, but should include developments in understanding of the genes that may influence abnormality, developments in brain scans, and improvements in accuracy in defining criteria for psychiatric conditions.

Self-assessment questions

Self-assessment questions 6.1

1   Abnormal psychology focuses on the classification, causes, diagnosis and treatment of impairments in important areas of normal mental functioning.

2   Rosenhan and Seligman's seven criteria for determining abnormality include whether:
   a   the person's behaviour involves suffering
   b   the behaviour appears to be the source of the person's troubles
   c   the person manages to communicate feelings in a rational and reasonable way

    d the person shows an unpredictable pattern in dealing with situations

    e the person experiences a particular situation in an unusual way

    f the behaviour causes awkwardness and embarrassment to others

    g the person is doing things in such a way that they are a violation of their accepted cultural standards.

3 Validity of diagnosis refers to the likelihood of it being correct. Reliability of diagnosis depends on the degree to which the diagnosis is independently supported by one or more of the psychiatrist's professional peers.

4 Problems affecting the validity of diagnosis include:

    a the clinical interviewer's personal perception of the patient's situation

    b the clinical interviewer's approach to the patient in terms of theoretical orientation, style and cultural background

    c the clinical interviewer's difficulties in distinguishing between normal and abnormal behaviour – exemplified by Rosenhan (1973)

    d cultural considerations in diagnosis – exemplified by the study of Zhang et al. (1998) on the occurrence of depression in China.

5 The following studies contributed to assessing the validity of diagnoses made in psychology:

    a Rosenhan (1973) highlighted a very high rate of psychiatrists' professional failure to distinguish between genuine and fake schizophrenia in patients. That study placed considerable doubt on the validity of the diagnosis process.

    b Jakobsen et al.'s (2005) study of 100 Danish patients with a history of psychosis indicates an overall improvement in the reliability of diagnosis in schizophrenia. The 98% concordance rate between two independent psychiatrists implies that modern criteria may be applied more accurately when two independent psychiatrists use the same diagnostic tool (DSM-5 or ICD-10).

    c Parker et al. (2001) studied cultural dimensions in ways that people of different cultures framed their feeling of depression when seeking help: Western people tend to describe symptoms in emotional terms; Chinese people tend to describe symptoms in somatic terms. Descriptors of symptoms of depression in professional manuals seem biased to psychological rather than somatic descriptors.

6 Ethical issues in diagnosis:

    a Possibility of stigmatisation, where a person with abnormal behaviour is devalued and discredited by their society. This can make a psychiatrist very cautious when weighing up the evidence of the condition and deciding whether or not to give the diagnosis.

    b Possible racial bias: for example, in the UK a patient is nine times as likely to be diagnosed as being schizophrenic if coming from an Afro-Caribbean background than from a white British one (Morgan et al. 2006).

    c Possible gender bias: for example, the research of Rosser (1992) argues that the higher rate of diagnosis of depression in women than men may be partly due to the large number of male psychiatrists in the profession, who might 'over-diagnose' and stigmatise a woman as being depressed.

Self-assessment questions 6.2

1 **a** Aetiology involves the explanation of the causes of abnormal behaviour.

    b Affective disorder is the generic term for mood-related conditions such as major depression and bipolar disorder.

    c Major depression is feeling continuously sad for at least two weeks without a clear reason. There is a lack of interest and pleasure in enjoyed activities.

    d Anorexia nervosa is loss of control and self-disgust over eating too much high-calorie food. Behaviour involves striving to lose weight by excessive dieting, laxative tablets and/ or excessive exercise.

2 Symptoms of major depression include:

a affective: feeling continuously sad for at least two weeks without a clear reason, lack of interest and pleasure in enjoyed activities

b behavioural: not wishing to be with other people, difficulty in sleeping at night, difficulty in getting through a normal day's work, observable agitated or unusually slow movements, self-destructive and even suicidal behaviour

c cognitive: problems in staying focused on what is going on, inappropriate feelings of guilt and negative attitudes to oneself and one's surroundings

d somatic: fatigue, loss of appetite, and significant weight loss or gain.

Symptoms of anorexia nervosa include:

a affective: disliking the shape of one's body, fear of putting on weight

b behavioural: desperate attempts to get rid of excess weight through under-eating and over-exercising

c cognitive: a negatively distorted body image and low self-esteem, often accompanied by a depressed mood

d somatic: nutritional deficiencies leading to hormonal imbalances, muscle cramping, tiredness, and with women probably, though not always, disruptions in the menstrual cycle.

3 Biological, cognitive and socio-cultural aetiologies of major depression:

Biological: genetic factors including high rates in biological concordance for depression (Nurnberger and Gershon, 1982), GWAS correlates with two short 5-HTT genes (Caspi et al., 2003).

Biological: hormone factors include cortisol levels, which are too high or too low, typically from long periods of chronic stress (Fernald et al., 2008).

Cognitive: faulty thinking resulting from negative schemas with automatic negative thoughts, reflected in the cognitive negative triad (Beck, various studies), negative depression-fostering schemas and negative cognitive biases.

Cognitive: learned helplessness when negative previous experiences have convinced a person of being powerless to handle similar situations even where they subsequently can cope (Seligman, 1974).

Socio-cultural: stressors from the environment and in one's personal circumstances (Brown and Harris, 1978).

4 Biological, cognitive and socio-cultural aetiologies of anorexia nervosa:

Biological: genetic factors including GWAS correlates showing higher frequencies of gene EPHX2 in genetic material samples from those with anorexia nervosa than in those without (Scott-Van Zeeland et al., 2014), and from significance concordance rates in MZ and DZ twin studies (Kortegaard et al., 2001).

Biological: biochemical imbalances in the brain, including dopamine receptor sites (Bailer and Kaye, 2010), and weaker feel-good pleasure responses due to weaker neural responses in the insula area of the brain (Oberndorfer et al., 2013).

Cognitive: faulty negative thinking on the reality of one's own body shape and body weight (Fallon and Rozin, 1985; Fairburn, 1997).

Cognitive: attentional bias, where the desire is to perceive a perfect body self-image while overlooking the dangers involved in self-starvation, including bone thinning, kidney damage and heart problems (Southgate et al., 2009).

Socio-cultural: social learning theory holds that social norms strongly influence the individual's behaviour patterns. Ideal body images of peers and people in the media frequently persuade young women in particular to work hard towards obtaining a similar 'ideal' body shape (Becker et al., 2002; Groesz et al., 2002).

Socio-cultural: culture creating the model for the disorder to be acceptable in terms of age and gender (Brooks-Gunn et al., 1988).

Self-assessment questions 6.3

1 Psychiatric treatment is medically based, involving types of drugs and other biologically-based interventionist procedures. Psychotherapeutic treatment is physically non-interventionist. It involves a series of one-to-one or group sessions with a therapist that strive to steer the individual towards normal functioning, taking into account past and present experiences.

2 Two biomedical treatments for disorders are SSRIs and ECT treatment.

SSRIs: for example, paroxetine and fluoxetine (Prozac) make each unit of neurotransmitter serotonin more pleasurable by enabling it to stay longer in the synaptic gaps. Placebos have been found to be less effective, though not ineffective (Leuchter et al., 2002).

ECT treatment: use of electrical stimulation to create a seizure in the patient's brain, which appears to relieve and even sometimes abate depression. The biological mechanism is unclear, and its use is based on the largely empirical evidence of its success. The more recently developed and less invasive TMS creates a magnetic field to induce a much smaller electric current in a specific part of the brain without causing seizure or loss of consciousness. The current is caused by a magnetic field created by an electromagnetic coil that delivers the pulses through the forehead.

3 Strengths of the biological approach in treating major depression include:
   a rapid if often short-term relief
   b unlikely to have long-term negative effects when applied professionally and carefully
   c can lower tension, enabling the patient to be responsive to psychotherapy.

Limitations of the biological approach in treating major depression include:
   a not clear how far depression is caused by low serotonin levels
   b risks of short-term side effects of drugs
   c difference in positive outcomes between SSRIs and placebos is relatively small (Kirsch et al., 2008)
   d both SSRIs and ECT treatment address the symptoms rather than the causes of the depression
   e medical suspicion that ECG can cause anasognosia.

4 Two cognitive treatments for disorders include CBT and group therapy.

CBT involves therapist-led cognitive restructuring for treating disorders that is designed to enable the client to:
   a identify what the negative beliefs and thinking patterns are
   b test out whether these beliefs are actually true
   c accept that parts of the thinking patterns are flawed.
It moves on to cognitive rehearsal, where the patient selects a past or current difficult situation and works with the therapist to structure a coping strategy to handle the problem. IPT is similar to CBT, but it focuses on the importance of improved human communication as a promoter of mental health.

Group therapy may include the use of CBT, IPT or other therapies. It involves therapist-led activities suitable to the participants' conditions, such as brain-storming, situation-simulation exercises, role-playing, giving feedback and building up trust within the group. There is often emphasis on developing bonds of trust and sharing of experiences between the participants, with the therapist acting as facilitator. It requires care in putting groups together in terms of compatible objectives and behaviours of the participants.

5 Strengths of the cognitive approaches in treating major depression:

The strengths of CBT/IPT are:
  a recognition of depression being caused by thinking
  b emphasis on erroneous schemas creating automatic negative thoughts
  c capacity to enable the client to work towards a more positive thinking process
  d being readily adaptable to the specific situation of the client
  e it can be effective where there is mutual trust between therapist and client.

The strengths of group therapy in treating major depression include:
  a the openness of the more communicative members of the group encouraging the shyer person to talk more frankly than in a one-to-one session with the therapist
  b its lower cost to each participant than one-to-one treatment
  c the comparable success rates with one-to-one based on outcome studies (Thimm and Antonsen, 2014)
  d even better overall rates of success (Toseland and Siporin, 1986).

Limitations of the CBT/ITP in treating major depression include:
  a the condition being of biological rather than thought-process in origin
  b the insufficient attention to operative socio-cultural factors
  c the improved condition likely to be due to positive changes in the patient's life during therapy rather than the therapy itself
  d the existing success ratings relying too exclusively on outcome-based rather than processed-based research
  e limited application of Western models of therapy to the cognitive patterns commonly found among Asians.

Limitations of the group therapy approach in treating major depression include:
  a fears of lack of confidentiality with proceedings in the group
  b higher drop-out rates than one-to-one therapy
  c incompatibilities within the group in form and intensity of depression
  d personality clashes and over-dominant individuals within the group
  e existing efficacy studies being outcome-based rather than process-based.

6 As a study of eclectic treatment, Riggs et al. (2007) investigated the effectiveness of combining CBT with SSRI medication or a placebo. One hundred and twenty-six teenage participants took part in the study, many already known to the social services and the juvenile courts. All had been diagnosed with depression as well as substance abuse or conduct disorder. Divided into CBT plus SSRI drugs, and CBT plus placebo drugs, the results after four months of treatment showed success ('improved' or 'much improved'): 76% for the CBT plus medication, and 67% for CBT plus placebo.

Exam-style questions – sample answers

Essay response question

Abnormality may be defined as an aspect of an individual's cognitive and behavioural state that impairs interpersonal functioning and/or creates distress for others. Validity in this context refers to the likelihood of the psychiatrist's diagnosis being correct according to criteria in the diagnosis manual, such as DSM-5 in the USA and ICD-10 of the WHO and generally used in the UK. The reliability of the diagnosis depends on how far the diagnosis is independently supported by one or more of the psychiatrist's peers.

The command term 'discuss' implies looking critically at a suitable range of factors influencing two elements, *in this case* that assess the professional accuracy of diagnosis: validity and reliability.

Key terms correctly defined.

Two elements considered here: self-reporting and clinical interviewer's perception. Both are supported by a relevant study.

In practice, the validity and reliability of the diagnosis depends on several factors beyond the definitions and classifications of the manual. Due to the fact that most abnormal behaviour patterns are not traceable to pathological origins, the diagnosis procedure is likely to involve the clinical interviewer's perception of the patient's condition. Most diagnoses given today rely on the degree to which the psychiatrist's personal impressions and observations, and the patient's guided self-reporting of the condition, satisfy the set criteria in the professional manual. Ideally, two different psychiatrists should reach the same diagnosis if they apply the same criteria and procedures. The perceptions of psychiatrists, however, may differ for many reasons. For example, the work of Cooper et al. (1972) sought to investigate reliability in the diagnosis of depression and schizophrenia. It involved American and British psychiatrists observing movies of clinical interviews of patients, whom they had to diagnose. Twice as many of those viewed were diagnosed as schizophrenic by the American psychiatrists as by the British psychiatrists, indicating a possible cultural bias to diagnosis affecting both validity and reliability.

More recent studies, however, indicate an overall improvement in the reliability of diagnosis. The research of Jakobsen et al. (2005) used ICD criteria in diagnosing schizophrenia in 100 Danish patients with a history of psychosis, and found a concordance rate of 98% between two psychiatrists working independently on each case, suggesting that modern criteria may be applied with much greater accuracy. However, it could be argued that a manual-based diagnosis of schizophrenia is not necessarily accurate because two psychiatrists concur in applying the same diagnostic tool. The diagnosis of schizophrenia depends on the presence of several symptoms being present at the same time, which could lead to over- or under-diagnosis. The diagnosis criteria also work on the basis that there is no state of co-morbidity, meaning that the patient has more than one abnormal condition.

This needs to be expanded: it might depend on the severity of the symptoms rather than the number of symptoms.

The point is correct and well-supported, but it needs to more explicitly place the ideas used within a framework of ethical practices in diagnosis.

In addition to the psychiatrists' perceptions of the patient's condition is the degree of willingness of psychiatrists to award a diagnosis. This can affect both the validity and reliability when fellow-professionals are independently involved in awarding the diagnosis. This is where the individual psychiatrist has to decide whether the degree of severity of the patient's symptoms actually meets the criteria for the diagnosis. For example, the psychiatrist may suspect partial and even unintended flaws in the patient's reporting of symptoms. That puts the responsibility of interpreting the patient's report on the psychiatrist, and it is in this area that such professional individuals are likely to differ. Psychiatrists are well aware that an invalid diagnosis could wrongly and negatively label the patient, affecting employment, medication and even hospitalisation. In reality, the individual may be enduring a difficult temporary phase coping with, for example, colleagues and clients at work. Conversely, the non-diagnosis of an under-reporting patient could result in that person not receiving vital support and treatment. In balancing these factors, professionals will vary on to how far to apply the official criteria in diagnosis.

Details of the research are correctly included as they advance the argument of the response. Here they are used to support the possibility of cultural bias in Western diagnostic manuals.

Finally, the validity and reliability of diagnosis may well have cultural elements. This is exemplified by the research of Parker et al. (2001) whose aim was to investigate cultural considerations in the diagnosis of the abnormal condition of major depression. This cross-cultural study included 100 participating outpatients seeking professional help for that condition in two contrasting societies: Australian patients of Western ancestry and culture, and Chinese patients living in Malaysia. The purpose was to investigate the ways in which each group of patients identified cognitive and somatic symptoms as reasons for seeking professional help. In this study, participants were asked to describe their symptoms by responding to a questionnaire, which required them to check the boxes that they believed had influenced their decision to seek help. There were two lists of symptoms: psychological and somatic. The somatic symptoms were those commonly observed by Singaporean psychiatrists with experience of Chinese patients. The study found that 60% of the Chinese patients stated that they sought help because they experienced a symptom that was somatic. In contrast, only 13% of the Australians described their major depression in somatic terms. Thus the Chinese patients had selected significantly fewer cognitive and emotional symptoms of depression. The study would therefore suggest that expressing depression in terms of personal thinking, emotions or any way that suggests mental problems, may be significantly less socially acceptable in Chinese culture than in Western culture. As a result, the depression of Chinese patients could be under-diagnosed because of the Western bias of the standard manuals emphasising psychological rather than somatic symptoms. The general under-diagnosis of depression of Chinese patients would make the Western-setting standard interview method less valid. There is also likely to be a lower level of reliability, as professionals with varying experiences of ethnic communities are likely to differ in their interpretation of the patient's reporting.

In conclusion, the validity of the diagnosis of abnormality on the basis of official professionally-determined criteria is subject to the individual professional's interpretation of the behaviour and reporting of the patient, the degree of willingness of the professional to award a diagnosis, and the professional's relative cultural awareness and experience when dealing with someone from a different culture. All these factors can affect diagnosis reliability, as peer psychiatrists differ in personality and experience. These issues in validity and reliability in diagnosis are likely to persist as most conditions are non-pathological in origin, and are thus unlikely to be detectable through brain scanning.

<aside>Suitable conclusion, incorporating the series of arguments in the body of the response.</aside>

Chapter 7

Theory of Knowledge

1 Possible approaches might include:
   a Biological evidence: changes within blood samples of hormonal oxytocin and vasopressin levels, changes in neurotransmitter serotonin levels, and changes in appetite levels and weight over a short period. The high degree of attraction may be supported by the presence of immune-complementing rather than immune-similar genes (MHC, Wedekind et al., 1995).
   b Cognitive evidence: e.g. perceived similarities in personality and outlook between oneself and the partner. Differences tend to be perceived as complementing rather than clashing with the other.
   c Socio-cultural evidence: pre-falling-in-love frequency of meeting tending to increase attraction and trust (e.g. Festinger et al., 1950), and cultural compatibility.

2 There are several possible ways of tackling the question. One is given below.

The reductionist approach is likely to be based on grounded theory, research already done in the field. Depending on the position of the psychologist, they are likely to apply existing theory from the biological, cognitive or socio-cultural level of analysis. The biological level is more likely to generate quantitative data, while the cognitive and socio-cultural levels will probably produce qualitative data. Reductionism will tend to emphasise one approach while minimising the others, though that might clarify rather than confuse the symptoms of falling in love.

A holistic approach will give the opportunities of assembling a wider variety of quantitative and qualitative data, each acting as a check and balance on the other and thus enabling triangulation in approach and analysis. It is particularly suited to where the focus is on the actual falling in love, with the phenomenological perspective likely to invite explanatory contributions from all three perspectives. However, the holistic approach may well give undue emphasis to data of lesser weighting where it conflicts with data of greater weighting.

Self-assessment questions

Self-assessment questions 7.1

1 a Accommodation in maintaining a relationship is the capacity to handle and adapt to the other's tolerance-straining behaviour, according to the degree of friendship or intimate relationship already present.
   b The Investment Model of Commitment Processes proposes that problems occurring within relationships are more likely to be proactively and effectively handled when there is interdependence between the couple.
2 a Biological explanations for physical attraction:
   i rise in neurotransmitter activity (e.g. serotonin)
   ii rise in hormonal levels (e.g. oxytocin, vasopressin)

      iii genetic compatibility (MHC complex) through complementary genes which promote immunity to disease (e.g. the MHC research of Wedekind et al. (1995) showing female preference for a man whose genes complemented rather than duplicated her own physical immune structure).

  b Cognitive explanations for physical attraction:

      i perceived personal similarities with potential partner (e.g. Markey and Markey (2007) showing a high degree of personality similarities between partners)

      ii the degree of self-esteem at the time of forming the relationship (e.g. Kiesler and Baral (1970) showing that those who feel good about themselves are particularly likely to start a conversation with an attractive member of the opposite gender).

  c Socio-cultural explanations may include:

      i increasing familiarity with the person (e.g. Jorgensen and Cervone (1978) giving higher ratings to the photographs of strangers the more times participants saw their photo)

      ii proximity (e.g. Festinger et al. (1950) showing high rates of occurrence of student relationships with partners living or studying nearby)

      iii cultural compatibility (e.g. Buss et al. (1990) within socially-approved criteria of age difference, and presence or lack of virginity).

3 Communication strategies that may help a relationship to continue successfully as listed by Canary and Stafford (1994) are:

  a positive, yet unpredictable surprises to partner

  b self-disclosure to partner

  c tuning into the feelings of one's partner

  d keeping a social network by doing things together with a wide circle of family and friends

  e sharing some of the household tasks together.

4 The interpretation of the partner's behaviour may enhance or deteriorate the relationship depending on whether it is perceived as dispositionally grounded or situationally grounded. Where the behaviour is positive, it is more likely to enhance the relationship if interpreted dispositionally. Where the behaviour is negative, it is less likely to upset the relationship if interpreted situationally.

5 **a** Gupta and Singh (1982) – based on work in the Indian community, love between couples is likely to be more enduring where the marriage is arranged rather than based on pre-marital romantic attraction.

  b Levine et al. (1995) – the likelihood of people marrying partners who have all the desirable qualities without love present is minimal in individualist societies, but commonly acceptable in a collectivist, traditional society.

Self-assessment questions 7.2

1 Deindividuation theory proposes that a person feels less accountable for violent conflicting behaviour where the victim is unidentifiable, faceless or part of the opposition crowd. Zimbardo's (1969) controlled experimental work showed a greater degree of inflictor-compliance in willingness to induce pain when the inflictor was masked or otherwise deindividuated.

2 Two socio-economic explanations on the origins of conflict other than deindividuation are:

  a power differences between social groups, where a stronger in-group activates its prejudices against the weaker out-group (e.g. British colonialists against native Tasmanians over scarce supply of land for farming)

  b subcultures with elements of conflict and violence (e.g. gang members who have been persistently exposed to violent role models seeking to assert their masculinity by girlfriend abuse (Totten, 2003)).

3 **a** Peer counselling is where fellow-students serve as trained mediators between the parties involved in inter-student conflict in schools, with the background support and supervision of the faculty; Houlston and Smith, 2007: some success, mainly in creating awareness of bullying though less evidence of actually reducing the bullying.

b Imposing super-ordinate goals is a framework that enables the antagonistic parties to co-operate in peace-making through a mutually beneficial task that promises rewards to all those who co-operate; Sherif's (1954) Robber's Cave scenario.

Self-assessment questions 7.3

1 **a** Social responsibility is where able people assist others who are experiencing difficulties.
  b Bystanderism is where the individual does not step forward to help a victim when others are present.

2 **a** Pro-social behaviour is generic: acting in a way that helps a person or group. Altruism is where the pro-social behaviour is specifically at one's own cost, without expectation of benefit or reward.
  b Diffusion of responsibility is the likelihood of a capable individual not volunteering to help where other similarly-able people are present. Pluralistic ignorance is where individuals and people look around at others to see their reactions, as cues for how to act in an emergency situation. The fewer the cues, the less likelihood of individual intervening.

3 Three theories for pro-social behaviour include:
  a Kin-selection theory: biologically-based theory focusing on the innate, evolutionary desire to promote the survival of the part of the human race that has the highest amount of shared genetic material as a means of promoting one's own virtual survival beyond death. The closer the person is related, the more intense that desire becomes. It is supported by Madsen et al. (2007) for example, whose work indicates that individuals are likely to show higher levels of unselfishness and self-sacrifice to those they are biologically related to, than to complete strangers.
  b Empathy-altruism theory: cognitive-based theory proposing that the observation of the suffering of another person creates personal distress and a consequent desire to help. That is evidenced in the findings of Toi and Batson (1982), which showed a greater willingness to help where the helper is clearly exposed to the other's personal distress circumstances.
  c Dispositional and situational considerations: socio-cultural-based theory. Dispositional motives propose that people behave altruistically because concern for others is part of their upbringing or religious practice. Situational motives propose that behaving altruistically is more likely to take place when the helper is in a moment of leisure rather than when in a hurry to get to somewhere. The work of Darley and Batson (1973) with theological seminary students showed a greater likelihood of altruistic behaviour when situationally not in a hurry than when being in a hurry, even when the hurried person was recently actually involved in learning about the importance of helping others.

4 Both Piliavin et al. (1969) and Levine et al. (1994) focused on the likelihood of an individual showing pro-social behaviour in helping strangers when other potential helpers are present. Piliavin et al. focused on pro-social behaviour in New York only. Levine et al. was a wider, cross-cultural study involving cities in other regions of the USA as well as in other continents. Piliavin et al.'s help situations included where the individual was in need of personal help (such as having fallen), but Levine et al.'s involved both personal help (help to a blind person in immediate difficulty) and property help (returning a dropped pen or fallen newspaper). Piliavin et al. showed a high degree of pro-social behaviour which declined slightly when the need for help appeared to be the fault of the needy person (the drunken man). All Levine et al.'s scenarios were situations where the person was either apparently genuinely needy (as with the blind person) or did something accidentally (dropped pen, fallen newspaper), and yet showed considerable regional and international variations in degree of positive response.

5 Pro-social behaviour might be promoted by any of the following three methods:
  a community involvement: peer counselling in schools (Houlston and Smith, 2007)
  b super-ordinate goals reducing conflicts and promoting co-operation to common, beneficial goals between previously conflicting groups (Sherif et al., 1961)
  c supporting legislation offering protection to those offering pro-social assistance (e.g. as being promoted today in China).

Exam-style questions – sample answers

Essay response question

The biology, cognition and socio-cultural elements involved in the excitement of falling in love and/or the novelty of being in a long-term relationship including marriage typically fade with time. The work of Duck (1982) shows that conflicts occur sooner or later, and are the norm in relationships.

It needs a sentence indicating the basis on which Duck reached those conclusions.

Relationships may change for the better or worse through the use of communication skills. Where communication is sub-optimum, the chances of breakdown and ultimately divorce will increase.

This sets a clear sense of direction in the response.

There are many reasons why relationships may change or end; every relationship is unique and no two people find themselves in precisely identical circumstances. Relationships can drastically change when children are born to the couple. This response, however, will focus on two other factors, which are problems with communication skills, and degree of accommodation skills in maintaining the relationship. In this context, accommodation is the capacity for one to handle and adapt to the other's tolerance-straining behaviour once a friendship or intimate relationship is already in existence.

Research study is used to support importance of communication strategies. The passage below could be used for critical analysis by limiting the findings of Canary and Stafford to, for example, where both partners are on the same level of communication.

These arguments could have been framed within the more generic attribution theory, presented in Chapter 5.

Whether the relationship survives and flourishes or goes into terminal decline depends to a great degree on the communication strategies used by the couple, and their capacity to accommodate the increasingly noticeable differences between them. Communication strategies that may help a relationship to continue successfully as listed by Canary and Stafford (1994) are positive-yet-unpredictable surprises to the partner, self-disclosure to the partner, tuning into the feelings of the partner, keeping a social network by doing things together with a wide circle of family and friends, and sharing some of the household tasks together. Ignoring those and similar other strategies can result in the couple becoming less focused on one another.

As well as communicating, the interpretation of the partner's communication may enhance or deteriorate the relationship, depending on whether it is perceived as dispositionally grounded or situationally grounded. Dispositionally grounded means that behaviour was perceived as deliberate, such as purposely arriving late to upset the other. Situationally grounded means that behaviour was perceived as happening irrespective of the relationship between them, and the reason for lateness was perhaps a traffic delay. Where the behaviour is negative, such as the late arrival, it will do minimum damage to the relationship if interpreted situationally; they were late because of the traffic. However, if that same behaviour is interpreted dispositionally, it could well harm the relationship, as they frame the lateness as personally directed.

This is a second line of argument. It is not a direct follow-on from problems with communication skills.

This idea is supported by …

This leads to the role of accommodation in maintaining a relationship. As partners get to know each other, they face annoying things about the other's behaviour patterns. Rusbult et al. (1991) experimentally investigated the relationship between the level of commitment within a relationship and the capacity to accommodate, if not actually tolerate, annoying aspects of the other's behaviour. With 144 male and female participating psychology students with relationship experience, the independent variable was the level of interdependence, meaning the degree of closeness between the two people. These were on four levels, going from low to high level of interdependence: casual acquaintance, casual dating, regular dating and seriously involved with each other. After each scenario, they answered questions on the dependent variable, which was how they would respond in adverse scenarios. They chose from a list of responses varying from exiting the relationship, letting the relationship deteriorate without exiting, keeping quiet and hoping that the relationship would improve, and actually getting together and talking about the problems.

Good coordination of the two strands of discussion: communication and accommodation.

Both poor communication and sub-optimum accommodation of adverse behaviour can accelerate the decline and become contributing factors to the end of the relationship. Indeed, the research of Levinger (1980) proposes that relationships frequently go through the five stages which are: initial attraction, building by dating and making the relationship permanent, continuation once things become routine, deterioration on finding interests outside the marriage framework, and finally ending the relationship in break-up or divorce.

His work suggests that the relationship becomes at risk when the continuation stage slowly and silently fades into the deterioration stage, especially where the couple feel unmotivated to make the effort but let the relationship just drift. Then, the threat to the relationship may increase through situational elements, such as pressure of work, clashes in working hours and availability of other partners.

Another element that psychologists draw attention to in explaining the breakdown in relationships is one partner feeling overburdened relative to the other. Hatfield et al's study (1979) of 2000 couples showed that those who felt that they suffered from an unfair division of duties were most likely to cheat on the relationship. Duck (1982), using a series of longitudinal studies, identified the following factors that put marriage and long-term relationships at risk. These range from pre-existing incompatibilities, which are not always obvious at the beginning of the relationship (e.g. carefully-hidden behavioural abnormalities) to mechanical failures, where a once-compatible couple becomes incompatible as each partner matures in a different direction, to a sudden distress-creating behaviour, such as infidelity or an argument escalating to physical violence.

Overall, relationships are susceptible to change and termination once they follow a predictable routine. Elements assisting the change and breakdown include, but are not restricted to, sub-optimal communication within the relationship, and patterns of accommodation including neglecting the relationship. The relationship is likely to move towards separation and divorce where other forces are present. These include internal factors such as wide differences in culture and socio-economic status, and external factors such as incompatible working hours and differences in ways of spending leisure time.

Predictable routine was mentioned, but not developed in the main discussion. It should not be heading the summary: that role should be left to the communication and accommodation.

These final two factors have not been discussed in the main body of the response.

Overall, develops two main themes and supports them with suitable research, but needs to make more use of opportunities for critical analysis.

Chapter 8

Theory of Knowledge

1   Responses may include:

- scale devised on an empirical basis

- scale devised on a cross-cultural basis

- stressors included that have been demonstrated to be stressors, though not readily perceived as such, such as getting married

- allows for a multi-variable and weighted analysis of stress.

2   Responses may include:

- data based on participant's self-reporting

- individuals differ widely in capacities to deal with stress

- does not address the individual's susceptibility to stress. Responses may bring in ideas from your own or others' experiences, or your own research (such as Type A or Type B personalities).

- does not measure the quality of the social and economic environment and resources available, which may exacerbate or alleviate the stress level experienced.

3   Responses may include:

- modification of the Holmes-Rahe Scale according to the individual's susceptibility to stress

- modification of the scale to include measures of the participant's environment, such as financial resources, education and degree of social support available

- alternative methods to self-reporting for stress measurement, ranging from brain scanning to observation of the participation.

- use of follow-up semi-structured interviews.

Self-assessment questions

Self-assessment questions 8.1

1   **a**   Determinants of health are the biological, socio-economic, environmental and psychological factors that influence the health status of individuals or populations.

      b   Self-efficacy is the degree to which the individual believes that they can participate in society in particular activities.

2   **a**   Stress is a reaction to a stimulus that disturbs a person's physical or mental equilibrium. Eustress is the normal degree of stress that is beneficial and positively motivational for the individual.

      b   Dispositional health attribution considers the degree to which people attribute their own health-detrimental realities to their own personality, and their persistence in taking necessary steps to maintain behavioural change. Situational health attribution is where the patient believes that the detrimental health situation is not within personal control.

      c   A risk factor is a condition or a variable that promotes undesirable health outcomes, whereas a protective factor is a condition or variable that promotes desirable health outcomes, or at least reduces the risk of negative outcomes.

3   The Holmes-Rahe Social Readjustment Scale measures the degree of stress-severity that individual stressors cause to the typical individual. It is on the basis of comparing the stressor with the stress of death of spouse, which is perceived to be the greatest stressor that an average person will face in life.

4   The Kiecolt-Glaser study indicates that chronic stress causes an increase in cortisol, which not only leads to depression and memory problems, but also a decrease in the number of T-cells that cause the immune system to weaken.

5   Dispositional factors positively affecting health belief:

      a   Perceptions of degree of stressor (primary appraisal) and self-efficacy in coping with it (secondary stressor): this is presented by the transactional model of stress (Lazarus and Folkman, 1984) which sees the cognitive stress-coping mechanism as a two-way transaction between the individual and the environment.

      b   Degree of capacity to relate to past-experienced stresses: the research study of Evans and Kim (2013) indicates that chronic stresses experienced through childhood may well create a high capacity to relate to childhood-experienced stresses, which in turn weakens dispositional elements that can promote a strong health belief. Conversely, an overall positive childhood experience is likely to strengthen the dispositional elements positively affecting health belief.

      c   Perception of enjoying social support: the research study of Graber et al. (2015) indicates that having an encouraging best friend can positively raise health belief, raising the degree of resilience to stress.

      d   Degree of autonomy a person feels in one's work: the Whitehall research studies found that the risk of death from coronary heart disease in the British civil service was twice as high among the lowest grades in jobs such as doorkeepers and messengers than at the highest levels with more senior policy-makers and administrators, as the latter had more job autonomy.

6   Two interventionist-based protective initiatives to reduce the risk of starting or continuing to smoke:

      i   School-based anti-smoking programmes with strong student input: Hanewinkel and Wiborg (2002) on primary prevention of child smoking showed that competitive social pressure has some significant success at preventing young people from beginning to smoke at the age they are judged to be most vulnerable.

      ii   Financial incentives for adults seeking to quit smoking, especially where the smoker makes a substantial personal investment of money with a view to getting a large financial return on succeeding to quit: Halpern et al. (2015).

Self-assessment questions 8.2

1 On the causes of obesity:

   a The work of Stunkard et al. (1990) on a biological-empirical basis indicates that genes determine the propensity towards obesity.

   b The work on Claussnitzer et al. (2015) on a micro-biological basis indicates that it is specifically the FTO gene that determines whether the fat-conserving mechanism is permanently switched on or not. Weight is harder to lose if the body is constantly in fat-conserving mode.

   c The work of Polivy (2001) on a cognitive basis indicates that overall weight gain can result from unrealistic expectations in dieting.

   d The work of Prentice and Jebb (1995) on a socio-cultural basis indicates that trends towards obesity are in line with an increasingly sedentary lifestyle in both the workplace and the home.

   e The work of Li et al. (2015) on a socio-cultural basis indicates that the recent rise in the standard of living specifically in China has been encouraging grandparents involved in child care to supply children with obesity-promoting foodstuffs.

2 In the field of health promotion, psychology attempts to understand the cognitive barriers to living healthily. It seeks ways to motivate the person to identify the barriers, deal with them, and attempt to overcome them.

3 In health promotion:

   a The Health Belief Model holds that addressing the combination of two simultaneous sets of forces motivates the individual to address behaviour adverse to health: the degree to which it is believed to be a threat and yet in one's control, and the degree to which quitting (for example, smoking) is reinforced by supportive messages from the environment.

   b The Stages of Change Model features the six stages a person goes though to change a habit adverse to health:

     i pre-contemplation

     ii contemplation

     iii preparation

     iv action

     v maintenance

     vi termination.

     Support should be available according to the stage being experienced.

4 **a** Quist-Paulsen and Gallefors (2003) supports the Health Belief Model. It indicates that successful rates of stopping smoking among heart patients rise substantially when the environment to stop becomes more powerful; in this case where counselling sessions are followed by the nursing staff's regular and frequent reinforcing phone calls home.

   b West and Sohal (2006) considerably modifies the Stages of Change Model on their empirical evidence that most smokers stop suddenly, without contemplation. It is the build-up of tension that suddenly triggers the act of stopping, and the treatment should focus on the person suddenly stopping having immediate access to physiological and psychotherapy support.

Exam-style questions – sample answers

Essay response question

A health promotion strategy is a programme that educates and motivates people to adjust their lifestyle towards achieving an improved personal physical condition. It can involve cessation of habits that are threats to health such as smoking, alcohol or drugs. It is supported by publicity, education and support staff.

Although all people want to have a quality physical lifestyle, many face considerable cognitive barriers, such as addictions to smoking, previous negative experiences with dieting, and unpleasant memories of physical education at school. In promoting physical well-being, health psychologists endeavour to identify the barriers and how they may be overcome. The two ways of health promotion we will —— Suitable introductory paragraphs with good lead into the foci of the response.

look at are youth-driven anti-smoking campaigns (exemplified by the Truth campaign of Florida, USA 1998–99), and financial strategies (exemplified by the work of Halpern et al., 2015).

Give more details on the location of the study.

The Truth campaign (brand name) was a public project designed to prevent young and mid-teenagers from starting to smoke. The aim of the Truth campaign was to get young people to believe that it was not cool to smoke. With $25m from state support, Truth used posters and TV commercials to convey the message that successful, young celebrity-types who enjoyed life and achieved things did not smoke. Smoking was for losers. The idea was that the teenage viewers would immediately see themselves as cool, and identify with the successful types and their non-smoking lifestyle. It also presented smoking as a money-making scheme at their expense: the cigarette companies didn't care about the young lives that they negatively affected as long as teenagers provided a market for their tobacco products.

This idea could be further developed with a sentence bringing in social identity theory (Chapter 5).

The strength of the Truth campaign was that it produced positive results. A telephone survey carried out six months into the campaign showed that the number of young smokers dropped by 20% in middle schools and 8% in high schools. It also showed that 80% of that age group knew about Truth, indicating that the methods used to target young people in that state were successful. It thus became a model for similar projects in other states.

This should link to the sentence 'The idea was that the teenage viewers would immediately see themselves as cool, and identify with the successful types and their non-smoking lifestyle.'

This health-promotion strategy was distinctive as it took place at grass-roots level. Being planned by teens for teens, it had the strength of speaking to teens in ways to which they could readily respond. Their passion for the campaign spread to others very quickly. It did much towards establishing a youth social norm: 'It's not cool to smoke'. It also made use of teens' own social networks, which were out of reach of more conventional approaches. It was indeed the teenagers who delivered the message. This highlights the potential of social media health-promotion programmes at grass-roots level.

Systematic and effective evaluation.

The main limitations were that the campaign was aimed at a subset of a particular population: non-smoking teenagers at risk from starting to smoke. In addition, the campaign lost power soon afterwards because of a lack of funding. Truth was re-launched in 2014 as 'Finish it' (enthusing today's youth to be the generation that completely stops smoking), but it has not been in action long enough for a realistic assessment.

Financial incentives have also been shown to be a valuable strategy for health promotion. This is exemplified by the work of Halpern et al. (2015). Compared to the scope of the Truth campaign, it was of a smaller scale study on one hand, but more intensely directed at the participants on the other. Like Truth, it was directed towards smoking, but to stopping smoking rather than deciding on whether or not to start.

The researchers used the following method. There were 2,500 participants who claimed that they were planning to stop smoking. All either worked or were connected to workers of healthcare company CVS Caremark. Each participant was randomly assigned to either one of four incentive programmes, or to a group that was given a basic level of support for stopping smoking; access to free aids and information on giving up smoking that included nicotine replacement therapy. Those allocated to the four incentive programmes were also able to access the basic support, but each received additional help of one type or another. Two of those programmes used one-to-one support, and two used groups of six people. In addition, one of the individual-based and one of the group-based programmes awarded a prize of $800 for permanently stopping smoking for as long as one year. The other two programmes required each participant to pay-in $150, which was they would lose if going back to smoking during the 12-month period. But if they managed to quit, they would get their $150 back, plus an additional $650 pay-out, giving $800 in total.

The results were that those who had invested the initial $150 showed a 52% success rate in quitting smoking, the highest in any of the conditions the participants were allocated to. But those who had not paid anything into the programme were only 17% successful, even though their total final payout was higher than those who had to put money into the system. Similar results were found for both one-to-one therapy and group therapy.

The strengths of this study are in the design. It used a large sample and it was ecologically valid: the setting was real-life, with as ordinary support for all, and different special supports for all of the incentive groups, which took place during the day-to-day normal functioning of the company. Also in two of the conditions each potential quitter paid in $150 of their own money, which was a real-life situation as they would never see it again if they didn't manage to give up smoking. In addition, this study exemplifies that employers can have the dual role of promoting employees' health and at the same time saving money on their health plans.

Its limitations are that such a set-up was not shown to be fully effective: many people had not been put off by the prospect of losing their deposited investment when tempted to smoke. Also, the value of such programs for companies to promote health care is restricted to those who can afford them.

In conclusion, health programmes appear to have a greater quality of success when structured towards elements that appeal to the individual. In the first study they are the culture exclusive to the age group, and in the second, the fear of failure associated with losing the deposit and associated sense of shame in the face of fellow workers. Their main limitations are limited budgets to keep those programmes going for a long enough period to achieve maximum effect, and the need for follow-up programmes in the event of relapse.

How far may the findings of Halpern be generalised?

—— Effective frame for the conclusion.

Final point not discussed in the body of the response.

Chapter 9

Theory of Knowledge

Knowledge by authority

Findings will vary. It may help if each student is given a copy of the following simple grid for recording responses.

Participant number	Type of parenting	Principles emphasised by parents	Participant's comments	Current view of parental beliefs
Example	**Authoritative**	1. Good grades are the key to success. 2. Honesty is the best policy. 3. No dating until you're 21.	1. That was true – in my case, looking back. 2. Yes, habitual liars can't deceive others for ever. 3. Well, I met my boyfriend in my first year of college. We've been happily married for 12 years.	**Rethinking of parental beliefs is dominant**
1				
2				
3				
4				
5				
6				
7				
8				
9				
10				

The student will determine whether any patterns emerge between the second and the fifth column. The results of all students can then be pooled and statistically tested for correlation.

Self-assessment questions

Self-assessment questions 9.1

1 a Play involves enjoyable activities that are unrelated to survival, production or profit.

   b Piaget proposed that play assists the assimilation of ideas at the child's age-bound level of processing information. Exploratory and role-playing activities involve consolidating ideas in a pleasurable way rather than learning something new. Also, the social benefits of play include the experiences of working in groups, dealing with conflicts and learning to speak up for themselves.

   Vygotsky proposed the idea that play can promote as well as consolidate development, in a rich zone of proximal development where children learn when mixing with relatively dynamic and experienced peers close by.

   c Ladd (1990) investigated the degree to which the quality of children's peer relations can affect their adjustment to school at kindergarten level. It concluded that the more positive the peer relationships (often rooted in playtime when peers interact more freely) at both pre-school and kindergarten level, the better the cognitive and social development within the kindergarten school setting.

2 a Childhood trauma involves the experience of a sudden and adverse change in circumstances such as the death of the primary caregiver, war and dislocation as a refugee, and physical and sexual abuse. Childhood deprivation is where a child is not receiving the level of care, attention, sustenance, and education that are needed for physical, mental, and moral well-being.

   b Childhood trauma (effects not always obviously distinguishable from childhood deprivation):

   i PTSD – fMRI-based research of Carion et al. (2009) showing PTSD's characteristic symptoms of decreased hippocampus activity. Those individuals also demonstrated poorer memory skills, and appeared to feel more isolated and emotionally apathetic.

   Childhood deprivation:

   i reduced childhood brain growth – Perry and Pollard (1997) based on CT scans of deprived children being significantly smaller in brain size than average for that age group.

   ii cognitive impairment and attachment disturbance – Rutter et al. (2004) based on observation, cognitive testing, and adoptive-parent interviews of recently UK-adopted infants from Romanian orphanages).

   c Hodges and Tizard (1989) showed that children deprived of attachment until the age of eight years were able to make attachments when placed in homes where they were loved and wanted. This was a more common situation when they were adopted than when they were returned to their biological parents. However, both adopted and returned children found considerable difficulties in forming close relationships with peers, and tended to desire adult attention and approval beyond the level typical for their age group.

3 a Resilience is the ability to thrive, mature and increase competence in the face of adverse circumstances, and to recover from conditions of deprivation and trauma.

   b Factors favourable to promoting resilience include:

   i Schoon and Bartley (2008), meta-study based in the UK: support from family and social environment, child sensing achievement and confidence in their own learning and social abilities

   ii High/Scope Perry Pre-school Project: high-quality and regular pre-school programme incorporating parental support and involvement.

4 Pollitt's longitudinal study indicated that protein deficiencies typical of villagers in Guatemala are only one of several factors adversely affecting cognitive progress in the early years of schooling.

Self-assessment questions 9.2

1 **a** Attachment is where the bond between two people is strong and long-lasting, with substantial separation causing distress.

b Bowlby's theory is that the intense mother and child attachment made in the first three years of life sets the nature of the child's future attachments throughout life.

c Ainsworth identified three early-years attachment types between the child and the mother, based on her observations in her 'Strange Situation' research. Type B (70%) were securely attached to the mother, Type A (20%) were detached from the mother and Type C (10%) were ambivalent towards the mother.

d Type B children are emotionally close to their mothers. Type A children are more likely to feel emotional distance and less responsiveness to the mother. Type C children are more likely to experience inconsistencies in maternal responsiveness and attention.

e Hazan and Shaver's work on the quality and nature of adult romantic relationships indicates that their nature and quality are significantly correlated with early life experiences with the mother figure.

2 **a** Sex is a person's chromosome-based biological determinant. Gender is defined as the social and psychological characteristics of being male or female. Gender roles are the norms that dictate the types of behaviour that are considered to be acceptable within a given society, in terms of the sex of the individual.

b Factors influencing gender role include:

i Biological: evolutionary theory claiming that the gender roles that developed out of the early needs of society are genetically supported to this day. Also, the higher levels of testosterone for males and oestrogen for females result in both genders tending to choose activities that typify their gender stereotype (Money (1972): andrenogenital syndrome girls showed preference for activities fitting the male rather than female stereotype).

ii Cognitive: gender schemas developing out of affirming or disapproving feedback in infancy when showing gender-based behaviours (Martin and Halverson (1983) young children's inaccuracies in recalling pictures with gender content were connected with their gender-role schemas).

iii Socio-cultural: social-learning theory claiming that gender roles are learnt and developed through interacting with the environment and modelling those of the same gender. However, a child will use a person of the opposite sex as a role model when seeking to become involved in an activity associated with the opposite gender (Bussey and Bandura, 1992).

3 **a** Empathy is the capacity to understand and share the feelings of the other even when not in agreement. Theory of mind enables a person to be empathic: humans have the capacity to attribute thoughts and understand the mindset and feelings of others in order to interact with them, and also to predict their behaviour.

b Wimmer and Perner (1983) indicates that theory of mind starts to develop between the ages of four and six at normal rates of child development.
Baron-Cohen et al. (1985) indicates that lack of development of theory of mind helps to explain the phenomenon of autism.

Self-assessment questions 9.3

1 A cognitive approach considers a person's understanding in terms of mental representations. The cognitive approach becomes a cognitive developmental approach in viewing how mental representations change and become more mature with age and experience.

2 The fundamental principles in Piaget's theory of cognitive development are:

a Biologically-driven mental development precedes learning.

b The child's intellectual development occurs as a series of processes.

c The child's intellectual development may be promoted through active interaction with the world.

d The child assists their learning progress by being actively involved in the learning process.

3 The four ways in which schemas adapt in scope and complexity according to Piaget:
   a Assimilation – application of an existing schema to incorporate a new object or situation.
   b Disequilibrium – the existing schema is found not to work in a given situation. The schema needs to be modified or enlarged to deal with it.
   c Equilibration – the person's existing schema becomes sufficiently adjusted and expanded to deal with most similar situations.
   d Accommodation – the person's expanded schemas have developed to such a level of complexity that the person can handle similar objects and situations without thought.

4 As in the table below:

Stage 1 – Sensory-motor stage (ages 0–2)	Transition from Stage 1 to Stage 2: Sense of object permanence
Stage 2 – Pre-operational stage (ages 2–7)	
Stage 3 – Concrete operational stage (ages 7–11)	Transition from Stage 2 to Stage 3: Sense of conservation, and capacity to see from the physical viewpoints of others
Stage 4 – Formal operational stage (11+)	Transition from Stage 3 to Stage 4: Capacity to reason abstractly; without visual support

5 **a** Zone of proximal development: identifying the area between what the child can achieve without help, and what can be achieved under the appropriate guidance of a teacher or more advanced student.
   b Scaffolding: where the educator breaks down the new concept, skill or task into suitably structured units for the student to grasp.
   c Use of language: the capacity to think by verbalising thoughts even when not communicating, typically between the ages of three and seven. Thoughts are shaped by the degree of sophistication and cultural aspects of the language that the child has learnt through the continuous interaction with others.

6 The spiral curriculum means that programmes of work are designed so that students revisit concepts and ideas at intervals throughout their schooling, each time at a more sophisticated level. Learning becomes an upward climb on the same base. In contrast to Piaget, Bruner claims that even a very young student can learn almost any material as long as it is suitably developed, scaffolded and revisited.

7 **a** **i** Maturing in the prefrontal context and the age-related increasing complexity of the folds of the surface of the brain affect its capacities for impulse control, decision-making, planning and assessing evidence. These continue to mature until the mid-20s.
      ii The neurons' development of myelin covering means that older children can react more quickly as it is that which accelerates the speed of transmission of information within the nervous system.
      iii The life-long present phenomenon of brain plasticity indicates that differences in personal learning experiences affect the rates of growth of different learning-associated networks in the brain.
   b On a biological basis, Waber et al. (2007) indicates that the increase in the effectiveness of learning capacity in a wide range of domains is age-bound in normally healthy children. Barkley-Levenson and Galván (2014) indicates that it is the heightened range of expectations and emotions within the teenage VS neural stage of development that prompts teenagers to advantageously take risks to a higher degree than adults.

Exam-style questions – sample answer

Essay response question

Gender includes the social and psychological characteristics of being male or female. Gender roles are the norms that dictate the types of behaviour that are considered to be acceptable within a given society, in terms of the sex of the individual.

Psychologists accept that gender roles do exist. Some are virtually universal throughout humanity, and others vary according to different socio-cultural norms. However, the more influential causes of differences in gender roles are debated between psychologists. For example, does a boy who demonstrates the masculine stereotype do so largely because it is within his hormonal structure, or predominantly because he was brought up that way?

We will consider two theories for the development of gender roles. They are the biologically-based theory of gender development, and the socio-cultural theory of gender development.

The biologically-based theory of gender role development holds that males and females have differences in physiology that are in turn suited to the traditional male and female behaviors, activities, and roles in society. These include hormones. Males have higher levels of testosterone, and females have higher levels of oestrogen. The testosterone tends to stimulate rough and tumble play amongst boys, and the oestrogen influences the complex and emotive social relationship amongst girls. This view holds that testosterone-fired boys' play helps to prepare the male for the real world where he has to compete for scarce resources, including for desirable members of the opposite sex. The girls' oestrogen-fired complicated relationships with one another help to prepare them for the traditional adult real-life in bringing up their own children. These are far more important in gender-role development than social influences such as culture and gender-associated parental and school expectations.

Biological explanations in gender identity also point to evolutionary theory, which claims that gender roles developed out of the needs of early societies. Males were physically powerful. Men had to be tough and competitive, and show females that they could supply food and protection to any children who were born. Otherwise few, if any, women would be interested in them, and they would therefore not have the chance to pass their genes down to the next generation. Women concentrated on taking care of their health and looks to the highest possible level in order to attract the best possible male. Together, their lives would continue according to those roles. Women stayed at home, to bring up and care for their children. Men continued to use their physical and mental strength to find, hunt, and gather food and other items that the family needed and wanted.

Biologists also argue that these gender roles are genetically supported, even though the needs of modern society have changed. Most jobs (in Western society) are open to both men and women. In some marriages, the wife even earns more while the husband stays at home, brings up the children, and does the household tasks.

The strength of the biological approach in the promotion of gender roles is that hormone-driven differences in these roles may also be observed in non-human species, such as in dogs.

In addition, hormone-driven differences in the womb also appear to affect gender roles in life.

This is supported by the longitudinal study of Money and Ehrhardt (1972), which studied 25 girls with adrenogenital syndrome whose symptoms show a higher-than-normal level of male-associated hormones. The study showed their preferences for doing things that fitted the male, rather than the female, stereotyped gender role.

However, the link between higher testosterone levels and male aggressive behaviour is correlational. It may be the male gender-associated activities that promote higher levels of testosterone, rather than higher levels of testosterone encouraging those activities. Also, the variations in different societies' male and female gender roles (such as whether the man or the woman does the shopping) suggest that biological elements may be greatly modified by socio-cultural expectations.

The command term 'discuss' means looking critically at the validity of two relevant theories.

Needs to be placed in the context of gender identity.

The masculine stereotype needs to be behaviourally exemplified, such as preferring to play with toy cars than with dolls.

The theory is rather general up to here.

Evaluates study, relates to theory.

In contrast with biological theory, socio-cultural-based theory of gender role development tends to connect with social learning theory. Social learning theory holds that gender roles are learnt and developed through interacting with the environment and modeling those of the same gender. In the case of gender role development, the theory accepts that children observe role models of the same sex and will imitate their behaviours if they can see them leading to gender-role-associated desirable consequences.

On what basis?

The study of Bussey and Bandura (1992) subsequently extended this theory to include the child's more active participation in gender-role development. It is not that society gives cues for the desirable roles for each gender, but that the child decides what role they would like, and chooses the role models to imitate. For example, a six-year-old girl is passionate about fast cars and desires to be a Formula 1 racing driver. She observes male racing champions on television and declares that she wants to be one when she grows up. As a result, she may pick up cues from the people she chooses to emulate even if they are of the opposite sex rather than people of her own gender. This can be true even where she may face some social disapproval from her own peers, particularly if she is in the pre-teen age group (Sroufe et al., 1993).

Needs to present this as a limitation of social learning theory model.

Does this cross-gender involvement modify gender roles in developing a personal identity?

The strength of the socio-cultural influence is reflected in the importance of changing gender roles, such as fathers becoming more involved in child-rearing where they have participated in parenting and child-development programmes (Engle and Breaux, 1994). The socio-cultural influence may also be supported empirically, such as by the success of the rising number of women in traditionally male professions.

However, in contrast to biological theories, the socio-cultural approach does not easily account for gender roles being a constant and driving force behind the individual's behaviour. Additionally, social factors may be biologically influenced, such as Mead's findings in traditional tribal societies in New Guinea which indicated that the men were more forceful than women in almost all cultures.

Needs elaboration: how may Mead's findings be explained in biological terms?

In conclusion, it appears that both biologically-based and socio-cultural-based theories contribute to the reality and nature of gender roles. Neither wholly determines gender roles, and the relative importance of each set of theories is debated by psychologists.

Chapter 10

Theory of Knowledge

Your answer may contain the development of the following themes illustrated by suitable research studies:

Approaches in psychology resemble methods used in natural sciences:

- use of quantitative methods and statistical analysis
- use of controlled laboratory experiments
- use of correlation research
- designs often resemble natural sciences (e.g. independent measures, matched pairs)
- generate data to which descriptive and inferential statistical analysis may be applied
- research may be evaluated in terms of reliability, credibility and categories of bias.

Approaches in psychology differ from methods used in natural sciences:

- use of interview methods which rely on self-reporting feelings
- need to take possible researcher bias into account
- analysis of qualitative data (interviews, observations, case studies) can be subject to bias
- participant behaviour can be influenced by the research process (e.g. interviewer effect, Hawthorne effect)
- results obtained in one environment might not generalise/transfer to another one.

Self-assessment questions

Self-assessment questions 10.1

1 Five quantitative methods commonly used in psychological research include the following:
   a laboratory experiments: where the researcher manipulates the IV in a non-real-life environment; for example, Loftus and Palmer (1974)
   b field experiments: where the researcher manipulates the IV, but within a real-life environment; for example Rosenthal and Jacobson (1968)
   c quasi-experiments: where the IV being studied occurs naturally, the variable is pre-existing, and no experimenter manipulation takes place; for example, Baron-Cohen et al. (1985)
   d natural experiments: where the experimenter is not able to manipulate the IV as it occurs in circumstances beyond researcher control; for example, Charlton et al. (2002)
   e correlation research: where the experimenter seeks to find a statistically significant relationship without determining cause and effect between two or more quantitatively measured variables; for example, Bouchard et al. (1990).

2 Three qualitative methods commonly used in psychological research include the following:
   a interviews: may be unstructured, semi-structured, and focus-group interviews, all designed to gain an insight into people's thoughts, opinions and feelings; for example, Totten (2003)
   b naturalistic observations: involving precise measurement of naturally-occurring behaviour, typically using field notes and coding (may be used for quantitative as well as qualitative investigations) (for example, Charlton et al. (2002)), which may also be covert, and participant observed (for example, Rosenhan (1973).
   c case studies: involving the detailed analysis of one individual or a small group, usually over a period; for example, Curtiss's study of Genie (1977).

3 Possibilities of bias in psychological research include the following:
   a interviewer effect: where the interviewer's attitude and demeanour could bias participant responses
   b Hawthorne effect: where behaviour of those observed improves significantly from the norm when they perceive that they are being watched
   c Rosenthal effect: where perceived higher expectations lead to a higher level of performance than the norm while being watched
   d researcher bias: where the investigator's beliefs, ideals and hoped-for findings influence the analysis of the data
   e confirmation bias: over-considering information and interpretations that confirm pre-existing opinions and expectations, and under-considering those that contradict them
   f lack of reflexivity: where the researcher does not sufficiently reflect on their own background and beliefs, and how these could influence the research process
   g participant bias: the possibility that those taking part may be influenced by demand characteristics, answering or behaving in the way that they think fits in with the researcher or with other participants
   h sampling bias: where the sampling procedure does not accurately represent the target population.

4 Three common quantitative, experimental research designs include the following:
   a the independent measures design using a test group(s) and a control group of randomly selected participants; for example, Loftus and Palmer (1974)
   b the repeated measures design using the same participants in both the control and test condition(s) of the experiment; for example, Harris and Fiske (2006)
   c the matched pair design involving different but similar participants being assigned to a different condition; for example, Kearins (1981).

5 Six methods of sampling include the following:

    a random sampling: where each member of the population has an equal chance of being selected

    b stratified sampling: where the target population is divided up for sampling purposes into different sections and samples are taken for each, such as age groups or income groups

    c opportunity or convenience sampling: where the selected sample is made up of participants who are able and willing to take part in the study at a given time

    d volunteer sampling or self-selected sampling: where the sample is made up of participants who wish to take part rather than being selected by the researcher

    e purposive sampling: where the sample is made up of participants who possess the particular characteristics that are being researched (tends to be the preferred method in qualitative research)

    f snowball sampling: where participants already in the study help the researcher to recruit more participants through their social networks.

6 Three main categories of ethical considerations include:

    a informed consent: where the participants know the purpose of the study, their roles in the study and that their agreeing to participate is entirely voluntary

    b the protection of participants from harm: by guaranteeing anonymity, confidentiality, protection of privacy and protection from anything that might cause discomfort or distress during the investigation

    c the protection of participants from being exploited: analysis must be conducted in good faith, with due attention to elements that might detract from the integrity of the study, such as researcher bias and reflexivity.

7 Inductive content analysis is a qualitative method of analysis that aims to generate new theory based on the research data. It typically involves:

    a working through the transcripts or field notes, using colour or other coding

    b identifying emergent themes

    c deciding how those themes relate to each other through placing them in clusters and hierarchies

    d producing a summary table of the themes and relevant details according to the interviewed participant(s).

8 Descriptive statistics are used for describing the centre and spread of the data, summarising the data, and graphing the data. They include measures of central tendency (mean, median, mode), measures of dispersion around the mean showing the degree that scores differ from the mean (quartiles) and measures of variance from the mean (standard deviation). Inferential statistics aim to identify and highlight relationships and patterns in the data, and their degree of significance. In correlation studies, they involve the calculation of the correlation coefficient and its significance, the method/test depending on the nature of the data. In experimental studies designed to generate two (or more) sets of data from the control group and from the test group, inferential testing is applied to determine whether there is a mathematically-determinable and significant difference between the data generated from the control, and the test groups. In all cases, the researcher:

    a sets a hypothesis

    b selects an inferential statistical test

    c uses the data and test's formula to calculate a value

    d looks up the value in a distribution table for that particular test to see whether differences have or do not have the mathematical support of being significant.

9 Validity assesses how accurately the study measures what it is designed to measure. A study is internally valid when the differences between the test and control samples have been caused entirely by the manipulation of the IV, with all extraneous variables rigorously controlled. A study is externally valid where the results of a study can be generalised or transferred to a different environment, population or time period. Reliability is the degree to which the study, in repeated trials using the same methods, design, and measurements, produces the same results. Credibility, used in qualitative research, serves the same purpose as internal validity in quantitative research and is maximised where the study produces the truest possible picture of what is being investigated, researcher reflexivity possibilities are suitably addressed, and the proceedings of the research are carefully documented.

Exam-style questions – sample answers

Short-answer questions

1 a The research method was the semi-structured interview. One of its characteristics is that the ideas to be explored are clear to the investigator before the interview takes place. Another feature is that it contains open questions as well as closed questions. The open questions enable the interviewer to invite the participant to give further details, while the closed questions ensure that the data includes the essential sought-after information.

   b The sample method was purposive sampling. A purposeful sample is made up of participants who possess the particular characteristics that are being researched. In this study, all 24 participants had dropped out of school between age 16 and the formal finish of high (secondary) school.
This purposive sample may have become a snowball sample if participants already in the study helped the researcher to recruit more participants through their social networks.

   c The researcher could have used focus group interviews with five or six people instead of interviewing all participants individually. That enables participants to respond to issues raised by others, which can help to identify areas of agreement and disagreement among group members.

2 Each individual's participation was emphasised as being entirely voluntary, with the option to withdraw from the study at any stage. In addition, the researchers emphasised that the data would be anonymous and used only for the stated purpose of the study. Furthermore, each participant indicated willingness to be involved by signing a consent form.

Other ethical considerations that could be applied are that the participants should be debriefed immediately after the study, especially as it is possible that they may have given data of a sensitive nature. Also, it may well have been desirable or even necessary to obtain parental approval for the participation of those under the age of 18. Finally, the study would need to obtain the favourable opinion of an academic ethics committee.

3 A content analysis of the data indicated that students dropped out of school mainly due to dissatisfaction with the school system or their own performance within it, with preferences for employment opportunities being given by a minority only. Three issues in generalising the findings from this qualitative study to school drop-out rates at ages 16–18 are credibility, follow-up possibility, and opportunities to develop theory.

Credibility, used in qualitative research such as this study, serves the same purpose as internal validity in quantitative research. It is supported where researcher reflexivity possibilities are suitably addressed and the proceedings of the research are carefully documented, making it possible for other investigators to critically follow the entire research process. It needs to address the possibilities of bias, such as confirmation bias with over-considering information

> Method correctly identified and two characteristics given as required. Other characteristics of the semi-structured interview could include the informal, participant-friendly setting that is typically used, and the possibility of professional rapport developing between interviewer and participant, making it easier to handle sensitive topics.

> Correct. The sampling method is correctly identified, and it is duly supported by two characteristics.

> Correct. The use of the focus group has been suitably justified. An alternative response could be the use of a quantitative survey.

> The maximum of three ethical points are duly identified. However, those points need to be fully justified to obtain maximum marks. Not all points were.

This response does contain the elements that would place it within the top mark-band level descriptor for this question. There is effective consideration of strengths and limitations, and the discussion is balanced. However, the second paragraph would be improved by relating the ideas more effectively to the stimulus material.

and interpretations that support pre-existing researcher opinions and expectations, and under-considering those that contradict them. It also needs to consider the possibility of participant bias, where those taking part may answer or behave in a way that they think fits in with the researcher or with other participants.

The findings were based on one medium-sized city only. Following up the investigation by repeating it with groups of different socio-economic status and in different districts may increase the possibilities of generalising the findings to other populations. In addition, the results of this study may form the basis of a quantitative follow-up that could support or limit the capacity to generalise the study.

Finally, the findings of the study being recognised by the researchers as contrary to expectations could open an investigation of a new area of theory influencing prevalence rates of school drop-out in this age group.

Glossary

A

Abnormal psychology: the classification, causes, diagnosis, and treatment of impairments in important areas of normal mental functioning.

Accommodation in maintaining a relationship: the capacity to handle and adapt to the other's tolerance-straining behaviour according to the degree of friendship or intimate relationship already present.

Accommodation (Piagetian concept): the existing schemas have developed to the level of complexity where the person can handle similar objects and situations without thought.

Acculturation: where people change or at least adapt due to contact with another culture, in order to fit in to that culture.

Acculturation stress: the psychological strain of striving to adapt to a different culture.

Acetylcholine: a neurotransmitter whose many functions include activating other neurons and hormones such as dopamine, creating a feeling of well-being.

Acute stressors: stress-causers that do not last long, and might require immediate attention.

Addiction: a compulsion to use the substance in order to avoid discomfort in its absence, such as the smoker's craving for a cigarette.

Adolescence: the development period between puberty and adulthood, typically between 12 and 20 years.

Adrenaline: a hormone produced by the adrenal glands. When released, it quickens up the heartbeat and deepens the breathing, preparing for fight, flight, fright or freeze.

Adrenogenital syndrome: where a female's endocrine system shows a higher-than-normal level of male-associated hormones.

Aetiology: the study of the causes of a disorder.

Affectionless psychopathy: inability to show affection; a likely consequence of deprivation or trauma.

Affective disorder: a category of mental abnormalities whose symptoms include mood disorders.

Affective symptom: an indication of a mood disorder.

Agency theory: putting the moral responsibility on people regarded as experts and superiors when carrying out their instructions. Connected to agentic state of mind.

Agentic state of mind: where a person obeys without question those accepted as experts or superiors, such parents, teachers and employers. Connected to agency theory.

Allele: an alternative form of a gene that can arise by mutation on the same place on the chromosome.

Alternative (experimental) hypothesis (H_1): alternative to the null hypothesis; proposes that the researcher's intervention will have an effect on the phenomenon being studied, for example human behaviour. It is a testable statement of what the researcher seeks to find.

Altruism: helping another person at one's own cost, without expectation of benefit or reward.

Amygdala: the part the brain that integrates basic emotions, emotional behaviour and motivation.

Anasognosia: where the individual suffering a disorder is unaware of having that disorder.

Anchoring bias: a heuristic where the individual relies on the first piece of information offered (the 'anchor') to make a decision, irrespective of its accuracy and relevance.

Anorexia nervosa: disorder evidenced by severely limited food intake, together with extreme concern about body image and body weight.

.. no

Anterograde amnesia: being unable to form new memories after brain damage, but still able to recall memories made before the brain damage.

Antigens: harmful bacteria, viruses and cancerous cells.

Anxiolytics: medication that reduces anxiety.

Arachnophobia: fear of spiders.

Articulatory suppression: participants are required to memorise and recall a random list of numbers or words, but at the same time have to constantly repeat a specified word while learning the list.

Assimilation (Piagetian concept): the applying of an existing schema to deal with a new situation.

Assimilation: where an individual strives to adopt the attitudes and behaviours of the majority culture and exits the original culture in the process.

Attachment: where the bond between two people is strong and long-lasting, and substantial separation causes distress.

Attentional bias: excessive focus on one element in a scenario, at the expense of another operative element.

Attribution theory: how the individual attempts to explain why people behave in a particular way.

Authoritarian parenting: characterised by high demands and low responsiveness. Parents have very high expectations of their children, yet provide very little in the way of feedback and nurturance. Mistakes tend to be punished harshly. When feedback does occur, it is often negative.

Authoritative parenting: characterised by high expectations and emotional responsiveness. It incorporates clear limits and fair discipline as well as warmth and support.

Autism: a mental condition involving difficulties in communicating and forming relationships with other people.

Automatic negative thinking: a false set of self-limiting beliefs promoted by a series of negative schemas.

Autonomic nervous system: this connects organs and glands to the central nervous system and deals with involuntary actions, such as breathing, hormone regulation and digestion.

Autonomous state of mind: where a person makes their own decisions and takes full responsibility for the consequences.

Availability heuristic: a person's assessment a situation being influenced by the amount of information instantly accessible, rather than on a balanced assessment of the situation.

B

Behavioural approach: focuses on studying observable elements in behaviour under the headings of stimulus and response.

Behavioural symptom: an indication of a mental abnormality based on the patient's behaviour.

Bias: supporting or opposing someone or something in an unfair way, due to personal opinion influencing judgement.

Bias (research): factors that can adversely affect the accuracy of a study.

Biochemical imbalances in the brain: where there is an abnormality in the degree of concentration of neurotransmitter receptor sites in the brain, for example a low concentration of dopamine receptor sites in the brains of anorexic patients.

Biological approach: focus on the ways that genetics, the nervous system and the endocrine system influence thoughts and actions.

Biological phenomena: the forms that a group or category of living organisms may take.

Biomedical approach: biologically-interventionist treatment to treat mental disorders, such as drugs or chemotherapy.

Biopsychosocial model: the psychological elements of thoughts, feelings and behaviours as well as the biological factors of health and disease influence the physical condition of a person.

Body-mass index (BMI) score: measure of a person's closeness to ideal weight. Calculated by dividing the weight of the person in kilograms by the square of the height in metres. A BMI of between 18.5 and 25 is ideal, above 25 is overweight, and over 30 is obese.

Bottom-up processing: the interpreting of new sensory information as being initially something new and then in stages integrating it with existing schemas.

Brain: the part of the central nervous system that is enclosed within the skull.

Brain function lateralisation: the tendency for specific neural and cognitive functions to be more dominant in one brain hemisphere than in the other.

Brain function localisation: the idea that different parts of the brain perform different functions.

Brain functions: the multitude of voluntary and involuntary roles that the brain carries out, ranging from controlling heartbeat rate to deep thinking and decision-making.

Brain plasticity: the capacity of the central nervous system to develop additional neurons in response to a person's persistent efforts to develop a specific skill.

Brain-scanning techniques: electronic technology making it possible for doctors and researchers to view activities within the brain without using invasive surgery.

Briefing: the information given to participants before taking part in the investigation. It is required by the ethical guidelines in psychology.

Broca aphasia: impaired ability to produce speech, yet able to understand speech.

Broca area: part of the brain responsible for speech production, located in the left frontal lobe of the brain.

Bullying: where a person is repeatedly exposed to negative actions of others, which may be physical, verbal or psychological.

Bystanderism: where individuals do not step forward to help a victim when others are present.

C

Case study: investigation involving a few participants or even one participant in depth, typically in a natural ecologically valid setting.

Caudate nucleus: site that has a role in the decision-making process.

Central executive (CE): sensory memory component of the working memory model. It selects the sensory information that is picked up and passed on to the suitable parts of the three-component working STM system.

Central nervous system (CNS): the part of the nervous system composed of the brain and spinal cord.

Chronic stressors: stress causers that are constant, create worry and last for a long time.

Cognitions: the ways in which the individual mentally processes stimuli and information.

Cognitive approach: focus on how behaviours relate to the way that the mind processes information.

Cognitive behavioural therapy (CBT): psychotherapeutic treatment based on the theory that thinking patterns strongly influence many behaviour patterns.

Cognitive developmental approach: where growing up and maturing results in mental representations changing and becoming more sophisticated.

Cognitive bias: the inaccurate processing of information due to the over-focus on some elements and the under-focus on others of equal or greater importance.

Cognitive rehearsal: a form of cognitive therapy where the client imagines being in a difficult situation that happened in the past. The therapist works with the client to practise effective management of the problem.

Cognitive restructuring: a form of cognitive therapy focusing on adopting more rational and constructive ways of dealing with stresses and problems.

Cognitive symptom: an indication of a mental abnormality based on the patient's reporting of their perception of the environment or an event.

Co-morbidity: where the patient is diagnosed as having more than one abnormal condition.

Compliance: adjusting behaviour to fit in with overt demands.

Computerised tomography (CT): scanning technique in which ionised dye is injected in the blood to highlight specific brain tissue. The tissue is then scanned to create an image.

Concordance rate: in genetics, the proportion of twins or relatives sharing similar physical or behavioural characteristics.

Concrete operational stage (seven to eleven years): Piagetian concept where the individual can perform mental operations, but only when the objects are physically present.

Confabulation: where memories are sincerely believed and declared by the person to be true even though they are contradicted by evidence.

Confirmation bias: a heuristic where the individual focuses on information and interpretations that confirm pre-existing opinions and expectations.

Conformity: adjusting thinking and behaviour to fit in with the perceived norms of the environment, without being told to do so.

Confounding variables: where extraneous variables not being adequately controlled could adversely affect and therefore invalidate the results of the study.

Conscious mind approach: the consideration of the images, sensations and feelings that the individual experiences to understand the way that a person is thinking.

Conservation: Piagetian concept where an object or substance is perceived as remaining the same in quantity even where it is worked into a different shape.

Content analysis: the finding of patterns within qualitative data.

Continuous variable: where a variable has an infinite number of possible values, even within a range.

Correlation coefficient: a value that shows the degree to which the variables correlate, and the likelihood of the found degree of correlation occurring by chance.

Correlation studies: collecting sufficient data on two or more variables to see if there is a direct or inverse relationship between them.

Correlational: having connection between two or more things, such as sets of data or situations.

Correlation research: where the research focuses on the degree to which two or more variables are related to each other, and how statistically significant that relationship is.

Cortisol: a neurohormone active in adapting to stress through pain reduction and improved physical and mental activity, although prolonged high levels weaken immunity to disease.

Covert observation: when those observed do not know that they are being watched.

Credibility: used in qualitative research, it establishes how far the results of the research are in agreement with the phenomenon under study, and with the participants' perceptions and experiences.

Cultural dimensions: the issues and perspectives of a culture based on cultural norms and values.

Cultural norms: behaviour patterns which are typical of specific groups.

D

Debriefing: the information given to participants after taking part in the investigation. It is required by the ethical guidelines in psychology.

Declarative memory: (also referred to as episodic memory) contains facts, concepts and ideas that have been consciously learnt and rehearsed. It divides into episodic memory and semantic memory.

Deductive (in etic/emic context): where research is conducted according to the theory and methods of the investigators' culture. It is then applied to a local culture, which may or may not be similar. Typically used in etic rather than emic studies.

Deep culture: the beliefs, values, thought processes and assumptions of a culture that are more easily understood by members of that culture but are less accessible to members of other cultures.

Deindividuation theory: a person feels less accountable for violent behaviour where the victim is unidentifiable, faceless or part of the opposition crowd.

Demand characteristics: the participant responds according to what he or she thinks that the researchers want to hear without it necessarily being true.

Dendrite: a long, very thin projection of the neuron, which carries electric impulses received from other neurons.

Dependent variable (DV): the variable in experimental psychology that is studied as being affected in both the test condition and the control condition.

Depressive episode: a period of symptoms of depression, which becomes major depression if it persists continually for at least two weeks.

Deprivation (child): where the child's basic physical, emotional and social needs are not taken care of.

Descriptive statistics: these describe the spread and range of the data. An efficient way of summarising and graphing the data.

Determinant of health: biological, socio-economic, environmental and psychological factors that influence the health status of individuals or populations.

Determinism: where a thought process or behaviour is considered to happen through processes beyond the individual's choice or control.

Diagnosis manual: a professionally-compiled and comprehensive collection of abnormalities with standardised guidelines and criteria for diagnosis.

Diathesis–stress model: model which holds that psychological abnormality and its associated behaviours are products of both genotype and environment.

Diffusion of responsibility: the likelihood of a capable individual not volunteering to help where other similarly-able people are present.

Discrete variable: where a variable has a limited number of possible values.

Discrimination: unjustifiably negative behaviour towards members of an out-group.

Disequilibrium: Piagetian concept, where a person finds that an existing schema does not work in a new situation, and that the schema needs to be modified to deal with it.

Dispositional attribution: the degree to which people attribute their own health-detrimental realities to their own personality.

Dispositional factors: where you understand a person's behaviour as being directed personally at you, and not a product of their own circumstances.

Dizygotic (DZ) twins: formed when two sperm cells pierce two separate ova. The resulting twins will be non-identical and may be of different genders.

Door-in-the-face: compliance technique asking a larger favour than required, getting it turned down and proceeding to the much smaller favour required.

Dopamine: a neurotransmitter that helps to control the brain's reward and pleasure centres. Increased dopamine levels in the brain mean increased pleasurable stimulation.

Dopamine receptor sites: located on the post-synaptic neuron. They receive the pleasure-giving dopamine neurotransmitter that is fired by the pre-synaptic neuron.

DSM-5: the diagnosis manual for abnormalities used in the USA.

Dual process model of thinking and decision-making: holds that individuals bring two systems of thinking to decision-making known as System-1 and System-2 thinking.

Ductless glands: glands that secrete hormones directly into the bloodstream; also known as endocrine glands.

Dyadic stage (of relationship break-up): secondary stage of relationship break-up involving confronting rather than avoiding partner over the benefits and losses involved in break-up, which might lead to reconciliation and a new beginning, but could also phase into complete break-up.

E

Eating disorder: a category of mental abnormalities whose symptoms include problems with food intake.

Eclectic treatment: where health professionals combine methods, such as medication and counselling, that together are likely to assist the patient's recovery.

Ecological validity: where the nature of the environment in which the research takes place enables the findings to be more readily applied to real-life situations.

Egocentric: thinking of yourself only, without consideration for others.

Electroconvulsive therapy (ECT): a controversial treatment where electrical stimulus is designed to promote chemical changes in the brain in order to abate the disorder.

Electroencephalography (EEG): a brain-scanning technique where a large number of electrodes are attached to the head, making it possible to record impulses from the top layers of the brain.

Emic approach: this approach views behaviour within one culture and examines it within the parameters of that culture rather than within a worldwide norm.

Empathy: the capacity to understand and share the feelings of others without necessarily being in agreement with them.

Empathy-altruism theory: the observation of the suffering of another person creates personal distress and a consequent desire to help.

Empirical approach: focus on findings based on observation, experience and experimentation with a suitably large number of people.

Empiricism: the view that the understanding of human behaviour needs to be based on findings that can be observed and counted.

Enactive representational stage: Brunerian concept where our mental encoding of a concept is in the elementary form of a physical action fundamental to that concept.

Enculturation: the acquisition of the necessary and appropriate norms and skills of your own culture of origin.

Endocrine system: the biochemical messenger system responsible for generating, releasing and distributing hormones.

Endowment effect: a heuristic where an individual is biased to overestimate the value of something simply because they own it.

Epigenetics: the study of the factors that switch genes on and off. Also known as gene regulation.

Episodic buffer: the part of the STM within the working memory model that processes narrative-type information.

Episodic memory: the part of explicit or declarative memory that holds the details of events and experiences of one's life.

Equilibration: Piagetian concept, where the person's existing schema becomes sufficiently modified and complex to deal with most situations.

Ethical guidelines: code of conduct for investigators in psychology to prevent unacceptable exploitation of participants. The guidelines must be satisfied in every piece of research.

Ethically acceptable: the research conforms to the professional guidelines binding on psychology investigators.

Ethnocentrism: the generalising of the findings on one culture to another culture.

Etic approach: this approach views behaviours across cultures, and attempts to find out if specific behaviours are culturally determined or universal.

Eustress: the normal degree of stress that is beneficial and positively motivational for the individual.

Exclusionary reactions: viewing globalised culture with suspicion and as a threat.

Experimental psychology: psychological research carried out under both test conditions and controlled conditions. These conditions are identical, except for the IV which is changed in the experimental condition.

Experimental study: where the researcher uses a test and control population, and has the capacity to manipulate the independent variable in the test population.

Explicit memory: (also referred to as declarative memory) contains facts, concepts and ideas that have been consciously learnt and rehearsed. It divides into episodic memory and semantic memory.

External validity: where the results of a study can be generalised or transferred to a different environment, population or time period.

Extraneous variables: variables other than the IV that might affect the DV.

F

False belief: being able to recognise that the other person has a different viewpoint even when certain that the viewpoint is wrong.

False memory: recalling an event that never happened and believing it is true.

Family studies: plotting the recurrence of a behaviour over several generations in order to assess the likelihood of it being inherited and passed to the next generation.

Faulty thinking: thinking based on schemas that do not match reality.

Field experiments: where the researcher manipulates the IV, but within a real-life environment rather than a laboratory.

Flashbulb memory: an emotional memory that relates to a specific powerful impression-creating event that reconstructs what the person did and felt at the time.

Focus groups: typically consist of a group of six to ten people where the researcher acts as discussion director and facilitator, aiming for data to be generated from several people at the same time.

Foot-in-the-door: compliance technique asking for a small favour which is easy to grant, with a view to requesting a much larger favour.

Formal operational stage (from 11 years): Piagetian concept where thinking and processes involving a combination of schemas can be carried out mentally without the support of representing objects being physically present.

Framing: a heuristic where decision-making is liable to be biased by the way the information is given or the request is made.

Functionalist approach: based on the idea that individuals seek to enable their continuation by successfully adapting to changing circumstances and situations: the survival of the fittest.

Functional magnetic resonance imaging (fMRI): brain-scanning technique that measures the energy released by haemoglobin molecules, using it as a means of determining the amount of blood and oxygen in specific parts of the brain.

Fundamental attribution error: overestimating the role of dispositional factors and underestimating the role of situational factors, or vice versa.

G

Gender: the social and psychological characteristics of being male or female.

Gender bias: the possibility that a diagnosis or means of treatment of abnormality may be wrongly influenced by perceived gender similarities or differences between the professional and the patient.

Gender roles: the norms that dictate the types of behaviour that are acceptable within a given society in terms of the sex of the individual.

Gender schema: the mental processing of a person's behaviour in terms of compatibility with their gender.

Generalisation (quantitative data): assessing how far what the researchers concluded from their sample study applies to the target population, and possibly wider populations.

Gene regulation: mechanisms that cells use to increase or decrease the production of particular proteins that can affect physical characteristics or behaviours.

Genetic expression: where a gene is switched on and thus can influence a specific behaviour to occur.

Genetic factors: the role that biological heredity plays in determining cognition and behaviour.

Genocide: violent behaviour with the ultimate objective of destroying a whole race of people.

Genome-wide association studies (GWAS): the study of specific genetic variants within a large number of individuals to investigate whether a genetic variant or set of variants is associated with a trait.

Genotype: the genetic make-up of a particular organism.

Globalisation: the growing interdependence of countries worldwide through the increasing volume and variety of cross-border transactions in goods and services and of international capital flows, and through the more rapid and widespread diffusion in technology.

Grave-dressing phase (of relationship break-up): the final phase of relationship break-up where typically each partner will produce their own story of the breakdown, commonly blaming the other for all that went wrong.

Genome-wide association studies (GWAS): the study of specific genetic variants within a large number of individuals to investigate whether a genetic variant or set of variants are associated with a trait.

H

Hawthorne effect: the research participants' responses are influenced by the knowledge that they are part of a research study.

Hazing: compliance technique requiring a newcomer to go through a difficult and seemingly pointless procedure to gain acceptance with the group.

Health Belief Model: a person is most likely to stop an anti-health practice when they have high self-motivation and receive powerful messages from the environment.

Health beliefs: the degree to which an individual believes they are capable of being able to make the necessary behavioural changes to improve personal health.

Heuristics: mental short-cuts that may or may not be suitable bases for particular decisions, developed in the hippocampus and only then in the amygdala.

Holism: the explanation of a phenomenon in terms of a variety of causes and/or approaches.

Holistic: dealing with or treating the whole of a phenomenon and not just a part.

Holmes–Rahe Social Readjustment Scale: the degree of stress-severity that specific stressors cause to the typical individual.

Hormonal activity: the work of chemical substances secreted by endocrine glands that determine the rate at which the body works.

Hormones: biochemical substances produced by glands within the endocrine system, carried in the bloodstream. Hormones bio-determine the way the body synchronises and adjusts to specific stimuli and conditions.

Hypothalamus: a small area at the base of the brain that regulates the endocrine system and the autonomic nervous system.

Hypothesis: a proposed explanation of something observed which may be supported or refuted by evidence.

I

ICD-10: the diagnosis manual for abnormalities used in the UK, as well as in the World Health Organisation.

Iconic representational stage: Brunerian concept where our mental encoding of a concept is in the form of a picture fundamental to that concept.

Idiographic: where the factors influencing a person's behaviour cannot be generalised to others in similar circumstances, but are specific to that individual.

Idiographic human development: where an individual's development processes are not easily explained by application of the standard models.

Imitation: where behaviour is learnt through observing and modelling the actions of other people.

Implicit memory: memory containing information acquired mainly without conscious effort.

Independent measures design: where each participant in the sample is involved in either the control condition or in the test condition.

Independent variable (IV): the variable in experimental psychology that is changed in the test condition, but held constant in the control condition.

Inductive (in etic/emic context): determining what research questions are to be investigated only after getting to understand the culture of the local people. Typically used in emic studies.

Inductive content analysis: a qualitative method of analysis that aims to generate new theory based on the data.

Ineptness schema: an individual's mental matrix of processing information that sees them incapable of competently handling a particular situation.

Inferential statistics: these aim to highlight relationships and trends in the data, and their degree of significance.

Informed consent: an ethical requirement where participants should normally be made fully aware of the content and context of the research. Their decision on whether or not to take part must be based on full knowledge of the purpose of the work, and where their contribution fits in.

In-groups: groups with which an individual identifies.

Insula: the part of the brain where taste is sensed and integrated with the neural reward systems.

Integrative reaction: where people welcome or at least accommodate globalised culture.

Intergroup behaviour: relating to someone as a member of the in-group would to an outsider, rather than as one human being to another.

Internal validity: this is achieved where the differences between the test and control samples have been caused entirely by the accurate manipulation of the IV, with all extraneous variables rigorously controlled.

Internal working model: where early-learnt schemas set the pattern for behaviours in later life.

Inter-observer reliability: reliability is assessed in observational studies by employing several observers and correlating their findings or scores.

Interpersonal behaviour: relating to someone as one human being to another, and not specifically as a member of an in-group would to an outsider.

Interpersonal therapy (IPT): psychotherapeutic treatment based on the theory that thinking patterns associated with current difficulties in relationships strongly influence some behaviour patterns.

Interpretative phenomenological analysis (IPA): a means of carrying out inductive content analysis, typically involving colour coding, identifying emergent themes and seeking to organise them into a framework from which theory may be generated.

Inter-quartile range: the range of the middle 50% of the scores Q3–Q1.

Interval data: where distance between the values within the data is known.

Interviewer effect: where the interviewer's attitude and demeanour could bias answers from the respondent.

Intra-physic stage (of relationship break-up): primary stage of relationship break-up involving private perception of being unhappy with the relationship, and focus on its negative aspects and the attractions of sharing life with someone else.

Investigator effects: where the researcher's attitude and demeanour influence the responses and behaviours of the participants.

Investment model of commitment processes: problems occurring within relationships are more likely to be proactively and effectively handled when there is interdependence between the couple.

J K

Kin-selection theory: the innate, evolutionary desire to promote the survival of the part of the human race that has the highest amount of shared genetic material. This is a means of promoting one's own virtual survival beyond death.

Knock-out: in genetics, where specific genes have been clinically removed.

L

Learned helplessness: where past experience of insoluble problems or inescapable and intolerable physical conditions has reduced the individual to apathy in facing similar situations in the future. Believed to be a possible cause of depression.

Lesion: a structural alteration to tissues or organs caused by disease or injury.

Linkage analysis: where the frequency of particular behaviours is matched up by polymorphisms or variations within the gene.

Longitudinal study: research continuing with the same participants for an extended period, typically months or years.

Long-term memory (LTM): the permanent human memory store with virtually unlimited capacity.

Low-balling: compliance technique getting the person initially committed, and then upping the requirement at the last moment, knowing that the person won't change their mind.

M

Magnetic resonance imaging (MRI): a brain-scanning method that monitors the electromagnetic energy released by the brain after it has been exposed to a magnetic field.

Major depression: where the mood disorder of depression continues for an uninterrupted two weeks or more.

Major histo-compatibility complex (MHC): sets of cell-surface proteins that help the immune system to recognise foreign substances. The immune system itself protects the body from invading organisms, such as viruses, bacteria and cancerous cells.

Majority influence: where the individual follows the thoughts, behaviours and attitudes that are the norms of the group.

Marginalisation: where the individual is excluded from the majority culture and cannot maintain the original culture.

Maslow's hierarchy of needs: the forces motivating our behaviour are those of the most basic need currently not being satisfied. From most basic to least basic, these are physiological survival, personal safety, love and belonging, esteem and self-actualisation.

Matched pair design: different but similar participants are used in each condition. Each participant of a matched pair is assigned to a different condition.

Maternal deprivation hypothesis: Bowlbyian concept, where the mother's being consistently inaccessible in infancy creates attachment-based disorders in later life.

McClintock effect: the hypothesised synchronisation of menstrual cycles that may develop over a time period when a large number of women live and work in close proximity.

Measures of central tendency: the degree to which scores differ from the mean (average), which may be expressed as the inter-quartile range or the standard deviation.

Medial prefrontal cortex: the front part of the frontal lobe of the human brain that fully develops during early adulthood. Functions include decision-making.

Melatonin: a hormone secreted by the pineal gland in response to darkness, which aids sleep.

Memory encoding: where attended-to information is mentally converted into a representation that can be stored in the memory and retrieved later on.

Memory retrieval: where information held in the memory is retrieved and brought into consciousness.

Memory storage: where information mentally converted into a representation is held in the short- or long-term memory.

Mental representation: an arrangement of internal cognitive symbols that seek to correspond to external reality.

Minority influence: where a persuasive minority group successfully exerts pressure to change the attitudes or behaviours of the majority.

Modelling: where behaviour is learnt from the example of someone else.

Modes of representation: Brunerian concept: the ways in which knowledge and understanding are encoded and stored in the memory, including enactive, iconic and symbolic stages. Each stage is readily transferable into the next.

Monozygotic (MZ) twins: formed where two sperm cells pierce the same ovum. The resulting twins will be of the same gender and identical.

Multi-store memory model: memory storage and recall are linear processes, involving the sensory memory, the short-term memory and the long-term memory.

N

Narrative interviews: the use of open questions to enable the participant to give detailed verbal responses. Used in qualitative research.

Natural experiments: where the background scenario for both the test and the control already exists within the environment – often associated with quasi-experimental investigations.

Naturalistic observations: a quantitative and qualitative research method, involving measuring naturally-occurring behaviour with as much precision as possible.

Negative schemas: an individual's mental matrix of processing information that interprets the environment as being hostile or non-negotiable.

Neural networks: a system of interconnecting neurons, for example within the brain.

Neurons: nerve cells found in both the central and peripheral nervous systems.

Neuroplasticity: the development of additional neurons, appropriate in nature to a person's persistent efforts to develop a specific skill.

Neurotransmitters: biochemical substances that travel across the synapses of nerve cells that carry the specific stimuli to the next cell. They are powered by the electricity that the body naturally generates.

Nicotine: a stimulating substance that attaches itself to the acetylcholine receptors, creating many more such receptor sites in the process and an accompanying craving for more nicotine.

Nominal data: where data is categorical; neither measured nor ordered, but placed into distinct categories.

Nomothetic: where the factors influencing a person's behaviour can be generalised to the behaviour of individuals in similar circumstances.

Normal distribution: where the distribution of particular attribute studies has a bell-shaped tendency; most scores of individuals are at or close to the mean, with the number of scores decreasing the further from the mean.

Normality: the enjoyment of mental health, whose parameters are to some degree culturally determined.

Normative human development: where an individual's development processes are within the normal range of the human experience, and may be explained by the application of the standard models.

Null hypothesis: where the hypothesis is expressed in terms of there being no statistical significance between two variables under study. Research involves attempting to discredit it.

O

Obedience: where a person yields to specific instructions or orders from an authority figure.

Obesity: severely overweight, typically with a BMI over 30.

Object permanence: understanding that objects still exist even when out of view.

Observation: in quantitative research this involves recording the nature and the frequency of a given behaviour or other phenomenon in a particular environment.

One-tailed hypothesis test: the direction of the relationship between the IV and DV is predicted, forming part of the hypothesis.

Operationalisation: a statement of how the IVs and DVs are to be measured.

Operations: where several schemas co-operate in carrying out a specific task.

Opportunity (convenience) sampling: where the selected sample is made up of participants who are able and willing to take part in the study at a given time.

Order effect: where the participants, responses or behaviour in the earlier stage are likely to influence those in the later stage.

Ordinal data: where data is ordered, but the distance between those categories is unknown.

Outcome-based study (in abnormal psychology): where the degree of improvement in the patient's condition is judged on completion of the treatment, rather than during the process of the treatment.

Out-groups: groups with which an individual does not identify.

Overt observation: when those observed have given their consent.

Oxytocin: a hormone that is discharged through the pituitary gland into the bloodstream, which promotes feelings of love, trust and acceptance of one another. It is also a neurotransmitter.

P

Paradigm: an over-arching way of thinking that accommodates a set of theories.

Participant bias: where those taking part may answer or behave in the way that they think fits in with the researcher or with other participants.

Participant observation involves the researcher(s) becoming part of the target group that is being studied. The investigator is working from within those being observed.

Pathological: the study of the nature of disease and changes that it can cause.

Peak-end rule: a heuristic where a person's recollection of an event is characterised by how it started, the best or worst thing that happened, and how it finished.

Peer counselling: fellow-students serve as trained mediators between the bully and the victim, with the background support and supervision of the teaching staff.

Peripheral nervous system (PNS): part of the nervous system that is outside the brain and spinal cord.

Permissive parenting: characterised by the setting of few rules and boundaries and a reluctance to enforce rules. These parents are warm and indulgent but they do not like to say no or disappoint their children who grow up lacking in self-discipline.

Personal models: people that you know who influence your behaviour, for example parents, teachers, peers and community leaders.

Phenotype: an observable physical or behavioural characteristic that is determined by the interaction of genetic and environmental factors.

Pheromones: chemicals that are produced and released into the environment by an animal species that can affect the behaviours of other members of the species nearby.

Phonological loop: (also referred to as articulatory loop) the part of the STM within the working memory model that processes auditory information. It consists of a short-term sound store with auditory memory traces that if left alone are quickly lost.

Pie charts: a circular graphic divided so that the relative size of each slice illustrates a numerical proportion.

Placebo: intervention that is designed to have no effect. Any effect that does take place is attributed to a person's expecting a change to take place.

Pluralistic ignorance: where people look around at others to see their reactions, as cues for how to act in an emergency situation. The fewer the cues, the less likelihood of an individual intervening.

Polymorphism: variations within an individual gene.

Pop-psychology: where popularly-accepted explanations of human thinking and behaviour claim to be supported by psychology, but are insufficiently supported by academic research.

Positional models: people that you do not know but who influence your behaviour, such as political leaders and celebrities.

Positive distinctiveness: what makes the in-group special, enabling its members to feel proud to belong to it.

Positivism: the view that theory on human behaviour has to be supported by scientific evidence.

Positron emission tomography (PET): an electronic technique that images processes in the brain. Its mechanism is based on the injection of radioactive material injected into the bloodstream, and the monitoring of the decay-emitted positrons in the brain.

Post-modern transcript: where the interview transcript does not only contain the words, but also the gestures, hesitations and fillers.

Post-traumatic stress disorder (PTSD): an abnormal condition that can develop after a person has suffered a traumatic event. Typical symptoms include feelings of isolation, poor memory skills and a sense of being emotionally dulled.

Power Distance Index: the measurement of the amount of deference shown by someone lower down the power pyramid to someone higher.

Prejudice: unjustifiably negative attitude towards members of an out-group.

Pre-operational stage (two to seven years): Piagetian concept where the child's thinking is limited by lacking the dimensions of conservation, and is unable to see a physical situation from the view of another person in a different position.

Procedural memory: part of the implicit memory, handling stages or motions of a particular operation or skill.

Pro-social behaviour: acting in a way that helps another person or group.

Protective factor: a condition or variable that promotes desirable health outcomes, or at least reduces the risk of negative outcomes.

Psychiatry: a branch of medicine that deals with mental and emotional disorders.

Psychoanalytical approach: a means of investigating mental disorders based on the interaction of conscious and unconscious mental elements.

Psychobabble: the application of the terminology of psychology in a manner that is academically unacceptable.

Psychology: the disciplined study of the mind and behaviour.

Psychopathological: concerning mental disorders and associated behaviours that may be the result of a mental abnormal condition(s).

Psychotherapy: an interactive conversation-based treatment of mental health problems based on the client's thoughts, feelings, moods and behaviours.

Purposive sampling: where participants are selected for having the characteristics that fit in with the research aim.

Q

Qualitative research: based on the more extended and descriptive data that typically comes from personal journal entries and interview transcripts. The information does not translate into figures.

Quantitative research: based on figures that come from surveys, interviews, observations and questionnaire responses. They can be statistically summarised, and statistically analysed.

Quasi-experimental investigations: the researcher imposes the situation of the test and control investigation using the pre-existing natural environment.

Quasi-experiment: where the IV being studied occurs naturally, for example gender, age group, race or scores on a depression-classification table. The variable is pre-existing. No experimenter manipulation takes place.

R

Random sampling: where each member of the researched population has an equal chance of being selected.

Ratio data: quantitative data that can be measured on a scale. It may be multiplied and divided, and has a non-arbitrary zero.

Reciprocal determinism: where individuals can communicate and influence new norms to society.

Reciprocity: where people comply out of feeling obliged to return a favour.

Reconstructive memory: where schemas, beliefs, imagination and gaps in recollection combine to create an individual's inaccurate recall of events.

Reductionist: explaining a phenomenon in terms of a single cause and/or approach.

Reflexive: where the research may be influenced by the viewpoint of the researcher.

Refutable: able to be rejected, for example where the analysis of data gathered in research has the potential of causing the rejection of the hypothesis.

Relatedness: the degree to which individuals are connected when they share common genetic material.

Relativist: a perspective which views psychological processes as being so different that they cannot be compared across cultural groups.

Reliability (of research): the degree to which the study in repeated trials using the same methods, design and measurements produces the same results.

Reliability of diagnosis: the degree that the diagnosis is confirmed by another independent psychiatrist.

Repeated measures design: the same participants are used in both the control and test condition(s) of the experiment. There is one group of participants only.

Replication: repeating a study with a view to investigating whether it likely to show the same significant relationships with different researchers, in a different location and/or at a different time of the year.

Research design: means of coherently and logically planning a study so that it addresses the research problem.

Research hypothesis: the theorising about a phenomenon that is justified on the basis of established psychological theory, related previous research or empirical evidence.

Research question: what a study is seeking to answer, but not in the form of a testable statement.

Researcher bias: elements that could influence the investigator to analyse the data in a non-objective manner.

Resilience: where a person successfully adapts to problem conditions or to a difficult environment.

Risk factor: a condition or variable that promotes undesirable health outcomes.

Rosenthal effect: where perceived researcher-communicated higher expectations lead to a higher level of performance than the norm while being watched.

S

Sampling bias: where the sampling procedure does not accurately represent the target population.

Sampling technique: method of sampling chosen so that it is most representative of the population being studied.

Scaffolding: where relatively difficult concepts can be made accessible by breaking them down into suitable units.

Schemas: individualised mental representations that guide behaviour.

Schizophrenia: a disorder that can involve delusions, hallucinations and disturbances in emotions and behaviour.

Screw-you effect: the participant, determined not to co-operate, gives the response that they think the researchers do not want to hear without it necessarily being true.

Seasonal affective disorder (SAD): a form of depression as a response to the changing amount of natural light available at the beginning and the end of the winter season.

Selective abstraction: focusing excessively on a particular aspect of a social interaction or event, ignoring other aspects that are of at least equal importance and could result in a different overall interpretation.

Selective memory: the ability to retrieve certain facts and events but not others, depending on how easily the inputs coded into memory fit into existing schemas.

Self-blame schema: an individual's mental matrix of attributing negative experiences to their own faults rather than to outside factors.

Self-concept: the way people think about themselves as individuals.

Self-efficacy: the degree to which the individual believes they can participate in particular social activities.

Self-evaluation schema: an individual's mental matrix based on how they judge themselves that is applied to interpreting interactions and events.

Self-limiting beliefs: patterns of thinking that prevent people from functioning at maximum potential, which are supported by negative schemas about oneself.

Semantic memory: the part of explicit or declarative memory that holds facts and concepts.

Semantic scale: questionnaire-survey descriptors are turned into numbers. The scale is arranged along a spectrum of possible responses to a question. The numbers cannot be added up.

Semi-structured interview: the use of both closed and open questions to enable the participant to develop responses made. Used in qualitative research.

Sensory memory: receives inputs from the environment. It processes attended-to inputs into the STM.

Sensory-motor stage (birth to two years): Piagetian concept; cognitive stage where the infant goes from reflex, instinctive actions such as breastfeeding to constructing a schema such as through the experience of what can and cannot be sucked.

Serotonin: a neurotransmitter which when fired causes feelings of pleasure. It is an inhibitory neurotransmitter, employed by the nervous system to medicate pain, control sleep and regulate mood.

Serotonin re-uptake inhibitors (SSRIs): medication enabling each unit of neurotransmitter serotonin to be more effective.

Short-term memory (STM): this holds a limited amount of information received from the sensory memory, for a maximum of 30 seconds. That information needs to be attended to in order to keep it longer within the entire memory system.

Significance level: probability level (α) set by the researcher at which the null hypothesis will be rejected.

Simple experiment: where only one IV is used in the experiment.

Situational factors: where you understand a person's behaviour as a product of their own circumstances, rather than being directed personally at you.

Snowball sample: where participants already in the study help the researcher to recruit more.

Social categorisation: a cognitive process where the individual divides the social world into those who belong to their particular group and those who do not.

Social cognitive theory: how people process information about the world (including other humans) on the basis of cognitive elements such as schemas, attributions and stereotypes.

Social comparison: determining where your in-group stands relative to rival out-groups.

Social identification: where individuals adopt the identity and behavioural norms of the in-group, or groups.

Social identity theory: the ways individuals think about who they are and evaluate themselves in relation to groups.

Social learning theory: the individual acquires behaviour patterns through observing, imitating and modelling the behaviour of others.

Social phase (of relationship break-up): tertiary phase of relationship break-up involving facing family, friends and communities with a socially acceptable narrative on why they are no longer together.

Socialisation: where the individual learns to behave compatibly with social and cultural norms, and through them acquires a sense of identity.

Socio-cultural approach: focus on how behaviour relates to the social and cultural contexts in which behaviour is learnt and occurs.

Somatic: relating to the body rather than to the mind.

Somatic nervous system: this is also called the voluntary nervous system and it enables the individual to choose how to react to stimuli and which movements to make, such as the decision to stand up or sit down.

Somatic symptom: an indication of a mental abnormality based on the patient's reporting of their physical feelings.

Spinal cord: the thick band of nervous tissue that extends downwards from the brain through the spine, forming the central nervous system together with the brain.

Spiral curriculum: Brunerian concept; designing a programme of learning to enable the regular revisiting of previously encountered concepts at more complex levels. The learning process is an upward climb on the same base.

Stages of Change Model: a person must go through six stages of change to permanently break an anti-health habit: pre-contemplation, contemplation, preparation, action, maintenance and termination.

Standard deviation: measure of deviance from the mean that is calculated by finding the square root of the variance.

Stereotype: a person being identified as belonging to a particular group, with the belief that they have the characteristics commonly attributed to that group.

Stereotyping: a cognitive process where an unknown individual is perceived to have the characteristics commonly associated with the group they belong to.

Stigmatisation: the devaluing of an individual or category of people whose behaviour differs from society's norms.

Stimuli: anything that may excite sensory receptors of the nervous system.

Stratified sampling: where the target population is divided up into different sections for sampling purposes, such as age groups or income groups.

Stress: a reaction to a stimulus that disturbs our physical or mental equilibrium. Ordinary stress is a higher level of stress than eustress.

Super-ordinate goals: where a goal requires the co-operation of two or more people or groups, which results in rewards to all the co-operating parties.

Surface culture: the behaviours, customs, traditions and communication patterns of a culture that can easily be observed.

Symbolic representational stage: Brunerian concept where our mental encoding of a concept is in the form of increasingly complex sets of codes based on flexible-to-apply language or mathematics.

Symptom: an indication of a disorder, which may be physical or mental.

Synapse: the gap between the points of connection between neurons.

Synaptic clefts: the tiny gap between the presynaptic neuron that fires the neurotransmitters and the postsynaptic neuron that receives the neurotransmitters.

System-1 thinking: the thinking is quick, automatic, involves little effort, and is more likely to be influenced by biases.

System-2 thinking: the thinking involves patience, logic, effort, careful reasoning and application to the particular goal.

T

Target population: the population being researched through a sample.

T-cells: subtype of white blood cells that have the power of locking themselves onto antigens, multiplying and destroying them.

Test-retest method: reliability is assessed by giving the same test to the same participants on two different occasions, and correlating the findings or scores.

Theory: a well-substantiated explanation for a phenomenon or relationship.

Theory of mind: the capacity to attribute thoughts, feelings and beliefs to other people that are different from our own thoughts, feelings and beliefs.

Thermogenesis: the capacity of the body to burn-off energy from nutrition rather than store and accumulate it.

Thin slicing: where judgements about the nature and quality of a human interaction are made on the basis of the expert viewing a very small part of the interaction.

Top-down processing: the bringing of models, ideas, expectations and schemas to interpret new sensory information.

Transactional memory: where the human encoding, storage and recall on command is delegated to a digital device.

Transactional model of stress: the cognitive stress-coping mechanism is viewed as a two-way transaction between the individual and the environment.

Transcranial magnetic stimulation (TMS): creation of a magnetic field to induce a small electric current, as treatment to the specific part of the brain associated with the disorder.

Trauma (child): where the child experiences a sudden and adverse change in circumstances.

Triangulation: in research, where more than one method is used to determine the relationship between the same two or more variables. This typically involves both quantitative and qualitative methods.

Two-tailed hypothesis test: it is predicted that a relationship between the IV and DV exists, but it could be in either direction.

Type 1 error: where the difference in data between two or more samples is accepted as being real, but is actually not. A true null hypothesis is rejected, when it should not be.

Type 2 error: where the difference in data between two or more samples is wrongly found to be insignificant. A false null hypothesis is rejected when it should not be.

U

Universalist: a perspective which assumes that cognitive and emotional psychological mechanisms are generally similar throughout the human race, even though they may be expressed behaviourally in different ways.

Unstructured interviews: designed to draw out in a conversational style how the individual thinks, behaves and would react in a particular scenario. Tend to be narrative in style.

V

Validity (of research): how accurately the study measures what it is designed to measure.

Validity (of diagnosis): how accurately the diagnosis procedures correctly identify the condition of the patient.

Vasopressin: a hormone released during sex that powers long-term commitment between the couple.

Ventral tegmental area (VTA): region that has a role in influencing the intense emotions involved in love.

Vicarious learning: a behaviour modelled on the example of others.

Violent behaviour: where aggression is used to dominate or harm another person or group.

Visual-spatial sketchpad: the part of the STM within the working memory model that processes visual information.

Volunteer (self-selected) sampling: where the sample is made up of participants who wish to take part rather than being selected by the researcher.

W

Wernicke area: the part of the brain that processes the meaning of language, located in the rear of the brain.

Wernicke's aphasia: impaired ability to understand speech, yet able to produce speech.

Working memory: theoretical framework referring to the structures and processes used for temporarily storing and manipulating sensed information.

X Y Z

Zone of proximal development: Vygotskian concept, referring to the area between what the child can achieve without help, and what the child can achieve when stretched by an educator or fellow-student with more knowledge and skills.

References

Ainsworth, M. D. S. (1969). Object relations, dependency and attachment: a theoretical review of the infant–mother relationship. *Child Development*; 40: 969–1025.

Ainsworth, M. D. S., Bell, S. M., & Stayton, D. J. (1971). Individual differences in strange-situation behavior of one-year-olds. In H. R. Schaffer (Ed.), *The Origins of Human Social Relations.* London and New York: Academic Press, pp17–58.

Ainsworth, M. D. S., Blehar, M. C., Waters, E., & Wall, S. (1978). *Patterns of Attachment: A psychological study of the strange situation*. Hillsdale, NJ: Erlbaum.

Aldwin, C. M., & Levenson, M. R. (2001). Stress, coping, and health at midlife: A developmental perspective. In M. E. Lachman (Ed.), *Wiley series on adulthood and aging. Handbook of Midlife Development.* Hoboken, NJ: John Wiley & Sons Inc, pp188–214.

Alter, A. L., Oppenheimer, D. M., Epley, N., & Eyre, R. N. (2007). Overcoming intuition: Metacognitive difficulty activates analytic reasoning. *Journal of Experimental Psychology: General*; Nov 2007; 136(4): 569–76.

Altman, I., & Taylor, D. A. (1973). *Social Penetration: The development of interpersonal relationships.* Oxford, England: Holt, Rinehart & Winston.

Ambady, N., Bernieri, F., & Richeson, J. (2000). Toward a histology of social behavior: Judgmental accuracy from thin slices of the behavioral stream. *Advances in Experimental Social Psychology*; 32: 201–71.

Andrade, L., Caraveo-Anduaga, J. J., Berglund, P., Bijl, R.V., De Graaf, R., Vollebergh, W., Dragomirecka, E., Kohn, R., Keller, M., Kessler, R. C., Kawakami, N., Kiliç, C., Offord, D., Ustun, T. B., & Wittchen, H. U. (2003). The epidemiology of major depressive episodes: results from the International Consortium of Psychiatric Epidemiology (ICPE) Surveys. *International Journal of Methods Psychiatry Research*; 2003; 12(1): 3–21.

Arcelus, J., Mitchell, A. J., Wales, J., & Nielsen, S. (2011). Mortality rates in patients with anorexia nervosa and other eating disorders. A meta-analysis of 36 studies. *Archive of General Psychiatry*; Jul 2011; 68(7): 724–31.

Argyle, M. (1988). *Bodily Communication*, 2nd ed. New York, NY: Methuen.

Ariely, D., Loewenstein, G., & Prelec, D. (2003). Coherent arbitrariness: stable demand curves without stable preferences. *The Quarterly Journal of Economics*; 1 Feb 2003; 118(1): 73–106.

Aronson, E., & Mills, J. (1959). The effect of severity of initiation on liking for a group. *Journal of Abnormal and Social Psychology*; 59: 177–81.

Asch, S. E. (1956). Studies of independence and conformity: I. A minority of one against a unanimous majority. *Psychological Monographs: General and Applied*; 70(9): 1–70.

Atkinson, R. C., & Shiffrin, R. M. (1968). Human memory: A proposed system and its control processes. In K. W. Spence and J. T. Spence (Eds), *The Psychology of Learning and Motivation*, Vol. 2. London: Academic Press, pp89–195.

Baddeley, A. D., & Hitch, G. J. (1974). Working memory. In G. A. Bower (Ed.), *Recent Advances in Learning and Motivation,* Vol. 8. New York: Academic Press, pp47–90.

Baddeley, A. D., & Hitch, G. J. (2000). Development of working memory: Should the Pascual-Leone and the Baddeley and Hitch Models be merged? *Journal of Experimental Child Psychology*; 77: 128–37.

Bailer, U. F., & Kaye, W. H. (2010). In R. A. H. Adan and W. H. Kaye (Eds), Behavioral Neurobiology of Eating Disorders, Current Topics in Behavioral Neurosciences 6, Heidelberg: Springer-Verlag Berlin, 2010, published online 11 September 2010.

Baillargeon, R., Spele, S., & Wasserman, S. (1985). Object permanence in five-month-old infants. *Cognition*; 20(3): 191–208.

Bandura, A. (1961). Psychotherapy as a learning process. *Psychological Bulletin*; 58(2): 143–59.

Bandura, A. (1965). Behavioral modification through modeling procedures. In L. Krasner & L. P. Ullman (Eds), *Research in Behavior Modification,* New York: Holt, Rinehart & Winston.

Bandura, A. (1977). *Social Learning Theory.* Englewood Cliffs, NJ: Prentice Hall.

Bandura, A. (1977). Self-efficacy: Toward a unifying theory of behavioral change. *Psychological Review,* 84(2): 191–215.

Bandura, A. (1995). Self-efficacy. In A. S. R. Manstead & M. Hewstone (Eds), *Blackwell Encyclopedia of Social Psychology,* Oxford: Blackwell, pp453–54.

Bandura, A. (1997). Self-efficacy and health behaviour. In A. Baum, S. Newman, J. Wienman, R. West, & C. McManus (Eds), *Cambridge Handbook of Psychology, Health and Medicine,* Cambridge: Cambridge University Press, pp160–62.

Bandura, A. (2001). The changing face of psychology at the dawning of a globalization era. *Canadian Psychology,* 42(1): 12–24.

Bandura, A., Ross, D., and Ross, S. A. (1961). Transmission of aggression through imitation of aggressive models. *Journal of Abnormal and Social Psychology*; 63(3): 575–82.

Bargh, J., Chen, M., & Burrows, L. (1996). Automaticity of social behavior: direct effects of trait construct and stereotype activation on action. *Journal of Personality and Social Psychology*; 1996; 71(2): 230–44.

Barkley-Levenson, E., & Galván, A. (2014). Neural representation of expected value in the adolescent brain. *Proceedings of the National Academy of Sciences of the United States of America*; 111: 1646–51.

Baron-Cohen, S., Leslie, A. M., & Frith, U. (1985). Does the autistic child have a 'theory of mind'? *Cognition*; 21: 37–46.

Barsky, A. J., Peekna, H. M., & Borus, J. F. (2001). Somatic symptom reporting in women and men. *Journal of General Internal Medicine*; 2001; 16: 266–75.

Bartlett, F. (1932). *Remembering: A study in Experimental and Social Psychology.* Cambridge: Cambridge University Press.

Batson, C. D., Duncan, B. D., Ackerman, P., Buckley, T., & Birch, K. (1981). Is empathic emotion a source of altruistic motivation? *Journal of Personality and Social Psychology*; 40(2): 290–302.

Bauman, Z. (1998). *Globalization: the human consequences.* New York: Columbia University Press.

Baumgartner, T., Heinrichs, M., Vonlanthen, A., Fischbacher, U., & Fehr, E. (2008). Oxytocin shapes the neural circuitry of trust and trust adaptation in humans. *Neuron*; 22 May 2008; 58(4): 639–50.

Beck, A. T. (1976). *Cognitive Therapy and the Emotional Disorders.* New York: International Universities Press.

Becker, A., Burwell, R., Herzog, D., Hamburg, P., & Gilman, S. (2002). Eating behaviours and attitudes following prolonged exposure to television among ethnic Fijian adolescent girls. *British Journal of Psychiatry*; 180(6): 509–14.

Bem, S. L. (1981). Gender schema theory: a cognitive account of sex typing. *Psychological Review,* 88(4), 354–364.

Bern, S. (1981). Gender schema theory: A cognitive account of sex typing. *Psychological Review*; 88: 354–64.

Berry, J. W. (1974). Psychological aspects of cultural pluralism: Unity and identity reconsidered. *Topics in Culture Learning*; 2: 17–22.

Berry, S. H., & Kanouse, D. E. (1987). Physician response to a mailed survey: An experiment in timing of payment. *Public Opinion Quarterly*; 51: 102–16.

Bertakis, K. D., Helms, L. J., Callahan, E. J., Azari, R., Leigh, P., & Robbins, J. A. (2001). Patient gender differences in the diagnosis of depression in primary care. *Journal of Women's Health and Gender-Based Medicine*; Sept 2001; 10(7): 689–98.

Bouchard Jr, T. J., Lykken, D. T., McGue, M., Segal, N. L., & Tellegen, A. (1990). Sources of human psychological differences: the Minnesota Study of Twins Reared Apart. *Science*; 12 Oct 1990; 250(4978): 223–28.

Bowlby, J. (1951). *Maternal Care and Mental Health*. Geneva: World Health Organization.

Bowlby, J. (1953). *Child Care and the Growth of Love*. Harmondsworth: Penguin.

Bowlby, J. (1969). *Attachment and Loss. Vol. 1: Attachment*. London: Hogarth Press.

Bradbury, T. N., & Fincham, F. D. (1992). Attributions and behavior in marital interaction. *Journal of Personality and Social Psychology*; Oct 1992; 63(4): 613–28.

Breggin, P. (1997). *Brain-Disabling Treatments in Psychiatry*. New York: Springer Publishing Company.

Broca, P. (1861). Nouvelle observation d'aphémie produite par une lésion de la troisième circonvolution frontale. *Bulletins de la Société d'Anatomie (Paris), 2e serie*; 6: 398–407.

Broca, P. (1865) Sur le siege de la faculté du language articulé. *Bulletin of Social Anthropology*; 6: 337–93.

Brommelhoff, J. A., Conway, K., Merikangas, K., & Levy, B. R. (2004). Higher rates of depression in women: role of gender bias within the family. *Journal of Women's Health* (Larchmt); Jan–Feb 2004; 13(1): 69–76.

Brooks-Gunn, J., Burrow, C., & Warren, M. P. (1988). Attitudes toward eating and body weight in different groups of female adolescent athletes. *International Journal of Eating Disorders*; 7: 749–58.

Brown, G. W., & Harris, T. (1978). *Social Origins of Depression*. London: Tavistock.

Brown, R., & Kulik, J. (1977). Flashbulb memories. *Cognition*; 5: 73–79.

Bruner, J. (orig. 1960, reprinted 1976). *The Process of Education*. Cambridge: Harvard University Press.

Buss, D. M., Abbott, M., Angleitner, A., Asherian, A., Biaggio, A., & 45 other co-authors, (1990). International preferences in selecting mates: A study of 37 cultures. *Journal of Cross-Cultural Psychology*; 21: 5–47.

Bussey, K., & Bandura, A. (1992). Self-regulatory mechanisms governing gender development. *Child Development*; 63: 1236–50.

Butland, B., Jebb, S., Kopelman, P., McPherson, K., Thomas, S., Mardell, J., & Parry, V. (2007). *Foresight. Tackling obesities: future choices. Project report* 2007; p155.

Byrnes, D. A., & Kiger, G. (1990). The effect of a prejudice-reduction simulation on attitude change. *Journal of Applied Social Psychology*; 20: 341–356.

Canary, D. J., & Stafford, L. (1994). Maintaining relationships through strategic and routine interaction. In D. J. Canary & L. Stafford (Eds), *Communication and Relational Maintenance*. San Diego, CA: Academic Press, pp3–22.

Cao, J., Galinsky, A. D., & Maddux, W. W. (2013). Does travel broaden the mind? Breadth of foreign experiences increases generalized trust. *Social Psychological and Personality Science*; 5(5): 517–25.

Carion, V. G., Hass, B. W., Garrett, A., Song, S., Reiss, A. L., et al. (2009). Reduced hippocampal activity in youth with posttraumatic stress symptoms: An fMRI Study. *Journal of Pediatric Psychology*, 2009. *Journal of Pediatric Psychology*; Jun 2010; 35(5): 559–69.

Caspi, A., Sugden, K., Moffitt, T. E., Taylor, A., Craig, I. W., Harrington, H., McClay, J., Mill, J., Martin, J., Braithwaite, A., & Poulton, R. (2003) Influence of life stress on depression: moderation by a polymorphism in the 5-HTT gene. *Science, New Series*; 301(5631): 386–89.

Champion, L. A., & Power, M. (1995). Social and cognitive approaches to depression: Towards a new synthesis. *The British Journal of Clinical Psychology / The British Psychological Society*; 34 (Pt 4): 485–503.

Chapman, L. S. (2005). Meta-evaluation of worksite health promotion economic return studies: 2005 update. *American Journal of Health Promotion*; Jul–Aug 2005; 19(6): 1–11.

Charlton, T., Gunter, B., & Hannan, A. (Eds). (2002). *Broadcast Television Effects in a Remote Community*. London: Routledge.

Charlton, T., Panting, C., Davie, R., Coles, D., & Whitmarsh, L. (2006). Children's playground behaviour across five years of broadcast television: a naturalistic study in a remote community. *Emotional and Behavioural Difficulties*; 2000; 5(4): 4–12.

Claussnitzer, M., Dankel, S. N., Kim, K. H., Quon, G., Meuleman, W., Haugen, C., Glunk, V., Sousa, I. S., Beaudry, J. L., Puviindran, V., & Abdennur, N. A. (2015). FTO obesity variant circuitry and adipocyte browning in humans. *New England Journal of Medicine*; 373(10): 895–907.

Cochrane, R., & Sashidharan, S. P. (1995). Mental health and ethnic minorities: A review of the literature and implications for services, NHS Centre for Reviews and Dissemination/Social Policy Research Unit. University of Birmingham and Northern Birmingham Mental Health Trust, February 1995.

Cockett, M., & Tripp, J. (1994). Children living in re-ordered families (review). *Social Policy Research Findings*; Feb 1994; No. 45: Joseph Rowntree Foundation.

Condon, R. G. (1988). *Adolescents in a changing world, Vol. 1. Inuit youth: Growth and change in the Canadian arctic*; Piscataway, NJ: Rutgers University Press.

Cooper, J. E., Kendell, R. E., Gurland, B. J., Sharpe, I., Copeland, J. R. M., & Simon, R. (1972). *Psychiatric Diagnosis in New York and London (US-UK Diagnostic Project)*. London: Oxford University Press.

Corkin, S. (2002). What's new with the amnesic patient H. M.? *Nat. Rev. Neurosci.*; 3(2):153–60.

Costrich, N., Feinstein, J., Kidder, L., Marecek, J., & Pascale, L. (1975). When stereotypes hurt: three studies of penalties for sex-role reversals. *Journal of Experimental Social Psychology*; 11(6): 520–30.

Currin, L., Schmidt, U., Treasure, J., & Jick, H. (2005). Time trends in eating disorder incidence. *British Journal of Psychiatry*; Feb 2005; 186: 132–35.

Curtiss, S. (1977). *Genie: A Psycholinguistic Study of a Modern Day 'Wild Child'*. New York, NY: Academic Press.

D'Esposito, M., Detre, J. A., Alsop, D. C., Shin, R. K., Atlas, S., & Grossman, M. (1995). The neural basis of the central executive system of working memory. *Nature*; 16 Nov 1995; 378(6554): 279–81.

Darley, J. M., & Batson, C. D. (1973). From Jerusalem to Jericho: A study of situational and dispositional variables in helping behavior. *Journal of Personality and Social Psychology*; 1973; 27: 100–108.

Darley, J. M., & Latané, B. (1968). Bystander intervention in emergencies: Diffusion of responsibility. *Journal of Personality and Social Psychology*; 8: 377–83.

Davis, J. L., & Rusbult, C. E. (2001) Attitude alignment in close relationships, *Journal of Personality and Social Psychology*; 81(1), 65–8.

Dawkins, R. (1976). *The Selfish Gene*. Oxford: Oxford University Press.

de Silva-Sanigorski, A., Prosser, A., Carpenter, L., Honisett, S., Gibbs, L., Moodie, M., Sheppard, L., Swinburn, B., & Waters, E. (2010). Evaluation of the childhood obesity prevention program Kids - 'Go for your life'. *BMC Public Health*; 2010; 10: 288.

Doherty, E. G. (1975). Labeling effects in psychiatric hospitalization. A study of diverging patterns of inpatient self-labeling processes. *Archives of Gen. Psychiatry*; May 1975; 32(5): 562–68.

Duck, S. W. (1982). A topography of relationship disengagement and dissolution. In S. W. Duck (Ed.), *Personal Relationships, 4,* New York: Academic Press, pp1–30.

Duck, S. W. (1998). *Human Relationships,* 3rd edition. Newbury Park, CA: Sage, pp1–30.

Dunbar, R. I. M. (1992). Neocortex size as a constraint on group size in primates. *Journal of Human Evolution*; 22(6): 469–493.

Egeland, J. A., & Hostetter, A. M. (1983). Amish Study, I: Affective disorders among the Amish, 1976–1980. *American Journal of Psychiatry*; Jan 1983; 140(1): 56–61.

Elkin, I., Shea, M. T., & Watkins, J. T. (1989). National Institute of Mental Health treatment of depression collaborative research program: general effectiveness of treatments. *Archives of Gen. Psychiatry*; 46: 971–82.

Engel, G. L. (1977). The need for a new medical model: a challenge for biomedicine. *Science*; 8 April; 196(4286): 129–36.

Engle, P. L., & Breaux, C. (1994) *Is there a Father Instinct? Fathers' Responsibility for Children.* New York/Washington DC: Population Council/International Center for Research on Women.

Evans, G. W., & Kim, P. (2013) Childhood poverty, chronic stress, self-regulation, and coping. *Child Dev Perspect*; 7: 43–48.

Fairburn, C. G. (1997). The management of bulimia nervosa and other binge eating problems. *Advances in Psychiatric Treatment*; Jan 1997; 3(1): 2–8.

Fallon, A. E., & Rozin, P. (1985). Sex differences in perceptions of desirable body shape. *Journal of Abnormal Psychology*; 94(1): 102–105.

Femlee, D. H. (1995). Fatal attractions: affection and disaffection in intimate relationships. First published 1 May 1995, Research Article, *Journal of Social and Personal Relationships*.

Fernald, L. C. H., Burke, H. M., & Gunnar, M. R. (2008). Salivary cortisol levels in children of low-income women with depressive symptoms. *Dev. Psychopathol.*; 2008; 20: 423–36.

Fernando, S. (1988). *Race and Culture in Psychiatry*, London: Croom Helm.

Festinger, L., Schachter, S., & Back, K. (1950). *Social Pressures in Informal Groups; A Study of Human Factors in Housing*. Oxford, England: Harper.

Feyerabend, P. (1975). *Against Method: Outline of an Anarchistic Theory of Knowledge*. London: New Left Books.

Fisher, H., Aron, A. & Brown, L. (2005). Romantic love: An fMRI study of a neural mechanism for mate choice. *The Journal of Comparative Neurology*; 493(1): 58–62.

Fiske, S. T. (2004). *Social Beings: A core motives approach to social psychology*. New York: Wiley.

Folkerts, H. W., Michael, N., Tölle, R., Schonauer, K., Mücke, S., & Schulze-Mönking, H. (1997). Electroconvulsive therapy vs. paroxetine in treatment-resistant depression – a randomized study. *Acta Psychiatr. Scand.*; Nov 1997; 96(5): 334–42.

Freud, S. (1909). *Analysis of a Phobia of a Five-Year-Old Boy*. The Pelican Freud Library (1997); 8: Case Histories: 169–306.

Gardner, B., Lally, P., & Wardle, J. (2012). Making health habitual: the psychology of 'habit-formation' and general practice. *British Journal of General Practice*; Dec 2012; 62(605): 664–66.

Gelstein, S., Yeshurun, Y., Rozenkrantz, L., Shushan, S., Frumin, I., Roth, Y., & Sobel, N. (2011). Human tears contain a chemosignal. *Science*; (6014): 226–30.

Gilman, S.E., Rende, R., Boergers, J., Abrams, D.B., Buka, S.L., Clark, M.A. et al. (2009). Parental smoking and adolescent smoking initiation: an intergenerational perspective on tobacco control. *Pediatrics*; 123: e274–e281.

Goel., V., Buchel, C., Frith, C., Doland, R. J. et al. (2000). Dissociation of mechanisms underlying syllogistic reasoning. *Neuroimage*; Nov 2000; 12(5): 504–14.

Graber, R., Pichon, F., & Carabine, E. (2015). Working Paper 425 Psychological resilience: State of knowledge and future research agendas; Oct 2015; Overseas Development Institute.

Groesz, L. M., Levine, M. P., & Murnen, S. K. (2002). The effect of experimental presentation of thin media images on body satisfaction: a meta-analytic review. *International Journal of Eating Disorders*; 31(1): 1–16.

Grossmann, K., Grossmann, K. E., Spangler, G., Suess, G., & Unzner, L. (1985). Maternal sensitivity and newborns' orientation responses as related to quality of attachment in Northern Germany. In I. Bretherton & E. Waters (Eds), *Growing Points of Attachment Theory and Research,* Monographs of the Society for Research in Child Development; 50(1–2, Serial No. 209), 233–56.

Gupta, U., & Singh, P. (1982). An exploratory study of love and liking and type of marriages. *Indian Journal of Applied Psychology*; 19(2): 92–97.

Haier, J. R., Siegel, B., Tang, C., Abel, L., & Buchsbaum, M. (1992). Intelligence and changes in regional cerebral glucose metabolic rate following learning. *Intelligence*; 16: 415–26.

Halpern, S.D., French, B., Small, D.S., Saulsgiver, K., Harhay, M.O., Audrain-McGovern, J., Loewenstein, G., Brennan, T.A., Asch, D.A., Volpp, K.G. (2015). Randomized trial of four financial-incentive programs for smoking cessation. *The New England Journal of Medicine*; 372: 2108–2117.

Harlow, H. F., & Harlow, M. K. (1962a). The effect of rearing conditions on behavior. *Bull. Menninger Clinic*; 26: 213–24.

Harlow, H. F., & Harlow, M. K. (1962b). Social deprivation in monkeys. *Sci. Am.*; 207: 136–46.

Harlow, J. M. (1848). Passage of an iron rod through the head. *Boston Med. Surg. J.*; 39: 389–93.

Harris, L. T., & Fiske, S. T. (2006). Dehumanizing the lowest of the low: neuroimaging responses to extreme out-groups. *Psychol. Sci.*; Oct 2006; 17(10): 847–53.

Hatfield, E., Traupmann, J., & Walster, G. W., Equity and extramarital sex. In M. Cook & G. Wilson (Eds), (1979). *Love and attraction: An international conference*, Oxford: Pergamon Press, pp309–22.

Hatfield, E., Utne, M. K., & Traupmann, J. Equity theory and intimate relationships. In R. L. Burgess & T. L. Huston (Eds), (1979). *Social Exchange in Developing Relationships*, New York: Academic Press, pp99–133.

Hazan, C., & Shaver, P. R. (1987). Romantic love conceptualised as an attachment process. *Journal of Personality and Social Psychology*; 52: 511–24.

Hendricks, T. J., Fyodorov, D. V., Wegman, L. J., Lelutiu, N. B., Pehek, E. A., Yamamoto, B., Silver, J., Weeber, E. J., Sweatt, J. D., & Deneris, E. S. (2003). Pet-1 ETS gene plays a critical role in 5-HT neuron development and is required for normal anxiety-like and aggressive behaviour. *Neuron*; 37(2): 233–47.

Heninger, G. R., Delgado, P. L., & Charney, D. S. (1996). The revised monoamine theory of depression: a modulatory role for monoamines, based on new findings from monoamine depletion experiments in humans. *Pharmacopsychiatry*; Jan 1996; 29(1): 2–11.

Hochstetler, S., Rejeski, W. J., & Best, D. (1985). The influence of sex-role orientation on ratings of perceived exertion. *Sex Roles*; 12: 825–35.

Hodges, J., & Tizard, B. (1989). Social and family relationships of ex-institutional adolescents. *J. Child Psychoi. Psychiai.*; 1989; 30(1): 77–97.

Hofstede, G. (2001). *Culture's Consequences: Comparing Values, Behaviors, Institutions and Organizations across Nations*. Thousand Oaks, CA: Sage (co-published in the PRC as Vol. 10 in the Shanghai Foreign Language Education Press SFLEP Intercultural Communication Reference Series, 2008).

Hofstede, G., & Bond, M. H. (1984). Hofstede's Culture Dimensions: An Independent Validation Using Rokeach's Value Survey. *Journal of Cross-Cultural Psychology*; 15(4): 417–33.

Holmes, T. H., & Rahe, R. H. (1967). The Social Readjustment Rating Scale. *Journal of Psychosomatic Research*; 11: 213–18.

Hong, T., & Johnson, C. (2013). A longitudinal analysis of adolescent smoking: Using smoking status to differentiate the influence of body weight measures. *Journal of School Health*; 83(5): 314–21.

Houlston, C., & Smith, P. K. (2007). The impact of a peer counselling scheme to address bullying in an all-girl London secondary school: A short-term longitudinal study. *British Journal of Educational Psychology*; March 2009; 79(1): 69–86.

Hughes, P., & White, E. (2010). The Space Shuttle Challenger disaster: A classic example of Groupthink. *Ethics & Critical Thinking Journal*; 3: 63–70.

Hunter, I. M. L. (1964). *Memory*, London: Penguin Books.

Hutchings, B., & Mednick, S. A. (1975). Registered criminality in the adoptive and biological parents of registered male criminal adoptees. In *Proceedings of the Annual Meeting of the American Psychopathological Association*; 63(105).

Jakobsen, K. D., Frederiksen, J. N., Hansen, T., Jansson, L. B., Parnas, J. & Werge, T. (2005). Reliability of clinical ICD-10 schizophrenia diagnoses. *Nordic Journal of Psychiatry*; 2005; 59: 209–212.

Jahoda, M. (1958). *Current Concepts of Positive Mental Health*. New York: Basic Books.

James, W. (1890). *Principles of Psychology*. New York: Holt.

Jaques, E. (1965). Death and the Mid-life Crisis. *Int. J. Psychoanal.*; Oct 1965; 46(4): 502–14.

Johnston, L. D., O'Malley, P. M., Miech, R. A., Bachman, J. G., & Schulenberg, J. E. (2016). *Monitoring the Future national survey results on drug use, 1975–2015: Overview, key findings on adolescent drug use.* Ann Arbor: Institute for Social Research, The University of Michigan.

Jorgensen, B. W., & Cervone, J. C. (1978). Affect enhancement in the pseudorecognition task. *Personality and Social Psychology Bulletin*; 4(2): 285–88.

Kahneman, D. (2011). *Thinking, Fast and Slow.* London: Allen Lane.

Kaufman, D. (1991). *Rachel's Daughters: Newly Orthodox Jewish Women.* New Brunswick, NJ: Rutgers University Press.

Kearins, J. (1981). Visual spatial memory in Australian Aboriginal children of desert regions. *Cognitive Psychology*; 13: 434–60.

Keel, P. K., & Klump, K. L. (2003). Are eating disorders culture-bound syndromes? Implications for conceptualizing their etiology. *Psychol. Bull.*; Sept 2003; 129(5): 747–69.

Kenrick, D. T., & Gutierres, S. E. (1980). Contrast effects and judgments of physical attractiveness: When beauty becomes a social problem. *Journal of Personality and Social Psychology*; 38(1): 131–40.

Kessler, R. C., Avenevoli, S., & Merikangas, K. R. (2001). Mood disorders in children and adolescents: an epidemiologic perspective. *Biological Psychiatry*; 49(12): 1002–14.

Kessler, R. C., Berglund, P., Demler, O., Jin, R., Merikangas, K. R., & Walters, E. E. (2005). Lifetime prevalence and age-of-onset distributions of DSM-IV disorders in the National Comorbidity Survey Replication. *Archives of Gen. Psychiatry*; Jun 2005; 62(6): 593–602.

Kiecolt-Glaser, J. K., Garner, W., Speicher, C. E., Penn, G. M., Holliday, J., & Glaser, R. (1984). Psychosocial modifiers of immunocompetence in medical students. *Psychosomatic Medicine*; 46: 7–14.

Kiesler, S. B., & Baral, R. (1970). The search for a romantic partner: The effects of self-esteem and physical attractiveness on romantic behaviour. In: K. J. Gerden & D. Marlow (Eds), *Personality and Social Behaviour,* Reading, MA.; 155–65.

Kirsch, I., & Sapirstein, G. (1998). Listening to Prozac but hearing placebo: A meta-analysis of antidepressant medication. *Prevention & Treatment*; 1(2): Article ID 2a.

Kirsch, I., Deacon, B. J., Huedo-Medina, T. B., Scoboria, A., Moore, T. J., & Johnson, B. T. (2008). Initial severity and antidepressant benefits: a meta-analysis of data submitted to the food and drug administration. *PLoS Med.*; 5: 260–68.

Kito, M. (2010). Self-disclosure in romantic relationships and friendships among American and Japanese college students. *J. Soc. Psychol.*; April 2005; 145(2): 127–40.

Kleinman, A. (1982). Neurasthenia and Depression: A Study of Somatization and Culture in China. *Culture, Medicine and Psychiatry*; 6: 117–90.

Kortegaard, L. S., Hoerder, K., Joergensen, J., Gillberg, C., & Kyvik, K. O. (2001). A preliminary population-based twin study of self-reported eating disorder. *Psychological Medicine*; 2001; 31: 361–64.

Kuhn, T. S. (1962). *The Structure of Scientific Revolutions.* Chicago, IL: University of Chicago Press.

Kulkofsky, S., Wang, Q., Conway, M., Hou, Y., Aydin, C., Mueller-Johnson, K., & Williams, H. (2011). Cultural variation in the correlates of flashbulb memories: An investigation in five countries. *Memory* (Hove, England); 19: 233–40.

Ladd, G. W. (1990). Having friends, keeping friends, making friends, and being liked by peers in the classroom: Predictors of children's early school adjustment? *Child Development*; 61(4): 1081–100.

Landry, P., & Bartling, C. (2011). Phonological loop and articulatory suppression. *American Journal of Psychological Research*; 7(1): 79–86.

Lazarus, R. S., & Folkman, S. (1984). *Stress, Appraisal, and Coping.* New York: Springer.

LeDoux, J.E. (1999). *The Emotional Brain: The Mysterious Underpinnings of Emotional Life*. London: Weidenfeld & Nicolson Ltd.

Leinenga, G., & Götz, J. (2015). Scanning ultrasound removes amyloid-beta and restores memory in an Alzheimer's disease mouse model. *Science Translational Medicine*; 11 Mar 2015; 7(278): 278.

Leu, J., Wang, J., & Koo. K. (2011). Are positive emotions just as "positive" across cultures? *Emotion*; Aug 2011; 11(4): 994–99.

Leuchter, A. F., Cook, I. A., Witte, E. A., Morgan, M., & Abrams, M. (2002). Changes in brain function of depressed subjects during treatment with placebo. *The American Journal of Psychiatry*; Jan 2002; 159(1): 122–29.

Levav, I., Kohn, R., Golding, J., & Weissman, M. (1997). Vulnerability of Jews to affective disorder. *The American Journal of Psychiatry*; 154: 941–47.

Levine, R.V., Martinez, T., Brase, G., & Sorenson, K. (1994). Helping in 36 U.S. Cities. *Journal of Personality and Social Psychology*; 67: 69–81.

Levine, R., Sato, S., Hashimoto, T., & Verma, J. (1995). Love and marriage in eleven cultures. *Journal of Cross-Cultural Psychology*; 26(5): 554–71.

Levine, R.V., Norenzayan, A. & Philbrick, K. (2001). Cross-cultural differences in helping strangers. Journal of Cross-Cultural Psychology; 32(5): 543–560

Levinger, G. (1980). Toward the analysis of close relationships. *Journal of Experimental Social Psychology*; Nov 1980; 16(6): 510–44.

Li, B., Adab, P., & Cheng, K. K. (2015). The role of grandparents in childhood obesity in China - evidence from a mixed methods study. *International Journal of Behavioral Nutrition and Physical Activity*; 2015; 12: 91.

Loftus, E. F., & Palmer, J. C. (1974). Reconstruction of automobile destruction: An example of the interaction between language and memory. *Journal of Verbal Learning and Verbal Behavior*; 13: 585–89.

Loftus, E. F., & Pickrell, J. E. (1995). The formation of false memories. *Psychiatric Annals*; 25: 720–25.

Lord, C. G., Ross, L., & Lepper, M. R. (1979). Biased assimilation and attitude polarization: The effects of prior theories on subsequently considered evidence. *Journal of Personality and Social Psychology*; 37(11): 2098–109.

Lueck, K., & Wilson, M. (2010). Acculturative stress in Asian immigrants: the impact of social and linguistic factors. *International Journal of Intercultural Relations*; 2010; 34(1): 47–57.

Lueck, K., & Wilson, M. (2011). Acculturative stress in Latino immigrants: the impact of social, socio-psychological and migration-related factors. *International Journal of Intercultural Relations*; 2011; 35(2): 186–95.

Madsen, E., Tunney, R. J., Fieldman, G., Plotkin, H. C., Dunbar, R. I. M., Richardson, J-M., & McFarland, D. (2007). Kinship and altruism: A cross-cultural experimental study. *British Journal of Psychology*; 98(2): 339–59.

Maguire, E. A., Gadian, D. G., Johnsrude, I. S., Good, C. D., Ashburner, J., Frackowiak, R. S., & Frith, C. D. (2000). Navigation-related structural change in the hippocampi of taxi drivers. *Proceedings of the National Academy of Science*; 97(8): 4398–403.

Markey, P. M., & Markey, C. N. (2007). Romantic ideals, romantic obtainment and relationship experiences: The complementarity of interpersonal traits among romantic partners. *Journal of Social and Personal Relationships*; 24: 517–34.

Markey, P. M., & Markey, C. N. (2010). Vulnerability to violent video games: A review and integration of personality research. *Review of General Psychology*; 14(2): 82–91.

Marmot, M. G., Rose, G., Shipley, M., & Hamilton, P. J. (1978). Employment grade and coronary heart disease in British civil servants. *Journal of Epidemiology and Community Health*; 32(4): 244–49.

Marmot, M. G., Davey Smith, G., Stansfield, S. et al. (1991). Health Inequalities among British civil servants: the Whitehall II study. *Lancet*; 337(8754): 1387–93.

Marsella, A. J. (1995). Urbanization, mental health, and psychosocial well-being: Some historical perspectives and considerations. In T. Harpman, & I. Blue (Eds), *Urbanization and Mental Health in Developing Countries*, Sydney: Avebury, pp17–38.

Martin, C. L. & Halverson, C. F. (1983). The effects of sex-typing schemas on young children's memory. In C. L. Martin, & C. F. Halverson Jr., *Child Development*; Jun 1983; 54(3): 563–74.

Marty, M. E., & Appleby, R. S. (1993). *Fundamentalisms and the State: remaking polities, economies, and militance.* The Fundamentalism Project.

Maslow, A. H. (1943). A theory of human motivation. *Psychological Review*; 50(4): 370–96.

McClintock, M. K. (1971). Menstrual synchrony and suppression. *Nature*; 229: 244–45.

McCrone, J. (2000). *Going Inside. A tour round a single moment of consciousness.* London: Faber & Faber.

McDonald, M. M., Navarrete, C. D., & van Vugt, M. (2012). Evolution and the psychology of intergroup conflict: the male warrior hypothesis. *Philosophical Transactions of the Royal Society, B. Biological Sciences*; 367(1589): 670–79.

McGrath, E., Keita, G. P., Strickland, B., & Russo, N. F. (1990). *Women and Depression: Risk Factors and Treatment Issues.* Washington, DC: American Psychological Association.

Mead, M. (1935). *Sex and Temperament in Three Primitive Societies.* New York: Morrow.

Mead, M. (1949). *Male and Female: A study of the sexes in a changing world.* Oxford, England: William Morrow.

Milgram, S. (1961). *Dynamics of Obedience.* Washington: National Science Foundation.

Milgram, S. (1963). Behavioral study of obedience. *Journal of Abnormal and Social Psychology*; 67(4): 371–78.

Milgram, S. (1974). *Obedience to Authority: An Experimental View.* London: Tavistock Publications.

Milner, B., Corkin, S. et al. (1968). Further analysis of Hippocampal Amnesic Syndrome - 14-year follow-up study of HM. *Neuropsychologia*; 6(3): 215–30.

Money, J. & Ehrhardt, A. A. (1972). *Man and Woman, Boy and Girl.* Baltimore, MD: Johns Hopkins University Press.

Morgan, C., Dazzan, P., Morgan, K., Jones, P., Harrison, G., Leff, J., Murray, R., & Fearon, P. on behalf of the Aesop study group (2006). First episode psychosis and ethnicity: initial findings from the AESOP study. *World Psychiatry*; Feb 2006; 5(1): 40–46.

Murdock, B. B. (1962). The serial position effect of free recall. *Journal of Experimental Psychology*; 64(5): 482–88.

Neisser, U., & Harsch, N. (1992). Phantom flashbulbs: False recollections of hearing the news about Challenger. In E. Winograd, & U. Neisser (Eds), *Emory symposia in cognition, 4. Affect and accuracy in recall: Studies of "flashbulb" memories*, New York, NY, US: Cambridge University Press, pp9–31.

Newcomer, J. W., Selke, G., Melson, A. K., Hershey, T., Craft, S., Richards, K., & Alderson, A. L., (1999). Decreased memory performance in healthy humans induced by stress-level cortisol treatment. *Archives of Gen. Psychiatry*; 56: 527–33.

Nolen-Hoeksema, S. (2000). The role of rumination in depressive disorders and mixed anxiety/depressive symptoms. *Journal of Abnormal Psychology*; Aug 2000; 109(3): 504–11.

Nolen-Hoeksema, S. (2001). Gender differences in depression. In Susan Nolen-Hoeksema, *Current Directions in Psychological Science*; 10(5): 173–76.

Norasakkunkit, V., & Uchida, Y. (2011). Psychological consequences of post-industrial anomie on self and motivation among Japanese youth. *Journal of Social Issues*; Dec 2011; 67(4): 774–86.

Nurnberger Jr, J. I., & Gershon, E. S. (1982). Genetics of affective disorders. In E. Paykel (Ed.) (1982), *Handbook of Affective Disorders.* London: Churchill Livingstone, 126–45.

O'Loughlin, J., Karp, I., Koulis, T., Paradis, G., & Difranza, J. (2009). Determinants of first puff and daily cigarette smoking in adolescents. *American Journal of Epidemiology*; 1 Sept 2009; 170(5): 585–97.

Oberndorfer, T., Simmons, A., McCurdy, D., Strigo, I., Matthews, S., Yang, T., Irvine, Z., & Kaye, W. (2013). Greater anterior insula activation during anticipation of food images in women recovered from anorexia nervosa versus controls. *Psychiatry Res.*; 30 Nov 2013; 214(2): 10.

Oettingen, G., & Mayer, D. (2002). The motivating function of thinking about the future: expectations versus fantasies. *Journal of Personality and Social Psychology*; Nov 2002; 83(5): 1198–212.

Okello, E. S., & Ekblad, S. (2006). Lay concepts of depression among the Baganda of Uganda: a pilot study. *Transcultural Psychiatry*; Jun 2006; 43(2): 287–313.

Pampel, F., Legleye, S., Goffette, C., Piontek, D., Kraus, L., & Khlat, M. (2015). Cohort changes in educational disparities in smoking: France, Germany and the United States. *Social Science & Medicine*; Feb 2015; 127: 41–50.

Parker, G., Cheah, Y. C., & Roy, K. (2001). Do the Chinese somatize depression? A cross-cultural study. *Soc. Psychiatry Psychiatr. Epidemiol.*; Jun 2001; 36(6): 287–93.

Parten, M. B. (1932). Social participation among pre-school children, *The Journal of Abnormal and Social Psychology*; 27(3): 243–269.

Perrin, S., & Spencer, C. (1980). The Asch effect – A child of its time. *Bulletin of the BPS*; 33: 405–6.

Perry, B. D., & Pollard, D. (1997). Altered brain development following global neglect in early childhood. Society For Neuroscience: Proceedings from Annual Meeting, New Orleans, 1997.

Piaget, J. (1932). *The Moral Judgement of the Child*. London: Kagan Paul.

Piaget, J. (1952). *The Origins of Intelligence in Children*. New York: International Universities Press.

Piaget, J. (1962). *Play, Dreams, and Imitation in Children* (original work published in French in 1927). London: Routledge and Kagan Paul.

Piaget, J., & Inhelder, B. (1956). *The Child's Conception of Space*. London: Routledge.

Piccinelli, M., & Wilkinson, G. (2000). Gender differences in depression. Critical review. *British Journal of Psychiatry*; Dec 2000; 177: 486–92.

Piliavin, I. M., Rodin, J., & Piliavin, J. A. (1969). Good Samaritanism: An underground phenomenon. *Journal of Personality and Social Psychology*; 13: 1200–13.

Polivy, J. (2001). The false hope syndrome: unrealistic expectations of self-change. *Int. J. Obes. Relat. Metab. Disord.*; May 2001; 25(Suppl. 1): S80–4.

Pollitt, E., Gorman, K. S., Engle, P. L., Rivera, J. A., & Martorell, R. (1995). Nutrition in early life and the fulfillment of intellectual potential. *J. Nutr.*; April 1995; 125(Suppl. 4): S1111–18.

Poongothai, S., Pradeepa, R., Ganesan, A., & Mohan, V. (2009) Prevalence of depression in a large urban South Indian population – The Chennai Urban Rural Epidemiology Study (CURES-70). *PloS One*; 4: E7185.

Popper, K. R. (1934). *The Logic of Scientific Discovery*, English translation, 1959. London: Hutchinson.

Prentice, A. M., & Jebb, S. A. (1995). Obesity in Britain: gluttony or sloth? *BMJ*; 12 Aug 1995; 311(7002): 437–9.

Prochaska, J., & DiClemente, C. (1983). Stages and processes of self-change of smoking: toward an integrative model of change. *Journal of Consulting and Clinical Psychology*; 51(3), 390–95.

Quist-Paulsen, P., & Gallefors, F. (2003). Randomised controlled trial of smoking cessation intervention after admission for coronary heart disease. *BMJ*; 29 Nov 2003; 327(7426):1254–57.

Reed, G. M., Kemeny, M. E., Taylor, S. E., & Visscher, B. R. (1999). Negative HIV-specific expectancies and AIDS-related bereavement as predictors of symptom onset in asymptomatic HIV-positive gay men. *Health Psychology*; 1999; 18: 354–63.

Riggs, P. D., Mikulich-Gilbertson, S. K., Davies, R. D., Lohman, M., Klein, C., & Stover, S. K. (2007). A randomized controlled trial of fluoxetine and cognitive behavioral therapy in adolescents with major depression, behavior problems, and substance use disorders. *Archives of Pediatric and Adolescent Medicine*; 2007; 161: 1026–34.

Rolls, B. J., Fedoroff, I. C., & Gutherie, J. F. (1991). Gender differences in eating behavior and body weight regulation. *Health Psychology*; 1991; 70(2): 133–142.

Rosenhan, D. L. (1973). On being sane in insane places. *Science*; 179: 250–58.

Rosenhan, D. L., & Seligman, M. E. P. (1984). *Abnormal Psychology*. London: WW Norton & Co.

Rosenstock, I. M., Strecher, V. J., & Becker M. H. (1988). Social learning theory and the Health Belief Model. *Health Educ. Q.*; Summer 1988; 15(2): 175–83.

Rosenthal, A. M. (1964). *Thirty-Eight Witnesses: The Kitty Genovese Case*. Melville House Classic Journalism.

Rosenthal, R., & Jacobson, L. (1968). *Pygmalion in the Classroom: Teacher expectation and pupils' intellectual development.* New York: Holt, Rinehart & Winston, p240.

Rosenzweig, M. R., Bennett, E. L., & Diamond, M. C. (1972). Brain changes in response to experience. *Sci. Amer.*; 1972; 226: 22.

Rosser, S. V. (1992). The gender equation. *The Sciences*; Sept-Oct 1992; 32(5): 42–47.

Rouse, G., Ingersoll, G. M., & Orr, D. P. (1998). Longitudinal health endangering behavior risk among resilient and nonresilient early adolescents. *Journal of Adolescent Health*; Nov 1998; 23(5): 297–302.

Rowland, C. V. (1970). Anorexia nervosa. A survey of the literature and review of 30 cases. *International Psychiatry Clinics*; 7, 37–137.

Rusbult, C. E., Verette, J., Whitney, G. A., Slovik, L. F., & Lipkus, I. (1991). Accommodation processes in close relationships: Theory and preliminary empirical evidence. *Journal of Personality and Social Psychology*; 60, 53–78.

Russell, W. M. S., & Burch, R. L. (1959). *The Principles of Humane Experimental Technique.* Wheathampstead (UK): Universities Federation for Animal Welfare.

Rutter, M. (1981). *Maternal Deprivation Reassessed,* 2nd edition. Harmondsworth, Middlesex: Penguin.

Rutter, M. (1995). Clinical implications of attachment concepts: retrospect and prospect. *J. Child Psychol. Psychiatry*; May 1995; 36(4): 549–71.

Rutter, M., O'Connor, T. G., & English and Romanian Adoptees (ERA) Study Team (2004). Are there biological programming effects for psychological development? Findings from a study of Romanian adoptees. *Dev. Psychol.*; Jan 2004; 40(1): 81–94.

Santos, P. S. C., Schinemann, J. A., Gabardo, J., & Bicalho, M. D. (2005). New evidence that the MHC influences odor perception in humans: a study with 58 Southern Brazilian students. *Horm. Behav.*; 2005; 47: 384–88.

Saraswathi, T. S., & Larson, R. W. (2002). Adolescence in global perspective: An agenda for social policy. In B. B. Brown, R. W. Larson & T. S. Saraswathi (Eds), *The World's Youth: Adolescence in eight regions of the globe.* New York: Cambridge University Press, pp344–62.

Sartorius, N., Davidson, H., Ernberg, G. et al. (1983). *Depressive Disorders in Different Cultures.* Geneva: WHO.

Schaffer, H. R. (2004). *Introducing Child Psychology.* Oxford: Blackwell.

Schoon, I., & Bartley, M. (2008). The role of human capability and resilience. *The Psychologist*; Jan 2008; 21: 24–27.

Schultz, P. W., Khazian, A. M., & Zaleski, A. C. (2008). Using normative social influence to promote conservation among hotel guests. *Social Influence*; 3: 4–23.

Schum, C., & Gold, R. J. (2007). The Birth of 'truth' (and What It Tells Us about the Importance of Horizontal Influence), Cases in Public Health Communication and Marketing, School of Public Health and Health Services, George Washington University, June 2007.

Schwartz, B. (2004). The tyranny of choice, *Scientific American*; 290(4): 70–75.

Scott-Van Zeeland, A. A. et al. (2014). Evidence for the role of *EPHX2* gene variants in anorexia nervosa. *Molecular Psychiatry*; 19: 724–32.

Scoville, W. B., & Milner, B. (1957). Loss of recent memory after bilateral hippocampal lesions. *J. Neurol. Neurosurg. Psychiatry*; 20(1): 11–21.

Seligman, M. E. P. (1974). Depression and learned helplessness. In R. J. Friedman & M. M. Katz (Eds), *The Psychology of Depression: Contemporary Theory and Research,* Washington D. C.: Winston-Wiley.

Seligmann, J., Rogers, P. & Annin, P. (1994). The pressure to lose. *Newsweek*; 123(18): 60–1.

Shakya, H. B., & Christakis, N. A. (2017). Association of Facebook use with compromised well-being: A longitudinal study. *American Journal of Epidemiology*; 1 Feb 2017; 185(3): 203–11.

Sharot, T., Martorella, E. A., Delgado, M. R., & Phelps, E. A. (2007). How personal experience modulates the neural circuitry of memories of September 11. *Proc. Natl Acad. Sci. USA*; 2 Jan 2007; 104(1): 389–94.

Shaver, P., & Hazan, C. (1987). Being lonely, falling in love: Perspectives from attachment theory. *Journal of Social Behavior and Personality*; 2: 105–124.

Shaver, P. R., & Hazan, C. (1988). A biased overview of the study of love. *Journal of Social and Personal Relationships*; 5: 473–501.

Shaver, P. R., Hazan, C., & Bradshaw, D. (1988). Love as attachment: The integration of three behavioral systems. In R. J. Sternberg & M. L. Barnes (Eds), *The Psychology of Love*, New Haven, CT: Yale University Press, pp68–99.

Sherif, M., Harvey, O. J., White, B. J., Hood, W. R., & Sherif, C. W. (1961). *Intergroup Conflict and Cooperation: The Robbers Cave Experiment (Vol. 10).* Norman, OK: University Book Exchange [Involves the Sherif et al. 1954 *Robbers Cave* research study.].

Sherman, P. W. (1980). The limits of ground squirrel nepotism. In: Barlow, G. W. & Silverberg, J. (eds.), *Sociobiology: Beyond nature/nurture?*: 505–544. Boulder, Colorado: Westview Press.

Singh, T, Arrazola R. A., Corey, C. G., Husten, C. G., Neff, L. J., Homa, D. M., King, B. A. (2016). Tobacco use among middle and high school students – United States, 2011-2015. *Morbidity and Mortality Weekly Report*; 65(14): 361–7.

Skinner, B. F. (1953). Some contributions of an experimental analysis of behaviour to psychology as a whole. *American Psychologist*; 8(2): 69–78.

Smith, K. W., Balkwill, L-L., Vartanian, O., & Goel, V. (2015). Syllogisms delivered in an angry voice lead to improved performance and engagement of a different neural system compared to neutral voice. *Frontiers in Human Neuroscience*; 12 May 2015; 9:273.

Southgate, L., Tchanturia, K., & Treasure, J. (2009). Neuropsychological studies in eating disorders. *Neuropsychological Studies in Eating Disorders*; 1–89.

Sowell, E. R., Thompson, P. M., Holmes, C. J., Jernigan, T. L., & Toga, A. W. (1999). In vivo evidence for post-adolescent brain maturation in frontal and striatal regions. *Nat. Neurosci.*; Oct 1999; 2(10): 859–61.

Sparrow, B., Liu, J., & Wegner, D. M. (2011). Google effects on memory: cognitive consequences of having information at our fingertips. *Science*; 5 Aug 2011; 333(6043): 776–8.

Sroufe, L. A., Bennett, C., Englund, M., Urban, J., & Shulman, S. (1993). The significance of gender boundaries in preadolescence: contemporary correlates and antecedents of boundary violation and maintenance. *Child Dev.*; April 1993; 64(2): 455–66.

Stanovich, K. E. (1999). *Who is rational? Studies of individual differences in reasoning.* Mahwah, NJ: Erlbaum.

Strober, M., Freeman, R., Lampert, C., Diamond, J., & Kaye W. (2000). Controlled family study of anorexia and bulimia nervosa: evidence of shared liability and transmission of partial syndromes. *American Journal of Psychiatry*; 157: 393–401.

Stunkard, A. J., Harris, J. R., Pedersen, N. L., & McClearn, G. E. (1990). The bodymass index of twins who have been reared apart. *New England Journal of Medicine*; 322(21): 1483–7.

Swing, E., Gentile, D. A., Anderson, C. A., & Walsh, D. A. (2010). Television and video game exposure and the development of attention problems. *Pediatrics*; 126: 214-221.

Szasz, T. S. (1971). From the slaughterhouse to the madhouse. *Psychother. Theory Res. Pract.*; 8: 64–67.

Tajfel, H. (1970). Experiments in Intergroup Discrimination. *Scientific American:* Springer Nature; 223: 96–102.

Tajfel, H., & Turner, J. C. (1979). An integrative theory of intergroup conflict. In W. G. Austin, & S. Worchel (Eds), *The Social Psychology of Intergroup Relations*, Monterey, CA: Brooks/Cole, pp33–37.

Thimm, J. C., & Antonsen, L. (2014). Effectiveness of cognitive behavioral group therapy for depression in routine practice. *BMC Psychiatry*; 2014; 14: 292.

Toi, M., & Batson, C. D. (1982). More evidence that empathy is a source of altruistic motivation. *Journal of Personality and Social Psychology*; 43(2); 281–292.

Torelli, C. J., Chiu, C-Y., Tam, K-P., Au, A. K. C., & Keh, H. T. (2011). Exclusionary reactions to foreign cultures: Effect of simultaneous exposure to cultures in globalized space. *Journal of Social Issues*; 67(4): 716-742.

Toseland, R. W., & Siporin, M. (1986). When to recommend group treatment: A review of the clinical and the research literature. *International Journal of Group Psychotherapy*; 36(2), pp171–201.

Totten, M. (2003). Girlfriend abuse as a form of masculinity construction among violent, marginal male youth. *Men and Masculinities*; 6: 70–92.

Tulving, E. (1989). Remembering and knowing the past. *American Scientist*; 77: 361–67.

Van IJzendoorn, M. H., & Kroonenberg, P. M. (1988). Cross-cultural patterns of attachment: A meta-analysis of the strange situation, *Child Development*; 59: 147–56.

Vandenberg, B. (1986). Play theory. In G. Fein, & M. Rivkin, (Eds), *The Young Child at Play*, Washington, DC: NAEYC, pp17–22.

Vygotsky, L. S. (orig. 1934, reprinted 1962). *Thought and Language.* Cambridge, MA: MIT Press.

Waber, D. P., Forbes, P. W., Almli, C. R., Blood, E. A., & The Brain Development Cooperative Group (2007). Four-Year Longitudinal Performance of a Population-Based Sample of Healthy Children on a Neuropsychological Battery: The NIH MRI Study of Normal Brain Development. *J. Int. Neuropsychol. Soc.*; Mar 2012; 18(2): 179–90.

Watson, J. B., & Rayner, R. (1920). Conditioned emotional reactions. *Journal of Experimental Psychology*; 3: 1–14.

Wayment, H., Silver, R., & Kemeny, M. (2006). Spared at random: survivor reactions in the gay community. *Journal of Applied Social Psychology*; 25: 187–209.

Wedekind, C., Seebeck, T., Bettens, F., & Paepke, A. J. (1995). MHC-dependent mate preferences in humans. *Proc. Biological Sciences*; 260(1359): 245–49.

Weiss, R. B., Baker, T. B., Cannon, D. S., von Niederhausern, A., & Dunn, D. M., et al. (2008) A Candidate Gene Approach Identifies the CHRNA5-A3-B4 Region as a Risk Factor for Age-Dependent Nicotine Addiction. *PLOS Genetics* 4(7): e1000125.

Wernicke, C. (1874). *Der Aphasische Symptomencomplex.* Breslau: Cohn and Weigert.

West, M. D. (2005). *Law in Everyday Japan: Sex, Sumo, Suicide, and Statutes.* Chicago: University of Chicago Press.

West, R., & Sohal, T. (2006). "Catastrophic" pathways to smoking cessation: findings from national survey, *BMJ*; 25 Feb 2006; 332(7539): 458–60.

Wiborg, G., & Hanewinkel, R. (2002). Effectiveness of the "Smoke-Free Class Competition" in delaying the onset of smoking in adolescence. *Prev. Med.*; Sept 2002; 35(3): 241–49.

Wilhelm, K., Mitchell, P. B., Niven, H., Finch, A., Wedgwood, L., Scimone, A., Blair, I. P., Parker, G., & Schofield, P. R. (2006). Life events, first depression onset and the serotonin transporter gene; *British Journal of Psychiatry*; Mar 2006; 188: 210–5.

Wimmer, H., & Perner, J. (1983). Beliefs about beliefs: Representation and constraining function of wrong beliefs in young children's understanding of deception. *Cognition*; 13: 103–28.

Wolfgang, E. M., & Ferracuti, F. (1967). *The Subculture of Violence: Towards an Integrated Theory of Criminology.* London: Tavistock Publications.

Wood, D. J., Bruner, J. S., & Ross, G. (1976). The role of tutoring in problem-solving. *Journal of Child Psychology and Psychiatry*; 17: 89–100.

Wu, Y., Yang, Y., & Chiu, C.-Y. (2014). Responses to religious norm defection: The case of Hui Chinese Muslims not following the halal diet. *International Journal of Intercultural Relations*, 39: 1-8.

Wundt, W. (1873). *Grundzüge der physiologischen Psychologie*; 2 vol. (1873–74); 3 vol. 6th edition (1908–11).

399

Yang, D. Y-J., Chen, X., Cheng, S. Y. Y., Kwan, L., Tam, K. -P., & Yeh, K. -H. (2011). The lay psychology of globalization and its social impact. *Journal of Social Issues*; 67: 677–695.

Yuille, J. C., & Cutshall, J. L. (1986). A case study of eyewitness testimony of a crime. *Journal of Applied Psychology*; 71: 291–301.

Zajonc, R. B. (1971). Attraction, affiliation, and attachment. In J. F. Eisenberg, & W. S. Dillon (Eds), *Man and Beast: Comparative Social Behavior*, Washington, DC: Smithsonian Institution Press, pp141–79.

Zhang, W. X., Shen, Y. C, & Li, S. R. (1998). Epidemiological investigation of mental disorders in 7 areas of China [in Chinese]. *Chinese Journal of Psychiatry*; 31: 69-71.

Zimbardo, P. G. (1969). The human choice: Individuation, reason, and order versus deindividuation, impulse, and chaos. In *Nebraska Symposium on Motivation*. University of Nebraska Press.

Zimbardo, P. G. (1971). Coercion and compliance: The psychology of police confessions. In R. Perruci, & M. Pilisuk (Eds), *The Triple Revolution Emerging*, Boston: Little, Brown, pp492–508.

Zucker, D., Hopkins, R. S., Sly, D. F., Urich, J., Kershaw, J. M., & Solari, S. (2006). Florida's "truth" campaign: a counter-marketing, anti-tobacco media campaign. *J. Public Health Manag. Pract.*; May 2000; 6(3): 1–6.

Human Genome Project. Coordinating scientific researchers worldwide between 1990 and 2004 https://www.genome.gov/12011238/an-overview-of-the-human-genome-project/

Louise Frechette, ex-UN Deputy Secretary-General, (Address to UN delegates, 1999). Press Release DSG/SM/70
https://www.un.org/press/en/1999/19991012.dsgsm70.doc.html

Office of the Surgeon General (US); Center for Mental Health Services (US); National Institute of Mental Health (US). Mental Health: Culture, Race, and Ethnicity: A Supplement to Mental Health: A Report of the Surgeon General. Rockville (MD): Substance Abuse and Mental Health Services Administration (US); 2001 Aug.

The Children's Act (2004)
https://www.legislation.gov.uk/ukpga/2004/31/contents

The *High/Scope Perry Preschool Project*. Greg Parks. The Office of Juvenile Justice and Delinquency Prevention.

The Plowden Report (1967) Children and their Primary Schools A Report of the Central Advisory Council for Education (England). London: Her Majesty's Stationery Office 1967.

Index

PET. *See* positron emission
    tomography (PET)
Pet-1 gene, 75
phenotype, 63
pheromones, 59
pheromones in human behaviour, 59–61
phonological loop, 91
Piaget, Jean, 286
    accommodation, 288
    applications and evaluation, 292
    assimilation, 268
    biologically-determined stages,
      289–290
    concrete operational stage (ages
      7–11), 289
    conservation, 289
    disequilibrium, 288
    equilibration, 288
    evidence of progression, 290–292
    preoperational stage (ages 2–7), 289
    sensory motor stage (ages 0–2), 289
    strength and weakness, 292–293
Pie charts, psychological research, 317
placebo, 46, 196
pluralistic ignorance, 228
PNS. *See* peripheral nervous
    system (PNS)
polymorphism, 63
pop-psychology, 17
positional models, 133
positive distinctiveness, 129
positive hypothesis, 8
positivism, 3
positron emission tomography (PET),
    49, 117
post-modern transcripts, 315
post-traumatic stress disorder
    (PTSD), 270
poverty, 181
Power Distance Index (PDI), 149
prejudice, 50
pro-active interaction, 161
procedural memory, 88, 89
pro-social behaviour
    definition, 221
    empathy-altruism theory, 224
    kin-selection theory, 223
    promotional strategies, 229
    situational considerations, 225–227
    socio-cultural psychology, 225–227
protective factor, health outcomes, 247
protein-based lesions, 76–77
Prozac, 76
psychiatry, 11, 190
psychoanalysis, 3
psychoanalytical approach, 5

psychobabble, 16
psychological analysis
    cognitive levels of, 85
    socio-cultural levels of, 85
psychology, 3, 7–9, 54
    approaches in, 3–6
    cultural issues, 10–11
    discipline of, 15
    general debates in, 9–10
    growth of, 21
    microscope analogy applied
      to IB, 6–7
    practical value of, 11
    principles and research in, 15
    research, 19
psychopathological conditions, 168
psychotherapy, 11, 190, 193
purposive sampling, 307, 313

Q

qualitative methods, 19
qualitative research, 307–310
    case studies, 310
    focus groups, 308
    interviewer effect, 308
    interviews, 307–308
    naturalistic observations, 308–309
    non-experimental methods, 34–36
    Rosenthal effect, 309
    semi-structured interviews, 308
    unstructured interviews, 308
quantitative research methods, 19,
    305–306
    experimental methods, 20–24
    non-experimental methods, 24–33
quasi-experiments, 22, 306

R

random sampling, 312
ratio data, 318
reciprocal determinism, 125, 142
reciprocity, 138
reconstructive memory, 96, 103–107
reductionist, 7
reductionist-holism debate, 9
reflexive, 36
refutable, 8
relatedness, 64
relativist perspectives, 147
reliability, 102, 319
    of diagnosis, 170, 170
    potential issues affecting, 170
repeated measures design, 310

replication, 321
research design, 305
researcher bias, 320
research hypothesis, 20
research methods
    analysing data, 315–319
    chi-squared test, 319
    conclusions, 320
    dependent variables, 312
    elements of, 310–314
    ethical considerations, 37–39,
      313–314
    evaluating theories and research in,
      36–37
    evaluation, 319–320
    hypotheses, 311
    independent t-test, 319
    independent variables, 312
    laboratory experiments, 305
    Mann-Whitney U test, 319
    natural experiments, 306
    Pearson product movement, 319
    qualitative methods, 307–310
      in non-experimental methods,
        34–36
    quantitative methods, 19, 305–306,
      316–319
      experimental methods in, 20–24
      non-experimental methods,
        24–33
    repeated t-test, 319
    research designs, 310–311
    sampling technique, 312–313
    sign test, 319
    Spearman's rho, 319
    traditional, 210
    vs. psychobabble, 15–18
    Wilcoxon, 319
research question, 154
research study
    Ariely et al. (2003), on System-1-
      type thinking, 109
    Barkley-Levenson and Galván
      (2014), on risk taking
      behaviour, 299–300
    Bartlett (1932), on constructive
      memory, 94–96
    Baumgartner et al. (2008), on
      workings of oxytocin, 58–59
    Bouchard et al. (1990), on role of
      genes in behaviour, 64–65
    Brown and Kulik (1977), on
      flashbulb memories, 113–114
    Cao, Galinsky and Maddux
      (2013), on effects of the
      interaction, 161

Acknowledgements

My thanks to the indefatigable work and devoted support of the team at Cambridge University Press. I have richly benefited from their insights, suggestions and patience throughout the stages of preparation of this work.

My thanks also to my colleagues and students: in particular to Dr. Barbara Zinn for her help with the final methodology chapter, and to Ms. Lour Al Raheb for advice with the illustrations.

And finally to my family: my wife Aviva and my two children, Jonathan and Daniella.

My work aims to make your journey in IB Psychology informative and thought-provoking, as well as helping you to achieve success in your course. I hope you enjoy it throughout!

The author and publishers acknowledge the following sources of copyright material and are grateful for the permissions granted. While every effort has been made, it has not always been possible to identify the sources of all the material used, or to trace all copyright holders. If any omissions are brought to our notice, we will be happy to include the appropriate acknowledgements on reprinting.

Thanks to the following for permission to reproduce images:

Cover wildpixel/Getty Images; *Inside* Fig 1.1 Imagno/Getty Images; Fig 1.2, 1.3, 2.16 Bettmann/ Getty Images; Fig 1.4 George Rinhart/Getty Images; Fig 1.5 Sam Falk/New York Times Co./ Getty Images; Fig 1.7 Richard Bailey/SPL/Getty Images; Fig 2.2 JGI/Daniel Grill/Getty Images; Fig 2.3, 5.1, 9.7 Westend6/Getty Images; Fig 2.8, 5.10, 6.7 Jan Rieckhoff/ullstein bild via Getty Images; Fig 2.9 Granger Historical Picture Archive/Alamy Stock Photo; Fig 2.10 Atlaspix/ Alamy Stock Photo; Fig 2.11 Handout/Getty Images; Fig 2.12 Time Life Pictures/US Signal Corps/The LIFE Picture Collection/Getty Images; Fig 2.13 Gideon Mendel/Getty Images; Fig 2.14 Compassionate Eye Foundation/Dan Kenyon/Getty Images; Fig 2.15*t* Matteo Colombo/ Getty Images; Fig 2.15*b* TommL/Getty Images; Fig 3.2 photo courtesy Dr. Nancy L. Segal; Fig 3.6 Monty Rakusen/Getty Images; Fig 3.12 'Brain in Love' illustration by Rachel Ignotofsky; Fig 3.14, 9.8 Flashpop/Getty Images; Fig 3.15 Ricardo DeAratanha/Los Angeles Times via Getty Images; Fig 3.16 Kirill Kukhmar/Getty Images; Fig 4.1 Cindy Prins/Getty Images; Fig 4.3 Jetta Productions/Getty Images; Fig 4.4 elenaleonova/Getty Images; Fig 4.8 Stolk/Getty Images; Fig 4.9 Keystone/Hulton Archive/Getty Images; Fig 4.10a Deco/Alamy Stock Photo; Fig 4.10b davidf/Getty Images; Fig 4.12 Don Tormey/Getty Images; Fig 5.2 Mario De Biasi/ Mondadori Portfolio via Getty Images; Fig 5.3 Keystone/Getty Images; Fig 5.4 Jon Brenneis/ Life Magazine/The LIFE Images Collection/Getty Images; Fig 5.5, 5.6 courtesy of Albert Bandura; Fig 5.7 PYMCA/Getty Images; Fig 5.8 Caiaimage/Chris Ryan/Getty Images; Fig 5.9 Konstantinos Tsakalidis/Alamy Stock Photo; Fig 5.11 Reproduced with permission, Copyright 1955 Scientific American, a division of Nature America, Inc. All rights reserved; Fig 5.16 Alex Ramsey/Alamy Stock Photo; Fig 5.17 image courtesy Geert Hofstede; Fig 5.18 based on illustration by Professor David Harvey in The Condition of Postmodernity, © David Harvey, 1990, Blackwell; Publishers; Fig 5.19 Kali9/Getty Images; Fig 5.20 Karl Johaentges/Getty Images; Fig 5.22 Greg Baker/Rex/Shutterstock; Fig 6.1 Michael Albans/NY Daily News Archive via Getty Images; Fig 6.2 Colin Davey/Getty Images; Fig 6.3 Mauro Fermariello/Science Photo Library; Fig 6.6 Barry Lewis/Alamy Stock Photo; Fig 6.12 Jonathan Nourok/Getty Images; Fig 6.13, Will McIntyre/Science Photo Library; Fig 6.14 Barry Rosenthal/Getty Images; Fig 7.1, 9.21 Klaus Vedfelt/Getty Images; Fig 7.2 Aurelien Meunier/Getty Images; Fig 7.3 BSIP/ Getty Images; Fig 7.4 AleksandarNakic/Getty Images; Fig 7.5 Halfdark/Getty Images; Fig 7.7 Markus Bernhard/Getty Images; Fig 7.8 PeopleImages/Getty Images; Fig 7.10 Chronicle/Alamy Stock Photo; Fig 7.11 Paul Fearn/Alamy Stock Photo; Fig 7.12 Tim Tadder/Getty Images; Fig 7.14 Archives of the History of American Psychology, The Drs. Nicholas and Dorothy Cummings Centre for the History of Psychology, The University of Akron; Fig 7.16 SAEED KHAN/AFP/ Getty Images; Fig 8.2 Caiaimage/Paul Bradbury/Getty Images; Fig 8.5 Manoj Adlukay/Getty Images; Fig 8.6 Martin Harvey/Getty Images; Fig 8.7 Oli Scarff/Getty Images; Fig 8.8 Gilaxia/